Y0-DLC-883

International Handbook of Education Systems

INTERNATIONAL HANDBOOK OF EDUCATION SYSTEMS

Volume I
Europe and Canada
Edited by Brian Holmes

Volume II
Africa and the Middle East
Edited by John Cameron and Paul Hurst

Volume III
Asia, Australasia and Latin America
Edited by Robert Cowen and Martin McLean

International Handbook of Education Systems

Editors: J Cameron, R Cowen, B Holmes, P Hurst and M McLean

Volume III
ASIA, AUSTRALASIA AND LATIN AMERICA
Edited by
Robert Cowen and Martin McLean
Institute of Education, University of London

JOHN WILEY & SONS
Chichester · New York · Brisbane · Toronto · Singapore

Copyright © 1984 by John Wiley & Sons Ltd.

Reprinted August 1985

All rights reserved.

No part of this book may be reproduced by any means, nor transmitted, nor translated into a machine language without the written permission of the publisher.

Library of Congress Cataloging in Publication Data:

(Revised for vol. 3)
Main entry under title:

International handbook of education systems.
   Contents: v. 1. Europe and Canada/edited by Brian Holmes—v. 2. Sub-Saharan Africa/edited by John Cameron. North Africa and the Middle East/edited by Paul Hurst—v. 3. Asia, Australasia, and Latin American/edited by Robert Cowen and Martin McLean.
   1. Education—Dictionaries.   I. Holmes, Brian.
II. Cameron, John, 1914–.   III. Hurst, Paul.
LB15.158   370'.321   82-17375

British Library Cataloguing in Publication Data:

International handbook of education systems.
   Vol. 3 Asia, Australasia and Latin America
   I. Cowen, Robert   II. McLean, Martin
   370.19'5   LA132

ISBN 471 90214 4

Printed in Great Britain

Contents

Preface

Section A

Introduction	1
Afghanistan	11
Australia	37
Bangladesh	71
China	99
India	129
Indonesia	161
Japan	209
Nepal	251
New Zealand	279
Pakistan	301
Peninsular Malaysia	335
Sabah	389
Sarawak	421
Singapore	455
Sri Lanka	479
Thailand	515

Section B

Introduction	559
Argentina	565
Brazil	601
Chile	629
Colombia	655
Cuba	699
Mexico	723
Peru	755
Venezuela	807

Preface

The need for this Handbook of Educational Systems was suggested by the success and usefulness of the profiles of educational systems compiled over the last ten years by the British Council, which is the major organisation supported by the British Government to promote the knowledge of British life and culture worldwide through cultural and educational activities.

The main headings under which data have been classified and the sequence in which the headings have been placed are the same in each of the national profiles. Sub-headings in general follow the same pattern in each case but where apropriate the headings have been changed to meet the particular circumstances of the national system described. Diagrams giving a simplified picture of the structure of each educational system have been standardised (and taken from the IBE/Unesco International Yearbook of Education, XXXII, 1980) but simplified diagrams showing how education in each country is administered have not been standardised. Statistics have been drawn from the latest Unesco Statistical Yearbook and standardised to facilitate comparisons; more detailed information about any of the systems can be obtained from the Unesco Yearbook itself. Further more detailed information about the organisation of educational administration can usually be obtained from national Ministries of Education; the address of each Ministry of Education and the address of the national documentation centre are given in the previously mentioned IBE/Unesco International Yearbook of Education, XXXII, Paris, Unesco, 1980.

The Editors of this Handbook have adopted the framework or headings of the British Council profiles for all the profiles included here, as far as the content will allow, and the Editors have drawn upon a variety of sources for information, data and first-hand experience. Although no such Handbook can hope to be entirely comprehensive it is hoped that future editions will include more countries as well as revising and updating the profiles of countries included here.

Although every effort has been made to ensure the accuracy of the information in the Handbook, no responsibility is implied or accepted by the Editors, the British Council or the Publishers for any errors or omissions. The British Council, in particular, is not associated with any opinions or interpretations which may be expressed or implied in the Handbook.

The Editors and Publishers also wish to express their thanks to those who have helped in the compilation of this volume, and especially the Embassies or High Commissions of the following countries: Chile, Cuba, India, Malaysia, New Zealand, Singapore, Sri Lanka and Thailand.

The China report was commissioned from and written specifically for this volume by Ruth Hayhoe and the Cuba report was written by Martin McLean. Robert Cowen revised the report on Brazil and wrote the introduction to Latin America. Martin McLean wrote the introduction to Asia and Australasia and revised the other reports. Each report includes an introduction and comparative perspective on the national education system.

SECTION A

Introduction

EDUCATION AND THE WIDER CONTEXT

Asia and Australasia, taken together, lack the homogeneity of the other continents and sub-continents of the world. Europe, though divided into East and West by political ideology, has a common Graeco-Roman and Christian tradition and a contemporary shared experience of industrial urban society. In Africa there have been attempts to foster a continental identity based upon common needs associated with underdevelopment and a shared history of European intervention. Both North and South America have each a cohesion linked to common cultural origins and similar kinds of social and economic development. In Asia, even excluding the Middle East, there are major cultural divisions, especially related to religious affiliations but also affected by different kinds of historical external intervention; there are both countries which are among the richest and most industrialised in the world and those which are very poor and agricultural; and there are instances of almost every kind of political system and ideology.

Education systems are affected by each of these cultural, economic and political conditions, so there are in Asia and Australasia great variations in educational practice and examples of almost every kind of educational organisation which is found in the world.

Yet despite the great diversity of the region, certain strands can be identified which apply to groupings of countries both in terms of education and the wider political social and economic context. In terms of economic development three kinds of country can be identified. There are the high income, industrial urban countries - Japan, Australia and New Zealand. There is then a band of middle income countries which experienced considerable economic growth in the 1970s and, though often retaining an agricultural/rural base, have begun to industrialise. These countries include, in the survey, Malaysia, Thailand, Singapore and, more marginally, Indonesia. Other countries in this group are Taiwan, Hong Kong, South Korea and the Philippines. Finally, there are the low income countries which are primarily agricultural and rural in population such as China, India, Pakistan, Sri Lanka, Bangladesh, Nepal and Afghanistan.

Variations in level of economic development are reflected in the extent of educational provision. In the industrialised countries of Japan, Australia and New Zealand universal and compulsory primary and lower secondary education has been a reality for some time and all three countries are moving towards mass upper secondary (already almost universal in Japan) and higher education. In these countries the areas in which there is felt to be need for further expansion of provision are mainly pre-school education and post-compulsory vocational and technical education.

The middle income countries are near to attaining or, in some cases, have already achieved universal primary schooling. The main policy issue in terms of provision is the attainment of higher participation rates in secondary schooling. Popular pressure is largely behind this expansion with governments concerned to try to channel this demand into types of secondary schooling which are more diversified than the traditional academic model.

In the poorer countries, levels of provision vary considerably and are not always directly related to levels of national wealth. China, India and Sri Lanka have high levels of participation in primary schools while Pakistan, Afghanistan and Nepal still are very far from achieving universal primary education. Bangladesh has had fairly high proportional participation but this has declined in response to economic difficulties and population growth. The countries with high levels of proportional participation are facing issues of how to reach particularly disadvantaged groups in society, of how to improve the quality and of how to absorb the demand for secondary education from primary school leavers which the economy cannot easily absorb. Countries with low participation rates are concerned largely with mass education schemes and with choices over the priority to be given to expanding formal primary schooling or to developing non-formal adult education schemes.

The cultural diversity of Asian countries has an impact on education in two ways. Firstly, there are major religious traditions - Islam, Hinduism, Buddhism, Confucianism and Taoism - which have to be reconciled with the generally secularist tendencies of modern education systems. Secondly, there is diversity of languages, religious affiliations and ethnic identities within countries which have important educational implications.

The impact of the major religious traditions varies between countries. In Islamic cultures there are often separate Muslim schools and institutions of higher learning which co-exist with state schools. In some countries - particularly Pakistan - the content and aims of state education have been given a stronger Islamic orientation in recent years. In other countries the response to the Islamic revival has been to give aid to Muslim schools. However, there are still political conflicts between Muslim traditions and government aims to provide universal education, especially for women and girls, which has sometimes led to open conflict as in Afghanistan.

Conflict between other religious traditions and state education have been less acute though residual Confucian attitudes have been an important factor in debates about education in China. Hinduism in India and Sri Lanka as well as Buddhism in Thailand and Sri Lanka have been reconciled with relatively secular education systems but these religious affiliations still have some impact on attitudes to education. In Japan, where the education system is highly attuned to a wealthy, industrial and technological society, traditional values are still maintained, by overt policy action, especially in the strong moral education element of the curriculum. The nature of the relations between the traditional and the modern, however, varies between nations and depends upon the strength and character of the cultures of each country as well as their political ideologies.

The education systems of many Asian countries are also affected by deep internal cultural divisions. There is diversity based on language, religion and a more general ethnic identity. Few countries have one national language which is the mother tongue of the overwhelming majority of the population. Problems associated with language diversity are those associated with national unity, with the autonomy of minority groups and with access to education. In some countries, particularly India but also Sri Lanka, Malaysia and Singapore, no one language has achieved a clear and recognised dominance. In India the position of Hindi as the official language has been difficult to establish in the face of demands of other substantial language groups. In Sri Lanka and Malaysia there are numerically large groups using a language other than the majority language while in Singapore the former colonial language has an important economic role. In these countries linguistic diversity has been linked to political disunity.

Elsewhere in Asia and Australasia, minority languages are used by economically and often politically deprived groups. As education has spread more widely so the schools have to cater for more children whose mother tongues have a limited currency. There has also been a widespread concern in the 1970s to recognise the cultural identity of minority language groups in countries as widely separated as Afghanistan and Australia.

Generally the education systems of Asian countries have provided for linguistic diversity. In India and Pakistan and other large countries where linguistic groups are geographically separated many languages have been used as the medium of instruction in educational institutions though only the most important languages have been used at the higher levels of education. In Singapore or Malaysia separate schools in the same geographical areas have used different language media according to the background of the pupils. Even in Australia and New Zealand with strong assimilationist histories, minority languages have received more attention in recent years.

The use of several languages in educational institutions increases costs and strains on educational resources, especially where educational provision has for long been at a low level. It is also likely to intensify political disunity. But the demands of linguistic groups are so strong that rarely have governments been able to resist them.

Despite the several major religious traditions of Asia, internal religious divisions have not had a major impact on general educational provision in most countries except where the religious identity is part of a wider ethnic affiliation as with the Chinese groups of the southern Asian peninsulas. European Christian mission schools have generally become less important and have in some cases been absorbed by the state system. The strongest private Christian religious education system is in Australia rather than in the areas where European settlement was slight.

Ethnic identity has had important educational implications especially whee there has been historical immigration from other Asian areas. This applies particularly to the Chinese community in Malaysia and that of the Tamils in Sri Lanka. In both areas there has been political conflict and violence based upon ethnic identity and in both instances, the relative educational success of the minority has been a factor in the hostility to them. Malaysia has responded by measures to increase educational opportunities for the Malay majority but such actions, as with attempts to improve educational facilities for underprivileged castes in India, have brought accusations of discrimination. In other areas, especially Australia in regard to Aborigines, recognition of the role of education in improving the status of groups suffering from discrimination has come only more recently.

Cultural division in society which has educational implications in many parts of Asia is linked also to the impact of historical colonialism. British influences remain strong on the education systems of India, Pakistan, Bangladesh, Sri Lanka, Malaysia, Singapore, Australia and New Zealand while Indonesian education still has a residual Dutch character. Even the countries which were not direct colonies have experienced foreign educational imports including China, Japan, Thailand, Afghanistan and Nepal.

This foreign influence is of two kinds. There is a continuing impact of the language and knowledge of the educational exporter. Educational institutions and philosophies have also been transferred. Language influences can be seen in the continued use of English as the medium of education in some higher level institutions in India, Pakistan, Bangladesh and Sri Lanka. In these countries, however, most education at most levels is carried out in indigenous languages while the dependence on knowledge created in the west is again found mainly in higher level institutions. In the smaller countries, the use of the former colonial language is more widespread. English is used in upper secondary schooling in Malaysia while the majority of schools at every level in Singapore has English medium.

The widespread use of English cannot be linked purely to colonial influences. English has gained at the expense of Chinese and Malay as the medium of instruction in schools in Singapore. This can be associated, both in Singapore and in other Asian countries, with the value of English in commercial and industrial life.

The other former colonial influences can be seen in educational philosophies, curricula and institutional arrangements. Educational philosophies in England traditionally have given great prestige to the humanities and the pure sciences and have often dismissed technical and vocational education as mere 'training'. Furthermore, importance is given to the specialised study of a limited range of subjects at upper secondary and higher education levels.

These English approaches can still be seen to be dominant in the former British controlled areas of Asia and Australasia. The humanities still have the highest status at upper secondary and higher education level in India, Pakistan, Bangladesh, Sri Lanka, Malaysia and Singapore. They also attract proportionally higher numbers of students. Early specialisation, similar to the English 'A' level upper secondary system is common in these countries. Such biases are seen to be antithetical to the development of broader courses including more technical and practical elements which the governments of these countries perceive to be important for more balanced national development.

Formal institutional links with Britain have been severed in most countries though in the smaller states such as Malaysia and Singapore there are still vestiges of the influence of the English School Examination Boards and these countries still send many students to British universities. In all the areas which were once under British control, however, the educational institutions have characteristics of their English counterparts. The English academic grammar school with its stringent selection procedures and the English university with traditions of autonomy and of single subject courses often remain the model. In several countries there are considerable selection hurdles placed in the way of those wishing to enter lower or upper secondary education. Technical institutions struggle to gain equal status. The function and responsibilities of universities, especially in the less developed countries, remain open to question.

Other Western influences, particularly from the USA and Western Europe, can be seen. But the extent of the surviving British colonial impact can be illustrated by comparison with countries such as Thailand where there was never Western colonial control and where the education system has a more diversified character.

The political and administrative background of Asia and Australasian countries which has relevance for education varies considerably. There are communist, Marxist-Leninist régimes particularly, among the countries of this survey, China and, so some degree, Afghanistan. There are authoritarian régimes in which parliamentary government has been suspended or weakened and there are parliamentary systems of government especially in countries such as India, Japan, Australia, New Zealand.

Communist governments have been noteworthy in attempts to spread mass education rapidly particularly to achieve the ideological mobilisation which is seen to be essential to socialist transformation. They have also given emphasis to a polytechnical, work-orientated study, and to ideological elements in the curriculum. These tendencies may differ in degree rather than kind from those of non-communist countries where the spread of education is seen to contribute to social transformation, where the aim is to relate education to local economic life and where the content of education is seen to contribute to the achievement of a strong national identity. Societal rather than individualist aims predominate in most countries though perhaps less so in the more democratic countries such as India and Australia. Some of the ethnically divided countries with a colonial history such as India, Singapore and Malaysia perceive a need to create a stronger national identity through education which, as yet, has been difficult to achieve.

Most of the countries in the survey have centralised systems of educational administration though there are differences between those countries where the administration is centred on the state in a federal structure and those which are nationally centralised. There are few examples of the kind of local control which has typified for instance the education systems of the United States, Britain or Denmark.

The control of education by central government in the capital city has been the rule in most of the countries in this survey. The Ministry of Education raises and allocates finance, appoints and places teachers and decides the subjects and content of the curriculum. This system is often thought to lead to favouritism in the distribution of educational resources to central and urban areas to the neglect of rural and remote regions. It is also thought to lead to a uniformity and inflexibility which inhibits programmes to make education more responsive to local social, economic and cultural needs. In several countries there were movements in the 1970s to devolve some powers of educational decision to local authorities.

Yet in some of the major countries of this survey national governments have little power in educational matters. This applies particularly in India and Australia where control over schools is exercised very largely at State rather than Federal level. In both countries, federal government has attempted to intervene to achieve greater consistency in standards, provision and policies between states. Where there is a high degree of regional control over education, as in these two countries, there are attempts to strengthen rather than devolve the powers of the national government.

Other contextual features, apart from the economic, cultural historical and political, have had an important effect on education systems of the countries of Asia and Australasia. Size of population and territory have had important influences. Asia contains the two most populous countries in the world – China and India – which differ so much in political ideology and culture. Yet their very size of population has made it difficult to achieve consistency and coherence in educational matters given the range of interests that such large populations contain. In India this has resulted in enormous variations in educational provision and great obstacles to radical reform. In China it has led to several violent swings in educational policy since the Revolution in the late 1940s.

In other countries such as Singapore or Hong Kong the relatively small and compact size of the territory has allowed for closely-knit education systems with less variation in quality associated with larger countries even though the ethnic diversity and cultural allegiances within the population have been given educational recognition. In few countries in Asia covered in this survey the populations are so small that the whole range of educational institutions from pre-school and higher education levels cannot be provided as is the case in some of the island states of the Pacific and Caribbean.

In several countries of Asia and Australasia, geographical factors are obstacles to the achievement of full educational provision. Even wealthy countries such as Australia and New Zealand have difficulties in making full and adequate provision for students in remote areas. In Nepal and Afghanistan the scattered nature of the population has proved a major barrier to the achievement of widespread education and helps to explain why these countries have among the lowest rates of participation in education in the world. Such geographical constraints on the spread of education are difficult to overcome using conventional education methods.

TRENDS IN EDUCATION

Despite the diversity of cultures, traditions and economic conditions in the countries of Asia and Australasia, certain common trends in educational development can be discerned. In the 1960s and early 1970s expansionist policies were widely adopted in countries of many different types. In the late 1970s the pace of growth slowed down, usually by deliberate government decision, and the aims of increasing educational provision on a wide front were replaced by more limited and selective objectives.

The way that this change occurred and the form it took differed in the various countries of the region. In some of the poorer countries, government endorsement of expansionist aims continued to be as strong as before but the actual achievement was reduced. In others, there was a shift in priorities from general education to specific technical preparation at particular levels. Yet in most areas there was a concern for quality rather than quantity. There was a bias towards disadvantaged minorities instead of the majority of the population. There was emphasis on pre-school education and in post-compulsory vocational training rather than on higher education.

The expansionist aims of the 1960s and early 1970s can be associated with the adoption of beliefs that education was a fundamental human right, that there should be equality of educational opportunity and that increased provision of education would bring economic benefits to the whole society. The international endorsements of such conceptions could be seen in statements such as the United Nations Declaration of Human Rights of 1948 and the report of the UNESCO Regional Conference at Karachi in 1959.

The implementation of these aims took different forms in the various countries. In the non-industrial countries there was an expansion of primary education so that in most of the poorer countries of this survey a majority of the age group were in primary schools and most had achieved or were near to achieving universal primary schooling. Only a few countries such as Afghanistan, Nepal and Pakistan failed to keep up with this movement. By the 1970s lower secondary education expanded in these non-industrial states to cater for around half the age group and there was proportional growth in higher education though it was still only available for a minority.

These developments to a large extent had been a response to popular demand for education as an avenue to social mobility. But governments responded by increasing funds for education which grew both as a proportion of total government expenditure and of Gross National Product. The achievement of political independence from colonial rule in many areas between the late 1940s and early 1960s intensified this process.

In the richer countries such as Japan, Australia and New Zealand where universal primary schooling was already a reality in the 1940s, expansion focused on secondary and higher education. As lower secondary education became universal, questions arose about how to adapt traditional, selective and academic secondary schools to cater for mass enrolment. The academic orientation remained in Australasian schools particularly at upper secondary level and relatively small proportions of pupils stayed beyond the age of 16. In Japan the secondary schools were more genuinely comprehensive in that the vast majority of the age group stayed to the end of secondary school. But differential status between different schools developed which the use of entrance examinations intensified. There was selection in relation to schools of the same kind rather than between schools of different types or within each school.

In these richer countries, higher education enrolments expanded greatly especially in the late 1960s and 1970s to reach between 25% and 40% of the relevant age group in 1980. In each of these countries — Australia, New Zealand and Japan — this expansion was achieved without radically changing the character of universities as elitist academic institutions concerned with the furtherance of knowledge. In Australia and Japan, however, non-university higher education institutions were set up or expanded to absorb some of the increased numbers of students while in New Zealand, as in many of the non-industrial countries of Asia, there were high drop-out rates. In Japan as in India differentiation in the popular esteem of various universities occurred. Selection within higher education occurred by some means in most countries.

The end of the expansionist era in most countries occurred towards the end of the 1970s. It was signalled by a change of governmental intentions rather than those of educational consumers. Generally, and especially in poorer countries, popular demand for education has continued though it has been modified, at least at lower levels, in the richer and some of the middle income countries by sharply falling birth rates.

Changes in governmental intentions could be measured by the falling or static proportions of government expenditure allocated to education. They are less easy to explain. There has been a loss of the confidence among policy makers that educational expansion would stimulate economic growth as was widely accepted in the 1960s. There has been alarm at the growth of demand for education − whether at primary level linked to rising population in some of the poorest countries or at secondary or higher level in countries which have already achieved widely available basic education. In both richer and poorer countries there has been concern about the content and quality of education and about the employability of school and higher education graduates.

There has been greater emphasis in most countries on improving teacher education or the school curriculum. There has been a strong trend towards more technical or vocational education in most countries both richer and poorer. This is associated with underemployment of those prepared by traditional academic means for older professions and occupations, with the need for skilled manual workers and technicians in many less-industrialised countries and with youth unemployment linked to the world economic recession in some industrial countries.

However, educational retrenchment has been a worldwide phenomenon since the late 1970s. In some parts of Asia, the slowing down of expansion has been less acute than in the world generally. This applies particularly in the south and south east Asia group of countries where economic growth has been higher than in any other region of the world in the 1970s. In Japan, Singapore or Malaysia expansionist attitudes still remain. But expansion in the 1960s and early 1970s created popular demand for education which cannot be fully met even in this rapidly developing countries.

Despite the more limited and restrictionist attitudes to educational expansion which have become more prevalent since the late 1970s, there has been increased concern for the education of some groups in society. Pre-school education has developed in most countries even though provision is very limited in the poorer states. In all countries there has been expressed concern for the education of disadvantaged minorities. In non-industrial countries the focus has been on providing education for the very poorest groups who often experience social prejudice such as the discriminated castes in India. Minorities who are socially distinguished and discriminated against in the richer countries such as the aborigines of Australia and the Maoris and Pacific Islanders of New Zealand have also been the centre for educational policy makers concerns. Also, in the richer countries there has been greater attention to the educational needs of physically and mentally disabled students.

The priority given to these groups does point out further

the retreat that has occurred in most countries' commitments to expanding provision for the majority of the population. Most governments have not yet found effective ways of managing educational retrenchment.

Afghanistan

CONTENTS

1	Geography	12
2	Population	15
3	Society and Culture	15
4	History and Politics	16
5	The Economy	17
6	The Education System	18
7	Educational Administration	25
8	Educational Fiannce	25
9	Development and Planning of the Education System	26
10	The System in Operation	26
11	Trends, Problems and Possibilities	28

Afghanistan is economically underdeveloped, Islamic in religion but otherwise culturally diverse. These characteristics are shared to a large extent with the neighbouring countries to the South, South-West and South East. The education system of Afghanistan reflects these economic, religious and cultural conditions and also has much in common with those of her southern neighbours. Educational provision falls behind in international norms as in other parts of western Asia. There is a continuing tension, expressed particularly in educational questions, between secular and Western orientated values and traditional beliefs, especially Islamic. Furthermore, educational policy and provision has to take account of considerable cultural (especially linguistic), social and geographical differences within the country.

But Afghanistan and its education system also differ in significant ways from its neighbours. Participation rates at primary and secondary school level have been among the lowest if not the lowest in the world. This is a product not only of poverty or, for instance, Islamic suspicion of female education since Bangladesh, which is equally Moslem and even poorer, has much higher rates of participation in education. The very low rates of access do seem to be related to the scattered nature of the population and the prevalent pastoral way of life. These obstacles are substantial and not easily surmounted.

Unlike the countries to the South-East, Afghanistan has not had a history of Western colonial control, though it has been a theatre of great power rivalry. The education system was not based on that of one European country though there were considerable foreign influences - French, German, British and Turkish since before the Second World War, America since 1945 and Soviet and Eastern European especially since 1979. There is less of an entrenched impact of any one foreign country on the education system to inhibit reform but the range of external influences tends to rob the education system of coherence.

The 1979 revolutions and Soviet intervention have produced some major changes affecting education. Contacts with the West have come to an end. Soviet and Eastern European educational practices have been introduced. In line with this there has been a greater emphasis on the expansion of mass basic education and of education related to productive activities.

On the other hand, the Marxist revolutionary government has reaffirmed the importance of Islamic beliefs in Afghanistani society and has given greater recognition in education to the diversity of languages used in the country.

As long as the Civil War persists, possibilities of educational expansion are limited. Hostilities have destroyed many schools or have prevented them from operating.

Mass education programmes have been seen as threats to Islamic values and have been opposed by those who resist the government. In the short term and in quantitive terms there has been clearly a decline in educational provision.

1 GEOGRAPHY

Topography

Afghanistan is a mainly mountainous country, remote from the sea, whose comparatively sparse population depends for its basic subsistence on an unreliable annual rainfall. Eighty-five percent of the people are engaged in agriculture and there is no significant industry. Its mineral resources are mainly too remote to be exploited profitably; exports of fruit, karakul pelts, hand-knotted carpets and natural gas account for most of its meagre foreign currency earnings. Poverty is general, but the necessities of life are available and cheap by Western standards.

The area of 250,000 square miles which comprises Afghanistan straddles the 700 mile long Hindu Kush range. The country shares common boundaries with the USSR, Iran, Pakistan and, for a short distance, China (an arrangement of the nineteenth century statesman to prevent the British and Russian empires from touching at any point). The country's three main rivers have their source about the mid-point of the Hindu Kush range where the peaks start to decline westwards from an average altitude of 13,000 - 20,000 feet (3,962 - 6,096 metres) to the low hills around Herat; the Kabul river flows to the east mostly through wide cultivated valleys among the southern offshoots

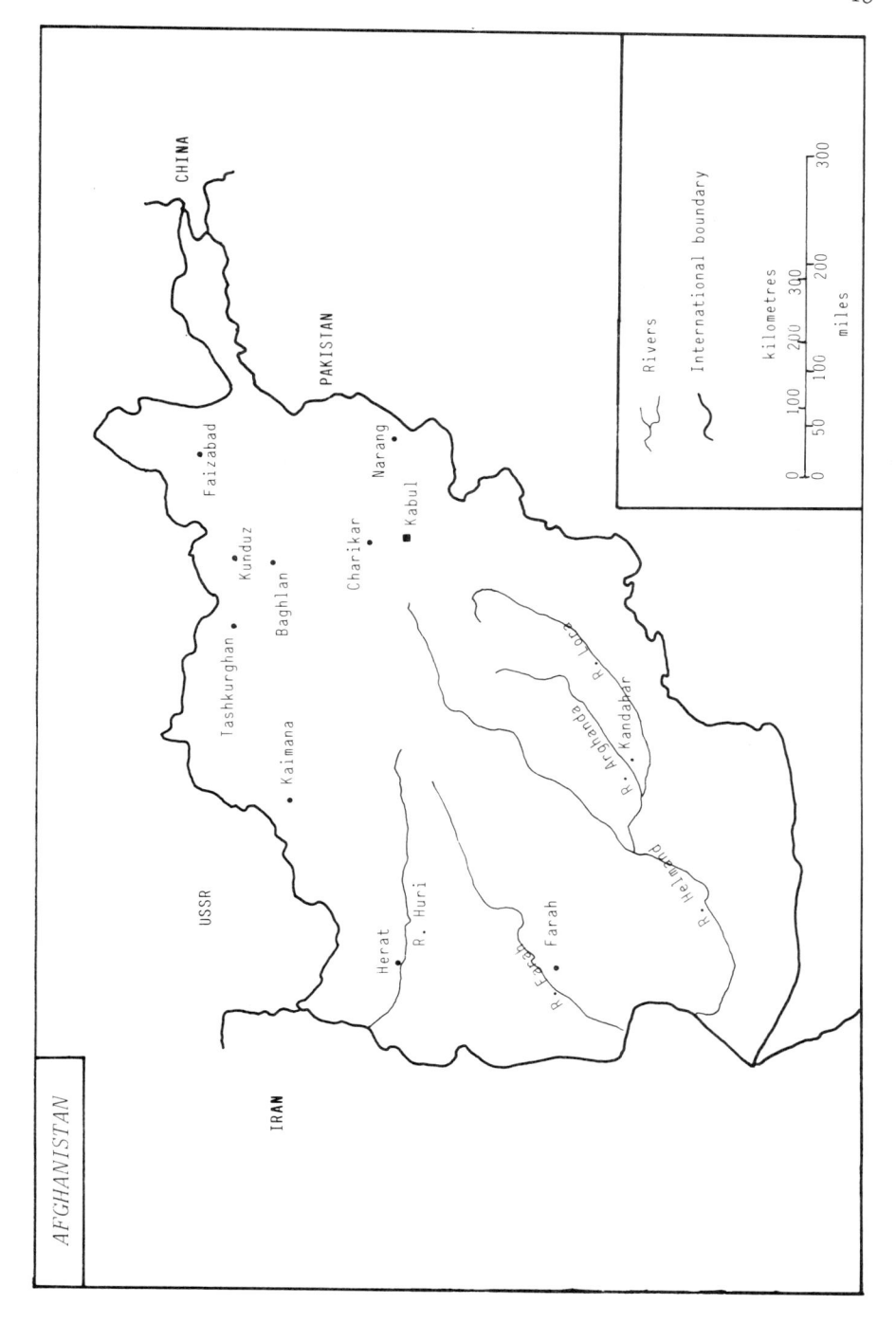

of the Hindu Kush before joining the Indus at Attock; the Helmand river flows south-west to lose itself in the vast desert that Afghanistan shares with Iran and Pakistan; the Hari Rud flows west through the fertile plains around Herat until it too loses itself in the desert beyond the frontier. In the north the Oxus forms for much of its length the boundary between Afghanistan and the USSR, and a broad plain consisting mainly of loess deposits or desert intervenes between the river and the mountains.

Climate

The climate varies between alpine or sub-arctic in the high north-east to total desert on the banks of the lower Oxus and Helmand rivers; but most of the country enjoys a dry continental climate which is particularly favourable to the cultivation of fruit and vegetables. The average annual rainfall of only 10 inches falls mainly on the steep slopes of the mountains, from which most of it is swiftly borne away before it can be used for cultivation. Slowly melting snow, however, provides some water throughout the year. The importance of an adequate annual snowfall can be understood from the catastrophic effect of two consecutive years of meagre snowfall in 1970-72 on agricultural production and animal husbandry, when large flocks of goats and sheep had to be slaughtered for lack of grazing.

Agriculture depends to a large extent upon man-made irrigation schemes tapping river water or underground sources. Little more than the usable land is under cultivation, 5.3 m of this being irrigated. There is evidence that the destruction of irrigation systems by invaders may have helped to turn south-west Afghanistan into a desert. Gradual deforestation must also have had its effect on the climate.

Fruit, rice, bread and tea form the staple diet, meat (a luxury for 90% of the people) and fat being provided by flocks of fat-tailed sheep. Afghanistan is virtually self-supporting except that in recent years wheat and sugar have had to be imported.

Communications

The Hindu Kush provides the only practicable access between Central Asia and India and from time immemorial its passes attracted the trader and conqueror. European development of maritime trade routes in the seventeenth century rapidly diminished their importance and today Afghanistan has no transit trade. Hard-top roads were built to link Kabul with Iran, Pakistan (providing a route for Afghan exports to India and access to Karachi port) and, northward across the Hindu Kush through a tunnel at 11,000 feet (3,353 metres), with the USSR. Though much of the country is still far from a metalled road the reduction in travel time between the main centres greatly assisted the political cohesion of the country and the distribution of commodities. Outside the main towns the telephone is virtually restricted to the needs of the local government authorities. Radio, on the other hand, is a great unifying factor and potential educator. Proposals to introduce television have not reached a serious stage. Soviet television can sometimes be received in the northern town of Kunduz; Soviet radio broadcasts in Persian and Tajik are received in many areas even more clearly than Radio Afghanistan from Kabul.

2 POPULATION

The population of Afghanistan was $15\frac{1}{2}$ million according to the 1979 census and is remarkable for the ethnic and linguistic diversity which it owes to the accidents of geography and history. The principal groups are: Pathans (perhaps 5% of the population), Pushto speaking, settled and nomad, concentrated in the south and east, with large scattered settlements elsewhere; Tajiks (30% of the population?), Persian speaking farmers, merchants and artisans; Hazaras ($\frac{1}{2}$-1 million?) with Mongol features that indicate a link with the hordes that garrisoned Afghanistan in the thirteenth century; the Turkic speaking Uzbeks ($\frac{1}{2}$-1 million?), horse and sheep breeders; and Turkomen (200,000?), stock breeders and carpet weavers, many of whom migrated across the Oxus in the face of nineteenth century Russian expansion or the consolidation of Bolshevik power in the 1920s.

Language

In these days, although over 30 languages (not dialects) of Indo-Iranian, Turkic, Semitic and Dravidean origin continue to be spoken in homes and villages, most of the population is fluent in Pushto and Dari (as the Persian language is called in Afghanistan). Both languages use a modified Arabic script, are the medium of administration and are the only native languages to be taught in schools. Pushto owes its status as the official language of the State to the numerical and political ascendancy of the Pathans. The Persian language is far more widely used and is one of the unifying factors in modern Afghanistan, due partly no doubt to the wealth of its literature which is a mine of quotations that come easily to the lips of a population which is over 85% illiterate.

3 SOCIETY AND CULTURE

Religion

Virtually all Afghans are Muslims, of whom 75-90% are Sunnis of the Hanafi school. The rest are Shiahs. In the past enmity between Sunnis and Shiahs was so keen that the Sunni Uzbeks of Kunduz, for instance, felt justified in capturing Hazaras to sell as slaves in Bokhara. Though sectarian bias is still latent, tolerance has been the general rule. Religious feeling is strong everywhere, and except among the small educated class, the veiling of women is still prevalent. With the introduction of Western-style education the mosque schools have lost their importance, but theology and Arabic (the language of the Koran) are still essential elements of the State school syllabus. Religion is a major factor in the Civil War since 1979 though government recognises the central place of Islam in the country.

Social System

Afghan society has been tribal rather than feudal. The main element was a fairly democratic structure of tribal and village headmen, who are responsible to the government authorities for local administration, settlement of disputes etc. The legal system was based on the Sharia (religious law) modified or extended by customary law and Western legal practices. Emancipation of women is encouraged officially but is restricted outside Kabul by conservative feeling. There is a conflict between the general awareness of the benefits of education on the one hand and, on the other, the low standard of schooling and the lack of jobs for graduates. A very small but sophisticated ruling class united by ties of blood retained power. A commercial and professional middle class emerged in the towns.

4 HISTORY AND POLITICS

The State of Afghanistan had its origins in the assumption by Ahmed Shah Abdali in 1747 of the hegemony of the Pathan tribes after the death of the Persian monarch Nadir Shah Afshar for whom he and his followers had been fighting. The Koh-i-Nur diamond, which he extracted from the Persian treasury at the time, later passed via Ranjit Singh to the British crown. He adopted the name Durrani for his tribe, and one or other of two branches of the tribe sat on the throne of Kabul until 1973. Insurrections of dissident chieftains were, however, only finally put down by the Amir Abdul Rahman Khan (1880-1901), by which time the encroaching empires of Russia and British India agreed to regard Afghanistan as a buffer state and demarcated its frontiers to their mutual satisfaction. To secure the compliance of Afghanistan's rulers the British twice invaded the country in the first and second Afghan Wars (1839/42) ending with the disastrous Retreat (1879/1881) famous for General Roberts' march from Kabul to Kandahar. After the Russian invervention in Panjdeh (the 'Panjdeh Incident' of 1885) the Amir ceded his control of foreign affairs to the British in return for subsidies. The third Afghan War (1919) led to Afghanistan's full independence. From 1926 the Amir Amunullah introduced too early a drastic programme of modernisation. The opposition of conservative and religious elements to his plans led to his downfall, and the lessons of this event have retarded the pace of reform up to the present time.

The downfall of the monarchy was brought about by its corruption, its weak administration and general unrest. The new President was a cousin and brother-in-law of the deposed king and the bloodless coup took place whilst the monarch was in Italy. President Daoud had the support of the army and in fact could not have carried out the coup without their support.

In April 1978, Daoud was overthrown and killed in a coup by the Armed Forces Revolutionary Council. This Council was expanded into the Revolutionary Council including members of the pro-communist and previously banned People's Democratic Party. Taraki became Prime Minister and later President. Closer relations with the Soviet Union developed and programmes of land reform and nationalisation began.

Between March and December 1979 there was further political instability and a civil war culminating in Soviet occupation in December 1979. Amin became Prime Minister in March. Heavy fighting began between the Army and Moslem rebels who declared a holy war against the régime. By August 20% of the population was under rebel control with a further 30% in disputed areas. On December 27th Amin, like Taraki, died in a coup which installed Balrak Karmal as Prime Minister. The coup was accompanied by an invasion of 85,000 Soviet troops who were deployed against rebels in a Civil War that showed no sign of abating by September 1982.

The Amin and Karmal régimes proposed socialist policies though the 1980 Constitution - together with other government statements - have reaffirmed official respect for Islam and greater recognition of cultural minorities, especially linguistic. Attempts to improve the position of women - especially in literacy campaigns - have, however, intensified the opposition to the régime.

After the 1978 coup, relations with communist countries strengthened while those with Western countries cooled. After the Soviet invasion international recognition and support for the Afghanistan régime has practically disappeared. Aid and trade since 1980 has come almost entirely from Eastern bloc countries.

5 THE ECONOMY

Development before 1978 was characterised by a lack of coordination of either aims or resources. It was President Daoud's declared policy to continue the development programme inaugurated during his tenure of office as Prime Minister in the first and second five-year economic plans, by building upon the 'infrastructural projects' completed then, mainly in the fields of agriculture, mining and industry. Reforms were initiated in the field of finance to encourage investment, protect local industry and enforce collection of taxes. Attempts were made to limit the widespread practice of smuggling.

Afghanistan has a largely agricultural economy although natural gas is found in the north of the country and exported almost entirely to the Soviet Union. There are large unexploited iron and copper deposits, the former in Hajigak and the latter in Logar Valley. A feasibility study was undertaken for the exploitation of both iron and copper; communication with these two areas is, of course, the problem.

Before 1979 the Karakul exports (Persian lamb furs) went almost entirely to the London auction markets and the export of dried fruit and nuts and fresh fruit were the largest export commodities. Raw cotton took on increasing importance before 1979. The British Government gave aid for the development of cotton processing.

Western involvement in the economic development ceased after the Soviet invasion. Foreign assistance since then has come entirely from Eastern bloc sources though economic development inevitably has suffered from the ravages of the war.

6 THE EDUCATION SYSTEM

Aims, Objectives and Implementation

Sher Ali, ruler of Afghanistan from 1869-79, is credited with founding the first State school in the country (half military and with courses in English) at Bala-i-Hisar, the citadel of Kabul. Previously the only education available had been the religious instruction given by the Mullas in *maktabs* and *madressahs* attached to the mosques, an education characterised by rigid orthodoxy and absence of intellectual enquiry. In Central Asia generally knowledge of the West and Western science was extremely limited before the second half of the nineteenth century. From the mid-century onwards British military intervention in Kabul and the modernisation with mainly Russian help of the armies of the neighbouring states of Persia, Khiva and Bokhara convinced the rulers of Afghanistan that their independence must depend upon their adopting Western military technology.

The name of Mahmoud Tarzi is indissolubly linked with the emergence of modern Afghanistan. Exiled to Turkey for 20 years he returned (1902) upon the accession of the Amir Habibullah, and as leader of an enlightened group known as the Young Afghans he championed the causes of Afghan nationalism and modernism. He founded the country's first newspaper, to promulgate his views and to educate the ruling class. He claimed that the neglect of education and science was the cause of Afghanistan's decline; that Afghanistan must not only borrow from Europe for purposes of defence but use European cultural, scientific and administrative ideas as the basis for its own development. In accordance with these views the Amir Habibullah inaugurated the present Afghan educational system with the foundation of Habibiya College (for boys only) in 1904. English and Urdu were the two foreign languages in the curriculum, and the school boasted the first public library.

The Department of Education was founded in 1913 and attempted to broaden the curriculum of the traditional schools, train elementary school teachers and issue uniform textbooks. These innovations and particularly the teaching of English and other modern subjects met with stiff resistance from the religious establishment. The succeeding Amir, Amanullah, founded three more modern schools in Kabul, Istiqlal (on the French model), Nejat (on the German model) and in 1927, Ghazi (where classes were taught in English). In 1921 a programme was started for sending graduates of these schools abroad for higher study; the first girls school (Malalai) was opened in the same year, under the patronage of Mrs Mahmoud Tarzi and the Queen. The problem of reconciling modern education with the tenets of Islam, as seen by the traditionalists, was not resolved, however, at the time of Amanullah's fall in 1929, and in the constitution of 1931 Nadir Shah upheld the central traditionalist element in the curriculum which his predecessors had tried to diminish. The King nevertheless supported education as paving the way to the people's acceptance of social reforms. What was to become the first faculty of Kabul University, the School of Medicine, was opened in 1932 under the supervision of French and Turkish professors.

If education was imported, at first as a prerequisite of military power and independence, then as the basis of modernisation, it was also seen as a means of promoting national unity. Very slowly during the succeeding years modern education was introduced to the towns and villages, unified textbooks were distributed to control the contents of the syllabus and the study of Pushto was introduced with the intention (never realised) that it should become the national language, replacing Persian.

The first Five Year Plan (1957-62) was aimed at the expansion of literacy (85% estimated illiterate even today) and primary education (the universal right to primary schooling confirmed in the 1931 and 1964 constitutions is still far from being achieved). The second Plan (1962-67) was supposed to give more emphasis to secondary and vocational education in order to provide the technicians and managers needed for economic development as well as to provide teachers for the primary stage. In the third Plan (1967-72) it was hoped to make the connection between education and manpower needs more realistic at the same time as improving the quality of education generally.

In January 1975 a new Education Policy was promulgated. Briefly the aims and objectives of the education reform were:

(i) to improve the quantity and quality of education by means of reforming the educational structure and creating conditions for its better organisation and coordination

(ii) to relate education to manpower training and requirements

(iii) to prepare the ground for the acquisition of permanent literacy during the period of primary education.

Great emphasis was laid on using education as a means of developing national unity and patriotism; of furthering the aims of an independent republican Afghanistan; of ending social discrimination and inequalities; of inculcating a respect for work etc. Much was made of the need to eradicate illiteracy, to develop new skills and training, to develop a questioning, scientific approach and to relate the school curriculum, especially in the new vocational secondary schools, to the local manpower needs and employment opportunities.

A new education policy was introduced in December 1979. Some elements were a development of the 1975 policy. But four striking changes were introduced:

(i) universal primary education was to be introduced immediately so that all 7 year olds would be in school in 1980. The length of full schooling was reduced from 12 years to 10 partly to accommodate expansion in numbers in the first grade

(ii) adult literacy schemes were to be expanded rapidly to cater for 8 million people

(iii) all secondary schools would have a vocational as well as general educational function. Separate vocational secondary schools would disappear

(iv) education would be available through the medium of five Afghanistan languages.

Primary

Primary education, both before and since 1979, has begun at the age of 7. Before 1979 there were no examinations up to Grade 4. Examinations in Grades 4-6 were taken by students with a 75% attendance rate. There was then a concours system whereby pupils completing primary education would sit an examination for selection to secondary education. This system was rather similar to that of schools in france before the 1960s.

Since 1979 there has been a movement towards Soviet-style school assessment and selection. Pupils in each class are given grades from 1 (poor) to 5 (very good). An average of 2 is required for promotion to the next grade. But all pupils completing the primary cycle successfully must be admitted to secondary education if they so wish. A provision was made in 1980 that pupils from disadvantaged areas could telescope four years primary schooling into two and then enter secondary schools.

Primary school buildings were modest and limited before the Civil War. Buildings of sun-baked brick with mud roofs were erected by local efforts or with Ministry assistance. But classes also were often held in Mosques and religious officials were frequently used as teachers even in State schools. Before 1979 classes were often held out of doors. The destruction of school buildings during the Civil War has limited physical provision even further.

Before 1979, the medium of instruction was either Pushto or Dari depending on the locality. The other language was a compulsory subject. The subjects of the primary school included the Koran, Theology, Arithmetic, Geometry, Geography, History, Drawing, Handicrafts, Calligraphy and Physical Education.

Since 1979 there has been a movement to mother tongue instruction. Primary education is to be given in one of five languages - Dari, Pushto, Uzbake, Turkmani or Baluchi. New curricula are being introduced systematically starting with Grade 1 and new textbooks are being prepared in the various languages. More emphasis is given in the curriculum to the practical implications of schooling for local economic life.

Secondary

Secondary education is administered centrally by the Department of Secondary Education in the Ministry. Principals and Vice-Principals are in charge of the administration of each school. Students may be admitted to Grade 7 after the successful completion of primary education provided they are not over the age of 17. A student who fails the end of year examination twice running or is over age (i.e. 23 years old in Grade 12) may be expelled.

The language of instruction is Pushto or Dari according to the area where the school is situated. Two of the original modern schools still teach some subjects in Grades 10-12 in French (Istiqlal Lycee) or German (Nejat Lycee) with the help of native speakers supplied by France and West Germany. These two schools have been recently rebuilt on a lavish scale by the governments concerned and attract pupils from the 'best families'.

The syllabus up to 1978 was as follows: Grades 7-9 in boys' and girls' schools studied Koran, Theology, Dari, Pushto, mathematics, history, manual work, chemistry, physics, biology, Arabic, foreign language English (plus French at Istiqlal and German at Nejat), economics, Geography. Koran and Arabic were dropped from Grade 10 onwards, as was manual work. Geology was added in Grade 10, religion and logic in Grade 12 (though the latter was apparently not considered suitable for girls). Girls did needlework in Grades 7-9, home economics in grades 9-12 and psychology (not suitable for boys, apparently) in Grade 12). There were 35 periods a week of 45 minutes each.

To utilize the available school buildings to the full, one set of students and teachers works a morning shift and another set an afternoon shift. Schools which include all kinds of educational establishments from primary to higher education in areas of Afghanistan which enjoy intense summer heat and mild winters have their annual three-month vacation in the summer and those which enjoy intense winter cold and moderately hot summers have their annual three-month holiday in the winter. This arrangement helps to conserve fuel and obviate the need for heating or air-conditioning. For instance schools in Kabul being in a 'cold weather area' are closed for the three severest winter months, and the school and university year starts shortly after the Afghan New Year holiday (Nauroz on 21 March).

The 1975 reform abolished the middle school and absorbed the first two years into primary school and the third year into secondary school. This extended secondary education from three to four years. Three types of secondary school were introduced: the general secondary lycee (largely the traditional academic type), vocational schools (agricultural, commercial or technical) and the Islamic Lycee for would-be theological students. Selection for the different type of school depended upon the results of the concours examination at the end of primary level. Special care was to be taken to ensure that there were no more academic lycees than the economy could maintain - an obvious attempt to cut down the number of unemployed high school graduates - and specialisation into science and the social sciences was to take place in Grade 12.

The introduction of vocational schools was an attempt to relate what goes on in the secondary schools with the projected manpower needs of the country. Much was made of the fact that graduates from these schools would be able to get jobs immediately. In order to increase the number of vocational schools a number of existing lycees were to be converted. Apart from straightforward agricultural schools there were to be veterinary schools, irrigation schools, agricultural machinery and equipment repairing schools and land survey schools. Under the general umbrella of technical schools there were to be technological, mechanical, textile, nursing and public health schools, and among the commercial schools will be schools specialising in public administration, accounting and secretarial work.

In all cases the curricula was either modified or introduced so as to conform to 'the economic, social, cultural and political needs of the society'.

The 1975 'Educational Reform' document stated that although 'there are many so-called lycees in every province, in reality they are only a name. Most of them are without adequate buildings, sufficient equipment, laboratories, and other necessary facilities and materials. Above all they are without qualified teachers'. The result is that school leavers reach the job market 'without adequate education and knowledge'. Without reform and without conversion of provincial lycees into vocational schools between 70-72% of the school leavers in 1977/78 would be unemployed (i.e. 65,500 students). The proposals were therefore for 50% in lycees for at least the next four years when the situation will be reviewed.

The 1975 reforms were far from being implemented at the time of the 1978 revolution. The 1979 reform changed much of what was proposed in 1975. The whole period of schooling was reduced from 12 grades to 10 and secondary education was to consist of two cycles - one of four years and the second of two years. Separate vocational secondary schools were to be abolished in favour of a vocational/technical element in all secondary schools - in line with Soviet practice.

The Afghanistan government claimed that the content covered in 10 grades of schooling will be greater rather than less than was available in 12 grades. The main addition is to be the vocational/technical courses though these programmes, it is admitted, are being introduced only slowly.

Teachers and Teacher Education

Teacher training courses are organised separately for each level of schooling.

Primary teacher training is provided in nine training colleges throughout the country. The course is for one year at Grade 13 level and is entirely professional.

Middle school teacher training is provided in five Higher Teachers' Colleges throughout the country. The course is for two years at the Grade 13 and 14 level and is partly professional, partly academic. Higher teachers' colleges are in joint institutions with primary training colleges with the exception of the institutions in Kabul which are separately housed. Entry to both the primary training colleges and higher teachers' colleges is by a common examination open to graduates of Grade 12.

Training for teachers in upper secondary schools is provided at the Faculties of Letters, Science and Theology in the University of Kabul. The course is for four years at Grade 13-16 level. Training is also provided for school supervisors and administrators. Selected graduates of higher teachers' colleges are admitted to the last two years of the Faculty of Letters' courses. Entry to the course at Grade 13 is by normal university entrance examination.

Teacher education training is provided at the Academy for Teacher Educators, Kabul. The course is for one year at the post-graduate level, Grade 17. On graduation educators are posted to the provincial training colleges.

Science supervisors are trained at the Science Centre, established in 1970 by the Ministry of Education in Kabul. Courses last for a few months. Graduates are sent to provincial Directorates of Education and provided with kits for demonstrating scientific experiments. Most teacher training institutions in the country have a 'laboratory school' under their direct adminstration or have an arrangement with a 'cooperating school'.

All teacher training colleges are coeducational.

A Central Teachers Retraining Institute was established in Kabul in 1981 to upgrade teachers' qualifications and expertise. Seminars have also been organised in Kabul for teachers to prepare them to teach the new syllabi.

More emphasis has been placed on the quality of teacher training. A Master of Education course was started in 1979 at the Academy of Teacher Educators in Kabul. It is to enrol 100 students a year who will work in teacher education.

Higher Education

The main institution of higher education is the University of Kabul. The other institutions (apart from Vocational Institutions, etc., offering instruction in Grade 13 which are mentioned above) are the Nangarhar Medical Faculty, the Higher Teachers' Colleges and the Academy for Teacher Educators, and the Institute of Industrial Management. All institutions of higher education are now administered by the Ministry of Education.

The University of Kabul may be said to have been founded in 1932 with establishment of the Faculty of Medicine; other faculties followed: Law 1938, Science 1942, Letters 1944. In 1947 the University was organised as a separate institution operating within the framework of the Ministry of Education. The Faculty of Theology opened in 1951, Engineering and Agriculture in 1962 and the Polytechnic Institute in 1968. Women first entered the University in 1960. Enrolments increased from 1,000 in 1956 to nearly 7,000 in 1972. The new campus, built with US aid, opened in 1964.

The medium of instruction is mainly Persian (Dari) though some faculties because of their affiliations with various foreign aid programmes used other languages of instruction in some classes:

      Engineering (US) English
      Agriculture (US) English
      Economics (FRG) German
      Law (France) French
      Architecture (US) English
      Medicine (France) French
      Polytechnic (USSR) Russian
      Science (FRG) German
      Theology (Saudi Arabian, Egyptian) Arabic

The University admits students who have completed their secondary education (Baccalaureate) and have passed the university entrance examination (concours). Students may enter the faculty of their choice if there are places available. It is more than probable, however, that the authorities will re-introduce the system of directing the students to faculties in accordance with national manpower requirements. The number of students applying for entry has in recent years far outnumbered the places available.

The University offers the following degrees: Bachelor of Arts, Bachelor of Science, and Doctor of Medicine. To obtain a degree a student must attend at least 75% of the total hours for each course he is taking and must reach a pass mark of 50 in each course. Examination practice varies from faculty to faculty.

Dormitories are provided for students from outside Kabul (including one womens' dormitory for 80 students).

The General Library contains about 120,000 books largely in English and other foreign languages. Faculties have their own specialist libraries, usually very small.

Freshman students have an orientation year of general studies (including English language) in most faculties followed by three years of specialisation (Polytechnic: two years of general study plus three years of specialisation; Faculty of Medicine: one orientation year, five years of specialist studies leading to graduation, followed by a year's internship).

The Polytechnic offers instruction in the following fields: geology and mining excavation, mine exploitation, geology and exploration of gas fields, chemical technology, roads and high-

ways, industrial and civil structure, hydrotechnic structure.
The Nangarhar Medical Faculty awards degrees of the University of Kabul. It is situated near Jalalabad and was intended to become the nucleus of a second university. It was founded in 1963 and until recently received US aid.

Non-Formal Education/Literacy

Though 85% of the population is illiterate, adult literacy classes were undeveloped before 1978. There were a small number of adult literacy classes organised by the Ministry while functional literacy programmes were encouraged by UN and other external agencies.

Since 1979 proposals for the rapid expansion of adult literacy classes have been introduced which it is hoped will cater for 8 million people. Particular attention is paid to women and out of work youth. Literacy programmes are conducted in the five languages of instruction. These literacy classes are often linked to teaching in practical and vocational skills.

7 EDUCATIONAL ADMINISTRATION

Administration of the education system in all its aspects from finance to curricula is very centralised. Even in the 1975 reforms, centralisation was emphasised. Authority lies with the Minister. Indeed, the President and his Central Committee are the real initiators of policy in this as in all other fields. This possibly accounts for the unhurried approach towards implementing reforms. Key posts in the Ministry include the Presidents of Primary Education, Secondary Education and Teacher Training.

There are 29 administrative areas which comprise 28 provinces plus the city of Kabul. Each province has a Director of Education. He acts as the administrative head for education but because policy is made centrally and money for educational development is allocated almost entirely by the central government (95.5%) he really does little more than implement official policies. Provincial Governors have overall responsibility in their provinces for the work of government departments and a Governor who takes a special responsibility in education can often help the Director of Education to make considerable improvements in the school administration and the teaching in his province.

8 EDUCATIONAL FINANCE

Education is financed entirely from central sources. In 1980, 11.5% of recurrent spending was allocated to education but only 1% of the development budget. This reflects the shift in emphasis to the expansion of mass education using limited physical resources. In 1972 only 8% of recurrent funds went to education and 7% of the development budget. However, total proportion of the government budget allocated to education has declined from 9% in 1972 to 7% in 1980 reflecting changed political and military conditions. Substantial Western aid to education has ended which in part accounts for the decline in the development budget.

9 DEVELOPMENT AND PLANNING OF THE EDUCATION SYSTEM

Major changes were made in the structure of the education system in 1975 and in 1979. Up to 1975 a 6+3+3 structure was in operation. Six year primary schools (though in remote areas there were also three year village schools) were followed by three year middle schools which led to three year lycees. In 1975 an 8+4 structure was proposed so that all primary schools would offer the eight years schooling which it was thought was necessary to produce permanent literacy. The four year secondary schools would include both general and vocational lycees.

The 1979 reform proposed a 4+4+2 structure. The four year primary schools for the first time would be compulsory for all, starting with Grade 1 in 1980. This would be followed by four years 'incomplete' secondary schooling and a further two years 'complete' secondary education. The whole period of schooling has been reduced to achieve maximum provision in the lower grades.

Pre-primary schooling is available in only a handful of kindergartens in Kabul and in one or two other towns. These schools are essentially outside the State education system, although teachers are supplied by the Women's Welfare Association which is itself under the supervision of and almost totally subsidised by the Ministry of Education. Parents must pay fees of Afs 100-200 per month per child which restricts their use to the wealthy.

10 THE SYSTEM IN OPERATION

Up to 1978 the development of the Afghan educational system was hampered by imprecise aims, lack of trained manpower and lack of financial resources, a situation not dissimilar from that prevailing in many countries.

"The objectives of the present system of education are not clear", says the introduction to the 1972 statistics issued by the Ministry of Education. "Moreover the curriculum is not well adjusted to the age of the students, their ability, or future needs of the country nor is the present system of education compatible with the country's social and economic requirements". this lack of clearly defined objectives or the inability to adhere to such principles as have been defined in, for instance, the Five Year Plans, led to considerable imbalance in the system and wastage of effort and money. The curricula appear to have been drawn up in an effort to accommodate many differing interests and consequently were overcrowded and rigid. The overwhelming majority of secondary pupils studied general and academic rather than vocational subjects. Enrolment in vocational schools dropped by 2% during the third Five Year Plan; even so it was difficult to place graduates not only because the rate of industrial expansion was lower than planned, but also because of the poor standard of the graduates and their unwillingness to work in the remoter areas.

There is a significant imbalance in student enrolment. although primary education reaches only a quarter of the age group, the bottom of the educational pyramid is very large in comparison with the top. Drop-out rate is high, reflecting not only the boredom of the students, but also low teaching standards and traditional illiteracy. Enrolment at secondary level grew much faster than had been allowed for in the third Five Year Plan, leading to increased demand for university places and to graduate unemployment. Political activists were able to take advantage of this situation, and for several years before the 1973 coup the authorities were forced to close the University for long periods in the face of student indiscipline.

Because of the lack of clear objectives foreign aid up to 1978 was uncoordinated and wasted. Sometimes projects in the same or closely related fields were pursued in isolation; at other times a project became the victim of personal rivalries, or a project was allowed to collapse when aid was terminated.

There is a shortage of trained teachers at each level. Over 75% of upper-secondary level teachers graduating from the faculty of education (recently incorporated in the faculty of letters) have found more lucrative positions in administration or outside the field of education. It follows that most secondary teachers have not received training for the level at which they are working. In 1972 only 9.2% of all teachers had a level of education above Grade 12, while 25.4% had attained Baccalaureate (Grade 12 final examination) and 41.3% had a lower level of attainment and had not attended a teacher training course.

Even the standard of trained teachers is low. Low salaries encourage teachers to take extra jobs or extra classes. This inevitably has its effect on the preparation of lessons and correction of written work, and teachers find it easier to base their lessons on rote learning. Teachers also set and correct the end-of year examinations for their own classes. The examinations serve little purpose but to weed out those who are unable, by fair means or foul, to pass them.

The teacher is further hampered by the conditions in which he works. Not only does he face a crowded classroom with insufficient desks and textbooks, but he may even lack such simple necessities as blackboard, chalk and duster. In practice he is seldom visited, let alone helped, by an inspector, and is lucky to be given any form of in-service training.

As is to be expected in one of the UN's list of 25 Least Developed countries, money is short, and the Ministry's budget is unable to keep up with either the expansion of the school system or rising costs generally. This leaves little for the building or maintenance of schools (a half of village schools are housed in mosques; a quarter of primary schools are rented; most village, primary and middle schools are housed in simple mud buildings), for the printing of textbooks, for the supply and maintenance of equipment (especially in vocational schools), even for the day-to-day running expenses.

Though there is a concentration of educational institutions in Kabul, schools are generally evenly distributed through the provinces, the more developed provinces being naturally more favoured. It is interesting to note that a recent survey found that English is not better taught in Kabul than in the provinces; the same survey concluded that "very little real English is being taught anywhere in Afghanistan". It is likely that a survey of other subjects would prompt a similar reflection.

11 TRENDS, PROBLEMS AND POSSIBILITIES

The Internal Efficiency of the System

A summary of educational problems that Afghanistan has faced is as follows:

(i)   lack of trained teachers at all levels

(ii)   inadequate recurrent budgets coupled with rising salaries and costs

(iii)   shortage of buildings, equipment, textbooks and all supplies

(iv)   a corrupt examination system relying mainly on memory work

(v)   teachers' efficiency often impaired by doing two jobs

(vi)   low student attendance rates

(vii)   high drop-out rate at primary level

(viii) crowded and academic curricula

(ix)   crowded classrooms

(x)   virtual absence of inspection

(xi)   low teachers' salaries without incentives

(xii)   primary education reaches only one quarter of the age group

(xiii) foreign aid projects numerous and uncoordinated

(xiv) absence of real libraries in the majority of schools; faculty and university libraries containing predominantly foreign language works are little used.

External Relevance

Curricula have been academic, non-practical and irrelevant to the needs of the economy or even to the personal requirements of a predominantly agricultural population.

There were few attempts to match secondary and higher education graduates with the labour market. Not only were too many arts or general studies graduates being produced, but the standard of graduates of the vocational schools was so low that they could not be used in developmental projects without extensive re-training.

While the government has made strong proposals since 1978 to expand and improve basic education both in and out of school, the economic and political conditions - and above all the Civil War - continue to be serious constraints. The shift of emphasis to lower levels of education may further reduce the quality of post-primary education despite proposed reforms in this area.

EDUCATIONAL FLOWCHART UP TO 1975 - AFGHANISTAN

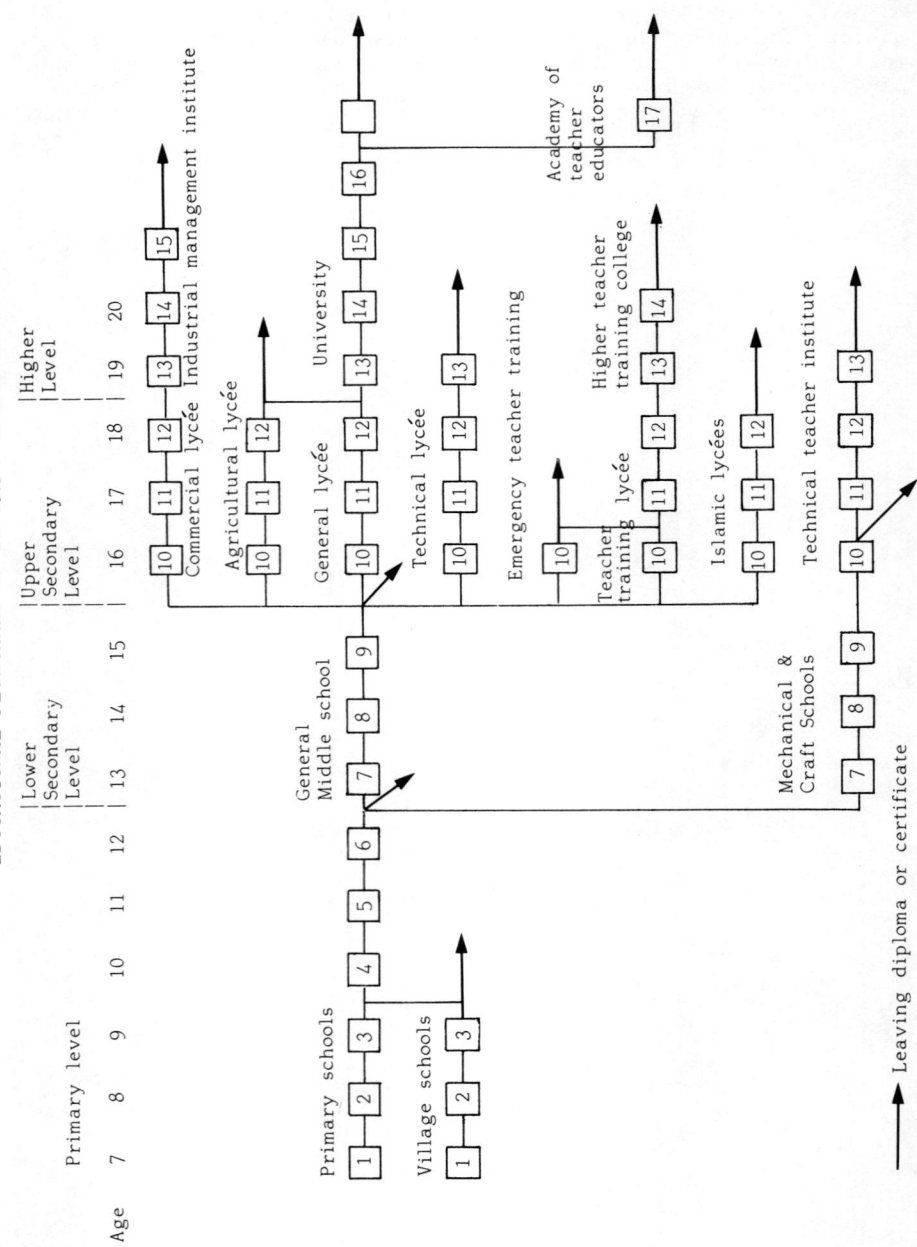

THE EDUCATIONAL STRUCTURE 1975-1979

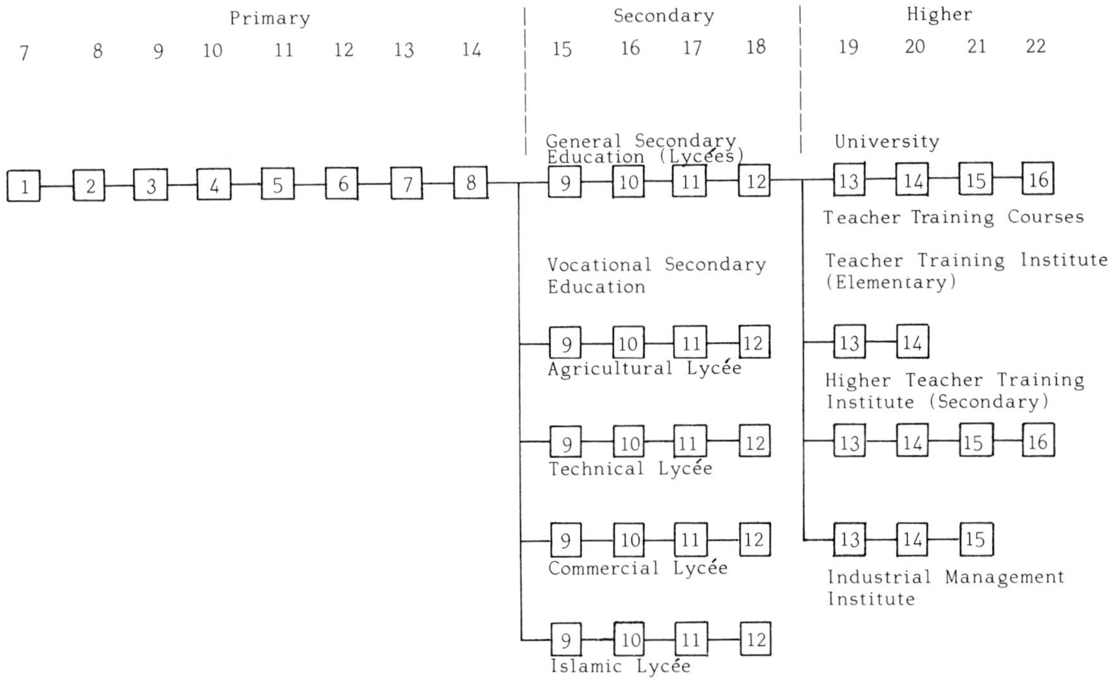

Level	Ages	Stages
Primary	7–14	1 – 2 – 3 – 4 – 5 – 6 – 7 – 8
Secondary	15–18	General Secondary Education (Lycées): 9 – 10 – 11 – 12
		Vocational Secondary Education:
		Agricultural Lycée: 9 – 10 – 11 – 12
		Technical Lycée: 9 – 10 – 11 – 12
		Commercial Lycée: 9 – 10 – 11 – 12
		Islamic Lycée: 9 – 10 – 11 – 12
Higher	19–22	University: 13 – 14 – 15 – 16
		Teacher Training Courses
		Teacher Training Institute (Elementary): 13 – 14
		Higher Teacher Training Institute (Secondary): 13 – 14 – 15 – 16
		Industrial Management Institute: 13 – 14 – 15

THE EDUCATIONAL STRUCTURE 1979 →

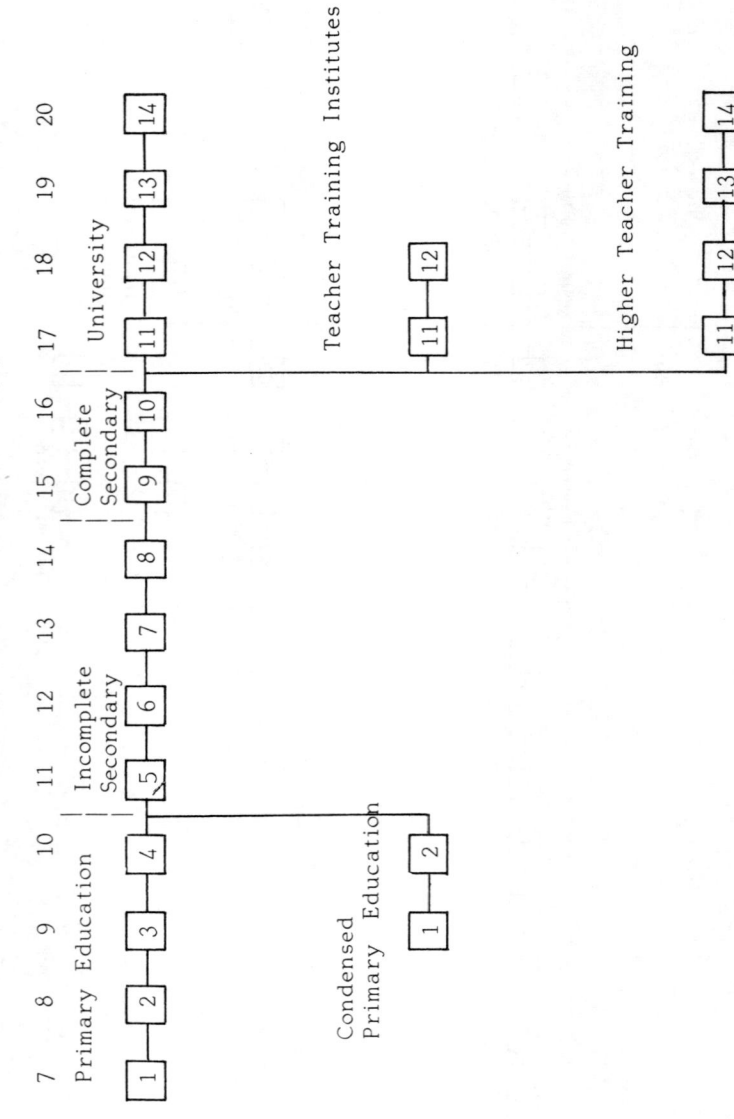

Age		Level
7 8 9 10	1 2 3 4	Primary Education
11 12 13 14	5 6 7 8	Incomplete Secondary
15 16	9 10	Complete Secondary
17 18 19 20	11 12 13 14	University
	1 2	Condensed Primary Education
	11 12	Teacher Training Institutes
	11 12 13 14	Higher Teacher Training

32

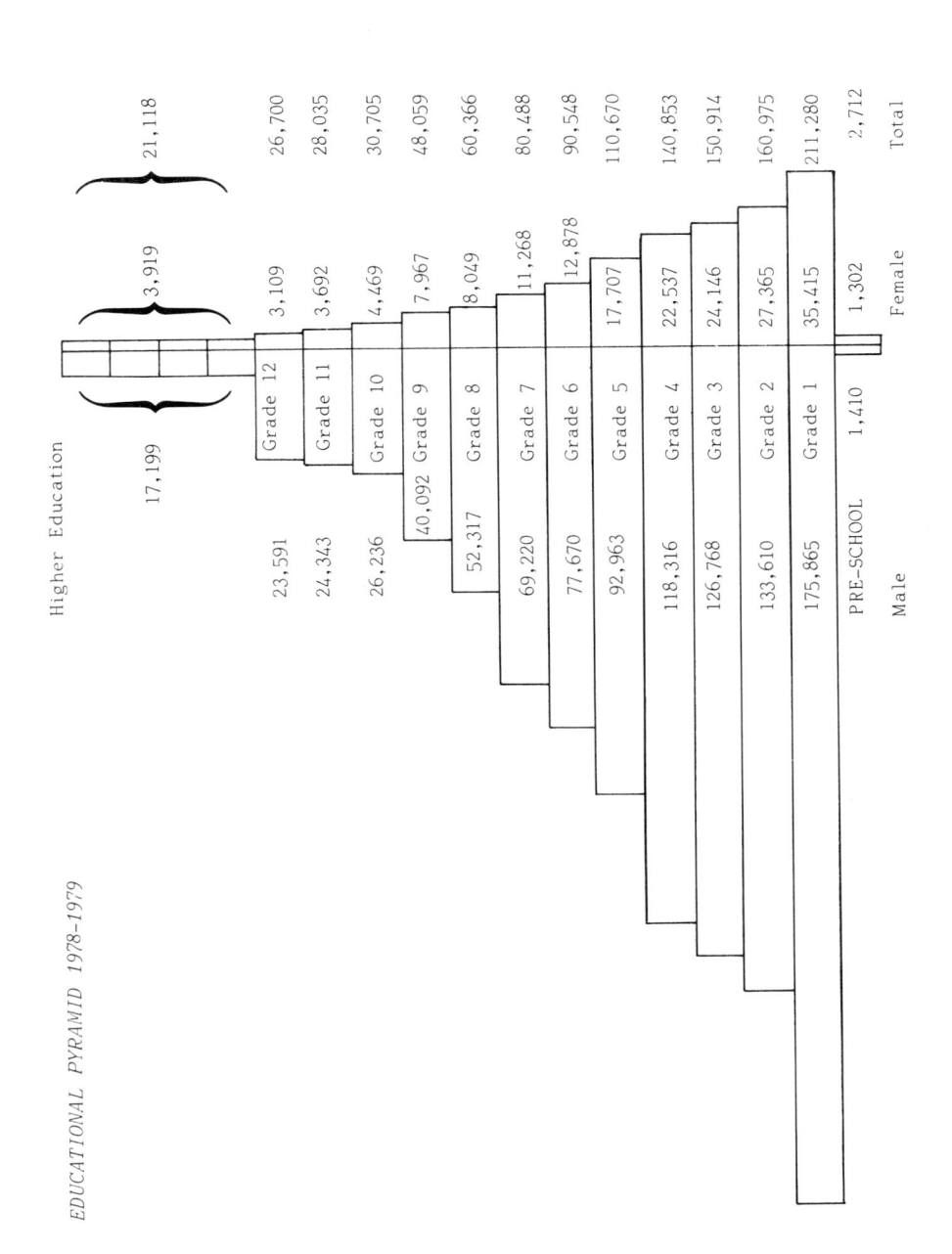

EDUCATIONAL PYRAMID 1978-1979

Male	Grade	Female	Total
17,199	Higher Education	3,919	21,118
23,591	Grade 12	3,109	26,700
24,343	Grade 11	3,692	28,035
26,236	Grade 10	4,469	30,705
40,092	Grade 9	7,967	48,059
52,317	Grade 8	8,049	60,366
69,220	Grade 7	11,268	80,488
77,670	Grade 6	12,878	90,548
92,963	Grade 5	17,707	110,670
118,316	Grade 4	22,537	140,853
126,768	Grade 3	24,146	150,914
133,610	Grade 2	27,365	160,975
175,865	Grade 1	35,415	211,280
1,410	PRE-SCHOOL	1,302	2,712

AFGHANISTAN BASIC STATISTICS

Expansion of the Education System

	\multicolumn{4}{c}{Enrolment}		
	Pre-School	Primary	Secondary	Higher
1951 (a)	–	89,156	5,523	456
1960 (a)	–	175,664	16,231	1,554
1970 (a)	979	540,685	116,174	7,732
1975 (b)	1,891	784,568	93,497	12,256
1979 (b)	2,712	1,006,094	133,498	21,118*

(a) Primary = Grades 1-6; Secondary = Grades 7-12.
(b) Primary = Grades 1-8; Secondary = Grades 9-12.
*1978

% of Pupils Repeating Grades 1978

% Repeaters	36	27	27	32	26	24	31	22	22	28	17	9
Grade	1	2	3	4	5	6	7	8	9	10	11	12

Branches of Study of Higher Education Students 1978

	Male	Female
Education and Teacher Training	4,603	1,940
Humanities and Tehology	1,657	480
Law	495	93
Commerce and Business	1,370	180
Natural Science	1,012	463
Medicine and Related Studies	2,288	344
Engineering	3,966	326
Agriculture	1,807	93
Totals	17,199	3,919

Schools, Teachers and Pupils 1980

	Schools	Teachers	Pupils
Primary (Grades 1-4)	3,812	33,871	1,076,014
Secondary (Grades 5-10)	423	6,339	117,665

Pupil/Teacher Ratio Primary Schools 1970-79

1970	1975	1979
41	37	31

Proportions of the Age Group in Education 1975 and 1979

(Gross Enrolment ratios = number of pupils as a percentage of total numbers of children and young people [estimated] aged 6-13 [primary] 14-17 [secondary] and 20-24 [higher].)

	Total	Male	Female
Primary			
1975	20	32	6
1979	22	36	7
Secondary			
1975	6	10	1
1979	7	12	2
Higher			
1975	0.7	1.2	0.2
1979	1.2	1.9	0.5

Expenditure on Education 1980

	% of Budget
Recurrent expenditure	11.5%
Development expenditure	1.0%
Total	7.0%

Current Expenditure by Level of Education 1970 and 1978

Level	1970	1978
Pre-primary	–	1.1%
Primary	28.5%	45.3%
Secondary	41.7%	20.0%
Higher	20.4%	19.1%
Other Types	–	2.4%
Not Distributed	9.3%	12.1%

Basic Social and Economic Data

Gross National Product per capita 1979: US$ 170

Annual average growth of GNP per capita 1960–79: 0.5%

Life expectancy 1979: 41

Proportion of the Labour force employed in:

Agriculture

1960	85%
1979	79%

Industry

1960	6%
1979	8%

Services

1960	9%
1979	13%

Australia

CONTENTS

1	Geography	38
2	Population	40
3	Society and Culture	42
4	History and Politics	44
5	The Economy	46
6	The Education System	47
7	Educational Administration	59
8	Educational Finance	61
9	Development and Planning of the Education System	62

Three aspects of Australia, past and present, may help to give an overall impression of the country's education system. Firstly, Australia is an industrial urban society with a political system similar to those of the states of Western Europe and North America. Educational provision and especially the trends of educational development over the last 20 years share common characteristics with these other industrial countries. Secondly, the Australian people, culture and system of government have British origins. There are many recognisably English survivals in Australian educational practice despite the increasingly greater gulf that has emerged between Australia and the former mother country. Thirdly, Australia has a federal system of administration and a federal system of education. The reference point for comparison here may be other federal nations such as the USA, Canada or West Germany.

Like most other industrial countries, Australia has universal primary and lower secondary education. Over the last 20 years there has been a movement to common secondary schooling for all pupils though there is still a considerable attrition rate after the age of compulsory schooling at 15 or 16. Higher education provision expanded considerably in the late 1960s up to the mid-1970s so that about a quarter of the relevant age group in universities or other higher education institutions – a participation rate much above that of Britain though still some way behind the United States. As in most other industrial states there has been educational retrenchment in the late 1970s and early 1980s with a cutback in expansion - especially at higher education level - a concern for efficiency and more attention to school to work transition programmes.

The education systems of industrial countries do differ often because of different historical experiences. The Australian education system still has close parallels with that of England and Wales. Secondary schools are comprehensive but are often streamed according to pupils' ability and there is still a strong academic ethos. High proportions of students, as in Britain, end their education at 16 rather than 18 or 19. There is a binary higher education system as in Britain with more vocationally orientated (and often lower status) Colleges of Advanced Education existing alongside more traditional universities. Formal selection and differentiation of students occurs at a relatively early age as in Britain but unlike the USA.

There has been some movement away from British patterns and towards those of the United States. There has been a greater emphasis on internal school assessment of pupils in lower and upper secondary level rather than on external examinations - though these still exist. The expansion of higher education has been linked to the provision of much more part time study of students who are in full time occupations.

Generalisations about Australian education are difficult after a certain point because of the federal system. Each of the seven states or territories has its own educational administration and different practices have developed in different areas. The federal government, as in the USA, has intervened mainly to provide money while decisions are made at State level. However, there are differences from the United States. Most funds are raised by federal government and some educational sectors - particlarly higher education - are under more direct federal control. Decision making within states is centralised without a separate level of powerful local educational authorities. But there is a very significant government supported private, religious school sector which adds to the diversity of Australian educational provision.

The major issues of Australian education are in the main similar to those of other industrial countries. But there are peculiar conditions facing Australian education. There is the education of immigrants - and an indigenous disadvantaged minority - in what is still in many ways a country of immigrants and there is the need to find a national identity as ties with Britain are increasingly relaxed.

1 GEOGRAPHY

Australia, the world's smallest continent and largest island, lies between latitude 10°41' and 43°39'S and longitude 113°9' and 153°39'E. (Comparable latitudes in the northern hemisphere are Nice, 43°42' and Port of Spain, 10°38'.) Sydney (33°55'S) lies on much the same latitude as Buenos Aires (34°40'), comparable in terms of the northern hemisphere with Casablanca (33°39'N). The maximum distance east-west is 2,400 miles (3,864 km) (compare 2,485 miles [4,000 km] which separates Liverpool

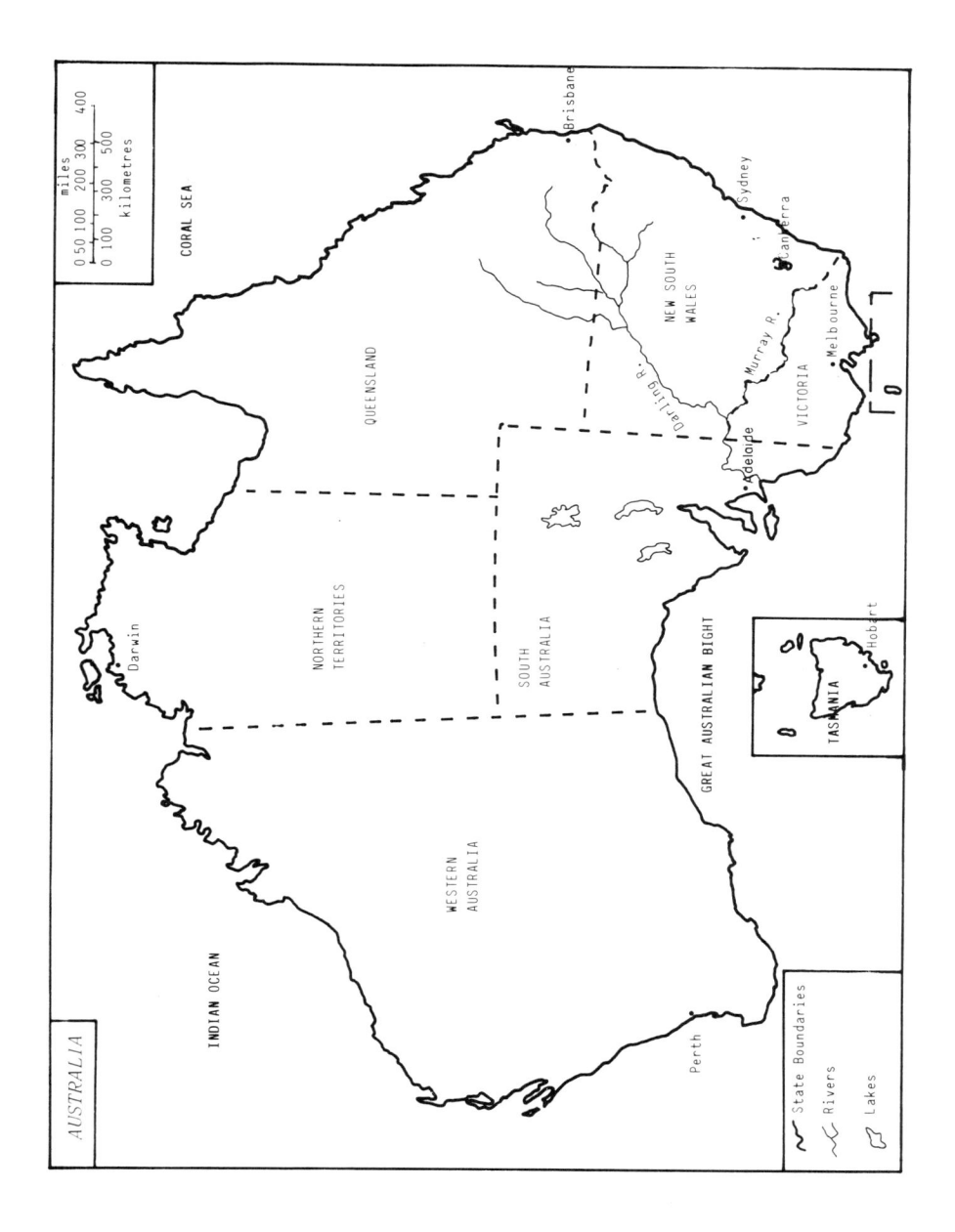

from Halifax, Nova Scotia) and north-south 1,970 miles (3,172 km). In area it is about the size of the United States of America (without Alaska) or three quarters the size of Europe i.e. almost 3,000,000 square miles (8,149,959 sq km).

It is an isolated continent having relatively close neighbours only to the north (Papua New Guinea being only about 90 miles [145 km] from Cape York, the northern extremity of mainland Australia, and Timor 400 miles [644 km] from Darwin). On all other sides it is surrounded by ocean with, except for New Zealand 1,200 miles (1,932 km) distant, nothing to the east until South America, to the west Southern Africa and to the south Antarctica. The distance from Sydney to London is 12,799 miles (20,606 km) via Vancouver or 12,688 miles (20,427 km) via the Panama Canal. Tasmania is separated from the mainland by Bass Strait, 140 miles (225 km) wide. These factors have given Australians a sense of isolation from the rest of the world.

One of the oldest of the Earth's land masses, Australia was hardly affected by the tertiary earth movements which caused the formation of the Alps or the Himalays. The greater part of the country consists of a vast, arid plateau, part of which is below sea level. A feature of this interior is the Lake region, the largest of which, Lake Eyre and Lake Torrens, can be over 100 miles long during a flood but in a dry season are little more than salty marshes. This barren plateau is bounded on the east by the Great Dividing Range in which is found Australia's highest peak, Mount Kosciusko, 7,327 feet (2,233 metres). Between the Great Dividing Range and the Pacific Ocean is a fertile, coastal plain, which is the part which most visitors to Australia see.

Because of the vastness of the country quite striking extremes of climate occur. For example, while 40% of the country receives less than 10 inches (25.4 cm) of rain per annum, 10% receives more than 40 inches (101.6 cm). The latter is mostly in the tropical area of northern Queensland and the Northern Territory (i.e. where the disastrous cyclone hit Darwin on Christmas Day 1974). The drought areas occur mainly in the inland plateau and often exacerbate the danger of forest fires. Snow and low temperatures occur in the Australian Alps and the temperate climate of Sydney and the southern Coastal regions is not unlike that of the Mediterranean.

There are rail links between all the major cities, Sydney-Melbourne taking 14 hours and Sydney-Perth about three days. Roads are good or adequate between the major cities and around the towns. However, because of the great distances involved, air is the most common form of travel. Telephone links between the major cities are good (there is a standard charge for calls between the State capitals) and long-distance calls are used more often than in Britain.

2 POPULATION

Australia is the most sparsely populated continent in the world with a density of only 4 persons per square mile. The population in 1969 was 12.5 million. It was estimated at 13.5

million in 1979 with an annual average rate of growth of 1.6% between 1970 and 1978, partly the result of natural increase, partly the result of immigration. Life expectation is one of the highest in the world. Some authorities have argued that Australia should aim at a considerable expansion of its population but difficulties arise because of the capacity to absorb large numbers of immigrants from alien linguistic cultures and to maintain non-working dependents. Others believe that Australia can only survive if it expands its population.

The paradox of being the most sparsely populated continent is that it is also one of the most highly urbanised countries in the world. Eighty percent of the population are concentrated in the south east corner of the country and 80% of these live in maritime cities. In fact 50% of the country's population live in State capital cities, all of which are maritime, and barely 20% live in so-called rural areas. Outside the State capitals few towns have populations of more than 50,000. New South Wales and Victoria are the most densely populated States, the Northern Territories the least populated. Australia is thus very suburban and its major problems are metropolitan ones.

Those who live in these areas are predominantly of British stock but immigration from other countries, particularly from South Europe since the Second World War, has influenced the traditional life style and has hastened the process of adaptation to life in a largely Mediterranean climate and environment. Inevitably conflicts have arisen between British traditions and East and South Europeans' views, between the aspirations of newcomers and old stagers, between English speakers and Romance or Latin speakers and the new Australia has had to come to terms with this new state of affairs. Officially the White Australia Policy no longer exists but in practice the majority of immigrants (called migrants in Australia) are from Europe or the Americas and few from Asia or Africa. Some live in depressed areas and take on the lower-paid jobs but many have integrated successfully into the society.

English is, of course, the national language and an important factor in the absorption of new arrivals, although many ethnic clubs exist where Italian, Greek or Spanish but very little English, is to be heard. Extensive resources have been made available for the teaching of English as a foreign language in which there is great interest at present. Materials such as 'Situational English' are internationally known. However, a report published in 1973 stated that 60% of children born of migrant parents in Australia have no English or a very poor command of the language. Another report published earlier the same year was severely critical of the lack of trained teachers, poor accommodation and large classes for migrants in Victoria. This report was taken very seriously by the Department of Immigration and steps were taken to improve the situation. A lively debate continues not only over facilities but also over materials and methods. The teaching of modern languages, both European and Oriental, has been seriously neglected in Australia but there has been an increase in the study of Asian languages as a result of the recommendations of the Auchmuty Advisory Committee in the Teaching of Asian Languages and Cultures set up in 1969.

Those who live in the rural areas, on the other hand, tend to be aborigines. When Australia was discovered by Europeans it was found to be somewhat sparsely inhabited by a nomadic, Stone Age people who have since become much reduced in numbers by a combination of factors, including actual extermination in the early days (completed in Tasmania by 1876) and the onslaught of diseases to which they had no resistance. At the 1971 census, 106,290 people described themselves as aborigines or as half or more than half aborigine. There is a large aboriginal reserve in Arnhem Land but this is being encroached upon and reduced by mining. The aborigines' way of life (in which the physical and the spiritual blend to a remarkable degree) requires a large area in which they can hunt, gather food and visit their sacred sites; money and other material alternatives are not an adequate substitute for this. They are natural artists and their bark paintings are recognised as being, in many cases, works of art of high quality, but they never made pottery in their original state and a scheme for developing this craft amongst them is one of the most successful of such ventures. Other specially funded projects designed to improve their material well-being or to promote their absorption into a European way of life have been less successful. Although genuine aborigines do not consider half-castes part of their society, it is from this class that thje vocal (often radical) 'stirrers' usually come and it is they who have, somewhat incongruously, raised the standard of Black Power. There is a growing awareness amongst white Australians that the aborigines are generally socially depressed and educationally deprived and that something should be done about them and, above all, about the question of land rights for the aborigines. In December 1973 a National Aboriginal Consultative Committee was set up to give a greater say to the aboriginal people in their own affairs.

3 SOCIETY AND CULTURE

'Middle Australia' generally holds to attitudes characteristic of the middle class in Britain a few years ago. Many expressions of opinion give a familiar, traditional but *autre temps* impression to the 'Britisher'. At the same time people have an open casualness in their way of life uncharacteristic of Europe and a get-up-and-go initiative more characteristic of the United States. This is, after all, a country historically connected to, but geographically separated from, the Old World and the influence of the United States is strong for both historical and geographical reasons. Attitudes are generally materialistic but the cultural life of Australia is extremely vigorous and reaches high standards, especially in painting, ballet and opera. The biennial Adelaide Festival has an international reputation and the growing importance of music and the theatre in Australia is reflected in the recent spate of new buildings for housing these activities, including the Adelaide Festival

Centre, the new Concert Hall in Perth and culminating in the Sydney Opera House.

Class distinction (based on money rather than origin), competition between the States and differences between the urban and rural population (reflected in the major political parties) exist, but none of these causes serious conflict. People cannot be placed regionally by the way they speak as in Britain and there is less variation socially.

Attitudes are probably best exemplified by standard remarks such as 'Give it a go', 'Fair dinkum', 'She'll be all right', all followed by 'Mate', a term dating back to the Gold Rushes and early settling in rural areas. Although less frequently heard than books on Australia might suggest, these phrases do express the Australian interpretation of Liberty, Equality and Fraternity, willing to try anything so long as it appears fair, and optimistic of the outcome but resentful of anything imposed from above, no matter what its virtues.

Social trends are similar to those of other developed nations but that Australia is a 'lucky country' in terms of natural benefits without the problems (particularly in regard to minorities) of, say, the United States or Britain is a widely held concept. The idols of the society are material success and the good (preferably outdoor) life.

Religious Background

Today Australia is nominally a Christian country. Most denominations and sects are represented and some are experiencing a period of growth and revival. Other religions, though having few adherents, are freely tolerated. There is a tradition of rivalry between Protestants and Roman Catholics, particularly in Victoria and the Roman Catholic Church has made its influence felt, politically, for example through the anti-communist movement led by B. A. Santamaria, but, more importantly, through its schools and educational lobbies. In fact, sectarian disputes and rivalries about the role of the Church in education hampered the early establishment of a uniform and satisfactory system of educational provision.

While the early governments of New South Wales and Tasmania were too occupied with the problems of settlement in a barren and inhospitable land they nevertheless recognised the right of the Church - in this case the Church of England and its missionary societies - to provide education and they wished to supplement Church provision out of local taxation. In 1826 therefore with the creation of the Church and Schools Corporation the Church of England was given a privileged position, and one seventh of the land of the counties of New South Wales was set aside for Church schools. The outcry from the Catholics was loud and bitter and in place of the corporation an Irish National System was introduced by Governor Bourke in 1833. This in turn led to strong Protestant opposition and ultimately both Catholics and Protestants were given equal subsidisation for building denominational schools though the Protestants refused to agree to denominational religious instruction. In

1848, however, a system not unlike that existing in Ireland was introduced, when government aid to education was channelled through a Board of Denominational Education and a Board of National Education (i.e. State controlled, non-denominational). The division lasted barely 20 years since the New South Wales Public Schools Act of 1866 abolished both boards and in their stead created a Council of Education with control over both public and denominational schools. Similar situations prevailed in other colonies and gradually Australia moved towards a unified, non-sectarian education system as denominational schools failed for lack of support.

4 HISTORY AND POLITICS

In terms of the society which now predominates, Australia is one of the youngest of countries. There had been a small aboriginal population from early times and there had been speculation in the West about the existence of a southern continent since the time of Ptolemy. The island is thought to have been known to the Chinese in the fifteenth century and may well have been circumnavigated by them at that period. Despite some rather hazy evidence suggesting that the existence of Australia was known to the Portuguese in the early sixteenth century, the honour of its discovery by a European (in the light of present day knowledge at any rate) belongs to a Dutchman, Captain Willem Janszoon, in 1606. However, the modern history of Australia is taken to date from 1770 when Captain James Cook landed on the east coast and, having travelled to the northern point of Queensland, took possession of eastern Australia in the name of the Crown on 23 August that year. It is important to remember that Cook, one of whose commissions for the voyage was to observe the transit of Venus from Tahiti, was accompanied by Joseph Banks, a wealthy explorer-naturalist subsequently President of the Royal Society for more than 40 years. Banks reported favourably on the prospects of settling Australia and it was he who first suggested before a House of Commons committee in 1779 the establishment of a colony to which convicts might be transported instead of to the former colonies in America. The First Fleet, carrying 717 convicts, of whom 180 were women, guarded by 119 marines under 19 officers, reached the east coast at the beginning of 1788. Some Australians are still sensitive about their lawless origins though most are justifiably prouder of their achievements. It is significant, incidentally, in view of Australia's later high reputation in the arts, that the first play was performed in Australia just over a year after the convicts first arrived.

Exploration of the continent was undertaken by both sea and land, and by 1875 all the main geographical features of Australia were known. From the early 1820s there were demands for more power to be exercised by the governors of New south Wales and less control from London. Gradually separate states emerged - Tasmania 1825, Western Australia 1829, South Australia 1834, Victoria 1851, Queensland 1859, the Northern Territories 1863, this latter being transferred to the Commonwealth in 1911, when the Australian Capital Territory was also formed. Federation was proclaimed in 1901. There is still, however, rivalry between the states, between the states and the central government, between north and south and east and west, and particularly between Sydney and Melbourne.

Australia's attitude to Britain is bitter-sweet. Many have links with Britain and Australia has proved a staunch ally in two world wars. Relations are bound to change as each country assumes a new role in world affairs. Churchill's depletion of the forces guarding Australia for other theatres of war was seen as confirmation that self-interest was stronger than family ties and Britain's entry into the EEC set the seal on this view of the relationship. Nevertheless the ties are still strong.

Government and Politics

Australia is politically a very stable country. If stability is to be measured in such a way, until the election of a Labour government in 1972, the previous Liberal-Country Party coalition administration had governed for 23 years. Such political longevity can also, of course, indicate conservatism. The major political parties - Labour, Liberal (cf. UK Conservative party) and Country - traditionally represent the urban workers, the urban middle class and rural interests respectively. The trades union movement is a powerful force, frequently in areas outside industrial relations.

There is no shortage of parliaments in the country of 13.5 million people. Each state has one consisting of two chambers (with the exception of Queensland which manages with one) and there are two Houses in Canberra. A major domestic issue is the States' right v. federalism, aggravated where the federal and State governments are of different political complexions. Every year the State Premiers go cap in hand to Canberra to tussle among each other and with the central government for their share of federal largesse. This affects many areas but is particularly important in education.

International Relations

As has already been pointed out, this most sparsely populated continent's closest neighbours are the populous countries of Asia. Until 1960 the motto of *The Bulletin*, Australia's weekly magazine of news and opinion, was 'Australia for the White Man' (previously it had been (Australia for the White Man; China for the Chows'). This sentiment dates back to the influx of Chinese during the gold rushes of the early nineteenth century. The threat from the north was seen even more acutely during the Second World War when Japanese aircraft attacked Darwin and Japanese submarines entered Sydney Harbour. In Papua New Guinea Australia shared a common land frontier with Indonesia, one of Asia's most populous countries. Some Australians will argue that since so much of Australia is inhospitable desert it cannot be considered as an area for

Asian Lebensraum but they seldom sound as if they have convinced themselves let alone the 'teeming hordes'.

Traditionally Australia's alliances have, through SEATO and ANZUK, been with the West. It is probably because of these alliances that Australia's attempts at involvement in a plan for the neutralisation of South East Asia, endorsed by Malaysia, Singapore, Thailand, the Philippines and Indonesia, have received only a lukewarm response. Nevertheless Australia has begun to see her future very much tied up with the destiny of South East Asia and the Pacific Islands, and she has begun to adjust her policies accordingly. One of the Labour government's earliest actions was to recognise the People's Republic of China thereby removing a running sore between the two nations and anticipating American recognition by more than two years. These policy changes have also had implications for the curriculum since South East Asian studies and Australia's place in the world have at last begun to be studied seriously.

5 THE ECONOMY

Australia is a rich country and the full extent of its natural resources is still unknown. Aridity and distance from markets prevent the commercial exploitation of 34% of the total land area, covering vast expanses of South Australia, Western Australia and the Northern Territories. Another 42% to the north, east and west of this region is suitable only for sheep and cattle. Of the remainder, because of mountainous topography or poor soils, only about 8% is suitable for cultivation and as much of this is used for livestock, only a little over 1% is actually used for raising crops. Australia produces about one third of the world's wool and sheep are to be found in areas receiving 15-20 inches (38-50 cm) of rain i.e. predominantly on the tablelands and plains of the east coast. Cattle are to be found in the drier interior, in the hot humid areas of the north and in the humid upland and coastal areas of the south-east. The major crops are wheat, oats, barley, maize, rice and sugar. Mechanisation, irrigation and refrigeration have had an important influence in expanding production and opening up markets.

About 3% of the total land area contains commercially exploitable forests. The major minerals are manganese, lead, zinc, bauxite, iron, copper and gold. Petroleum reserves are being explored and there is a great interest in developing this resource. Water has been harnessed for hydroelectric power and irrigation, the most famous example being the Snowy Mountain Scheme, and artesian bores are an important source of water in the interior. There has been speculation about towing icebergs from the Antarctic and producing solar energy in the central deserts but the expense of such a project has so far prevented it from being taken seriously.

Australia has a mixed economy with a very strong strain of private enterprise. Agriculture has been a staple industry from the beginning and is now an important export element. Gold was discovered in 1851 and today the full extent of

Australia's vast mineral resources is still a matter of conjecture (and speculation).

As in most other industrial countries, there has been a slow down in economic growth since the mid-1970s and a growth of unemployment. The expansionist attitudes of the period up to this time have been modified and have affected the provision of resources for education.

Australia's major trading partners are, for exports, Japan, the USA, the UK; for imports, the USA, followed by the UK, and Japan. Japan is seen as an increasingly important trading partner and economic connections are strengthening all the time. Australia is also a major influence in the exploitation of the islands of Oceania but, probably because they present no military threat, there is even less knowledge of them than of the South East Asian countries.

An analysis of Australia's position is full of antitheses: a wealthy, sparsely populated, advanced country whose closest neighbours represent the most populous and least developed areas of the world; a society whose cultural ties are with countries on another side of the world, anxious to preserve its standards and traditions but needing to come to terms with its neighbours. The answers to many of these problems rest with the educational system.

6 THE EDUCATION SYSTEM

Aims, Objectives and Implementation

The system in Australia is an example of education in a new pioneering country. It was based on the systems of Europe, especially those of England and Ireland, but has demonstrated the influence on education of an egalitarian democracy and the growth of central and State control. Characteristics of the 'new' society which affected education in the beginning were a persistent shortage of labour, encouraging short schooling, irregular attendance and a high proportion of infants in the schools; a shortage of capital, especially private capital, throwing reliance on the State and the Churches; demographic problems such as an early imbalance of the sexes, an uneven geographic distribution of population, periodic (and considerable) increases in the number of children. The nature of the frontiers, with a sparse and scattered population, gave rise to problems which still persist.

Because of similarities in geography, economy, society and politics, the history of the development of education in the different states has been fairly uniform. Change has normally been the product of financial considerations and pressure of numbers rather than of educational theory or public opinion.

In the early days one of the aims of education was to separate children from their vicious parents. Teachers were controlled by clergymen of the Church of England, answerable to the governor. Children went to school at an early age and often left early, when they were able to work. 'Higher schools' were opened as the number of merchants and farmers increased, the first being at Parammata in 1800. The first school for middle and upper class girls, providing an education in 'polite accomplishments', was established in 1807. The methods used were those current in England at the time. Gradually opposition developed to the Anglican monopoly over elementary education and, after the New South Wales Church Act of 1836 regularised government aid for denominational elementary education, four competing systems - Anglican, Roman Catholic, Presbyterian and Methodist - emerged. In 1848 a National Board of Education was set up in New South Wales to control State elementary education and allocate funds to the four church systems. By this time it had been realised that the class-based system of England was unsuitable for the colonies and the more democratic schools of Scotland or the Irish National System were advocated as models. In Tasmania there had been a general system of schools controlled by a Board of Education; in South Australia a voluntary system; in Western Australia two government schools and a few private ones until 1849 when separate Protestant and Roman Catholic systems, subsidised by the government, were established.

A State system of schools existing side by side with State-aided denominational schools gradually spread through the different provinces and increasingly became the normal pattern of schooling. It was certainly the State schools which were to take the lead in reform and improvement, opening up curricula in a way denied the lower classes in England and giving education in Australia a democratic hue. As hostility to denominationalism grew the desire for social cohesion also grew and 'free, compulsory and secular' education became the slogan for educational reform from the 1880s onwards though hardly anywhere did it entirely meet all these ideals because of lack of funds and staff. At the same time there was seen to be a need for an effective examination system to set standards in the democratic, educational systems of the colonies and this need was met in the first place by the public examinations of Sydney University and Melbourne University's matriculation examination.

Prosperity and reform alternated with depression and retrenchment, but by 1908 primary school fees had been abolished in all states; syllabi were broadened; literature and history were given a central place with the intention of developing social and moral education; the pupil-teacher system was abandoned in favour of pre-training in teachers' colleges; external examinations replaced testing by inspectors and opened avenues to the universities for able children. The aim was to extend educational provision to the secondary level but in practice concern for extending literacy at the primary level to as many as possible absorbed the majority of funds and teachers. Some 30 years later with economic expansion and the emergence of the welfare state, there developed a new emphasis on equality in education: all children were expected to go to secondary schools; there was a move to discard the discrimination between academic, commercial and technical subjects; external examinations were widely discarded in favour of internal ones; the school leaving age was raised - all encouraging an increase in the number of non-academic students in schools.

With rising aspirations and subsequent demands for better and more education schooling is now seen by a substantial proportion of the population as a means of vocational preparation and an avenue for social mobility. Technological changes have led to students staying longer in the system than previously and as class distinctions decline there is a growing influence, particularly from white collar workers, on the content and organisation of the educational system. Selective secondary schools have been widely replaced by comprehensives. The range of secondary school subjects has widened and science subjects have increased in importance. Nevertheless a system which aims to provide a 'free, compulsory and secular' education for all, a slogan reiterated in the preface to a recent NSW Department of Education Report, and to engender a cohesiveness to society, is still criticised as being too conservative, for failing to deal adequately with the problems of minorities and for failing to meet the technological requirements of Australia, all of which continue to be burning issues.

To sum up therefore the objectives of Australian education have been to improve the human welfare of its citizens; to improve standards of health, the ability to earn a living and to serve the common good; to develop social graces, knowledge and character; and to develop the ability to use leisure time profitably.

Since the mid-1970s there has been more attention in the statement of general aims to the education of disadvantaged and cultural minorities and to improving the efficiency of the system. There has been greater insistence that the cultural background and ancestry of various groups - including aborigines - should be given greater recognition within the education system while using educational means to discriminate positively in favour of the disadvantaged. At the same time there have been more demands in official federal statements for more clearly defined objectives in education, more uniform curriculum practice and for greater parent control over the choice of schools which their children attend.

The Structure of the System

As in most countries education in Australia is divided into pre-primary, primary, secondary and tertiary levels. In recent years there has been a considerable expansion of kindergarten classes and of technical education. Another development has been that of colleges of Advanced Education. All post-secondary education is classified as 'tertiary' and there is no distinction between further and higher education.

The school year in Australia begins in early February and ends in mid-December. The academic year for universities and other institutions of tertiary education begins towards the end of February or in early March and ends in December. The long vacation is taken in summer (December to February) and two other short vacations, around Easter and in the winter, break the academic year generally into three terms. (Some universities now base their year on semesters).

Education is compulsory throughout Australia until the age of 15 (16 in Tasmania). Some children are exempted by reason of isolation from a school or physical disability and in such cases they receive tuition by correspondence, Schools of the Air or school radio and television broadcasts.

About 18% of Australia's children attend non-government schools and 80% of these attend schools in the highly developed Roman Catholic system, which can thus be said to represent a seventh educational system running parallel with the six state systems. Other independent schools are run by the Anglicans or the non-conformists. A few are Jewish and a few non-denominational. Organisation of the Catholic primary schools is largely diocesan under the general direction of the bishop while the secondary schools are administered by Australia-wide religious orders. In all states except Queensland and Western Australia non-government schools are subject to government inspection, and in Victoria and Tasmania these schools and their teachers must be registered with the State education authorities. Because the students of the non-government schools sit the same public examinations as those from State schools, the courses in the two are generally similar, with the former naturally giving more time to religious instruction than the latter. All the universities of Australia (with the exception of the Australian National University in Canberra) were created by an act of State parliament. They are constitutionally autonomous institutions though government nominees are members of their governing bodies and State allegiances are strong. There are no denominational universities.

Pre-school

Pre-school centres for children below the age for admission to schools exist in all States. The Commonwealth Government provides facilities in the Australian Capital Territory and the Northern Territories. In most States these facilities are provided by kindergarten unions or similar organisations, often with a government subsidy. In Tasmania pre-schools are run by the State Education Department. The facilities, however, are inadequate, and early in 1973 following parental pressures the federal government appointed an Australian Pre-Schools Committee to recommend measures that might be taken to ensure a year of pre-school education for every Australian child. A programme of central government grants has also been established for research into pre-schooling.

All states have adopted policies to make pre-school education universally available for all children aged four (or five in Western Australia). Apart from one state with a 40% participation rate of four year olds, 80% or more of the age group is in pre-primary institutions.

Primary Education

Although primary education extends officially from the ages of 5 to 12, there is considerable variation from state to state. Thus, in Queensland, children attend school from 6 to 13, whereas in Victoria they attend from 4+ to 11+. The basic aims are the inculcation of skills in language and numbers and the development of basic knowledge and attitudes. Emphasis on reading skills is particularly strong and children are expected to read by the time they reach Grade 3.

Schools are provided where there is sufficient population to justify them (in NSW 12 students) and, in theory, whatever the size or location of the schools, standards of tuition are similar because all teachers in the state follow similar courses of training and are transferable between urban and rural areas; syllabi are state-wide. In practice some schools are inevitably better than others depending on the quality of the teachers, the enlightenment of the principal or the facilities provided.

With the removal of primary leaving examinations, as with the removal of the 11+ in England, there has been a greater experimentation in teaching methods, classroom organisation and curriculum development. The project or thematic approach with an emphasis on discovery methods and integrated studies has become commonplace in many schools. Mixed ability groupings, family groupings and other experiments in classroom organisation are becoming the pattern in many urban schools and self-teaching machines are in use in some schools. Open plan schools are to be found especially in South Australia and the Australian Capital Territory and team teaching has been practised with varying degrees of success. Greater use is being made of audio and visual material and in line with the concept of greater freedom corporal punishment is frowned upon. It must be stressed, however, that not all developments have been successful or beneficial, and not all teaching is either good or enlightened. Certain sectors, especially the independent preparatory sector, Roman Catholic primary schools and small rural schools still tend to be traditional in their approach.

Since, outside the large towns and cities, Australia is made up of many small, often isolated, rural settlements and since there are often vast distances between these settlements, education for children in remote areas has called for special provision. There are still one-teacher all-age primary schools where all primary classes are in one room under the supervision of one teacher. In fact, more than a quarter of the Commonwealth government schools in Australia come under this category. They are, however, rapidly declining as children are 'bussed' to larger, centrally located schools.

Another development has been that of correspondence schools. These began in 1916 and have been expanded and modified considerably since then. There are today correspondence schools in each State capital, but their work has been greatly eased by the Schools of the Air, the first of which began in 1951, when it was realised that radio broadcasts could be beamed through to isolated farmsteads attuned to the Royal Flying Doctor Service radio network. Since then Schools of the Air have grown in number. There are now 12 - five in Western Australia, three in Queensland, two in the Northern Territories and one each in South Australia and New South Wales - serving children in a total area of a million square miles, though the number of children is now declining as parents send them to boarding schools or move their families from the outback.

Secondary Education

As in Britain the provision of secondary education is immensely complex. Progression from primary to secondary school is usually automatic at the age of 12 or 13 and secondary courses vary in length from five years in most states to six years in New South Wales, the Australian Capital Territory and Victoria. Most schools are co-educational (though some in the capital cities, especially the denominational schools) are segregated) and the most common type is the comprehensive or multi-purpose high school.

Traditionally public examinations set by central examining authorities in each state at the junior and senior secondary levels have controlled the curricula to a large extent, though in recent years the junior level examinations taken at the end of the third, fourth or fifth year of secondary schooling have been abolished or soon will be and their place taken by internal assessment. While the senior level examination, taken in the final year and used for matriculation purposes, is still retained in most states, there is a trend towards the abolition of examinations at this level also. These developments are said to have allowed a broadening of curricula and experimentation to cater for the individual needs of students. This kind of advance naturally varies from school to school, depending on the teaching aids, libraries and science facilities but the increase in numbers places a strain on the limited financial and manpower resources available.

Since there are slight variations in each state, the following paragraphs will try to highlight these.

New South Wales

In 1957 the Wyndham Report recommended comprehensive schooling with a common core curriculum and since 1962 secondary schooling has consisted of six years, the first four years leading to the School Certificate Examination (now 75% internally assessed by the school) and the last two years leading to the Higher School Certificate examination. The first four years consist of the following 'core' subjects: English, mathematics, science and a social science together with art, music and PE. Courses are offered at different levels according to ability in different subject areas (i.e. 'advanced', 'ordinary' and 'modified'). The 'modified' course is designed for pupils of below average ability.

The change to the upper school is marked by more demanding and academically rigorous courses especially for those taking first level courses. Those taking third level courses would have some difficulty in passing the HSC.

It is fair to say that the emphasis in New South Wales' secondary schools is on a broadly based comprehensive school catering for all abilities and offering a wide selection of electives ranging from Bahasa, Indonesia, Dutch, Asian Social Studies, ceramics to weaving, sheep husbandry and wool science, before academic streaming and pressure are offered to those few aiming for higher education. There are, however, still a few selective secondary schools in Sydney and several specialised schools (e.g. 4 agricultural high schools, and the Conservatorium High School which specialises in music.) To qualify for the School certificate a student must be examined in at least five subjects and pass in four at one sitting, a situation reminiscent of the old British School Certificate.

Victoria

This state is not typical of other Australian states in several ways since there are still a number of higher elementary schools (i.e. secondary forms at the top end of primary schools), several junior technical schools and single sex (girls only) secondary schools. By far the majority of schools are high schools and the tendency is towards co-education, integrated studies and delay in specialisation. Since 1973 only two external examinations have been taken – the Higher School Certificate at the end of six years' secondary schooling, conducted by the Victorian Universities and Schools Examination Board, and the Technical Leaving Examination taken after five years in a technical stream.

A number of non-government secondary schools continue to exist, especially in Melbourne. The majority of these are religious foundations.

Western Australia

Western Australia offers up to a five year secondary course. Ten percent of pupils enrolled leave after the first two years but at least 90% stay until the end of their third year and 25% stay for the full five years. Like comprehensive schools in Britain, however, those in Western Australia are equally varied and range from junior high schools (additional to the primary schools), high schools (offering three-year courses) to senior high schools (offering the full five-year course leading to the State Leaving Certificate). As in New South Wales there are a number of specialist agricultural, music or art high schools of which Perth Modern Senior High School (Music) is possibly the most famous.

Queensland

Still regarded as the most conservative state educationally, though since 1962 it too has rapidly moved towards a co-educational comprehensive system. Because of sparsely populated areas there are still primary schools with secondary 'tops' and a number of children are catered for by correspondence schools, but in those areas that have five-year comprehensive high schools developments are towards common courses in the first year followed by electives thereafter set by and assessed by individual schools though externally moderated.

South Australia

South Australia's secondary education is a mixture of high schools, technical schools and area schools. Courses are still streamed or 'tracked', though, as elsewhere, internal assessment with external moderation is becoming more frequent.

Tasmania

Tasmania followed a tripartite system of secondary education until 1962. With the abolition of the Classification Test in that year it has had comprehensive, non-selective high schools. Recently it has experimented with sixth form colleges, called Matriculation Colleges, which cater for fifth and sixth year students studying for the Tasmanian Higher Scool Certificate. How far this experiment will spread to other parts of Australia remains to be seen.

The Northern Territory

This is the least populous region and as such has the smallest number of secondary schools. Before the cyclone of Christmas Day 1974 there were three government high schools in Darwin with another one in Alice Springs and four other government and non-government schools in different parts of the Territory. Courses and curricula were identical with those of South Australia whose examinations were also taken.

In recent years secondary education in Australia generally has undergone a marked change. The universities, for long the restraining influence on the school curriculum and examinations, have begun to experiment with new forms of assessment, including recommendations and reports from individual schools. The result has been a move away from external examinations towards greater freedom in curriculum innovation and internal courses and assessment. Experiments with thematic approaches and mixed ability groups have also gained in importance. Owing to rising enrolments many new buildings have been put up and not unnaturally these have reflected architectural changes. The fact that each state system is centralised and relatively uniform means that ideas and experiments in one state are quickly transmitted to another, while children in one state have the same 'equality of opportunity' as those in another.

Non-Government Schools

Since these cater for 20% of all secondary enrolments they require a special mention. A cross between the British independent and direct grant schools the non-government schools are styled grammar schools, colleges or high schools. Many have religious foundations and the majority are single sex institutions, though this pattern is also changing. Many are also boarding institutions which aim at giving a broad cultural training as well as a more academic curriculum. All non-government schools and their staff must register with the various state departments of education, though it is not common for them to be subject to a full scale inspection unless there are pressing reasons for this to take place.

Technical Education

Technical education has frequently been regarded as the 'Cinderella' of Australian education but following the Martin Report (1964) there has been a considerable expansion especially with the creation of technological universities in New South Wales and Victoria.

Some technical subjects are taught as part of the general curriculum of secondary high schools or, in some states (e.g. South Australia and Victoria) in separate technical high schools, but most technical education takes place in technical colleges controlled by State Departments of Education except in New South Wales and South Australia where separate departments are responsible. Some technical training courses are also provided by private industry and government departments or organisations.

In the past courses have generally been part time; 'learn as you earn' ones, but the trend recently has been towards more full time sandwich and even day release courses. It has also been towards more mature students going in for training. Courses range from technician/craftsmen courses, through apprenticeships to post-graduate diplomas. At a higher level, courses are offered by the Institutes of Technology in South Australia and Western Australia and by the New South Wales Univesity of Technology. However, as the whole question of technical education is being looked at by the Technical Education Commission set up by the central government, it is probable that the whole scope of technical education will be reformed.

Tertiary Education

Tertiary education in Australia is carried out in universities, colleges of advanced education and technical and further education colleges. In spite of the widening base for higher education there is still great selectivity at the universities. The Committee on the Future of Tertiary Education in Australia recommended that in 1965/66 capital grants be made by the state and federal governments to 12 specified institutions in five states, preliminary to an expansion of tertiary education outside the universities to provide degree level education oriented to the needs of industry, commerce and government. Administrative changes have taken place in the states to coordinate the activities of these Colleges of Advanced Education. In New South Wales an Advanced Education Board has been established; in

Victoria the powers of the Victoria Institute of Colleges have been strengthened; in Tasmania a Council of Advanced Education has been set up and in Queensland and South Australia Boards of Advanced Education. In some states provision is being made for the coordination of all tertiary education, notably through the Higher Education Authority in New South Wales, the Tertiary Education Commission in Western Australia and the Joint Consultative Council in Tasmania.

Universities

Students wishing to enter a university must have passed the matriculation examination in one of the states (i.e. after five or six years of secondary education) and each university has its own regulations specifying the number and combination of subjects to be passed or the level of performance required. In spite of a tremendous increase in the number of university places over the past decade places are still not available for all matriculated students who wish to enrol and several universities have quotas on enrolments in their courses.

Most university courses are full time day courses taking from three to six years but two significant categories of Australian students are those studying part time and those following courses offered by the external studies departments of a few of the univesities, e.g. Queensland and New England. Post-graduate study and research can be undertaken at all the universities. Bachelor degree courses last three or four years and can be followed by post-graduate diplomas (usually one year), masters degree (two years) or doctorates (three or four years).

Enrolments in Australian universities rose dramatically in the 1970s. However, the number of full time students fell slightly between 1977 and 1980 though the increase of part time and external students in the same period compensated for this fall. The arts faculties take about 28% of enrolments, science 20%, medicine 12% and engineering 10%. Within these broad areas however, most universities have a larger number of faculties than their British equivalents. Concern for standards of teaching has led to the establishment of research units and tertiary teacher training centres, and concern for the high rate of drop outs or repeaters has led to reform in examination systems, the introduction of continuous assessment, etc. There has likewise been an increase in taught master's courses.

The harsh financial realities of recent years have weakened the so-called autonomy of universities and the Australian Universities Commission has gained considerably in power and influence. The AUC arranges finance for universities on a triennial basis but it also scrutinises course reorganisation, buildings and university government. Although in the midst of change, it is fair to describe Australian universities as cautiously progressive rather than revolutionary.

Colleges of Advanced Education

The Colleges of Advanced Education are a fairly recent creation. Following the Martin Committee's recommendations (1964) for the expansion of tertiary education into a non-university sector supported by Federal funds Victoria established the Victoria Institute of Colleges. Other states quickly followed and CAEs are now part of the tertiary education scene. Their nearest equivalents are the polytechnics in the UK - i.e. they are an amalgamation of technical or technology colleges and other colleges (e.g. agricultural colleges, the National Institute of Dramatic Art, the NSW Conservatorium of Music) plus new foundations - offering degree level courses orientated towards industry, commerce and government, and in some cases the teaching profession. The Australian Commission on Advanced Education sees the CAEs as being "to increase the range of opportunity for tertiary education having a strong emphasis on practical application . . . The performance of its graduates in industry and society rather than their qualifications will be the criterion by which the community judges the college system". The emphasis is therefore more on teaching than research.

The Colleges of Advanced Education almost caught up the universities in numbers of students enrolled with 159,476 students in 1980 compared to 163,156 in universities. The 1974 figures were 107,202 in Colleges compared to 142,859 in universities. However, the Colleges absorb a smaller proportion and declining proportion of public resources than the universities (8% in 1979 compared to 9% in 1975, while the university proportion of government educational spending has been steady at 12% throughout the late 1970s). The growth of enrolments in the Colleges has been mainly among part time and external students - 38.2% and 12.8% respectively in 1980 compared to 33.2% and 6.0% in 1974. The number of full time students has fallen from a peak of 84,894 in 1977 to 78,229 in 1980.

Courses offered range from a two-year diploma to three- and four-year degree courses. In some institutions like the royal Melbourne Institute of Technology, the NSW Institute of Technology in Sydney, post-graduate masters' and doctoral degrees are also offered.

At this point it is worth referring to the Australian Council on Awards in Advanced Education which has been established by joint action of the six states and the federal government. One of the functions of the Council is to promote consistency throughout Australia in the nomenclature and standards used for awards in advanced education. This body might assume greater importance if Australia were to set up an open-type university, a project under consideration at present by a Committee of Enquiry of the AUC.

Technical and Further Education Colleges

These institutions grew rapidly in the late 1970s. They offer courses in professional, para-professional, trades, other skilled, adult and further education. They have six streams. The first two lead to a diploma or associate diploma; the third and fourth streams follow courses for a certificate; while the other two streams have shorter courses which do not lead to a formal qualification. Over 90% of the students are part-time combining study with employment. In 1979 42% of the students were following general, preparatory and adult education courses, 38% skilled trades programmes and 21% professional or para-professional courses (888,228 students in all).

Teacher Education

Specialist teacher colleges have been absorbed into Colleges of Advanced Education (except for some non-government denominational colleges). Most primary teachers are trained in three year courses in the Colleges of Advanced Education, while secondary teachers are prepared through four-year courses which take place mainly in universities (though both types of teacher are trained in both kinds of institution). There are proposals to extend the four-year course to all kinds of teachers.

In August 1972 it was announced that the Commonwealth would extend the present financing arrangements applying to universities and colleges of advanced education to include the state teachers' colleges which are being developed as self-governing tertiary institutions (and also to pre-school teachers' colleges). Trainee teachers are recruited mainly from students leaving school on the results of their final secondary examination. Infant and primary teachers follow a three-year course which includes teaching theory, educational psychology, physical education, hygiene, crafts, art and music as well as subjects intended to broaden their own educational background. Secondary school teachers should be graduates with a professional qualification such as a diploma in education. At some universities students can take a four-year bachelor of education course, which includes professional training.

Trainee teachers are paid a living allowance and the education department bears the cost of tuition, some incidental expenses and, in most states, textbooks. In return for this assistance the trainees are required to enter into a bond to serve the department for periods varying in most states according to the length of training. There are a few non-governmental teachers' colleges.

Innovations include experiments in curriculum, breaking away from traditional education areas like philosophy, sociology, psychology and developing broader interdisciplinary subject areas such as 'Man in a Scientific and Technological World', or 'Education in Australian Culture and Society'. At university level experiments are being made with taking education electives alongside main degree subjects. Even the non-government sector is taking seriously the question of teacher training for new recruits and in-service training for those already in the non-government schools. In order to overcome the teacher shortages in mathematics and science special teaching scholarships have been awarded by the federal government, teachers have been recruited from overseas and salaries have been improved. Induction programmes for beginning teachers have also been introduced as well as plans to train aboriginal teachers and those for colleges of technical and further education.

7 EDUCATIONAL ADMINISTRATION

With the constitution creating the federation in 1901 responsibility for education was retained by the states. As a result school systems differ from state to state, although for reasons mentioned earlier there is a remarkable similarity between the six states. However, although the constitution might not have changed, the realities of life have, and with the need for larger sums of money the federal government has begun to play a larger part in state education.

The establishment of a Commonwealth Office of Education in 1946 led to an increased interest in and involvement in educational problems and policy (e.g. equality of educational provision). By 1955 the Office of Education was already in control of international matters affecting UNESCO and other international bodies, immigration insofar as it affected education, the Commonwealth Scholarship Scheme, etc. It was reorganised in 1966 as the Commonwealth Department of Education and Science to advise the federal government on educational matters and to administer various federal schemes of financial assistance. It was renamed the Australian Department of Education in 1973 by the Labour government, and Science is now a separate department.

In 1959 the Australian University Commission was created to act as a liaison body between the federal and state governments and the universities; to report every three years on university development; and to make recommendations on university finance to the governments concerned. (Because of the federal structure of Australia the AVC cannot be equated with the UGC in Britain.) In 1964 the Martin Report recommended federal assistance to other forms of tertiary education and the Australian Commission on Advanced Education cooperates with the AUC in advising the federal government on the development and financial requirements of the universities and colleges of advanced education.

Other federal bodies have been established to deal with aspects of education other than at the university level. The Australian Schools Commission, for example, was established by the federal government to investigate the needs of students in all schools at all levels and an Australian Pre-Schools Commission was set up to develop and administer a comprehensive pre-school and child care programme. The Australian Council for Educational Research, a non-government body with a wide range of educational research activities, receives financial support from both the federal and state governments. The Australian College of Education, a loosely-structured body founded in 1959, aims at bringing together leaders in education for their mutual benefit and the benefit of education throughout Australia. There is also a Curriculum Development Centre to advise on school curriculum and a National Aboriginal Education set up in 1977. Nevertheless, in spite of greater federal involvement, especially at the tertiary level, education is still very much a state matter. Policy is determined by the state cabinet or the federal parliament but the finance available for school level education is approved by the state in the annual state budget.

State Departments of Education are responsible for primary, secondary and teacher training levels of education as well as for adult education and leisure time activities. Each Department is divided into a head office in the state capital and into area offices, each under its own Director of Education. These Directors are responsible for provision of education at local level and for supervision and inspection through District Inspectors. The latter wield considerable power as it is impossible to be promoted in any teaching appointment with the approval of an Inspector.

The pattern of centralised control at state level is part of Australian history but in the past 25 years attempts have been made to decentralise, especially in New South Wales and Queensland. In New South Wales, for example, the state was divided into 11 administrative areas as early as 1948. Since then other states have to a greater or lesser extent moved detailed administrative matters to the area offices, thus leaving the State Departments of Education to consider policy matters in a wider context.

As part of this move towards decentralisation there has also been a change in curriculum revision and innovation. The traditional pattern, as in all centralised systems, has been for curriculum statements to be issued centrally but increasingly, teachers at the grass roots level have been encouraged to initiate change and teachers' centres, as in the UK, are being used to disseminate information.

Planning

From the foregoing it can be seen that educational planning is primarily a state responsibility though the influence of the federal government and national educational bodies is considerable and is growing fast. This influence can naturally be expected to increase as the states request more and more financial assistance from the centre.

Each State Department of Education has a Division of Planning under a director. The Division is sub-divided into an economic planning section, chiefly concerned with the demand for and supply of educational resources (e.g. buildings, staff, equipment); an information section; a demographic planning section or unit concerned with school mapping and the placement of children especially at secondary level; and a survey section which undertakes various surveys and research.

Research and planning go hand in hand and it is not uncommon to have separate research centres as, for example, in New South Wales where there is a Centre for Research in Learning and Instruction, mostly concerned with practical problems in the classroom, and a Centre for Research in Measurement and Evaluation, primarily concerned with assessment of aptitudes and achievement. Curriculum developments and planning are left to Secondary Schools Boards and Boards of Senior School Studies.

8 EDUCATIONAL FINANCE

Public expenditure on education in Australia was relatively low in real terms compared to other industrial countries before the 1970s. In 1970 13.3% of total government expenditure (federal and state) was devoted to education which amounted to 4.2% of GNP. In the 1970s there was a rapid expansion of public resources allocated to education so that they reached 16.2% of total government expenditure and 6.6% of GNP in 1977. More recently there have been a cut-back so that the proportion of GNP spent on education declined to 5.9% in 1979/80.

Public educational expenditure was split in the proportion of 63% on schools (including pre-schools), 20% on higher education and 10% on technical and further education in 1979-80. The proportion on technical and further education increased from 7% in 1975-76 while the percentage absorbed by higher education has fallen from 21% in the same year.

No special tax is levied for education and each state determines what part of its total income is to be spent in the education sector. Finance comes mainly from two sources. *Current running expenditure* comes from consolidated revenue funds made up of tax rebates from the federal government, revenue receipts and indirect taxes levied at state level. *Capital expenditure* comes from Commonwealth-raised loan funds. Because state governments surrendered their rights to levy direct taxation during World War Two (1942) they are now largely dependent on the federal government for funds. This situation highlights a burning issue in Australian education – the clash of interest between the Commonwealth and the States.

Commonwealth involvement began with the power to make awards to students, firstly at post-graduate level, later at upper secondary level. Its real involvement, however, has come about because of the increasing cost of providing tertiary education. In 1950 universities appealed to the Commonwealth government for assistance and the Murray Report (1957) and the Martin Report (1964) recommended that federal funds should be allocated to universities. This has been on the basis of A$1 for A$1.85 in the case of recurrent expenditure. Perhaps the biggest increase in federal funding in the 1970s came as a result of the creation of Colleges of Advanced Education (CAE) following the Martin Committee's recommendations. These are Commonwealth institutions under State auspices (except for Canberra CAE which is entirely financed by the Commonwealth government) and are financed on the same basis as universities.

Sizeable Commonwealth contributions are also made to independent schools and new state schools. In fact, some Roman Catholic and rural schools have only survived as a result of federal support. Although Commonwealth funds are welcomed - and 20% of all educational expenditure comes from the Commonwealth - States fear that the Commonwealth government may begin to demand how these funds are spent. As a result States are introducing a series of checks and balances to protect their own rights but these rights in education are now very fluid and constitutionally obscure and it seems inevitable that the moves towards centralised control will increase.

Tuition fees are not charged in government schools, though parents are expected to buy their children's textbooks, personal equipment and uniforms. As described earlier the non-government schools are financed by fees, government grants and private contributions. The federal government makes special grants for school libraries and science facilities. Large numbers of scholarships are awarded.

9 DEVELOPMENT AND PLANNING OF THE EDUCATION SYSTEM

Since 1977 the quantitative growth of provision has slowed, stopped or, in some cases, been reversed. Education has ceased to be favoured by politicians as it was in the mid-1970s. The contraction represents the consequence of changed attitudes as well as of declining rates of population growth. There are major problems within the education system in adjusting to contraction of resources and teachers which are psychological as well as material.

The emphasis since the late 1970s has been on qualitative rather than quantitative improvement. Parents freedom of choice of schooling for their chidlren has been widened so that good schools can attract more students. The federal Curriculum Development Centre proposed a core curriculum for schools in 1980 to encourage greater uniformity of standards. From 1982 the federal government began a programme of rationalisation and consolidation of colleges of advanced education to produce greater efficiency. Each of these measures, though designed to promote efficiency, are seen by many in the education system as further attacks on the gains made in the 1970s.

There have been areas of expansion within this general framework of rationalisation and contraction. More attention has been paid to the educational needs of students from cultural minorities - both in terms of transmitting the home culture and in expanding provision for the teaching of English as a second language. Vocational and Technical education programmes for school leavers and projects within the Transition from School of Work Programme initiated in 1979 have tackled the problems associated with rising youth unemployment. There has been more concern with the education of the handicapped.

These approaches still are only beginning to deal with the problems involved. Australia has important growing and hitherto neglected non-British cultural minorities. As in other industrialised countries - in recession - the problems of young unemployed have proved so intractable that educational courses appear often little more than marginal palliatives.

Australian education has undergone expansion in the 1970s which has widened the range of educational opportunties open to many children, young people and adults. The percentage of children receiving pre-school education has increased considerably, as have the proportions of young people staying in education beyond the minimum age required by law, of students going on to higher education, of women in higher education and of adults receiving part time education. The achievements of the decade up to 1977 were very considerable.

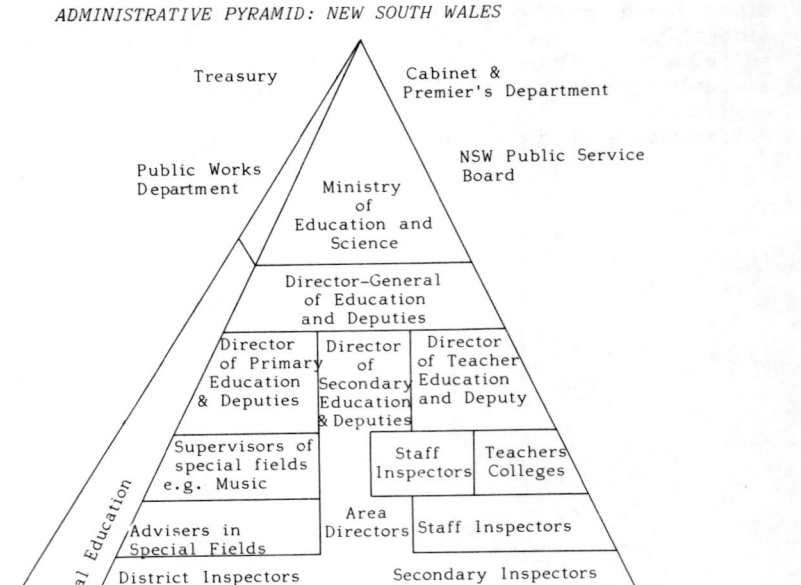

ADMINISTRATIVE PYRAMID: NEW SOUTH WALES

- Treasury
- Cabinet & Premier's Department
- Public Works Department
- NSW Public Service Board
- Ministry of Education and Science
- Director-General of Education and Deputies
- Director of Primary Education & Deputies
- Director of Secondary Education & Deputies
- Director of Teacher Education and Deputy
- Supervisors of special fields e.g. Music
- Staff Inspectors
- Teachers Colleges
- Advisers in Special Fields
- Area Directors
- Staff Inspectors
- District Inspectors
- Secondary Inspectors
- School Principals, Teachers and Clerical Assistants

Department of Technical Education

SPECIAL SERVICES	ACCOMMODATION	CURRICULA	ADMINISTRATION
Division of Planning Centre for Learning & Instruction Centre for Measurement and Evaluation Guidance and Special Education School Library Service Audio-visual Centre Automatic Data Processing	School Sites Buildings Furniture Stores and Equipment	Secondary Schools Board Board of Senior School Studies Examinations & Scholarships Directorate of Studies	Finance Teacher Personnel Secretariat Industrial Relations

Administrative machinery of a state education system. The bureaucratic pyramid is supported by many centres, divisions, branches and other offices. The third face of the pyramid is represented by miscellaneous Department of Education and Science activities, e.g. NSW Universities Board, Advanced Education Board. Policy proposals emerging from the edifice are sometimes clouded by the attitudes expressed by the other departments shown.

Source: Education in Australia, P.E. Jones (David & Charles 1974).

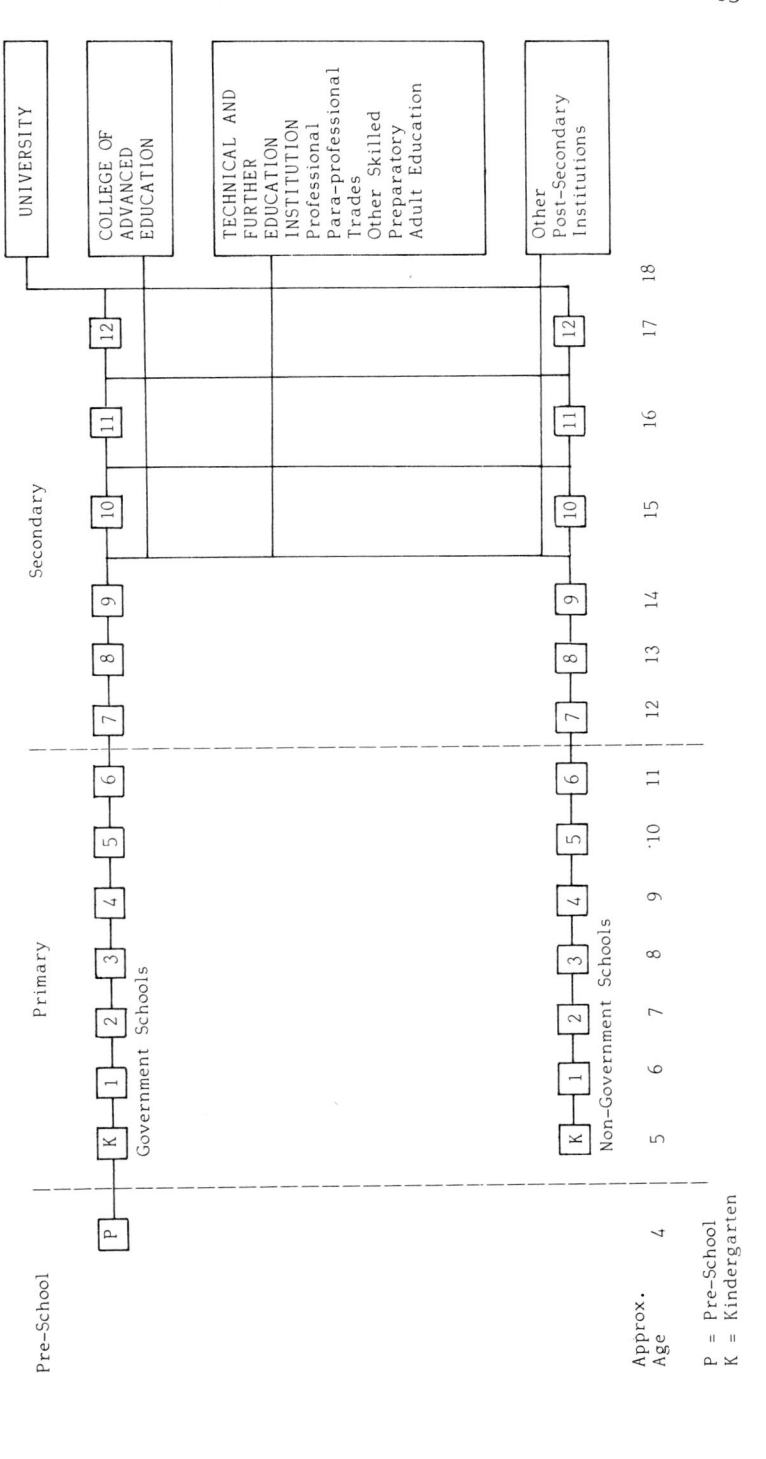

65

DIAGRAM OF THE GENERAL EDUCATION SYSTEM

Pre-School	Primary	Secondary	

Pre-School: P

Government Schools: K 1 2 3 4 5 6 7 8 9 10 11 12 → UNIVERSITY, COLLEGE OF ADVANCED EDUCATION

Non-Government Schools: K 1 2 3 4 5 6 7 8 9 10 11 12 → Other Post-Secondary Institutions

TECHNICAL AND FURTHER EDUCATION INSTITUTION
Professional
Para-professional
Trades
Other Skilled
Preparatory
Adult Education

Approx. Age: 4 5 6 7 8 9 10 11 12 13 14 15 16 17 18

P = Pre-School
K = Kindergarten

Grades in Australian Schools 1972

The grade terminology follows, as nearly as possible, that used in government primary and high schools in each State in 1972. It is not necessarily used in all types of schools. The guides have been written in to agree with the age-scale shown on the diagram in order to indicate differences in age-grade patterns between States. However, age-grade information is not precise enough to allow determination of accurate average age of students in each grade and the age indications are therefore only approximate. The diagram should not be taken as a comparison of academic standards of grades between States.

AGE	ACT	NSW	NT	QLD
18-	Higher School Certificate — Form VI	Higher School Certificate — Form VI	Matriculation Secondary School Cert. — 5th year	
17-	Form V School Certificate — Form IV	Form V School Certificate — Form IV	5th Year Leaving Certificate Secondary School Cert. 4th year	Senior Cert. — Grade 12
16-				Grade 11 Junior Cert.
15-	Form III	Form III	4th Year	Grade 10
14-	Form II	Form II	3rd Year	Grade 9
13-	Form I	Form I	2nd Year	Grade 8
12-	6th Class	6th Class	1st Year	Grade 7
11-	5th Class	5th Class	Grade VII	Grade 6
10-	4th Class	4th Class	Grade VI	Grade 5
9-	3rd Class	3rd Class	Grade V	Grade 4
8-	2nd Class	2nd Class	Grade IV	Grade 3
7-	1st Class	1st Class	Grade III	Grade 2
6-	Kindergarten	Kindergarten	Grade II	Grade 1
5-			Grade I(b)	

AGE	SA	TAS	VIC	WA
18-	Matriculation Secondary School Certificate, 5th year	Higher School Certificate	Higher School Certificate & Matriculation	Leaving Certificate and Matriculation
	5th year Leaving Certificate	6th Year (a) Higher School Certificate	6th Form	5th Year
17-	Secondary School Certificate, 4th Year	5th Year School Certificate	5th Form	4th Year Achievement Certificate
16-	4th Year	4th Year School Certificate (Preliminary)	4th Form	3rd Year
15-	3rd Year	3rd Year	3rd Form	2nd Year
14-	2nd Year	2nd Year	2nd Form	1st Year
13-	1st Year	1st Year	1st Form	
12-	Grade VII	Grade 6	Grade VI	Grade 7
11-	Grade VI	Grade 5	Grade V	Grade 6
10-	Grade V	Grade 4	Grade IV	Grade 5
9-	Grade IV	Grade 3	Grade III	Grade 4
8-	Grade III	Grade 2	Grade II	Grade 3
7-	Grade II	Grade 1	Grade I	Grade 2
6-	Grade I(b)			Grade 1
5-				

(a) In Tasmania many students study for the Higher School Certificate over a two-year period

(b) Preparatory grades are attached to some schools in South Australia and the Northern Territory

(c) Pre-school centres for children below the age for admission to schools have been established in many localities in all States. The Commonwealth Government provides pre-school facilities for children in the ACT and NT.

AUSTRALIA BASIC STATISTICS

Population

1969	1979
12,500,000	13,500,000

Enrolment Ratios

Primary
Enrolments as a percentage of the population aged 6-11

Secondary
Enrolments as a percentage of the population aged 12-16

Higher
Enrolments as a percentage of the population aged 20-24

(Figures in brackets are the enrolments of students of the relevant age group as a percentage of the total population of these ages)

	Primary	Secondary	Higher
1970	115	82	16.6
1979	111 (100)	86 (78)	25.7

Participation rates in upper secondary and higher education

Secondary
Pupils aged 15 and over as a percentage of the age group 15-18

Higher
Students in Universities and Colleges of Advanced Education as a percentage of the 17-22 age group

	Secondary	Higher
1975	36.5%	18.1%
1979	37.1%	19.5%

Institutions, Teachers and Students

	Schools	Teachers	Pupils
Primary			
1975	3,590	78,746	1,810,344
1980	3,466*	90,667*	1,884,081
Secondary			
1975	–	74,041	1,099,922
1980	–	84,529*	1,100,481

* = 1979

Students in Further and Higher Education

	Universities	Colleges of Advanced Education	Technical & Further Education
1975	148,338	122,557	–
1980	163,136	159,476	888,228*

Higher Education Students by Field of Study 1977

		% female
Education and Teacher Training	75,750	65.7
Humanities	46,233	59.3
Fine and Applied Arts	6,349	58.5
Law	10,593	27.1
Social and Behavioural Science	20,954	37.0
Business and Commerce	35,751	17.3
Natural Science	28,267	29.4
Mathematics and Computer Science	5,469	22.1
Medicine and related fields	21,144	49.4
Engineering	22,801	1.9
Architecture	6,925	14.5
Agriculture	6,461	21.2
Other	14,179	59.8

Public Expenditure on Education

	As a % of total government spending	As a % of GNP
1970	13.3%	4.2%
1979	16.2%*	5.9%

* = 1977

Public Expenditure on Education by Level

	1975	1979
Pre-Schools	2%	1%
Primary & Secondary Schools	61%	62%
Universities	12%	12%
Colleges of Advanced Education	9%	8%
Technical & Further Education	7%	10%
Other	9%	7%

Basic Social and Economic Data

Gross National Product per capita 1979 - US$9,120
Average annual growth of GNP per capita 1960-79 - 2.8%
Life expectancy 1979 - 74 years
Proportion of the labour force employed in:

Agriculture
1960   11%
1979   6%

Industry
1960   40%
1979   33%

Services
1960   49%
1979   61%

Bangladesh

CONTENTS

1 Geography 72
2 Population 74
3 Society and Culture 75
4 History and Politics 75
5 The Economy 77
6 The Education System 78
7 Educational Administration . . . 85
8 Educational Finance 87
9 Development and Planning of
　the Education System 91

Bangladesh is the poorest of the countries of the Indian subcontinent and has the most precarious economic position. It has struggled to find national and political cohesion since seceding from Pakistan in 1971. These social, economic and political constraints place great difficulties in the way of achieving a fully efficient and dynamic education system. Yet the reform of education is seen by governments as one of the means of escape from chronic economic, social and political problems.

Despite the gravity of the situation, Bangladesh does have some advantages, both cultural and economic, which are not enjoyed by some other Third World countries with somewhat less acute economic and political difficulties. One language – Bengali – is used by 98% of the population and can be used in all educational institutions at least at the lower levels. There is a high degree of religious unity in a population which is 85% Muslim, and though there has been official reassertion of Islamic values there have been fewer conflicts with secularist ideology than has characterised some other predominantly Muslim states.

The education system, quantitively, is relatively well developed in relation to the economic level of Bangladesh. By 1975 over 70% of children of primary school age were in school (including 90% of boys). Universities and secondary schools are also relatively well developed.

The major problems in education firstly are those not only of improving present levels of provision but of maintaining them in the face of economic difficulties and rates of population growth. Though a programme to achieve 90% enrolment in primary schools by 1985 was launched in 1980 this goal was adopted in the context of a significant decline in the proportion of the age group in primary schools between 1975 and 1979. The economic and demographic causes of this decline are likely to obstruct any further expansion. The obstacles to widespread provision of primary schooling for the poorest sections of society and for girls remain formidable.

The second major problem in primary schooling is qualitative. Standards - as measured by the provision of buildings, equipment and books and by the teacher:pupil ratio - are very poor. In these conditions, primary education is likely to remain rigid and narrow. It is not capable of leading a transformation of Bangladeshi society from below. Educational policy makers are in a quandary of trying to increase provision while standards in existing schools are too low to make primary education effective.

Secondary and higher educational provision increased proportionately more than primary schooling in the 1970s as measured both by numbers and financial allocations. This can be seen to be a result of popular demand but the relatively greater expansion of post-primary education has tended to create an unbalanced education system and to reinforce patterns of social stratification.

While secondary schools and universities are relatively developed and efficient, they maintain an academic/literary ethos inherited from the British colonial period. The curriculum and examinations are similar to those that operated in the colonial period and they have strong parallels with historical practice in England.

The continued bias towards literary/academic studies at upper secondary and higher education levels in part may be attributed to the colonial legacy. But it is reinforced by popular demand and is difficult to change as long as the Bangladesh economy does not offer more diversified employment opportunities.

1 GEOGRAPHY

Topography

Bangladesh is located around the intersection of the 90° east meridian and the Tropic of Cancer, lying south of the Himalayas. It has an area of 55,126 square miles (141,122 sq km). Its southern shores front the Bay of Bengal and apart from a small area in the south-east, adjacent to Burma, the land frontier is almost totally shared with the Republic of India. Physiographically the country consists of alluvial plains, a coastal region of saline soil, and hilly regions in the east and north-east (there are no mountains). The country's natural resources include the great fertile plains, river fish, some 8,500 square miles (22,015 sq km) of forest, natural gas and probably offshore oil.

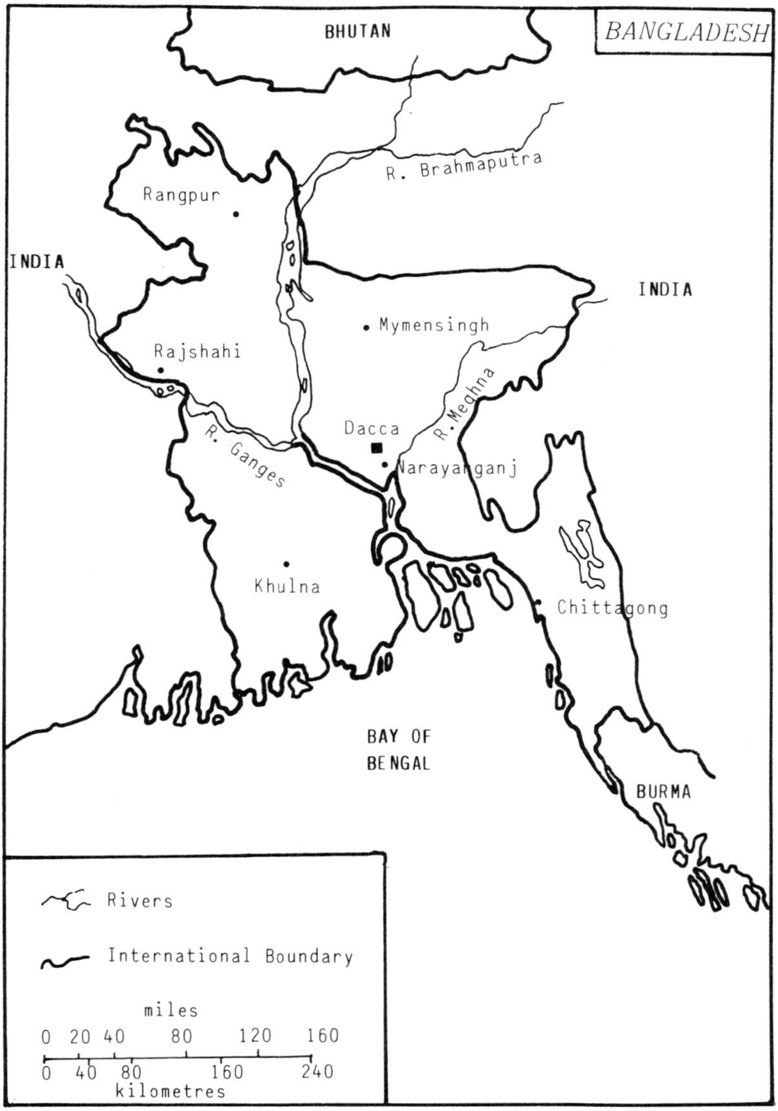
BANGLADESH
BHUTAN
R. Brahmaputra
Rangpur
INDIA
INDIA
Mymensingh
Rajshahi
R. Meghna
Dacca
R. Ganges
Narayanganj
Khulna
Chittagong
BAY OF
BENGAL
BURMA
Rivers
International Boundary
miles
0 20 40 80 120 160
0 40 80 160 240
kilometres

Climate

For 8-9 months of the year the climate is hot, being rarely lower than 13°C in winter and rising above 20°C in summer (April until the end of October). High humidity, 90-100% in summer, is linked with the long monsoon. Monthly rainfall averages 50 mm for 8 months of the year. The north of the country (Rajshahi District) is marginally hotter and drier in spring, and Sylhet District in the east is wetter and cooler, but there are no hill stations where relief from the trying climate can be found.

Communications

The country is a vast complex of rivers based on the Ganges, Meghna and Brahmaputra which inevitably serve as the main routes of inland transport for people and goods. The road link between the capital, Dacca, and the main port Chittagong, has three ferry crossings, while the railway takes an extensive detour to link the two places. Transport is thus slow, and while motorable roads are kept in reasonable repair after the annual monsoon rains, structural track weaknesses and single-line working limit train speeds to 35 m.p.h. Regular flights by the State airline link several towns with Dacca, reducing, for example, the 180 mile (290 km) journey Dacca-Chittagong to 40 minutes from 8 hours by train or 6 by road.

2 POPULATION

Growth

Between 1901 and 1961 the population rose from 29 million to 59 million. The provisional result of the 1974 census gives 71 million but estimates of international agencies of 80 million plus are more realistic and this figure is often cited by government. The 1979 estimate was 84,700,000 million with an annual growth rate of 3% between 1970 and 1979.

Distribution

The country has 19 district towns (i.e. district administrative 'capitals'), 61 local towns (i.e. sub-divisional 'capitals'), 3 ports (one inland), and 65,000 villages in which 92% of the population live. In 1951 Dacca had 500,000 inhabitants. This has grown to over 1.5 million. The other major towns which are referred to as cities are Chittagong (population about 900,000), Khulna (population about 450,000) and Narayanganj (population about 270,000). Inevitably, most of the illiterates are village or city slum dwellers.

Groups

The people of Bangladesh form a compact homogeneous racial group. The European presence in India, beginning with the Portuguese in the sixteenth century and continued by the British in the eighteenth, left no trace in the colour or physique of its inhabitants. Today's folklore, art, literature, and philosophy stem from and continue the indigenous cultural traditions. Census figures indicate that at least 98% of the population speak Bengali.

Health

In 1950 life expectancy for a Bengali was 30 years. In 1979 it was 49. Tuberculosis, cholera, dysentery (and until 1975 smallpox) are endemic and malnutrition, dense housing and the absence of effective sanitary provision ensure that they will continue to be. A 1971 estimate quoted 7,600 doctors, 250 midwives and 6,000 hospital beds for 70 million people.

3 SOCIETY AND CULTURE

Social Patterns

Since such a high proportion of the population live in villages, the village as a social force and unit has a special importance. Most city workers maintain regular contact with their villages, often owning land which is worked by relatives or leased to other villagers. They usually go home for annual holidays and, if possible, religious festivals, discarding city clothes for the ubiquitous *lunghi*. Bangladesh remains a largely peasant society without a sophisticated upper class. In towns a certain superiority over the labouring classes is assumed and asserted by the beneficiaries of university education, and by those who have secured posts in the civil service.

Religion

It was the predominance of Muslims in eastern India which led to their grouping as the east wing of Pakistan in 1947. Currently 85% of the populace are a Muslim, 12% Hindu and the remainder Christian and Buddhist. Although in 1971 the Hindu community suffered at the hands of both the Pakistan Army and some Muslim Bengalis, most of the 10 million refugees who fled to India returned. Islamic principles were recently reasserted in place of the previous constitution's secularism.

4 HISTORY AND POLITICS

Genesis of East Pakistan

This lay partly in Muslim resentment at two centuries of Hindu social and economic domination in eastern Bengal. Hindus were landlords, merchants and administrators: Muslims were cultivators. Thus in 1947 there was support for Mr Jinnah's policy of creating an Islamic state at the partition of India. East Pakistan became one of five provinces, the other four comprising West Pakistan. But with no more than a common faith to cement this political union of people separated by 1000 miles (1,610 km) of alien India – people of different race, language, habits and temperament – it proved as difficult to sustain as would a union of Catholic Austria and Ireland.

Growing Unrest

By 1952 East Pakistan found itself in economic subservience to West Pakistan. Jinnah's declaration in 1948 of Urdu as the official national language and script led to 'language riots' in Dacca and the shooting of students in 1952. In October 1955 Pakistan was reorganised in two nominally equal wings with equal representation in a central assembly. But under Ayub Khan's authoritarian rule the feeling of exploitation and discrimination grew. Eventual secession from Pakistan was presaged in 1966 when Sheikh Mujibur Rahman's Awami League adopted his '6 Point Programme' as its creed. This proposed retention by each wing of its own resources and autonomy in everything except defence and foreign affairs. Mujibur Rahman was imprisoned and not released until 1969.

The Struggle for Independence

After Ayub was replaced by President Yahya Khan national elections were held in December 1970. Mujib's party gained 160 of the 303 seats in the National Assembly and Yahya Khan, declaring that the Awami League was secessionist, decided in March 1971 to use repressive measures. He arrested Mujib and began a massive security operation in East Pakistan which led to millions fleeing to India. Armed Indian intervention resulted in liberation in December 1971 and the establishment of the independent state of Bangladesh. Mujib returned from imprisonment in Pakistan in January 1972 as leader of the new country.

Since Independence

On its creation on December 16, 1971, Bangladesh was proclaimed a secular state with a parliamentary constitution. Elections confirmed Sheikh Mujib as Prime Minister with 291 of the Assembly's 300 seats. Without foreign exchange or reserves of food, with crippled communications and few trained administrators, and with a multitude of loyal followers to reward, he faced enormous difficulties. In 1972 alone the country absorbed $1,000 million aid; 1973 was a year of floods, famine, rampant corruption and unrest. Continuing lawlessness, administrative inefficiency and widespread agitation led in early 1975 to Mujib's proclamation of a one-party government and assumption of total power and eventually to his downfall and death in August. After his death martial law was declared and in November 1975 governmental power was assumed by an appointed president and a council of three service chiefs. There were no ministers, only advisers. In April 1977 General Ziaur Rahman, who was already Chief of Army Staff and Chief Martial Law Administrator, assumed the Presidency.

Political unrest and instability have continued since 1977. There was an unsuccessful military coup in October 1977 which led to the imposition of martial law until April 1979. In May 1981, following strikes and demonstrations, President Ziaur Rahman was killed in another unsuccessful coup. A state of emergency was re-introduced.

International Relations

Bangladesh follows a non-aligned foreign policy. In 1976 it established diplomatic relations with Pakistan and China, thus normalising relations disrupted by the independence struggle of 1971. The geographical position of Bangladesh inevitably means that relations with India are very important, but are sometimes subject to strains because of conflicting interests. As members of the Commonwealth, Bangladesh and Britain maintain close contact, not least through Bangladeshis who have settled in Britain. Representatives of Bangladesh attend the meetings of Islamic states and in 1974 Bangladesh was admitted to the United Nations.

5 THE ECONOMY

Economic Situation

In 1901 the country was fairly prosperous by the standards of that time, but is now one of the poorest in the world. As recently as 1960 a family of 6 persons was supported by 2.5 acres of available cultivable land; by 1980 this was reduced to 1.1 acres. Bangladesh is thus apparently a textbook case of Malthusian stagnation, its central problem being whether resources available for consumption can grow faster than population. However, recent assessments suggest that with the proper use of fertilisers, irrigation, improved seeds, etc., agricultural production could increase by as much as five-fold. The balance of payments has been critical. While the Gross National Product has risen by 3.3% per year between 1970-1979 per capita GNP has declined 0.1% per year between 1960-1979. Bangladesh has been one of only ten countries in the world to experience negative GNP per capita growth between 1960-1979 and all the others have populations of less than 13 million.

Employment

Much of the rural population lives at little more than bare subsistence level, yet the labour force rises by 600,000 a year. Creating work for these, together with the estimated 2 to 3 million already unemployed, is an unsolved problem.

Agriculture

Bangladesh has always been, and is likely to remain, a primarily agricultural country. It has been estimated that in 1979 74% of the working population were engaged in agriculture, 11% in manufacturing, and 15% in services. Such concentration on agriculture reflects the limited resource base of the country. Rice is the staple cereal diet, and its production is the main target of the so-called 'Green Revolution'. Yet floods and other problems affecting agricultural production led to the import of grains. Even so, famine and malnutrition continued. The decline in grain production was attributed to short supply of seeds, fertilisers, pumps and pesticides, inefficient distribution and administration, as well as hoarding, widespread corruption and smuggling to India. Tea is an export commodity, but jute is the most important cash crop and biggest exchange earner. However, production has fallen. Poor quality, low yield per acre as well as faulty pricing policy contributed to this. Atempts are now being made to develop the export of raw and finished hides.

Industry

Steelmaking at Chittagong is based on melted scrap and imported pig-iron. There being no stone, cement must be importex or made from imported clinker. Natural gas in Sylhet is piped to various places, including Dacca, and is a source of power in the manufacture of fertiliser. Almost all capital equipment must be imported. Nationalised industries, which account for 85% of all industries, have run at a loss due to under-utilisation of capacities in jute, cotton, sugar, steel, paper and chemicals. Lack of managerial experience, political patronage, shortages of imported spare parts, labour unrest and low credit were contributing factors. A subsidiary result was to lessen the scope for increasing employment. Recently the government has begun a programme of selective denationalisation.

6 THE EDUCATION SYSTEM

Pre-Primary

This sector of education is insignificant in extent. These schools are mainly private kindergartens for middle-class children.

Primary

The government is responsible for managing all recognised primary schools and paying the salaries of primary teachers. There were 36,665 government and 7,271 non-government primary schools in 1980. Primary education is free but not complsory. Children can join at the age of 5 and the primary course lasts five years (Classes I-V). The curriculum comprises Bengali, mathematics, general science, social studies, religion and, nominally, arts and crafts. (Compulsory physical education consisting in the main of 'drill' exercises has recently been introduced in all primary schools.) Children can begin schooling up to about age 8, and rural classes often only cover a three-year age range. All primary schools are co-educational, except for the few that are attached to secondary schools. The total primary enrolment in 1980 was 8.24 million (6.96 million in government schools).

Junior Secondary

The three-year junior secondary course (Classes VI-VIII) is basically an extension of the primary curriculum, but to be admitted to Class VI pupils usually have to pass an entrance examination which is conducted by individual schools. One major difference in the course is that English is introduced as a second language. Until recently children could begin English in Class III, and appropriate textbooks were provided by the Textbook Board. Recent indications are that English will become a compulsory subject from Class III. Nevertheless, it seems probable that for most students English will become a 'foreign language' rather than a 'second language'. After Class VIII some students leave school, but about 90% enrol in the high school course and a few enter vocational training institutes. In 1980 300,000 students were enrolled in 2,557 junior secondary schools. There were also 700,000 students in junior secondary courses within full secondary school.

Senior Secondary

After the successful completion of Class VIII, pupils may seek enrolment for the two-year course leading to the Secondary School Certificate (SSC) examination taken at the end of Class X. Each school offering this course has the authority to select its own pupils. Three main courses are offered: humanities, science and commerce. Other courses, mainly in agricultural subjects, are taken by fewer than 2% of the students. In all courses, Bengali and English are compulsory subjects. Some secondary schools offer science in addition to arts courses and some of which are called 'multilateral' because they also run courses in commerce or agriculture. There were 8,776 high schools in 1980. Only 157 of these schools are 'government schools', i.e. less than 2%. The total number of teachers in 1980 was 85,067,387 being employed in government schools.

Higher Secondary

Students who pass the SSC examination may apply for entry to a two-year higher secondary (or 'intermediate') course. These courses for Classes XI and XII are mainly offered by 'intermediate colleges'. However, some high schools extend as far as Class XII, and some degree colleges also offer courses for the Higher Secondary Certificate (HSC). English and Bengali are compulsory subjects for all the courses. A student following the humanities course or the science course must study three other subjects chosen from five or six. Students may also take one optional subject. Similar courses are offered in commerce.

THE EDUCATION SYSTEM OF BANGLADESH

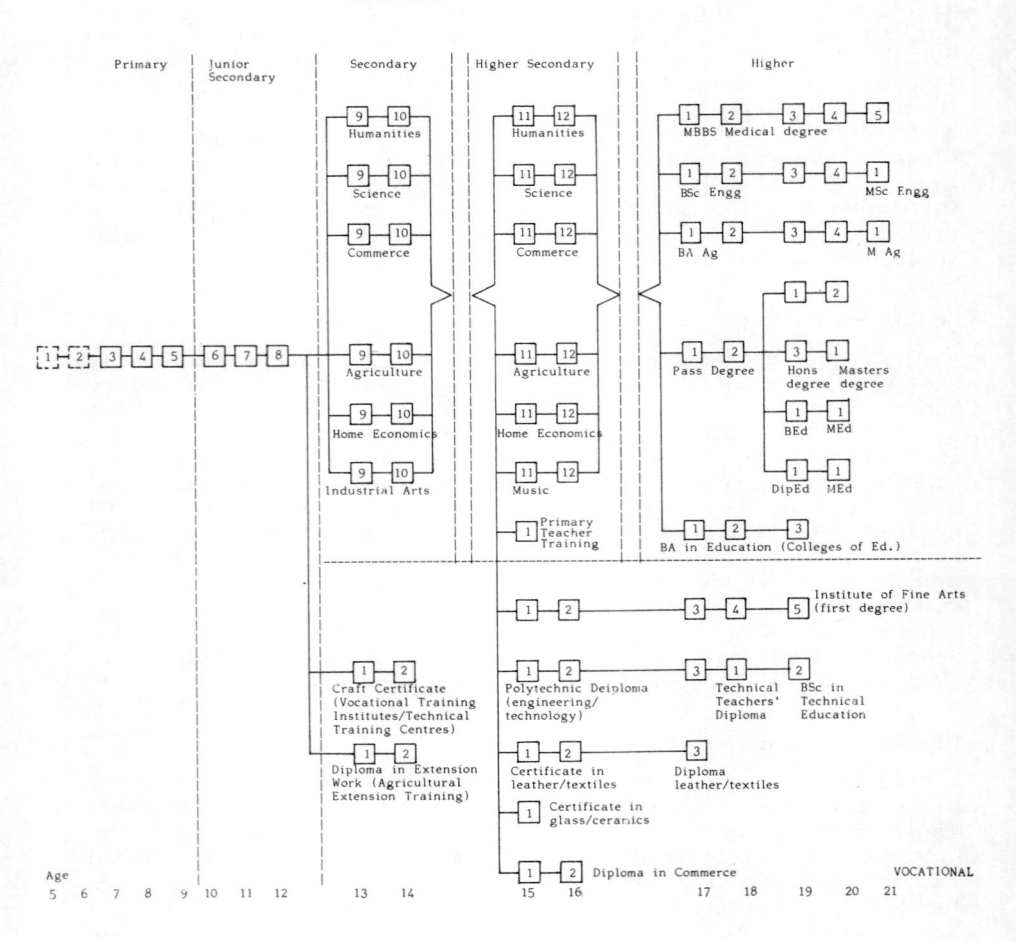

Madrasahs

The first school officially sponsored by the British authorities in Bengal was a *madrasah*, established by Warren Hastings in an attempt to win support from the Muslims and to give them the knowledge and skills necessary for government service. However, when in 1837 English replaced Persian as the tate language, the *madrasahs* continued to use Persian, and subsequently Arabic and Bengali. Ever since then they hae formed a relatively small but significant education system parallel to the mainstream of government and private education. Traditionally they have concentrated on Islamic instruction, preparing boys for religious duties. In the last few years, however, there have been moves to give greater emphasis to general education in the *madrasahs* so that their 'graduates' are prepared and qualified for general employment. The final examination at the *madrasahs* is considered equivalent to the Secondary School Certificate. Students who achieve satisfactory results can then apply for admission to Class XI in a general college. Official statistics showed that in 1980 43,650 students were attending 2,259 *madrasahs* of various categories.

Technical and Vocational Education

In 1947 the only institution within the formal education system offering technical or vocational courses in what is now Bangladesh was the Ahsanullah School of Engineering in Dacca. This school had an enrolment capacity of 125 and conducted diploma courses in civil engineering. Since then a good many more institutions for this kind of education have been opened, mainly during the 1960s. There are now four levels of technical course: certificate, diploma, first degree and post-graduate.

Degree Courses in Technical Subjects

Degree and post-graduate courses are run by the Bangladesh University of Engineering and Technology (BUET) in Dacca. In addition there are four colleges of engineering with 2,520 students in 1980 which conduct first degree courses in various branches of engineering. All engineering BSc courses last four years. The colleges of engineering are at present affiliated to the local university (Dacca in the case of Khulna).

Polytechnic and Similar Institutions

Bangladesh has 17 polytechnics, plus the Bangladesh-Swedish Institute of Technology at Kaptai. These offer three-year diploma courses in various branches of engineering and technology, civil engineering being the most popular. The minimum qualification for entry is a second division pass in the SSC examination. Three-year diploma courses are also organised by monotechnics specialising in leather and textile technologies. These two institutions are in Dacca, as are the Institute of Graphic Arts and the Commercial Institute. The commercial courses last only two years. The Institute of Glass and Ceramics, also in Dacca, runs a one-year certificate course. There are also two-year certificate courses in leather and textile technologies. There were 13,588 students at polytechnic institutes in 1980.

Craft Courses

Craft courses at the 'certificate level' are organised by the Vocational Training Institutes (VTIs). The courses at the VTIs are for prospective automobile and farm mechanics, joiners, bricklayers, etc. Candidates must have completed basic education to at least Class VIII standard. Other certificate courses are run by some of the polytechnics operating a 'second shift'. There are also a few training centres which offer commercial and secretarial training for women. There are one or two private vocational schools, notably St Joseph's School of Industrial Trades, which is in Dacca. In addition, however, there are several other institutions involved in technical and vocational education. Each of the four technical training centres has an annual enrolment of about 80 for a two-year certificate course for various types of craftsmen. The Bangladesh German Technical Training Centre offers similar training. There are at present eight agricultural extension training institutes each offering two-year diploma courses. The marine diesel training centre at Narayanganj organises apprenticeship courses which do not lead to a formal paper qualification. There are a few similar courses for motor mechanics.

Teacher Training

There are four main kinds of pre-service teacher training establishments and four corresponding levels of teacher training: 47 primary training institutes (PTIs) run eight-month certificate courses for primary teachers; 10 teacher training colleges (TTCs) provide a one-year course leading to a BEd; the Institute of Education and Research (IER) at Dacca University organises Diploma, MEd and PhD courses; and the technical teachers training college in Dacca offers two courses, one for a diploma in technical education and one for a BSc in technical education.

Primary Training Institutes

Candidates for the PTI course must have a Secondary School Certificate. PTI instructors usually have a first degree and a teaching certificate. In 1975 the Ministry of Education decided that the 'one academic year' course should be condensed to eight months, without any 'long holiday' between successive courses. In 1980 there were 47 PTIs and 8,978 students.

Teacher Training Colleges

The TTCs train university graduates to teach in secondary schools. The BEd courses are validated by the universities to which the colleges are affiliated. In 1980 there were 2,600 students in these colleges.

Institute of Education and Research

The diploma courses of IER are the equivalent of BEd courses at the TTCs. Both diploma and BEd holders may be accepted for the one-year MEd course.

Specialist Teacher Training Colleges

Candidates for the Technical TTC courses must have at least a diploma in engineering. The maximum enrolment for the one-year diploma course under the Board of Technical Education is 60; there are 30 places for each year of the two-year degree courses which is validated by Dacca University. There are also three other specialist teacher training colleges in Dacca: the college of physical education, the college of arts and crafts and the college of home economics.

In-Service Training

The Bangladesh Education Extension and Research Institute in Dacca organises residential in-service training courses which usually last four weeks and are intended for teachers in secondary schools (mainly) and colleges. Each of the 20 or so subject based courses arranged each year has an enrolment of 20 to 30 teachers.

Higher Education

Higher Education was provided in 1980 by six universities, 113 government and 475 private degree colleges, and several specialist colleges.

Universities

There are general universities at Bangladesh are Dacca, Rajshahi, Chittagong and Jahangirnagar. The last is located about 20 miles from Dacca and is still in the early stages of its development. Dacca is by far the largest, and is the only one to have been founded before 1947. Since the early years of this century it has played a significant part in the political and social development of this region. A high proportion of the leaders of all aspects of national life are Dacca graduates.

There are also specialist universities: the Bangladesh University of Engineering and Technology (BUET) in Dacca, and the Bangladesh Agricultural University (BAU) in Mymensingh. BUET developed out of the Ahsanullah Engineering College. Initial capital outlay and staff training for both universities depended to a large extent on aid from the USA. Total enrolment at universities in 1980 was 27,553 (about 0.4% of the age group) and a fifth of the students are women.

Degree Colleges

The government colleges offer a wide range of first degree courses. In recent years they have begun to offer an increasing number of masters' courses also. The number of private degree colleges has increased greatly since independence. The main specialist degree colleges, apart from teacher training institutions, are eight medical colleges with 7,024 students, 11 law colleges with 6,421 students, the College of Agriculture at Dacca and the College of Social Welfare. There are about 420,000 students in all degree colleges.

Enrolment

To enrol on a first degree course a student must have a Higher Secondary Certificate. In addition, it is customary for university departments to set selection examinations and hold interviews when applications are being considered. Candidates with good qualifications may be admitted direct to three-year honours courses; others will study for two years for a pass degree, after which, if their results are good, they can attempt a two-year masters course. Students with a good honours degree can complete a masters degree in one year. A few students are then accepted for research degrees to PhD level. Most successful students, however, aspire to PhD training abroad.

Other Points

Many of the senior teachers in the universities have been trained abroad, and a good proportion have PhDs. In Dacca, Rajshahi and Chittagong the teacher-student ratio is about 1:24; in the two specialist universities it is 1:10. The universities are arranged on a faculty-department pattern, and in general each department sets annual 'comprehensive' examinations. A few departments have recently introduced 'credit courses'. BUET follows an 'extended semester' form of programme. Some masters courses include a thesis to be written on a limited topic of research; others are entirely by instruction.

Since 1972 Bengali has been increasingly used as the medium of instruction in higher education. Most standard textbooks, however, and almost all the reference books used by students are in English.

Non-Formal Education and Literacy work

In 1974 26% of the population was literate: 37% male and 13% female. Since independence much interest has been expressed in non-formal education and in literacy work. Most ministries run training courses of some kind which are designed to help people take part in development programmes. In addition, several independent or voluntary agencies are involved in small-scale non-formal education and literacy programmes. The Adult Education Programme has about 1,300 Centres, including 500 or so for women. However, it seems to be making little headway in the attempt to reduce illiteracy. A large scale literacy programme was initiated by the Second Five Year Plan (1980-85) with the aim of eradicating illiteracy in the age group 11-45 by 1985.

Use of Mass Media

The government has announced plans to make increasing use of radio and television for educational purposes. In general, however, limited resources have so far prevented large scale use of radio, or television. Very few schools or colleges have radios, and only a small number of educational programmes are broadcast, and then outside school hours. There are better prospects for radio being used on an increased scale to assist development schemes.

Academic Year

The academic year varies according to the level of education. For primary and secondary levels it begins in January and ends in December. In educational institutions for study beyond Class X, courses begin in July and end in June. There are three main periods of holiday: the winter break (2-3 weeks in January), the summer break (May-June), and the Ramadan holiday. (It is customary to take 2-6 weeks holiday at the time of the Muslim fasting month.) In 1976 this began on 27 or 28 August; in subsequent years Ramadan will occur earlier by ten days a year, following the lunar calendar.

At present most university courses are considerably out of phase with the official academic year. Recently classes have begun in October/November rather than in July. And, because of the disruptions caused by the liberation struggle, the students admitted in 1975 should have formed the 1974 or even 1973 intakes. The final dates of courses have been considerably delayed with examination dates being deferred several times in some cases. Degrees are referred to by the notional date of completion (e.g. 1974) rather than by the year in which they were finally awarded (e.g. 1976).

7 EDUCATIONAL ADMINISTRATION

Centralised Control

In Bangladesh, education has been centrally controlled and administered with the Ministry of Education is responsible for all basic policy decisions, the processing of development plans, the allocation of funds, the appointment and transfer of senior officers, and the selection of candidates for awards offered by foreign agencies. It has also coordinated and supervised the work of various 'autonomous' educational bodies. This highly centralised form of administration was largely a legacy from the colonial past, and in essence was based on a system devised in the last century. In the main, it was not equipped to deal with present problems. However, it was tied into the general administrative system of Bangladesh, and partly for this reason was very resistant to change. However, since 1978 proposals have been made to decentralise the control particularly of primary education.

Boards of Secondary Education

In each of the four administrative divisions of the country there is a BISE (Board of Intermediate and Secondary Education). These Boards are responsible for all matters pertaining to curricula and examinations for the Secondary School Certificate (SSC) courses (Classes IX-X) and for the Higher Secondary certificate (HSC) courses (Classes XI-XII). The old names for the SSC (Matriculation) and the HSC (Intermediate) are still occasionally used. The work of these Boards is coordinated through their chairmen and through a committee established by the ministry, but they still have a considerable degree of autonomy. Theoretically, BISEs are responsible for granting recognition to High Schools (Classes IX-X) and Intermediate Colleges (Classes XI-XII).

Textbook Board

The Bangladesh Textbook Board is also an 'autonomous body'. It is responsible for commissioning, printing and distributing textbooks for Classes I-X. There are no set texts for HSc courses, except for literature courses, and these are published by the Boards of Intermediate and Secondary Education themselves.

Universities

The universities are autonomous, self-governing bodies, established by an act, ordinance or order. They are free to conduct their own affairs within the limits of the ordinance; they are not subject, within these limits, to legislative control or executive or ministerial directive. However, they depend on the State for nearly the whole of their finances and funds. Degree colleges are under the administrative control of the DPI but are affiliated to one of three universities (Dacca, Rajshahi and Chittagong). They are subject to periodic inspection by the universities which are responsible for ensuring that adequate academic standards are maintained.

University Grants Commission

The University Grants Commission (UGC) was established in 1973. It comprises three full-time members, including a chairman (all appointed by the government), and nine part-time members, six of whom are from the universities, the other three being high-ranking officials from the Ministry of Planning, the Ministry of Education and the Ministry of Finance. The main function of the UGC is to determine the financial needs of the universities and receive funds from the government and then allocate and disburse them to the universities for their maintenance and development. The UGC is also concerned to promote research or investigations which are aimed at the healthy development of tertiary education. To this end it has set up committees on social science, science, agricultural education, libraries etc. It also plays an important role in helping the government with the coordination of aid offered to universities by foreign agencies. In all this work it acts as an intermediary between the government and the universities.

8 EDUCATIONAL FINANCE

Education Budget

The proportion of Gross National Product spent on education has fallen in the course of the 1970s. In 1972, 24% of current government expenditure was allocated to education. This proportion fell to 19% in 1975 and to 13.6% in 1978. This is in part a reflection of acute economic and financial difficulties. Educational spending is cut when revenue does not match up to estimates. Yet an increasing proportion of national wealth is spent on education. In 1975 1.4% of Gross National Product was spent on education by government. In 1978 this proportion reached 2.2%.

A considerable amount of finance comes from private funds to private grant-aided institutions. The Second Five Year Plan (1980-1985) estimated that 10% of finance for primary education and 8% for secondary education would come from the private sector.

Allocation of Funds

In 1978 the distribution of government recurrent funds between the sectors of education was as follows: Primary Education 51.2%, secondary education 24.8% and higher education 21.3%. The bias towards higher level education has become more pronounced. In 1975, 17.4% went to higher education; 16.5% to secondary and 57% to primary. The 1980 Plan proposes allocations similar to those of 1978.

Foreign Aid

A recently issued (1977) directory lists 131 voluntary agencies in Bangladesh, representing many religions and nations, and covering many functional areas. The directory also lists seven UN agencies and 37 diplomatic missions who are almost all involved in aid programmes of one kind of another. Most of the aid donors are geared to appraise projects only in terms of capital costs, leaving to the Bangladesh authorities the onus of labour and recurrent costs. Not all of the agencies are directly involved in aid to education, but many of their projects have training components. Some few are involved in non-formal, functional education: e.g. the locally controlled but externally funded Bangladesh Rural Advancement Committee has a large commitment to materials development for adult functional literacy and numeracy. Several others have extensive programmes for vocational (mainly handicraft) training, and

ADMINISTRATIVE AND
OF EDUCATION

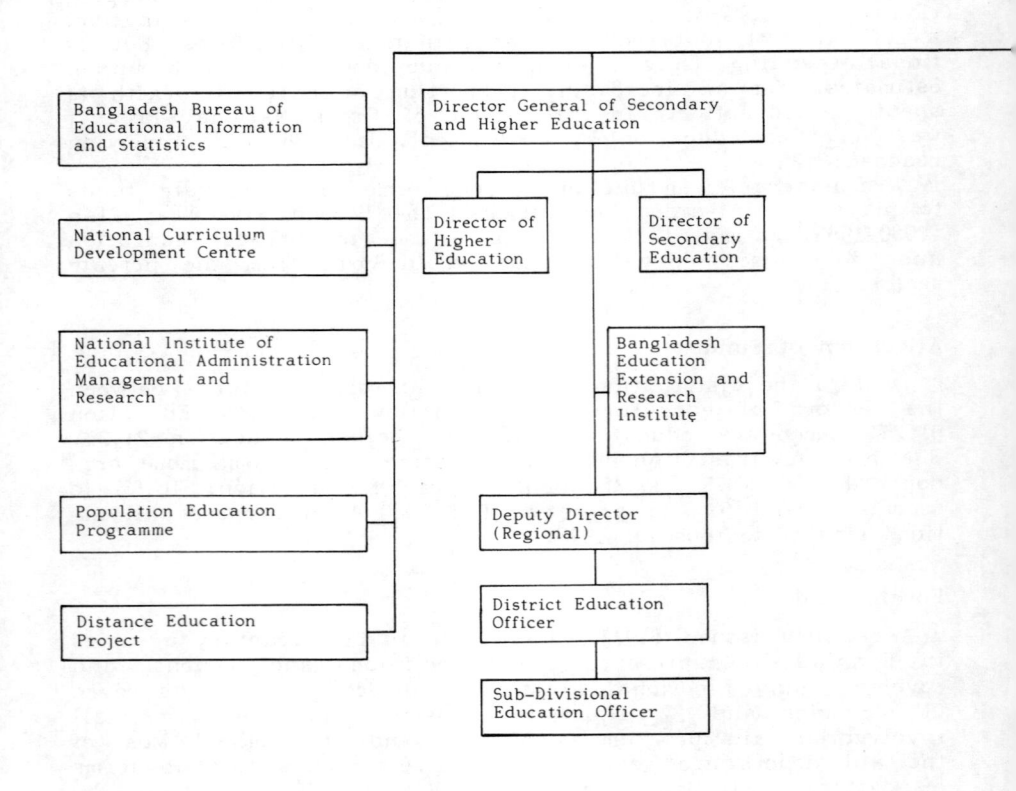

```
                                    ┌─────────────────────────────┐
                            ┌───────│ Director General of Secondary│
                            │       │ and Higher Education        │
┌─────────────────────────┐ │       └──────────────┬──────────────┘
│ Bangladesh Bureau of    │ │              ┌──────┴──────┐
│ Educational Information │─┤              │             │
│ and Statistics          │ │     ┌────────┴──────┐ ┌────┴────────┐
└─────────────────────────┘ │     │ Director of   │ │ Director of │
                            │     │ Higher        │ │ Secondary   │
┌─────────────────────────┐ │     │ Education     │ │ Education   │
│ National Curriculum     │─┤     └───────────────┘ └─────────────┘
│ Development Centre      │ │              │
└─────────────────────────┘ │     ┌────────┴────────┐
                            │     │ Bangladesh      │
┌─────────────────────────┐ │     │ Education       │
│ National Institute of   │ │     │ Extension and   │
│ Educational Administration│─┤    │ Research        │
│ Management and          │ │     │ Institute       │
│ Research                │ │     └─────────────────┘
└─────────────────────────┘ │              │
                            │     ┌────────┴────────┐
┌─────────────────────────┐ │     │ Deputy Director │
│ Population Education    │─┤     │ (Regional)      │
│ Programme               │ │     └────────┬────────┘
└─────────────────────────┘ │              │
                            │     ┌────────┴────────┐
┌─────────────────────────┐ │     │ District Education│
│ Distance Education      │─┘     │ Officer         │
│ Project                 │       └────────┬────────┘
└─────────────────────────┘                │
                                   ┌────────┴────────┐
                                   │ Sub-Divisional  │
                                   │ Education Officer│
                                   └─────────────────┘
```

MANAGEMENT STRUCTURE IN BANGLADESH

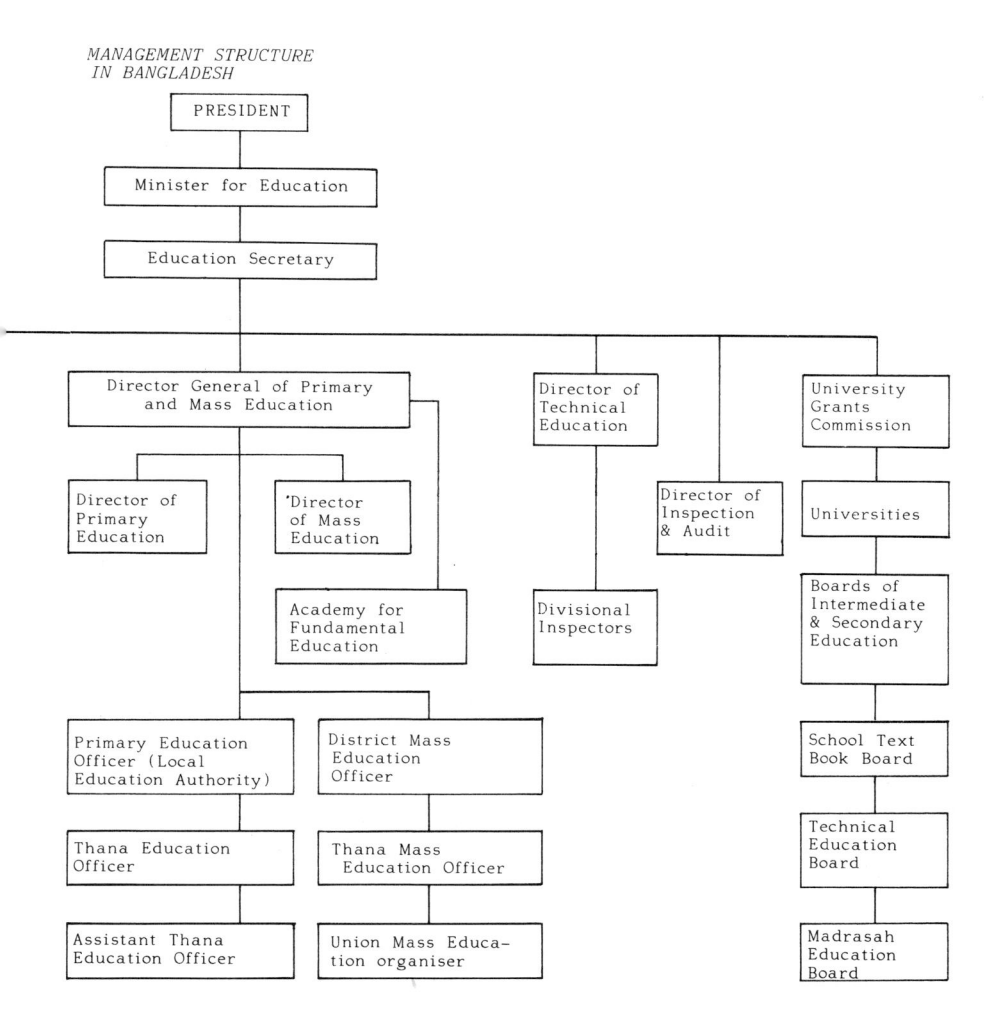

```
                           PRESIDENT
                               │
                      Minister for Education
                               │
                       Education Secretary
    ┌──────────────────────────┼──────────────────────────┐
    │                          │                          │
Director General of      Director of              University
Primary and Mass         Technical                Grants
Education                Education                Commission
    │                          │                          │
    ├─────────────┐       Director of              Universities
    │             │       Inspection                      │
Director of   Director    & Audit                  Boards of
Primary       of Mass         │                    Intermediate
Education     Education   Divisional               & Secondary
              │           Inspectors               Education
              Academy for                                 │
              Fundamental                          School Text
              Education                            Book Board
    │                                                     │
Primary Education    District Mass                 Technical
Officer (Local       Education                     Education
Education Authority) Officer                       Board
    │                    │                                │
Thana Education      Thana Mass                    Madrasah
Officer              Education Officer             Education
    │                    │                         Board
Assistant Thana      Union Mass Educa-
Education Officer    tion organiser
```

89

others are involved in health and community education and family planning.

Foreign aid in the formal sector is dominated by the UN agencies and by various forms of bilateral aid. UNICEF projects since the creation of Bangladesh in 1971 include the restoration of physical facilities in 6,000 primary schools, the provision of basic equipment to all government primary schools, a programme of agricultural training for primary school teachers, and capital and equipment aid to teacher training institutions (with particular emphasis on women trainees). There has been considerable Swedish, West German and IDA aid for technical education, especially by way of capital and equipment costs for for the vocational training institutes and polytechnics and the agricultural extension training institutes have received Japanese capital. Many other nations and agencies are involved in other institutions and levels. British aid to education concentrates mainly on the exchange of persons and the printed word.

It has been said that between 1971 and 1975 foreign donors provided about £15 million to assist in rehabilitating the educational sector: mainly school reconstruction and the provision of textbooks, equipment and in-country training. This amount, expended over 3 years, almost equals the amount of foreign assistance to education over the previous 20 years which was spent largely on scholarships and training abroad (25%) and capital projects at the post-secondary level. Recurrent expenditure for these institutions must now be found from local sources.

Students' Contribution

It is estimated that at least 60% of the recurring income of non-government institutions comes from student fees. These range from Tk 7 per month in secondary schools to Tk 20 in degree colleges. Although the State meets most of the costs of university, teacher training and technical education, students at these institutions have to pay monthly tuition fees which vary from Tk 10 to Tk 20. If they live in hostels they must also pay boarding fees of about Tk 150. In addition they have to buy textbooks (if they are available), writing materials, etc. (Students in TTCs and colleges of education receive a monthly grant of Tk 80.) It has been estimated that the average monthly costs to be met by a university student amount to Tk 300-400; that is about five times the per capita income of Bangladesh. Primary school children pay no fees, and primary textbooks are subsidised by the government. Nonetheless parents have to buy textbooks, and writing materials, and meet other incidental expenses. A very small number of secondary students are awarded talent scholarships on the basis of competitive examinations. Likewise a tiny proportion of university students receive awards, but the relative value of these has declined recently and the scholarship holders still have to meet most of their study costs.

Funding of Private Institutions

Primary schools, universities, teacher training institutions and technical education institutions are government financed; secondary and college education, however, is mainly supported by private finance, since only 2% of secondary schools and 6% of colleges are within the government system. Apart from fees the remainder of the income of these institutions comes from government grants (if they are recognised), local grants and taxes, and interest from property or endowments. Support by local philanthropists has greatly declined over the last few years.

9 DEVELOPMENT AND PLANNING OF THE EDUCATION SYSTEM

Origins

The system of government schools and colleges which developed from the middle of the nineteenth century provides the basic skeleton of the present system. It was initially intended to supply the manpower required by the colonial government. The curriculum was mainly based on the humanities. Recognising the advantages to be gained through education, various private bodies established other schools and colleges. In general the Hindus took a more active interest in this 'foreign' education, while the Muslims preferred the *madrasahs*.

Effects of 1947 Independence

Independence in 1947 brought several changes, with effects that are still felt. Many Hindus left and this produced a considerable gap in the most highly educated group. Yet, of course, there was an even greater need for trained people to fill high positions in all aspects of national life. Inevitably there was a rapid expansion of secondary, college and university education, while primary education relatively stood still. Education became the escape route from the realities of peasant farming to more congenial and secure employment in government service. Initially the expansion was linear, with very little curriculum development or diversification. It was not until the 1960s that science and technology were given more emphasis. But then, in an attempt to redress the balance, the expansion was perhaps too rapid, and technical education was largely academic, institutional and unrelated to industry and development. This two-stage expansion, first of general and then technical education, has led to problems which the authorities are now attempting to tackle.

Planning Since 1947

Since 1947 there have been several official investigations intended to lead to suitable plans for educational development. The findings and recommendations of these education commissions have been implemented only in a piecemeal fashion. If anything this has led to greater distortions because those sectors which had benefited most in the past had influence and so acquired a large share of the available resources. This is especially true of the universities.

Bodies Involved in Planning and Reform

Before 1971 there was only a provincial administration in East Pakistan, and so the Bangladesh Ministry of Education did not inherit any effective planning section. Nonetheless all proposals and schemes for educational development have to be considered by the Ministry. In recent years four agencies have been involved in educational planning. One was the National Education Commission which was set up soon after independence to examine all aspects of education and to recommend measures to bring about the fundamental reforms which were commonly acknowledged to be long overdue. It was disbanded in 1974. The other three are permanent bodies within the central administrative system: the Ministry of Education; the Education and Manpower Section of the Ministry of Planning; and the small Planning Section of the Directorate of Public Instruction. These last three have been mainly concerned with preparing and assessing specific programmes or projects. In March 1976 a National Committee on Curricula and Syllabi was formed. This body has produced a programme for curriculum and syllabus reform for courses below degree level. If this programme is accepted by the government of Bangladesh, its implementation will probably be supervised by a Bureau for Educational Development which the Ministry of Education is about to constitute for purposes of implementation, supervision and evaluation.

Report of Education Commission

In June 1974 the Education Commission produced its report but for various political reasons it was not published until October 1975. Its recommendations may be summarised as follows:

(i) Education should embody the 'State principles'; nationalism, democracy, socialism and secularism; it should be 'mass-oriented' and 'scientific'; the medium of instruction at all levels should be Bengali

(ii) There should be a change of emphasis from general education to curricula which give due weight to science and technology and to vocational training. work oriented education should be introduced at all levels of education so that education is relevant to the needs of the country and no longer alienates students from such vital occupations as farming

(iii) Primary education should be free and compulsory; illiteracy should be eliminated. Ideally the authorities would like to extend 'basic' or 'fundamental' education from Class I to Class VIII and make it free and compulsory by 1983

(iv) Greater emphasis should be given to the education of girls and women; special schemes for recruiting and training women teachers should be devised

(v) Secondary education should be designed to be terminal for most. It should be diversified to include vocational training. It was hoped that by 1978 20% of secondary students would be on vocational courses and that this proportion would thereafter increase to 50%

(vi) Education should not neglect the cultural attainments of the nation; rather it should enrich them.

Five Year Plan 1973-78

Although the government has not yet officially commented on these aims, the Five Year Plan for 1973-78 included a section on educational objectives which in outline were very similar to those of the Education Commission. However, at the halfway stage of the Plan period few of these objectives had been achieved or even systematically tackled.

Planning Difficulties

One major difficulty is that none of the existing 'educational planning' bodies is adequately staffed to deal with large-scale planning and research. And, equally important, they lack the means and the manpower to supervise the implementation of such planning. They are swamped by detailed administration, and often have to give urgent and continual attention to 'aid schemes' which may be excellent and necessary in themselves but tend to encourage a piecemeal approach to educational development.

In addition, the tiny Education and Manpower Section in the Ministry of Planning has no initiating executive authority. Its main task has been to scrutinise education projects prepared by other bodies. It assesses the extent to which these projects fit in with agreed plan objectives. Each June an Annual Plan is published which allocates funds for specific projects during the succeeding 12 months.

Another important consideration is that over the period 1972-75 there were no formal procedures for coordinating the work of the Education Commission, the Education and Manpower Section of the Planning Commission and the Planning Section in the Directorate of Education. Specific projects tend to be proposed and approved when interested groups exert pressure on the administration. Thus, the University Grants Commission and individual universities have proposed various ad hoc development schemes within their own sphere of interest, and several of these have been completed. Likewise, some schemes supported by funds provided by outside agencies such as UNICEF and the World Bank, have been implemented.

All planning is made more difficult by the lack of coordinated information and statistics. It is hoped that the recently established Bureau for Educational Information and Statistics will be in a position to provide the essential figures on which planning can be based.

Trends

The Second Five Year Plan 1980-1985 has placed emphasis on mass education.

> "The Plan aims at the development of low cost functional education by making different levels of education consistent with production process as far as possible. Efforts will be made to broaden the base of primary education, link education with employment, make science technology a basic component of education system, accelerate the development of women's education and reduce the rural-urban gap."

The major objectives more specifically were:

1   Introduction of universal primary education (90% by 1985)

2   Launching of national mass education programme

3   More financial support to rural institutions and individual talents

4   Introduction of selectivity in higher education.

The objective is that educational development should respond to the poverty, disadvantage and economic decline of the majority of the population. However, the aims have not been followed by any major redistribution of financial resources between education sectors. Even if they were there are difficulties in achieving change linked to the aspirations of students and their families and the major role that private institutions play in post-primary education.

BANGLADESH - EDUCATIONAL PYRAMID 1979

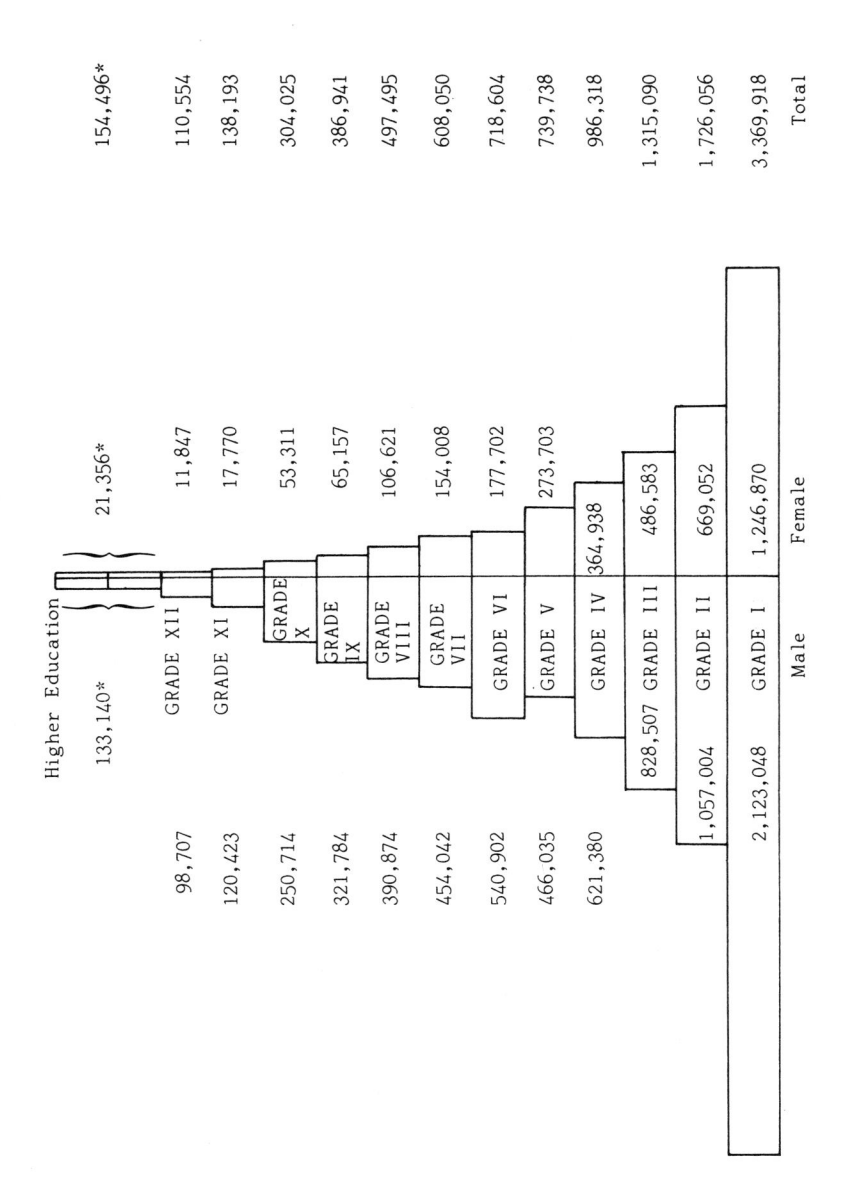

Male		Female	Total
	Higher Education		
133,140*		21,356*	154,496*
98,707	GRADE XII	11,847	110,554
120,423	GRADE XI	17,770	138,193
250,714	GRADE X	53,311	304,025
321,784	GRADE IX	65,157	386,941
390,874	GRADE VIII	106,621	497,495
454,042	GRADE VII	154,008	608,050
540,902	GRADE VI	177,702	718,604
466,035	GRADE V	273,703	739,738
621,380	GRADE IV	364,938	986,318
828,507	GRADE III	486,583	1,315,090
1,057,004	GRADE II	669,052	1,726,056
2,123,048	GRADE I	1,246,870	3,369,918

BANGLADESH BASIC STATISTICS

Population

1970	1975	1979
68,117,000	78,961,000	86,643,000

The Literate Population 1974

Total	Male	Female
25.8%	37.3%	13.2%

Enrolment Ratios

(Children in primary schools as a proportion of all aged 5–9, pupils in secondary schools as a proportion of all 10–14 year olds, higher education students as a proportion of the 20–24 age group).

		Primary Schools	Secondary Schools	Higher Education
1975	Total	71%	25%	2.3% *
	Male	91%	38%	3.9% *
	Female	50%	11%	0.6% *
1979	Total	65%	25%	2.1% †
	Male	79%	38%	3.5% †
	Female	49%	11%	0.6% †

* = 1976   † = 1978

Schools, Teachers and Pupils 1970 and 1979

	Primary (Grades I–V)		Secondary (Grades VI–XII)	
	1970	1979	1970	1979
Schools	28,731	43,739	–	–
Teachers	117,275	187,504	–	111,927
Pupils	5,293,787	8,219,313	–	2,763,862

Teacher:Pupil Ratio in Primary Schools

1970	1975	1979
45	51	44

Higher Education Students by Fields of Study 1978

	Total	% Female
Educational Teacher Training	3,495	25%
Humanities and Religion	40,468	20%
Law	6,633	4%
Social and Behavioural Sciences	33,771	19%
Commerce and Business	18,059	4%
Mathematics	3,211	11%
Natural Science	28,374	11%
Medicine and Related Studies	8,335	19%
Engineering	3,826	1%
Agriculture	2,656	2%
Other	5,668	5%

Expenditure on Education 1975 and 1978

		As a % of government expenditure	As a % of Gross National Product
1975	Total	13.6%	1.4%
	Current	15.9%	1.0%
1978	Total	10.1%	2.2%
	Current	13.6%	1.4%

Expenditure on Education by Sector 1975 and 1978

	Primary	Secondary	Higher	Not distributed
1975	57.0%	16.5%	17.4%	9.1%
1978	51.2%	24.8%	21.3%	2.7%

Basic Social and Economic Data

Gross National Product per capita 1979 = US$90

Average growth of GNP per capita 1960–1979 = –0.1%

Life expectancy at birth 1979 = 49

Distribution of the labour force:

Agriculture 1960 = 87%
Agriculture 1979 = 74%

Industry 1960 = 3%
Industry 1979 = 11%

Services 1960 = 10%
Services 1979 = 15%

China

CONTENTS

1 Geography 102
2 Population 103
3 Society and Culture 103
4 History and Politics 105
5 The Economy 108
6 The Education System 111
7 Educational Administration 119
8 Educational Finance 121
9 Development and Planning of
  the Education System 122

With her vast land mass and long cultural tradition, China is probably best understood in relation to the Soviet Union to the north and India to the south. The Russian Revolution of 1917 made a very strong impact on young Chinese in despair over their country's inability to eradicate feudalism and weakness in the face of the imperialist powers. Soviet Communist representatives contributed to the early Communist movement in China, though the definitive shape of Chinese Communism matured under the leadership of Mao Tse Tung in the remote rural areas. When the Revolution was achieved in 1949, Chinese leaders first followed Soviet patterns very closely in political organisation, economic policy and educational planning, especially at the tertiary level. However, from 1957 the Maoist model, shaped in Yanan, re-emerged and since then Chinese education has oscillated between a stress on expertise along Soviet lines, and a concern with redness or correct political orientation which was most strongly felt during the Cultural Revolution of 1966-76. The Cultural Revolution model with its focus on rural education, learning from the peasants and joining with them to build up the country through grassroots initiative rather than dependence on either money or ideas from the developed world, has provided inspiration for many Third World countries struggling to free themselves from a vicious dependency cycle.

China's relationship with India to the south has much deeper roots than that with the Soviet Union, as in Buddhism China embraced the only external religion which penetrated the whole country and every level of society. While Indian spirituality is far more radical than that of traditional China, where Daoism maintained a dialectical balance between the spiritual and the material, these two ancient cultural traditions of the East share certain common characteristics which stand in strong contrast to western civilisation and its patterns of dominance. China's economic development may also be compared with that of India as both share the problem of a huge population and the inadequacy of traditional agriculture to feed it and generate capital for industrialisation. Chinese leaders have taken more vigorous, even ruthless, political, economic and cultural measures to ensure both faster economic growth and a fairer distribution of resources among their vast population, yet GNP per capita is still not much higher in China than in India. Recently Chinese educational researchers have commented on the fact that a higher proportion of the national budget is devoted to education in India than in China, which may be a way of putting pressure on the government for higher educational spending. The reluctance on the part of the government to invest heavily in education may reflect a persisting lack of confidence in intellectuals, particularly teachers, who tend to ensure the preservation both of traditional educational values and those foreign influences which have left their mark on Chinese education over the century.

The Chinese themselves often compare their own development with that of Japan, which received its high culture from China in the sixth century AD, and whose remarkable economic success has been both an inspiration and a cause for deep soul searching to the Chinese. Since the Japanese succeeded, they are convinced that China, the mother culture with a social and political system superior to that of capitalist Japan, must also be able to achieve rapid modernisation. Their first modern education system was patterned after the Japanese version of western models at the turn of the century. At the same time the Chinese do not forget that their severest traumas in this century resulted from the expansionist aggression that was a part of Japan's industrial success.

One of the fascinating issues to watch in future will be the effects of the newly revived interaction between China and the West, much of which is mediated through educational channels. The power of progressive Chinese ideas left their impact on the West both in the eighteenth century European emulation of the Chinese selective examination system and in the democratisation of western universities in the 1960s in response to the demands of students inspired by Maoism. The West also gave to China several models for a modern education system and the Chinese are still working at the task of adapting these models to a Chinese framework of values. Future cultural interaction has the potential for mutual enrichment, yet may always be somewhat precarious because of deep-rooted differences in worldview that can spark off explosive misunderstanding.

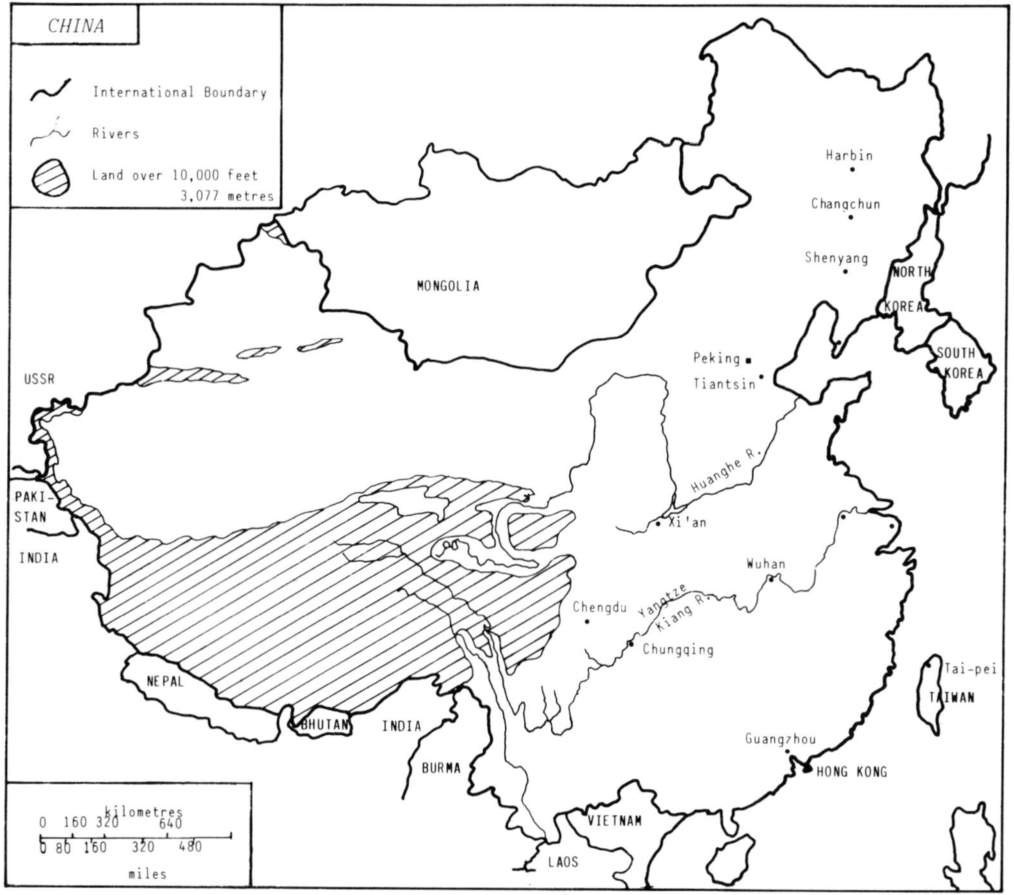
CHINA
International Boundary
Rivers
Land over 10,000 feet
3,077 metres
MONGOLIA
USSR
PAKI-
STAN
INDIA
NEPAL
BHUTAN
INDIA
BURMA
LAOS
VIETNAM
HONG KONG
TAIWAN
Tai-pei
NORTH
KOREA
SOUTH
KOREA
Harbin
Changchun
Shenyang
Peking
Tiantsin
Huanghe R.
Xi'an
Wuhan
Chengdu
Yangtze
Kiang R.
Chungqing
Guangzhou
kilometres
0 160 320 640
0 80 160 320 480
miles

1 GEOGRAPHY

Topography

China has a land area of 9.6 million square kilometres (3,706,560 square miles), one fifteenth of the total land area of the earth, one quarter of Asia. It is the third largest country in the world, next to the Soviet Union and Canada. With respect to slope and relief, the land of China may be classified as plain (14%), basin (16%), plateau (34%), hill (9%), and mountains (30%). Plains and basins provide the richest areas for agricultural production; also a wide variety of crops and trees are grown in hilly areas through terracing. Plateaus and mountains are found mainly in western and central China. Irrigation systems have been developed from ancient times based on control of the great rivers, the Yangtse, the Yellow River, the Huai River, etc. In spite of continued attention to this great task of engineering, flood control remains a serious problem.

Climate

In such a vast country the climate is naturally diversified. Temperatures in north and south differ by only about 8°C in summer, when it is very hot throughout the country, but differences are extreme in winter with a range as great as 34° between Guangzhou in the south and Harbin in the north. Rainfall varies greatly, being highest in the south east and decreasing as one moves towards the northwest, where the huge province of Xinjiang is so dry that it depends for its water supply on the melting of snow from the Tian mountains. Rainfall also varies greatly from season to season and from year to year, with about 80% normally falling between May and October.

Communications

China has an extensive railway network which is undergoing continual development. Other forms of transport include highways, waterways (rivers, canals and sea coast), and civil aviation. For short distances, the bicycle is the ubiquitous method of travel, and China manufactures the largest number of bicycles in the world. For 1980 the volume of passenger transport was as follows: (units: 100 million person-kilometre) railways: 1,381; highways: 729; waterways: 129; air transport: 40. The figures for cargo transport in the same year are: units: 100 million ton-kilometre) railways: 5,717; highways: 764; waterways: 5,053; civil aviation: 1.4. Telegraph and telephone networks are well developed; television's 38 stations reach an estimated 20-30 million viewers, while radio reaches the majority of the population.

2 POPULATION
Growth

China's population has grown from about 550,000,000 at the time of Liberation in 1949 to an estimated 982,550,000 at the end of 1980 (excluding Taiwan), about 22% of the world's total. The first official census after Liberation was conducted in 1953 (587,960,000), the second in 1964 (694,581,759), and the third in July 1982 (1,031,882,511). About 60% of China's population are under 29 years of age. In the 1950s and 1960s government population policies fluctuated between encouraging large families and emphasis on the need for birth control. Since 1970, however, there have been consistent efforts to control growth with the result that births were reduced by 56 million, and the birthrate dropped from 33.59 per thousand to 17.9 per thousand by 1979.

Distribution

The area of the 22 provinces in eastern China along or near the sea amounts to 40% of the total land area but contains 90% of the population, with only 10% in the vast tracts of Northwest and Southwest China. China's 216 cities contain about 15% of the total population. The three largest cities are Beijing, the capital (9,230,687 in 1982), Shanghai, the great commercial and industrial centre (11,859,748 in 1982) and Tianjin, also an important industrial centre (7,764,141 in 1982). These three cities have a distinctive status as municipalities on an equivalent level to provinces in the administrative system. Urban growth has been controlled through several intense ideological campaigns designed to mobilise the urban population, particularly in the young, to go to the countryside and settle in remote regions where they could contribute to development.

Groups

The Han nationality make up 94% of the population. In addition there are 55 minority nationalities spread all over the country, but mainly concentrated in the Northwest and Southwest.

3 SOCIETY AND CULTURE
Cultural Traditions

China's rich cultural heritage goes back several millenia, with historical and literary records dating back to the early part of the first millenium BC. Chinese culture has been dominated by the teachings of great masters such as Confucius (551-479 BC) whose ethical teachings became the main basis of both family and political relations from the Han dynasty until the last imperial dynasty, the Qing, which fell in the Revolution of 1911. Daoism, the teaching of another great philosopher, Lao Zi (circa 590 BC) formed a more anarchic thread of Chinese philosophy which focused on man's relation to nature, and which encouraged remarkable scientific experimentation. Buddhism was introduced to China from India in the first century AD and became deeply embedded in Chinese culture, flourishing particularly in the Tang dynasty (619-907 AD). China's remarkable cultural achievements had a profound influence on the surrounding nations, forming the basis of Japan's high culture from the sixth century AD, and also influencing Korea and South East Asia. Many of China's minority groups also have distinctive languages and highly developed cultural traditions, but Han culture has tended to be a dominating force.

Language

Chinese culture is inextricably linked with the ideographic language in which each character, originally derived from pictograms, represents a unit of meaning and is capable of being pronounced in hundreds of different ways according to regional dialects. There are as many as 60,000 characters in the most exhaustive of dictionaries, but about 3,000 to 5,000 are needed in order to be able to read Chinese newspapers with ease. The beautiful and controlled brushwork involved in traditional calligraphy is the basis of most Chinese art, so that the written language is at the same time one of the highest art forms. The complexity and difficulty of the language has meant that a large percentage of the population have remained illiterate until recent years, and mastery of the language and its literature was the main requirement for those who were to become rulers in traditional society.

Great efforts have been made in this century to simplify the language, by abandoning the classical written style 'wenyan' and adopting the spoken idiom 'baihua' in writing, by simplifying the stroke content of the characters and reducing the number in common use, and by popularising one spoken dialect, 'putonghua', to prepare the way for the possible future adoption of a phonetic script.

Religion

Religion has never played a central part in traditional Han culture, as both Confucianism and Daoism are essentially philosophical systems, although both have had religious ceremonies associated with them. Confucian temples were closely linked with the imperial bureaucracy and legitimated the Emperor's rule. Buddhism had a very widespread influence at certain periods and was able to coexist harmoniously with Daoism so that many temples contain both Buddhist and Daoist features. Islam came to China in the seventh century, and it is the religion of ten of China's minority nationalities, as well as several million Han Chinese, mainly in the far West. Christianity was brought to China first by Nestorians in the seventh century, when it made little impact, and again under the Jesuits in the sixteenth century. The nineteenth century was the main period of both Catholic and Protestant missions, resulting in a Christian population of about 3-4 million, but having far greater proportional influence on social and educational institutions during China's painful modernisation process than these figures suggest. Since Liberation in 1949 the Chinese constitution has protected the rights of all religious believers to religious freedom, while at the same time atheism has been officially propagated through the education system.

Social Patterns

In Chinese feudal society the main classes were scholars, farmers, craftsmen and merchants, having that order of social prestige. Commerce was despised so that no extensive merchant class arose until the nineteenth century. Women were kept in strict subjugation under what were called the 'three obediences': to the father when young, to the husband when married, to the son when a widow. The ideal was a harmonious unchanging society in which all exercised restraint in the use of the produce of the land. Against these tenacious traditional values, determined efforts have been made in this century to increase agricultural productivity and develop industry and commerce in a society where workers and peasants are supposed to be the leading classes. Women have gained equal rights before the law and form an important part of the labour force, yet they still tend to be kept in subordinate positions due to traditional family patterns. Minority nationalities have been encouraged to preserve and develop their own cultures yet they are often overshadowed by the Han.

4 HISTORY AND POLITICS

Origins

Chinese history goes back to a legendary era from 2550 to 2205 BC in which five wise emperors supposedly created the first laws and religious rituals; also the tools of warfare, agriculture and the arts. The Xia dynasty (2205-1766 BC) marked the beginning of China's hereditary monarchies. In the subsequent Shang (1766-1122) and Zhou (1122-221) dynasties a feudalist society developed and in its latter years the great philosophers Confucious and Lao Zi taught under the patronage of feudal lords. The whole empire was united under a centralised administration by Qin Shi Huang Di, nicknamed the Tiger of Qin, whose brief Qin dynasty (221-206 BC) saw the standardisation of the Chinese written language, currency, weights and measures, the promulgation of a uniform system of laws, and the extensive building of roads. This emperor was also responsible for consolidating and lengthening the Great Wall as a barrier against incursions of the nomads of the Mongolian steppes. The Han dynasty which followed (202 BC to 220 AD) established the patterns of Chinese culture which were to last until the early twentieth century, the most significant feature being the imperial examination system which selected scholar-officials to rule on the impartial basis of their knowledge of the Confucian classical canons. In this way China evolved one of the earliest meritocratic forms of government, one which was to prove the enduring value of the Confucian teachings for the maintenance of a stable, harmonious imperial order. The Tang dynasty (618 to 907 AD) was a golden age of economic and cultural expansion marked by the celebrated poetry of Li Bai and Du Fu, and by inventions such as the printing press and gunpowder. The Song dynasty (960 to 1279 AD) has been described as an age of refined artistic tastes and stimulating philosophical debates. Of the last three dynasties, Yuan (1279-1368), Ming (1368-1644) and Qing (1644-1911), two saw the ascendancy of foreign rulers from the north, the Mongols in Yuan and the Manchus in Qing, with Ming as a period whose chief goal was the restoration of traditional values. However, both Mongol and Manchu rulers were fully assimilated to Confucian cultural norms, and ruled successfully through the bureaucratic system dominated by Confucian scholar-officials, a tribute to the universal validity of Chinese culture.

The Nineteenth Century and the Impact of the West

The nineteenth century was a period of crisis for the Chinese empire with one of the most extensive peasant revolts in Chinese history, the Taiping Rebellion (1851-1864) and the increasing incursion of western traders and missionaries bringing severe dislocation to China's traditional political and economic order. Through a whole series of wars, the two Opium Wars with the British (1840 and 1856), the Franco-Chinese War (1884-5) and finally the Sino-Japanese War (1894-5), China was brought to utter humiliation and forced to open more and more treaty ports to western trade under terms set by the western powers and Japan. The Manchu rulers slowly responded to this enforced and bitter modernisation by establishing military and naval academies and finally by adopting plans for a modern education system in 1902, when they finally faced the fact that western military techniques could not be imported without the study of western science and the social and political institutions of the West. However, the reform movement proceeded too slowly to ward off the forces of revolution led by Sun Yat Sen and the Guomindang Party which overthrew the Qing dynasty in 1911. This first revolution was followed by 15 years of near anarchy with the country divided under conflicting warlord interests before a reorganised Guomindang Party succeeded in establishing a national government in Nanjing in 1927. Meanwhile the Chinese Communist Party was born in 1921, and worked steadily first to form a basis among urban workers, later more successfully to mobilise peasants to revolutionary action. The Sino-Japanese War of 1937-45 gave the Communist Party an opportunity to demonstrate both its skill in agricultural renewal and its ability to inspire the whole nation to struggle against the Japanese invaders. It emerged greatly strengthened from the war years, and able to overthrow the corrupt Guomindang government, in spite of strong American support for the latter. The Guomindang rulers took up residence in Taiwan after being defeated by the Communists in 1949, and have succeeded in developing it as a prosperous rebel province, supposedly representing the whole nation, with the help of considerable American economic and military aid.

The Present Political System

The People's Republic of China defines itself as a people's democratic dictatorship under the leadership of the Chinese Communist Party. The highest organ of State is the National People's congress (NPC) to which delegates are elected from the lower level Provincial or Municipal People's Congresses, below which are the Local People's Congresses at the county level. The NPC is supposed to be convened yearly, but because of its unwieldy size much of its responsibility is carried out by its Standing Committee. It is the main legislative organ of the people's government, and is headed by the Chairman of the People's Republic, which it elects. The State Council is the highest executive or administrative organ of State power, consisting of the Premier, the Secretary General, a number of vice-premiers and the ministers and chairmen of commissions. The Supreme People's Court is the main juridical organ of State government, its president being elected by the NPC. Below it are provincial and local level people's courts which relate appropriately to local government organs. Since the end of the ten year Cultural Revolution period (1966-1976) and the purge of radical leftist leaders, great emphasis has been put on strengthening the socialist legal system and six important new laws have been adopted.

The Chinese Communist Party (CCP) has a nationwide pyramidical structure, resembling the administrative hierarchy of government, so that there are Party organisations parallel to all government bodies, beginning with the Central Committee of the CCP and its politbureau at the top. Often interlocking leadership patterns are used to strengthen Party guidance over government organisations, although at present emphasis is being placed on the separation of Party and State functions. While eight other political parties, mainly democratic parties founded in the 1930s and 1940s, are allowed to exist, their membership is an ageing one, and they have little political influence.

International Relations

In its early years the People's Republic of China relied on very close relations with the Soviet Union and borrowed extensively from Soviet political and educational patterns. The Chinese benefited from a major injection of Soviet technical expertise and industrial aid in the 1950s. However, increasing tensions with the Soviets over border disputes and disagreements about basic issues of socialist development strategy resulted in the complete withdrawal of all Soviet economic and technical aid in 1960. This rupture has never been healed and present Chinese foreign policy stresses the need to counter the threat of Soviet hegemonism. In the 1960s China did much to enhance her relations with Third World nations of Africa and Latin America, and established herself as the champion of self-reliant nations standing up to the threats of the superpowers. The most significant foreign policy development of the 1970s was the visit of American President Richard Nixon to China in 1972, which led eventually to the normalisation of Sino-American relations in 1979, and a flourishing cultural and economic exchange situation between China and both America and Europe. China regained her seat in the United Nations in 1971 with the withdrawal of Taiwan, but American military support of Taiwan remains a serious obstacle to the further improvement of Sino-American relations.

5 THE ECONOMY

Pattern of the Economy

China has a planned socialist economy whose policies were largely patterned after the Soviet model in the early years. After the Revolution, the years from 1949 to 1952 were given to restoring the productive capacity which had been paralysed due to war. The first Five Year Plan, 1953-57, followed a Soviet model in which rapid industrialisation through comprehensive planning was the most important objective. Priority in the allocation of investment and resources went to heavy industry where Soviet aid provided the basis of the industrialisation process. Agriculture continued to execute its role as provider of essential consumption and supplier of raw materials and exports. After 1960 and the withdrawal of Soviet aid, the guiding policy for economic development changed to an emphasis on agriculture as the foundation with light and heavy industry as the leading factors. Both industry and agriculture were brought under total socialist ownership during the 1950s with industries transformed into State or joint State and private enterprises, and agriculture collectivised. Since 1976 economic policies have increasingly stressed greater autonomy and self-management for individual enterprises and a controlled use of market mechanisms to guide investment and raise quality in what is called the 'responsibility system'.

Natural Resources

China is relatively richly endowed with mineral wealth and is already a significant world producer of many mineral products. Intensive programmes of geological investigation have led to the discovery of even further resources which indicate enormous potential for industrial growth. At present China stands third in the world in coal resources, eighth in petroleum, and sixteenth in natural gas. There are rich water power resources and valuable uranium deposits which are now being used for nuclear power development. However, the rapid rise of agricultural production desirable for investment in industry has proven elusive due to the limited amount of arable land and the intensive traditional methods of cultivation which could not easily be improved for higher productivity.

Agriculture

About 72% of China's labour force are engaged in agricultural work, as against 88% in 1950. Major farm products include grain (rice, wheat, barley, oats and maize), cotton, peanuts, rapeseed, sesame, silk, tea and sugar cane. China's total agricultural produce in 1978 was worth 158.1 billion yuan, as against a total industrial output of 459.1 billion yuan. Because traditional agriculture was so highly developed it has been difficult to achieve rapid growth in agricultural production parallel to industrial growth, in spite of persistent efforts to develop improved fertilizers and new seed strains. Mechanisation of agriculture has also proceeded slowly due to the difficult terrain in many areas, and the efficiency of traditional labour intensive methods. There has been considerable development of rural industry related to lower level agricultural mechanisation, which provides jobs for young people in the countryside. Also, recent policies have encouraged the use of small private plots for sideline production of fruit, vegetables and meat to be sold in free markets, and a responsibility system which gives peasants greater control over their productive work and correspondingly greater responsibility to improve efficiency. Grain still has to be imported to meet the needs of the major cities, and this trend is likely to continue and increase.

Industry

China's major industries include coal, crude oil, steel, electricity, heavy machinery, and light industries such as textiles, silk, TV and radio sets, bicycles, sewing machines, wrist watches, etc. A growing emphasis is being put on light industry recently to meet the needs of a vast and expanding internal consumer market. Industrial growth since 1949 has been remarkable as the following indices suggest:

Year	Agricultural Production	Industrial Production
1949	53	20
1959	83	173
1969	112	266
1978	156	651

Source: CHINA: Facts and Figures, Annual, Vol. 3 (1957=100)

In spite of this impressive growth record urban industry is still not growing fast enough to absorb the large number of urban school leavers who do not find a place in higher education and who are no longer willing to go down to the countryside and labour with the peasants for protracted periods.

Efforts are being made to absorb them into small cooperatives or private enterprises often involved in service industries such as restaurants, repair shops, tailoring, etc.

China's remarkable achievements in space technology have been demonstrated in 14 nuclear and two satellite tests since 1964. In early 1980 the Chinese announced that training for a manned space programme had begun. However, the Chinese continue to reiterate their commitment to the peaceful development of space technology.

Overseas Trade

Because of China's vast size and huge internal market, overseas trade has had a relatively small role in her development. Chinese leaders have oscillated between policies of self-reliance and a minimal involvement in the international market on the one hand and greater stress on the development of foreign trade with the Soviet Union and the socialist world in the 1950s, and increasingly with industrialised countries of the West in the 1970s and 1980s. This has led to the consciousness of the need to develop more modern management skills, to do research in world marketing trends and to utilise more sophisticated techniques for participation in international commercial deals. The creation of joint-venture enterprises between Chinese and foreign firms is a new strategy being used by China's leaders to speed up the industrialisation process and attract more foreign capital. These new trends, sometimes described as an open door policy, make important demands on the education system to produce the kind of skilled young people needed for these tasks.

China's main exports are cotton, tea, silk, handicrafts, foodstuffs, hides, skins, bristles, also crude oil, especially to Japan. Her imports include heavy machinery, in some cases whole plants, and large quantities of grain. Her balance of payments has remained good. The following figures show both her growing involvement in world markets, and balance of payments:

Year	Imports	Exports	Currency
1977	6,337.3	6,792.9	million US$
1978	10,874	9,726	million US$
1979	15,300	13,500	million US$
1980	18,466*	17,933*	million US$

Source: CHINA: Facts and Figures Annual, Vols. 2, 3, 4

*Converted from yuan at US $1.00 = 1.50 yuan)

6 THE EDUCATION SYSTEM

The Academic Year

The academic year in China has two terms, the first running from early September to mid-January, followed by a three-week vacation for Chinese New Year. The second begins in February and runs to mid-July leaving about six weeks for summer vacation.

Structure of the Education System

The structure of the regular school system in China follows a 6-3-3-4 pattern: 6 years primary schooling, 3 years junior middle school, 3 years senior middle school and an average of four years for higher schools. Parallel to the regular system is a highly developed informal system of part time institutions which are run by agencies such as factories, communes and local councils, and are flexible in timetabling and curricula to suit local production needs. During the Cultural Revolution, 1966-1976, the regular schooling system was greatly shortened and integrated with the productive system along the lines of the informal schools. Primary schooling was reduced to five years, middle schooling to four years in all, and higher schooling to two or three years. All students had to spend at least two years working in the countryside before they could be recommended for higher education. However, since the fall of the radical leaders in 1976, the old system has come back, with primary schooling gradually being lengthened to six years again. Most junior middle schools are now three years, and senior middle schools are being lengthened to three years at the moment. Higher education is now four years. There is a move at present to lower the age for entering primary school from seven to six years of age.

Examinations

Examinations have once again come to play a major role in Chinese education as a means of articulating the movement of students from each level of education upwards. During the Cultural Revolution examinations and the academic orientation which they stood for were severely criticised, and other means such as popular recommendation were used to select students for higher levels of education. But in December 1977 nationwide higher education entrance examinations were reinstated in order to select the most talented young people. At lower levels examinations have also come to play an important role. In urban areas city-wide examinations are held at the end of junior middle school on the basis of which students are promoted to senior middle school, the top candidates being admitted to 'keypoint' middle schools whose task is to set higher educational standards. At the end of primary school examinations are organised on the level of the district or county for deciding the movement of graduates to appropriate middle schools.

Pre-Primary Schools

As the majority of Chinese women work full time, nursery care is provided for children from 1½ to 3 years old in nurseries that are usually attached to the place of work and staffed by nurses. About 50% of children in the cities are cared for in this way, a lower percentage in the countryside. Day care centres operate from Monday to Saturday, and are subsidised by public funds but mainly supported by funds from the workplace. Parents pay for food and a general fee of 4-6 yuan a month.

Kindergartens may be run either by communes and factories, or under local bureaus of education, and are usually situated in residential areas. They are staffed by specially trained teachers and cater to children aged 3-6. Their curriculum focuses on group activities such as singing, dancing, and drawing. Children learn how to carry out simple tasks such as hanging up towels, folding quilts, sweeping floors in a collective spirit. Some number work is begun but reading is not supposed to be taught in the kindergarten, although in some cases a beginning is made with simple Chinese characters.

Primary Schools

Great efforts have been made to universalise primary education and by 1978 it was estimated that almost 95% of the school age population was attending primary schools, in contrast to a figure of 40% in the cities and 5% in the countryside before Liberation. Primary school enrolments rose from 24.5 million in 1949 to 146.27 million in 1980.

The aim of Chinese education is that children should develop morally, intellectually and physically to become workers with socialist consciousness and culture. Thus political education plays an important part in the curriculum, not only through classes in politics but through the tone and presentation of all subjects in the curriculum, especially language and literature. The main subjects at the primary level are politics, Chinese language, common knowledge (including science, geography and history), mathematics, physical training, music and art. The difficulty of the Chinese language requires that one half to one third of the curricular time be given to language lessons.

During the Cultural Revolution period great attention was given to adapting the curriculum to local needs and involving the children in productive labour through the development of small school farms and participation in simple factory work, often done on school premises. While the integration of labour and learning is still an important principle in Chinese education, in recent years more emphasis has been placed on raising academic standards beginning from the primary level. From 1978 a number of keypoint primary schools were designated in each county or district to lead the way in promoting excellence, but since 1982 this distinction has been abandoned at the primary level. In 1978-9 a nationwide series of new textbooks were produced at the Ministry of Education in Beijing, designed to be used throughout the country and to stimulate improved standards. Foreign language teaching is now begun in the third or fourth years of primary school with English and Japanese as the most widely taught languages.

Secondary Schools

Secondary school enrolment has increased from just over one million in 1949 to about 58 million in 1980. In the mid-seventies it was estimated that about 80-90% of urban primary school graduates went on to middle school, but only 60-75% of rural children did the same. A much smaller percentage are able to complete the five to six years of secondary schooling, especially in rural areas where many middle schools only provide three years of schooling.

Curriculum

Middle schools were even more radically affected by the Cultural Revolution than primary ones, and the traditional academic curriculum was abandoned in favour of one focusing on three main study areas: language and literature, politics (the study of Mao's thought and CCP history), and industrial or agricultural production, which encompassed all the natural science teaching needd for a practical understanding of local industrial or agricultural conditions. In addition military training and physical education were emphasised. Schools were to open their doors to society, and students often spent one day a week in industrial production and another day in agricultural work. At certain times in the year whole classes would go to the countryside for several weeks of agricultural work. This productive labour was supposed to contribute both to the shaping of correct proletarian attitudes and to a better intellectual grasp of scientific theory as applied in practice to production.

Since 1976 middle schools have returned to a more traditional academic curriculum with the following main subject areas: Marxist-Leninist philosophy, economics and CCP history; mathematics, physics, chemistry; hygiene, physiology and population studies; English, Japanese or another foreign language; geography, history and physical culture. Art and music are stressed differently in different schools. Students still take some part in productive labour usually in small school factories but much less time is given to it. Standardised textbooks produced by the Ministry of Education in 1978-79 are used in most middle schools, but teachers are encouraged to supplement these with locally oriented material suited to the aptitude of the class. Keypoint middle schools have been designated to lead the way in striving for academic excellence, and graduates of these schools are likely to have a much higher success rate in the competitive examinations for higher education entrance. In rural areas keypoint middle schools tend to be those located in county towns. In practice this has meant the concentration of the most talented students in these schools and a consequent lowering of talent in more remote schools which in some cases has led to the closing of senior middle schools in rural areas. The same tendency is noticeable in cities although Chinese commentators account for it in terms of demographic changes.

Diversification of Types of Middle School

During the Cultural Revolution distinctions between ordinary, vocational, technical and agricultural middle schools virtually disappeared, as all schooling was linked with productive labour. Now than an academic curriculum has re-emerged, middle schools are put under great pressures in preparing students for the intensely competitive higher education entrance examinations, in which only about 10-15% of those who participate are offered places. The danger of an examination-oriented curriculum which will leave the majority of school leavers ill prepared for productive or socially useful tasks has been recognised. Efforts are being made to introduce vocational subjects into many senior middle schools for those who are unlikely to go on to higher education. Also some ordinary middle schools are being changed into technical or vocational schools. In addition there are agricultural middle schools focusing on specialised training related to local agricultural needs, and professional middle schools training middle level personnel such as kindergarten and primary school teachers, nursing assistants and clerical workers.

Schools for National Minorities

China's 55 minority nationalities have the right to education in their own language if it has a developed written form. They then study Chinese as a second language from the first year of primary school. In 1978 there were 7,685,000 students in minority primary schools, and 2,526,000 in minority secondary schools. At the tertiary level efforts are made to integrate national minorities into the mainstream higher institutes, but there are also about ten special minority institutions of higher learning.

Schools for the Handicapped

The education of the handicapped received only limited attention during the early years of the present régime, and little is known about special schools during the Cultural Revolution period. Chinese sources have recently reported the existence of 292 schools for the blind and deaf throughout the country, and the establishment of a research centre for research into special education at Beijing Normal University.

Higher Schools

Chinese higher education has seen remarkable expansion from about 117,000 enrolment in 1949 to 1,144,000 in 1980. Universities and other higher institutions were centres of revolutionary activity during the Cultural Revolution, and most were closed for all educational purposes from 1966 to 1971, when they reopened with reduced enrolments and a brief to make higher education serve proletarian politics. However, since 1976, policies quite similar to those of the 1950s have been followed, with an emphasis on raising academic standards.

Curriculum

Higher education is very diversified in types of institution, roughly following the Soviet pattern of having a small number of comprehensive universities offering a broad curriculum in arts, social sciences and pure sciences, a some-what larger number of polytechnical institutions offering a wide range of applied sciences, and even more specialised institutions giving professional training in such fields as engineering, medicine, teacher training, finance, trade, foreign languages etc. Even in comprehensive and polytechnical institutions students tend to take all their courses within one specialisation under one department and receive a rigorous but somewhat narrow professional training. Efforts are now being made to strengthen general theory courses and broaden students' cultural education by inter-departmental cooperation and the limited use of the credit system in some universities. It is more difficult to achieve these goals in the specialised institutions but some cooperation among institutions is being tried out.

Methods of Expansion

Great attention has been paid to the expansion of higher education in recent years with a concern to maintain and improve quality at the same time. One of the ways this has been done is for established institutions to set up branch campuses which have totally separate administration and funding but which are able to benefit from the teaching resources, libraries and equipment of the parent institutions. The branch schools are mainly day schools which recruit from the locality and do not provide housing for students as is common in all the established higher schools. Another way in which enrolments have been expanded is for regular institutions to enrol day students who take most of their classes in the afternoons and who do not live on the campuses. At the same time quality is maintained through the special status given to 96 keypoint institutions whose main task is to raise standards to international levels in their respective fields. These institutions are able to select the most talented young people from all over the country, and they receive some priority in funding and capital construction.

Academic Degrees

For the first time since Liberation China has recently adopted a system of academic degrees, with the first bachelors' degrees being conferred on graduates in the spring of 1982. Only established higher schools offering four-year courses are qualified to confer degrees, as stipulated by the Academic Degrees Committee of the State Council. (About 450 out of 675 institutions have been designated as qualified so far).

Graduate Schools

Graduate education has been reorganised since 1978 and a limited number of university departments and professors have been given the right to recruit candidates for MA and PhD degrees, the first of which were conferred in the Spring of 1982. Graduate students are also recruited by the research institutes under the Chinese Academy of Science and the Chinese Academy of Social Science. In 1980 there were 22,600 post-graduate students in the whole country, in contrast to a total of 16,000 graduate students between 1949 and 1966, when all graduate education stopped with the Cultural Revolution. Of the 11,792 post-graduates selected in Spring 1982 to begin their study in the autumn, it is expected that over one thousand will be sent to do PhD degrees in the West, mostly in the pure and applied sciences.

Fees

No fees are required for higher education, and most students are given State stipends which cover minimum living expenses. Mature students who have worked for five years before entering university are able to draw their regular salary while in higher education.

Women in Higher Education

Only 24% of China's full time higher education students are women, which contrasts with a much higher percentage during the Cultural Revolution period when students were recommended for places in higher institutions. It is difficult to account for this except in terms of the traditional pressures put upon women through their family ties and general social expectations of them which result in a lower ratio of success in the competitive entrance examinations.

Teacher Education

With China's enormous educational expansion over the last 30 years, teacher training has remained a pressing and unfinished task. This has been compounded by the fact that teachers were severely attacked during the Cultural Revolution as conservative elements, and their traditionally low social position fell even further, making it difficult now to recruit talented young people to the profession.

There are three levels of teacher training institutions:

1 higher teacher training institutes with a four-year programme training senior middle graduates to teach in senior middle schools

2   teacher training schools with a two-year programme training senior middle graduates to teach in junior middle schools

3   secondary teacher training schools with a three year programme training junior middle graduates for teaching in primary schools or kindergartens.

Curricula in teacher education tend to stress basic academic subjects. Pedagogical subjects have not been highly developed, although at present efforts are being made in this direction. The following percentages indicate the critical shortage of adequately trained teachers in China's present system:

Year	1965	1973	1977	1979
1 Percentage of qualified primary school teachers with secondary normal education or above	47.4	28.0	-	47.0
2 Percentage of qualified lower middle school teachers with specialised senior middle school education or above	71.9	-	14.3	10.6
3 Percentage of qualified senior middle school teachers with academic senior middle school education or above	70.3	-	33.2	50.8

Source: Billie Lo, 'Teachers and Teacher Training in China, 1977-Present', Working Paper No. CC31, Centre of Asian Studies, University of Hong Kong.

In-service teacher education is being stressed at present to upgrade the teaching corps, but much more emphasis needs to be put on pre-service training.

Spare Time Education

China has a fully developed system of spare time schools mostly run by factories, farms or other enterprises to raise the cultural and scientific level of their workers while they are on the job. Originally most of these concentrated on basic literacy training, but now they provide education up to the highest levels and are an important supplement to the regular system. In 1980 it was reported that 455,000 people were enrolled in spare time universities.

Other efforts being made to provide educational opportunities for young people who have not been able to enter the regular higher education system include the recently organised television universities which had an enrolment of 324,000 in 1980, and various self-study programmes associated with libraries. In both cases students are able to take examinations organised

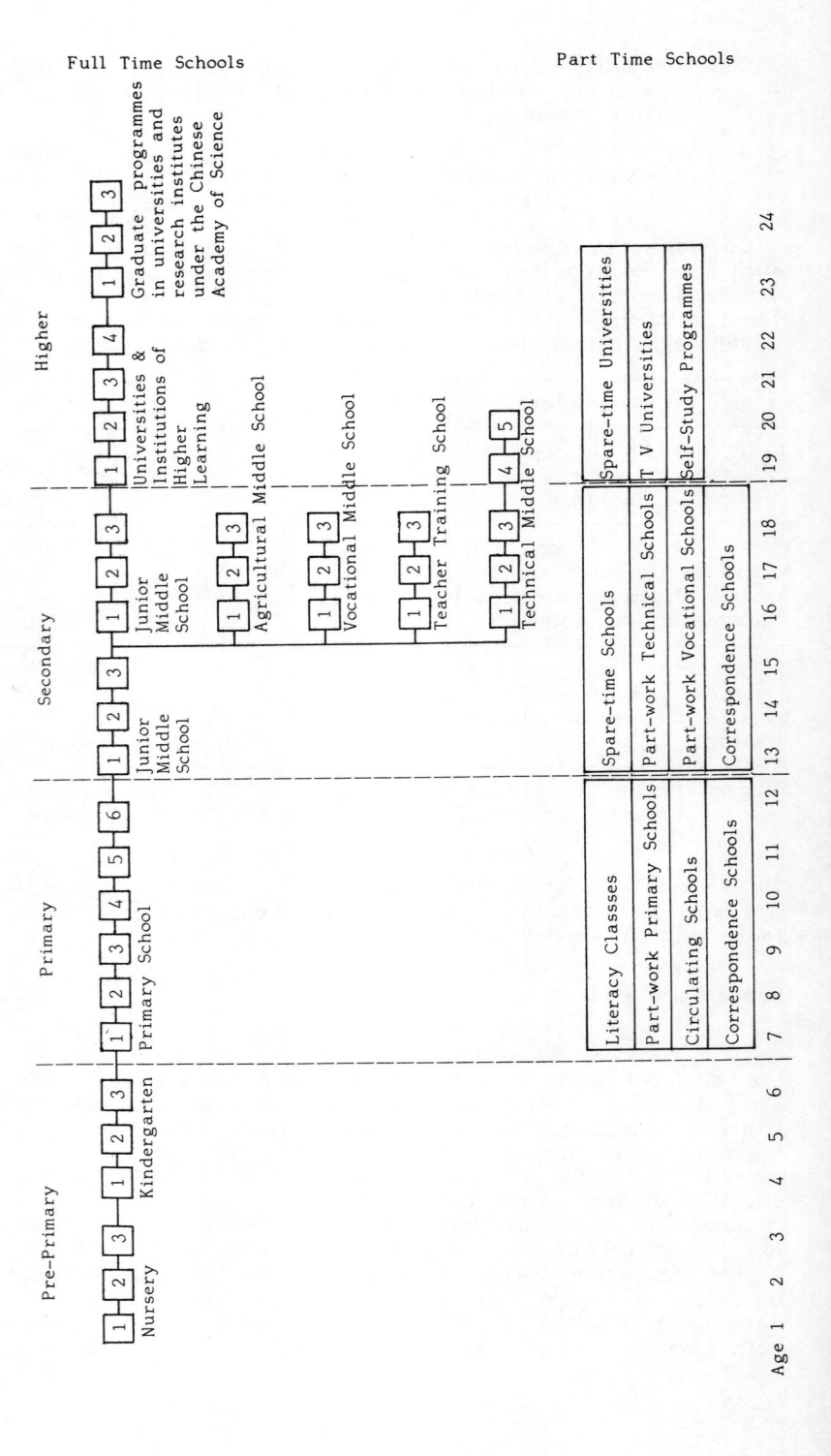

CHINA - THE SCHOOL SYSTEM

by the Ministry of Education and receive appropriate qualifications and job assignments.

7 EDUCATIONAL ADMINISTRATION
State Organs

The main bodies responsible for the education system are the Ministry of Education at the national level, which is under the State Council and responsible for implementing general policy formulated and adopted at the National People's Congress, bureaus of education at the level of the 21 provinces, 3 municipalities and 5 autonomous regions, responsible to provincial and municipal people's councils, and bureaus of education at the country or urban district level, responsible to local people's congresses.

National

The Ministry of Education in Beijing has recently strengthened its guiding function over the content of education at all levels through the nationwide textbooks for all subjects and levels which were prepared in committees directly under its control in 1978-79. This was seen as essential for standardising the content of education after the disruption of the Cultural Revolution years, and for raising quality in all areas. In cooperation with other ministries and the Academy of Science, the Ministry of Education is also responsible for planning research, drafting quotas of manpower, and over-seeing the allocation of graduates to various sectors of the economy. In addition it administers the nationwide higher education entrance examinations. However, it has direct control of only a small number of educational institutions, mainly in higher education, including 38 comprehensive universities and teacher training colleges, and a few national level keypoint secondary schools. A majority of the higher education institutions, mainly polytechnical or specialised schools, are either under the control of other State ministries appropriate to their subject content, or under provincial bureaus of education.

Provincial

Provincial or municipal bureaus of education exercise direct control over 411 of China's 675 institutions of higher learning. In addition they may control a small number of keypoint secondary schools which may recruit students from the whole province or municipality. Although the nationwide entrance examinations for higher education are organised at the national level, much of the marking and regional assignment of places is done at the provincial level. The provincial bureau may also organise examinations at the end of junior middle school to decide the movement of students to senior middle school. It provides in-service training courses for teachers, and exercises a general supervision over the implementation of educational policies within the province.

System of Management of Institutions of Higher Learning in China

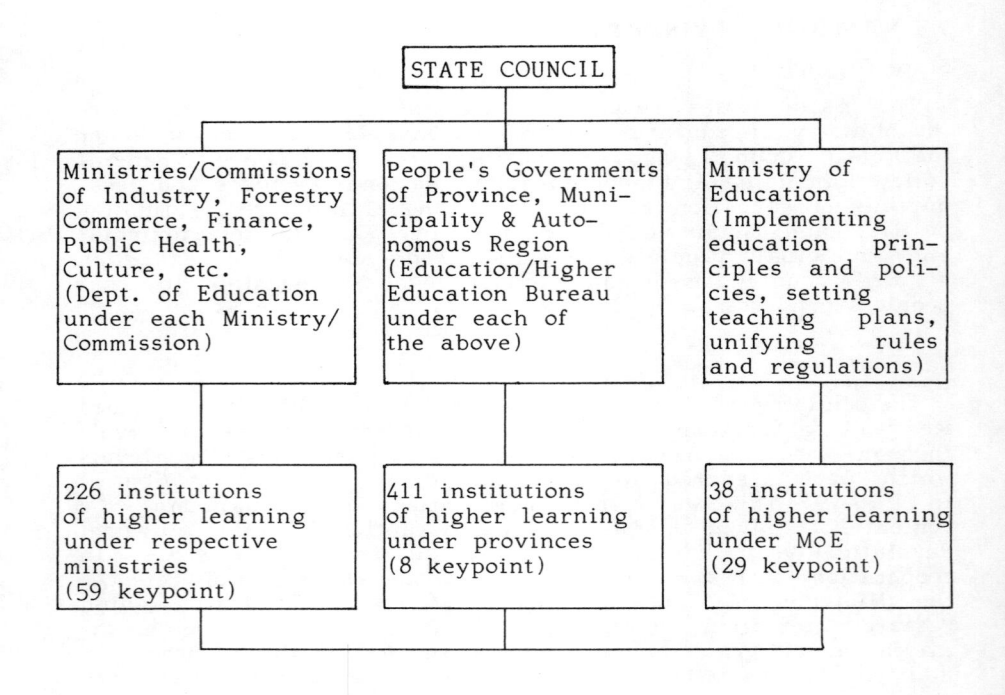

```
                        ┌─────────────────┐
                        │  STATE COUNCIL  │
                        └─────────────────┘
                                 │
        ┌────────────────────────┼────────────────────────┐
        │                        │                        │
┌───────────────────┐  ┌───────────────────┐  ┌───────────────────┐
│ Ministries/       │  │ People's          │  │ Ministry of       │
│ Commissions       │  │ Governments       │  │ Education         │
│ of Industry,      │  │ of Province,      │  │ (Implementing     │
│ Forestry          │  │ Municipality &    │  │ education prin-   │
│ Commerce,         │  │ Autonomous Region │  │ ciples and poli-  │
│ Finance,          │  │ (Education/Higher │  │ cies, setting     │
│ Public Health,    │  │ Education Bureau  │  │ teaching plans,   │
│ Culture, etc.     │  │ under each of     │  │ unifying rules    │
│ (Dept. of         │  │ the above)        │  │ and regulations)  │
│ Education under   │  │                   │  │                   │
│ each Ministry/    │  │                   │  │                   │
│ Commission)       │  │                   │  │                   │
└───────────────────┘  └───────────────────┘  └───────────────────┘
        │                        │                        │
┌───────────────────┐  ┌───────────────────┐  ┌───────────────────┐
│ 226 institutions  │  │ 411 institutions  │  │ 38 institutions   │
│ of higher learning│  │ of higher learning│  │ of higher learning│
│ under respective  │  │ under provinces   │  │ under MoE         │
│ ministries        │  │ (8 keypoint)      │  │ (29 keypoint)     │
│ (59 keypoint)     │  │                   │  │                   │
└───────────────────┘  └───────────────────┘  └───────────────────┘
```

675 Institutions of Higher Learning in total (96 keypoint)

Source: The Chinese Education Association for International Exchanges, 1980.

County/District

The county of district level bureau of education exercises direct control over all State primary and most State secondary schools within its area. It organises examinations which guide the movement of pupils from primary to junior middle schools. It has a staff of curriculum advisors, one or two for each subject taught at primary or secondary level, who liaise with teachers and help them in planning appropriate locally oriented material to supplement the national curricula and textbooks used. It also runs teacher enrichment courses in various fields to upgrade the teaching corps.

Non-State Organs of Administration

In addition to State schools administered at the three levels described above, a large number of full time primary and secondary schools as well as part time schools at all levels are set up and administered directly by such units as communes, production brigades and factories. These schools follow national guidelines in organisation, curricula and textbooks, but they recruit their own teachers and finance themselves out of their own budgets.

Guidance of the Chinese Communist Party

Communist Party branches exist at every level of education from the individual institutions and departments within them up to the National Ministry of Education, and in some cases Party Secretaries also hold key leadership posts in administrative organs, although this practice is now being discouraged. The task of the Party Branches at each level is to ensure that Party guidelines for education are followed, and to be responsible for the political education of administrators, teachers and students.

8 EDUCATIONAL FINANCE

No statistics are available at present for the financing of Chinese education, although it is generally known that State funding is drawn upon at national, provincial and local levels for all State schooling, while all other schools are financed by the organisations which control them, in some cases with a limited State subsidy.

Chinese educational researchers have only recently been exposed to the literature of the 1960s on education as an investment, due to their isolation from the world community during the Cultural Revolution. As a result many articles have appeared recently in the Chinese press deploring the low level of budget allocation for education in China in comparison with other developed and developing countries. In one such article in June, 1980, it was reported that 1.59% of China's total income wenjt towards education in 1971, and 2.09% in 1980 (*Guangming Ribao*, June 15, 1980).

9 DEVELOPMENT AND PLANNING OF THE EDUCATION SYSTEM

Origins

Traditionally Chinese society put a very high value on education from early times, as shown in the system of imperial examinations begun in the first century BC, which ensured the selection of scholar-officials versed in the classical canons for all important positions in the bureaucracy. These examinations were adminstered by the State at the national, provincial and local level through State schools which, however, had no teaching function. All teaching and learning was done through individual master-disciple relations, through small family or clan schools, and private colleges endowed by wealthy gentry. Only in 1902 were plans for a modern system of schools adopted in principle by the Qing imperial government, and these were slow to materialise due to political upheavals and inadequate funding. However, from the establishment of the Republic after the Revolution of 1911 until the Communist victory of 1949, remarkable progress was made under very difficult circumstances in setting up a modern system of primary schools, secondary schools and universities. From 1902 to 1921 Japanese influence was predominant, from 1922-1928 American influence was strongly felt, and after 1927 a strong European influence was added to the shaping of China's modern education system. Residues of American and European influence can be noticed in the structure and curricula respectively of China's primary and secondary system in the 1950s.

Educational Legislation

The right of all citizens to education and the responsibility of the State to provide it were clearly laid down in the Common Programme adopted in 1949, and in the first constitution of the People's Republic adopted in 1954. Recent changes in legislation reflect the drastic changes in educational policy that have been made in the last decade:

1975 Constitution (adopted during the Cultural Revolution period)
Article 12: The proletariat must exercise all-round dictatorship over the bourgeoisie in the superstructure, including all spheres of culture. Culture and education, literature and art, physical education, health work and scientific research work must all serve proletarian politics, serve the workers, peasants and soldiers and be combined with productive labour.

Article 27: Citizens have the right to work and the right to education. (*Peking Review*, Jan. 24, 1975.)

1978 Constitution (adopted after the fall of the 'Gang of Four')
Article 13: The State devotes major efforts in developing education in order to raise the cultural and scientific level of the whole nation. Education must serve proletarian politics and be combined with productive labour, and must enable everyone who receives an education to develop morally, intellectually

and physically and become a worker with both socialist consciousness and culture.

Article 51: Citizens have the right to education. To ensure that citizens enjoy this right, the State gradually increases the number of schools of various types and of other cultural and educational institutions and popularises education. (*Peking Review*, Mar. 17, 1978.)

1982 Revised Draft of the Constitution (to be adopted by the fifth session of the Fifth National People's Congress)
Article 20: The State promotes the planned, socialist development of education, science, public health and sports, culture and art . . . The State operates and encourages non-government bodies to operate various types of schools in order to wipe out illiteracy, universalise primary education and develop secondary, vocational and higher education. The State increases various types of cultural and educational facilities and promotes political, cultural, scientific and professional education among the workers, peasants and other working people.

Article 21: The State, in a planned way, trains intellectuals who serve socialism, increases their number and gives full scope to their role in socialist modernisation.

Article 22: The State promotes the virtues of love for the motherland, the people, labour, science and socialism; it educates people in the ideas and ethics of patriotism, collectivism, internationalism and communism; and it opposes the influence of capitalist ideas, the remaining feudal ideas and other decadent ideology.

Article 44: Citizens of the PRC have the right and obligation to receive education. The State promotes the all-round development - moral, intellectual, physical - of young people and children. (*Beijing Review*, May 10, 1982).

There are two significant additions to the 1982 Draft of the Constitutions that appear for the first time in post-Liberation Chinese educational legislation. The first is that education is not only the right but obligation of all citizens, the first legal statement of compulsory education. The second is the inclusion of a separate article devoted to intellectuals, who were severely attacked during the Cultural Revolution, but now are given legal protection for their important role in contributing to socialist modernisation. Another important change is the more exhaustive attention given to education, and the fact that it is no longer seen as the servant of proletarian politics but is given a more autonomous role in the nurturing of a wide range of socialist virtu , as well as intellectual skills needed for modernisation. The State is to take an active part in developing education in order to overcome the continuing problems of illiteracy and inadequate primary schooling.

Development Trends – an Emphasis on Quality

Chinese education has made remarkable, if somewhat erratic, progress in the expansion of provision at all levels. A glance at the growth statistics shows that the greatest expansion of primary schooling occurred between 1957 and 1965, whereas huge gains in secondary provision were made during the Cultural Revolution years from 1966 to 1976. Higher education, where enrolments fell during the Cultural Revolution period, has benefited from a thrust to expand since 1976. However, now Chinese leaders are focusing concern on the task of raising the quality of education, as indicated in Vice-Premier Deng Xiao-ping's speech at the National Educational Work Conference in April, 1978. A number of measures are being taken for this purpose, some of them controversial.

Teacher Training

The status of teachers fell to an all-time low during the Cultural Revolution, when much teaching work was taken over by workers and peasants. It is not surprising then that only an estimated 10% of teachers at the junior secondary level were qualified in 1979. Now efforts are being made to expand pre-service training and to extend greatly all channels of in-service training. Some observers feel too much attention is being given to the latter, and not enough to the urgent needs of pre-service training. Also other measures are being taken to enhance the social status of teachers, including special citations and campaigns among students to respect their teachers. However, until salaries, which are now lower than those of factory workers, are raised to a reasonable level, the teaching profession is likely to have little attraction for talented young people.

Keypoint Schools

In 1978 the practice of designating a small number of keypoint schools at each level and in each area which receive priority in funding and a concentration of talented teachers and students was revived and developed from its pre-Cultural Revolution use in the late 1950s and 1960s. This practice has proven less controversial than one might expect. Although it seems antithetical to socialist egalitarian norms, it is easily accepted by the many Chinese still deeply influenced by traditional Confucian norms. At the primary level, keypoint status is now being de-emphasised, but secondary and tertiary level keypoint institutions are likely to play an important role in Chinese educational development for some time to come.

International Educational Exchange

Great hopes for raising the quality of education are being pinned on the present opportunities for lively educational exchange with the West which are unprecendented since Liberation. There are now several hundred European and North American teachers in China, mainly teaching in tertiary institutions, but some in secondary ones. Also China has sent about 13,000 teachers and students, mainly of tertiary level institutions, for advanced scholarly work in western universities and research institutes. International organisations such as the World Bank and UNESCO are involved in projects to develop Chinese education. The great challenge facing Chinese educators is how to adapt these inputs of western educational expertise to the needs of China's modernisation process. Foreign educational influence has not proven easily digestible in China's past experience, neither the European and American pre-Liberation inputs, nor the Soviet influence of the 1950s. However, China's present economic and political situation and the value structures of her educational workers may be better suited to absorbing this foreign input than in the past.

Educational Research Bodies

As education has always been highly politicised and closely integrated with the political system in both traditional and modern China educational research has not been seen as important for the making of educational policy. However, this may be changing. In 1963 a centre for Scientific Research in Education was established by the Ministry of Education in Beijing, then closed due to the Cultural Revolution in 1966. In 1978 it was reopened, and now research is being carried out in the following areas: educational theory, education history, educational systems, school management, teaching materials and methods, infant education, foreign education systems. Most research topics are decided by the Ministry of Education on policy related issues. Educational research is also being carried out in the major teachers' universities. However, it remains to be seen what impact research done by these bodies will have on Chinese educational policy in future.

CHINA BASIC EDUCATIONAL STATISTICS

Population Trends

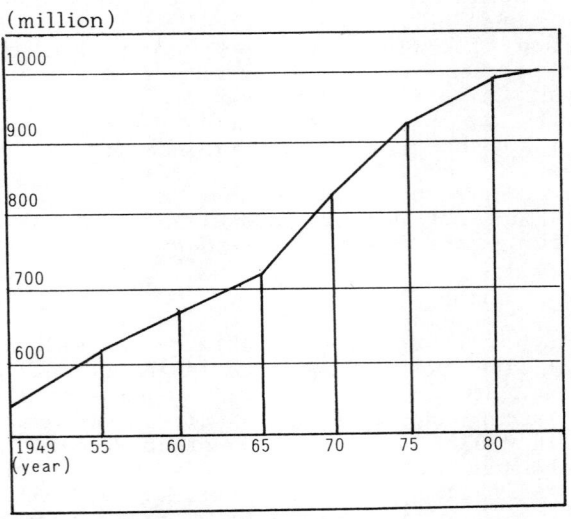

Growth of Chinese population

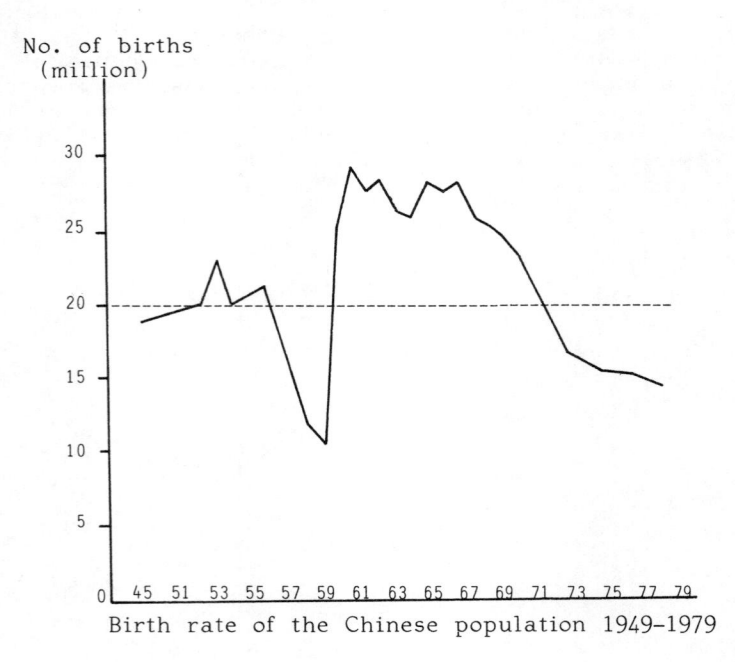

Birth rate of the Chinese population 1949-1979

Growth in Enrolments, Numbers of Institutions and Teachers

Pre-Primary

Year	Schools	Teachers	Pupils
1949	–	–	–
1957	16,400	50,000	1,088,000
1965	19,200	62,000	1,713,000
1980	170,400	411,000	11,508,000

Primary

Year	Schools	Teachers	Pupils	% Female
1949	346,000	836,000	24,391,000	28.0*
1957	547,300	1,884,000	64,283,000	34.5
1965	1,681,000	3,857,000	116,209,000	39.3
1980	917,300	5,499,000	146,270,000	44.6

*1951

Secondary (Ordinary)

Year	Schools	Teachers	Students	% Female
1949	4,045	67,000	1,039,000	31.9*
1957	11,096	234,000	6,281,000	30.8
1965	18,102	457,000	9,338,000	32.2
1980	118,377	3,020,000	55,081,000	39.6

*1951

Secondary (Agricultural, Technical and Vocational)

Year	Schools	Teachers	Students	% Female
1949	1,732	23,000	306,000	31.9*
1957	2,106	102,000	1,282,000	25.4
1965	63,762	296,000	5,377,000	37.0
1980	8,435	243,000	2,458,000	35.0

*1951

Secondary (Teacher Training)

Year	Schools	Teachers	Students	% Female
1949	620	9,000	152,000	26.0*
1957	592	15,000	296,000	28.4
1965	394	11,000	155,000	48.6
1980	1,017	38,000	482,000	26.0

*1951

Higher Education

Year	Schools	Teachers	Students	% Female
1949	205	16,000	117,000	22.5*
1957	229	70,000	441,000	23.3
1965	434	138,000	674,000	26.9
1980	675	247,000	1,144,000	23.4

*1951

Source: Education in China, Compiled by the Education in China Group of the Ministry of Education, Beijing, 1981.

Curriculum Emphasis in Tertiary Education 1949–1966

Subject Area	Number of Graduates	Percentage
Engineering	577,840	34%
Natural Sciences	98,387	6%
Medicine	184,868	11%
Education	468,417	27%
Finance and Economics	85,140	5%
Other	159,199	9%

Source: CHINA: Facts and Figures Annual, Vol.2.

India

CONTENTS

1 Geography 132
2 Population 133
3 Society and Culture 133
4 History and Politics 135
5 The Economy 137
6 The Education System 138
7 Educational Administration . . . 145
8 Educational Finance 151
9 Development and Planning of the
   Education System 152

India has one of the lowest levels of economic development in the world yet she has a rich and varied education system. Universal primary education is within sight. Universities are well established and include some institutions of outstanding merit. But the variations in character and quality within the education system are great. These differences reflect the complexities of Indian society. If education has a role in removing the conflicts and contradictions in Indian society, then the present education system has many weaknesses in that it mirrors the distortions within Indian society.

The Indian constitution at independence in 1947 declared that there should be universal, free, and compulsory education up to the age of 14. For long this was an aim rather than a reality but by the end of the 1970s almost 80% of children were in primary schools. The 1980 Five Year Plan shifted the objective from universal primary education to primary education for disadvantaged minorities, particularly the oppressed castes and tribes.

Though primary education has become more widely available, the quality of resources available for it is often low. While the majority of primary teachers are trained, their social and economic position is poor which remains a major obstacle to the overall improvement of the system. Furthermore there are continuing conflicts over the objectives of primary schooling. Mahatma Gandhi's ideal of basic education which would strengthen the traditional social and economic base of rural communities still has some official support. But the British colonial tradition of literacy schooling to prepare clerks lingers on while the priority of Nehru after 1947 to industrial development still has the effect of orientating even rural primary schooling to preparationfor higher level education and employment in modern industry.

Secondary and higher education are well developed in the context of overall Indian economic conditions. The proportions of the age group in secondary schools and universities are high compared to other economically under-developed countries. But, as with primary schools, there are problems related to the quality and orientation of post-primary education. The British tradition of academic and literary secondary and higher education is well entrenched. There is an over-production of secondary and higher education graduates in the humanities especially so that unemployment or under-employment among these groups is high. Similarly, while there are centres of excellence at both secondary and higher education level, there are also many poor quality institutions. Popular pressures for a literary and higher level education are difficult to resist especially when India has a federal government and education administration is largely decentralised.

India has achieved a relatively high degree of industrialisation even though the rural agricultural sector together with the economically marginal populations of the great cities still predominate. There is a commendable provision of technical and scientific education though it does not compete with the traditional humanistic education in size. But even technical and scientific education, which has developed in response to a succession of Five Year Plans, does not always match economic requirements. There is unemployment among certain types of graduate engineers. The Indian economy is so large and complex that it appears to have defeated the intentions of educational planners.

In comparison to education systems of some of her neighbours, Indian education lacks cultural and ideological coherence though it perhaps provides for greater individual choice and freedom. The linguistic diversity of the country is reflected in a school system which allows for much basic education to take place in the pupil's mother tongue. Secondary and higher education in the major Indian languages is also well-developed though the objections of some major groups to Hindi as the official language together with the preponderance of literature in Western languages in many technical and scientific subjects means that English still has a major place, especially at higher education level.

The Indian education system is secular. This contrasts with the strong ideological orientation in education in some neighbouring countries. But the relative cultural tolerance and neutrality of Indian education perhaps intensifies the cultural diversity and ambiguity of Indian society. Traditional and Western values co-exist and sometimes compete. Regionalism is strong. This is consistent with the strong democratic tradi-

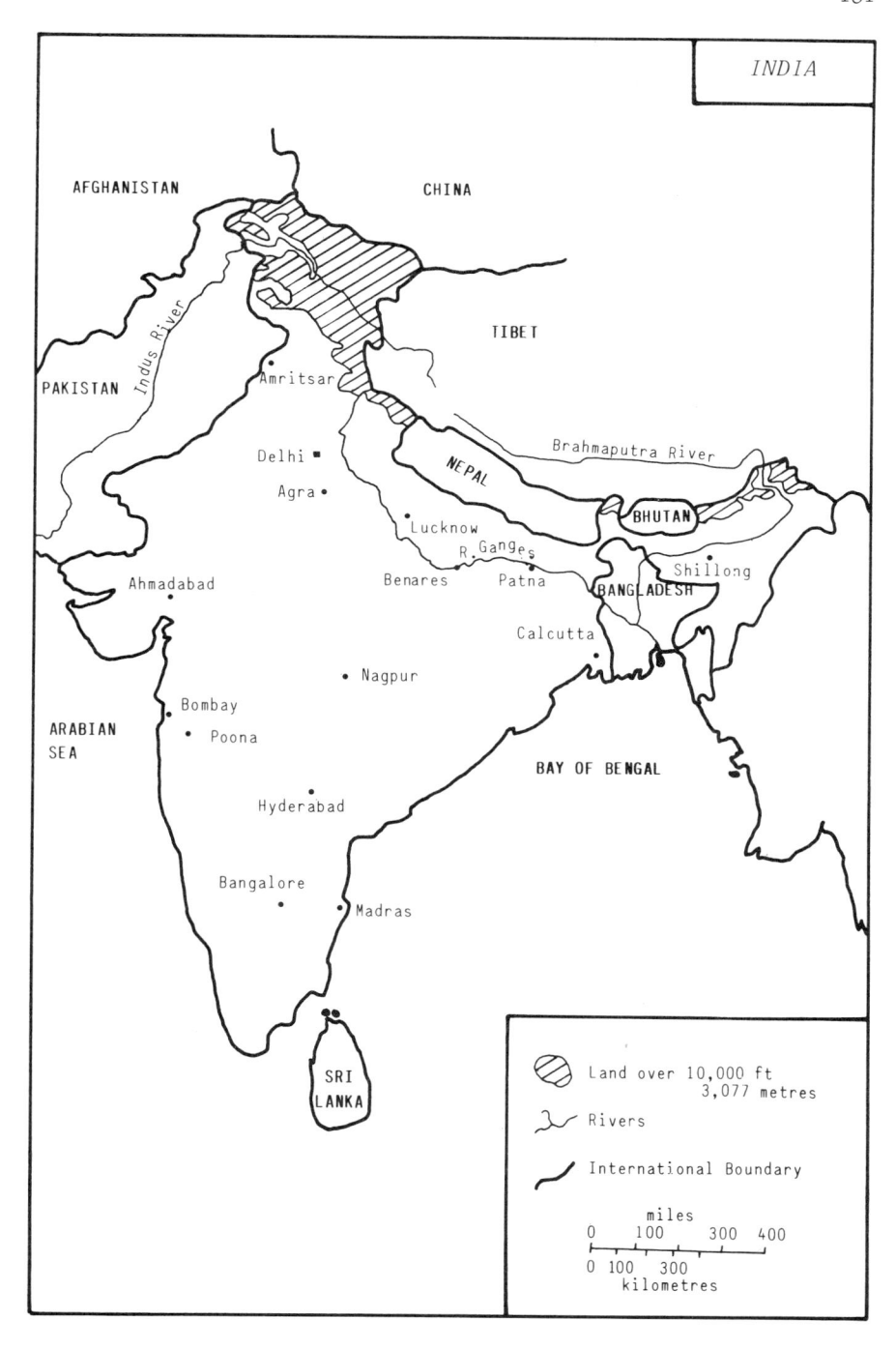

INDIA

- Amritsar
- Delhi
- Agra
- Lucknow
- Benares
- Patna
- R. Ganges
- Shillong
- Ahmadabad
- Calcutta
- Nagpur
- Bombay
- Poona
- Hyderabad
- Bangalore
- Madras

AFGHANISTAN
PAKISTAN
CHINA
TIBET
NEPAL
BHUTAN
BANGLADESH
SRI LANKA

Indus River
Brahmaputra River

ARABIAN SEA
BAY OF BENGAL

Land over 10,000 ft / 3,077 metres
Rivers
International Boundary

miles
0 100 300 400
0 100 300
kilometres

tions of India since 1947 but does not help to alleviate the lack of cohesion in Indian society which has been seen as one of the major obstacles to its development.

1 GEOGRAPHY

Topography

India is the seventh largest (3,268,090 sq km) and the second most populous country (an estimated 684 million in 1981) in the world. The mainland consists of three regions: the great mountain zone, the Gangetic Plain, and the southern Peninsula. India has substantial deposits of heavy metals, including high grade iron ore, alloy materials, fluxes and refractories, a virtual monopoly of mica, and good sources of fissionable materials. While some of these natural resources are being exploited, there is often a lack of the capital investment and expertise required for their full utilisation. Certain states and areas are either less well endowed with such resources or have not yet developed their industries. These include States such as Rajasthan, Madhya Pradesh and Orissa, which rely mainly upon agriculture.

Climate

There are four seasons in India: (i) cold weather – December to March; (ii) hot weather – April to May; (iii) rainy season – June to September; and (iv) the season of the retreating south-west monsoon – October to November. These seasons vary, however, in different parts of India. The hot season throughout much of India is very hot indeed and temperatures of over 100°F are common. Three of the four major cities, Bombay, Calcutta and Madras, are situated near the sea and high temperatures are accompanied by high humidity. The hot season ends in torrential downpours of rain during the north-east monsoon, which is usually followed by cool, and on occasions, cold weather.

Communications

India possesses a network of rail, road, river and air routes. Communications between the major cities are by and large good though the weight of traffic is such that the main trunk roads are frequently congested and domestic air flights fully booked. A vast railway network is spread throughout India, but again the demand upon its sevices is extremely heavy. Communications in the more remote rural areas are often poor and natural calamities such as extensive flooding during the monsoon period can disrupt large sections of railways and roads. One problem in improving communications is the vast distances which have to be covered. The distance, for example, between the northern border and the southern tip of India is 3,200 km (1,987 miles). Though domestic air services have reduced travel time between the major cities, it is normally a three-day journey by road, or a one- or two-day journey by rail, from Delhi to Calcutta or to Bombay.

2 POPULATION

The people of India originate from many different races, chiefly the Dravidian, Aryan and Mongol. There have also been influxes of refugees and conquerors throughout Indian history. Settlers have come to India from countries such as China, Persia and Nepal, some of whom maintain their own distinctive customs and traditions. Differences of racial origin as well as of environment have contributed to the cultural pattern of India.

According to the 1981 Census there are 683.8 million people in India. The rate of population growth has been 2.5% per annum 1961-1981. This increase has given rise to numerous problems resulting from excessive demands being made upon limited natural and social resources and has undermined to some extent India's socio-economic development programmes. These problems have been accentuated by the increase in the percentages of non-productive sections of the community. State and Central Government have launched large scale birth control programmes which have had some impact upon but not greatly reduced the rate of population growth. The pressure of population allied to limited employments prospects has resulted in emigration to the United Kingdom, the United States, Canada and Australia. The emigrants include professional and other qualified workers who constitute the 'brain drain', a debilitating factor in terms of India's socio-economic development.

There are very few areas in India which are entirely uninhabited. Over-population and the system of land tenure are such that the arable landscape of India is a patchwork of small farms, many of which provide an inadequate livelihood. The majority of the population, approximately 80%, live in villages and rely upon subsistence farming, but natural calamities, floods or drought may result in mass migrations to the towns. The absence of job opportunities in rural areas together with the favourable image of city life have also contributed to an increase in urban dwellers.

Many factors have therefore combined to produce a rapid growth of towns and cities throughout India. The migration is both from country to town and from town to city. Calcutta and Bombay have populations of over 7 million, Delhi and Madras over 3 million. One result is that the infrastructure of cities, the medical services, transport systems, schools, even the pavements, are overwhelmed by sheer numbers of people. Efforts are being made in both urban and rural areas to alleviate these problems and to improve living conditions but resources are inevitably limited.

3 SOCIETY AND CULTURE

Differences in language, religion, culture and stages of socio-economic development make India a land of contrasts. The traditional social structure was based upon caste and community. The old divisions between Hrahman, Kshatriya, Vaishya and

Shudra still persist in certain sections of the community, particularly in rural areas. In the middle class urban situation, however, caste is being replaced by 'class' to some degree as a result of the pressure generated by industrialisation and modernisation. The joing family still prevails in rural areas but is tending to be replaced by the nuclear family in the cities. The family is of great social importance in India. The family usually makes decisions on virtually every aspect of the individual's life, including employment, education and marriage and provides the main form of social security for its members. Arranged marriages related to caste and community are common. India has an abundance of traditions, customs and religions which contain and direct the individual's life from birth to death. There have, however, been modifications in these traditional lifestyles as a result both of the spread of education and the influx of new concepts resulting from economic and industrial development. The impact of modernisation has been felt mainly in urban areas and there exists a wide social gap between rural and urban communities. This is to some degree reflected, for example, in the position of women. Traditionally Indian women were restricted mainly to household affairs and rarely received any education. In urban areas, however, the marriage prospects of women are generally improved if they are educated. A small number seek work before and after marriage and a few achieve high positions in government and other services.

Religion

A further fundamental element of Indian culture is that India has been the home of many of the world's religions. The Hindu religion embraces approximately 83.5% of the Indian population, the Muslim 11%, the Christian 2.6% and there are, in addition, Buddhists, Sikhs, Jains, Parsis and Jews. Communities based upon these religious groupings have been active in founding hospitals, schools, youth organisations and charitable institutions, to which they have given certain distinctive characteristics. There exist Catholic and Protestant mission schools and colleges as well as Hindu, Sikh and Muslim educational institutions, the latter including Universities. India is a secular State, and freedom of worship is a fundamental right under the Constitution.

Language

Allied to this variety of religions and communities is the variety of languages spoken in India of which there are an estimated 826 grouped languages and dialects. Fifteen languages are recognised as official languages by the Indian Constitution, Hindi being the official national language which is being actively promoted by Central Government. Each State, however, has its own official State language. The result has been the implementation of the 'three-language formula' in schools under which children study the official State language plus English plus one other Indian language, i.e. Hindu in the non-Hindi States and in the Hindi States a further Indian language. In practice the Hindi States do not teach a third language and in Tamil Nadu there is officially only a two-language formula (Tamil and English). English is often used as a lingua franca among the educated and is retained as an official associate language ultimately to be replaced by Hindi.

Among the factors contributing to changes in traditional attitudes is the spread of literacy. The percentage of literates increased from 24% in 1961 to 29.45% in 1971 and to 36.17% in 1981. Again, however, the increase in population has been such that though the actual percentage of illiterates has decreased, the number of illiterates has actually increased. Literacy, like other forms of education, is often seen as a means of improving one's social status and personal fortunes. The traditional structure of society was such that social mobility was vitually non-existent. Many communities lived without any expectation or hope of personal or social advance. The Government of India has deliberately used education as a means of breaking down these barriers. Special provisions are made for backward classes, including the Harijans, such as scholarships, and more lenient entry requirements to higher studies. A percentage of places in Government service and the public sector are also reserved for members of these communities.

4 HISTORY AND POLITICS

Historical Development

It is clearly impossible to encapsulate the history of India in a few lines. Among the salient features is the rule of the Hindu Emperors which laster till 1200 AD and extended over much of the territory which is now modern India, creating a period of prosperity often referred to as the 'golden age'. About 1300 AD the Pathans and Moghuls began their invasion of India and by 1500 controlled most of the country. Their rule was finally broken by the British who, having earlier established control over Madras, Bengal and Eastern India, had by 1850 established control over the whole sub-continent. India achieved Independence from Britain in 1947 and assumed republican status in 1950.

Politics

India is a federal union of 21 States and 9 Union Territories. Executive power is formally vested in the President in whose name all executive action of the Government of India is expressed. There are two Houses of Parliament and in each of the States there is an elected Assembly. The members of the Rajya Sabha (Upper House) are elected by the State Assemblies, while the members of the Lok Sabha (Lower House) and State Assemblies are elected directly by the people. There is universal adult suffrage. The Lok Sabha is elected for a maximum period of five years. The Constitution provides for a strong central government. In the event of a breakdown in a State government there is a constitutional provision for the imposition of President's Rule from the Centre. Local government mainly takes the form of municipal corporations or boards and Zilla Parishads which have certain responsibilities for educational and welfare services.

Both the Central and State Governments have a bureaucratic system which is often huge and slow moving. Complex systems of controls exist at all levels. The process of decision-taking is time-consuming because of the tradition that this prerogative belongs to the man at the top. Hence, for example, it is not unusual for the head of a State Education Department to be inundated with administrative trivia. A further complication is the frequent reference to the law courts of both major and minor decisions which aggrieve any particular party or individual. Attempts are being made to reform the administrative machinery, in particular the civil service, through the implementation of modern management techniques.

The Congress Party, having led the country to Independence in 1947, has governed the country ever since. In 1969 the party split and Mrs Gandhi's wing of the party went on to win a resounding victory in the 1971 mid-term General Election. In the 1972 elections to the State Assemblies (following the Bangladesh war) the Congress Party was returned to power in every State in which elections were held except Tamil Nadu. However, elections in February 1974 in four states revealed a significant decline in the popularity of the Congress Party. There are a number of opposition parties but they are wakened by disunity and regionalism. To the left of Congress there are two Communist parties and a Socialist party; to the right the Jana Sangh and a new coalition called the Bharatiya Lok Dal (BLD). There are many other minor parties. The Congress Party and Mrs Gandhi lost power in elections in the mid-1970s but both regained their former positions in the elections in January 1980.

International Relations

India is a member of the Commonwealth. Interest in Britain is still great, and relations are generally friendly. Indian immigration to Britain is an important new factor in the relationship, and though frictions are generated, they are not at present serious. Throughout the life of Jawaharlal Nehru, India pursued a foreign policy of non-alignment and was a leader of the non-aligned group of nations. The government remains committed to this policy, and does not regard the Indo/Soviet Treaty of 9 August 1972 as a breach of it. Relations with the United States, which worsened as a result of events at the time of the 1971 war with Pakistan, are improving. Relations with China have remained difficult since the war of 1962. Relations with Pakistan are uneasy, but despite setbacks, progress towards 'normalisation' under the Simla agreement of 1972 continues. Relations with Bangladesh are cordial, but subject to strains on economic grounds. Other smaller nations in South Asia also remain suspicious of India's preponderant power, but the Government of India tries hard to avoid the impression of 'bullying' them.

5 THE ECONOMY

India has acute economic and development problems, including at present an extremely high rate of inflation and a shortage of foreign exchange. Attempts have been made to bring about progress in a number of areas. Since 1951 India has produced a series of Five-Year Plans intended to both direct and accelerate economic growth. The economy is a mixed one; the public sector, which produces about 7% of the national income, includes companies with a large role in such basic sectors as steel, coal, heavy engineering and fertilizers. This reflects India's commitment to a 'socialistic pattern of society'. Industrial production in India has trebled since 1951 and certain manufactured goods are now exported to overseas countries. These figures have to be interpreted against a background, however, of high rates of inflation and of population growth.

The improvement in India's economic position has brought relative prosperity to some and a lifestyle similar to that of advanced countries. For the vast majority of the population, however, the improvements in living standards have been marginal, and stark contrasts exist between plenty and poverty. Over the years 1960-1979 national income rose at 3.4% per annum but population in the same period grew at 2.2% per annum, so that per capita income rose only 1.4% per annum between 1960 and 1979. The average per capita income according to the World Bank is the fifteenth lowest in the world, US$190 in 1979. Efforts are being made to channel resources through agencies such as the Small Farmers Development Agency to the more needy areas which are mainly inhabited by subsistence farmers. Schools, public health centres and public utility services are being developed and, for example, one out of every eight villages in the early 1970s had electricity as against one out of every 100 in 1951. Attempts are also being made to provide more and better facilities for the urban poor.

India is still basically a land of agriculture rather than industry and about 38% of the national income accrued from agriculture and allied activities in which the bulk of the population is employed. Foodgrain crops take up 80% of the total cultivated area of 149 million hectares, the main crop being rice, wheat, maize and barley. The production of foodgrains in the 1950s (particularly in the latter years under the influence of the Green Revolution) reached a peak in 1970/71. Since then production difficulties have increased and in each successive year there has been a shortfall. Imports were resumed in 1973 and in 1974 the overall supply position remained tight. As an exporter of agricultural products and raw materials, India remains vulnerable to fluctuations in world prices.

6 THE EDUCATION SYSTEM

Aims, Objectives and Implementation

One of the major influences shaping the traditional aims of Indian education was the cultural impact of, and the control exerted by, Britain during the colonial era. This was reflected both in the demands made upon the system and the manner in which these were met. On the one hand, the traditional system was partly designed to cater for the children of the wealthier and more influential sections of society, providing a small but powerful Indian educated elite. On the other, the aim was to provide a basic education sufficient both in size and quality to produce the relatively small number of clerks and craftsmen required for government service and the industrial and commercial sectors. The result of the former demand was the creation of English medium public schools closely modelled on the British system. The Christian missions also established schools, including the 'Anglo-Indian', the more prestigious of which followed the public school pattern. The type of education provided then, and to some extent now, emphasised the 'Humanities', the building of character, and sport. The syllabi and textbooks were often imported direct from Britain and bore little relation to the Indian context - the Magna Carta, Shakespeare, and British flora and fauna loomed large. Similarly, while the wealthy preferred to send their children to Britain for higher studies, the early Indian Universities looked to Oxbridge for inspiration, standards and courses of study. Schools at the lower end of the social spectrum, the missionary craft schools and orphanages and those established by local authorities, often lacked funds and were a relatively neglected and deprived sector, with the major exception of Southern India.

At Independence, committed to a democratic form of government and faced with an immense popular demand for education, the Indian Government made a crucial choice which profoundly affected the traditional system. Unlike certain African states, for example, which opted for controlled and systematic development related in some way to manpower requirements, the policy was adopted of massive expansion at all levels of the educational system. In many States this involved placing a degree of responsibility on private enterprise in the establishment and maintenance of schools and colleges. The traditional aims of a two-tier system, those of producing a small elite and a basically-educated labour force, were replaced by socio-political goals such as the equalisation of educational opportunities and the inculcation of Indian values and beliefs.

The aims of education in India have been stated in many official documents since Independence. These statements contain strong continuities as well as innovations. The goals stated in the Sixth Five Year Plan 1980-1985 are typical

(i) to guarantee to all equality of opportunity for education. . .

(ii)   to afford all young people and adults . . . the means for ample self-fulfilment . . .

(iii)   to provide for a continuous process of life-long education for physical, intellectual and cultural development of people and for inculcating in them capabilities to cope with and influence social change

(iv)   to establish dynamic and beneficial linkages between education, employment and development . . .

(v)   to promote respect for and belief in value of national integration, secularism, democracy and dignity of labour

(vi)   to sensitise academic communities to the problems of poverty, illiteracy and environmental degradation . . .

(vii)   to facilitate development . . . and utilisation of the youth to . . . participate in the process of national development

(viii) to support the growth of arts, music, poetry, dance and drama . . .

The breadth of these aims covering individual and society perspectives as well as economic, political, social and cultural concerns is unusual for an economically under-developed country. They also indicate the wide divisions of opinion about the function of education.

The inherent conflicts between traditional and post-Independence aims, between social and economic demands, between an imported and an indigenous culture, have not been fully reconciled. There has been, in general, a failure to couple traditional Indian modes and values with modern educational objectives. Those institutions which are most successful in educational terms are sometimes the most socially divisive. While there have been attempts at reform and reconciliation, charges of elitism are still levelled at the public and some Anglo-Indian schools to which the ambitious and relatively wealthy aspire to send their children. At many Indian universities, particularly in the 'Humanities', there has been little change in the methods of teaching or courses of study. The personal demand for job opportunities in the still relatively small modern sector as opposed to the traditional rural subsistence economy, echoed in the country's political life as a demand for equal opportunities, has resulted in a rapid and vast expansion of the educational system at all levels. Often personal expectations have been thwarted due to the very much slower expansion of the modern sector and hence of job opportunities. Possibly pre-eminent over the conflicts between varying cultures and values, often reflected in disputes over the language of instruction, is that between meeting the socio-political aims as well as the economic and developmental. The influence of local politics, for example, may be such that there are deviations from plan targets and key educational institutions fail to realise their full potential contribution.

Planning

Following Independence, the Government of India undertook the planning of all major aspects of national development, including education. The First Five-Year Plan was initiated in 1951-52, and apart from an inter-regnum of three years (from 1966-1969), there have been successive plans leading up to the Sixth Five-Year Plan (1980-85). Educational Planning at the national level is the responsibility of the Union Ministry of Education through its own planning division, advised by a Central Advisory Board of Education (CABE) and specially-constituted advisory commissions appointed by Government of India Resolutions (for example the Kothari Commission whose report, published in 1966, has had considerable influence on subsequent educational plans). The overall coordination of plans in the various sectors is undertaken by the Planning Commission which also has a division concerned with education. Education in India, however, is primarily the responsibility of the State Governments which produce their own educational plans through State planning units advisory boards and Institutes of Education.

National plans therefore have no mandatory force as such. The coordination of national and State plans is largely the result of State representation in national plan formulation and the allocation of centrally-controlled funds to State projects conforming to the national programmes. It is not unknown, however, for a State Government to establish new universities from its own resources, for example, in spite of the national plans stipulating a check on university expansion. Educational planning is subject to numerous restraints; educational statistics are often outdated and possibly inaccurate; the targets set are not always achievable within the resources allocated; local priorities may distort the plan frame and budgets be cut as a result of economic crises. The main function of national educational plans is more to give an indication of which developments Indian educationists and administrators would like to see implemented than of those which will actually be undertaken.

Administration

As education in India is decentralised, there are at present two levels of control:

(i) The Union Government is concerned with the coordination of educational facilities, determination of standards of higher education, technical education research, promotion of Hindi and the development of all Indian languages. The Union Government is also responsible for the running of 6 Central Universities (Delhi, Jawaharlal Nehru, Aligarh Muslim, Benares Hindu, Visva Bharati [Santiniketan], and North Eastern Hills University, Shillong) and "such other institutions of national importance as Parliament may by law declare"

(ii) State Governments control primary and secondary education within the municipal and State systems, including curricula, examinations, and finance and the training of primary teachers (that of secondary being mainly under the auspices of the universities). There are, however, a large number of private schools in India, over which more control is being sought by some State Governments.

The universities of India occupy a special position within the administrative framework in that traditionally they enjoy a relatively high degree of autonomy. The obligations of the Union Government are discharged through the University Grants Commission (UGC). The UGC is responsible for the development and maintenance of the Union Territories Universities and for providing grants towards the cost of approved development programmes in all other universities. Its powers over State universities are therefore limited. Changes in curricula and examinations are almost entirely in the hands of the Boards of Studies, i.e. the academic and administrative staff, though their decisions will in some cases be influenced by the UGC. The UGC receives its funds from the Ministry of Education and has collaborative arrangements with the Ministry supported para-university institutions, but no control. Many decisions made at the Ministry and UGC levels are extremely difficult to implement because of faulty administration.

Other responsibilities of the Union Government are discharged by the Department of Education through organisations such as the following:

The National Council for Educational Research and Training (which undertakes research, the publication of model textbooks and teacher in-service training programmes)

All-India Council for Technical Education

The National Council for Science Education

The National Council for Teacher Education

The National Council for Women's education

The Central Board for Secondary Education (which controls examinations in Union Territories and affiliated schools throughout India such as the Central Schools Organisation [CSO]).

In addition, the Centre works through organisations such as the National Institute of Education, the four Regional Colleges of Education, the Central Institute of English and Foreign Languages, which is associated with Regional and States Institutes of English, and assists through the Technical Teachers Training Institutes in the training of teachers for the State Polytechnics.

India has a complex administrative structure within which overlaps or changes in responsibility are frequent. State Government administration often parallels the national system. Each may have a Department of Education, a Department of Technical Education, State Institutes of Education and Science Education (responsible for in-service teacher training and educational research) and State Boards of Secondary Education Schools may use textbooks produced either by private publishers and approved by the State, or by State authorities independently or in conjunction with NCERT. Responsibility for in-service teacher education through Extension Services Departments based in Colleges of Education has recently been transferred from NCERT to the State Institutes of Education.

Pattern of Education

There is some variation in the structure within the different States, some of which have a ten-year pattern of school education, others 11-year. The Education Commission (1964-66) led to a Resolution on the National Policy on Education which aimed to provide a broadly uniform educational structure in all parts of the country, the '10+2+3' pattern. This would consist of ten years of schooling, two years of higher secondary education (either in schools or colleges) and a three-year period of higher education for a first degree. This involved many States in additional expenditure. By 1981, 16 of the 22 States and 8 of the 9 Union Territories had implemented the policy. The school year varies in different parts of India, but usually runs from July to April with brief breaks in October and December.

Pre-Primary Education

Pre-primary education is voluntary and in 1977 covered 690,352 of the 3-5 age group. Apart from private and self-help schemes, the programme is concentrated mainly on the under-privileged sections of the community, including in some instances the provision of welfare facilities.

Primary Education

Primary education in India is divided into a lower and upper stage, the latter sometimes being referred to as the 'middle school' level. Children normally enter the lower primary school at the age of 6 years and complete this stage at the age of 11 (Standards I to V). Upper primary consists of a three-year course for the 11-14 age band (Standards VI to VIII) though in some states primary education terminates at Standard VII. Though there are some variations from State to State, the syllabus normally includes the traditional subjects such as the three Rs, supplemented by some elementary history, geography and general science. In some States the study of English as a second language begins at Standard III but others will delay this until Standard V or Standard VI. Examinations at the lower primary level are set by either individual schools or Municipal Boards and are usually held at the end of each term and the school year. This also applies in the upper primary schools except that in some States public examinations are introduced in Standards VII or VIII. Both lower and upper primary schools are administered and financed mainly by municipal authorities or similar local bodies. There are, however, a number of private schools. In 1979-80 there were 71 million children in lower primary and 19.5 million children in upper primary schools.

Secondary Education

Secondary education usually covers a period of three years (Standards IX to XI) and caters for the 14 to 17 year old age band. Many schools, in fact, do not go beyond the Standard X examination and the term 'higher secondary' is often used to designate the eleventh year of school, i.e. Standard XI. There is, however, a proposal to add an additional year, the higher secondary covering Standards XI and XII. The curricula, which are determined by State and Central Boards of Secondary Education, comprise the traditional subjects, e.g. mathematics, science, history, geography and a more detailed study of English as a second language. Various different types of school leaving certificates are issued by these examining boards, including the Secondary School Leaving Certificate (SSLC), the Higher Secondary Certificate (HSC) and the Indian School Certificate (ISC). At the secondary level, schools can be sponsored and supported by local municipal authorities or by State governments. The position in individual States may vary, Tamil Nadu, for example, having a high percentage of government schools, whereas in West Bengal there are approximately only 40 out of 4,000, the latter indicating the importance of private enterprise institutions in some States. There are also distinctions between the curricula and standards of school in different States and in comparison with schools affiliated to central bodies such as the Central Schools Organisation.

Vocational Education

There were proposals in the Fifth Five Year Plan to introduce work experience into primary education and to vocationalise secondary education. The bulk of vocational training, however, is conducted by Industrial Training Institutes at the craftsman level. There are 495 ITIs in India, six of them being for women only and the others taking both sexes. There are also 336 private ITIs. This training may be of one year to two years' duration which is often followed by apprenticeship. The entry qualifications depend on the trade the entrant wishes to pursue, but for technical subjects the entry requirement may be as high as a pass in the Standard X with mathematics and science as a compulsory requirement. The language of instruction in the ITIs is the local language but in some trades such as radio servicing English terminology is widely used. Approximately 180,000 trainees pass out of the ITIs every year. Some sectors are less well catered for than others, for example, agricultural education in West Bengal. There are also polytechnics which enrol students for various diploma courses of three years' duration in vocational subjects.

Higher Education

Students usually enter higher education at the age of 16 or 17 years, either having completed Standard XI at school or a one year pre-university course. Though there is some variation between universities, many students will spend two years reading for a general degree and three years for an honours degree. First degree courses are generally conducted in affiliated colleges, i.e. a network of private and State-sponsored institutes recognised by a specific university which undertakes direct responsibility for post-graduate studies. The curricula and examinations are controlled by some 92 fully fledged universities. In addition to the traditional universities, there are nine specialist institutes of higher learning which are recognised as having the status of universities, e.g. the Central Institute for English and Foreign Languages, Hyderabad. Institutes such as the four Indian Institutes of Technology, the Regional Engineering Colleges, the Indian Institutes of Management, and various medical colleges also provide a specialist education at the graduate and post-graduate level. There were 4.5 million students (4.2% of the 20-24 age group) enrolled in higher education institutions in 1977.

Teacher Education

There are basically three types of training for teachers in India depending upon whether they are destined to teach in the lower primary, upper primary or secondary school. The minimum qualification for admission to the course for lower primary school teachers, which may last one or two years depending upon State regulations, is a pass in the Standard X examination, whereas for upper primary school teaching the minimum requirement is usually a pass at Standard XI for admission to a course which again may last one or two years. Teacher education institutes at these levels are controlled and financed by State departments of education. Secondary schools are staffed usually by graduates who have completed a one year Bachelor of Education course at a college affiliated to a university. In addition, there are certain centrally-funded institutions such as the four Regional Colleges of Education which offer a combined four-year course leading both to a subject degree and a Bachelor of Education, and the National Institute of Education in New Delhi which receive financial assistance from Central Government funds through the National Council for Educational Research and Training. Studies at the MEd and PhD levels are undertaken at a number of universities including the Centre of Advanced Study in Baroda. Teacher trainees constitute about 2% of the total student population.

Non-Formal and Adult Education

The social demand since Independence has been mainly for forms of institutional education. Non-formal education is a relatively undeveloped sector. There are a large number of programmes of adult education, often linked to the achievement of functional literacy, organised by the Ministry of Education and by State governments, but these represent a patchwork of efforts rather than an organised all-India programme. Research and training in adult education is undertaken at a number of centres, including the Department of Adult Education at Rajasthan University. A number of universities and other institutions conduct correspondence courses leading to either a degree or different vocational qualifications. There is, for example, a project in Maharashtra intended for the training of untrained teachers. The general tendency is for non-institutional forms of education to lead to formal qualification. The Fifth Five Year Plan envisaged a serious attempt to create an alternative system to formal education, including the development of correspondence courses, an 'Open University', and a system of continuous education.

7 EDUCATIONAL ADMINISTRATION

Enrolment Patterns

The most significant fact in Indian education is the phenomenal expansion which has taken place at all levels since Independence. Total enrolments have almost quintupled between 1950 and 1980, in the case of lower primary education, for example, rising from 42.6% to 83.6% of children of lower primary age. The rapid expansion of primary education is in accordance with the Directive within the Constitution that there should be free, compulsory and universal primary education up till the age of 14. One of the most dramatic increases in enrolment has been in higher education, the number of students increasing from 0.74 million in 1960 to 5 million in 1979-80. This rapid and often uncontrolled growth of the system has imposed serious strains on resources, and some would argue that it has resulted in a dilution of standards.

Disparities

The system of education is one in which there are many disparities. The limited resources available are often unevenly distributed because of the inability or unwillingness of particular States to invest in educational development or because certain types of institutions enjoy a privileged status. An Indian Institute of Technology may be housed in lavish buildings, while affiliated colleges or colleges of education are accommodated in what have been called 'educational slums'. The vast majority of educational institutions operate within very limited budgets. There is often a noticeable disparity between the provision made for education in rural and urban areas. The task of providing educational services for hundreds of thousands of small villages with populations as low as 300 to 400 is a formidable one, and the majority of primary pupils are in single teacher schools. The urban sector, however, is in general provided with better facilities. A further major disparity is between the educational system itself and its socio-economic context. There has been little real attempt to link schools and colleges to the demands of the labour market and the problem of the educated unemployed is extremely serious in India.

Primary Education

The high enrolment percentages in terms of age groups at the primary level can be deceptive in that there is an extremely high drop-out rate. The reasons for this are many and complex. One is certainly the hard economic facts of life: children are needed to assist the family in making a living (the herds of cattle are mainly tended by children). The enrolment of girls compares unfavourably with that of boys, and here again the drop-out rate is high because of social barriers and social values, as well as the necessity for young girls to assist in household chores (e.g. 63% girls enrolled in comparison to 92.0% boys in 1977 in the age group of 5-9 years). A further cause for the high rate of drop-out is rooted in the education system itself. Primary education in India tends to be dominated by the examination. The approach to teaching is rigid, formal and authoritarian and the idea of child-centred education is to a large extent alien. Children who fail the examination at Standard I are refused promotion to the next class in certain States. The effect of the examination system is evident in the high rate of stagnation. Some attempt is being made on a limited scale to develop an ungraded school system designed to reduce stagnation and wastage which are among the most serious problems within Indian primary education.

Examinations

The percentage of age groups enrolled in upper primary and in secondary schools steadily declines. Secondary schools generally have a higher standard of resources than primary, even though there may be acute shortages of well trained teachers in some states. The approach to education is rigidly geared at this level to the formal examinations set by the State and Central Boards of Secondary Education. Certain schools pride themselves on the percentage of Grade I passes obtained by their pupils, and it is sometimes alleged that in order to maintain their high record they will ruthlessly shed children who appear unlikely to reach this level. The examination system also results in long hours of homework and in the use of private tutors. 'Blood money', as private tuition fees are called, can amount to more than the teacher's actual pay which many consider inadequate. Secondary education can be an exhausting and soul destroying round both for the teacher and for the pupils because much depends on the final examination results.

Prestige Attached to 'Degree'

The situation at the higher education level has caused general concern among educationists. Rapidly expanding universities experience a host of administrative problems. The student follows a course of study which is often based upon out-dated texts and formal lectures to large groups. Sometimes the medium of instruction is a language which has only been partially learnt at school, an example being English. Again, the system is geared to examinations, failure in which can mean the end of student's and family's hopes of better prospects. Invariably, in such circumstances, many students rely on rote learning of set texts and model answers. Since success in the examinations means so much, there is widespread mass copying. A further common phenomenon is mass student protest, directed against 'hard questions' and intended to persuade the authorities to waive the examinations or agree to grace marks. Examinations, in consequence, are frequently postponed and examination invigilators will sometimes themselves agitate for 'danger money' or insurance. Some universities, it must be emphasised, however, manage to largely avoid such excesses and achieve a high level, particularly in the post-graduate departments of universities such as Bombay and Madras.

Status of Teachers

Part of the problem at the school level is attracting sufficient high calibre recruits into the teaching profession which, in comparison with professions, often earns a very low salary. The monthly salary of a teacher at lower primary level can be less than half that of the lowest grade clerk within government service. The supply of qualified teachers is uneven and the proportion of untrained teachers in each State varies considerably. Certain States may have a glut of trained teachers giving rise to problems of unemployment. One major problem for States with a high percentage of untrained teachers is to find the resources to enable them to be trained. The unqualified teacher, frozen at the very bottom of the salary scale, often with a poor level of general education, is a major obstacle to educational development. A number of schemes are now being tried out in India to provide low cost training, ranging from the Maharashtra correspondence course project to a large in-service upgrading progamme in West Bengal. Even where teachers are qualified, however, the type of training which they have received is likely to have many deficiencies. Teacher education institutes at all levels tend to have outdated, traditional curricula making heavy demands in terms of theoretical knowledge, and unrelated to practical teaching. There are, however, exceptions in that certain of the teacher education colleges attract good staff and good students and are prepared to accept innovations. The teaching profession is becoming increasingly attractive to women, though by and large the number of women teachers is relatively small (24% in primary school in 1977). Moreover, just as the degree obtained by a woman student is often regarded as an asset on the marriage market, so also the possession of a teaching qualification is not necessarily a passport to the classroom, but rather to an early marriage.

Curriculum Reform

Curricula and programmes of study are determined for the most part by external institutions or organisations, and teachers in India are not often involved in the formulation of curriculum development projects. In the case of schools, there will be the textbooks prescribed by the municipal or State authorities. The other controlling mechanism is the examination which is again determined by external organisations e.g. State Boards of Secondary Education and State Departments of Education. The system as such can be extremely rigid and teachers, not unnaturally, are reluctant to depart from the standard text or to introduce anything which is not of direct relevance to the examination. This control exists even at the university level in the sense that the affiliated colleges follow texts and examinations prescribed by universities mainly involved in post-graduate education. The great difficulty in introducing curriculum reform is that this is likely to be rejected unless simultaneous changes are made in, for example, the prescribed texts or examinations. A number of institutions are attempting to bring about educational reforms including the University Grants Commission and the network of State Institutes of Education and Science Education.

Status of Institutions

Both at the school and university level, there are differences in the prestige and status of individual institutions. The prestige schools, often using English as a medium of instruction, consist in the main of public and Anglo-Indian schools (the latter, however, also includes some schools catering for very deprived areas). Similarly, there is a hierarchy or pecking order within the universities, certain of which are well established, have attracted high calibre staff, and have more ready access to Central funds, whereas others are new, relatively unknown, and have difficulty in attracting State funds. There is thus a spectrum of attainment ranging across both the departments within a university, some of which may be given a special status and additional funds, and the affiliated colleges and universities. Some departments enjoy national and even international repute but others are less favourably regarded.

Choice of Courses

The students' choice of subject and programmes of study, greatly influenced by the family, is determined mainly either by traditional family occupations or by an assessment of what job opportunities exist, and personal preferences or aptitudes may count for little. Subjects such as science have been extremely popular amongst girls and boys at the school level, not necessarily because the students have any inherent ability or interest, but simply because these subjects appear to open more doors. Similarly, the prospects for graduate engineers seem good and there is a massive rush of students seeking admission to engineering courses. The result is that the labour market is ultimately flooded and increasing numbers find themselves unemployed. A reaction sets in and students shift their preference elsewhere. In general, the Humanities tend to attract students who cannot gain admission to other courses more directly related to job opportunities.

Education and National Development

There are clearly imbalances between the different levels of the system caused in part by the massive expansion brought about by personal and social demands rather than economic needs. There is, for example, the disproportionate expansion of university education which, being among the most expensive forms, now absorbs about 22% of all the expenditure on education in India and produces a vast number of unemployed graduates. Unemployment is most acute among the Arts graduates. Again, the proportions vary according to the State. Science graduates, by and large, enjoy better prospects but even here there are unemployed graduates and post-graduates. It might be anticipated that certain vocational forms of training at the university level would result in better employment prospects and to some extent this is true. But there are unemployed agricultural post-graduates in a country where agriculture is of great importance to national development. Similarly, there were also engineering and technical diplomates and graduates out of work. The fault does not lie entirely in an overproduction by the universities. It is sometimes the case that the type of education given is not related to the needs of industry, commerce and agriculture. It might appear from this depressing picture that the demand for university places would drop since the majority of parents are obliged to pay fees. In point of fact, however, university education is heavily subsidised and the rate of return to the individual remains high because the expenditure incurred by the parents or student is comparatively low. In addition, most organisations, both government and private, tend to stipulate minimum qualifications which are in excess of normal requirements as a means of reducing the number of applicants. Paradoxically, the ratio of professionals to technicians compares very unfavourably with most other countries. The demand for a degree, however, is unlikely to diminish and, in fact, the devaluation of the first degree because of excess supply to the labour market has tended to generate pressure for more places at the postgraduate level.

The government of India is very much aware of the many shortfalls and deficiencies within the educational system. Attempts are being made to find suitable remedies, but it is most essential that these be low-cost solutions if they are to be widely applied. The constant restraint on Indian education is that resources are extremely limited. There is a commitment in the Sixth Five Year Plan to expanding even further the primary sector with a view to achieving universal enrolment in the age range of 6 to 11 by 1985. This objective is possibly based less on economic considerations, though there may be advantages in providing some basic education for rural children who will be employed mainly in subsistence agriculture, than on the need to provide equal opportunities for all, including the socially under-privileged. This principle of egalitarianism underpins much of the official policy on education. The planners, however, have also sought to put a check on expansion at the other levels. It is not proposed to increase enrolment at the secondary level to any large degree. Efforts would also be made to check university expansion. These include an attempt to make secondary education terminal through vocationalisation. The objective is to divert up to 20-30% of students into vocational courses. While this is in itself intended to reduce the pressure on the universities, expansion at the undergraduate level will also be halted. Post-graduate education, on the other hand, will receive increased funding and support. It is difficult to determine how effective these controls will be. Much will depend upon the degree to which the States will exercise their prerogative and create new universities, or to which the universities will permit the opening of new colleges.

Internal Efficiency of the System

Among the major factors affecting the efficiency of the educational system are:

(i) an explosion in demand and rapid expansion at all levels

(ii) limited financial and other resources which are often unequally distributed

(iii) high drop-out, repeater and failure rates, particularly at the primary level

(iv) lack of 'articulation' between the levels of the system

(v) poor coordination between different State education systems and limited contact between educational innovators in the different States

(vi) high proportions of untrained teachers (in some States), low salaries, supplementation of income by private tuition, rigid methods for training teachers based on academic rather than pedagogical criteria, and promotion based on length rather than quality of service

(vii) outdated and irrelevant curriculum in many sectors of the system

(viii) formalistic teaching methods and examinations that encourage cramming

(ix) the adherence to educational aims and concepts inappropriate to socio-economic development

(x) social and political pressures on decisions in education at all levels.

External Relevance

Much of the curriculum is outdated and irrelevant, though attempts are being made to make education more development orientated. Similarly, the attitudes cultivated through education are often not directly helpful to development in that, for example, they reflect a disdain for the practical application of knowledge to solving social and economic problems.

The expansion of the Indian educational system is related less to the needs of the labour market than to personal and social demands. An academic degree, for example, is seen as a passport to social status (particularly among would-be brides) and students from families with no tradition of higher education now flock to the degree colleges. As many of the graduates prefer jobs in the modern sector, a sector which has expanded as a much slower rate than was originally hoped, there is a high percentage of educated unemployed. Many potential employers in all sectors operate small scale businesses and often these do not provide scope for employing graduates, or because they cannot (and do not need to) pay the higher salaries expected and demanded. The 'fit' between market and education might be made more satisfactory if the educational system were reorientated more towards the needs of the labour market, in terms of the numbers educated and the level and direction of their studies, and if industry, commerce and agriculture included more large scale enterprises. Like so much else in Indian society, change has occurred due to private, social and political demands which have undermined a systematic development within State and national plan frameworks.

8 EDUCATIONAL FINANCE

The principles of Indian educational finance are as complex as its administration. Due to various historical factors, finance comes from a variety of sources: Union Government, State Governments, local authorities, fees, endowments and voluntary contributions. About 70% comes from government sources, 16% from fees, 8% from 'other sources' and 6% from local bodies. These national averages do not reflect, however, a situation in which one university will receive 76% of its funds from the State whereas another will receive only 22%. Some institutions are privately owned, relying on fees and grants-in-aid from State governments, others are State-controlled and sponsored, the relative percentage of each varying from State to State. The situation is such that some institutions seek to increase the income from fees and capitation grants by crowding in students (this, it has been suggested, is the root malaise of many Colleges of Education). This complex system of funding makes it difficult to obtain reliable data on educational expenditure.

The percentage of the national income spent on education increased from 1.2% in 1950-51 to an estimated 2.9% in 1977. From the formulation of the First Plan, the Ministry of Education has pleaded for an allocation of 10% of the total plan outlay to be devoted to education, though the figure has usually been about 7%. These statistics have to be viewed in the light of an increase of total student enrolments at all levels from 23,684,000 in 1951/52 to an estimated 103,300,000 in 1979/80. Much of the expenditure has been on quantitative expansion programmes, rather than on qualitative improvement. The emphasis is likely to continue.

As education is primarily a State responsibility there are often large differences between the financial provisions made in different areas. Kerala, for example, spends over 35% of its total State budget on education, as opposed to little more than 10% in Jammu and Kashmir. In some States the educational system is starved of financial (and often human) resources, in others the position is favourable for financing programmes of educational innovations. Similarly, there are differences in the provisions made for the different levels. Higher education receives approximately 0.76% out of 3.3% of the national income devoted to education. Plan expenditure on primary and university education in 1950/51 was 56% and 9% respectively of the total plan expenditure on education: by the Fourth Plan (1969/74) this had evened out to 28.5% and 22.3%. There was a shift back to primary education in the Sixth Plan (1980-85) with a 36% share compared to 19% for higher education.

9 DEVELOPMENT AND PLANNING OF THE EDUCATION SYSTEM

The most discernible trend in formal education has been the expansion and overcrowding of many educational institutions, in particular in the higher education sector. There has been a shift in popularity from arts to science and subsequently to commerce, and a drop in the number of engineering students. Women's education has developed significantly. There is a growing interest in formal and non-formal education for adults. The non-formal sector is still at a rudimentary stage but is attracting more attention among educationists and educational administrators. Hopes are also being placed in the development of non-institutional forms of education such as correspondence courses and a possible Open University.

The priorities identified in the Sixth Five Year Plan (1980-85 are two-fold. At primary level, as universal education comes into sight - and has been achieved in some States - there is a concern for the economically poor and the socially disadvantaged. The low (scheduled) castes and tribes have very unequal access to education. Thirty-eight percent of scheduled caste children and 56% of scheduled tribe children are not in elementary schools. The aim is to expand provision for these under-privileged groups.

At secondary and higher education level, the priority is to diversify the kinds of education to relate them to economic needs and employment prospects. The aim is to reduce the very considerable unemployment among some groups of secondary and higher education graduates.

In spite of the serious and wide-ranging problems within the Indian educational system there is also considerable potential for educational development. Some States, for example, have made substantial progress in improving their educational facilities. The network of Central and State agencies involved in educational innovation, though these vary in effectiveness, are providing some support for reforms. Within any one sector it is often possible to find institutions and individuals which are receptive to new ideas and capable of achieving results which are impressive when seen against the background of limited human and material resources. In particular, the qualitative improvement projects within the national and State plans, even where these are cut back due to lack of funds, are likely to make some contribution both to educational development *per se* and to the solution of India's socio-economic problems.

EDUCATION SYSTEM OF INDIA BASED ON THE 10+2+3 SYSTEM

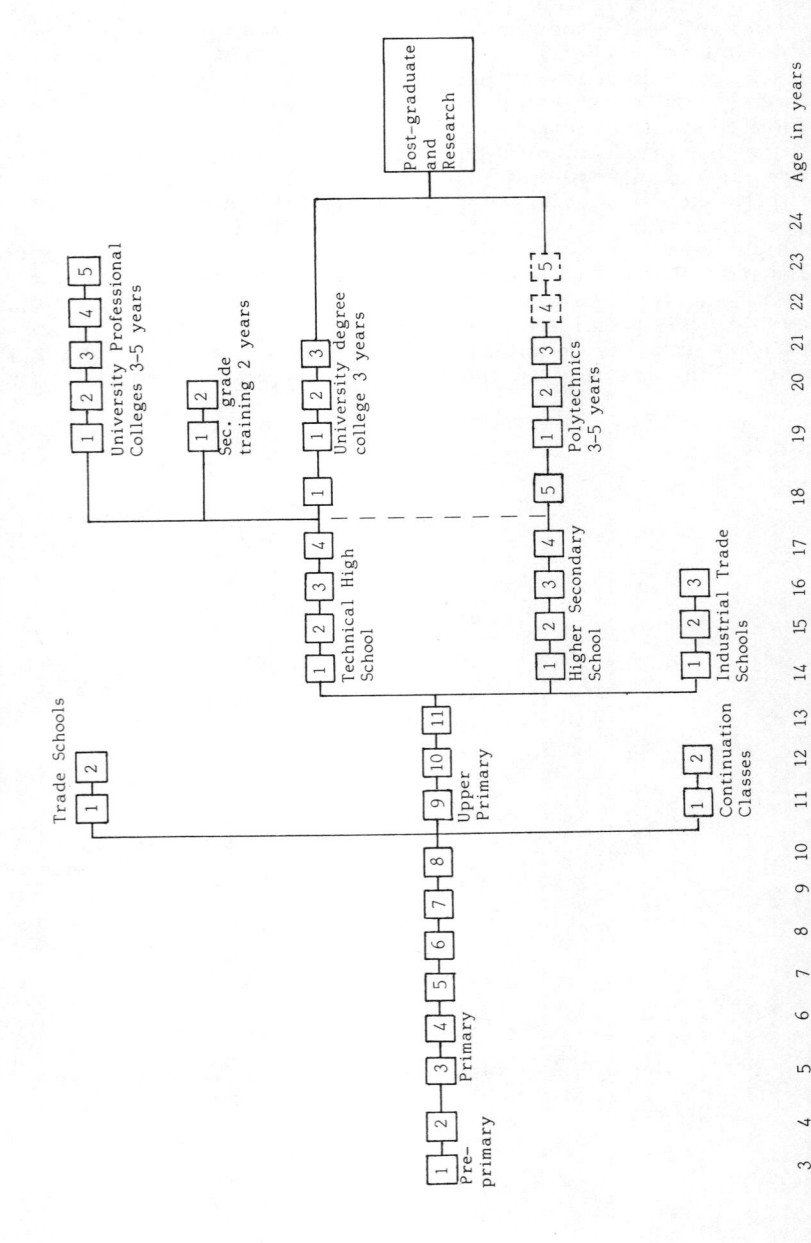

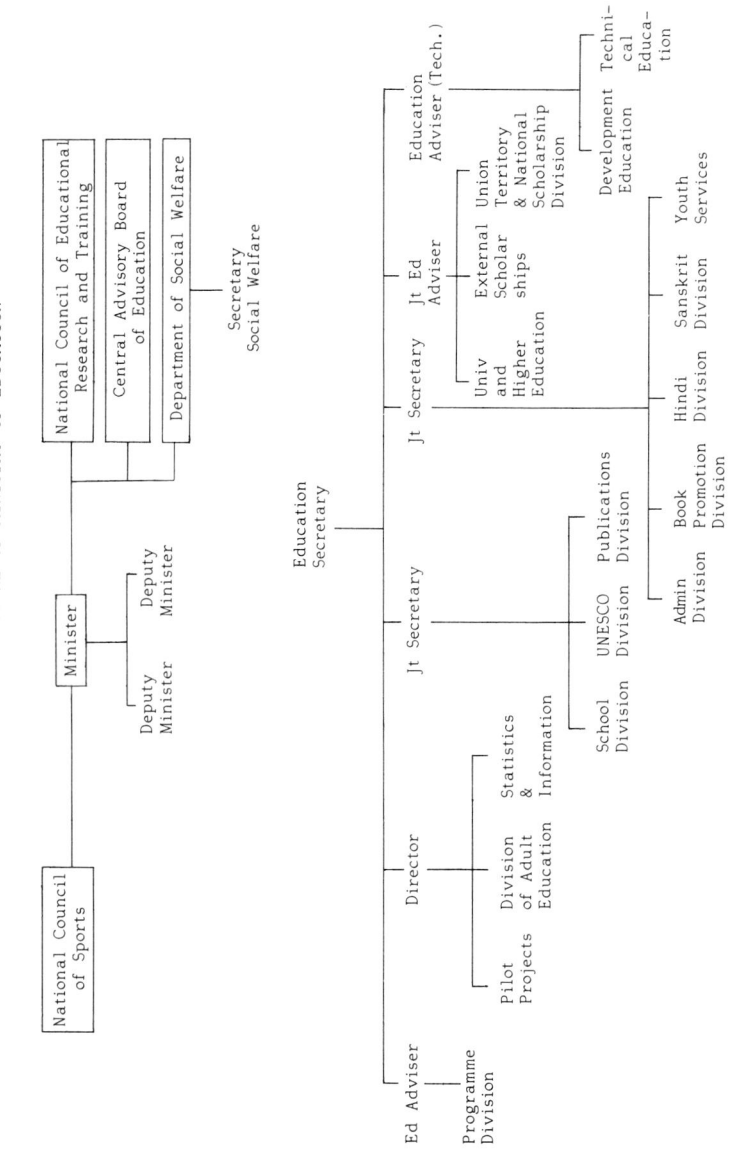

ADMINISTRATIVE STRUCTURE OF MINISTRY OF EDUCATION

156

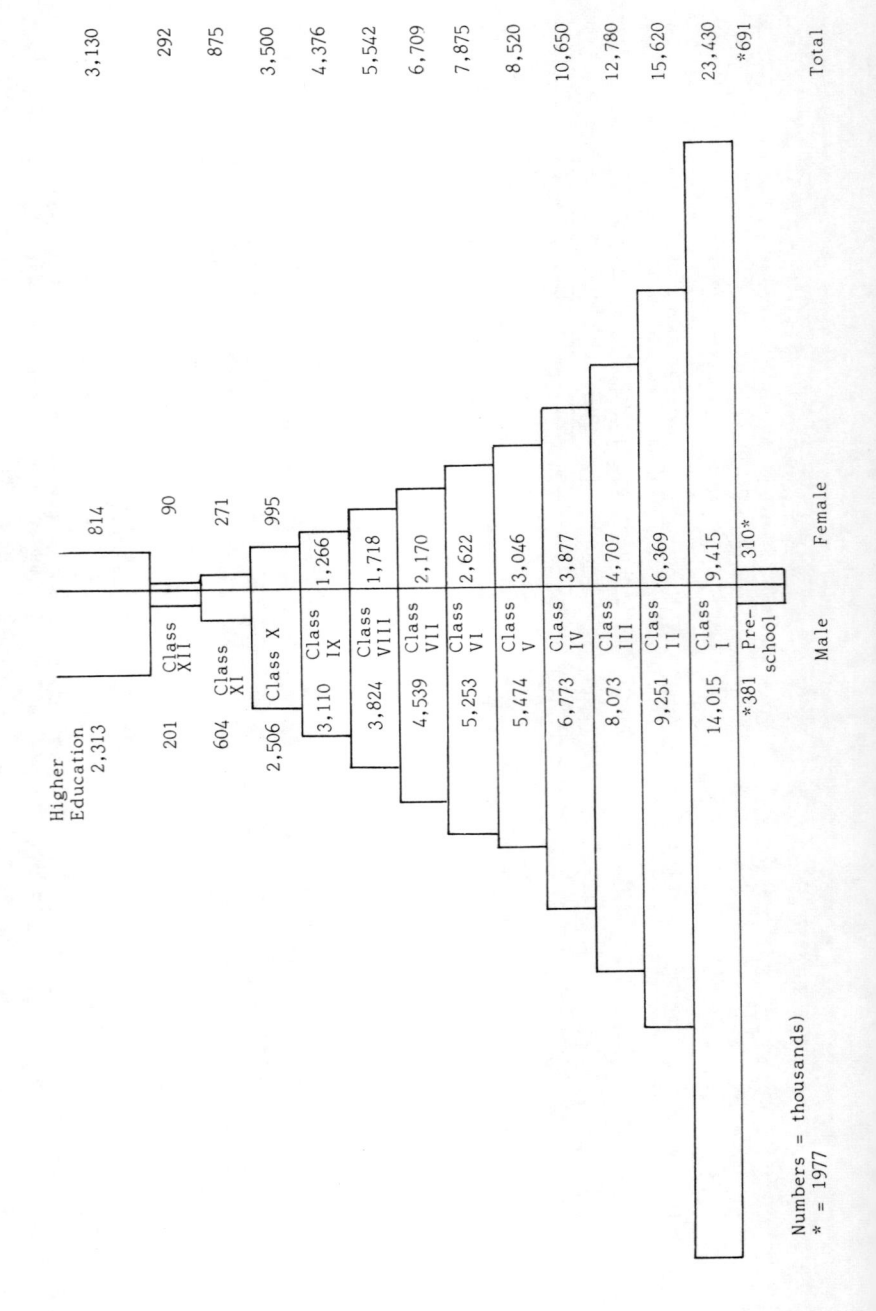

INDIA EDUCATIONAL PYRAMID 1979-1980

Male		Female	Total
2,313	Higher Education	814	3,130
201	Class XII	90	292
604	Class XI	271	875
2,506	Class X	995	3,500
3,110	Class IX	1,266	4,376
3,824	Class VIII	1,718	5,542
4,539	Class VII	2,170	6,709
5,253	Class VI	2,622	7,875
5,474	Class V	3,046	8,520
6,773	Class IV	3,877	10,650
8,073	Class III	4,707	12,780
9,251	Class II	6,369	15,620
14,015	Class I	9,415	23,430
*381	Pre-school	310*	*691

Numbers = thousands
* = 1977

INDIA BASIC STATISTICS

Population

1970	1975	1981
539,075,000	600,763,000	683,810,000

Proportion of Illiterates in the Population

1971			1981		
Total	Male	Female	Total	Male	Female
66.6%	53.2%	81.1%	63.8%	53.3%	75.1%

Enrolment Ratios

(Pupils in Classes I–V as a percentage of all aged 6–11, Pupils in Classes VI–VIII as proportion of all 11–14 year olds, Pupils in Classes IX–XII as a percentage of all 14–17 year olds, students in higher education as a proportion of all 17–23 year olds).

		Classes I–V	Classes VI–X	Higher Education*
1970	Male	90%	36%	–
	Female	56%	15%	–
1977	Male	92%	36%	12.2%*
	Female	63%	17%	4.2%*

* Proportion of all aged 20–24 in 1976

Schools, Teachers and Pupils 1979–1980

Grade	Schools	Teachers	Pupils
Lower Primary (I–V)	478,249	1,311,931	71,000,000
Upper Primary (VI–VIII)	114,720	835,292	19,500,000
Secondary (IX–XIII)	46,043	859,359	9,670,000

Proportion of Teachers with Training

Year	Lower Primary (I–V)	Upper Primary (VI–VIII)
1966	70.5%	76.9%
1980	86.8%	88.9%

Pupil:Teacher Ratio in Lower Primary Schools

1970	1977
41	41

Distribution of Students in Higher Education by Field of Study 1976

Discipline	Total	% Female
Education and Teacher Training	180,289	40.0%
Humanities	2,124,624	32.2%
Law	141,111	5.8%
Social & Behavioural Sciences	2,808	41.5%
Commerce and Business	615,095	9.9%
Natural Science	954,011	22.6%
Medicine & Related Subjects	139,886	24.5%
Engineering	322,878	6.3%
Agriculture	38,692	3.3%
Other	35,607	3.4%

Expenditure on Education

Year	As a percentage of Gross National Product	As a percentage of Total Government Spending
1970	2.8%	10.7%
1977	2.9%	9.9%

Expenditure on Education by Level (%)

Level	1970	1975
Pre-primary	0.2	0.2
Primary	22.2	21.2
Secondary	42.5	40.3
Higher	24.6	22.0
Non-distributed	10.6	16.3

Basic Social and Economic Data

Gross National Product Per Capita 1979: US$190
GNP per capita Annual Rate of Growth 1960-1979: 1.4%
Life expectancy at birth 1979: 52
Labour Force employed in Agriculture 1960: 74%
　　　　　　　　　　　　　　　　　　1979: 71%
　　　　　　　　　　　　　　Industry 1960: 11%
　　　　　　　　　　　　　　　　　　1979: 11%
　　　　　　　　　　　　　　Services 1960: 15%
　　　　　　　　　　　　　　　　　　1979: 18%

Indonesia

CONTENTS

1 Geography	162
2 Population	164
3 Society and Culture	165
4 History and Politics	166
5 The Economy	169
6 The Education System	171
7 Educational Administration	181
8 Educational Finance	186
9 Development and Planning of the Education System	189

Indonesia has yet to break through the barriers to industrialisation which some other countries of South-East Asia have begun to achieve. Despite high levels of production of minerals such as oil and tin, an impressive rate of economic growth in the 1970s and the existence of very large urban centres such as Jakarta, Indonesians remain a primarily rural and agricultural society with a Gross National Product per capita closer to those of India and Pakistan than to Malaysia or even Thailand.

Indonesia's education system, on the other hand, is relatively well developed. Over 90% of the relevant age group is in primary schools while lower secondary education has become available for over half the pupils who complete primary schooling. Upper secondary and higher education are provided for smaller proportions of the population but are relatively well developed. This achievement is considerable since educational provision when Indonesia gained formal independence from the Netherlands in 1949/1950 was very meagre. Yet continuing educational expansion to achieve universal primary schooling and substantial provision at post-primary levels is threatened both by increasing population and a loss of impetus in government plans.

Despite Indonesia's colonial history, the education system does not reflect Dutch practice and Dutch culture to the extent that former British colonies still follow British models. Indonesian language and culture are well entrenched. There is a relatively balanced educational structure of general education in primary and lower secondary schools followed by diversified upper secondary and higher education which cater for both general education and technical/vocational courses. However, further expansion is required for the transformation of Indonesia into an industrial economy.

The diversity of Indonesian culture and society has created some difficulties for educational planners. While there is a high degree of religious unity based upon Islam and less conflict than in some other countries between religious beliefs and secular eduction, there is great linguistic diversity which is likely to create difficulties in the achievement of universal primary and lower secondary education. Outside the main centres of population, there are many scattered and diverse communities. The provision of education for these groups involves logistic difficulties as well as potential cultural conflicts.

1 GEOGRAPHY

Topography

Indonesia is an archipelago forming a bridge between Asia and Australia and connecting the Indian and Pacific aceans. The total land area is 1,903,650 sq km (735,000 square miles), which is about one fifth of the total land area of Europe, or one quarter of Australia. However, the total area (land and sea) is over 8,000,000 sq km, as large as Australia. The whole territory extends 4,800 km (3,000 miles) from east to west and 2,000 km (1,250 miles) from north to south, and covers 17° of latitude (6°N to 11°S) and 48° of longitude (95°E to 144°E). There are at least 3,000 inhabited islands among a total of about 14,000, varying enormously in size. However, the five largest — Java, Sumatra, Kalimantan (Borneo), Irian Jaya and Sulawesi — account for about 92% of the land area. The archipelago is grouped into four regions:

(i) the Greater Sundas, comprising Sumatra (473,606 sq km), Java (132,608 sq km), Kalimantan (539,460 sq km) and Sulawesi (189,216 sq km)

(ii) the Lesser Sundas *(Nusa Tenggara)*, including the islands from Bali to Timor

(iii) the Moluccas *(Maluku)* including all those islands between Irian Jaya and Sulawesi

(iv) Irian Jaya (412,781 sq km).

Indonesia shares the island of Kalimantan with Malaysia and Brunei and the island of Irian with Papua New Guinea. East Timor, a Portuguese colony, was annexed by Indonesia in 1977.

There are considerable differences between the various regions. Western Sumatra, two thirds of Java, Madura and Bali have fertile soil but the rest of Java and Sumatra and Kalimantan have poor soil. The rich soil is volcanic, and a very large part of the archipelago consists of mountains and

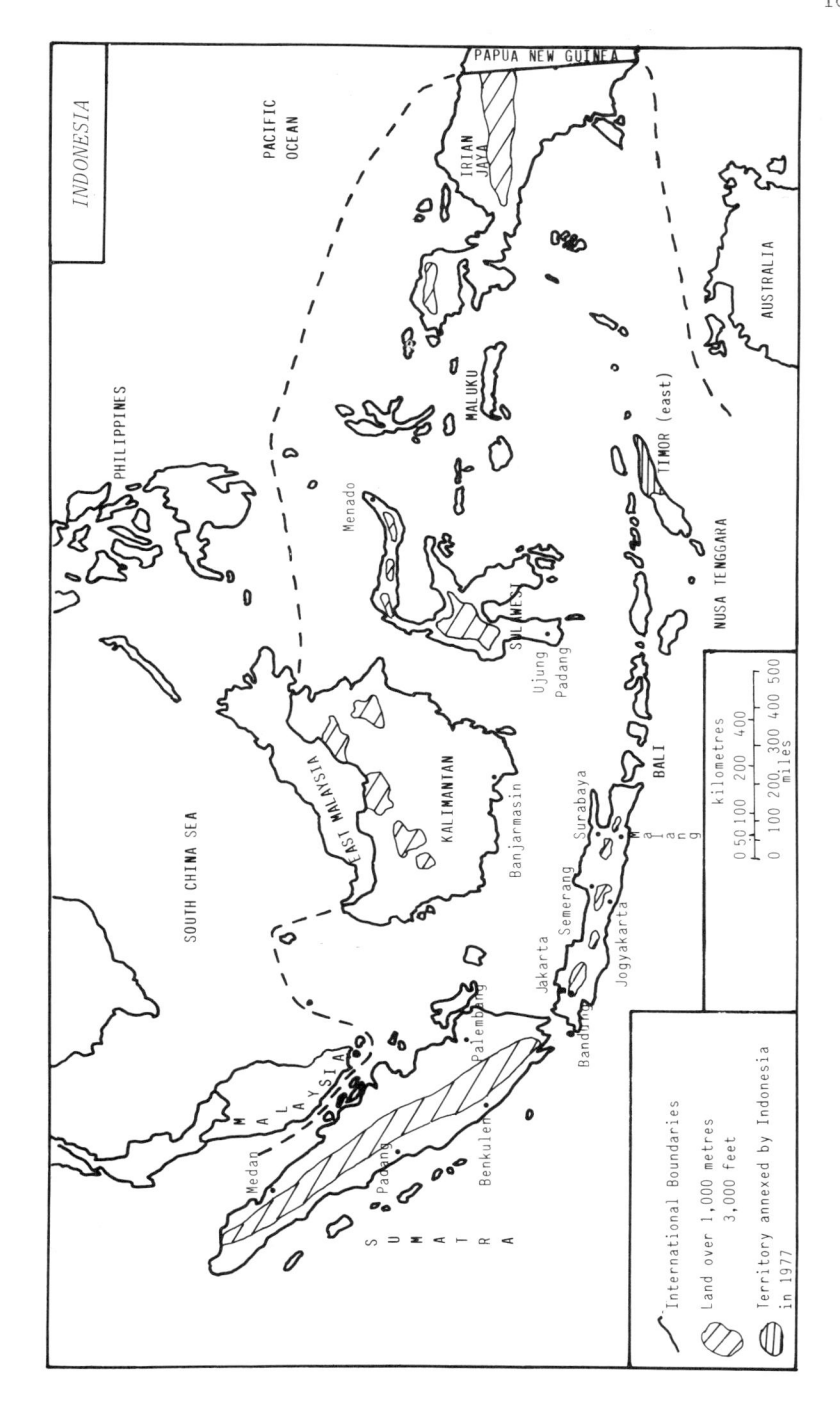

INDONESIA

volcanoes. Some of the alluvial coastal plains are well drained and fertile but the lowland areas of eastern Sumatra, west Java and southern Kalimantan consist largely of swamp which cannot be used for cultivation. Much of the land is covered by forest in the islands other than Java and Bali (e.g. 60% of Sumatra and 70% of eastern Indonesia).

Climate

The equator runs through Indonesia which is therefore situated in the tropical zone. There are two seasons: a drier season from May to October, and a wetter season from November to April. Rainfall is plentiful, with most of the country receiving between 1,500 mm (59 inches) and 3,000 mm (118 inches). West Sumatra receives over 4,000 mm. On the coast the temperature ranges between 24°C (75°f) and 30°C (86°F), but there can be great variations in the mountains. Humidity is rarely less than 75% and can rise to 97%

Communications

In 1975 there were 85,000 km of road, over 25% of which was surfaced. Roads on Java are adequate, but are poor on the other islands, and many parts of the interior of Kalimantan, Sulawesi and Irian Jaya are inaccessible to motor traffic. Considerable improvements have been made, including a trans-Sumatran highway under construction, but provision still falls far short of needs. There is about 6,500 km of railway track of Java, Sumatra and Madura; rivers are a means of communication in Kalimantan and Sulawesi. The main inter-island communication is by air and sea but it has so far proved impossible to operate an efficient and low-cost inter-island transport system. There are sea and air links with all the neighbouring countries - Singapore, Malaysia, Thailand, the Philippines, Hong Kong and Australia. Communications problems obviously hamper the spread of education and exacerbate the difficulties when students transfer from primary to secondary, and secondary to tertiary educational institutions.

2 POPULATION

Growth

At the census taken in 1971 the total population was 115,014,282 - an increase of 18% on the census figure of 1961. The 1979 estimate was 148,470,000. In terms of population Indonesia is the fifth largest country in the world. The average annual growth rate in 1978 was 2%, which will produce a population of 205 million by the year 2000. Between 1965 and 1970 there were 44.9 births per 1,000 of population every year; between 1970 and 1975 this had decreased slightly to 42.9 per 1,000 and continues to decline. It is estimated that 55% of the population is under the age of 25. This fact has important consequences for the longer term planning for employment and educational opportunities despite the steadily declining birth rate. By 1984 it is expected that there will be 25.3 million school age children between the ages of 7 and 13. The government is pursuing a vigorous family planning campaign, but various social and traditional factors affect the regional success of such campaigns.

Distribution

Though Java, Madura and Bali together constitute only one thirteenth of the total land area, they contain two thirds of the population. In 1974, as many as 79 million people were living on the islands of Java and Madura with an average density of 598 per sq km, the equivalent figures for other parts of Indonesia being 22.6 million on Sumatra (48 per sq km), 5.5 million on Kalimantan (10 per sq km), 8.9 million on Sulawesi (47 per sq km) and 9.1 million elsewhere (16 per sq km). The overall population density figure is 65 per sq km.

About 80% of the population still lives in rural areas, and the towns in the less populated areas are quite small; the largest, Medan (in Sumatra) has a population of less than 650,000. On Java, however, there are no less than three cities with over one million inhabitants; apart from Jakarta (now with a population of 5 million+), these are Surabaya (3 million) and Bandung (1.3 million).

Groups

Indonesia has approximately 300 different ethnic groups. People of Chinese origin are to be found everywhere, especially in urban areas and more particularly in certain trading cities e.g. Medan.

3 SOCIETY AND CULTURE

Social Patterns

Most Indonesians live in villages of a few hundred inhabitants, and the village community is the centre of life. Farming is usually communal. Social relationships are very clearly defined; the family is a hierarchy and relationships within the community tend to extend from this. There is a general veneration for age and traditional authority. However, having said this, there are marked differences between Javanese, Sumatran etc. societies, according to the islands' different cultures. But in spite of the dispersed nature of the country, communication difficulties and ethnic differences, Indonesia has successfully maintained itself as a unitary State.

Language

About 25 different languages and 250 dialects are spoken in the archipelago. Because of the early commercial influence of the Sriwijaya Empire in southern Sumatra, a dialect of Malay, Bahasa Indonesia, is spoken nearly everywhere. Since

Independence, priority has been given to developing Bahasa Indonesia as the national language.

Religion

The main religion in Indonesia is Islam. A current estimate is that 94% of the population is of this faith; however, this is not the pure Islam of the Middle East but an Islam transmuted by traditional animist and Hindu/Buddhist beliefs. Hinduism and Buddhism preceded Islam and both have left their mark. Bali remains almost exclusively Hindu. There are sizeable Christian communities (about 5% of the total population is Christian) but these tend to be concentrated in small areas. They include the Batak group on Sumatra, the Ambonese of Maluku, and the Minahasis of Sulawesi. There are still large numbers of animists in inland areas, especially in Kalimantan and Irian Jaya. The tenet concerning religion in the *Pancasilia*, the national philosophy, states there should be 'belief in God' but there is no State religion, religious tolerance being the government's official policy. There are Islamic and Christian schools and universities.

4 HISTORY AND POLITICS

Origins

Indonesia is a country with a long history. In earliest times Java was inhabited by 'Java Man' - *Pithecanthropus erectus*. From about 3000 to 500 BC there were Malay immigrants of early Mongoloid stock from South China and Tonkin. They inter-married with the indigenous people and settled in villages. From 206 BC to 24 AD navigational and commercial contacts were laid with South China. The first Hindu immigrants, mostly from South East India, came during the first century AD. This influx continued up to the seventh century and Hinduism gradually spread over the whole country. This peaceful 'Hinduisation' lasted about 14 centuries, creating a synthesised Indonesia-Hindu civilisation and culture. The first Buddhists from India arrived between 100 AD and 200 AD and the influence of Buddhism spread in Java and Sumatra. There were many Hindu and Buddhist kingdoms in Indonesia, notably the thirteenth century Sriwijaya Empire and the 14th Century Hindu Majapahit Empire. The latter finally disintegrated between 1513 and 1520 AD. In the meantime Moslem traders from Persia and Gujarat, and later from Arabia, introduced Islam from the twelfth and thirteenth centuries, although the first Moslems had visited Indonesia as early as the seventh century. In the sixteenth century Moslem kingdoms arose in central and west Java, Sumatra, Sulawesi, Kalimantan and Maluku.

Colonial Rule

In 1602 the United Dutch East India Company was founded in the Netherlands and eventually gained control over the spice and coffee exports in Indonesia and established suzerainty over Indonesian potentates and territories. In 1621, the Dutch Governor changed the name of the trading port which became Indonesia's capital from Sunda Kelapa to Batavia and the Dutch colonial period really began. The Dutch gradually established their rule, although the British built a fort on the west coast of Sumatra at Bengkulu named Fort Marlborough in 1714 and maintained a presence there until 1825. During the Napoleonic Wars when the Netherlands were occupied by France, Indonesia fell under the British East India Company's rule (1811-1816) with Sir Stamford Raffles as Lieutenant Governor of Java. In 1816 the Dutch resumed their possessions and after suppressing a series of widespread Indonesian revolts, in the next decades maintained their authority.

Independence

In the early twentieth century there were various national movements for independence. In March 1942 the Japanese invaded, and occupied Indonesia until August 1945; with their agreement, the Indonesians proclaimed their independence on 17 August 1945 when Sukarno was elected President and Dr Hatta Vice-President. A cabinet was formed on 5 September 1945. The actual declaration of independence was made a few days after the Japanese had surrendered to the Allies. Technically they were no longer in power at the time and the Dutch did not recognise the validity of the proclamation. This led to a bitter struggle by the Dutch to reimpose their colonial rule. After two bloody 'police actions', the UN Security Council engineered a cease-fire on 28 January 1949. After a United Nations conference the sovereignty over the whole territory of the former Netherlands East Indies was recognised to be in the hands of the United States of Indonesia on 27 December 1949. On 15 August 1950 the unitary Republic of Indonesia was established.

Since Independence

During the period 1949 to 1957 an attempt was made to develop a system of multi-party parliamentary government and in 1955 the first elections were held. But some 20 parties emerged and parliament proved to be deadlocked. In 1957 President Sukarno replaced Western-style democracy with a system known as 'guided democracy'. The elected parliament was replaced by an appointed legislature, the power of the executive was extended and the President progressively assumed control of the administration. Conflict between the army and the Communist party came to a head and after an attempted coup (allegedly Communist-inspired) in 1965, the army gained control under General Suharto and the Indonesian Communist Party was banned. In 1967 Sukarno resigned as President.

The 1970s

The 'New Order' of General Suharto met opposition from various sections of society including Islamic leaders and students in the early 1970s but in the elections of May 1977 the government-supported party won 232 of 350 elected seats in the legislature. President Suharto was re-elected to office in 1973 and 1978.

In 1975 Indonesia became involved in the independence movement in Portuguese Timor joining the side of those opposing a future left-wing government. In July 1977 Timor was absorbed into Indonesia, although the movement *Fretelin* continued to oppose this. The United Nations has yet to recognise the inclusion of East Timor in Indonesia.

Government Organisation

Government structure is centralised, and it is based on four main constituents; the President, the People's Consultative Assembly *(Majelis Permusyawaratan Rakyat)*, the House of People's Representatives *(Dewan Perwakilan Rakyat)* and the Supreme Advisory Council *(Dewan Pertimbangan Agung)*. The People's Consultative Assembly is the highest organ of State, and elects the President every 5 years. It therefore sits at least once during this period and includes all members of the House of Representatives plus regional delegates and members of functional groups within society (920 members in all). However, in practice the President and the army are the most powerful forces in the country. The Supreme Advisory Council, whose members are picked by the President, fulfils a purely consultative role. The People's Consultative Assembly has 460 members of whom 360 are directly elected and 100 appointed. The country is divided into 27 provinces (including East Timor). There are provincial legislatures which submit nominees to central government for the appointment of provincial governors.

International Relations

Indonesia adheres to the principle of non-alignment in foreign policy, though during the presidency of Sukarno it had close ties with both the Soviet Union and China. In the last ten years Indonesia has taken more account of the West and also its neighbours in South East Asia. In 1966 diplomatic relations were re-established with Malaysia and Singapore, and Indonesia took the lead in establishing the Association of South East Asian Nations (ASEAN), a politico-economic grouping comprising Indonesia, Malaysia, the Philippines, Singapore and Thailand. In 1966 Indonesia also rejoined the United Nations and related agencies.

Indonesia belongs to the South East Asia Ministers of Education Organisation, the other active members being Malaysia, Singapore, Thailand and the Philippines. SEAMEO is a consortium for regional educational development formed in 1965. It has a council and secretariat. There are six SEAMEO centres located as follows:

The Regional Centre for Tropical Biology (BIOTROP) in Bogor/Indonesia

The Regional Centre for Educational Innovation and Technology (INNOTECH) in Manila, Philippines

The Regional Centre for Education in Science and Mathematics (RECSAM) in Penang, Malaysia

The Regional English Language Centre (RELC) in Singapore

The Regional Centre for Graduate Study and Research in Agriculture in the Philippines

The Tropical Medicine and Public Health Project in Bankok, Thailand.

5 THE ECONOMY
Agriculture and Forestry

Agriculture continues to be the main sector of the economy, estimated in 1976 to employ about 60% of the labour force and to earn about 40% of GDP. It is a mixture of smallholding subsistence agriculture and large scale estate production. The main export and cash crops are: rubber, coffee, palm oil, palm kernel, tea, sugar, pepper, tobacco and copra. Maize, rice, cassava, tapioca, peanuts and soybeans are grown for domestic consumption. A major government objective is the achievement of self-sufficiently in rice production. Fishing is important and, with the increased use of modern equipment, production has grown.

As two thirds of the land area is covered by forest, timber production is substantial and Indonesia is now the leading supplier of Asian hardwood. Timber is the second most important foreign exchange earner after petroleum and in 1976 timber exports earned the equivalent of US$782 million. A major government afforestation programme is now under way aimed at planned exploitation and substantially increasing the plantation of teak, mahogany, eucalyptus and pine.

Natural Resources

The main mineral resource is high-quality petroleum with exports earning the equivalent of US$5,453.8 million in 1976. Indonesia is the major producer of oil in the Far East with estimated reserves of 15,000 million to 17,000 million barrels. Indonesia also has substantial reserves of natural gas which is exported to Japan and the western USA. Oil and gas exports are crucially important to the economy, providing 45% of foreign exchange earnings and 60% of domestic government revenue. Oil production has fallen slightly in recent years, but the Indonesian authorities are confident that current and future exploration will enable production to increase again. Indonesia is the world's third largest producer of tin, and also has deposits of copper, bauxite, nickel, coal, iron ore and kaolin.

Industry

At present industry contributes only about 10% to GDP and in general depends on imported machinery and components. However, progress has been made especially in the production of steel, fertilisers, batteries, car and TV assembly; although there are signs of domestic market saturation in the last two areas. It is intended to develop industry further, especially petro-chemicals and plastics. One of the problems of industrialisation is the relatively under-developed technical education system which at present is not turning out sufficient craftsmen or technicians with adequate skills for the modern industrial sector. Industry usually has to undertake some retraining, but there are three World Bank projects to improve the capacity of the public education system to produce skilled people in sufficient numbers. The fostering of small scale labour intensive industry and appropriate technologies for it are important objectives in industrial policy.

Economic Situation

Indonesia organises her economic development by means of Five Year Plans. The first of these Repelita I (1969-73) emphasised the development of agriculture and the infrastructure in order to encourage foreign investment and facilitate the development of industry. There is now large scale foreign investment amounting to US$5,160 million in 1976. Japan is the largest single investor. Repelita II (1974-78) has been modified, partly because in 1975 the government was forced to take over management of the national oil corporation Pertamina, which fell into serious financial difficulties. The second plan continued the work of its predecessor and also sought to stimulate more employment and foster a more equal distribution of wealth. The implementation of the first, and to a much lesser extent of the second, depended to a considerable extent on external financing in the shape of the Inter-Governmental Group on Indonesia (IGGI), the World Bank, the International Monetary Fund, and the Asian Development Bank. This means that the country has incurred a heavy debt burden. During the early 1970s Indonesia suffered from serious inflation which rose to 50% in 1973/74. This was subsequently reduced to 14% in 1976 and was below 10% before the devaluation of the Rupiah (from US$1 = 415 to US$1 = 625) on 15 November 1978. Unemployment and under-employment are serious problems, especially amongst the young (of which there are increasing numbers). Employment generation is an important facet of development plans. A third Five Year Plan, Repelita III, for the period 1979/84, has the theme of 'growth with equity'.

6 THE EDUCATION SYSTEM

Academic Year

The academic year used to run from January to December. From 1978 the new school year from July to June was introduced. The academic year is divided into two semesters of approximately five months each.

Pre-Primary

Pre-schools or kindergartens *(Taman Kanak-kanak - TK)* are usually only found in the larger towns, are private, and available only to the few relatively wealthy parents able to afford them. The government is beginning to show more interest in this level of education, planning to establish model kindergartens during Repelita III, and possibly a training/materials centre.

Primary

Primary education is officially a six-year course (classes I-VI) beginning at the age of 6. However, due to early and late starters and repeaters, many children in primary schools *(Sekolah Dasar - SD)* are actually younger than 6 or older than 12. Where possible the medium of instruction is Bahasa Indonesia but in classes I and II outside cities, the local language is frequently used. School fees (SPP) were abolished at this level in 1978 but parents often contribute money in other ways. A new curriculum, introduced in 1975 and highly structured, includes the usual primary school subjects: reading and writing in Bahasa Indonesia, and sometimes the vernacular, mathematics, social studies (IPS), science (IPA), art and craft, physical and health education, religion, and moral education (PMP) based on the national philosophy of *Pancasila*. Enrolment in 1978 was said to be 19.2 million, approximately 85% of the age group. By the end of Repelita III, if the goal of universal primary education has been achieved, it is expected that 25.3 million children will be in primary schools.

Junior Secondary (SLTP)

Junior secondary schools accept pupils at approximately the age of 13/14 for a three-year post-primary course. At this level there are both academic and vocational schools. In 1978, 58% of students completing class VI of primary school entered junior secondary schools, and it is projected that this figure will rise to 85% by 1984, though not all children who began primary school complete class VI. As more and more children have been completing primary school, so the pressure on the junior secondary schools has been steadily increasing. An 'open school' *(Sekolah Terbuka)* system is now in the planning stage, based on distance learning techniques and it is estimated that it will take 7.1% of the junior secondary enrolment by 1984.

Academic junior secondary schools, known as SMPs, are the most popular and take approximately 85% of junior secondary students (2,207,803 out of a total junior secondary enrolment of 2,673,976 in 1978). Entry to these schools is determined by performance in leaving examinations set individually by primary schools, but the more popular SMPs set their own examinations. It is proposed that during Repelita III, a standardised national examination will be introduced country-wide, replacing the one which was abolished several years ago. The new curriculum, on a similar pattern to that of the primary schools, was introduced in 1975 and comprises: 'general' education (compulsory for all students and including religion, moral education - PMP, sport and health, and art); 'academic' education (compulsory for all students and including Indonesian, the local language where necessary, English, social studies, mathematics and science); 'skill' education (in which students can choose from a number of options e.g. agriculture, practical science, handicrafts); and population education which should be integrated with other fields of study.

Those children who do not enter the academic schools may attend a variety of technical and vocational schools; at junior secondary level these include: commercial (SMEP), home economics (SKKP) and technical (ST) schools (presently being phased out). In 1978 there were enrolments of 166,702, 44,373 and 192,098 respectively in these schools.

Senior Secondary

Senior secondary schools accept pupils at approximately the age of 16/17 for a three-year post-junior secondary course. At this level too there are academic and vocational schools including, commercial (SMEA), home economics (SKKA), technical (STM), primary teacher training (SPG) and sports (SGO) schools; these between them accounted for 53% of senior secondary students in 1978. The remaining 47% (603,757 students) went to academic secondary schools, known as SMAs. Entry to senior secondary schools is determined by the pupils' performance in the leaving examination at the end of junior secondary school, sometimes also by an examination set by the senior secondary school, and by the ability of the student to pay. In 1979, 87% of students completing the SMP course went on to SMAs but it is projected that this figure will fall to 81% in 1984 (although absolute numbers will, of course, increase).

The '1975 curriculum' of the SMAs makes it compulsory for all students to follow courses in 'general' education, which includes religion, moral education (PMP), sport and health, and art, 'skill' education and population education; 'academic' education is common for the first semester for all students and includes mathematics, Bahasa Indonesia, English, science and social studies, but allows, for the second and remaining semesters, an option to specialise in science, social studies or languages, although it is compulsory for all students to continue with mathematics, Bahasa Indonesia and English. At the conclusion of the course, pupils take an examination in the general subjects and their specialisation, success in which determines their ability to proceed to higher education.

Special

Five categories of children are recognised as needing special education: the deaf, blind, physically handicapped, mentally handicapped and socially malajusted (roughly equivalent to children who would be sent to an approved school in Britain). Approximately 7,000 pupils were enrolled in 172 special schools (SLB) in 1978. Only 15 are government institutions, 9 administered by the Ministry of Education, and 6 administered by the Ministry of Social Affairs and the Ministry of Justice. Most of the provision is therefore by private institutions, run by voluntary organisations (known as *Yayasan*). Some schools, especially those for the blind, deaf and physically handicapped, are residential, with facilities provided by the Ministry of Social Affairs, in a system of dual control with the Ministry of Education.

Technical and Vocational

As has been pointed out there are technical and vocational schools at junior secondary and secondary levels. And as well as those schools under the Ministry of Education, there are senior secondary vocational schools run by other ministries such as: legal secondary schools, police schools, schools for nurses, medical auxiliaries and junior pharmacists. There is also a music school and a school of fine arts. Technical education is also provided at craft and technician levels.

Craft/Tradesman Level

During Repelita II, there was massive expansion of technical education with money provided by the World Bank, the Asian Developent Bank, Indonesian and bilateral sources, including Britain. The first major effort was the establishment of five centralised workshops known as technical training centres (TTCs) in Jakarta, Bandung, Surabaya, Medan and Ujung Pandang. These serve several nearby secondary technical schools (STMs), providing the practical facilities and training in which these schools were largely deficient. Mechanical, electrical, electronic, building and automotive are the trades for which these centres provide the technical training. A further four TTCs are currently being built in Semarang, Jogyakarta, Palembang and Padang. The TTCs receive British Technical Cooperation support in the form of consultants, VSOs and library development. The Ministry of Education has been seeking foreign aid to upgrade a further 80 STMs for which centralised workshops cannot be provided due to geographical factors. The Asian Development Bank and the Dutch have agreed to develop approximately 40 of these schools.

On the campus of the Institute of Technology Bandung (ITB), a 'mechanical polytechnic' has been established with the help of Swiss Aid. This institution is concerned with the training of toolmakers and maintenance mechanics. Although the intake is from SMA/STM and the course lasts three years, the level of output is craft or tradesman, not higher technician as would be expected in the British context from an institution called a polytechnic.

Technician Level

During the early 1970s, a pilot group of 12 development technical schools (STMP) was erected solely with Indonesian government funds. These schools provide a four-year post-junior secondary course which enables the students to reach what roughly equates to a trade technical level, that is, above the tradesman level to which the STMs aspire. Given the rapid development of technical education during the decade, the purpose and role of the schools within the overall pattern of technical education may be redefined. However, it is planned to establish several more STMPs which will offer a normal three-year STM course with an additional year open to all STM graduates to enable them to reach trade technician level.

During Repelita III, starting in 1979, six polytechnics will be established with World Bank aid on the university campuses of North Sumatra (Medan), Sriwijaya (Palembang), University of Indonesia (Jakarta), ITB (Bandung), Diponegoro (Semarang) and Brawijaya (Malang). These polytechnics will take SMA/STM leavers for a three-year course leading to a sub-degree level diploma equivalent to higer technical level, in the fields of civil, mechanical and eletrical engineering. The first enrolment of students will be in 1981 and the first output in 1984. A technician education development centre (TEDC) will be established on the ITB campus to provide professional leadership for the project, including: development of curriculum and materials; provision of pre- and in-service training for polytechnic staff; the monitoring of polytechnic operations; and carrying out employment and manpower research related to industrial technicians. Technical consultancy and possibly further aid for polytechnic development will be provided by the Swiss.

Higher

Tertiary education is diverse and in a state of transition. The most common pattern is for institutions to offer a three-year course leading to the degree of *Sarjana Muda* (a Bachelors' degree), and a further two years leading to the *Sarjana* (a Master's degree). Some degree level courses are longer, e.g. in medicine. In addition, a four-year Baccalaureate has recently been introduced. Two- to three-year diploma level courses are also offered (c.f. polytechnics above). In practice, the number of calendar years specified for a degree or diploma programme is generally exceeded, due both to repetition and part time study. There are five main types of tertiary level institution:

(i) universities which have a number of semi-autonomous faculties offering the *Sarjana*, *Sarjana Muda* and a limited number of diploma programmes

(ii) institutes which comprise a number of faculties in a single professional field and offer the *Sarjana* and *Sarjana Muda* degrees

(iii) teacher training colleges which until recently have offered only *Sarjana* and *Sarjana Muda* degrees but, in the future, will offer certificate and diploma level programmes also (see **Teacher Training** below)

(iv) academies which consist of a single faculty and a grant diploma/certificate for technician level courses

(v) other post-secondary schools which provide diploma level courses.

Universities are regarded as having three primary responsibilities: teaching, research and servicing the development of the communities in which they are located.

Enrolment

Those who pass the secondary school leaving examination are eligible to proceed to tertiary institutions. However, there is fierce competition for places at the more prestigious institutions and the five top ranking universities – University of Indonesia, Institute of Technology Bandung (ITB), Agricultural University Bogor (IPB), Gajah Mada University Jogyakarta, and Airlangga University Surabaya, have recently joined together to set one combined entrance examination for their own institutions.

In 1976, 285,000 students were enrolled in 460 post-secondary institutions. This represents 2% of the relevant age cohort, with approximately two thirds in public and one third in private institutions. Of these 55% were enrolled in degree granting institutions, 45% in diploma granting. About 37% of tertiary level enrolments are in the social sciences and humanities, 3% in basic sciences, 13% in engineering and 6% in agricultural sciences. The lower development of diploma level programmes in the sciences and engineering in comparison with degree level programmes is indicated by the figures for engineeering: only 7,800 students were enrolled in diploma programmes compared with 30,400 in degree programmes.

Exansion of tertiary level enrolments has continued at the rate of approximately 4% per year since 1970. However, senior secondary school enrolments during the decade 1967 to 1976 have been increasing at the rate of approximately 8% per annum with a consequent increase in demand for tertiary level places. The number of students in tertiary education is projected to double during Repelita III.

Overseas Study

Although some wealthy parents send their children overseas for undergraduate and even secondary school study, most students overseas are in post-graduate courses. The USA takes by far the largest proportion, but Britain, Holland, Australia and Japan also accept substantial numbers.

Reforms

Moves are presently under way to reform the structure of higher education. The *Sarjana Muda* degree will be abolished and the official length of a normal *Sarjana* course reduced from five years to four. An intermediate degree between *Sarjana* and PhD has already been introduced, the *Pasca Sarjana* (Master's degree). This is supposed to take two years post *Sarjana*, while a PhD will take a further two years. A system of semester credits will also be introduced (e.g. for a *Sarjana*, a student would require 140-160 credits), allowing greater comparability between different institutions. An examination system will be used to moderate the semester credits.

To strengthen coordination between institutions at tertiary level, subject oriented consortia (e.g. in technology, science, economics, agriculture and education) have been established. They meet regularly and consist of personnel from public and private institutions, and they discuss (among other things) curricula, and planning.

Teacher Training

Teachers in Indonesia are trained in different institutions and at different levels according to the type of school in which they intend to teach. The two major types of institution for per-service training are primary and secondary teachers' colleges, though there are also separate faculties for teachers in special schools and technical institutes. In-service training is also developing.

Primary

The teacher training college for primary school teachers (SPG) is a secondary level institution, approximately parallel to the SMA. It accepts students from the SMP for a three-year course. In 1975, there were 585 SPGs with an enrolment of 202,000 students, taught by 13,000 teachers. During the period of Repelita III, 125,000 new teachers will be required in addition to 96,500 to replace those retiring.

Secondary

The teacher training college for secondary school teachers (IKIP) is a tertiary level institution. It accepts students from senior secondary schools, usually from the SMA, for three-year *Sarjana Muda* and five-year *Sarjana* courses. The expectation is that teachers in the senior secondary schools will possess a *Sarjana* degree and in junior secondary schools a *Sarjana Muda* degree, but in practice this does not necessarily happen: teachers in the SMA do not always possess a full *Sarjana* degree. In addition to IKIPs, 13 public universities have faculties of education and teacher training which perform essentially the same function. There are now ten government IKIPs which, in 1977, enrolled 41,000 students and had nearly 2,500 staff. For the universities, there is a consortium on teacher education which was established in 1970 and advises on curricula, long term planning, textbooks and staff training.

Special

Teachers for special schools are trained at a teacher training college for special education (SGPLB) notably at Bandung, Jogyakarta and Solo; also certain IKIPs, notably Jakarta, Bandung and Jogyakarta, have departments of special education where research and training of teachers for SGPLBs is carried out.

Technical

The rapid expansion of facilities for training craftsmen has created an urgent need for more and better technical teachers which has led to the strengthening and development of technical teacher training courses. Faculties of technical teacher training (FKITs) exist at 7 IKIPs; two of these are presently being upgraded and expanded at Jogyakarta and Padang, with World Bank support and technical assistance provided through UNESCO. It is anticipated that these FKITs will eventually become key centres for the training of technical manpower at this level.

In-Service

At primary level, the main thrust has been through the Primary Education Project (P3D) which has been in operation for five years with World Bank and Canadian government support. It came to an end in 1979. As well as training teachers it has also produced textbooks. A 'cascade' system of teacher training has been adopted in which mobile trainers (TPK) selected from among SPG staff and the inspectorate are upgraded on a regular basis. They, in turn, run upgrading courses for primary teachers at 'SD centres' back in the provinces. As many as 220,000 educators and teachers have been upgraded in this way although doubts have been expressed on the impact of this type of project on the quality of the teaching in the classroom itself. This mode of in-service training has been adopted in the 17 inner provinces, but in the nine outer provinces, where communications are difficult, an attempt has been made to reach teachers through radio programmes. It is unclear what system of in-service training will be adopted during Repelita III but the draft plan expects that 400,000 will be affected.

At secondary level, a network of regional upgrading centres (BPGs) has been established, loosely attached to IKIPs. They provide in-service training for secondary school teachers in key areas of the curriculum (Bahasa, mathematics, science, social studies). These regional centres are, in turn, linked to national upgrading centres which specialise in certain subject areas. Thus the old science teaching centre in Bandung has now become the National Teachers' Upgrading Centre for Science (BPG-IPA) while the equivalent national mathematics centre is to be established in Jogyakarta, the language centre in Malang and a social studies centre in Jakarta. To cope with the immediate need for staff with practical technical skills to teach in the TTCs, a national in-service training centre known as the Technical Teachers' Upgrading Centre (TTUC) has been established in Bandung. This provides short term (three-month) training for staff from TTCs and the upgrades STMs. Technical assistance is being provided by UNESCO and Australia. A further four regional upgrading centres are planned for Medan, Jakarta, Surabaya and Ujung Padang, the Medan Centre being financed by the Asian Development Bank.

Recent Developments

With World Bank financial support, and technical assistance from the Oslo based consultants, IMTEC (funded by the World Bank), a massive project (P3G) to re-structure and improve pre-service teacher education in both IKIPs and SPGs is presently under way. One hundred and forty 'Master' teacher trainers, about one third of whom went on an extended overseas tour for about four months in 1978, are now engaged in curriculum development, materials writing, and planning the programme of in-service training for IKIP and SPG lecturers which will continue during Repelita III. This project has, up to the begionning of 1979, concentrated on the four key curriculum areas (Bahasa, mathematics, science and social studies), but further assistance is being sought from UNESCO to extend the coverage of the project to art, skill, moral education and other areas.

Abolition of those schools, known as POGSLP, which provided 'topping-up' for SPG or SMA leavers to enable them to teach at SMP leve, and abolition of corresponding 'crash' courses in IKIPs, is being carried out as part of a major overhaul of the structure of courses provided at IKIPs. A more flexible system of certificate and diploma courses, allowing multiple entry/exit and encouraging graduates who have not been through an education faculty of a university or IKIP to become teachers, will be introduced during Repelita III. As described above a feature of this system is that the *Sarjana Muda* will no longer exist, the *Sarjana* will be a four-year course, and an intermediate degree between *Sarjana* and doctorate, the *Pasca Sarjana* will be introduced.

Non-Formal and Adult

In 1977, it was estimated by the Ministry of Education that there were 17 million children and youths between the ages of 7 and 18 who were not attending school, and 23 million illiterate adults. During Repelita II, there has been increased attention to out-of-school and adult education. The most important agency involved in PENMAS, the directorate of the Ministry of Education chiefly responsible for out-of-school education. However, the extension departments of the Ministries of Social Affairs, Manpower, Home Affairs and Agriculture and certain other semi-autonomous agencies including BUTSI (the National Graduate Volunteer Corps) and *Pramuka* (the scouting movement) are also involved in non-formal education activities.

PENMAS

This organisation was established in 1946, and initially served a mainly adult clientele; but by 1972 it was providing a variety of courses for about 600,000 youths and adults annually. Reorganisation of the Ministry of Education in 1975 resulted in a reduction of staff from 11,000 to 6,500 and a further reduction to 2,500 by 1977. However, the government's determination to strengthen PENMAS is illustrated by their signing of a loan of US$15 million from the World Bank in 1977, now known as the Sixth Education Project. The objectives of the Project are to strengthen the management capability of PENMAS; establish a system of regular in-service training for its staff; create institutions which can develop appropriate learning materials; and create a system of direct and flexible funding of village level learning activities. The Project will publish over 300 pamphlets, distributing 11 million copies; and it was estimated that by 1982, PENMAS would be catering for 830,000 participants in 41,000 learning groups. Technical assistance funded from the loan is being provided by the University of Massachusetts.

Pamong

Under the auspices of the SEAMEO regional centre for innovation in education (ENNOTECH), an experiment known as Pamong has been conducted since 1973 in two villages near Solo. The experiment attempts to use the primary school as a learning centre which can be more flexible than a regular primary school in terms of clientele, teachers, methods and involvement with the community. Modular self-instructional materials, peer-group teaching, 'programmed teaching' of younger children by older children and teaching by members of the community have all been features of the system. Limited replication of the experiment is being attempted at a village in Bali, and it is proposed that, during Repelita III, the experiment should be further disseminated to small isolated schools in Kalimantan, possible with the assistance of New Zealand. It was planned that by 1983, the system would cater for 400,000 new pupils and 200,000 'dropouts'. Pamong has received technical cooperation support from several sources, including USAID and Canada.

Other

UNICEF's chief involvement in education during Repelita II was support for the production of a series of booklets and audio-visual aids designed for out-of-school children and youths on a variety of topics ranging from basic literacy and numeracy to certain types of skill education (Package 'A'). The first series of ten booklets appeared in 1978 but it is proposed that 100 will eventually be published. Integration with the PENMAS project is anticipated. The Ministry of Education's Research and Development Unit (BP3K), in cooperation with IPIP Ujung Pandang, has been involved in an action research study on community learning in two villages in South Sulawesi and West Java, attempting to find out how well learning resources are matched to learning needs, and to develop a prototype community learning system.

Islamic

The Islamic religious schools continue alongside the secular education system. The schools are run by private organisations and are guided, and to some extent subsidised, by the Department of Religious Affairs. Efforts are being made to provide these schools with the official text-books and to encourage them to follow the official curriculum. Some of these schools offer practical courses in animal husbandry and agriculture with practical experience provided by a school farm. It seems likely that there will be significant attempts during Repelita III to harness more effectively the potential of these schools. It was estimated that by 1983, the enrolment in *Madrasah Ibtidayah* Schools (Islamic SD schools) would be approaching 3.25 million.

Private

At all levels of the education system, there are private alternatives to State maintained education run by religious and private foundations *(Yayasans)*. It is difficult to generalise about private institutions because they vary enormously in quality from prestigious high schools in the main urban centres (often Protestant or Catholic) to which the elite aspire to send their children, to catchpenny private vocational and language courses. Private institutions for primary and secondary education are required to conform to centrally determined curricula and are subject to inspection and control. All private institutions, of which the largest sector by far is the English language schools, are required to register and are also subject to inspection. There are, however, many unregistered institutions. Private universities exist and these again vary enormously, some having parity with State institutions in at least some faculties (one is even designated as a SEAMEO centre of activity), others being universities only in name.

Educational Broadcasting

The Ministry of Information controls the chief broadcasting networks, RRI for radio, TVRI for television. RRI has been designated by the government as responsible for technical matters while the Ministry of Education and other interested ministries (e.g. Agriculture) are responsible for programme content. Within the Ministry of Education, a media section (TKPK) loosely attached to the Research and Development Unit of the Ministry (BP3K) has been operating since the early 1970s. Considerable resources, both financial and human, have been committed to developing educational broadcasting, with support especially from the USA. A domestic satellite (Palapa) was launched in 1976 with channels to be set aside for educational purposes. During Repelita III, facilities will be developed for television production at a site on the outskirts of Jakarta (Ciputat). In the meantime, TKPK has borrowed facilities from the Institute of Technology Surabaya (ITS), mainly for training purposes. Many staff have been trained overseas, chiefly in the US, Britain and the Federal Republic of Germany.

To date, the main achievement of TKPK has been the production and broadcasting of radio programmes for primary school teachers in remote areas. The units in Jogyakarta and Semarang are producing the radio programmes and correspondence texts in support of the new textbooks produced in association with the Primary Education Project (P3D). It is likely that during Repelita III, the emphasis will shift towards production of software for the open SMP. Considerable interest is also being shown in the possibility of an Open University system which would certainly make demands on the media section.

With support from the Federal Republic of Germany, a rural farm broadcasting unit has been developing radio programmes for farmers in the rural areas. Cassettes are distributed to many small local stations which re-broadcast them and the Agricultural Extension Service is said to have promoted the organisation of 12,000 listening groups throughout the country.

7 EDUCATIONAL ADMINISTRATION

Agencies for Education

Although the Ministry of Education has been designated by Presidential decree as the chief authority for education and training, many other ministries including Religious Affairs, Health and Home Affairs run their own education and training institutions, and programmes. The Ministry of Religion is particularly important in this respect, running a separate but parallel system of religious education from primary to tertiary level. The Ministry of Manpower and the National Institute of Administration (LAN) share with the Ministry of Education operational responsibility for education and training. The main discussion in this section will, however, refer to the Ministry of Education.

Ministry of Education

The Minister of Education, who is appointed by the President, is in turn responsible for appointing the heads of the seven main sections of the Ministry: Secretariat-General, Inspectorate-General, Research and Development Unit (BP3K), and Directorates General of Culture, Out of School Education, Primary and Secondary Education and Higher Education. In 1978, a junior Minister of Youth Affairs was also appointed. Although he is technically not under the Minister of Education, he frequently deputises for him at public functions. The Secretariat-General is responsible for the internal administration of the Ministry, for external relations with foreign agencies and governments, for medium-term planning in its *Biro Perencanaan*, and for public relations. The Inspectorate-General audits the accounts and performance of the rest of the Ministry but is not concerned with professional quality control in the sense that HMIs are.

The Directorate-General for Primary and Secondary Education (PDMU) is the executive section of the Ministry primarily concerned with the administration of schools. As can be seen from the chart overleaf, its directorates are: Primary Education, which includes responsibility for special education; Secondary Education: Skill and Vocational Education; Teacher Education; and Educational Facilities *(Sarana)* which includes responsibility for books and equipment. A new directorate has recently been established with responsibility for coordinating private schools at this level. Some idea of the importance of this Directorate-General is indicated by the fact that three Project Implementation Units (PIUs) for the World Bank Education projects are located here: P3D (Development of Primary Education); P3G (Development of Teacher Education); and the technical education project for the establishment of technical training centres. The Directorates are responsible for the management of the sector with which they are concerned including executive responsibility for curriculum matters, the curriculum planning and development functions lying with BP3K.

The Directorate-General for Higher Education *(Pendidikan Tinggi)* is responsible for all higher education institutions and is divided into directorates for: academic affairs (the key department); research and university public services; private higher education; and student affairs.

Centralised Control

The Ministry of Education controls the school system from Jakarta with the power to appoint, promote, transfer or dismiss teachers (except at primary level); and to create, expand or improve schools (except primary). For primary schools a complex system of dual control operates with the Ministry of Home Affairs responsible for teachers, buildings and equipment in primary schools, while the Ministry of Education is responsible for professional standards and supervision. The situation is further complicated by the Ministry of Religion which administers its own parallel system of education. The National Assessment of Education set up during Repelita I suggested three possible solutions to the problem of dual control and it appears probable that during Repelita III, unification of control under the Ministry of Education will take place.

Local Responsibilities

A long administrative chain separates the schools from the Ministry of Education. At the provincial level, the head of the provincial office, the *kepala kanwil*, is directly responsible to the Minister for educational matters in his province although on day-to-day matters he corresponds directly with senior officers of the department. He is responsible for secondary schools in the province.

Although central Ministry control is likely to be the dominant feature of the system for some time to come, signs of decentralisation can be seen. Provincial integrated planning units in Padang and Surabaya operated throughout the mid-1970s and have led the way towards the establishment of provincial planning units in several other areas of the country. At the same time, the establishment of research 'networks' in the regions, and the way in which the teacher education project is being managed, are healthy indications of the growing realisation that not everything should be managed from the centre.

Inspectorate

Professional supervision at primary level is carried out by an inspector *(penilik)* based at a district *(kecamatan)* office of education. He is responsible to the provincial office of education *(kanwil)*, through a branch office located in every regency *(kabupaten)*. At secondary level, inspectors are based on the provincial office but they do not have subject area responsibility. They are usually called *pengawas*.

Higher Administration

The Ministry of Education has direct control over 40 universities, institutes of teacher training colleges but no direct authority over 80 public academies and other post-secondary institutions. Through its coordinator for private higher education, the Ministry loosely administers 340 private institutions but many unregistered private institutions operate without any government supervision.

Universities and IKIPs are administered by a rector, assisted by deputy rectors, responsible for such matters as academic affairs, student affairs and administration. Academic affairs are controlled by a senate on which sit the deans of the faculties. Within faculties, subject departments are controlled by the head of department. All officers, from rector down, are

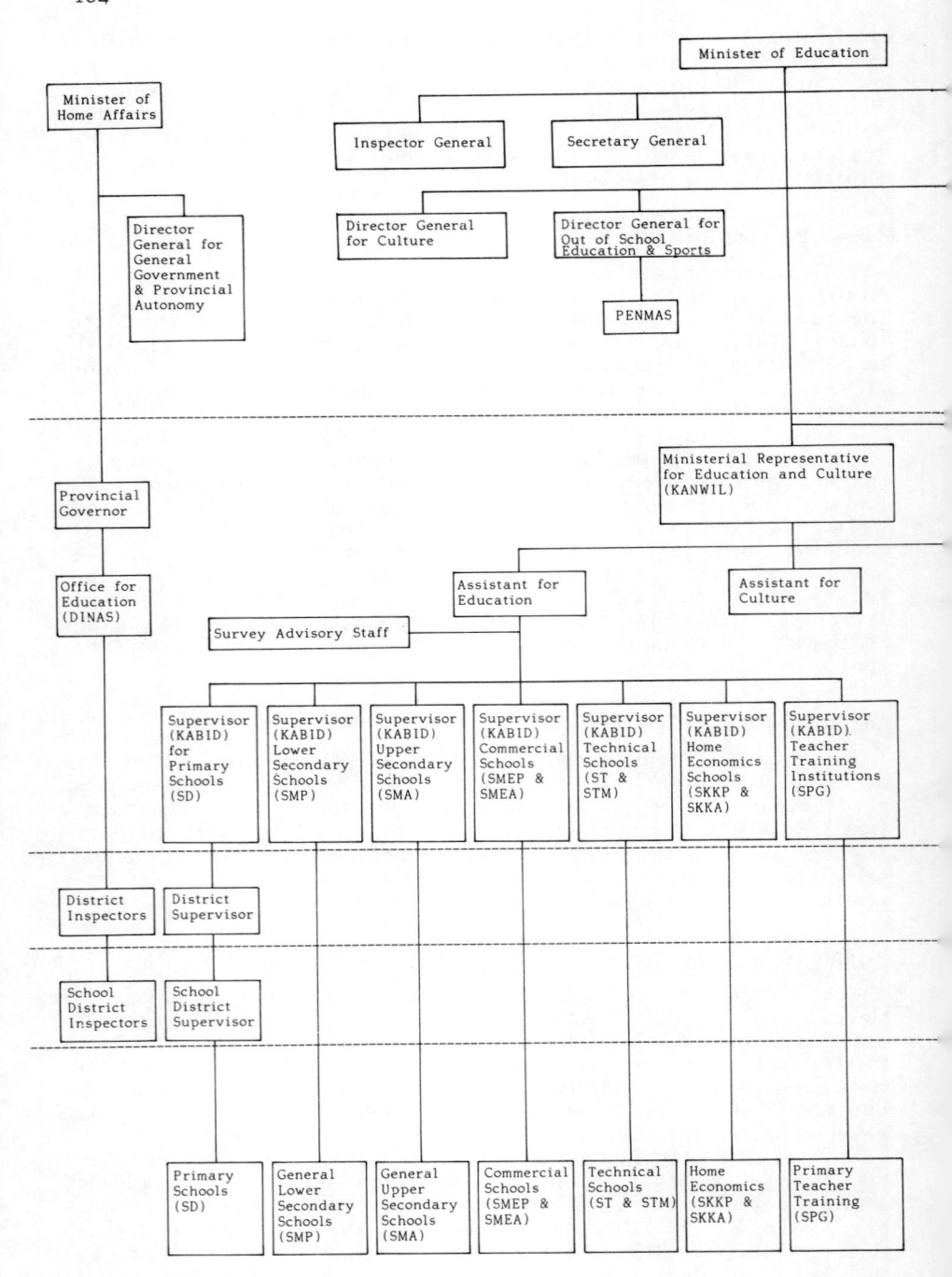

```
                                                                    ┌──────────────────┐
                                                                    │ Minister of Education │
                                                                    └──────────────────┘
┌──────────────┐              ┌──────────────────┐  ┌──────────────────┐
│ Minister of  │              │ Inspector General│  │ Secretary General│
│ Home Affairs │              └──────────────────┘  └──────────────────┘
└──────────────┘
                              ┌──────────────────┐  ┌──────────────────────┐
         ┌──────────────┐     │ Director General │  │ Director General for │
         │ Director     │     │ for Culture      │  │ Out of School        │
         │ General for  │     └──────────────────┘  │ Education & Sports   │
         │ General      │                           └──────────────────────┘
         │ Government   │                                    │
         │ & Provincial │                              ┌──────────┐
         │ Autonomy     │                              │  PENMAS  │
         └──────────────┘                              └──────────┘
```

```
                                                    ┌────────────────────────────┐
                                                    │ Ministerial Representative │
                                                    │ for Education and Culture  │
                                                    │ (KANWIL)                   │
┌──────────────┐                                    └────────────────────────────┘
│ Provincial   │
│ Governor     │
└──────────────┘
                            ┌────────────────┐      ┌────────────────┐
┌──────────────┐            │ Assistant for  │      │ Assistant for  │
│ Office for   │            │ Education      │      │ Culture        │
│ Education    │            └────────────────┘      └────────────────┘
│ (DINAS)      │    ┌──────────────────────┐
└──────────────┘    │ Survey Advisory Staff│
                    └──────────────────────┘
```

| Supervisor (KABID) for Primary Schools (SD) | Supervisor (KABID) Lower Secondary Schools (SMP) | Supervisor (KABID) Upper Secondary Schools (SMA) | Supervisor (KABID) Commercial Schools (SMEP & SMEA) | Supervisor (KABID) Technical Schools (ST & STM) | Supervisor (KABID) Home Economics Schools (SKKP & SKKA) | Supervisor (KABID) Teacher Training Institutions (SPG) |

```
┌──────────────┐  ┌──────────────┐
│ District     │  │ District     │
│ Inspectors   │  │ Supervisor   │
└──────────────┘  └──────────────┘

┌──────────────┐  ┌──────────────┐
│ School       │  │ School       │
│ District     │  │ District     │
│ Inspectors   │  │ Supervisor   │
└──────────────┘  └──────────────┘
```

| Primary Schools (SD) | General Lower Secondary Schools (SMP) | General Upper Secondary Schools (SMA) | Commercial Schools (SMEP & SMEA) | Technical Schools (ST & STM) | Home Economics (SKKP & SKKA) | Primary Teacher Training (SPG) |

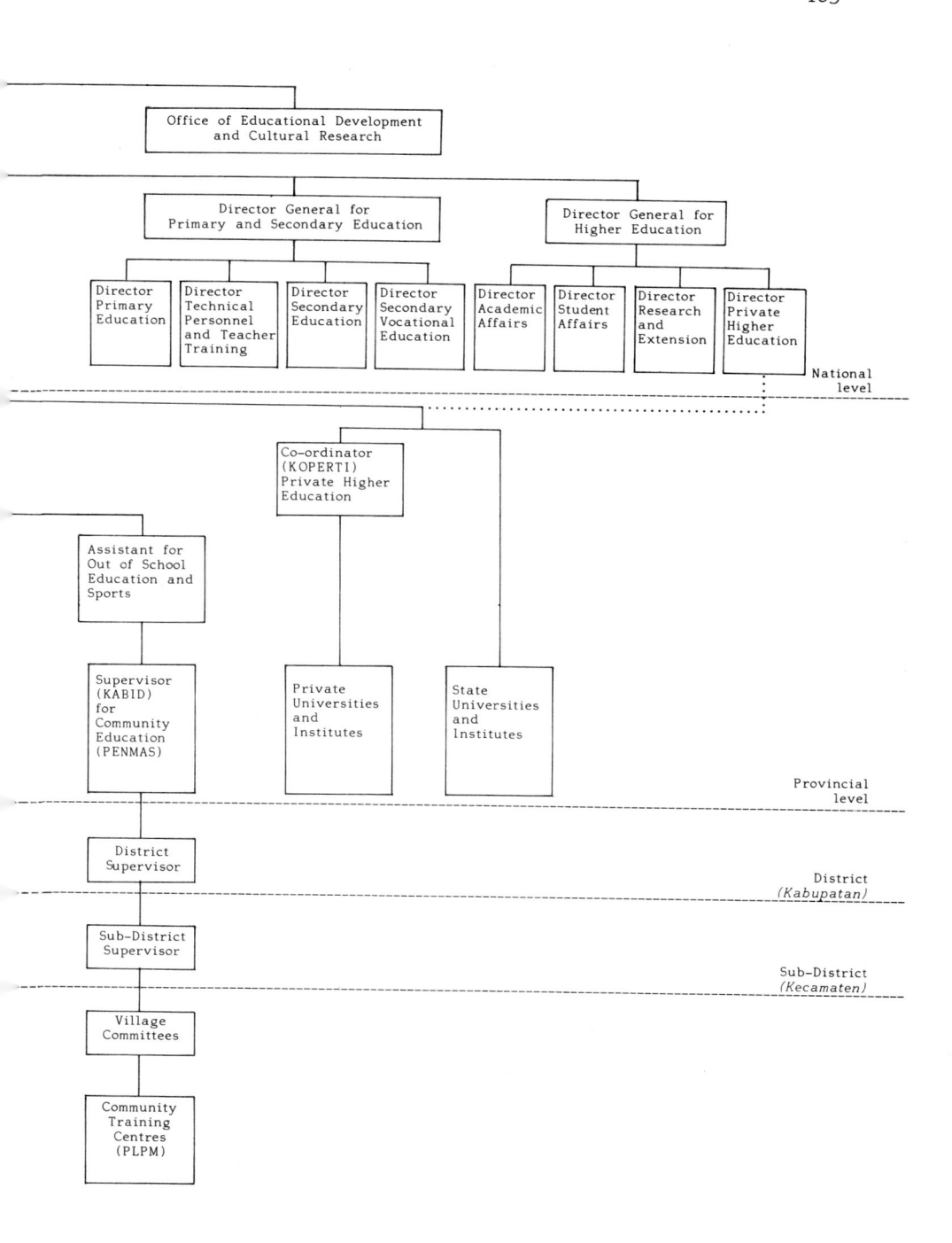

```
                        ┌─────────────────────────────┐
                        │ Office of Educational Development │
                        │    and Cultural Research    │
                        └─────────────────────────────┘
              ┌──────────────────┴──────────────────┐
    ┌─────────────────────┐              ┌─────────────────────┐
    │ Director General for│              │ Director General for│
    │ Primary and Secondary│              │  Higher Education   │
    │     Education       │              │                     │
    └─────────────────────┘              └─────────────────────┘
```

| Director Primary Education | Director Technical Personnel and Teacher Training | Director Secondary Education | Director Secondary Vocational Education | Director Academic Affairs | Director Student Affairs | Director Research and Extension | Director Private Higher Education |

National level

| Co-ordinator (KOPERTI) Private Higher Education |

| Assistant for Out of School Education and Sports |

| Supervisor (KABID) for Community Education (PENMAS) | Private Universities and Institutes | State Universities and Institutes |

Provincial level

| District Supervisor |

District (Kabupatan)

| Sub-District Supervisor |

Sub-District (Kecamaten)

| Village Committees |

| Community Training Centres (PLPM) |

elected for a fixed period, usually five years for rectors, and two years for deans. In the case of the rector, and sometimes deputy rectors, the appointment must be ratified by the Ministry of Education who may recommend if a candidate is not acceptable that the post be filled by nomination.

8 EDUCATIONAL FINANCE

Education Budget

The proportion of total (public and private) expenditure devoted to education has increased from about 2% of GNP in 1969 to about 3.5% in 1976/77. A distinction is usually made between 'routine' and 'development' budgets. These terms approximately correspond to the more usual recurrent and capital budgets, with the important qualification that experimental or innovative projects are financed from the development budget. A term frequently encountered is DIP *(Daftar Isian Proyek)* which is a proposed breakdown of a budget for a project. It becomes DUP *(Daftar Usulan Proyek)* when the project has been approved.

Allocation of Funds

Overall the proportion of central government funds allocated to the different levels of education for 1975 was as follows: 69% to primary, 21% to secondary and 10% to tertiary. However, these figures mask the corresponding development budget figures for central government which are approximately 5% to primary, 55% to secondary and 40% to tertiary. In the routine budget, expenditure on salaries is by far the largest element, around 90%, even at those levels of education where it might reasonably be expected that expenditure on materials and maintenance would be higher. In 1971, expenditure on personnel was 82% in secondary technical schools and 81% in higher education.

Per capita expenditure at various levels shows wide regional variations reflecting the relative financial strengths of provinces. As in most education systems, per capita expenditure in universities is many times greater than at primary level. In 1971, per capita costs for a university student were 50 times greater than for a pupil at a poor primary school. In 1976, recurrent costs for a student at a government university were Rp 66,000 per year while capital costs were Rp 1.78 million per place for science students and Rp 580,000 per place for students in other subject areas.

Sources of Funds

The system of financing education in Indonesia is extremely complex with respect to both the way in which funds are raised and used. There exist special subsidies and programmes, such as the INPRES (instruction-of-the-President) project where additional money is made available to certain sectors at the discretion of the President. In education, such money has been used especially for building new schools, but also for providing textbooks. These programmes, together with the existence of intermediate fiscal agencies make it almost impossible to give reasonable estimates as to the volume and composition of sources of educational finance and expenditure.

Approximately 0.8% of total educational expenditure is from private sources. The most important source of money is the central government: 11% of its budget was allocated to education expenditure in 1975/76. However, the share of education and training expenditure for all Ministries in the total central government budget has been slightly under 20% for the routine budget and almost 5% for the development budget. These figures are below the international average and indicate the importance of other sources of finance, especially the private sector. In 1975/76, only about 47% of government expenditure on education was channelled through the Ministry of Education and 53% through education programmes of other Ministries, in particular Home Affairs, which is responsible for the payment of primary teachers' salaries. At government schools, most routine expenditure is financed from the central government budget in the range 60-90%. The same pattern appears to apply to the development budget although it is difficult to determine the volume of provincial, local and private contributions.

Fees

Students' fees are another important source of finance for schools, until recently contributing not less than 10% to over 30% of their budgets. In 1971, a complex system of voluntary and compulsory fees was replaced by a single fee known as SPP. This is uniformly applied but varies according to level and branch of education, parental income, number of children and the location of the school. It is expressed as a percentage of the parents' income. However, in 1977 the SPP was abolished for the first three grades, and in 1978 throughout all six grades of the primary school. Nevertheless, education is not 'free' to parents of primary school children for they still contribute in other ways, for example through purchase of school uniforms and books, or to special funds established by schools. At secondary level, SPP is still payable and the supplementary costs may be considerably more than the fees. For example, in 1976 it was estimated that the school fee and entrance fee for a student was about Rp 11,000 at SMP level but the additional costs incurred by the parent might amount to another Rp 32,000 per annum. The corresponding figures for a student at SMA level were Rp 19,000 and Rp 67,000. Fees at government secondary schools are partly returned to the *kanwil* (35%) which uses 5% for supervision and 30% for redistribution to schools; and partly retained by the schools to improve the salaries of teaching staff and to pay for materials.

Private Institutions

Private institutions range from those which are wholly private *(swasta)*, through those which receive government financial support *(bantuan)* to those which receive both financial support and teachers paid for by the government *(subsidi)*. The latter have a considerable advantage over government schools as they can fix their own level of fees.

Overseas Aid

It is difficult to give a reasonable estimate of the amount of foreign aid to education partly because of the way in which agencies operating in the education sector classify their activities, and partly because of the periods over which finance is made available. In 1974, a crude estimate was that 5-6 billion rupiah was flowing in annually, but it is very much more than that now. All foreign aid in all sectors is coordinated by the State Economic Planning Board (BAPPENAS). Each year it publishes a list (the so-called 'Blue Book') of projects, both for capital and technical cooperation, for which Indonesia is seeking overseas financial support. Every project must be listed in this book before it has official government support and counterpart rupiah funding is released.

By far the largest donor is the World Bank, providing credits and loans on a massive scale. For the first three education projects, credits of US$4.6 million, US$ 6.3 million, US$13.5 million were made available; for projects 4 to 7, loans of US$37 million, US$19 million, US$15 million and US$49 million have been negotiated. A further US$85 million is presently being sought for the development of higher education. The Asian Development Bank has also provided substantial loans for the development of the institute of Technology, Surabaya, for Hasanuddin University, Ujung Pandang, and for secondary technical education. Other major donors include the UN family of agencies, especially UNESCO (although its operation has been scaled down since the UNDP financial crises in 1975/76), and UNICEF which concentrated on non-formal education during Repelita II. USAID has made available credits and loans for the development of educational media, a PhD training scheme and certain non-formal education projects. Other bilateral aid comes from Britain (chiefly technical cooperation training both overseas and in-country, English language teaching, technical education and books), the Netherlands (especially higher education), the Federal Republic of Germany (science equipment development), and Japan. Philanthropic and charitable organisations are also highly active, including Oxfam, and the Rockefeller and Ford Foundations. The latter has provided support for the National Assessment and technical expertise for educational research and provincial educational planning.

9 DEVELOPMENT AND PLANNING OF THE EDUCATION SYSTEM

Colonial Period

In common with other newly independent countries Indonesia inherited a system of education based on a colonial pattern and designed principally to serve the needs of the colonial power. Before the coming of the European colonial powers such formal education as existed was confined to the Koranic schools or *pesantren* which instructed children in the Islamic faith. With the coming of the Portuguese and Spanish, schools were opened which besides teaching religion – their aim being to obtain converts to Christianity – also taught reading and writing in Roman script and arithmetic.

From 1600-1800 when the Dutch East India Company controlled the country, schools were opened where the company had its 'factories' with the purpose of promoting Christianity and of training local employees for the company. Little change occurred when the Dutch government took over control in 1800, but in 1848 under the influence of more liberal ideas, schools for the native population were established offering a three-year course in the local vernacular, reading, writing and arithmetic. Under the Dutch a system of elite education was also developed based on the metropolitan pattern and using Dutch as the medium. This provided a full primary and secondary course which could lead on to university education but only for a tiny minority of the population. Linking schools were established to permit transfer from the vernacular school to the Dutch medium secondary school. The chief change brought about under the Japanese occupation was the replacement of Dutch by Indonesian as the medium of instruction.

Throughout this period the Chinese in the main attended Chinese medium schools which were privately established and maintained and designed to preserve the link with the Chinese mainland. For a small and select group of Chinese the Dutch government established the Dutch-Chinese school which followed a metropolitan pattern of education. Chinese schools were permitted to continue during the Japanese occupation and indeed increased in number.

Since Independence

With the Declaration of Independence on 17 August 1945 Indonesia had a largely illiterate population and only a handful of qualified personnel. When the unitary Republic of Indonesia came into being in 1950 Indonesia's new government embarked on a programme intended to provide education for all in a unified school system. Education was regarded as the right of all citizens and the government made heroic efforts to provide it, despite being hampered by shortage of funds, teachers, buildings and books in the national language, now officially the medium even at the tertiary level.

By 1972, the Ministry of Education was able to list the following among its achievements:

(i) abolition of State examinations

(ii) restoration of academic freedom in universities

(iii) establishment of academic standards for higher education

(iv) upgrading of teachers and university teachers

(v) replacement of teachers dismissed for subversive activities

(vi) rebuilding of schools and offices

(vii) establishment of proper budgeting procedures

(viii) reorganisation of the Department of Education and Culture

(ix) establishment of an Inspectorate General and of BPP (Research and Development Unit), now re-titled BP3K

(x) decentralisation of authority.

At independence the Chinese school system was strongly entrenched and it continued to look outside Indonesia. With the fall of the Kuo-Mintang government, the Chinese schools which had always had a strong political orientation were divided in their allegiance, some continuing to support the Kuo-Mintang, others looking to the new Chinese government. With the overthrow of the Sukarno government and the outlawing of the Indonesian Communist Party (PKI) the new military government ruled that all schools in Indonesia not expressly under the protection of a foreign diplomatic mission should use Indonesian as the medium of instruction and conform to the curriculum laid down by the Ministry of Education. This meant the end of the Chinese schools, all of which were compelled to conform to the new ruling.

Educational Planning

Planning on a national scale is conducted by the State economic planning board BAPPENAS. In the Ministry of Education, the planning function is divided between different sections of the Ministry, namely: the *Biro Perencanaan* (Planning Bureau) of the Secretariat-General; BP3K; and the *bagian perencanaan* (planning section) of the various Directorates-General. Under the decree establishing BPP (now BP3K) in 1969, one of its major responsibilities was to be the preparation of annual development plans and medium range five-year plans, albeit subject to the final authority of the Minister and BAPPENAS. However, the routine Ministry budget is controlled by the Secretary-General working with the Directorates-General. In 1974, the responsibility for preparation of the annual development budget was transferred to the Secretary-General, the long range planning function residing with BP3K.

Provincial Level

Pilot projects in provincial educational planning (PROPPIPDAs) were established in West Sumatra (Padang) and East Java (Malang) to help the provincial authorities with the planning and management of education, and to see how such a unit might become a permanent part of the government structure. Largely as a result of their activities, planning sections *(bagian perencanaan)* were created in 1975 in provincial offices of education *(kanwils)*. Their three major functions are: data collection and processing on educational institutions in the province; the programming of budgets; and the supervising of the implementation of projects (e.g. reviewing of tenders and progress of building).

National Assessment of Education (PPNP)

It was apparent that the piecemeal approach to educational planning which resulted in the first Repelita plan for education needed overhaul. During Repelita I, therefore, a National Assessment was set up to provide a better base for planning Repelita II. It was not expected to produce a plan, nor a survey nor recommendations. Rather, it was to be used to develop guidelines for educational decision making over a period of years. Its prime purpose was to assess the situation: to show where major policy decisions had to be made, to discuss alternative courses of action and arguments for and against each. It produced valuable information, brought people together to give them a wider perspective on their work and resulted in a report which has had considerable influence on educational planners.

Five-Year Plans

Repelita I (1969-1973)

This was seen as period of rehabilitation and stabilisation following the political upheavals in the mid-1960s. With an emphasis on economic development, it is not surprising that support for technical and vocational education was one of the clearest priorities in the education sector. Otherwise, everything was to go on much as before, except that there should be more and better education.

Repelita II (1974-1978)

Political goals for education for Repelitas II and III are based on the *Garis Besar Haluan Negara* (GBHN or Guidelines for State Development). Essentially these are:

(i) education should be based on the *Pancasila* or five Principles: belief in one God, Indonesian nationalism, humanitarianism, democracy, and social justice

(ii) education should contribute to economic development
(iii) education should be provided for all citizens both in and out of school
(iv) education should be the joint responsibility of parents, the community and the government.

From these essentially political goals, educators have derived their own goals in which four major themes can be discerned: educational opportunity, pursued through expansion of enrolments at primary and secondary level; improvement in quality through more and better books and equipment, and teacher training both pre- and in-service; increased relevance through curriculum development and expansion of vocational education; and greater effectiveness and efficiency through improvement of the structure and organisation of educational management.

Repelita III (1979-1983)

The same goals as in Replita II are emphasised but the programmes outlined are more coherent and logical. In summary, the major emphases are: greater attention to moral education through the *Pancasila*; increasing enrolments at all levels, especially primary where universal primary education is anticipated by 1983; more textbooks and teacher training greater involvement of the private sector; and increased participation by employers in vocational education. The total budget for education in Repelita III is 3.7 times greater than for Repelita II.

Research and Development

This function is based on the Ministry's Research and Development Unit, BP3K, with a Chairman who is directly responsible to the Ministry of Education. During the early and middle 1970s, BP3K was responsible for the National Assessment of Education, of which a summary work has been published. Follow-up surveys of achievement of children in grades 6 (end of SD), 9 (end of SMP), and 12 (end of SMA) have been carried out and reports on grades 6 and 9 have been published. Technical assistance for these surveys has been provided by New Zealand. Partly because of its necessary contacts with other sections of the Ministry and partly due to its function as a 'think-tank', BP3K has received considerable technical cooperation in recent years, especially from UNESCO, although there are signs that this is decreasing.

There are four main sections within BP3K, shown on the following chart.

MAIN SECTIONS WITHIN BP3K

```
                    ┌─────────────────┐
                    │    Chairman     │
                    │ Research & Development │
                    │   Unit (BP3K)   │
                    └─────────────────┘
                            │
    ┌───────────┬───────────┼───────────┬───────────┐
    │           │           │           │           │
                                    Secretariat ─ ─ ─ ─ ─ ─ ┐
                                                            │
Research    Curriculum   Data         Innovation      Task Force on
& Evaluation Development Collection,  - especially    Communication
(PUSLIT)    (PUSKUR)    Processing   NFE projects    Technology
                        and          (INNOTEK)       and Education
                        Statistics                   Media (TKPK)
                        (P2DSK)
```

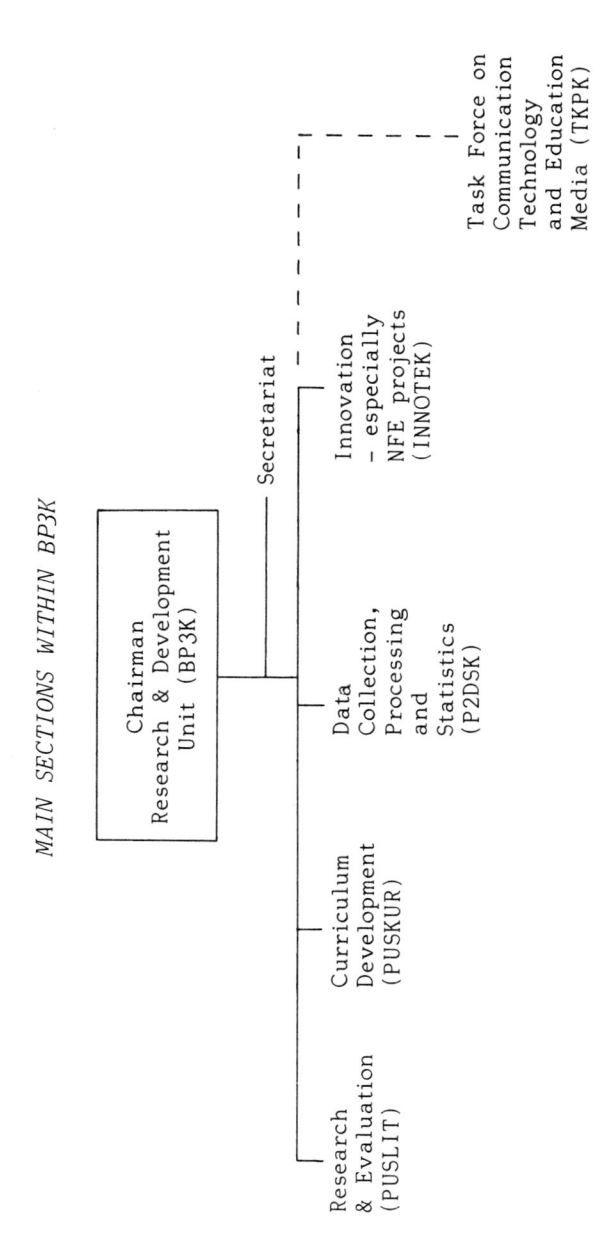

193

Research and Evaluation

The section is responsible for fundamental educational research, and for the evaluation of projects conducted by other parts of the Ministry of Education. A notable development is the establishment in Surabaya and Padang of research networks *(jaringan)* which make use of personnel in local education offices, IKIPs and universities. Ford Foundation has provided special support for this project.

Curriculum Development

The section was responsible for development of the '1975 curriculum' and for ideas concerned with teaching methods for its implementation. However, its main concern has been with eight development schools (PPSP) based on certain IKIPs, where modular instructional materials have been tested and revised. Approximately 25 pre-dissemination schools are now also using the materials. It is unclear what will be the future of the project during Repelita III. With so much of its resources devoted to the project, it has been impossible for the Curriculum Centre to provide much assistance to the writers who have been producing the primary and secondary textbooks in huge numbers for the ordinary schools.

Data Collection and Processing

Although the executive directorates-general of the Ministry are responsible for collecting statistical data on the system, it is BP3K's function to collate, analyse and publish the data. With the help of a small computer, school statistics are now being published remarkably promptly, although higher education statistics are less up-to-date.

Educational Innovation and Technology

This centre has been mainly involved with the Pamong and other non-formal education projects. However, it also has responsibility for miscellaneous other functions including career development of Ministry personnel.

ACRONYMS AND THEIR MEANING

BAPPENAS	State Economic Planning Board
BPG	In-service upgrading centre for teachers
BP3K	Office of Research & Development for Education and Culture
BUTSI	National Graduate Volunteer Corps
DIP	Project budget
DINAS	Office for education under provincial governor; (also means 'service')
DUP	Approved project budget
FKIT	Technical teacher training faculty of an IKIP
IKIP	Teacher training college for secondary teachers
IMTEC	Oslo-based educational consultants providing technical assistance for fifth education project
INPRES	Instruction-of-the-President
IPA	Science
IPB	Agricultural University, Bogor
IPS	Social studies
ITB	Institute of Technology, Bandung
ITS	Institute of Technology, Surabaya
KABID	Head of section
KANWIL	Provincial office of education
KKN	student work study progrmame
LAN	National Institute of Administration
LIPI	Indonesian Academy of Sciences
PALAPA	Satellite
PAMONG	Trial innovative programme for primary education using modular instructional materials, peer-group teaching, etc.

PANCASILA	National State Philosophy
PIMU	Directorate-General of Primary and Secondary Education
Penilik	Inspector or supervisor
PENMAS	Non-formal education, section of Ministry
PGSLP	Teacher training schools preparing junior secondary teachers (now being phased out)
PIU	Project implementation unit
PLPM	Community training centre
PMP	Moral education through the *Pancasila*
PPNP	National Assessment of Education
PPSP	Development school project
PROPPIPDA	Pilot project in provincial educational planning
P3D	Textbook and in-service teacher training programme
P3G	Pre-service teacher training programme
Repelita	Five Year Plan
RRI	Radio Republik Indonesia: radio broadcasting system in Indonesia
Sarjana	'Master's' degree
Sarjana Muda	'Bachelor's' degree
SD	Primary school
SEAMEO	South East Asian Ministers of Education Organisation
SGPLB	School for teachers of the handicapped
SKKA	Home economics senior secondary school
SKKP	Home economics junior secondary school
SLB	School for handicapped children
SLTA	Senior secondary school

SLTP	Junior secondary school
SMA	Academic senior secondary school
SMEA	Commercial senior secondary school
SMEP	Commercial junior secondary school
SMOA	Sports senior secondary school
SMP	Academic junior secondary school
SPG	School for primary teachers
SPP	School fees
ST	Junior secondary technical school
STM	Senior secondary technical school
STMP	Development senior secondary technical school
TEDC	Technician education development centre
TK	Kindergarten; pre-school
TKPK	Task Force for Educational Technology
TPK	Mobile teacher training team
TTC	Technical training centre
TTUC	Technical teacher upgrading centre
TVRI	National Television Broadcasting System

THE EDUCATION SYSTEM OF INDONESIA

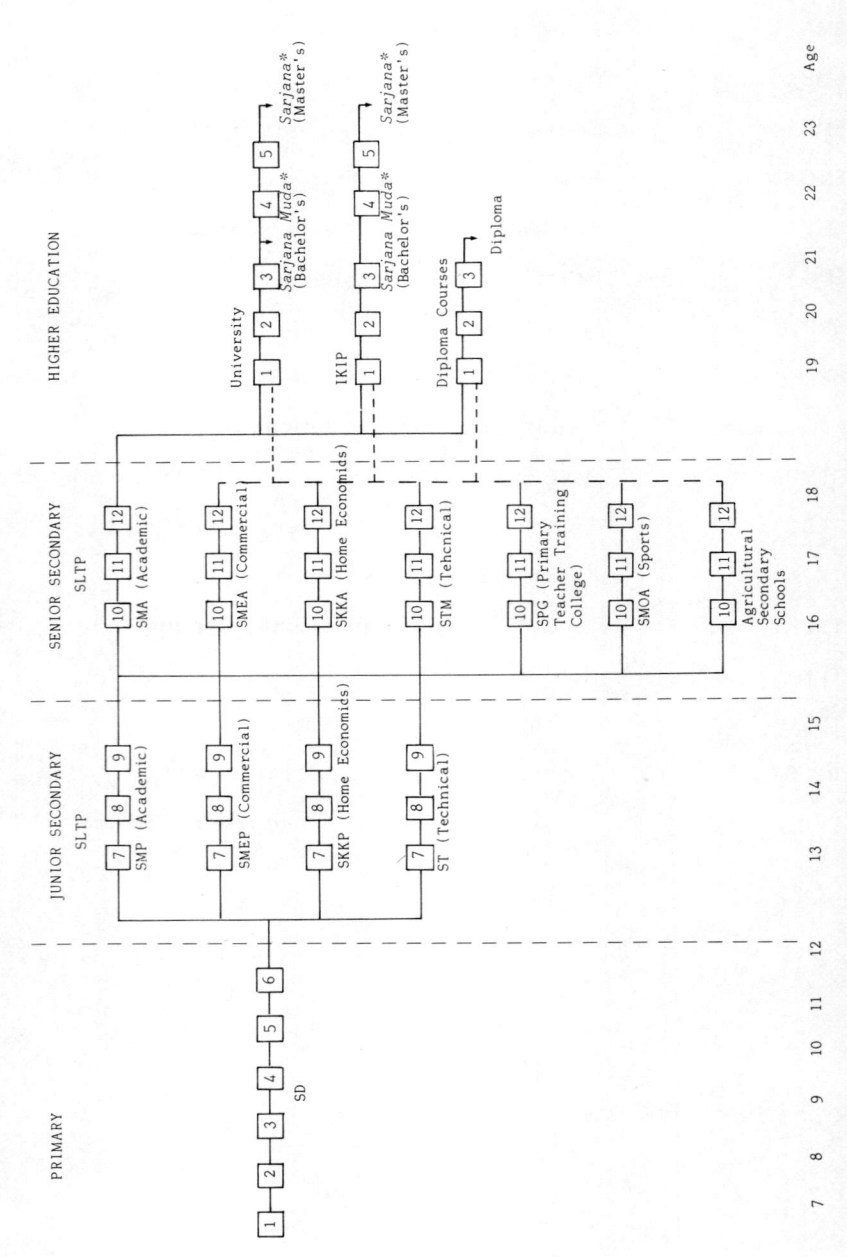

PRIMARY	JUNIOR SECONDARY SLTP	SENIOR SECONDARY SLTP	HIGHER EDUCATION

Primary: SD, grades 1–6

Junior Secondary (SLTP):
- SMP (Academic), grades 7–9
- SMEP (Commercial), grades 7–9
- SKKP (Home Economics), grades 7–9
- ST (Technical), grades 7–9

Senior Secondary (SLTP):
- SMA (Academic), grades 10–12
- SMEA (Commercial), grades 10–12
- SKKA (Home Economics), grades 10–12
- STM (Tehcnical), grades 10–12
- SPG (Primary Teacher Training College), grades 10–12
- SMOA (Sports), grades 10–12
- Agricultural Secondary Schools, grades 10–12

Higher Education:
- University: 1, 2, 3 Sarjana Muda* (Bachelor's), 4, 5 Sarjana* (Master's)
- IKIP: 1, 2, 3 Sarjana Muda* (Bachelor's), 4, 5 Sarjana* (Master's)
- Diploma Courses: 1, 2, 3 Diploma

Age: 7, 8, 9, 10, 11, 12, 13, 14, 15, 16, 17, 18, 19, 20, 21, 22, 23

*see text for discussion of recent changes

PYRAMID OF SCHOOL ENROLMENTS 1978

Total numbers of pupils per grade	Grade	Level
348,000	III	Senior High School } SLTA
418,000	II	
525,000	I	
739,000	III	Junior High School } SLTP
876,000	II	
1,059,000	I	
1,698,000	VI	Primary School } SD
2,225,000	V	
2,747,000	IV	
3,436,000	III	
3,923,000	II	
5,203,000	I	

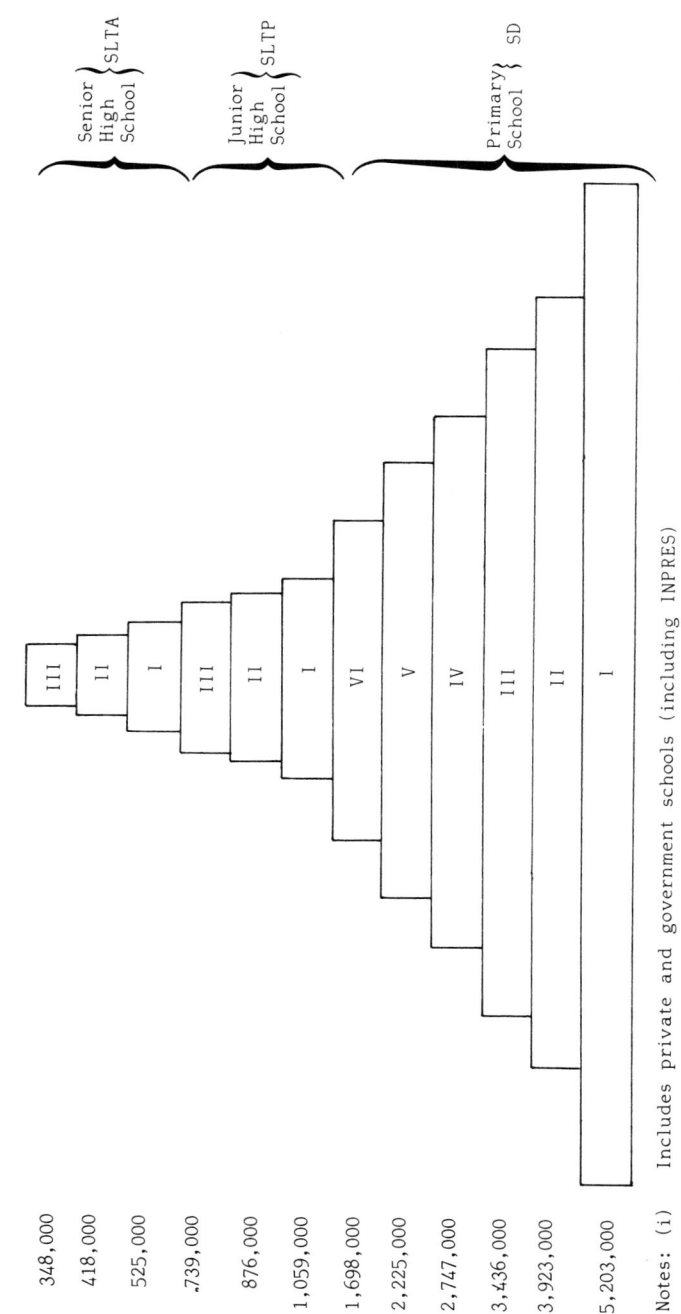

Notes: (i) Includes private and government schools (including INPRES)

(ii) Figures for higher education are not given due to the complexity of the system. The total figure for students in universities and IKIPs is approximately 173,000.

199

INDONESIA BASIC STATISTICS

Population	
1970	1979
119,467,000	148,470,000

Enrolment Ratios

Primary = enrolments as a percentage of the population aged 7–12
Secondary = enrolments as a percentage of the population aged 13–18
Higher = enrolments as a percentage of the population aged 20–24

	Primary	Secondary	Higher
1970	78%	16%	2.8%
1978	94%	22%	2.5%*

* = 1977

Enrolment Rates at Different Levels: 1979

	Institution*	1979
Percentage of age group enrolled	Primary (SD)	87.4%
	Junior Secondary (SLTP)	24.4%
	Senior Secondary (SLTA)	14.6%
	Tertiary	1.95%

*Figures for private and Islamic institutions are included.

Enrolments by Total Numbers, Numbers of Institutions and Numbers of Teachers for 1974 and 1978

Level and type of school	Total Enrolment 1974	Total Enrolment 1978	No. of Schools 1974	No. of Schools 1978	No. of Teachers 1974	No. of Teachers 1978
Pre-primary* *(Taman Kanak-kanak)*	N/A	674,292	N/A	14,840	N/A	27,223
Primary (SD)	13,469,650	19,232,872	68,903	92,246	N/A	592,539
Junior Secondary School (SLTP)	1,565,052	2,673,976	7,453	9,586	102,598	149,364
of which:						
General JSS (SMP)	1,232,317	2,270,803	5,519	7,728	72,698	119,999
Commercial JSS (SMEP)	108,184	166,702	769	712	10,819	10,569
Home Economics JSS (SKKP)	49,708	44,373	360	412	4,237	4,362
Technical JSS (ST)	174,843	192,098	775	734	14,824	14,434
Senior Secondary School (SLTA)	691,380	1,290,044	2,866	3,681	59,829	85,939
of which:						
General SSS (SMA)	300,903	603,757	1,178	1,579	25,194	36,812
Commercial SSS (SMEA)	145,647	210,586	622	702	11,240	13,914
Home Economics SSS (SKKA)	21,526	25,162	135	160	2,321	2,750
Technical SSS (STM)	146,876	238,208	468	611	12,867	18,457
Teacher Training (SPG)	76,428	201,577	463	585	7,747	12,962
Teacher Training for physical education (SGO)	N/A	10,754	N/A	44	N/A	1,044

*Figures for 1977

NB: Only seven of these schools are government

Student Flow Rates from one Level of the System to Another

	1979
From primary (SD) to junior secondary (SLTP)	58.2%
From junior secondary (SLTP) to senior secondary (SLTA)	87.1%
From senior secondary (SLTA) to tertiary	72.7%

Some Statistics from the Draft Repelita III Five Year Plan 1979–1984

Primary

By the end of the Plan period, there will be school facilities for 25.29 million elementary school children and 3.25 million children in *Madrasah Ibtidaiyah* schools. The Pamong system will cater for 400,000 new pupils and 200,000 dropouts from the system.

Buildings

New primary school buildings to be built (government schools): 89,430. New private primary school buildings to be built: 18,000 (half by government). Also a major replacement programme.

Teachers

125,000 *new* teachers will be required.
96,500 more teachers will be required to replace retiring/resigning ones.
400,000 teachers to be upgraded.

Textbooks and Equipment

255 million 'core' subject books to be produced.
18 million 'curriculum' books to be produced.
50 million readers to be produced.
100,000 sets of equipment to be produced for each of Bahasa Indonesia, mathematics, science, and social studies (175,000 for *Pendidikan Moral Pancasila*).

Community Education (Non-Formal)

Eradication of illiteracy	10 million
Primary school dropouts	4 million
Primary school leavers not continuing	1 million
Junior secondary school dropouts	750,000
Junior secondary school leavers not continuing	350,000
Senior secondary school dropouts	300,000
Senior secondary school leavers not continuing	1 million

Higher Education

Number of Institutions and Students Enrolled 1976

Type of institution	Number of institutions	Enrolment
Universities		
Public	27	109,000
Private	78	49,000
Institutes		
Public	3	12,000
Private	6	3,000
Teacher Training Colleges (IKIPs)		
Public	10	33,000
Private	24	7,000
Academies		
Public	59	11,000
Private	180	26,000
Other post-secondary		
Public	22	22,700
Private	50	12,000
Totals		
Public	121	187,700
Private	338	97,000
Total public & private	459	284,700

Post-Secondary Enrolments by Field of Specialisation 1976

	Public Institutions	Private Institutions	Total	% of Total
Basic Sciences	6,000	2,000	8,000	3
Social Sciences, Humanities	64,000	41,000	105,000	37
Health Sciences	14,000	4,000	18,000	6
Agro sciences	14,000	3,000	17,000	6
Economics*	27,000	22,000	49,000	17
Teacher education	33,000	7,000	40,000	14
Engineering, industry, mining	26,000	11,000	37,000	13
Others	4,000	7,000	11,000	4

* includes accounting and business adminstration

Central Government Expenditure on Education and Training, 1970/1971 and Budget for 1973/74 in Type of Expenditure and Department (Rps billion)

Ministries	Expenditure in 1970/71				Budget for 1973/74			
	Routine	%	Development	%	Routine	%	Development	%
Education & Culture	16.7	34	5.3	62	25.0	27	8.6	29
Religion	8.2	17	0.6	7	11.3	12	0.6	2
Defence	2.0	4	–	–	3.5	4	–	–
All others	1.1	2	2.6	31	4.0	4	4.6	16
Transfers*	21.0	43	–	–	49.6	53	15.8+	53
TOTALS	49.0	100	8.5	100	93.4	100	29.6	100

* Primary education subsidies from Ministry of Home Affairs to the Provinces

+ Extraordinary allocation for primary school buildings

Routine and Development Budgets for Ministry of Education and Culture
1969/70 to 1978/79
(Rps 000s)

	Routine Budget	Percentage of all Routine Government Expenditure on Education Spent by the Ministry of Education	Development Budget
1969/1970	13,459,003	–	5,213,000
1970/1971	16,700,893	–	5,320,000
1971/1972	20,904,615	–	6,120,000
1972/1973	27,758,476	–	7,919,703
1973/1974	32,122,855	–	9,705,000
1974/1975	61,533,142	75.6%	26,048,000
1975/1976	90,374,262	74.8%	50,544,000
1976/1977	95,022,164	70.5%	68,234,000
1977/1978	133,534,000	73.6%	90,487,000
1978/1979	166,819,000	71.6%	117,553,000

*Central Government Budgets for Education
by Level of Education
1973/74* (1976/77 in brackets)*

Level of Education	Routine Budget Rps billion	%	Development Budget Rps billion	%
Primary	49.6 (N/A)	71	16.3† (N/A)	68
Secondary	13.7 (38.3)	20	4.4 (34.2)	19
Higher	6.4 (17.6)	9	3.1 (14.3)	13
TOTALS	69.8	100	23.8	100

*Figures refer to Ministry of Education Schools only
† Including an extraordinary allocation of Rps. 15.8 billion.

*Annual Expenditure by Parent for Sending a Child
to Different types of Secondary School - 1976
(in Rupiah)*

Type of School	School Fee *Entrance Fee	Additional Expenses	Total
SMP	10,700	32,400	43,100
SMEP	5,400	32,400	37,800
ST	6,000	26,100	32,100
SMA	19,400	67,000	86,400
SMEA	21,700	50,200	71,900
STM	25,300	70,600	95,900
SKKA	29,400	90,800	120,200
SPG	14,000	58,100	72,100

*Includes: transport, books, uniform and shoes, examination fee, pocket money, equipment and handiwork.

Finance

% of Total Public Expenditure on Education, etc.

% GNP devoted to education (public expenditure only): 3.9% (1975)

% Total public expenditure devoted to education: 11.0% (1975)

Further Details of Public Institutions at Tertiary Level 1975

	University category*			Total
	A	B	C	
Universities (includes ITB, IPB, etc.)	5	9	15	29
Teachers' Colleges (IKIPs)	4	4	3	11
Enrolment	50,000	57,000	27,000	134,500
Staff (full time)	4,750	3,300	1,700	9,750
Staff with PhD	280	29	5	331
Graduates *(Sarjana)*	3,572	1,901	588	6,061
Research projects	760	270	155	1,185
Applicants for study	47,000	26,300	8,700	82,000
Accepted	9,300	10,700	6,000	26,000

*Category A universities are the most prestigious, category C the least.

Basic Social and Economic Data

Gross National Product per capita 1979: US$ 370

Average annual growth of GNP per capita 1960-79: 4.1%

Life expectancy 1979: 53 years

Proportion of the population employed in:

Agriculture
1960   75%
1979   59%

Industry
1960   8%
1979   12%

Services
1960   17%
1979   29%

Japan

CONTENTS

1 Geography 210
2 Population 212
3 Society and Culture 213
4 History and Politics 216
5 The Economy 220
6 The Education System 224
7 Educational Administration . . . 233
8 Educational Finance 240
9 Development and Planning of the
  Education System 243

Japan has had a faster rate of economic growth than any other large country in the world over the last twenty years. It has become in this period a major industrial and technological nation. Yet Japan has retained many elements of a traditional and cohesive social order in the midst of this rapid economic change. Her education system reflects both the pressures of industrial changes and the traditions of social conservatism.

Quantitively, Japan's education system matches her economic performance. Universal primary and lower secondary education has existed throughout the post-war period. But the proportions of the relevant age groups attending pre-school, upper secondary and higher education have increased rapidly in the 1960s and 1970s so that Japan by 1980 has higher proportional levels of enrolment at each level than any other non-communist industrial countries except France and Belgium (pre-school education) and the USA and Sweden (higher education).

This growth of provision has reflected pressure of demand in a competitive industrial society. The demand has not been completely satisfied and where it has, elite and prestigious institutions have emerged above the others at each level. The educational structure is punctuated by severe competitive hurdles which regulate entry, especially to the most desirable higher educational institutions but also to high status schools at secondary level. The pressures on children and parents are often considerable.

Yet the internal arrangements of Japanese schools are diversified and flexible. American type curriculum and assessment arrangements prevail which encourages students to continue their courses and to choose between a range of options. This is as much a response to the character of the Japanese economy as to the American attempts to reorganise Japanese education during the occupation after 1945. There is still a high degree of centralised control over educational provision, despite American moves to decentralise the system after 1945, and a high degree of central direction over the school curriculum.

The traditional elements of Japanese society are also reflected in the education system. Moral and social education have key roles in the curriculum in an attempt to preserve the cohesion (and traditional hierarchical and authoritarian character) of Japanese society at times of rapid economic change. Some of these traditional practices, however, are not easily reconcilable with the otherwise open nature of Japanese society. Girls and women have markedly lower rates of participation especially at the higher levels of education than is common in other industrial countries. The curriculum of schools - and of the Junior Colleges which higher proportions of women attend rather than the more prestigious universities - still emphasise subjects such as home-making and home economics which are consistent with a traditional role for women.

1 GEOGRAPHY

Topography

Japan, 'Nihon' in Japanese, which means 'the origin of the sun', comprises four large islands and more than 2,000 smaller ones, which lie in an arc off the east coast of Asia. Japan's distinctiveness from its continental neighbours is comparable to Britain's with the difference that the closest point to Japan on the Asian continent - the south coast of Korea - lies across more than 100 miles of stormy sea. The land area, 377,619 sq km (145,799 sq miles), is $1\frac{1}{2}$ times that of the United Kingdom. However, nearly 70% of the country is made up of precipitous mountains, whose economic exploitation is restricted to forestry, mining and hydroelectric power. The great bulk of the population live and work in the one-fifth of the country which is level. This consists of one large plain - the Kanto plain around Tokyo - and many small floodplains near the sea, as well as narrow river valleys and a few basins in the mountains. These parts of the country are exploited very intensively indeed. Agriculture shares the flat land with industry, which is concentrated with particular density along the Pacific coast. The coastal strip between Tokyo and Nagoya is almost entirely built up, and forms virtually a single strip city. Japan lies in an area of earthquakes and volcanoes, many of which are still active, and the country is dotted with natural hot springs.

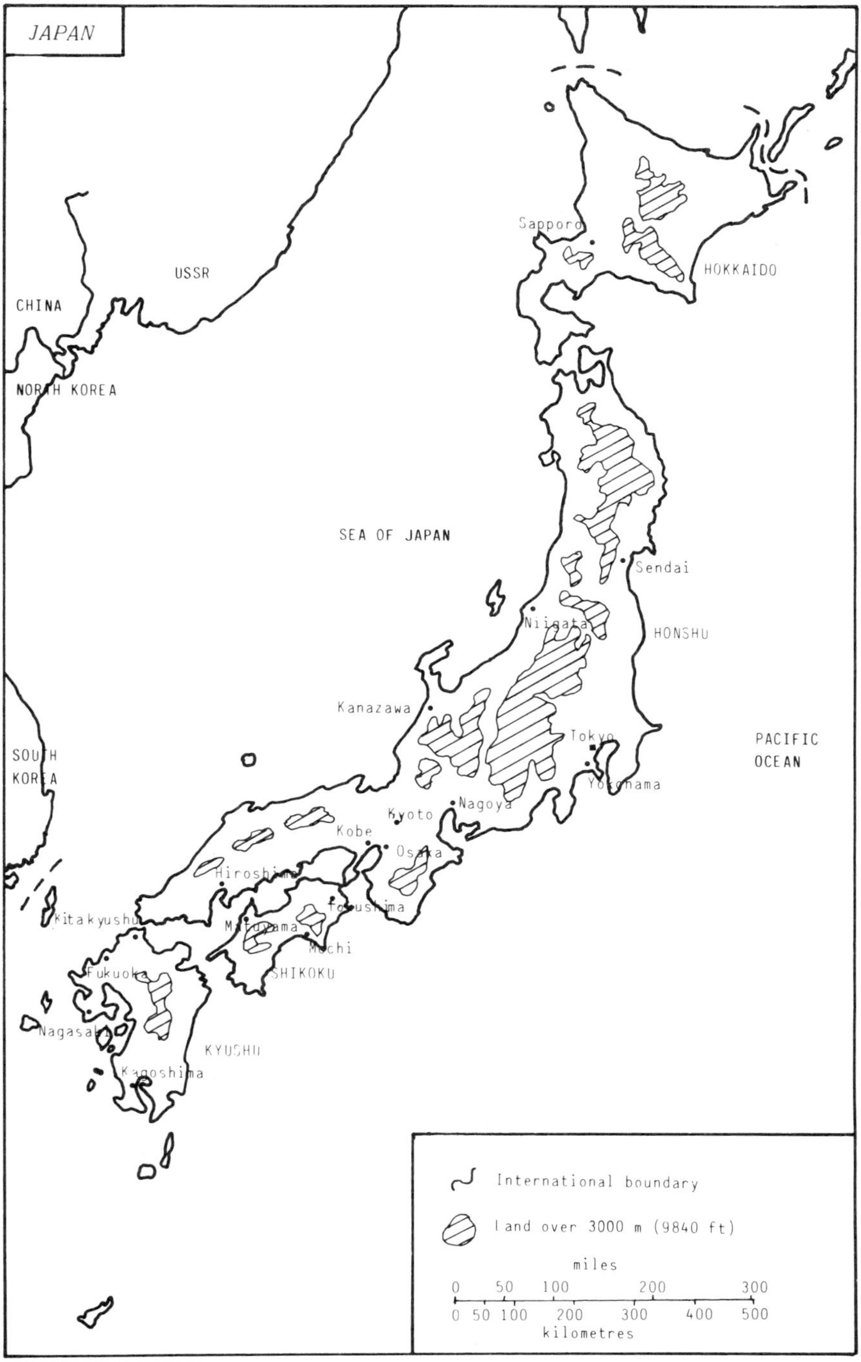
JAPAN
USSR
CHINA
NORTH KOREA
SOUTH KOREA
SEA OF JAPAN
Sapporo
HOKKAIDO
Sendai
Niigata
HONSHU
Kanazawa
Tokyo
Yokohama
PACIFIC OCEAN
Nagoya
Kyoto
Kobe
Osaka
Hiroshima
Tokushima
Kitakyushu
Matuyama
Kochi
SHIKOKU
Fukuoka
Nagasaki
KYUSHU
Kagoshima
International boundary
land over 3000 m (9840 ft)
miles
0 50 100 200 300
0 50 100 200 300 400 500
kilometres

Climate

Japan stretches from 43°N to about 28°N and consequently there are wide variations in temperature between the extremities of the country. The seasons are very clearly distinct one from the other and both summer and winter are more extreme than is normal in temperate zones. Spring is followed by a rainy season of about one month after which the fiercely hot, humid and wet summer sets in. Autumn stretches from September almost to December, and is dry and mild. Late summer and early autumn are frequently disrupted by typhoons which are strongest in the south and usually blow themselves out before they reach Tokyo. The summer wind is from the south-east but in winter it veers to the north-west and brings snow from Siberia which on the Pacific side of the country is lighter. Winters are not very severe, except in Hokkaido and on the Japan Sea coast and, like the autumn, the winter is generally dry and clear.

Communications

The impassability of the mountains, the shortness of the rivers and the division of the country into islands meant that, until recently, internal communication was fraught with difficulty. However, due to political centralisation followed by industrialisation during the twentieth century, internal communications are now excellent. A complex and efficient railway network stretches across the country and the metropolis and big cities are served by commuter railways. The *shinkansen* or bullet trains travel to many of the major cities, sometimes at speeds of over 100 m.p.h. Fast 'linear motor trains' are currently being developed and multi-lane highways are spreading rapidly to most areas. The water breaks between the main islands are being overcome by giant bridges and tunnels. These already connect Kyushu with Honshu, a tunnel to Hokkaido is being built, and bridges are being started across the inland sea to Shikoku. Planes are also widely used for internal and international transport.

2 POPULATION

Growth

The population of Japan was 115.9 million in 1979. This is more than twice the population of the biggest European countries, and the seventh largest in the world, just below Indonesia and Brazil. Economic growth in the seventeenth century allowed the population to soar to between 25 and 30 million. It then stablised, allowing an increase in living standards, and has since risen steadily. In recent years the growth rate has been about 1% per annum. It is thought likely that the population will stabilise at about 135 million in the year 2000. In 1977, taking into account all educational institutions from kindergarten to university, the student population of the country was 26,187,386.

Distribution

Per square mile of land, Japan's population density is 705 which, although very high, is not as high as Belgium or Holland. However, if only the habitable area of Japan is taken into account the population density rises to 4,922 per square mile, which is among the highest in the world. With a population of more than 15 million the Kano plain area in which Tokyo and Yokohama are situated probably contains the second biggest agglomeration of people in the world after New York. The Kansai region, which constitutes the second great centre, has over 12 million people. About three million live in Osaka, while the port city of Kobe and the old capital, Kyoto each have about 1.5 million. four other cities have populations greater than one million. In all, nearly 60% of the population is concentrated in the Kanto and Kansai regions and the Aichi region, which contains Nagoya and is located between the two. With the industrialisation of Japan there has been a depletion in the population of the countrywide. Migration to the cities has been in progress for about 100 years. Between 1955 and 1975 the agricultural population decreased from 27 million to 23 million, despite a 12.7% increase in total population.

Minority Groups

Despite differences of climate and dialect between the northern and southern extremities of the country, the Japanese are a strikingly homogeneous and unified people. The European visitor soon notes the paucity of foreigners, whether from Western or from other Asian countries, in their midst. There are a few thousand Chinese and Westerners resident in Japan but the only significant foreign minority are the Koreans, of whom there are about 600,000. The other minority that should be mentioned is the group of 'Japanese untouchables', or *Burakumin* (hamlet-people) as they are known nowadays. Before the Meiji Restoration they were the people engaged in butchery, leather-work and other trades involving dead animals which were stigmatised by Buddhism. Emancipated in the Meiji period, the *Burakumin*, who may constitute 2% of the population are now legally equal with other Japanese, but prejudice against them still exists, and non-*Burakumin* families are generally unwilling to accept marriage ties with them.

3 SOCIETY AND CULTURE

Social Development

The similarities between modern Japan and the advanced countries of the West are much more striking than the differences. The rural population is small; the urban population is large. Education standards are very high and literacy is universal; car ownership is widespread, as is possession of household durables such as colour television sets, refrigerators, washing machines. The differences, however, though largely invisible are very great and originate deep within the structure of society. To appreciate this it is necessary to take a brief look at the nature of Japanese society before the rapid economic and technological changes of the past century.

Throughout the Edo Period (1603-1868) Japanese society was rigidly divided into four classes. At the top of the warrior class were the Samurai. Next in status, though not in wealth, came the farmers, the bulk of the population, who occupied this position because the Samurai depended on their rice. Below the farmers were the craftsmen and below the craftsmen, at the bottom, the merchants. Not only the occupations but also the style and standard of living of each of these classes were quite different. This society has been described as 'one of the most restrictive and carefully enforced hereditary systems that the world has ever seen'. Within each class, the government exerted further control over people's lives by means of a system of responsibilities, through which any group might be punished for the misdeeds of one of the members. Along with the centralisation of government authority, the breaking up of the class system was one of the most important actions of the polticians behind the Meiji Restoration of the Emperor in 1868. The imported Western education system replaced the old hereditary system almost overnight; from this time onwards, function and place in society came to be decided by formal educational achievement. The class system disappeared and there is little of it to be found in modern Japan. But the system of hierarchical authority and orientation towards groups remain very strong to this day.

The Present

Hierarchies and Groups

Japan has been described as a 'vertical society', in contrast to 'horizontal societies' as typified by America. The family, the school, the company and also the myriad organisations and groups to which Japanese devote their leisure time are arranged in a tight hierarchical manner. Where a rigid structure is absent, for example in the egalitarian mass membership of agricultural cooperatives, a scrupulous respect for age distinctions remains. Vertical ties are further reinforced by the Japanese language; by choosing the correct level of respect language, the nature of one's relationship to the person addressed is confirmed. The use of status appellations is extensive, even within the family, and the Japanese bow comes in a variety of angles, depending on the degree of respect that is due. Nonetheless the strictness of formal hierarchies in Japan does not mean that authority within the hierarchy is harshly or autocratically applied, and a search for consensus is the general practice.

Women

Historically and by Western standards, women have been oppressed members of Japanese society. Although there has been educational provision for women since early times, this was often directed more towards preparing girls for early marriage and a confined married life than to enabling them to take jobs. Since the end of World War Two the role of women has changed markedly, though equality of the sexes is still less emphasised than in Western countries. Formally arranged marriages are still quite common but well educated or well travelled young women often reject their mothers' attempts to pair them off. Most working women still do comparatively menial jobs outside the career structures of their companies, receiving relatively low wages and with no chances of promotion: the average wage for women was still less than half that for men in 1971. However, career women are not at all uncommon, especially in teaching, the mass media and the arts, where career structures are not weighted against them, and there were six women members of the lower house of the Diet (Parliament) in 1977.

Religion

The two major religions of Japan are Shinto and Buddhism. Shinto is the ancient and animistic natural religion which has no particular ethical standpoint. Mahayana Buddhism arrived in Japan from China in the seventh century and flourished greatly, generally coexisting easily with Shinto. However, during the seventeenth century its importance began to wane, and it has become even less significant in the last hundred years. The proportion of the people to whom either religion has much spiritual significance is now probably rather small. In fact, Japan's tendency to secularism started at least 300 years ago. Since then, a greater influence has been exerted on the ethics of the people by Confucianism than by any religion. The teaching of Confucianism has not been studied in school for more than a hundred years, but its precepts of loyalty towards the ruler, filial piety and obedience to a strict social code are deeply ingrained in Japanese behaviour. The most recent religious phenomenon in Japan is the prodigous growth of literally hundreds of eclectic 'new religions' that has occurred since the end of World War Two. Since 1947 the teaching of religion in government administered schools has been forbidden by law.

Christians in Japan are relatively few in number - about 800,000 - but often holding good positions, they exert a disproportionate effect on society. Japanese interest in Christianity is part of the continuing nationwide fascination with things western, but it has not persuaded many to abandon their now traditional nonchalance concerning the invisible world. Christianity played a major pioneering role in secondary and girls' education in the Meiji Period, and a large percentage of private secondary schools, women's universities and some other private universities are of Christian foundation. Christians also led in the development of social work for the underprivileged and people with disabilities, and in the foundation of the Socialist Party.

Language

Japanese is said to have some distant connection with Korean and Mongolian but is probably unrelated to any other language in the world. A prerequisite for success would seem to be fluency in a foreign language. Thus the Japanese throw great energy and considerable sums of money into their study of foreign languages, especially English. Almost all students study English for six years in secondary school, and many continue these studies at university. In Tokyo, conversation schools flourish in great numbers and gruelling English immersion courses attract hordes of students. Some companies make employees take regular English classes during working hours and many more are encouraged to attend English classes in their own time. The net result is that the Japanese speak English no better than the English speak French. A number of observers have concluded that it is a problem of will. Whatever the truth of this, the grammar and examination orientation of English teaching in schools and the students' lack of contact with foreigners, are sufficient to explain much of the problem.

Modern Culture

Modern Japanese culture exhibits both traditional and modern elements but is in fact quite distinct from both it native and its western roots. The original homogeneity of the people has created a monolithic mass culture which is disseminated by the efficient and all-pervading mass media to every corner of the country. American-style TV participation shows and western-derived pop music command very large television audiences. Western classical music is no more foreign inJapan than Beethoven is in Britain. Meanwhile, in virtual isolation from all this, the old arts and crafts for which Japan is famous continue to prosper quietly. Noh theatres, for example, have increased in number since the last war; the Kabuki theatres draw capacity houses; and pottery, calligraphy, flower arranging and the other crafts are still attracting large numbers of people to their ranks.

4 HISTORY AND POLITICS

Origins

The symbol of the modern Japanese State is Emperor Hirohito, who has been on the throne since 1926. He has no power; indeed no emperor has had any real power for well over 1,000 years, but the uninterrupted rule of his family has provided a solid basis of tradition and continuity. Whatever the actual origins of the imperial line, it was firmly established by the sixth century AD. And by this date too, the self-identity of the Japanese was fixed. Most had arrived from north east Asia reaching the archipelago by way of the Korean peninsula. Some probably came from South China by the same route. But by the eight century AD immigration had effectively ceased, never again to resume.

Chinese Influence and After

By the sixth century Japanese military ambition had created a bridgehead on the tip of the Korean peninsula, and the cultural influence of China began to flow into Japan. One borrowing of special importance was the Chinese concept of civilisation as centering around a political, rather than a religious, authority. This tendency distinguished Japan and China from the Buddhist states of South East Asia. Japan developed rapidly along Chinese lines until about the tenth century. Then as this influence began to wane a synthesis of native and foreign elements produced eventually, in art, craft and literature a culture which was both developed and distinct. By the twelfth century the centralised structure of government borrowed from China had begun to break up. Vigilante bands of Samurai warriors sprang up all over the country, many led by cadet branches of the imperial family. The leader of one of the bands, Yoritomo Minamoto, set up his capital at Kamakura and named himself *shogun* or generalissimo. He and his successors managed to exert authority nationally through knights loyal to them who were sprinkled thinly throughout the country. This system never worked properly, and chaotic civil warfare broke out in 1467 and continued for a century. The emperors, impoverished and half-forgotten, continue the traditions of court life in Kyoto.

The first Europeans to reach Japan were the Portuguese who arrived in the 1540s. They introduced Catholicism and firearms into the country, and the latter speeded the process of national reunification under three successive military leaders. There followed more than 200 years of peace. Japanese culture developed untroubled by the political, industrial and scientific developments which occupied the world outside. The economy prospered, education advanced and the arts flourished, catering especially for the growing merchant class.

Japan's Modern Century

The increasing naval might of the western powers finally obliged Japan to open its harbours, first in 1853. The ruling shogun was compelled to sign the unequal treaties which the representatives of the western powers presented to him. Their admission to the country as highly unpopular and the power of the shogun began to founder as more and more of his tributary lords rallied to the slogan 'restore the emperor and expel the barbarian'. In 1868, after nearly 15 years of political confusion and a brief war, the shogunate fell, and the emperor was restored to his former glory - though he was quite as impotent as most of his ancestors had been before him. The country's real leaders, who were mostly lower ranking Samurai, began the transformation of Japan into a modern state. The first essential was to learn from the enemy, and with diligence and thoroughness the Japanese began to learn and to borrow from the West. The navy was modelled on the then pre-eminent British navy and the constitution on the highly authoritarian version of Germany; the favoured education system was the French and agriculture benefited from the example of the USA.

Among the countries threatened by the economic and military power of the West in the last century, Japan's response was uniquely fast, appropriate and successful. Politically, economically and militarily the country developed at a great speed. By annexing Taiwan, Korea and Manchuria in the 1890s and 1900s a start was made on the building of an empire. But an alliance was signed with Britain in 1902; in 1921 agreement was reached with the US and Britain on limiting the size of each country's navy, and in 1924 Japan reduced the size of its army. To all appearances, the country seemed set on a course of purely mercantile expansion. However, Japan did not escape the effects of the worldwide slump of the late 1920s and suffered from competition with the colonial powers who had access to unlimited and very cheap raw materials. A changed national and political mood occurred, leading in 1931 to the invasion of Manchuria by the Japanese army. After this turning point, the power of parliament began to decline as the power of the military rose, and Japanese power on the Asian continent increased until in 1937 war broke out between the Japanese and the Chinese government of Chiang Kai Shek. In 1940 the US, in an attempt to stifle the Japanese war effort in China, announced a ban on shipments of oil. The government decided to fuel its military effort with the oil of Indonesia but to be sure of seizing this it had first to put the US navy out of action. Thus occurred the famous bombing attack on Pearl Harbour and the simultaneous declaration of war on the US, and five years later, the total submission of Japan to American atomic bombs.

Japan was then occupied by US troops and for six years was governed by the Allied Command under the supreme authority of General MacArthur. In 1951, Japan and the United States signed the San Francisco Peace Treaty, and a security treaty which permited the retention of US military bases in Japan. The occupation forces were withdrawn in March 1952. In 1972 Okinawa (which had been retained by the US) was returned to Japan. In the intervening period, the country developed dramatically, especially in the economy. Almost as striking as the growth of the economy was the leap in education levels. Japan is now one of the world's leading democracies, with a poltical and social stability which many would envy.

Government and Politics

The Allied Command introduced a number of reforms. A new Constitution, which defined the Emperor as no more than a 'symbol of national unity' and stated that war was to be forsworn by Japan forever, was written and accepted by the Japanese administration through which the Allied Command exercised its power. The Constitution also extended the franchise to women, and replaced the House of Peers with an elected House of Councillors. A long list of popular rights was written into the Constitution, the judicial system was made as independent of the executive as possible and a radical reform of the land took place, by which agricultural land was handed over to the tenants who worked on it.

Japan's legislative body, the Diet, has two chambers: a House of Representatives of 511 members, and a House of Councillors of 252 members. The former, the Lower House, controls the budget and approves treaties with foreign powers. The political parties were revived in 1945. During the 1950s the leftist vote began to rise and two parties joined to form the Liberal-Democratic Party. In 1979 there were 248 Liberal-Democrats and 244 opposition members in the House of Representatives: the opposition was divided between seven parties, the largest being the Japan Socialist Party with 116 members. The Liberal-Democratic Party, which has been governing continuously for nearly 30 years, is generally conservative in its policies and is comparable in some respects to the British Conservative Party. It lacks a popular membership of any great size; instead, many politicians have large personal followings. The party itself is split into several factions. The faction is the basic unit of power within the party, and it is between opposing factions, voting in block, that the party leadership, and hence the premiership, is decided. According to rules adopted in 1971, the Premier can lead the party for a maximum of six years. The Liberal-Democratic Party receives large financial contributions from big business. And the government takes important decisions only after close consultation with the leaders of business.

Regional Government

The country is divided into 46 prefectures, and further subdivided into 3,256 municipalities, comprising 645 cities, 1,985 towns and 626 villages. The category 'city' indicates a town with population greater than 50,000 while the category 'village' may include several village-like hamlets. Each prefecture has its governor, elected by the local voters. Each prefecture, city, town and village also has an assembly of representatives elected by the same franchise as in national elections. The occupation authorities gave local governments greatly increased powers, and they were responsible for the post of prefectural governor being made elective, as the post of municipal mayor had long been. Local government appears to retain considerable autonomy in present-day Japan, but it is in fact very much subject to the influence of the central authorities. Local legislation is often based on models supplied by Tokyo, while governors and mayors maintain offices in the capital and spend a lot of time in Tokyo negotiating with central government.

International Relations

The treaties of 1952 determined Japan's status as an ally of the world's industrialised capitalist nations. Since 1956 Japan has been a member of the United Nations, and since 1964 of the OECD. During the 1970s it has commonly taken part in summit conferences of leading nations, the latest of which was held in Tokyo in July 1979. However, its active role in international relations has been small in relation to its global importance as a trading nation. Throughout the post-war period, economic advancement was given the top priority in Japan's foreign relations. Increasing strains between Japan and its trading partners became apparent; other Asian countries became resentful of the Japanese exploitation of local resources, which industrial nations complained about dumping and of the tight control of imports into Japan. Aware of the realities, the government has taken certain steps. In 1972 the Japan Foundation, a cultural organisation modelled on, and with functions comparable to, the British Council, was established. And official development aid, the 1977 level of which was third in the world, below the US and France, is expected to double by 1980. The United Nations University, largely funded by Japanese money, was invited to set up its headquarters in Tokyo.

Many Japanese, including a majority of the parliamentary opposition, were opposed to alignment with the US and continued involvement with its defence policies after World War Two, and the controversy over whether Japan should remain aligned or become neutral raged throughout the 1950s and 1960s. The Vietnamese War and America's continued occupation of Okinawa were issues which brought resentment of this alliance into sharper focus. However, the end of the war in Vietnam, the return of Okinawa in 1972, and President Nixon's advances towards China in the previous year, weakened the controversy.

New interpretations given in textbooks approved by the Ministry of Education for use from 1982 of Japan's war record have produced considerable hostility from countries that experienced Japanese occupation.

5 THE ECONOMY

The Pattern of the Economy

In 1868, the year of the Meiji Restoration, Japan's population was largely rural and its economy largely agricultural. During the intervening century industrialisation was both rapid and thorough. At the end of World War Two the Japanese economy was in chaos and at first recovered only slowly. However, a great national effort, aided in the early stages by American money, effected a complete recovery by the mid-1950s when pre-war per capita production levels were attained. By the end of the decade the economy was growing at around 10% per annum. It is still growing though at a much slower rate.

Government and industry are very close allies in Japan. Through the Ministry of International Trade and Industry (MITI) the government sets goals for specific industries, supervises the acquisition of foreign technology, encourages competition between rival companies, and in other ways gives direction to much of Japan's economic growth. Another government body, the Economic Planning Agency (EPA) has the task of formulating braod economic objectives and forecasts. The various sectors of large scale business and industry are organised into associations and these are brought together under the *Keidanran* (the Federation of Economic Organisation) which provides business with a unified voice in its discussions with the government.

The bulk of Japanese industry consists of very large public corporations. Their export drives are managed by independent 'general trading companies'.

Natural Resources

Japan has a great deal of rainfall, and water is the only natural resource the country possesses in really large quantities. The most important resource for industry is petroleum, 99.8% of which is imported, mostly from the Middle East. Japan's only energy-producing resource is its rivers but hydroelectric power accounts for only about 5% of the nation's energy requirements. Japan is not richly endowed with minerals. About one-third of its coal requirement is produced domestically, and in the past it was an exporter of copper, though now five sixths of its requirements are imported. It is the world's greatest importer of oil, coal, iron ore, cotton, wool, lumber and many other commodities. The sea surrounding the country is a great economic asset; Japan is the leading fishing nation in the world in terms of value, and second in terms of the bulk of the catch, and also harvests a great deal of seaweed for use as a food.

Agriculture

Less than 15% of the working population is employed in agriculture, and the percentage is still diminishing. Agriculture occupies 16% of the total area of the country, but despite its great efficiency per acre, the result of irrigation and double-cropping, agriculture contibutes less than 5% to the total GNP. For social and political rather than economic reasons, the price of rice is artificially kept above the world market price and strict import controls are enforced. As it is, Japan imports the great bulk of its food, mainly from the US. In particular, wheat, which the modern Japanese consume in the form of bread, and soybeans, which have occupied a central place in the diet for centuries, are almost wholly imported. Despite the diminishing importance of agriculture in the national economy, farming families generally hold on to their land; not only because the protection of central government ensures that their standard of living rises at roughly the same rate as that of city-dwellers, but also because of its phenomenally high value.

Industry

Twenty-five and one tenth percent of the Japanese workforce is employed in manufacturing, and another 9.4% in construction. Since the recovery of the economy in the early 1950s, the output of Japanese factories has changed several times. Beginning with labour intensive light goods, focus shifted to capital intensive heavy goods and chemicals and then on to technically sophisticated products. Most recently, world demand for cars has become sluggish while demand for ships has very largely dropped away; and the Japanese export drive has come to concentrate on computers and other 'knowledge intensive' industries which require a lot of skill but comparatively few raw materials. These rapid changes in the substance of industrial production were superintended by the Ministry of International Trade and Industry, whose functions were described briefly above. MITI not only encourages growing industries but also helps to phase out those industries which have become uneconomic, e.g. textiles.

Overseas Trade

Japan's overseas trade at the end of World War Two was at a standstill. Starting in 1954 with Burma, Japan made a series of reparation settlements with the countries of that area which were designed in such a way as to develop markets for Japanese products. Trade with other third world countries, notably those of Latin America, has also been of growing importance. In early post-war years, banking capital flowed from the United States into Japan, while from the outset the Americans were willing to accept exported Japanese goods. Trade with the US accounted for one-third of Japan's total trade in the early post-war years and was still as high as one fifth in the 1970s. For some years after the war the countries of Western Europe imposed severe import restrictions on Japanese goods. These have now largely disappeared, but the European trading relationship is as delicate as it is important. The communist countries did not participate in the San Francisco peace treaty of 1951; Japan had no treaty relations with them and consequently trade was slow to develop. However, in 1956 normal diplomatic ties were re-established with the USSR, and trade began to improve. Japan's great neighbour China is seen by Japanese businessmen as having great economic potential, both as a source of raw materials and as a huge new market for Japanese goods. Although relations have at last been normalised expectations have yet to bear much fruit. For example, China exports oil to Japan, but in quantity it does not exceed 2.5% of Japan's annual oil imports.

Japan's economic growth was more than twice the world average during the 1950s and 1960s. The existence of severe import controls in Japan itself, which prevented foreign traders from making inroads into Japan's economy caused some degree of resentment. In apparent retaliation to these controls, President Nixon in 1972 imposed a 10% temporary surcharge on imports to the USA. Though this was later removed, it did lead to the speeding up of the liberalisation of investments and industrial imports. This action has not led to foreign traders making great inroads into the Japanese market although imports have risen steadily.

Employment

When young workers, blue or white collar, join a large company, usually on completion of their secondary or university education, it is no casual undertaking. In return for loyalty and very hard work they are offered the likelihood of regular promotion, regardless of actual ability, with equally regular rises in pay, and full security until retirement at 55. After official retirement they may very possibly take a part time position in a different section of the same firm. This trading of loyalty for security may account in part for the comparatively low incidence of strikes, the still prevalent six-day week and the brevity of holidays. Unemployment in Japan has usually been less than 2% for the last two decades and changes of employer are much less common than in the West. Though nationwide, the system of lifetime employment is, however, by no means universal in Japan. It is restricted to the larger, more securely-based companies, and to the male employees within those companies. Women, and workers in smaller firms, can experience conditions as changeable and hazardous as those in any other industrialised country. Although unemployment has been kept at a relatively low rate in Japan, anxiety about jobs runs high; and competition for white collar jobs in the most famous and most paternalistic companies is very fierce.

Current Economic Situation

The Japanese economy was severely shaken by the oil crisis of 1973, as a result of which the price of oil quadrupled. Like other industrialised nations it suffered from a sudden rise in inflation, a marked deterioration in the balance of payments, and the worst recession since the war. Real GNP growth, which topped 10% in 1973, plummeted to nothing in the following year. Recovery was rather slow, and 1978 was a crucial year. The plan for 1978 had been to achieve domestic demand-oriented growth of about 7%, which was expected to contribute to an improvement of the employment situation and a decline of the current account surplus. This strategy seems to have been a success. The econmy enjoyed a recovery based on domestic demand, not exports, and GNP growth was 5.5%.

The government is aware of the long term need to encourage energy and resource-saving practices. The shift away from heavy industry to 'knowledge intensive' industry is in line with this thinking. For the present, Japan has the highest GNP growth rate of any of the OECD countries; and fuelled by this growth other indices of national well being such as per capita income and ratio of home ownership are also increasing. The development of post-compulsory and higher education, which runs roughly parallel with the development of the economy has also reached a very high level. It is intended that the Japanese economy should continue to grow at a rate of a little less than 6% per annum.

6 THE EDUCATION SYSTEM

The Academic Year

The academic year in Japan corresponds with the fiscal year; it begins on 1 April and ends on 31 March. Compulsory schools, that is, elementary and lower secondary schools, have three terms in a year: from April to July, from September to December, and from January to March. This pattern also holds for most upper secondary schools. Unversities on the other hand generally have two terms, or semesters, in a year with a summer vacation from mid-July to early September.

Schools and Colleges

All children who have reached the age of 6 are required to attend a six-year elementary school *(shōgakkō)*. From this they must proceed to a lower secondary school *(chūgakkō)* for another three years of compulsory schooling. They must attend until the end of the school year during which they have reached the age of 15. Nine years of schooling is compulsory. Lower secondary schools are usually referred to as 'junior high schools', and upper secondary schools *(kōtōgakkō)* as 'senior high schools'. Educational institutions in Japan are of three types by source of funding:

>   National   – financed directly by central government
>   Public   – financed by local authorities (prefectures, municipalities)
>   Private   – financed by private organisations.

All national and publicly provided schools, including upper secondary schools and most universities, are coeducational.

Pre-Primary

Pre-school education is not compulsory. Often the parents are charged tuition fees even in publicly controlled institutions. There are two types of institutions. Kindergartens *(Yochien)* cater for children aged 3-6. Day nurseries *(Hoikusho)* cater for children from birth to six years. They are run by the Ministry of Social Welfare and are for children who are deemed to need institutional care. In pre-school institutions as a whole 73 per cent of enrolments in 1980 were in private schools. However, the Ministry of Education, Science and Culture regulates the overall pedagogical character of all pre-school education.

There were 14,893 kindergartens with 2,407,093 pupils in 1980. The proportion of children in the first grade of elementary schools who had completed a kindergarten course was 64.4% in 1980. This proportion rose considerably in the 1960s and early 1970s but has been almost static since 1976. It was 28.7% in 1960, 41.3% in 1965, 53.8% in 1970 and 63.5% in 1975.

JAPAN - ORGANISATION OF THE EDUCATIONAL SYSTEM

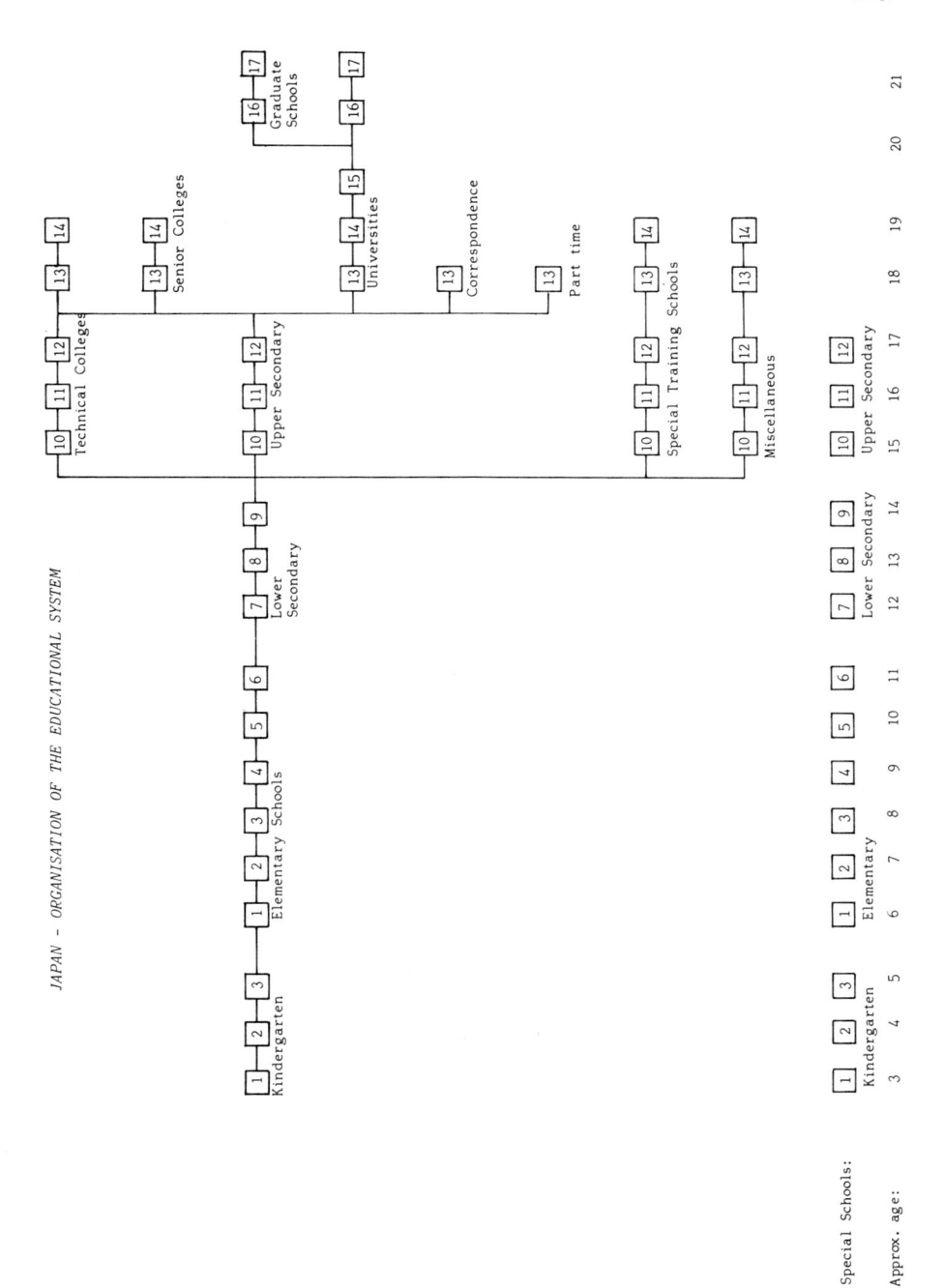

Kindergarten: 1 2 3

Elementary Schools: 1 2 3 4 5 6

Lower Secondary: 7 8 9

Upper Secondary: 10 11 12

Technical Colleges: 10 11 12 13 14

Senior Colleges: 13 14

Universities: 13 14 15 16 17

Graduate Schools: 16 17

Correspondence: 13

Part time: 13

Special Training Schools: 10 11 12 13 14

Miscellaneous: 10 11 12 13 14

Special Schools:

Kindergarten: 1 2 3
Approx. age: 3 4 5

Elementary: 1 2 3 4 5 6
Approx. age: 6 7 8 9 10 11

Lower Secondary: 7 8 9
Approx. age: 12 13 14

Upper Secondary: 10 11 12
Approx. age: 15 16 17 18 19 20 21

Primary

Parents are required by law to enrol their children in locally controlled public elementary and lower secondary schools between the ages of 6 and 15 unless they are admitted to nationally controlled or private schools. Over 99.6% of the 6-12 age group has been enrolled in elementary schools in every year since 1948. Because of high demand, national and private elementary schools (which accounted for 0.4% and 0.5% of total enrolments respectively in 1980) apply entrance examinations or other selection procedures. Total enrolments in primary schools in 1980 was 11,826,573.

Pupils are taught usually the whole range of subjects by one class teacher, though there are also some specialist teachers. The nationally determined curriculum decrees the subjects to be taught as Japanese, social studies, arithmetic, science, music, drawing and handicrafts, physical education, moral education, special activities and (for the final two grades only) home-making. Each subject is allocated a standard number of hours per year depending on the grade.

Lower Secondary

Children attend these schools between 12 and 15 and receive an education on the basis of their primary school studies. Instruction here is departmentalised to a large extent and the majority of teachers are specialists in one or two subjects. There is no selection procedure for entrance to municipal lower secondary schools, but children intending to enter private or national ones must take an entrance examination. Compulsory education finishes at 15, but the proportion of children continuing their studies in upper secondary schools has been rising at a phenomenal rate, from 42.5% in 1950 to 94% in 1980. In 1980 enrolment in lower secondary schools was 5,094,402.

The prescribed subjects of the lower secondary school are Japanese, social studies, mathematics, science, music, arts, health and physical education, industrial arts and home-making, moral education, special activities and elective subjects (including foreign languages).

Upper Secondary

Ninety eight per cent of those who applied to enter upper secondary schools in 1975 were successful. Entry to local upper secondary schools is by means of an achievement test set by the local authorities, while the national and private schools set their own entrance examinations. All three types of school also take into account reports from the principal of the applicant's lower secondary school. The full time upper secondary course takes three years. Within the schools both general and specialised courses are offered. Students enrolled in general courses account for 60% of the total. Specialised courses are further classified as vocational and non-vocational ones. Vocational courses include agriculture, fishery, home economics and nursing, while the non-vocational include science, mathematics, music and fine arts. These various options are encountered in different permutations from school to school. Some schools only provide the general course, while others offer a variety of specialisations; others again are specialised vocational schools offering training in one or more fields. Since 1973 all students, whatever courses they are enrolled in, must cover the following fields of study; Japanese language, social studies, mathematics, science, health and physical education and fine arts. Girls are required to study homecraft as well. A foreign language is a required subject, and in practice nearly 100% of students study English in both lower and upper secondary school.

There are three types of upper secondary schools: full time, part time and correspondence. The full time course lasts three years and the part time and correspondence courses take four years or more. Part time courses are of two types: day courses and evening courses. The majority of them are evening ones. Both part time and correspondence courses lead to a diploma equivalent to that available to students in the full time courses. Over half of all students in upper secondary education take these part time and correspondence courses. Of the students who graduated from upper secondary schools in 1979, 37.4% went on to universities, junior colleges, etc., 38.46% took employment, which 24.14 did not find employment or fell into other categories.

Special

Before starting their school lives Japanese children undergo a medical examination which identifies those who have physical or mental disabilities. These children enter special schools *(tokushu-kyōiku-gakko)* where they receive special education to help them overcome their disabilities, as well as a regular education. Special schools for blind and deaf children have been compulsory since 1948. Other schools which cater to children with mental and physical disabilities have been established and these became compulsory in 1979. There are special schools for each age group: pre-school, elementary, lower secondary the upper secondary. In 1980 there were 860 special schools of all types with a total of 91,812 students. Special classes in ordinary and elementary and lower secondary schools take care of children with comparatively mild disabilities.

School Curricula

The subjects to be offered and the standard number of school hours per year for each subject in elementary and lower secondary schools are provided for in an ordinance of the Ministry of Education, Science and Culture entitled 'Enforcement Regulations for the School Education Law'. For upper secondary schools, the same ordinance lays down the kind of subjects only. The basic framework for school curricula, including the objectives and standard contents of teaching in different subjects is outlined in the national 'Course of Study', which is compiled by the Ministry of Education, Science and Culture for each of the three school levels, i.e. elementary, lower secondary and upper secondary, on the basis of the recommendation of the Curriculum Council, an advisory body to the Minister. Each school organises its own curricula on the basis of the Course of Study, taking into consideration the actual conditions of its local community and school, and the development and characteristics of its pupils. In practice, however, the compulsory use of recognised textbooks and the requirements of the examination system lead to little curriculum variation between schools. The three areas of regular subjects, moral education and special activities are always supposed to be covered in the curricula. 'Special activities' includes such things as club activities, cultural performances and school excursions. The standards for lower secondary schools allow several hours for elective subjects and individual schools decide what to teach in these hours.

The 'Course of Study for Upper Secondary Schools' was revised in August 1978 and was enforced in April 1982. This revised course of study was drawn up on the basis of the following four guidelines:

(i) to respect the independent initiative of individual schools so that they maintain and develop their distinctive education

(ii) to ensure that the contents of teaching may be better adapted to differing abilities and aptitudes of individual students

(iii) to ensure that students may lead a relaxed and full school life

(iv) to ensure that students may obtain a better understanding and experience greater enjoyment of their working lives as a result of learning in an experience-oriented way; and to lay emphases both on moral and physical education, with the aim of developing the students fully.

School Textbooks and Equipment

Clearly the nature of school curricula, and the degree of variety or uniformity between different schools, depends to a large extent on the system of selection, authorisation and use of textbooks. In Japan the system operates as follows. On the basis of recommendations by the Textbook Authorisation Research Council, which is made up of schoolteachers and others with solid academic experience, the Minister of Education authorises textbooks which have been privately written and edited. In the case of textbooks to be used in lower secondary schools, the Minister then chooses the publisher, after receiving applications from different publishing firms. However, there is no particular system for choosing the publisher of books to be used in upper secondary schools. The School Education

Law prescribes that schools must use Ministry-authorised textbooks, unless they are unavailable or inadequate. Lists of authorised books are sent to schools by way of prefectural boards of education. Those to be used in local schools are then adopted by competent boards of education, while school principals adopt books to be used in national and private schools. The books are then distributed free to students in primary and lower secondary schools. As well as determining the curricula of the schools, the Ministry of Education also enforces standards for the provision of instructional aids and equipment, which were revised in 1978. The use of aids is very widespread: nearly all schools are equipped with slide projectors, overhead projectors and cassette tape recorders, and over two thirds have colour TV and film projectors. Aids such as language laboratories, VTRs and response analysers are increasingly being supplied, while the use of computers is being developed in some schools.

New textbooks approved for use for the new curriculum guidelines implemented in 1982 have provoked hostile reaction in other East Asian countries because of the interpretation they give of Japanese activities during the war which ended in 1945.

Higher

Universities *(daigaku)* offer courses of at least four years in duration, six in the cases of medicine and dentistry. Junior colleges *(tanki daigaku)* offer courses of two or three years. Both types of institution require candidates to have completed upper secondary education or its equivalent. A national university entrance preliminary examination was instituted in 1979 and aspiring entrants to universities sit for this before taking the entrance examinations of individual institutions. The results of the national examination are eliminatory as far as national universities are concerned (at least for the year in question) but even candidates thus eliminated may proceed immediately to the entrance tests of private universities. Private universities do not invariably take account of a student's results in the national preliminary examination. Practically all the universities and junior colleges limit the number of students to be admitted each year, so admission is obtained on a competitive basis. A growing number of institutions select a certain proportion, up to 20%, of the entrance solely on the basis of the recommendation of school principals, or occasionally on the basis of upper secondary school records. Of the entrants into higher education in 1979, 407,635 were admitted to undergraduate courses in universities and 176,979 to junior colleges. Comparing these figures with those for 1960, there were over twice as many university entrants and over four times as many junior college entrants. The percentage of students advancing from secondary to higher education has increased almost fourfold to nearly 40% in the 20 years to 1980. The proportion of women students enrolled in higher education has also been increasing steadily; it rose from 20% in 1960 to 33% in 1979. Besides the regular courses, short term courses and correspondence courses are also offered at some universities and junior colleges. Usually, as is the case with correspondence courses connected with upper secondary schools, these correspondence courses are of longer duration than the regular ones, but lead to a similar qualification.

Universities

In 1980 there were 446 universities. The majority – over 300 – were private while of the public universities around 90 were national and about 30 local. Seventy five percent of undergraduates were in private universities compared to 22% in national and 3% in local public universities.

Efforts have been made to standardise the quality of universities throughout the country, but great differences still exist, and a small number of national and private univesities stand well above the rest in terms of prestige. The most prestigious national universities, formerly known as the Imperial Universities, are: Tokyo, Kyoto, Tohoku University in Sendai, Kyushu University in Fukuoka, Hokkaido University in Sapporo, Osaka and Nagoya. Close behind these in prestige are a number of private universities of high standing, such as Keio and Waseda, both of which are in Tokyo.

There is great inequality in the geographical distribution of the universities: Tokyo alone has one-third of the total numbers and one-half of the students. Competitive pressure to pass the entrance examinations which open the door to the more prestigious universities is extremely heavy, and this pressure has resulted in *ronin* students who, having failed to pass the entrance examination for the top ranking schools, spend years cramming for a resit rather than enter an inferior institution. One striking contrast between national and private universities is in the matter of teacher-student ratios. In private universities in 1975 there were more than 40 students to one lecturer, and this ratio was increasing steeply. In national universities there were roughly 11 students to one lecturer, and the ratio was showing only a slight increase.

For the first two years of a university undergraduate course students study subjects of general education, in the humanities, social science and natural science; foreign languages; health and physical education and professional subjects. The first degree, known as *gakushi*, is obtained after four years' study. The faculties of medicine and dentistry differ from the other university faculties in that two years of compulsory general education are followed by four years of professional training. Although there are no final examinations, graduation, which depends on obtaining a proper number of credits, is by no means automatic. Of students admitted to four-year undergraduate courses in April 1969, those who graduated in March 1973 after four years of study accounted for 79.1%, while 8.8% graduated in March 1974 after repeating one year. The remaining 12.1% comprise drop outs and those who expect to graduate after six years or more. The proportion of students graduating after four years has shown a tendency to slip further since then - it stood at 97% in 1975. Almost half of the universities support graduate schools which offer advanced study in a number of fields leading to the master's and doctor's degrees. The master's degree takes an extra two years to study, while the doctoral course takes give years. Like the student body and the universities themselves, graduate schools are growing fast. Enrolment in master's courses doubled between 1965 and 1975, while enrolment in doctoral courses increased by 30% in the same period.

A university education in Japan must be paid for. But while the fees of private universities are often very high, those of the national universities are modest. Nearly half of all university students live at home while they are studying, while more than 40% of the rest live in boarding houses. About 7% live in university dormitories.

Junior Colleges

In 1980 there were 517 junior colleges offering two- or three-year courses, and nearly 90% of the students were women. Most courses offered in these colleges are in the fields of humanities, social sciences and home economics. None of these courses result in degrees, but the credits obtained may be counted towards the bachelor's degree. Ninety-one percent of these colleges are private, 4% are national and 5% are local public. The proportion of private colleges rises every year. As with the universities, a high proportion of junior colleges is located in Tokyo.

Vocational and Technical

Miscellaneous schools *(kakusho-gakkō)* provide young people with vocational and practical courses in dressmaking, cooking, book-keeping, typing, automobile driving and repairing, computer techniques, etc. Most courses in these schools require only the completion of lower secondary schooling for entrance, though some stipulate the completion of upper secondary schooling as well. The length of courses varies, the minimum being three months and the normal length being one year. Most of these schools are privately run. As more and more young people stay on at regular schools after the end of their compulsory education, the number of entrants into miscellaneous schools has been dropping. However, entrants aged 18 or over have been increasing gradually, suggesting that these schools have a new role to play as institutions of post-secondary education. In 1975 the total number of entrants into miscellaneous schools was 730,000. Since 1976 the Ministry of Education, Science and Culture has been reclassifying miscellaneous schools which have, or will soon come to have, a prescribed level and scale of systematic education as 'special training schools' *(senshu gakkō)*. In 1980 there were 2,520 special training schools with 432,914 students and 5,302 miscellaneous schools with 724,401 students.

Technical schools *(kōtō-senmon-gakkō)* first came into being in 1962. There were 65 colleges in 1975, 77% of them run by the State. In contrast to universities and junior colleges, the entrance requirement is the completion of lower secondary schooling, after which candidates must pass an achievement test before being accepted as students. Technical schools offer five-year courses in the various branches of engineering and graduating students should have a technician's standard of competence. On graduating, students are entitled to apply for admission to the upper division of an undergraduate course at university. Slightly different from the technical schools are the merchant navy colleges, which came into existence in 1967. All of these are administered by the State and the length of study is 5½ years which includes 12 months' training at sea. In both types of technical college, teaching time is divided between general and professional education. In 1980 there were 62 technical colleges with 46,388 students of whom 98% were men.

Social

'Social education' *(shakai kyōiku)* means 'organised educational activities for young people and adults, other than those provided in the curricula of elementary and secondary schools or institutions of higher education'. It takes a variety of forms. Activities are organised by both governmental, and non-governmental bodies and take place in public facilities such as 'citizen's public halls', 'youth houses', children's nature study centre, museums and public libraries. Training courses, correspondence courses, nature study sessions, lectures and art exhibitions as well as regular classes are among the activities which fall into the 'social education' category. In 1974-75, social education classes organised by local boards of education involved over 2,700,000 participants who took part in more than 51,000 classes.

Teacher Training

There are no distinct teacher training schools in Japan: would-be teachers follow teacher training courses of universities and junior colleges approved by the Minister of Education. The majority of elementary school teachers are trained at four-year elementary teacher training courses in national universities. The rest take the four- or two-year courses which are available at a small number of local and private universities and junior colleges. As lower secondary schools are compulsory, the national government is committed to train a certain number of lower secondary school teachers in national institutions. At present about 40% of these teachers are trained at four-year training courses in national universities. The minimum length of these courses is in fact two years, but most of those who go on to become teachers stay for four years. Upper secondary school teachers come from different undergraduate and post-graduate courses in local, private and national universities. In 1977, 83% of upper secondary teachers, 63% of lower secondary teachers and 43% of elementary teachers had completed an undergraduate or graduate course at a university, while most of the rest had completed a two-year course beyond the end of secondary education. Sixteen percent of elementary school teachers, however, had had no training beyond upper secondary school level. Special correspondence and summer courses for the upgrading of such teachers are organised by a number of universities.

Teaching certificates for lower and upper secondary school teachers are awarded to all university and college graduates who have acquired a minimum number of credits in both teaching subjects and professional subjects at a university or junior college. Regular certificates for teachers are of two classes, first and second. In order to become school principals, teachers must hold first class certificates, but otherwise there is no great economic or legal distinction between the two classes. Certificates are granted by prefectural boards of education which hold examinations for the purpose, and are valid in all prefectures and for life. Teachers employed in national schools are national public officials, and those in prefectural and municipal schools are local public officials; public school teachers are granted permanent tenure after six months' probationary service.

7 EDUCATIONAL ADMINISTRATION

National

Education in Japan has many elements of centralisation despite the formal powers of local education authorities. The central education authority is the Ministry of Education, Science and Culture, which is responsible for the integrated administration of governmental service at the national level relating to the promotion and dissemination of education at all levels, and of science and culture. The Ministry operates a number of national educational establishments including universities, junior colleges, technical colleges and museums and research designated primary and secondary schools attached to national universities of education. It supervises, advises and gives financial assistance to local education authorities and requires reports upon the educational activities under the jurisdiction of the local authorities. When necessary, it also holds inquiries and gives orders for necessary improvements or corrections to local education authorities. The Ministry also approves the establishment of local, public and private institutions of higher education and provides administrative supervision and advice.

Prefectural

Japan's 47 prefectures, one of which is the national capital, Tokyo, are each subdivided into municipalities. In every prefecture and every municipality there is a board of education which serves as local education authority. The prefectural board of education consists of five members appointed by the elected governor with the consent of the prefectural assembly. The members hold office for four years. The prefectural superintendent of education, chief executive officer responsible to the board of education, is appointed by the board with the approval of the Minister of Education, Science and Culture. This officer's major functions are as follows:

(i) to administer prefectural educational establishments (mainly primary and secondary schools and special schools for children with disabilities) other than universities or junior colleges

(ii) to supervise, advise and give financial assistance to the municipal boards of education within the prefecture

(iii) to require municipal boards of education to submit pertinent reports and, when necessary, to give them orders for improvements or corrections in their activities

(iv) to appoint and dismiss teachers of elementary, lower secondary and part time upper secondary schools established and operated by municipalities, and to pay the salaries of these teachers.

(v) to issue certificates for teachers

(vi) to coordinate school lunch programmes.

Distinct from those of the prefectural board of education, prefectural governors have some responsibilities of their own on education. They include the following:

(i) to administer prefectural universities and junior colleges

(ii) to undertake the general supervision of private elementary, secondary and miscellaneous schools and kindergartens. (Private institutions of higher education are under the general supervision of the Ministry of Education)

(iii) to prepare the prefectural budget for all sectors, including education, and to submit it to the prefectural assembly

(iv) to acquire and dispose of prefectural educational properties.

Municipal

The municipal board of education consists of three or five members appointed by the mayor with the consent of the municipal assembly. As in the case of the prefectural board, members hold office for four years. The municipal board selects a municipal superintendent of education, who serves as its chief executive officer, from among the board members with the approval of the prefectural board. Among the major functions of the municipal board are:

(i) to administer municipal educational establishments, mainly elementary and lower secondary schools, citizens' public halls and other educational establishments for adults and out-of-school youth

(ii) to appoint and dismiss teachers of municipal educational establishments other than elementary, lower secondary, part time upper secondary schools, junior colleges, or universities

(iii) to organise curricula for the municipal elementary and secondary schools administered by the board

(iv) to select from the Ministry of Education approved textbook list textbooks to be used in municipal elementary and secondary schools.

Municipal mayors also have some responsibility for education. Their main functions include the following:

(i) to administer municipal universities and junior colleges

(ii) to appoint and dismiss teachers of municipal universities and junior colleges

(iii) to acquire and dispose of municipal educational property

(iv) to prepare the municipal budget for all sectors including education, and submit it to the municipal assembly.

Supervisors

As has been pointed out above, the central Ministry of Education retains responsibility for such matters as curricula and choice of textbooks; respect for the independent initiative of individual schools is one of the desiderata of the revised Course of Study, but it is probably a long way from realisation yet. In such a closely supervised system, inspectors of the British type are not considered necessary; but there are supervisors and subject specialists attached to all three levels of administration whose job is to keep an expert eye on the schools. The supervisors attached to the Ministry are responsible for elementary and secondary education in general. They supervise the local boards of education, whose job it is to supervise the schools themselves. The Ministry-employed subject specialists conduct research and study on the standards of curricula for the school level and subject area to which they are assigned. They give advice on matters concerning the curriculum to the local boards. The supervision sections in prefectural boards of education give guidance and advice to municipal boards of education, conduct conferences and workshops for principals and teachers, and publish handbooks for teachers, based on the central policy for supervision and taking into consideration

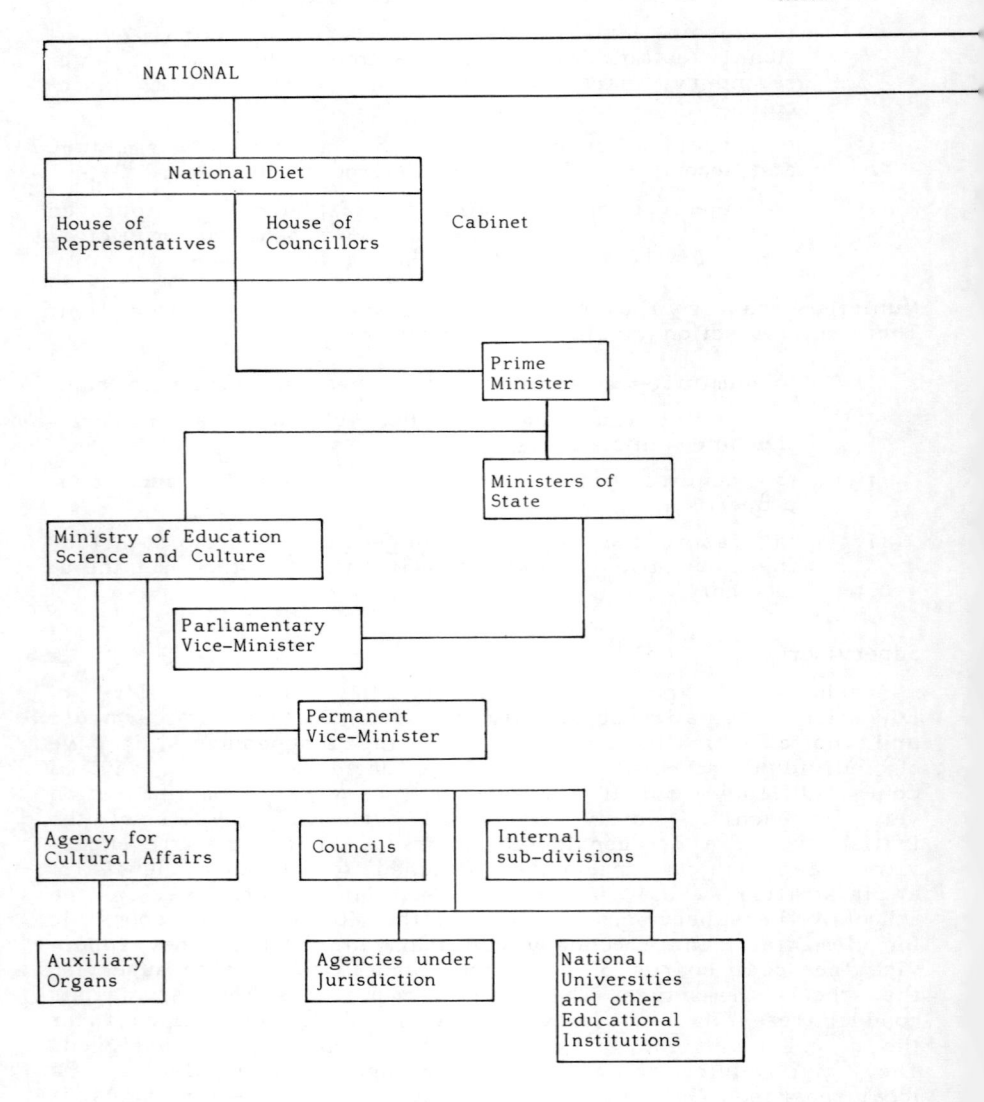

JAPAN -

```
NATIONAL
├── National Diet
│     ├── House of Representatives
│     └── House of Councillors
│           Cabinet
│           └── Prime Minister
│                 └── Ministers of State
│                       ├── Ministry of Education Science and Culture
│                       │     ├── Parliamentary Vice-Minister
│                       │     ├── Permanent Vice-Minister
│                       │     │     ├── Councils
│                       │     │     └── Internal sub-divisions
│                       │     │           ├── Agencies under Jurisdiction
│                       │     │           └── National Universities and other Educational Institutions
│                       │     └── Agency for Cultural Affairs
│                       │           └── Auxiliary Organs
```

STRUCTURE OF EDUCATIONAL ADMINISTRATION

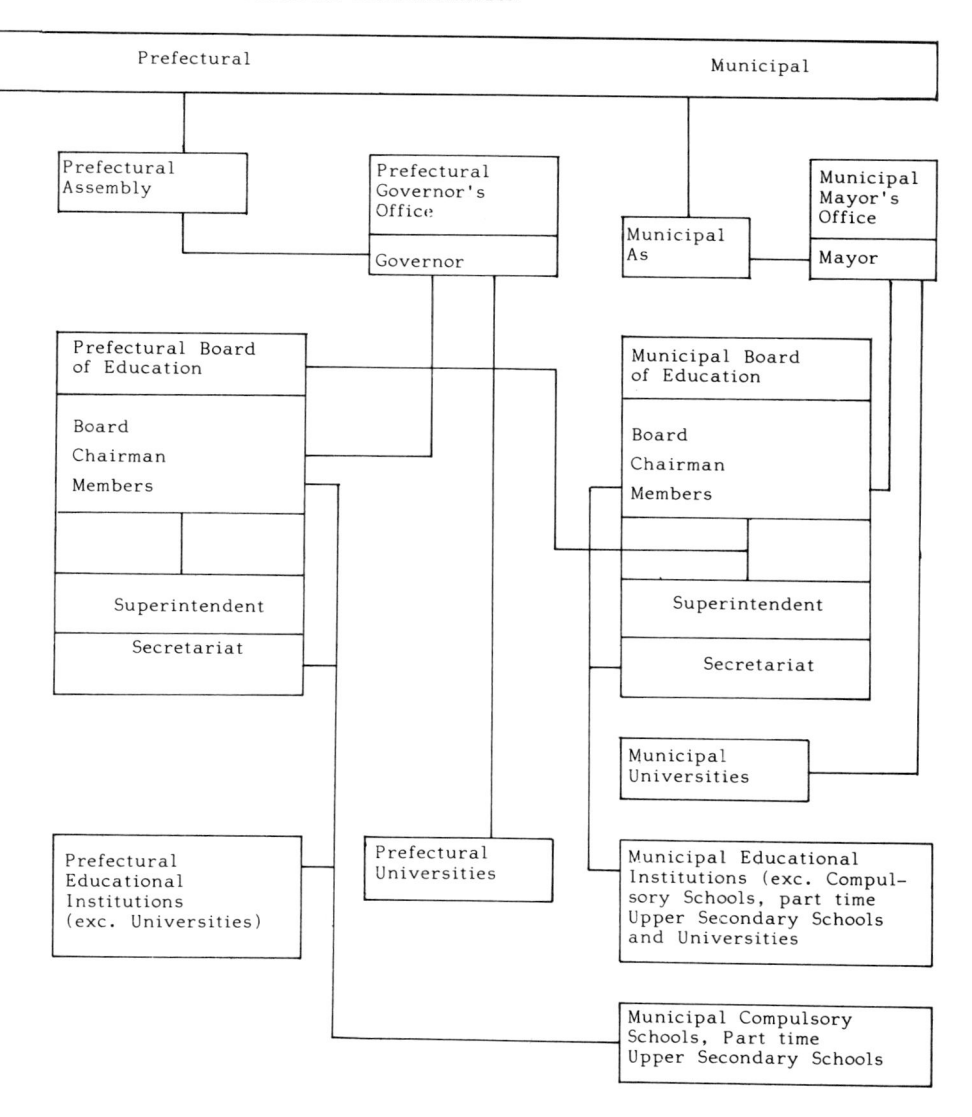

Prefectural		Municipal

- Prefectural Assembly
- Prefectural Governor's Office / Governor
- Municipal As[sembly]
- Municipal Mayor's Office / Mayor

Prefectural Board of Education
- Board Chairman
- Members
- Superintendent
- Secretariat

Municipal Board of Education
- Board Chairman
- Members
- Superintendent
- Secretariat

- Municipal Universities
- Prefectural Educational Institutions (exc. Universities)
- Prefectural Universities
- Municipal Educational Institutions (exc. Compulsory Schools, part time Upper Secondary Schools and Universities)
- Municipal Compulsory Schools, Part time Upper Secondary Schools

ORGANISATION OF THE MINISTRY

- Minister of Education Science & Culture
  - Parliamentary Vice-Minister
  - Permanent Vice-Minister of Education Science & Culture
    - Minister's Secretariat
      - Personnel Div
      - General Affairs Div
      - Budgeting & Accounting Div
      - Planning & Research
        - Planning Div
        - Research & Statistics Div
        - Information Management Div
    - Elementary & Secondary Education Bureau
      - Financial Affairs Div
      - Local Affairs Div
      - Educational Innovation Div
      - Kindergarten Education Div
      - Elementary School Education Div
      - Lower Sec. School Education Div
      - Upper Sec. School Education Div
      - Vocational Education Div
      - Special Education Div
      - Textbook Authorisation Div
      - Textbook Administration Div
    - Higher Education Bureau
      - Higher Education Planning Div
      - University Education Div
      - Technical Education Div
      - Teacher Training Div
      - Medical Education Div
      - Student Affairs Div

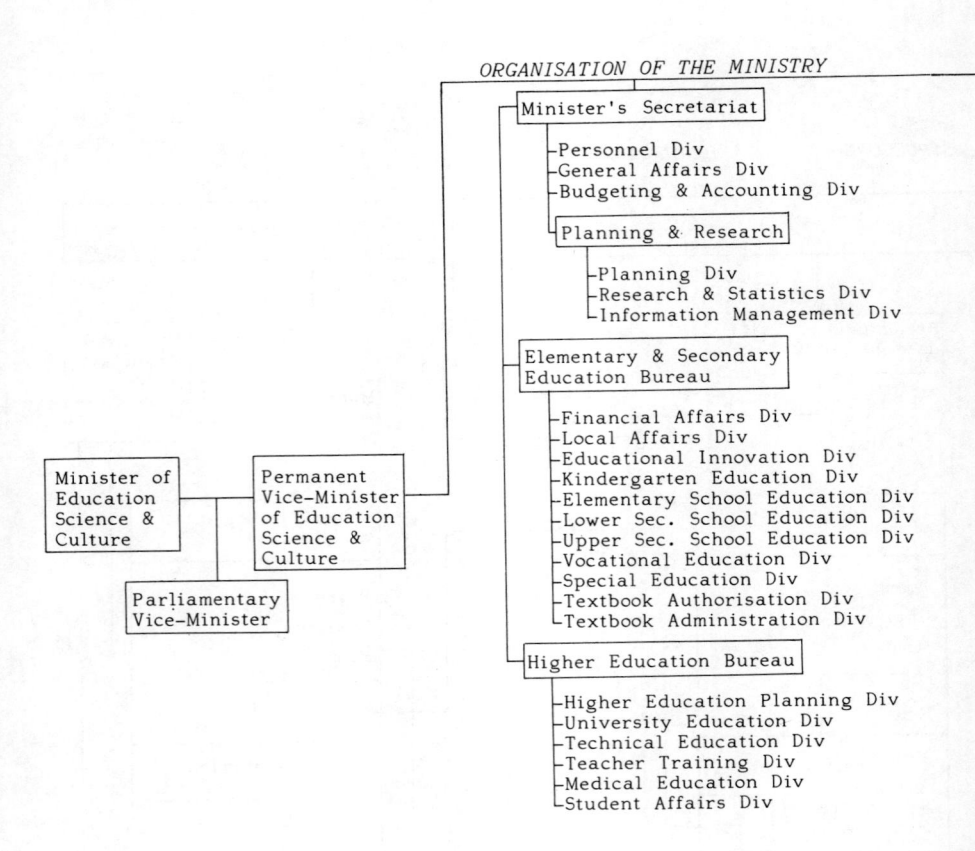

Councils (Advisory Bodies to Minister)

Central Council for Education
Selection of Persons of Cultural Merits
Curriculum
Health & Physical Education
Science Education & Vocational Education
Educational Personnel Trg
Science
Geodesy
Social Educational
Private University
University Chartering
University Problems (Temp)
Technical College
Textbook Authorisation Res.

Organs under Jurisdiction of the Ministry

Japanese National Commission for Unesco
National Institute for Educational Research
National Institute for Special Education
National Science Museum
National Trg Institute for Social Education
International Latitude Observatory
Institute of Stat. Maths
National Inst. for Genetics
Japan Academy
National Youth Houses (13)
National Children's Nature Centre (2)

OF EDUCATION, SCIENCE AND CULTURE

- **Science & International Affairs Bureau**
  - Science Div
  - Research Institute Div
  - Research Aid Div
  - Infn & University Lib Div
  - **UNESCO & International Affairs**
    - Planning & Coordination Div
    - Educational & Cult Ex Div
    - International Science Div
    - Student Exchange Div
- **Social Education Bureau**
  - Social Education Div
  - Youth Education Div
  - Women's Education Div
  - Audio-Visual Edn Div
- **Physical Educuation Bureau**
  - Physical Education Division
  - Sports Div
  - School Health Div
  - School Lunch Div
- **Administrative Bureau**
  - Private School Planning Div
  - Private School Promotion Div
  - Educational Personnel Welfare Div
  - **Educational Facilities Dept**
    - Planning Div
    - Facility Planning Div
    - Construction Subsidy Div
    - Contract Management Div
    - Construction Management Div
    - Local Construction Offices (7)

- **Commissioner Agency for Cultural Affairs**
  - **Commissioner's Secretariat**
    - General Affairs Div
    - Budgeting & Accounting Div
  - **Cultural Affairs Dept**
    - Cultural Diffusion Div
    - Art Promotion Div
    - Japanese Language Div
    - Copyright Div
    - Religious Affairs Div
  - **Cultural Properties Protection Dept**
    - Cultural Property Admin Div
    - Monuments & Sites Div
    - Fine Arts Div
    - Architecture Div
    - Intangible Cultural Properties and Folk Culture Div

National Educational Institutions, etc.

National Universities (88)
(with 47 kindergartens, 71 elem. schools, 76 lower sec. schools, 17 upper sec. schools, 31 special schools and 30 jun. colls. attached)
National Junior Colleges (1)
National Tech. Colleges (54)
National School for Handicapped Children (1)
National Laboratory for High Energy Physics
National Inst. of Japanese Literature
National Inst. of Polar Research
National Inst. for Molecular Science
National Museum of Ethnology

Organs attached to the Agency

National Museums (3)
National Museums of Modern Arts (2)
National Museum of Western Arts
National Lang Res Inst
National Research Inst of Cultural Properties (2)
Japan Art Academy

Councils (Advisory Bodies on Cultural Affairs)

Copyright
Religious Juridical Persons
Protection of Cultural Properties

the specific situations of the prefectures concerned. The supervisors themselves give guidance on curricula, teaching and so on within their prefecture. Other supervisors are attached to the municipal boards of education and supervise the local schools directly. All supervisors must be experienced professional educators.

8 EDUCATIONAL FINANCE

Government Budget

The national income of Japan has increased rapidly in recent years, and so has the proportion of it devoted to educational costs, if less dramatically; the percentage of the national income devoted to education increased from 5.3% in 1960 to 11.1% in 1979. In 1979 the national government contributed 47.9% and local authorities the remainder of the total public expenditure on education. The responsibility for the financial support of public education is shared by the national, prefectural and municipal governments with the Prefectures providing 28% and municipalities 24% of further expenditure on education in 1979.

National Government

Educational expenditure of the national government may be classified into two categories:

(i) expenditure for national educational establishments and services

(ii) subsidies earmarked for education which are made to prefectures, municipalities, private educational establishments and other bodies.

In addition to these subsidies, the government makes 'local allocation tax' grants to prefectures and municipalities. The government designates a certain proportion(32% in 1976-77) of the income tax, corporation tax and liquor tax as 'local allocation tax', which is distributed in grants among prefectural and municipal governments. These grants are intended to reduce the inequality in financial ability among the different prefectures and municipalities. Although these grants are not earmarked for any specific government services, a part of them is spent on education. The following are the main categories of educational expenditure which are subsidised by the national government:

(i) salaries of teachers in public compulsory education schools

(ii) construction of buildings and gymnasiums of kindergartens and public compulsory education schools; reconstruction of school buildings destroyed or damaged by natural calamities; reconstruction of superannuated school buildings

(iii) instructional equipment in public compulsory educational schools and nursery schools; equipment for science and vocational education; equipment for school lunch programmes

(iv) Social education programmes; facilities for social education activities including physical education and sports

(v) Aid to needy pupils in compulsory education schools (school supplies, lunch fees, medical care, etc.); special provisions for nursery school attendance, for the education of pupils with disabilities, for education in isolated areas and for part time and correspondence upper secondary schools.

The largest proportion of these subsidies goes for the salaries of teachers and for the construction and reconstruction of school buildings. The national government acknowledges the important role played by private educational establishments, and in view of that, subsidises their current expenditure to a certain extent.

Prefectural and Municipal Governments

Educational expenditure of the prefectures includes expenditure on prefectural educational establishments and services, salaries of teachers in municipal elementary, lower secondary and part time upper secondary schools and subsidies to municipalities for educational purposes. Educational expenditure of the municipal governments includes expenditure for municipal elementary and lower secondary schools (other than teachers' salaries), and expenditure for other municipal schools and social educational facilities, including sports facilities.

Funding of Higher Education

National universities and other educational institutions directly funded by central government account for 12.9% of such expenditure. National universities derive some 70% of their income from central grants, and the balance from fees and other receipts: the proportions are almost exactly reversed in the case of private universities.

Income of Public Schools

The main sources of income of public schools have been described above. In addition, schools receive a small proportion of their income in the form of donations from parents, either directly or through Parent-Teacher Associations, and from other citizens. In 1973, these donations came to 2.5% of the total in the case of full time upper secondary schools, and 0.5% of the total in the case of compulsory primary and lower secondary schools. In addition, parents also pay a share of the cost of school lunch fees and excursion fees for their children, and a share of the cost of instructional supplies and equipment and so on.

Tuition Fees

While instruction is free in public elementary and lower secondary schools which provide compulsory education, tuition fees are charged to students in public upper secondary schools (1980: Y3,800 per month) and in public institutions of higher education. The tuition fees which are collected from the students of an institution are incorporated into the revenue receipts of the government department operating the institution, and not earmarked for educational purposes. While tuition fees in national institutions are uniform throughout the country, those charged in prefectural and municipal schools are determined by individual local authorities. Fees in the private sector are higher and vary greatly. The average 1980 annual fee levels are given below (in yen):

	National Institutions	Local Public Institutions	Private Institutions
Kindergartens	33,600	38,840	121,494
Upper Secondary Schools	45,600	59,643	166,863
Technical Colleges	80,400	76,500	241,000
Junior Colleges	132,000	112,680	251,831
Universities	180,000	157,412	355,156

In addition, outside compulsory education, entrance fees, educational equipment, laboratory fees, etc., are payable. These vary greatly from university to university and according to academic specialisation. In 1980 the average annual equipment/ laboratory fee at a private university is Y140,000. Official figures published by the Ministry of Education gave the average annual expenditure of a university student in 1976 as Y742,000 of which the parents provided 78%, scholarships 4%, the remainder coming from part time jobs, etc. These averages conceal the wide disparity in cost between types of institutions. Predictably, fees in the private sector are significantly higher than in national and local institutions. For example, the annual fees for private nursery schools are over Y90,000, while those for the public sector are Y18,000. Tuition in private universities costs from about Y180,000 a year for humanities courses to as much as Y700,000 for medicine and dentistry; while annual fees for national universities are Y96,000, whatever the course. It must be remembered that these fees are actually paid by students or their parents. Study-loan schemes do exist, but not grants on the British model. Interest free loans are available; and are taken out by some 10% undergraduate and 50% or more of post-graduate students. Repayment of loans is waived in the case of graduates who enter the teaching profession.

9 DEVELOPMENT AND PLANNING OF THE EDUCATION SYSTEM

Before World War Two

The introduction into Japan of a modern education system, took place in 1872. Before this date, there were already many schools in existence in Japan. There were schools of a sort as far back as the Muromachi period (1336-1573), and during the Edo period (1602-1867) they were further developed and came to form the rudiments of a school system. Reform of education was given a very high priority by the leaders of the Meiji reformation and immediately they were established in power they began to consider what measures they should take. On 3 August, 1872, the government promulgated by cabinet decree the new education system which was to be imposed on the whole country. It was modelled on French practice, and besides centralising control over education it aimed at a high degree of standardisation. The school system was divided into three stages: elementary school, middle school and university. The aim of a minimum 4 years' schooling for all was realised with great speed, despite the initial unfamiliarity of the concept. Forty-six percent of all children received an elementary education in 1886; 61% in 1896; and 95% in 1906. In the decade after 1897, schools also aimed at providing a secondary education for women, business and advanced vocational education were introduced in quick succession, and colleges were organised. In 1907, the period of compulsory schooling was extended by two years, making the ordinary elementary school a six-year course and the upper elementary school a two-year course. From this time until the reforms which followed World War Two, the basic school system remained unchanged. The University Edict of 1918 authorised the establishment of private and municipal universities and colleges, and in 1926 the Kindergarten Edict was promulgated. A system of approval for textbooks was adopted, but after 1897 the texts were compiled by the government. Government-written textbooks were in use until after World War Two. The private schools and colleges established in the early decades of the Meiji Period took firm root. The founders of these institutions were often Christians, or Japanese who were opposed to the standardising education policy of the government. The non-conforming tendencies of some of the more illustrious universities caused the government some anxiety; it was probably to counteract these tendencies that Tokyo Imperial University was given such a marked official character. It was also at this time that Japanese education acquired its bias towards the learning of huge quantities of facts, which is still evident today.

After World War Two

Desiring to bring the Japanese system into line with American practice, the Occupation authorities in 1947 introduced the so-called 'single track' 6-3-3-4 school system. Elementary schooling was cut to six years, the two-year upper elementary course became a three-year lower secondary school; while the three kinds of secondary school - middle school, girls' school and vocational school - were combined into a three-year upper secondary school. As a rule schools were coeducational. The somewhat bewildering array of university institutions were all reorganised into four-year universities, and these were coeducational too. Graduate schools were established and the first two-year Junior Colleges were set up. These were the major changes, and it was these which determined the present character of the education system. Firmly set on these tracks, education has developed since the war at a speed which parallels the growth of the national economy. In 1947, 61.7% of 15-year olds went on to upper secondary schools; in 1978, the figure had risen to 96.2%. In 1947 only 5.8% of upper secondary school leavers went on to tertiary education; the figure for 1978 was 39.0%. Only in the United States do a higher percentage of school students go on to university, or college, and if current trends continue, Japan will soon overtake the United States.

Future Plans

The basic guidelines for the third reform of education - succeeding those of 1872 and 1947 - were submitted to the Minister of Education by the Central Council for Education, an advisory organ to the Ministry, in 1971. In this report the challenges Japan has to meet in education are summarised as follows:

(i) quantitative expansion of education to provide education for more people

(ii) equal opportunity for education to all

(iii) improvement of the quality of education to meet a variety of social needs

(iv) remodelling of the system and structure of education, as necessary for the improvement of the quality of education.

Curriculum Revision

The Curriculum Council, an advisory organ to the Minister of Education, Science and Culture, has been reviewing the curricula of elementary and lower and upper secondary schools since 1973 and revised curriculum guidelines were published in 1979. Consistency between the different levels of school, reduction of the students' memory-load and more diversity and elasticity in the curriculum have been the Council's main aims.

These guidelines were implemented in 1980 in elementary schools, 1981 in lower secondary schools and 1982 in upper secondary schools.

Kindergartens and Special Schools

The enrolment ratio in kindergartens was 64% in 1975. The Ministry of Education intends that by 1982 all children at the ages of 4 and 5 will be admitted to kindergarten, if their parents so wish. Special schools for children with disabilities will also be extended and improved.

Higher Education

There are wide divergences in academic standards between different institutions of higher education. The government intends to reduce these. University curricula are being made more flexible and the transfer of credits is being facilitated, to promote cooperation between institutions of higher education at home and abroad. Attempts are being made to create a new structure for universities, in place of the traditional form of the faculty. The University of Tsukuba, established in 1973, which is organised on a cluster basis, is put forward by the government as a model for future university education in Japan. Other innovations include the opening, in 1976, of a university of technology and science, which offers an education at graduate school level, leading to the Master's degree to technical college graduates, and an undergraduate education to the upper secondary school graduates of industrial courses. Other plans include a teacher training university, to train teachers from elementary school to graduate school level, and a university of the air.

However, the first stage of the plan proposed by a government plan on higher education in 1976 urged the restriction of the establishment of new institutions or the building of additional facilities in existing institutions. This had been achieved in the period between 1976 and 1981.

The second stage, which was to be achieved between 1981 and 1986, emphasised qualitative improvement. To this end mutual recognition of credits has been urged. Also a University of the Air was to be set up following a Law of 1981.

Special Training Schools

Established in 1976, these are intended to do the job of the vocational 'miscellaneous schools' described above. There are several courses of study, one of which is open to anyone, regardless of his or her level of educational attainment.

Private Education

Private education plays an important role in Japanese education, particularly at kindergarten, junior college and university level, but mainly for financial reasons, standards are not always satisfactory. To remedy this situation, the Ministry of Education has, since 1970, been giving financial assistance to private colleges and universities. This policy will continue.

Teachers

To ensure a supply of suitable teachers, a law was enacted in 1974 to fix teachers' salaries at a higher level than that of other national public service personnel. Since 1973, people experienced in other fields have been enabled to become teachers, by passing a special examination. With the aim of broadening teachers' horizons, overseas study programmes have been fostered: since 1973, 5,000 teachers have been sent abroad to study every year.

Lifelong Education

The continuing rapid changes in society demand great adaptations in people's living and thinking. With this in mind the Ministry of Education has been promoting 'social education' in the following ways:

(i) improvement of facilities such as libraries and museums

(ii) training of 'social education leaders'

(iii) opening of university extension courses, and special classes for women, families and the aged.

International Education Exchanges

In 1974, the Central Council for Education submitted a report to the Minister urging the improvement and expansion of international exchange and cooperation in edcuation. In response, the Ministry established a Science and International Affairs Bureau. Since then the number of Japanese students enrolled in higher education institutions abroad and funded by Japanese government scholarships has increased substantially, from four students in 1970 to 246 students in 1977. This remains, however, a very tiny proportion of the undergraduate population, slightly more than 0.01%. Meanwhile the number of Japanese students receiving foreign government scholarships remained almost stable between 1965 and 1977, at about 360 students.

JAPAN BASIC STATISTICS

Population

1970	1980
104,345,000	115,870,000

Proportion of the Relevant Age Groups Enrolled at each Level of Education

	1950 %	1960 %	1970 %	1980 %
Pre-primary*	8.9	28.7	53.8	64.4
Elementary	99.6	99.8	99.8	100.0
Lower Secondary	99.2	99.9	99.9	100.0
Upper Secondary	42.5	57.7	82.1	94.2
Higher	–	10.3	23.6	37.4
Post-graduate†	–	–	4.4	3.9

* Proportion of first grade elementary school children who had completed a kindergarten course

† Proportion of university graduates entering directly to graduate courses

Sex of Students in Post-compulsory Education 1980

	% female
Upper Secondary	49.6
Special Training Schools	66.5
Miscellaneous Schools	52.5
Technical Colleges	2.0
Junior Colleges	89.0
Universities	22.1

Institutions, Teachers and Students 1980

	Schools	Teachers	Pupils
Pre-Primary	14,893	100,958	2,407,093
Elementary	24,945	467,953	11,826,573
Lower Secondary	10,780	251,279	5,094,402
Upper Secondary	5,208	243,592	4,621,930
Special Schools	860	33,491	91,812
Vocational (Special Training & miscellaneous)	7,822	46,689	1,157,315

	Institutions	Teachers	Students
Technical Colleges	62	3,692	46,348
Junior Colleges	517	10,052	371,124
Universities	446	102,989	1,889,304

Upper Secondary Students by Course of Study 1980

	Percentage
General	68.2
Business	12.5
Industry	10.3
Agriculture	3.8
Homemaking	3.5
Welfare	0.6
Fishing	0.4
Other	0.7

Higher Education Students (Undergraduates)
by Field of Study 1980

	Universities	Junior colleges
Social Sciences	40.5%	9.1%
Technology	19.4%	5.5%
Humanities	13.8%	21.6%
Education	7.6%	24.4%
Medicine & Dentistry	4.1%	4.3% (Health)
Agriculture	3.4%	1.1%
Pharmacy	2.3%	–
Home Economics	1.8%	26.7%
Others	3.9%	5.3%

Public Expenditure on Education

	As a % of total government spending	As a % of GNP
1970	20.4%	3.9%
1978	16.1%	5.7%

Public Expenditure on Education by Level

Year	Pre-Primary	Primary	Secondary	Higher	Other
1970	0.9%	37.6%	37.3%	12.7%	11.5%
1978	1.3%	38.8%	35.6%	11.0%	13.3%

Basic Social and Economic Data

Gross National Product per capita 1979 – US$ 8810
Average annual growth of GNP per capita 1960–1979 – 9.4%
Life expectancy at birth 1979 – 76 years

Proportion of the labour force employed in:

Agriculture	1960	33%
	1979	13%
Industry	1960	30%
	1979	38%
Services	1960	37%
	1979	49%

Nepal

CONTENTS

1 Geography	252
2 Population	254
3 Society and Culture	255
4 History and Politics	256
5 The Economy	257
6 The Education System	259
7 Educational Administration	264
8 Educational Finance	267
9 Development and Planning of the Education System	268

Nepal can be compared, in both socio/economic and educational terms, with other mountainous countries to the north of the Indian sub-continent - particularly Afghanistan and to some extent Pakistan. All three countries have low incomes, largely rural and agricultural societies and very low participation rates in education. Nepal shares with Afghanistan one of the lowest levels of educational development in Asia.

The main indicators of the low level of educational provision are the proportions of the relevant age groups in primary and secondary education. In 1970 little more than a quarter of 6-10 year olds were in school and only about 10% of the 11-15 age group. By the end of the 1970s, almost 90% of 6-8 year olds and 20% of 9-15 year olds were in primary and secondary schools respectively. These figures represented a considerable expansion. But they still lagged behind those of most other countries with similar levels of economic development when it is considered that the three-year primary school and four-year lower secondary schools provided only slightly more education than was available in primary schools alone in other countries.

The lack of educational provision cannot be attributed simply to Nepal's level of economic development or to religious constraints. Though Nepal is primarily Hindu in religion - and Hindu societies have not been antipathetic generally to secular education - the relative participation of girls in education is lower than in many Islamic countries. Nepal's economic position has been relatively static since 1960 so that low educational development cannot be attributed to extreme proverty in former times.

The major constraints on educational expansion seem to be topography and demographic distribution. The scattered and geographically isolated nature of Nepal's population together with the lack of major urban areas create major logistic obstacles to the expansion of educational facilities which are reinforced by the lack of interest in modern education among remote rural communities. The lack of sustained economic growth in Nepal over the last 20 years inhibits any government initiatives – even if the will was there – to expand educational provision at a rapid rate.

Nepal has not experienced the distortions that long colonial rule has elsewhere created in education systems. But there are tensions between secularist educational aims and traditional Hindu culture and education which have restrained the development of education related to modern manpower requirements. This Hindu traditionalism may have discouraged the development of technical and vocational education but also created the conditions in which government and people do not give a very high priority to the expansion of modern educational institutions.

1 GEOGRAPHY

Topography

Nepal is situated along the arc of the Himalayas and surrounded by India and the Tibetan region of China. It is approximately 800 km (500 miles) wide from east to west and 160-240 km (100-150 miles) long from north to south. The total land area is 140,300 sq km (54,363 square miles). The physical differences are sharply marked; in less than 160 km the country changes from jungle on the Gangetic plain to Tundra in the high Himalayas. Elevation ranges from 60 to 8,683 metres (200 to 29,000 feet). Seven major water systems cut through the mountains in a north-south direction flowing into the Ganges.

There are three main geographical regions:

(i) in the south the Terai, a strip of the Gangetic plain with an even elevation of 60 metres which with its adjoining northern foothills forms a distinct region running 30-50 km south of the Siwalik range. It is partly cultivated and partly dense forest

(ii) in the centre the Middle Hill Areas (including the Kathmandu Valley) which consists of hundreds of valleys at an elevation of 600 to 1,500 metres (2,000 to 5,000 feet) and surrounding hills and foothills, at 1,800 to 3,000 metres (6,000 to 10,000 feet)

(iii) in the north the Himalayan highlands, a 25 to 30 km strip of the highest mountains.

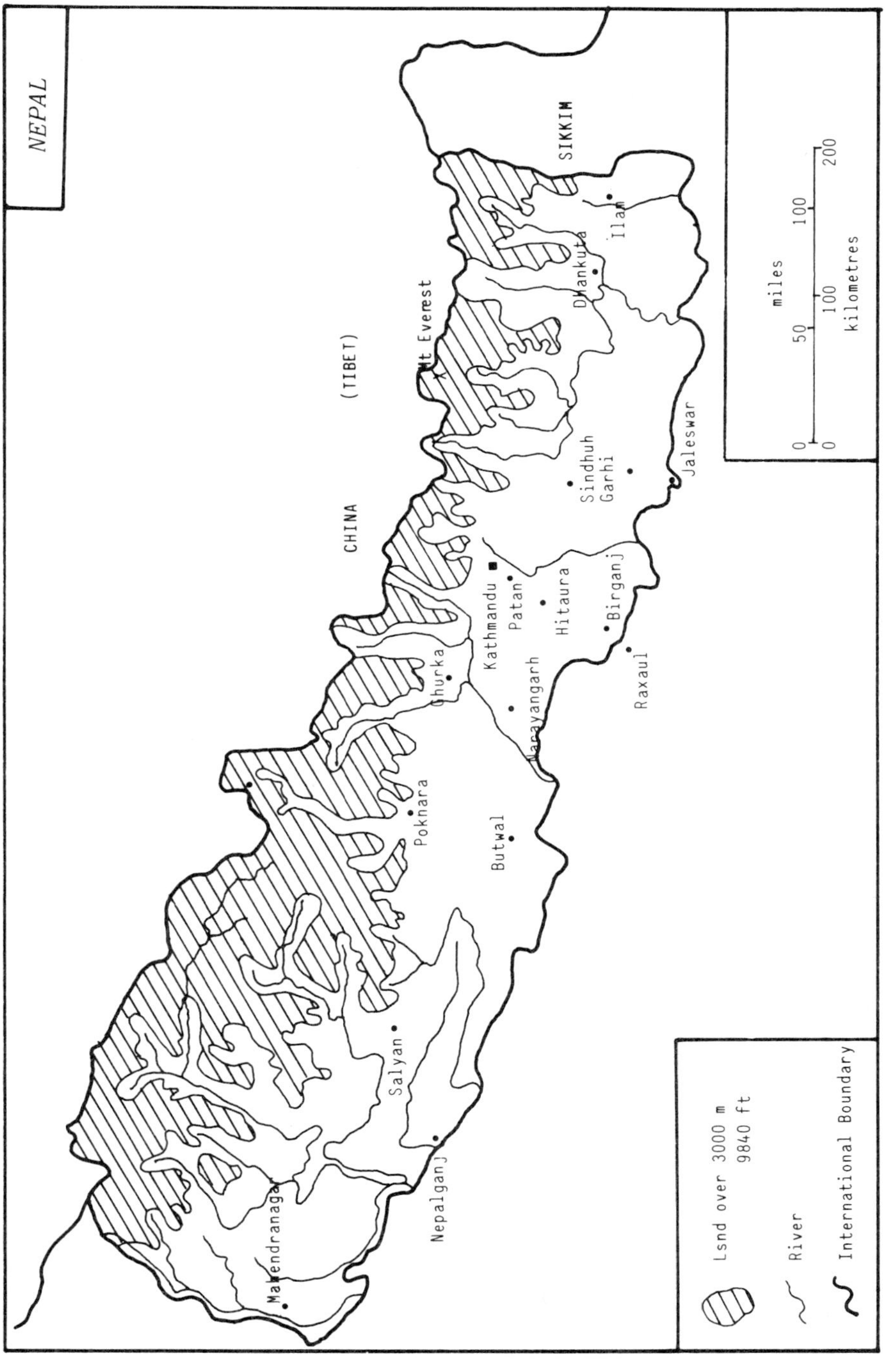
NEPAL
CHINA
(TIBET)
SIKKIM
Mt Everest
Ilam
Dhankuta
Sindhuh Garhi
Jaleswar
Kathmandu
Patan
Hitaura
Birganj
Raxaul
Ghurka
Narayangarh
Poknara
Butwal
Salyan
Nepalganj
Mahendranagar
miles
0 50 100
0 100 200
kilometres
Lsnd over 3000 m 9840 ft
River
International Boundary

Climate

The climate varies sharply with altitude. The Terai region is sub-tropical and the Himalayan highlands arctic. The Middle Hills region is generally temperate. The Kathmandu Valley is warm and wet in summer with an average temperature of 27°C (80°F). But in winter the temperature falls below 0°C at times in January. Rainfall ranges between 90 and 180 cm per year (35 to 70 inches) with 80% falling during the monsoon (June to September).

Communications

Communication by road is extremely difficult and there are virtually no roads in the western half of Nepal. A mountain road links Kathmandu with the Indian railhead at Rauxaul, and some other major roads have been built in the east, notably sections of the east-west highway in the Terai, the Kathmandu-Pokhara-Butwal road and the Kathmandu-Chinese border road. There are only two sections of railway with a total length of 100 km. In the flat areas of the south, torrential rivers debouching on to the plain present severe difficulties, while elsewhere the mountain ranges and unstable geological structure make road building both difficult and expensive. Most communication with outlying areas is by air and there is a fairly well developed internal air network using STOL aircraft. Helicopters are increasingly used for charter work. However, large areas of the country are completely accessible only on foot. In accessible areas communications are severely restricted during the monsoon season.

2 POPULATION

Growth and Distribution

The population was approximately 14 million in 1979 with a growth rate of about 2% per annum in 1977-78. There is an active government sponsored population control programme. The majority of the population live in the overpopulated Middle Hills area and the Kathmandu Valley alone contains over one million people, with an anticipated 3.6 million by the year 2000. There is a steady exodus to cleared areas of the Terai and to the Terai towns, which are sited where trade routes emerge from the mountains on to the plain and which have become centres of industrial expansion in a modest way. Although there is some transhumance in the high valleys the population is mostly settled in villages which may be dispersed in the Middle Hills, but are nuclear in other areas. New settlements are appearing on the developing road system, particularly where old foot tracks cross or meet new roads. Preferred sites are on south and west facing slopes providing maximum hours of sunlight and houses are often high above valley floors well away from water supplies. There are few large cities. Kathmandu, the capital, had a population of 395,000 in 1976. The other major towns were Patán (150,000) and Bhadgoón (100,000).

Groups

The population is of three basic types: the ethnically Tibetan group predominant in the north, which includes the Sherpa people from the mountains; the Middle Hills people, the traditional 'Gurkha' of British mythology; and the people of the Terai who are indistinguishable from North Indian peasants. Most Nepalese people are racially a blend of the Mongolian and Aryan types.

3 SOCIETY AND CULTURE
Social Patterns

The topography of Nepal has always kept its people in pockets of isolation. Physical and social mobility are difficult and tribe, caste and family are still significant features in the lives of most people. There are probably about 30 'tribes' identifiable often by the common occupations their members pursue, the location of their villages, the kind of architecture they practice, etc. The dominant group socially and politically are descendants of high-caste Hindus originating from India. some live in Kathmandu, others throughout the Middle Hills area, never settling at an altitude above 1,800 metres. Everywhere they form an elite group, dominating local politics. Another important group, the Newari, populate the Kathmandu Valley. They are urban dwellers with a high literacy rate. They tend to be bureaucrats, traders or skilled artisans and have contributed largely to Nepali culture. Apart from the various Nepalese communities there are still several camps for Tibetan refugees who have not been absorbed into the community although there are many Tibetan shops and restaurants in Kathmandu often run by people of aristocratic background. There appear to be no serious tensions between the groups though inter-marriage and social mobility are very limited.

Language

In the last language census 36 different languages were recorded. There is little in common between any of them but they do fall into two main groups: Indo-Aryan and Tibeto-Burman. Nepali was originally spoken in the Gurkha area of the country but since the eighteenth century the policy of the ruling groups has been to use Nepali as the official language and it has achieved the status of a lingua franca in much of the country. In 1971 52% of the population was recorded as speaking Nepali as a second language. Other important languages are Maithili (spoken by 11.5%) and Bhojpuri (7%).

Religion

The principal religions, Hinduism and Buddhism, have existed side by side in Nepal for many centuries, influencing each other and working together harmoniously. Hindus constitute the largest group; about 90% of the population is Hindu with 7.5% Buddhist. The royal family practice Hinduism but the King does preside over some Buddhist rituals. There is also a small Moslem community (about 2.5%). The propagation of Christianity is forbidden, though missionary societies have been allowed to establish a number of projects – schools, hospitals and some technical training – which are now gradually being taken over by the government.

4 HISTORY AND POLITICS

Historical Development

The present nation was created only 200 years ago when Prithvi Narayan Shah, then King of Gorkha, conquered the kingdoms of the Kathmandu Valley in a protracted campaign and subdued the tribes further east. His successors extended their territory by conquests to the north and west. The house of Gorkha ruled for less than a century. In 1846, the Prime Minister, Jang Bahadur Rana, usurped the power of the King and established a family oligarchy which governed Nepal for the next 100 years. In 1951 the Rana family was overthrown and political power was restored to the throne under King Tribhuvan. After a few years of experimental parliamentary democracy, the Nepalese Congress Party government was dismissed in 1960 by King Mahendra who banned political parties and established personal rule. In January 1972 King Mahendra died and was succeeded by his son who was crowned King Birendra Bir Bikram Shah Dev in February 1975. In 1972 King Birendra appointed Dr Tulsi Giri (later Prime Minister) as a political aide with cabinet rank to advise on strengthening democracy.

Panchayat System of Government

A new constitution was introduced by King Mahendra in 1962 which, with amendments in 1967 and 1976, provides for a *panchayat* (council) system of democracy under the Crown. The base of the system is the village or town assembly, a meeting of adult members of the community, which elects the village or town *panchayat*. These *panchayats* send members to the 75 district *panchayats*, which meeting at 14 zonal assemblies elect 112 members of the National Assembly *(Rashtriya Panchayat)* every four years. The King nominates the remaining 23 members and appoints from the *Rashtriya Panchayat* ministers of the Crown, who act as the Council of Ministers under the Prime Minister, form the chief executive body of Nepal. The King is also advised by a non-executive *Raj Sabha* or Privy Council. Executive authority is exercised by ministries through regional directors in four regions to district officers in 75 districts to *panchayat* heads at village and town level.

One reason for the adoption of the *panchayat* system was the need to decentralise government. The constitution was amended in 1967 to include a 'Back to the Village Campaign' under a central committee which works to 'lay down, interpret and propagate' political principles at grass roots level. There is also a Ministry of Home and Panchayat Affairs to implement this policy, part of which is the training of *panchayat* workers with administrative and developmental roles. A women's training programme is provided.

International Relations

The aim of Nepal's foreign policy is to maintain a non-aligned sovereign independence. There are consistent attempts to have the country declared 'a zone of peace', a policy endorsed by China. Nepal has been a member of the United Nations since 1955. In 1973 King Birendra was elected chairman at the conference of non-aligned nations in Algiers and he made State visits to India and China in 1975 and Russia in 1976.
The relationship between China and India is critical to Nepal. Indian policy in Sikkim and Bhutan is a matter of concern and China is currently regarded as an essential counterbalance. India played an important role in the overthrow of the Rana régime in 1951 but the imposition of the *panchayat* system of political organisation since 1960 has meant that India has provided a refuge for members of the Nepalese Congress Party. Relations with India are not always easy and there is a recurrent minor problem with people who have dual Indian/Nepalese nationality. The current regulation is that people of Nepali origin must be resident for two years before they can claim citizenship after a stay in India. The Indian government in 1976 imposed some restrictions on cross-border movement of people but these seem to be relaxing in practice. It is still too early to assess the effects of the recent change of government in India.

5 THE ECONOMY

Agriculture

Nepal is essentially an agricultural economy and is likely to remain so. Much of the country is heavily forested or too steep for cultivation; with the added effects of soil erosion 30% of the land is already unsuitable. Nonetheless, an estimated 93% of the population depend on agriculture mostly in the form of subsistence farming. Agriculture provides 66% of GDP and about 60% of total export earnings. Rice, maize, wheat, millet and barley are the principal crops and only a few districts outside the Terai produce a surplus. Jute, sugar cane, tobacco and oilseeds are grown as cash crops in the Terai while hill farmers sell potatoes and other vegetables and a little fruit. Tea and timber are exploited commercially. There is a small surplus of exportable foodstuffs but jute and timber are the major foreign currency earners. However, the forest is disappearing at an annual rate of 8% (and deforestation for fuel and fodder is a major problem). The Five Year Plan (1975-80) envisaged an expansion of 20% in agricultural production largely based on increased irrigation. Cotton growing in the Terai region was to be exploited and foreign aid would provide 45% of the total outlay.

Industry

Natural resources other than water power are limited, although there are some mineral deposits, notably mica which is mined east of Kathmandu, with small amounts of low grade copper, iron ore and cobalt. Persistent efforts to develop hydroelectric power are complicated by technical problems, by difficulties of distribution, and by India's unwillingness to be dependent on any large scale supply of power from Nepal. However, two projects are under way costing US$1,000 million in international aid. Tourism has been the most successful industry and the largest single earner of foreign exchange (over 100,000 people visited Nepal in 1976). Other industrial development has been patchy. There are medium sized factories producing cigarettes, textiles, strawboard, shoes and plastic buttons. The New Industrial Development Policy begun in 1974/75 was to encourage new industries in the private sector. The 1975-80 Five Year Plan aimed to develop new industries in both sectors, including the production of vegetable oil and paper products.

Trade

The major trading partner is India. Nepal still provides a large market for Indian manufactured goods and she is dependent on transit facilities through India and port facilities at Calcutta. In 1974 India increased prices to Nepal and the two countries did not renew their trade agreement in 1976. Nepal imports petroleum from the USSR and has trade agreements with China and North Korea.

Economic Situation

Nepal, with an average annual per capita GNP of US$130 in 1979 (including the notional value of subsistence production), is one of the poorest countries in the world. With an average annual growth rate of 2.7% between 1970 and 1979 the situation at present is not promising. Nepal is heavily dependent on foreign aid for development and the major contributors are the USA, China and India (in that order). But India's attitude to industrial development in Nepal has traditionally been ambivalent. Gurkha pensions are still significant in the national economy. A major problem for industrial expansion has been a lack of trained technical personnel and recent educational planning has placed appropriate emphasis on vocational and industrial training. But inevitably the coordination of education and training with the country's manpower needs will be a slow process.

6 THE EDUCATION SYSTEM

In 1970 the government drew up the National Education System Plan which aimed to establish for the first time a uniform system of education over the whole country. The recommendations of this plan have been and still are being implemented.

Academic Year

All levels of education work a six-day week (10.00 a.m. to 3.00 p.m. in schools and 5.00 p.m. at higher levels). In schools the long break in the academic session is taken in winter in the hills and in the summer in the Terai. There are many other religious and national holidays but the only other substantial break is two weeks for the main religious festival Dasain in September/October. The university also closes for Dasain and the long two-month break is taken in July and August.

Pre-Primary

At present there is scarcely any pre-primary education in Nepal and none outside Kathmandu. There is one English medium school in Kathmandu with pre-primary classes. The National Education System Plan does not propose to introduce pre-primary schools but says that they will be permitted with the approval of the appropriate authority. The government will assume responsibility for curricula and teacher-training for such schools but will not itself be responsible for the opening of schools. As a result private pre-primary schools appear and disappear from time to time.

Primary

The first three years of schooling (ages 6-9) constitute the primary stage. It is not compulsory but has been free throughout the country since 1975; (textbooks are also provided free in remote areas and to some poor families in other districts). The curriculum at this level concentrates on basic literacy and arithmetic, and the medium of instruction is Nepali, though mother tongue explanation is permitted in non-Nepali speaking areas. Curricula and syllabi are nominally the same in all primary schools.

There was a considerable expansion of primary school enrolments in the 1970s. The numbers of children in school grew from 390,000 in 1970 to 1,013,000 in 1979. The proportion of the 6-8 age group in primary schools rose from 51% in 1975 to 88% in 1979. These percentages give an over-favourable picture since there are primary school pupils outside the 6-8 age group but it was probable that about three quarters of children were in school.

The overwhelming majority of boys are in school. Less than half the girls of the 6-8 age group attended school in 1979 though the figure was less than 16% in 1975. There has been an expansion of provision for both sexes in the 1970s but the disparities between boys and girls are still very great.

Secondary

The 1970 Plan provides for a four-year lower secondary course (Classes IV to VII) which like the primary course is standard throughout the country. The lower secondary curriculum concentrates on character building, loyalty and pre-vocational training. Also included from Class IV is 'one of the UN languages'. In practice, this is English. From Class VIII (the beginning of the three years of secondary or high school education), students have a choice of a general academic course, a technical vocational course or a Sanskrit course concentrating on the Hindu classics; however, all the courses contain a vocational element. There is an admission test for entry to this stage of secondary education and students are advised on their choice of course in accordance with the country's needs. The aim of this stage is to produce productive vocation-oriented students. In 1961 the government began to convert some high schools into vocational schools. But little real progress has been made and in 1977 the government sought aid to set up a model vocational school in each of the four regions. In non-vocational schools general subjects receive 80% of school hours and vocational teaching 20%; in the vocational schools, however, 40% of the timetable is given to vocational subjects. On completion of the secondary course students take the School Leaving Certificate examination (SLC). In 1971/72 the pass rate was 29%; in 1974/75 it was 40.5%. The language of instruction throughout secondary education is Nepali.

Enrolments in secondary schools have risen from 282,000 in 1975 to 449,000 in 1979. However, this still represented a very small proportion of the age group. Nineteen percent of 9-15 year olds were in secondary schools in 1979 compared to 13% in 1975. Less than a quarter of all secondary pupils (23%) were in upper secondary schools in 1979.

The disparity in enrolments between the sexes is even greater in secondary education than in primary schools. Only 19% of secondary school pupils were girls in 1979 compared to 14% in 1975.

Private Schools

The most important private schools are the Jesuit St Xavier's (for boys) and St Mary's (for girls), both of which are in Kathmandu and have the highest academic standards. Formerly, they ran courses leading to the Senior Cambridge Overseas School Certificate; the last regular group sat for this examination in 1976. These schools and a few other mission schools in other parts of the country have now been affected by the National Education System Plan, which decrees that instruction must be given in Nepali. However, although absorbed into the national system to the extent of being required to take the SLC examination, the private schools have now been permitted to organise one-year post-SLC English medium courses (Class XI)

THE EDUCATION SYSTEM OF NEPAL

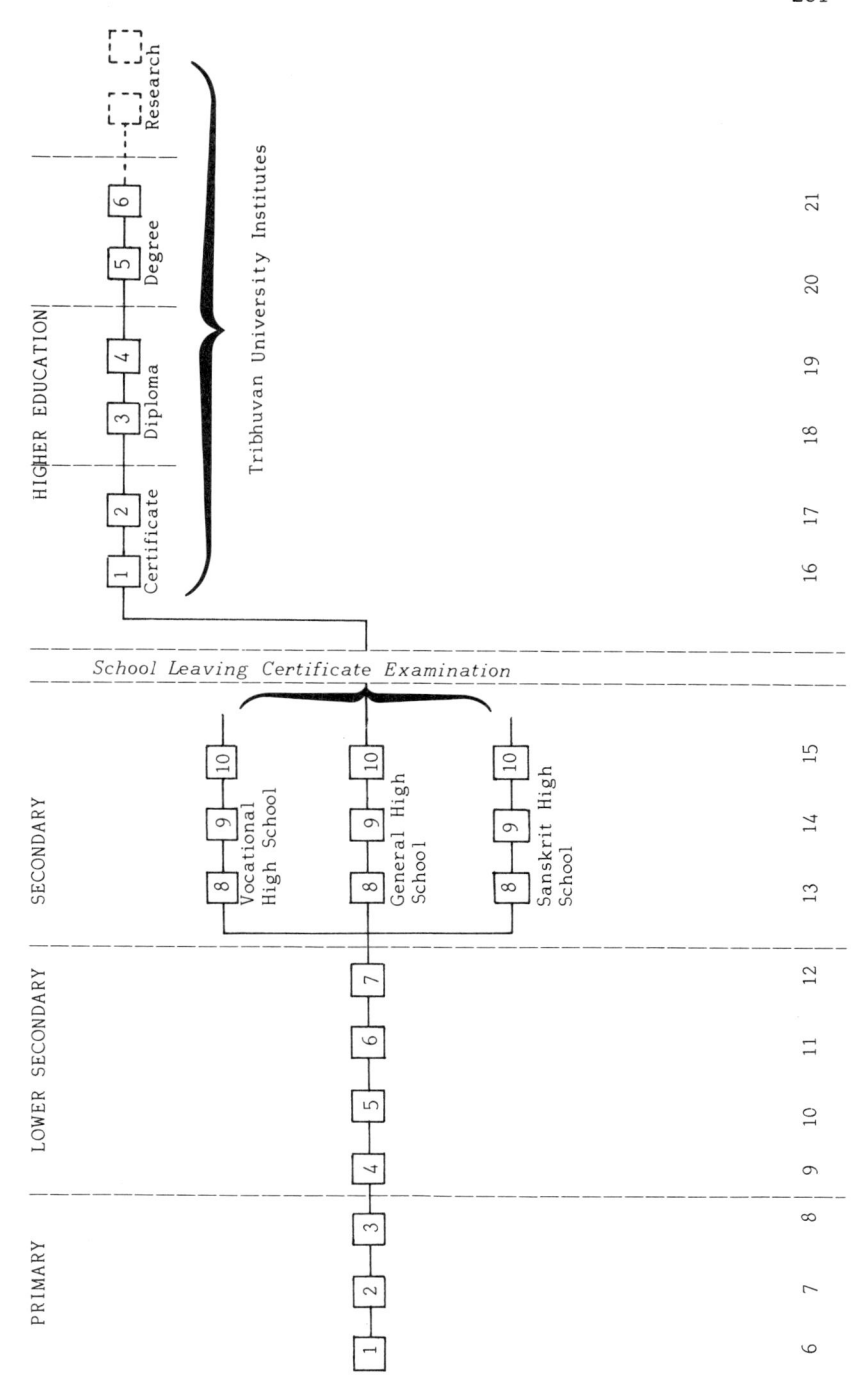

PRIMARY | LOWER SECONDARY | SECONDARY | HIGHER EDUCATION

Primary: 1, 2, 3
Lower Secondary: 4, 5, 6, 7
Secondary:
- 8, 9, 10 — Vocational High School
- 8, 9, 10 — General High School
- 8, 9, 10 — Sanskrit High School

School Leaving Certificate Examination

Higher Education (Tribhuvan University Institutes):
- 1, 2 — Certificate
- 3, 4 — Diploma
- 5, 6 — Degree
- Research

Ages: 6, 7, 8, 9, 10, 11, 12, 13, 14, 15, 16, 17, 18, 19, 20, 21

261

for the Cambridge examination. These schools still have a high reputation and are fully subscribed. The United Mission Boys Boarding School in Pokhara offers the best model so far for vocational schools.

Budhanilkantha School

This British aid assisted project - originally intended to be a model school on British public school lines - was started in 1966 and opened with its first intake of 80 pupils in May 1983. The aim now is to create a school which will be a realistic model for general high schools rather than one which is beyond their scope for imitation. Entry is on merit, with a system of zonal quotas to reduce the danger of elitism. A scholarship scheme provides free places for at least one third of the total number of pupils. The school will eventually have 480 pupils, mostly boarders. The senior staff are British. All other staff are Nepali. By a special compromise agreement the medium of instruction is English for mathematics, science and English; Nepali for all other subjects.

Tertiary

Tribhuvan University is the only degree-granting institution in Nepal. It consists of the following ten institutes or faculties covering the various subject areas:

(i) Business Administration, Commerce & Public Administration

(ii) Arts, Humanities & Social Sciences

(iii) General Sciences

(iv) Law

(v) Sanskrit Studies

(vi) Agriculture & Veterinary Science

(vii) Forestry

(viii) Medicine

(ix) Engineering

(x) Education

Formerly there were 12 institutes but during the academic year 1976/77 the university decided to build up a network of research oriented centres. thus the Institute of Applied Science and Technology was split, part going to the Institute of General Sciences and the remainder becoming the Centre for Applied Science and Technology. The Institute of Nepalese and Asian Studies became the Centre for Nepalese and Asian Studies. There already existed the Centre for Economic Development and Administration. The university operates through 79 campuses. Formerly independent intermediate or degree colleges offered undergraduate courses but these have now been amalgamated with the university. The official enrolment target for tertiary education is 19% of high school enrolment. In 1975/76 with approximately 67,000 pupils in high school education, 24,000 or 35% went on to tertiary education.

The pattern of higher education formerly consisted of three stages, each lasting two years; the first stage extended from the end of secondary schooling to the Intermediate examination, the second to the Bachelor degree and the third to Master's degree. The first two stages were taken in the colleges, and the third in the university itself. Under the National Education System Plan this basic structure has been maintained but with some changes. The Intermediate stage has been renamed Certificate, the Bachelor is now Diploma and the former Master's degree keeps its title. Beyond the Master's degree comes research, but there are still few facilities for study at this level.

National Development Service

From 1975 students at degree level have been required to work in a village for one year at the end of the fifth year of higher education. They are paid for this work by the ministries concerned. A major part of this service consists of teaching, both in schools and in adult literacy classes. The scheme may be extended to Diploma students at a later date.

Teacher Training

In 1971 the existing College of Education was absorbed by Tribhuvan University as the Institute of Education. The Institute has two large campuses in Kathmandu and six outside the Kathmandu Valley at Birgunj, Butwal, Dhankuta, Ilam, Nepalganj and Pokhara; a seventh is planned for Gorkha. The training may be summarised as follows:

(i) Primary level teachers — 2 semesters (1 year) pre-service for SLC holders; 1 semester (6 months) in-service for non-SLC holding practising teachers

(ii) Lower secondary level teachers — 4 semesters (2 years) pre-service for SLC holders; 2 semesters (1 year) pre-service for Intermediate or Certificate holders; 1 semester (6 months) in-service for practising teachers with Intermediate or Certificate qualification; 7 months pre-service training for SLC holders from vocational schools

(iii) Secondary level teachers — 4 semesters (2 years) pre-service for Intermediate or Certificate holders; 2 semesters (1 year) pre-service for Bachelor or Diploma holders; 1 semester

(6 months) in-service for practising teachers with Bachelor or Diploma qualification.

For ten years the British Council assisted first the Ministry of Education and then the Institute of Education with in-service training of English teachers. There was until 1975 an ODM Category IV contract adviser in English teaching attached to the Institute, solely concerned with in-service training. In 1973 the Institute produced a three year plan for in-service training in which English at secondary level (Classes VIII-X) was given an important place, in that it was the only subject to be given specialist treatment alongside the vocational subjects. The plan provided in-service training for 900 secondary English teachers in the course of three years.

Non-Formal and Literacy Work

At the time of the 1961 census the literate population of Nepal was said to be 9% of the total population over the age of 10 (16% of men; 2% of women). In 1956 a literacy campaign was started run by the College of Education. A 1969 estimate still rated the literate population as probably not exceeding 10% though a UNESCO document published in late 1973 suggested that the literacy figure was 14% (about 22% of men, 2% of women). In 1976 the Ministry of Education claimed a figure of 19% literacy. Literacy programmes are being encouraged both through the National Development Service and local educational institutions. There is a small budget for functional literacy classes in each district. The most successful programme so far has been Radio Nepal's weekly broadcasts for non-literate smallholders sponsored by the Ministry of Agriculture. Educational radio programmes for adults began in 1958 but as yet attempts to develop full scale distance learning programmes by radio have made minimal progress.

7 EDUCATIONAL ADMINISTRATION

Ministerial Control

The responsible minister at cabinet level is the Minister for Education advised by the National Education Committee under the chairmanship of the King or his delegate. This committee is ultimately responsible for all matters of planning and policy. Primary and secondary education are administered by the Ministry of Education headed by the Secretary for Education, assisted by four Joint Secretaries who control the four divisions of the ministry (Planning, Administration, Technical, Evaluation). Other ministries control some technical training in their respective fields. To decentralise the control of primary and secondary schooling, four regional directorates have been set up for eastern, central, western and far western Nepal under the ministry; subordinate to the regional directors are 75 district education officers. However, a long history of centralised decision-making is not quickly overcome by a structural change.

ADMINISTRATIVE ORGANISATION OF THE EDUCATION SYSTEM

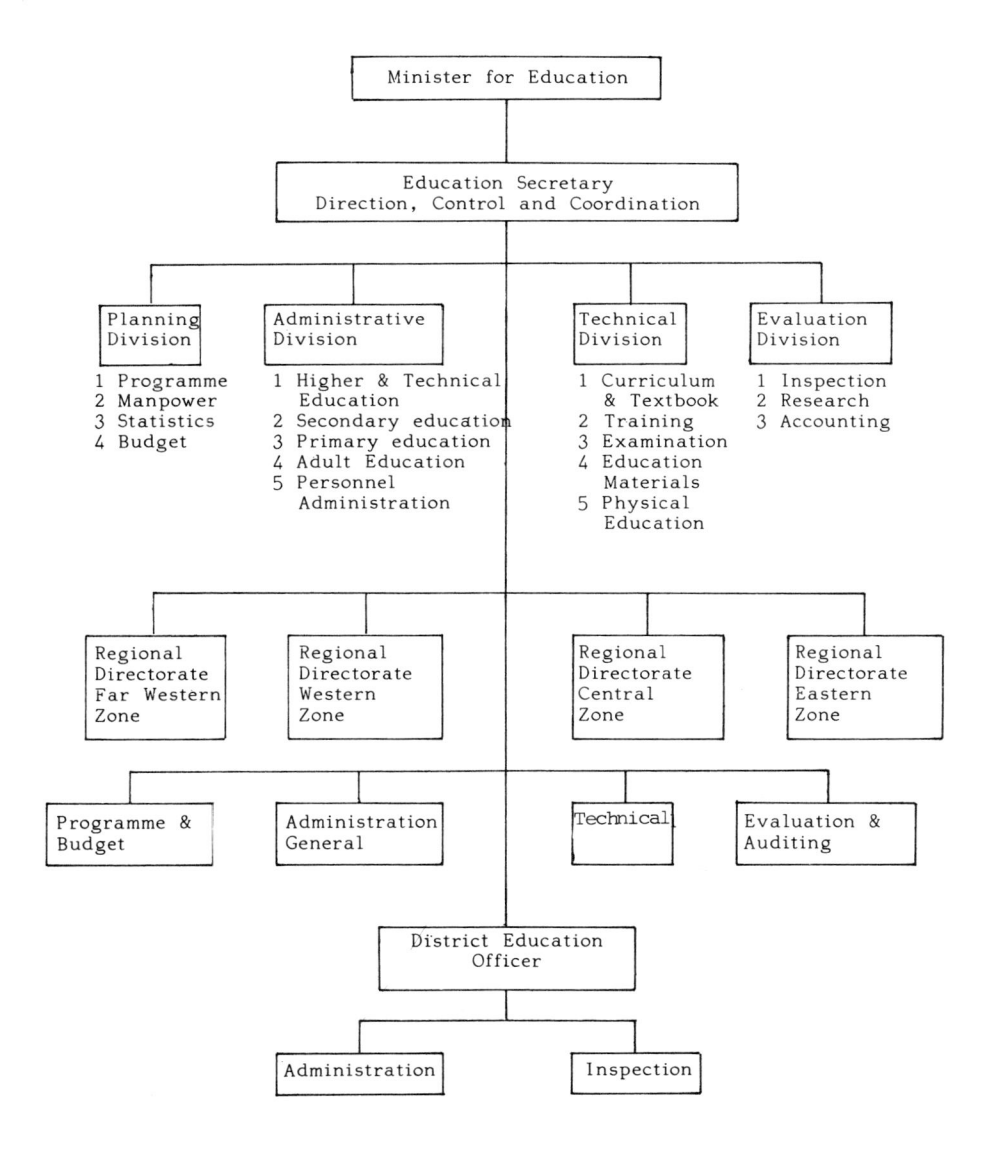

```
                          ┌─────────────────────┐
                          │ Minister for Education │
                          └──────────┬──────────┘
                          ┌──────────┴──────────────────────┐
                          │      Education Secretary         │
                          │ Direction, Control and Coordination │
                          └──────────┬──────────────────────┘
```

Planning Division	Administrative Division	Technical Division	Evaluation Division
1 Programme 2 Manpower 3 Statistics 4 Budget	1 Higher & Technical Education 2 Secondary education 3 Primary education 4 Adult Education 5 Personnel Administration	1 Curriculum & Textbook 2 Training 3 Examination 4 Education Materials 5 Physical Education	1 Inspection 2 Research 3 Accounting

Regional Directorate Far Western Zone	Regional Directorate Western Zone	Regional Directorate Central Zone	Regional Directorate Eastern Zone

Programme & Budget	Administration General	Technical	Evaluation & Auditing

```
              ┌─────────────────────┐
              │ District Education  │
              │      Officer        │
              └──────────┬──────────┘
                ┌────────┴────────┐
         ┌──────────────┐   ┌──────────┐
         │ Administration│   │Inspection│
         └──────────────┘   └──────────┘
```

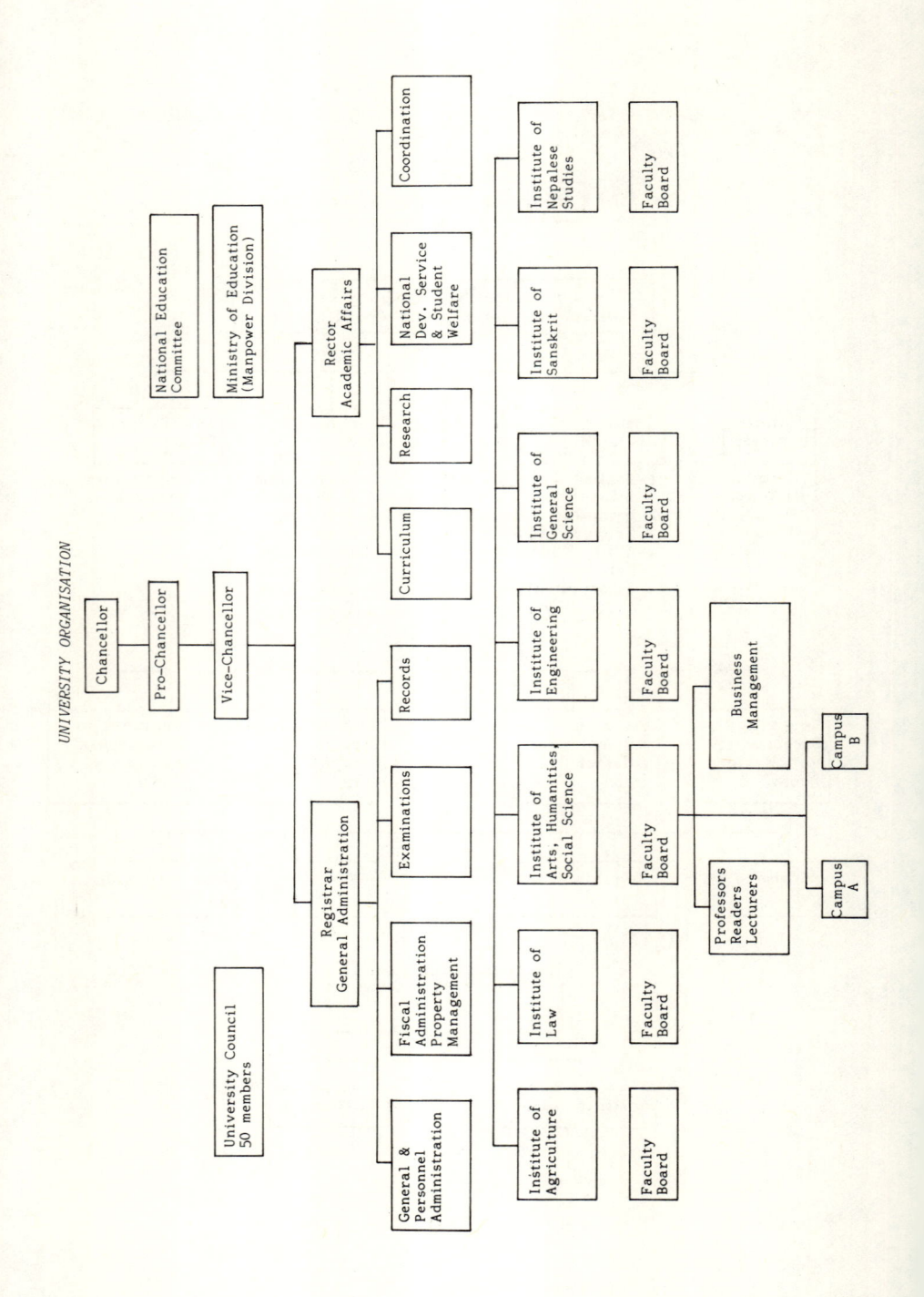

UNIVERSITY ORGANISATION

Curricula and Equipment

Under the National Plan, curricula and syllabi are controlled by the Minister of Education through the Central Curriculum Development Centre. Although established in 1972 it had only advisory powers until 1976 when it was given executive authority. Materials are produced and distributed by the Educational Materials Centre (JEMC). The current range of English textbooks was produced by an ODM-funded textbook specialist.

University Administration

Tribhuvan University, with guidance from the National Committee and the 50-member University Council, is responsible for higher education, and the university senate has a reasonable degree of autonomy. Each campus is headed by a campus chief. The institutes, which may be represented on each of the campuses, are headed by deans, who are responsible in turn to the rector and vice-chancellor of the university. The institutes have a large measure of independence in determining academic matters.

8 EDUCATIONAL FINANCE

Education Budget

The central government budget for education is derived from general revenue supplemented by local government contributions and overseas aid. In the decade from 1960 to 1970, although expenditure on education increased fivefold, the percentage of the national budget remained fairly constant between 7% and 8%. The percentage rose to 10.7% in 1975 and 10.9% in 1976 but fell to 8.3% in 1979 which represented 1.6% of GNP. The principal allocations in the Ministry of Education budget to July 1977 were:

	Millions of Rupees	%
Primary	64.6	28.4
Secondary	44.0	19.4
Vocational	4.3	1.9
University	89.7	39.4
Adult	2.0	0.9
Not by level	22.5	9.9
	227.1	99.9

Financial Administration

Under the National Plan, the district education committee supervises an education fund derived from government grants-in-aid, education tax, local school fees, donations, and income from other sources such as property. Grants-in-aid are recommended by the district inspector on the basis of student and teaching staff numbers, the educational programme and examination results. Government contributions vary from level to level and area to area. At the primary level, for example, all teachers' salaries are paid from government funds while all other expenses must be met locally; in specified remote areas, however, the government will meet the whole cost of primary education.

Overseas Aid

During the middle 1960s overseas aid (USAID and the Indian government providing by far the largest contribution) accounted for almost half of the education budget. Since then the proportion of overseas aid has declined considerably but remains important. On the multilateral front UNDP has financed an eight-year project (1969-77) to develop education, concentrating especially on primary teacher training, while another UNDP sponsored teacher training programme, aimed specifically at women was mounted between 1972 and 1975. During 1975/76 UNICEF made a grant of US$230,000 for hostel and primary school construction, supplies and equipment and over the period 1975-80 UNICEF has committed substantial funds for local support to primary teachers. UNESCO has supported the setting up of the Curriculum Development Centre at Tribhuvan University and continues to provide training, latterly especially in broadcasting.

The United States remains a major source of bilateral aid. A project was implemented between 1972-78 to improve the development and testing of educational materials in science and mathematics in conjunction with appropriate teacher training. A four-year programme 1976-80 was introduced to improve educational management skills. Other assistance is being given to secondary level mathematics and science and to the teaching of agriculture. Among other countries Canada has provided financial support for school building and NORAD has given partial sponsorship to Norwegian specialists working in the development of university curricula. Substantial British aid continues for the Budhanilkantha School and the British Council has been administering ongoing programmes for Nepal since 1960.

9 DEVELOPMENT AND PLANNING OF THE EDUCATION SYSTEM

Origins

Traditional Nepalese scholarship was a product of the Sanskritised Hindu and Buddhist priesthood. It reached its highest levels in the tenth and eleventh centuries in the

Kathmandu Valley (the only part of Nepal to have a comparatively continuous tradition of culture and education and a relatively literate population). At its height, the Valley was a centre of learning with influence on India, Tibet and China. There still exist in Kathmandu and Patan *bahals* (of a slightly later date) or quadrangles of civil settlement which were formerly centres not only of traditional Buddhist learning, but also of philosophy, rhetoric, grammar, literature and medicine. In addition to such academic pursuits, they were centres of apprenticeship in crafts such as painting, bronze-casting and jewellery and associated with them were highly developed skills in building and allied crafts such as brick and tile making, woodworking and brass casting and working. Alongside the Buddhist centres of learning, Brahmin tutors conducted the *varnashram* system of Hindu education. Both Buddhist and Hindu priesthood were connected with the court, had considerable authority and propagated a conservative orthodoxy in belief and behaviour, and both Hindu and Buddhist teaching traditionally emphasised rote-learning.

Nepal's first contact with western education came on the return of Jang Bahadur Rana (the ruler) from his European tour in 1853. He set up a small class under the tutorship of an Englishman, who gave lessons in English, mathematics and history to Jang Bahadur's brothers and nephews. Even after this informal class was institutionalised 30 years later as Durbar School, the main aim of education was to maintain the Rana ascendancy and schooling was therefore restricted to members of the clan and the client families who formed the bureaucracy. The first Nepalese citizen to go to Calcutta and pass the entrance examination for the school leaving certificate was Chandra J B Rana in 1884, who as Prime Minister 34 years later inaugurated Nepal's first modern college, reputedly with the words "This is the beginning of our end".

Development

The end was slow in coming. When it did come in 1951 Nepal had 11 secondary schools and Trichandra College was still the only source of higher education. It is estimated that there were about 1,000 people who had completed high school and perhaps 300 with a college qualification. Education was restricted to an administrative elite and was available only to a very few people of privileged background. In the following 20 years there was a rapid but uncontrolled increase in the number of schools.

Planning

The importance of planning in education had been recognised from the setting up of the National Education Planning Commission which produced its first long range plan in 1954/55. Much of what was planned was sound, but little of what was recommended was realised. For example, the Planning Commission recommended limited development in higher education, with a rate of 5% of secondary school enrolment. Unfortunately higher education was a powerful political and popular issue. Despite the advised target, the number of colleges grew from one in 1950 to 33 in 1961, by which time enrolment had shot up to 25%. The government's inability to resist popular pressure for education and its reliance at primary and secondary levels on commercial interests to provide it, led to a system in which schools were unevenly distributed, untrained teachers were in the majority and expensive technical subjects neglected in favour of the cheaper humanities. This situation in turn led to a reappraisal of the aims of education in terms of economics and development and the present attempt to reorganise the system in a more relevant form.

National Education System Plan

In 1970 the government drew up the National Education System Plan which aimed to establish a uniform system of education over the whole country, recognising the problems contributing to previous failures and making a number of provisions to overcome them. It was drawn up entirely without foreign aid, although it drew a good deal on the results of various aid projects and surveys. The Plan was implemented on a phased basis over a period of five years (1971-76). Its stated aims were:

(i) to strengthen devotion to the Crown and to the nation

(ii) to establish and maintain national unity and loyalty to the *panchayat* system of democracy

(iii) to establish a uniform national education system of a comprehensive range

(iv) to encourage the development and use of Nepali as the national language

(v) to stimulate financial and social mobility throughout the country

(vi) to meet the manpower requirements for optimum national development.

These aims were intended to fulfil the general purpose of transforming a geo-political unity into a realistic feeling of national solidarity and stimulating an active flow of life into the social and economic sector.

The Plan included the following specific proposals:

(i) decentralisation of administration of primary and secondary education and incorporation of all post-secondary education into the university

(ii) reform of the structure of the education system

(iii) placing of emphasis on vocational education at all levels

(iv)   regulation of opportunities for higher education according to the manpower requirements of the national development programme

(v)   standardised curricula at all levels, with Nepali as the medium of instruction and communication

(vi)   reform of the examination system to allow both internal and external evaluation at every level

(vii) maintenance of an appropriate balance between quantitative and qualitative progress

(viii) priority to be given to the production and distribution of suitable educational materials for all schools

(ix)   establishment of national standards and tests for the selection of students for post-secondary education and for advanced studies

(x)   increased provision of teacher training and an improvement in the status of the teaching profession by establishing standardised entry qualifications and awarding higher remuneration on a par with other professins

(xi)   establishment of scholarships for deserving students where family resources are insufficient to meet the expense of further study.

FORMATION AND IMPLEMENTATION OF THE NATIONAL EDUCATION SYSTEM PLAN 1970

REFORMS

Innovation

(i) *A Curriculum Development Centre* will be established for revising and reviewing curricula at all levels. The centre will be responsible for textbook research and reform and will maintain close relationships with the university, college of education and teacher training centres and the textbook production centres

(ii) *Teaching Methods* will be developed for each subject in accordance with the nature of the subject and the findings of modern pedagogical studies and research

(iii) *The Janak Education Materials Centre* will be made an autonomous organisation for the writing, printing, publication and distribution of all approved educational materials

(iv) *Textbook Distribution Centres* will be strategically sited throughout the country and the district education offices will be responsible for controlling distribution and utilisation of the textbooks in the schools within their respective districts. Textbooks will be made freely available to all primary school children in the remote areas and to the needy primary school children in other areas.

(v) *Science Education* Provisions will be made for the supply of suitable science equipment to all schools. There should be a science laboratory in every high school and adequate facilities for teaching science in lower secondary schools.

Teacher Training

(i) The general aim is to have only trained, qualified teachers in all schools, starting with the schools in the two pilot districts, Kaski and Chitwan

(ii) Those teachers working in schools who have the minimum academic qualifications will receive their additional professional training at an in-service course

(iii) The curricula in colleges of education and primary teacher training centres will be revised in accordance with the requirements of the new Plan

(iv) Research in teacher training methods will be encouraged and all teachers will receive training in physical education and health and in methods of internal testing and evaluation

(v) Arrangements will be made for special training courses for headmasters and district inspectors

(vi) Trained teachers, as available, will be assigned to schools by the Ministry of Education. The education inspectors will supervise and report on their performance in the schools

(vii) Refresher courses (in-service) will be arranged at regular intervals for practising teachers

(viii) There will be special standardised training courses in the various branches of vocational education for the teachers from the high schools

(ix) Teacher training stipends will be gradually phased out.

Teaching as a Professional Career

(i) Under the Ministry of Education, the appointment, promotion, transfer, discharge of all teachers will be controlled by a district education service commission

(ii) Similarly payments of salaries of teachers will be made from a district education fund drawn from grants-in-aid, school fees and other sources available to the schools of that district

(iii) Salary scales will be increased from 50% to 100%, the maximum being RS 155 a month for primary teachers and the maximum of Rs 600 a month for the headmasters of the high schools

(iv) Pupil-teacher ratios will be improved

(v) On retirement a teacher's pension will take the form of a lump sum to be determined by his ranking and years of service.

The Examination System

(i) Internal testing of pupils will be carried out every three months

(ii) Teachers will be responsible for keeping records of pupils' progress and achievement

(iii) Teachers' guides will include examples of testing procedures

(iv) Standardised tests will be developed in some subjects

(v) Criteria will be established for the rational, standardised grading of answers

(vi) Promotion from primary to lower secondary schools will be determined by the results of district-wide examinations

- (vii) Promotion from lower secondary to high schools will be determined by the results of zone-wide examinations
- (viii) The SLC (high school graduation) examination will be conducted on a district basis, with nationally standardised marking and grading
- (ix) An examination reform and research section will be established within the office of the Controller of Examinations
- (x) Provision will be made to allow up to 25% of the total marks in the SLC examination to be based on the school's internal assessment of the pupil
- (xi) Examinations in higher (tertiary) level education will be decentralised and given every six months instead of every two years. Internal evaluation will be gradually increased in weighting from 20% to 50%. Detailed reports of progress will be regularly made and given to the students
- (xii) Discrepancies between internal assessment and external (examination) evaluation of any student will be investigated and adjudicated by the University Examination Board. Consistent discrepancies will constitute evidence of the need for inquiries into the methods and procedures of the institution concerned.

IMPLEMENTATION OF THE PLAN
Phased Development

1971/72 Experimental	2 districts only (Kaski and Chitwan) for pilot testing
1972/73	13 districts on a 1 district per zone basis (there are 14 zones)
1973/74 Middle Phase	15 districts
1974/75	20 districts
1975/76 Permanent phase	25 districts
	75 districts in 14 zones

Total Five-Year Expenditure Summary

(i)	*Salaries*			NC Rs 205,000,000
	(a) primary	93m		
	(b) lower secondary	52m		
	(c) high school	60m		
(ii)	*Grants-in-Aid*			NC Rs 136,000,000
	(a) schools	53m		
	(b) vocational training centres	74m		
	(c) university	9m		
(iii)	*Development*			91,000,000
	(a) advanced vocational training	44m		
	(b) general higher education	21m		
	(c) teacher training	16m		
	(d) scholarships	10m		
(iv)	*Educational Materials*			41,000,000
(v)	*Research*			7,000,000
(vi)	*National Student Service*			10,000,000
(vii)	*Administration (Ministry)*			75,000,000
(viii)	*Contingencies*			13,000,000
		TOTAL		Rs 578,000,000

Say US$60,000,000

Estimate of Yearly Budget Requirements

1971/72	NC Rs	72m
1972/73		91m
1973/74		115m
1974/75		140m
1975/76		160m
		578m say US$60,000,000

NEPAL BASIC STATISTICS

Population

1960	1970	1979
9,245,000	11,230,000	13,421,000

Illiteracy Rate among Adults 15+ 1975

Total	Male	Female
80.8%	66.6%	95.0%

Enrolment Ratios

Primary = enrolments as a percentage of the population aged 6-8
Secondary = enrolments as a percentage of the population aged 9-15
Higher = enrolments as a percentage of the population aged 20-24

		Primary	Secondary	Higher
1970	Total	26% *	10% †	–
	Female	8% *	3% †	–
1975	Total	51%	13%	2.3%
	Female	16%	4%	0.9%
1979	Total	88%	19%	2.8% §
	Female	49%	8%	1.2% §

* As a percentage of the population aged 6-10
† As a percentage of the population aged 11-15
§ 1978

Schools, Pupils and Teachers

	1970	1975	1979
Primary:			
Schools	–	8,314	9,886
Teachers	17,988	18,874	26,384
Pupils	389,825	542,524	1,012,530
Secondary:			
Schools	–	–	–
Teachers	–	9,947	14,801
Pupils	–	281,816	449,038

Higher Education Students by Field of Study 1978

	Students	% female
Education & Teacher Training	6,198	17.0
Humanities & Religion	11,110	30.0
Law	1,966	6.0
Commerce & Business	5,242	8.1
Natural Science	2,786	14.7
Medicine & related fields	1,717	49.0
Engineering	1,673	0.1
Agriculture	1,160	0.0

Government Expenditure on Education

	As a % of total government spending	As a % of GNP
1970	6.7%	0.6%
1975	10.7%	1.4%
1979	8.3%	1.6%

Government Spending on Education by Level

	Primary	Secondary	Higher	Other
1971	23.0%	23.2%	31.6%	22.2%
1978	66.0%		32.4%	1.7%

Basic Social and Economic Data

Gross National Product per capita – US$130

Average Annual Growth of GNP per capita 1960–1979 – 0.2%

Life expectancy 1979 – 44 years

Proportion of the Population employed in:

    Agriculture
      1960   95%
      1979   93%

    Industry
      1960   2%
      1979   2%

    Services
      1960   3%
      1979   5%

New Zealand

CONTENTS

1 Geography	280
2 Population	282
3 Society and Culture	283
4 History and Politics	283
5 The Economy	285
6 The Education System	286
7 Educational Administration	291
8 Educational Finance	294
9 Development and Planning of the Education System	294

New Zealand is a wealthy and developed country with a mature education system. Yet she faces some of the educational problems more commonly associated with non-industrial countries. There are issues of rural education for scattered populations, of accommodation of indigenous as well as immigrant cultural minorities and, most crucially, of a persisting British influence.

The majority of New Zealanders have access to an education system which, in its quantative provision, matches or excels those of most industrial countries. Elementary and lower secondary education have been universal and compulsory for many years. Participation rates in upper secondary and especially higher education are greater than those of Britain. There is an extensive system of further education.

Yet much of the school system is British in origin and has been in danger of ossifying into a traditional British pattern. While lower secondary schools are open to all, they prepare pupils for an examination system very similar to the academic, single subject based English GCE system. The continuing academic and elitist orientation of this form of assessment is reflected in low pass rates and a concentration on traditional academic subjects. Universities are also traditionally British in their emphasis on pure disciplines. There is no technical/vocational sector of higher education except for teacher education which takes place entirely outside universities.

The British influence is part English and part Scottish. The Scottish legacy is seen in relatively open access to universities (though with highly competitive scholarship schemes) and a high drop out/failure ratio in contrast to the highly selective English system. Though English conceptions of pure education have been adopted, a more equalitarian view of access to education prevails. However, issues of relating the education system to economic needs still remain unsolved.

New Zealand has significant social minorities for whom the educational system is required to provide equal opportunities. There is the important rural farming population which plays a major role in the production of national wealth but which has not enjoyed full educational equality because of difficulties in providing adequate educational facilities for a scattered population. Correspondence and boarding education are well developed but there are still difficulties in creating large enough schools which can offer the full range of educational opportunities in rural areas.

New Zealand historically has enjoyed a reputation for an effective policy of providing the indigenous Maori minority with real choices between a majority or minority orientated education. However, there has been greater pressure for the recognition of Maori culture in recent years, at the same time as providing full equality of educational opportunity. The minority group issue has shifted perhaps further towards educational opportunity with the considerable and recent influx of Pacific islanders.

1 GEOGRAPHY

Topography

New Zealand comprises two main islands, North and South, Stewart Island, the Chatham Islands and a number of adjacent islets with a total area of 266,700 sq kms (103,000 square miles). Its overseas territories are the Tokelau Islands, Nieu and the Ross Dependency. The Cook Islands achieved the status of self-government in free association with New Zealand in 1965. The main islands, with high central ridges running south-west to north-east between 38°-48° latitude south, have a combined length of just over 1,600 km (1,000 miles) and a width not exceeding 450 km (280 miles) at the broadest point. There are areas of great natural beauty with snow-covered peaks rising to 2,762 metres (12,343 feet), forests in their natural state, glaciers, lakes and rivers and beaches. The islands are in an earthquake belt.

Climate

The climate is temperate with rainfall varying between 6,400 mm (252 inches) and 334 mm (13 inches). The capital, Wellington, averages 1,200 mm. Mean temperatures decrease steadily southwards from 15°C in the far north to about 12°C at Cook Strait, then to 9°C in the south. January and February

NEW ZEALAND

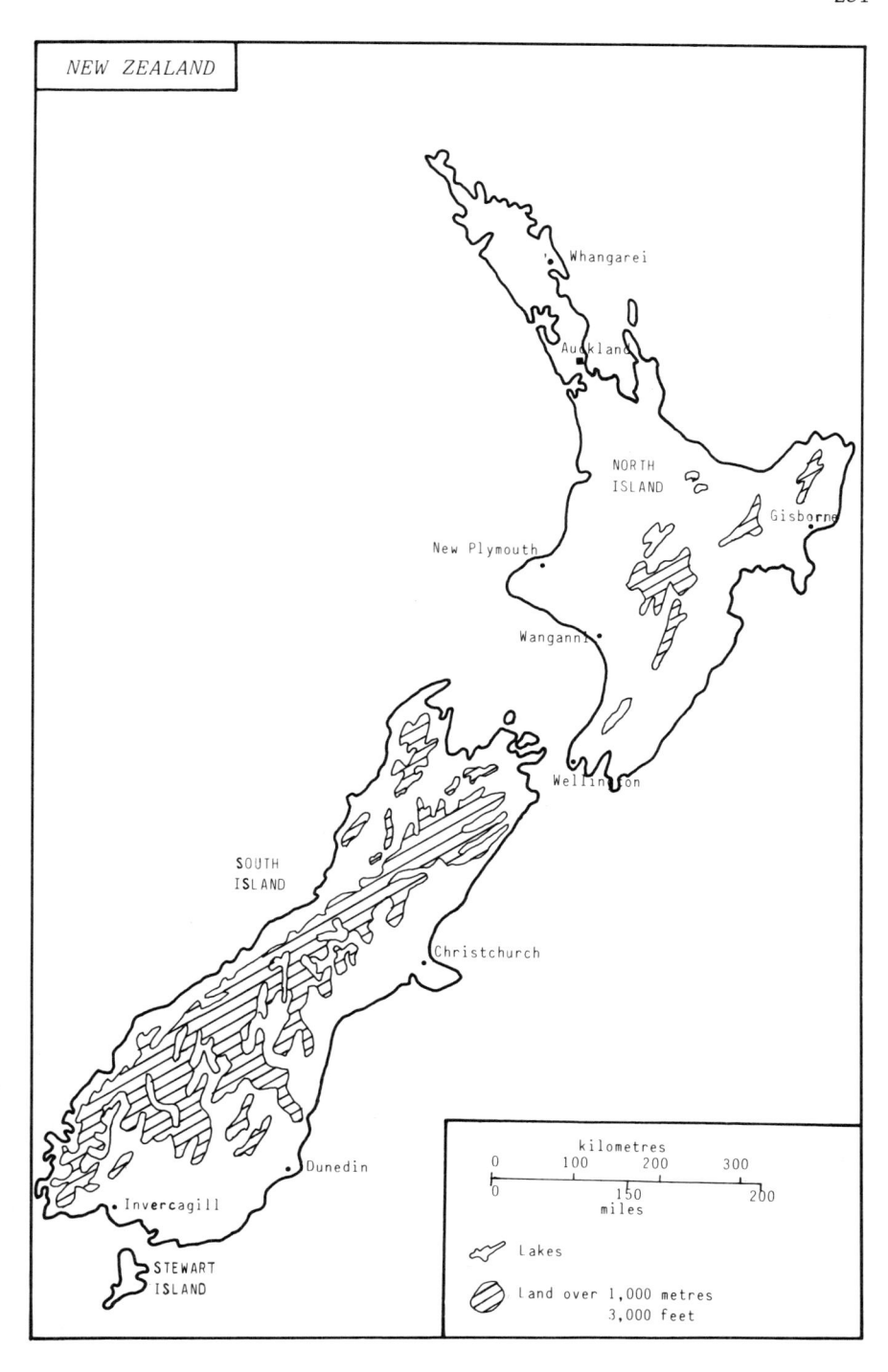

are the warmest months, and July is the coldest.

Communications

Communications with other countries are by sea and air with regular services across the Tasman to Australia and to Europe both via south-east Asia, India and the Middle East and by way of the Pacific islands and America. The international airports are at Auckland and Christchurch. Internal communications are by road, rail, inter-island ferries and air, the latter being used extensively because of the distances between centres of population.

2 POPULATION

Growth

The population in 1979 was estimated at 3,096,000. The rate of population growth over the past 20 years has averaged 2%. The government encourages controlled immigration; at the moment emigration figures are higher than immigration figures, but the gap between the two is narrowing, and the government has made projections of population by 1986 of 3,237,000 (assuming a net annual immigration of zero by 1984) or of 3,309,000 (assuming a net annual immigration of zero by 1982).

Distribution

The bulk of the population is concentrated in urban areas where the most rapid growth rates are occurring, owing to the development of manufacturing and tertiary industries and better social, cultural and educational opportunities in these areas. In 1956, 74.2% of the population were in urban areas and in 1976 the percentage was 83%. There is also a drift of population from south to north particularly into the Auckland area which has the most rapid rate of growth. The main urban areas are Auckland (population 805,900 in 1979), Wellington (349,900), Christchurch (327,300), Hamilton (159,800) and Dunedin (119,400).

Groups

Most of the 3.1 million inhabitants are of British descent, but there are significant groups originating from other European countries, especially Scandinavia, Netherlands and Yugoslavia, and of Indian, Chinese and Lebanese descent. There are about 275,700 Maories whose ancestors came from Polynesia in or before the fourteenth century.

3 SOCIETY AND CULTURE

Social Patterns

As a democratic state modern New Zealand encompasses a diversity of life styles and permits a wide variety of beliefs, attitudes and values to co-exist. Cultural traditions are mainly British with a strong and increasing influence from the United States. Sixty percent of imported radio and television programmes are from the USA. New Zealanders pride themselves on their egalitarianism and freedom from racism. There are, however, considerable variations in the standard of living (although this is very high on average) between the wealthy and the poorest sections of society. Maories assert that they are treated as second class citizens and there are few in managerial and professional classes. The strong accent which is emerging on the rights of all cultural groups has implications for the formulation of the aims of education. The Social Security system provides cash benefits and subsidised medical and hospital benefits such that there is reciprocity with Britain.

Language

English is the national language and Maoris and immigrants from the Pacific islands are at a disadvantage as English is not their native language. There is a growing realisation that more attention should be given to the Maori language.

Religion

The bulk of the population professes the Christian religion: Anglican (35%), Presbyterian (22%), Roman Catholic (16%), and Methodist (7%), with the rest spread thinly over a wide range of denominations. Victorian puritanism still lingers among the elderly, but the young people, as in Western countries, are tending to throw off the shackles of dogma and strict codes. The majority of the private schools, catering for 11% of school pupils, are run by religions organisations with Catholicism predominant.

4 HISTORY AND POLITICS

Development

First discovered by Europeans in 1642 and mapped by Captain Cook in 1769, New Zealand was regularly visited by whalers from 1792 onwards and numerous mission stations had been established in North Island by 1840, when a treaty was signed with the Maoris ceding sovereignty to the British Crown. Following this there was a steady stream of settlers to the new colony who brought with them British traditions which shaped society and education and remain deep rooted. New Zealand was given the title of Dominion in 1907 and was granted complete autonomy under the Statute of Westminster of December 1931, as a self-governing member of the Commonwealth, although it was not until 1947 that the New Zealand government formally adopted the Statute of Westminster. Ties with Britain remain strong but the younger generation no longer think of Britain as 'home'.

Government and Politics

New Zealand is a monarchial state, the Queen being represented by a Governor General. The legislative authority is the General Assembly, which consists of the Governor General and the House of Representatives. There are two main parties, Labour and National, which compete for votes in elections every three years. There is universal suffrage from 18 years of age (New Zealand gave women the vote in 1893). There are 92 constituencies, 88 European and 4 Maori. The system of government and parliamentary procedures are based on British precedents and traditions. In 1977 there were 239 territorial local authorities comprising 132 city and borough councils, 5 town councils and 98 county councils varying greatly in type, area, resources and population. A local government commission prepared area and local schemes of reorganisation and rationalisation of local government which are gradually being implemented.

International Relations

In recent years New Zealand has adopted an increasingly independent role in international affairs, becoming more confident and assertive in the United Nations (UN) and the Commonwealth. Considerations of defence and diversification of trade and export markets caused New Zealand to direct more attention to her neighbours in the Pacific and South East Asia as Britain drew closer to the European community. New Zealand plays an active part as a member of most of the specialised agencies of the UN and also of regional alliances and organisations, especially the Australia, New Zealand and US Defence Pact (ANZUS), the Australia, New Zealand and UK Defence Task Force based in Singapore (ANSUK), the South East Asia Treaty Organisation (SEATO), the Asian and Pacific Council (ASPAC), the Economic Commission for Asia and the Far East (ECAFE) and the South Pacific Commission. New Zealanders have had an increased sense of involvement in South Pacific countries are more territories in the area achieved self-government and looked to New Zealand for leadership, encouragement and aid.

The distribution of New Zealand government aid to overseas countries totalled $53.5 millions in 1979/80, of which $30 million was in the form of bilateral aid to the South Pacific and $12 million was in bilateral aid to South and South East Asia (including Colombo Plan aid).

5 THE ECONOMY

Economic Situation

New Zealand has a mixed economy, mainly agrarian. GNP grew from NZ$8,636 million in 1974 to NZ$12,786 million in 1977. The National Development Council had set a target growth rate of 4.5%. Other targets included increasing the proportion of GNP used for investment (around 25%) and growth of exports of 6.6% annum.

Agriculture

New Zealand is a farming country and one of the largest exporters in the world of meat, dairy produce and wool. About 65% of the total area of land is occupied farmland and there are probably more farm animals in proportion to population than in any other country. The pattern is one of intensive farming with improved management practices, heavy investment in land improvement and machinery and substantial growth of contracts services in harvesting, maintenance, shearing, etc.

Industry

Recent industrial developments include pulp and paper manufacture, aluminium smelting and semi-fabrication, light aircraft manufacture, textiles, leather goods and steel production. Exports of domestic produce in 1977/78 were valued at NZ$3,134,593 thousand, a rise of NZ$37,875 thousand from 1976/77. The government is now giving regional development an important place in planning and is encouraging the development of industry in priority regions to provide employment opportunities and restrain outflow of population from these regions. Mineral resources are limited, but a large natural gas project and iron and steel works are under development. Hydroelectric power is widely available, but needs to be expanded. The growing manufacturing industries are protected by import tariffs.

Employment

The labour force totalling 1,230,100 in 1977 was distributed as follows:

Primary industries	145,500
Manufacturing	308,400
Construction	91,200
Commerce	192,900
Transport and communication	110,800
Services, administration and professions	271,300
Armed forces	11,000
Unemployed	4,100

Trade

The value of trade in 1977/78 is shown below (in NS$ 000s):

Total imports	Export of domestic products	Re-exports	Total merchandise exported
3,001,508	3,134,593	174,520	3,308,113

Britain is traditionally the main export market for meat, milk products and wool, but recently there has been marked success in diversification. Imports are mainly of machinery needed for industry and manufactured goods for the growing population.

6 THE EDUCATION SYSTEM

The division between primary and secondary education is not uniform throughout New Zealand. The structure that most widely prevails is of an eight-year primary school followed by a five-year secondary school. In rural areas, however, different arrangements often apply. There are six-year primary schools which lead to one of the following: two-year intermediate schools followed by five-year secondary education; seven-year secondary schools; or to the secondary branches of all age district high schools or area schools. Some children receive both primary and secondary education in thirteen-year district high schools or area schools.

There is also a correspondence school providing classes, by radio as well as visiting teachers and other distance education activities for pupils from the pre-school stage to the end of secondary education as well as part time adults following secondary level education. Many pupils live in areas too far from a regular school though children living overseas, those with medical problems and those with whom normal schools cannot cope are also enrolled.

Private schools provide over 10% of school places but, since an Act of 1975, have been integrated into the State system.

Pre-Primary

Children below the age of 5 are not enrolled in State primary schools, but may be enrolled in free kindergartens or at play centres controlled by local associations. There were 35,560 children in 474 kindergartens in 1977 and 570 recognised play centres for approximately 21,396 children.

Primary

At the age of 5 a child may, and at 6 must, enter a primary school, or if living in an isolated area, must enrol with the primary department of the Correspondence School. Education in State primary schools is free and secular. After six years the top two years of the primary course, Forms I and II, may be provided in an intermediate school. On completing 8 years school attendance a child usually enters Form III of a secondary school or the secondary department of a district high school.

In 1980 there were, 2,179 schools (including 145 intermediate schools or departments) with 452,892 pupils (38,317 of whom were in intermediate schools or departments). There were also 314 private primary schools (or primary departments of private secondary schools) with 47,746 pupils. The majority of private schools were Roman Catholic.

The curriculum of the primary and intermediate schools covers oral and written language, mathematics, social studies, arts and crafts, science, physical education, health education, music and in Forms I and II woodwork and metalwork, homecraft and sewing and sometimes French and Maori. Teachers have the assistance of specialist teachers in many subjects and for children with special needs visiting teachers and advisers are available. Textbooks are issued free to pupils in all schools both State and private.

Secondary

Secondary education is compulsory up to the age of 15. The different types of secondary schools in 1980 were as follows:

State Secondary		District High Schools and Area Schools		Private Secondary	
		(Secondary Departments)			
Schools	Pupils	Schools	Pupils	Schools	Pupils
265	195,045	35	2,753	96	31,256

There were also 920 pupils in the secondary department of the Correspondence Schools.

Two hundred and two of the State secondary schools were coeducational but most of the private schools were single sex.

Students are admitted automatically to secondary education from primary schools. After three years in secondary schools, pupils take the School Certificate Examination run by the Ministry (or Department) of Education. This is similar to the English School Certificate in that it is a subject examination in which pupils may take any number of subjects up to six and is credited with passes in individual subjects though there are three compulsory subjects. The low pass rate per subject (49.6% in 1979) meant that only 24% of pupils leaving secondary schools in 1979 had completed the full five-year course.

In the fifth year students sit for the Higher School Certificate and for University Entrance Examination (as well as for compettive examinations for University Scholarships) though most students gain entry to university on the basis of school assessment.

There is a core curriculum – English, social studies, general science, mathematics, music, arts and crafts, and physical education – in the first two grades (with a presented number of units for each subject) – followed by specialisation in final three years.

Special

Special education services have been developed so that students with various kinds of disabilities can be enrolled with other students in ordinary classes wherever possible. There are also a large number of classes in schools, hospitals and clinics for students whose needs cannot be met in the ordinary way. In 1980, 13,082 children were enrolled in special schools and classes.

Maori Education

In 1980 there were 78,376 Maori children in State primary schools (3,387 in private primary schools) and 27,458 in State secondary schools (2,347 in private secondary schools). The teaching of the Maori language has been expanded so that 43,087 primary school children and 14,747 secondary pupils received Maori language teaching in 1980 – mainly from specialist and itinerant teachers. Two thousand and seventy-one pupils sat the School Certificate examination in Maori. There is also provision for more liberal staffing in schools with high proportions of Maori pupils.

Technical and Vocational

Technician training was established in 1960 with the inauguration of a part time course for engineering assistants; the Technicians Certification Authority was established in 1960, and its membership includes representatives of the Department of Education, the technical institutes, the universities and the sectors of industry and commerce most involved. The standards required for a pass in most of the subjects taken in the first and second year of the five-year part time courses are generally considered comparable to those attained in the School Certificate and University Entrance Examination Certificate respectively. In 1980 there there were 18 technical institutes, some of which are called polytechnics. They offer a wide range of part time as well as full time courses, not only in technical subjects but also in other fields of adult education. For young people who do not have access to a technical institute the technical correspondence institute provides a full range of trades technician training by correspondence, linked with periodic face-to-face practical instruction. There are four community colleges and others are being established in provincial centres where there is considered to be a need for technical education. These colleges are similar to the technical institutes

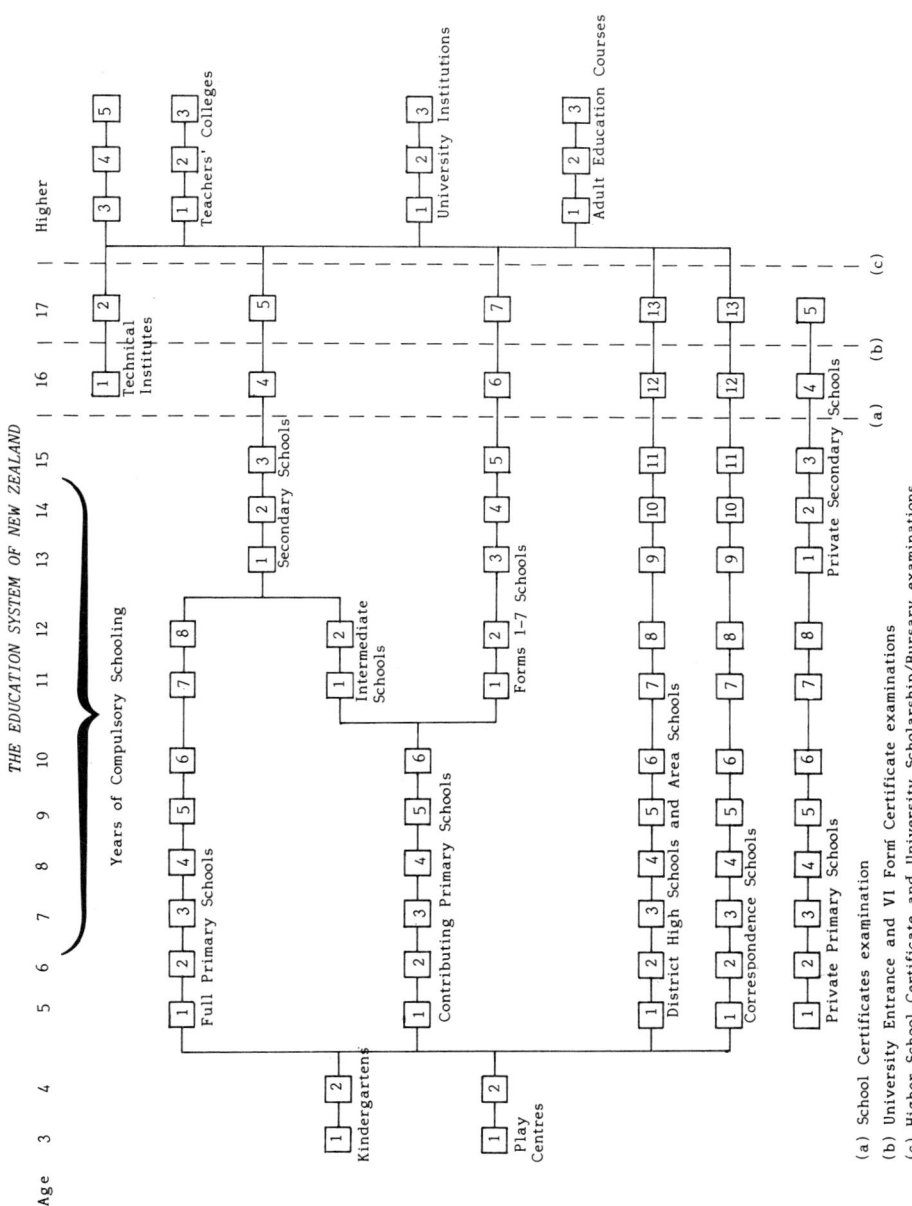

THE EDUCATION SYSTEM OF NEW ZEALAND

(a) School Certificates examination
(b) University Entrance and VI Form Certificate examinations
(c) Higher School Certificate and University Scholarship/Bursary examinations

but also fill the broader role of further education to meet the education needs of adults in each particular community. In 1980 there were 145,075 students in technical institutes and community colleges of whom 138,233 were part time.

Apprenticeship training is generally taken over five years, although a reduction may be given to those who have gained the School Certificate or passed trade examinations. Apprentices are required to pass written and practical examinations before the completion of their contract, and these examinations are set by the New Zealand Trades Certification Board. The Board also awards Advanced Trade Certificates on examination after completion of a post-apprenticeship year in specified trades. Apprentices in some trades who have gained an Advanced Trade Certificate may enter direct into the third year of the five-year course of technicians training.

Higher

Higher Education in New Zealand is provided in six universities and one university college of agriculture. In 1980 there were 51,608 students of whom 20,310 were part time or extramural. Student/teacher ratios are high in the universities, particularly during the first year, but become lower in subsequent years because of the number of students who leave at the end of the first year. A university education is open to anyone with University Entrance (UE). Those without this qualification may be admitted if they are over 21 years and are considered to have a good chance of succeeding. Besides offering courses in the usual faculties each of the six universities specialises in certain fields: Otago - medicine, dentistry, mineral technology, home science and physical education; Canterbury - engineering and fine arts and agriculture at Lincoln College; Auckland - architecture, engineering and medicine; Victoria University of Wellington - public administration and social science; Waikato - education; and Massey - agriculture, horticulture and veterinary science. A number of older students attend university, and Massey University provides correspondence courses for degrees and diplomas, mainly for mature students who have finished their formal education some years previously. The type of degree most commonly awarded is the three-year pass degree requiring 8 or 9 'units' (a 'unit' being a year's work in a subject) in at least two subjects, and study at all three levels or stages. There is cross-crediting between the universities so that students can move from one university to another. Some faculties in certain universities have been moving away from the unit system, and degree structures are being increasingly designed to permit flexibility in the make up of each student's course of study. Honours degrees are of at least four years' duration, except for those students who are admitted to the second year of a course in some degrees due to outstanding performance in the entrance scholarships examination. Other first degrees are mainly professional in character, and are preceded by an intermediate course of one year. Masters degrees are of

1-2 years' duration, and may be taken by course work, thesis, or a combination of both. The PhD degree involves supervised research for a minimum of two years.

Teacher Training

Teacher training in New Zealand is organised in five divisions. The sixth form certificate is required for admission to Division A (primary teacher training) which consists usually of three years at a teacher training college and a probationary year as an assistant in a State primary school; Division B provides three years of concurrent training at a university or technical institute and at a teacher training college; Division C is a one-year course for graduates; Division U consists of holders of secondary teacher studentships who are attached to teacher training colleges while attending universities as part-time students as part of their teacher training and Division S is for holders of primary teacher studentships in the same position as those in Division U. In 1980 there were 8 teacher colleges with 7,627 students.

Audio-Visual Services

The National Film Library has branches in Auckland, Christchurch and Wellington. In its 16 mm film section the library has over 44,000 prints of some 11,00 titles, and each week over 12,000 films are issued to some 3,000 educational institutions and over 4,000 community organisations. As well as films the Wellington branch also has a record and cassette loan service, an audio-tape reel/cassette copying service through which recorded cassettes are sold to schools at cost price, and a sample sheet music service. These services at present are limited to educational institutions only.

7 EDUCATIONAL ADMINISTRATION

The Department of Education

The Department of Education determines educational policy, sees that standards are maintained throughout the country on an equitable basis, and is responsible for curricula in State primary and secondary schools. Curriculum revision is a continuing process originating with an expert team in the Department and evolving by consultation with practising teachers through curriculum committees, trial procedures and evaluations. The department controls the inspectorate, supervises the staffing of schools and conducts the School Certificate Examination. It directly administers the Correspondence School and State special schools. All State and registered private schools are inspected regularly. The Department administers the capital expenditure voted for school buildings through its regional offices in Auckland, Wellington and Christchurch, and makes substantial grants to private schools on the basis of teachers' salaries.

Pre-School

The salaries of kindergarten teachers are paid by the Department of Education. Loans are made by the government for one-third capital cost of land, buildings and equipment, the remaining two-thirds being contributed by direct government grant. Play centre associations receive maintenance and a small establishment grant from the government.

School

Ten statutory Education Boards administer State primary schools and the governing bodies of secondary schools. They are the employing authorities of the teachers and disburse the grants received from the Department of Education for buildings, maintenance, equipment and teaching materials. No local rates are levied for education by municipal or local education authorities. Each State primary school controlled by an education board has its school committee, a statutory body, charged with management of property and other matters on behalf of the Board. School committees are elected by the parents of pupils and by adults resident in the school district. Members of the school committees elect the Education Board members and one teachers' representative is appointed to each Board. Secondary schools are controlled and administered by their own boards of governors which have a measure of autonomy in the control and management of the schools. Governors are elected by parents or are representatives of local groups and organisations together with one elected teacher representative.

Teacher

The nine teachers' colleges are administered by councils, which are made up of representatives from education boards, the universities, the Department of Education and from teachers' organisations.

Higher

The University Grants Committee (UGC) advises the government on the nation's needs for university education and research, determines the allocation of funds which it recommends for appropriation by parliament to meet these needs and reviews expenditure by the universities of this money. The UGC is also responsible for the distribution of research grants, for the award of scholarships, for the development of courses for degrees and diplomas, and for prescribing the conditions of examinations for entry to universities.

ADMINISTRATIVE ORGANISATION OF EDUCATION

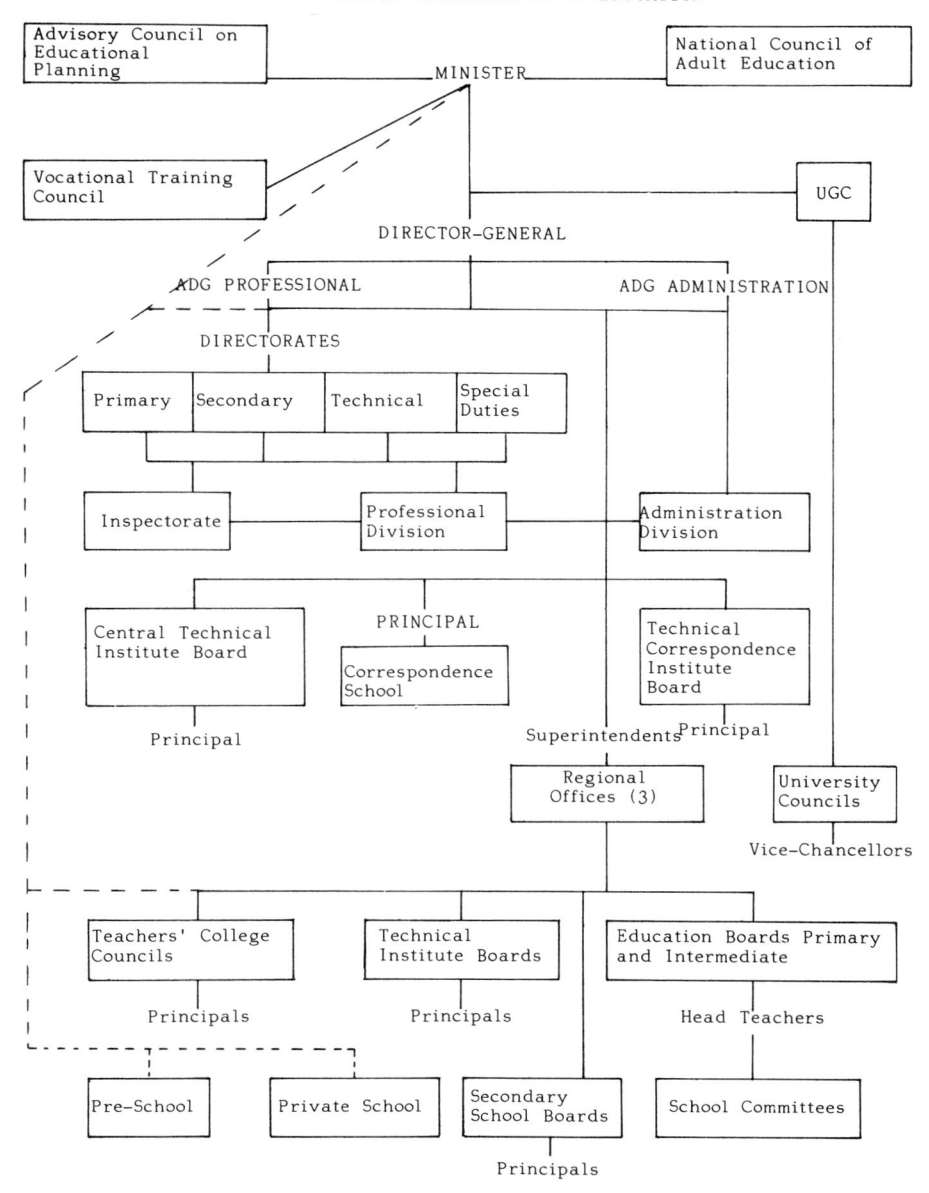

Advisory Council on Educational Planning			National Council of Adult Education
		MINISTER	

Vocational Training Council			UGC
		DIRECTOR-GENERAL	

ADG PROFESSIONAL — ADG ADMINISTRATION

DIRECTORATES

Primary	Secondary	Technical	Special Duties

Inspectorate	Professional Division	Administration Division

Central Technical Institute Board	PRINCIPAL Correspondence School	Technical Correspondence Institute Board

Principal — Superintendents — Principal

Regional Offices (3)	University Councils

Vice-Chancellors

Teachers' College Councils	Technical Institute Boards	Education Boards Primary and Intermediate
Principals	Principals	Head Teachers

Pre-School	Private School	Secondary School Boards	School Committees

Principals

8 EDUCATIONAL FINANCE

Education is financed from central government funds. Since 1970 private schools have been subsidised on the basis of 50% of teachers' salaries. Educational expenditure as a proportion of total government spending fell from 15.8% to 13.3% in 1980. The proportion of GNP devoted to education has also fallen - from 5.5% to 5% in the same period.

The distribution of funds to various levels of education in 1980 was as follows: pre-schooling 1.5%; primary schools 29.8%; secondary schools 19.3%; teacher education 5.4%; technical and community education 7.9%; special education 1.6%; universities 17.7%. The rest went to assistance to private schools (3.1%), school buildings (6.6%) and administration and support services.

9 DEVELOPMENT AND PLANNING OF THE EDUCATION SYSTEM

Development

The 1964 Education Act provided for free and secular education in State primary and secondary schools and compulsory education for all children between the ages of 6 and 15 years. In 1945 technical education was a variant form of secondary education, but over the last 15 years it has been transferred to the tertiary sector and vocational education and training is now provided by 18 technical institutes. This transformation is the result of a number of policy decisions to meet the demand for skilled workers and technicians in industry. Under the University Act 1961 a Federal University with constituent colleges was changed to a system of separate and autonomous universities, of which there are now six, to meet the demand for higher education. In recent years the education system has been characterised by numerical expansion, steady development of the curriculum, continuing rise in expenditure and a tendency to decentralisation of the administration. The levelling off in the growth of primary school rolls was expected to continue until at least 1982 and this combined with a higher retention rate of teachers is expected to result in a much improved teacher/pupil ratio in both primary and secondary schools.

Objectives

It may be said that the New Zealand system aims to provide equality of educational opportunity freely at all levels in the liberal humanist tradition and to meet the trained manpower needs of the country. The advisory Council of Educational Planning has recently provided a report for the Minister of Priorities in Education and in this connection has attempted to define the aims and objectives of education taking into account the nature of New Zealand society, the extent of the training task and areas of special competence. It is suggested that the aims of school education are:

    (i)   to lay the foundation for the educated and productive citizen by introducing the young person to deeper study in a range of humanities and sciences

(ii) to further the talents of each individual through appropriate studies and thus give a firmer basis for a later vocation

(iii) to encourage habits of rational thought and industry

(iv) to provide the young person with opportunities to learn how to be at ease and to work and play with members of the opposite sex as persons

(v) to further the growth of higher moral and social values.

Planning

In 1969 the National Development Conference made a number of recommendations on education and the Advisory Council on Educational Planning was set up to advise the Minister on implementation. The Council conducted a seminar in 1972 in conjunction with the National Commission for UNESCO, on educational planning which was attended by representatives of many educational interests and included distinguished overseas visitors. Three major themes are being pursued as a result of the seminar; educational planning in relation to national economic planning; planning the structure and content of education; techniques and information required for educational planning.

The Research and Planning Unit in the Department of Education is concerned with upgrading the statistical information required for planning and cooperates with the NZ Council for Educational Research in many projects. The research programme of this Council includes projects related to educational planning, the supply of qualified people in the community, teaching methods, services for children with special needs, pre-school education and Maori education. In addition, all educational planners are now laying particular emphasis on the education of Maori and Pacific Island children, and programmes in teacher education, special scholarships and trade training courses have been set up. Programmes in other fields are also being carried out, including a programme for five-day hostels at certain rural secondary schools which is intended to strengthen rural secondary education. A standing committee on relationships in tertiary education has been set up to consider the questions of placement on courses and rationalisation of teaching in technical and vocational education.

'Growing, Sharing and Learning', the report of the Committee on Health and Social Education, published in August 1977 discussed six main topics:

(i) the importance of ensuring a well balanced all round development of children

(ii) greater involvement of parents and community with the school

- (iii) the importance of the climate of human relationships in a school
- (iv) expanded teacher education
- (v) the need for more physical and human resources
- (vi) the greater availability of support services.

This report has been extensively circulated for public comment with a view to initiating planning in the fields which it discusses.

New Zealand has become a member of the International Curriculum Organisation and is to participate in the network for the exchange of curriculum materials and methods and undertake investigations of educational problems found in a number of countries. New Zealand also takes part in the work of the OECD's Centre for Educational Research and Innovation and the programme on educational building.

NEW ZEALAND BASIC STATISTICS

Population

1970	1979
2,816,000	3,096,000

Enrolment Ratios

Primary = Enrolments as a percentage of the population aged 5-10
Secondary = Enrolments as a percentage of the population aged 11-17
Higher = Enrolments as a percentage of the population aged 20-24

	Primary	Secondary	Higher
1970	110 (100)	77 (76)	27.8*
1979	107 (100)	81 (79)	29.1

(Figures in brackets are enrolments of students of the appropriate age range as a percentage of the total population in these age ranges).
* = 1975

Institutions, Teachers and Students

	Schools	Teachers	Pupils
Pre-Primary	–	1,133	55,522
Primary (inc. Special)	2,179	20,943	506,601
Secondary (inc. Special)	396	13,527	226,346

	Institutions	Teachers	Students
Technical & Community	20	2,256	145,075
Teacher Colleges	8	539	5,919
University	7	3,074	51,608

Higher Education Students by Field of Study in 1980

		% female
Education and Teacher Training	2,759	73
Humanities	12,600	64
Law	3,256	34
Social and Behavioural Sciences	1,045	64
Commerce and Business	6,899	24
Natural Sciences	6,708	30
Medicine and Related Fields	3,290	33
Engineering	2,958	6
Agriculture	2,339	23
Other	3,648	36

Public Expenditure on Education

As a % of total government spending		As a % of GNP
1976	15.8%	5.5%
1980	13.3%	5.0%

Public Expenditure on Education by Level 1980

Pre-school	1.5%
Primary	29.8%
Secondary	19.3%
Technical	7.9%
Teacher Education	5.4%
University	17.7%
Other	18.4%

Basic Social and Economic Data

Gross National Product per capita 1979 US$5930

Annual Annual growth of GNP per capita 1960-1979 - 1.9%

Life expectancy 1979 - 73 years

Proportion of the labour force employed in:

    Agriculture
        1960   15%
        1979   9%

    Industry
        1960   37%
        1979   35%

    Services
        1960   48%
        1979   56%

Pakistan

CONTENTS

1 Geography 302
2 Population 304
3 Society and Culture 305
4 History and Politics 306
5 The Economy 308
6 The Education System 312
7 Educational Administration 320
8 Educational Finance 321
9 Development and Planning of the
  Education System 326

Pakistan's educational system, educational policies and current educational problems are products of three salient features of the country's economy, history and culture. Pakistan is one of the five poorest states in the world measured by per capita GNP (if countries with populations of less than 10 million are excluded). This, on the one hand, has proved an obstacle to the achievement of the goal of universal primary education to which Pakistan like most poor countries, has given priority yet, on the other hand, has meant that plans for the expansion of educational provision have been linked to proposals that the education that is provided should contribute to the basic economic development of the other country.

Secondly, Pakistan's education system, like many other institutions, has been affected by centuries of British colonial rule. This has meant that academic secondary schools and universities, on the British model, have survived in ways that are not entirely relevant to Pakistan's economic and social conditions. Institutions which had the function of training general administrative cadres at various levels before and immediately after political independence still absorb a high proportion of government expenditure on education when official policy is to expand basic education and to make it relevant to social and economic conditions.

These two features also characterise the education systems of Pakistan's neighbours - India and Bangladesh. They are found also in several countries in Africa and have some importance in the somewhat richer countries to the south east of Pakistan such as Sri Lanka, Malaysia and Singapore. The third important characteristic - though having some bearing on conditions in Bangladesh, Sri Lanka and Malaysia - has particular significance in Pakistan. This is the influence of Islamic values and an Islamic ideology on the education system.

Pakistan's raison d'etre as a State was and is the Islamic affiliation of its people. The education system ever since the State was created in 1947 has had the role of preserving and strengthening Islamic values as an essential feature of the State ideology. This has produced some conflict with conventional models of economic and social development adopted by many countries of the world including Pakistan since the 1940s. These models are predominantly secularist and materialist. The adoption of educational policies associated with them has to some degree been antithetical to Islamic beliefs.

Since 1978, Pakistan's educational policy has swung decisively towards the reaffirmation of Islamic values seen not only in changes in school curricula but also in government support for mosque schools. The Islamic movement may be a reflection of international tendencies and also of a will to give a particular political and social character to Pakistan. But it is also consistent with policies to give priority to the mass of the people and their traditional values rather than simply to create Westernised elites.

Whether Islamicisation will ensure mass education is open to doubt. Pakistan only had 54% of the age group in primary schools in 1978 compared to 44% in 1970. The obstacles to universal primary education are still immense. The rates of female participation are even lower - 30% in 1978 compared to 24% in 1970. Islamic precepts do not give high priority to reducing this disparity.

Secondary and higher education institutions are often of a high standard by the criteria of the British models on which they are based. However, policies to give them lower priority - in terms of proportions of the age group in attendance and of the percentage of available resources available to them - are understandable in light of Pakistan's economic and social conditions. However, they are still almost as well attended and as liberally financed as they were in the early 1970s. Pressures from parents and students for traditional high level education remain great and are difficult to resist.

1 GEOGRAPHY

Topography

Pakistan has an area of 496,640 sq km (310,400 square miles), and also controls 83,807 sq km of the disputed territories of Jammu and Kashmir. The country came into existence in 1947 by the Indian Independence Act as one of the successor states to the British Indian Empire, and originally consisted of two separate Muslim majority areas, the present Pakistan and East Bengal. In 1971 East Bengal seceded from Pakistan to become

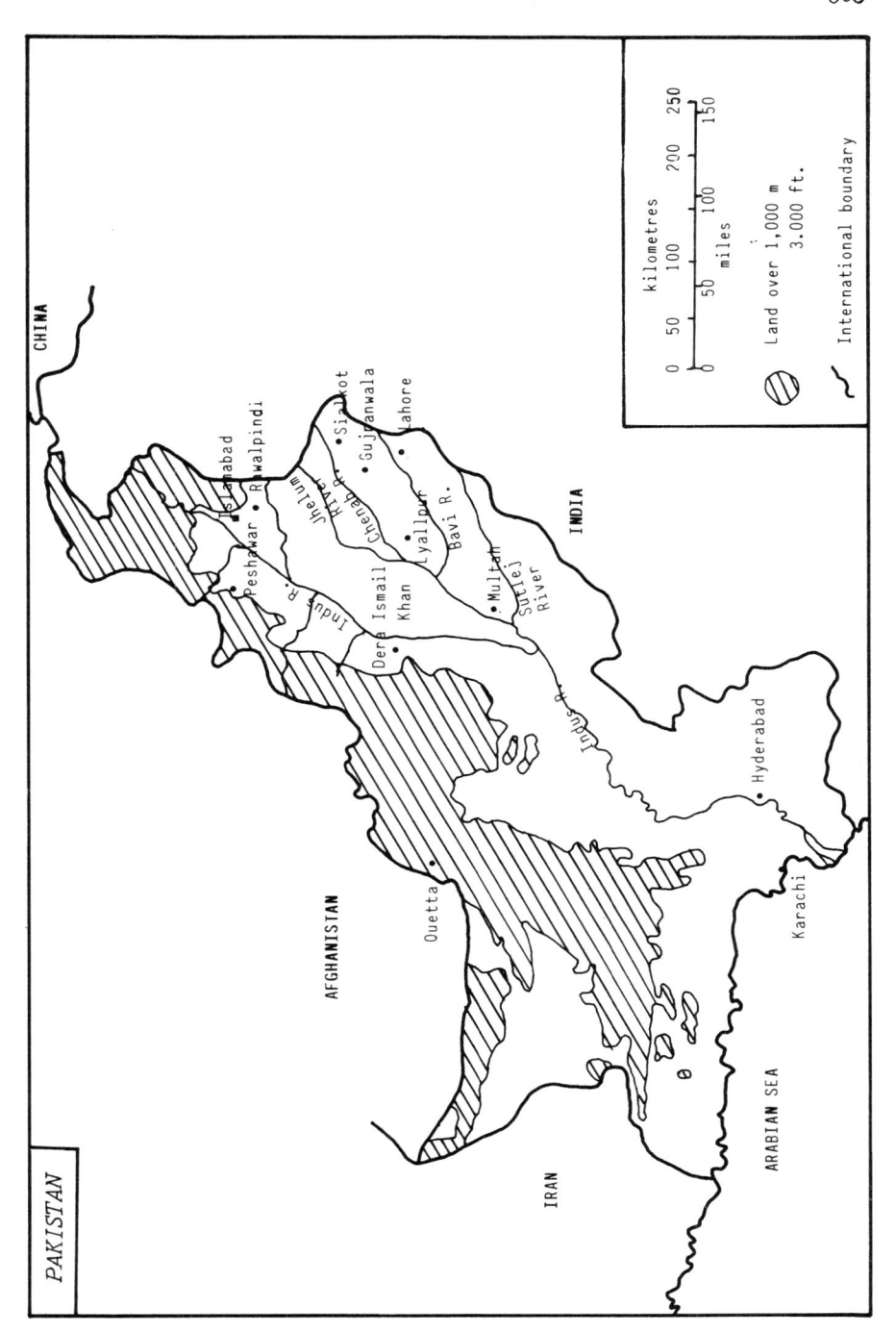

303

PAKISTAN

the independent State of Bangladesh. What is now Pakistan remains a large country, about the same size as Nigeria – containing great physical variety ranging from the Himalayan Mountains in the north through the fertile plains of the Punjab to areas of desert in Sind and thence to the Arabian Sea on which the great sea port of Karachi is situated. Pakistan is, in some places, fertile and well watered by a major river system of which the Indus river is the most important, and by a very extensive irrigation network, considerably improved since the completion of the Mangla Dam Project, but now giving rise to quite serious and widespread problems of salinity and waterlogging.

Climate

The climate has considerable variations throughout the year, parts in the north being almost Mediterranean, others in the south almost tropical. Over most of the country the winter from about November to March is a pleasant season while the summer from April to September is very hot with temperatures in June reaching 44°C (120°F) in certain parts. Rainfall is low and the country is very dry, although there is usually flooding during the monsoon which breaks around July.

Communications

Communications are uneven. There is an internal air service which covers many of the secondary towns as well as the major cities, a rail network and a reasonable road system. A highway links Karachi to Sinkiang in China. Radio services cover the country, and television services cover large areas.

2 POPULATION

Growth

According to the 1972 census the population was then just under 62 million; the 1979 estimate was 79.8 million (excluding Jammu and Kashmir). The growth rate is 3% per annum. Some alarm has been expressed in the press and in official quarters at this rapid increase and at the comparative ineffectiveness of government family planning programmes.

Distribution

Of the four provinces which make up Pakistan, Punjab has 65% of the population and with Sind is the most densely populated. The North West Frontier is mainly tribal, and Baluchistan mainly desert. The largest cities are Karachi (7,000,000) and Lahore (2,500,000).

The federal capital, Islamabad, dates only from 1960 and is still being constructed in the north, just under the foothills of the Himalayas. Its population is 235,000 (including environs).

Groups

Most of the people of Pakistan are Aryan, though there are tribes of Dravidian stock in part of Baluchistan. All, Baluchi, Pathan, Punjabi, Sindhi, are fiercely conscious of their tribal heritage.

3 SOCIETY AND CULTURE
Religion

The major factor in Pakistan's creation and probably the most important single fact about the country is that it was created for the Muslims of the sub-continent. It is known officially as the Islamic Republic of Pakistan, and Islam is the State religion. Freedom of religious worship for non-Muslims is guaranteed in the Constitution. Of the population, 88% are Muslims, most of whom are Sunnis, though there is a significant number of Shi'as and other sects. There is a Christian minority (4.5%), many of whom come from the poorest sections of society, and some Hindus (5.7% of the population) remain in Sind. There is also a very small Parsee minority, largely active in trade, and a small number of Buddhists.

Social Patterns

It is difficult, unless one has lived and worked in Pakistan, to appreciate the importance of Islam in the national life. It is immediately visible in the small proportion of women who go about out of doors and the smaller number without veils; western type dresses are not worn by Pakistani women. The fasting month of Ramazan is widely observed. It is very rare for schools to be coeducational, although at university level there are some mixed classes. However, many women in the upper educated echelons of society and the poorer nomadic tribes do move quite freely socially, and some women have attained senior posts. A clause of the Constitution reads "steps shall be taken to secure more fully participation of women in all spheres of national life". The forces for and against modernisation are strong. With little hope of political stability and economic development in the near future the situation is likely to remain confused; the importance of Islam as a founding and continuing factor in Pakistan's life will, however, remain.

British Legacy

Another major factor moulding Pakistan is the fact that for about a century before independence the area was under British rule. It contained in the Punjab (partitioned in 1947 but the greater part going to Pakistan) one of the richest and most developed provinces of British India, often referred to as 'the Granary of India', and in the North West Frontier Province, still known by that name, one of the most famous. The administrative and educational structures were British and even now, a quarter of a century and three military coups later, serious efforts to alter those structures encounter many difficulties.

Language

An obvious legacy of British rule is the place of the English language which remains in a remarkable position. This, and the fact that Western techniques came to Pakistan from Britain, are factors of major importance. English is a compulsory subject in all schools beyond primary level and as education expands is being studied by more people than ever before. There is a flourishing English language press. According to the 1973 Constitution Urdu is the official language but English may be used for official purposes until 1988. Urdu itself is the mother-tongue of a comparatively small proportion of the population (9%), the vernaculars being Punjabi (65%), Sindhi (11%), Pushtu, Baluchi, Gujarati and Brahui.

Perhaps this is the appropriate point to mention the position regarding language in education. In the great majority of schools Urdu (but Singhi in parts of Sind) is the medium of instruction up to matriculation level. There do, however, remain a number of English medium schools (about 100 in the Punjab alone, mostly nationalised) going up to matriculation or in some cases intermediate level, but these will have been phased out by 1988. In theory English is the language of all higher education but there has been a considerable swing towards Urdu and at many degree colleges answers can be written in that language. At university and post-graduate level English remains the actual language of instruction, as it does in professional (e.g. medical) training. Often a considerable amount of instruction in English is given to first year students to bring their knowledge of the language up to the standard required. However, a decision has recently been made to end English medium education by 1990.

4 HISTORY AND POLITICS

Origins

The area which is now Pakistan has known Islam from the seventh century. It became part of British India during the eighteenth and nineteenth centuries and always contained the bulk of the Muslim population in the sub-continent. Especially after 1857 the Muslim peoples felt themselves to be in the position of a disadvantaged minority in relation to the indigenous Hindu culture and population. In the early 1930s the idea of a Muslim state was first mooted; it was accepted in 1940 by the All-India Muslim League who subsequently won the 1946/47 state elections. Pakistan achieved Independence on 14 August 1947 after the Muslim provinces and princely states in the north-east and north-west had voted to join it. The exception was the predominantly Muslim Jammu and Kashmir whose Hindu maharajah decided to join India. The new state challenged his decision and fighting continued until 1949; since then Pakistan has controlled 'Azad Kashmir', the area west and north of the cease-fire line.

Post-Independence

From 1947 to 1971 Pakistan therefore included both the area of the present country and also East Bengal, known as East Pakistan. As long as East and West Pakistan remained a united country there were acute problems in trying to reconcile the needs of the two wings separated by over 1,000 miles of India. There was no really successful government in this period despite the fact that for some time it looked as though Ayub Khan's military régime would prove successful in modernising and developing the country. In 1971, however, after bitter fighting and with considerable support from India, the East broke away to become the independent state of Bangladesh. These traumatic events and the complete discrediting of the Yahya Khan military régime in the unsuccessful war with India resulted in the coming to power of the People's Party government under Zulfikar Ali Bhutto. This government launched a reformist left wing programme which applied in education as in other spheres. The years between 1973 and 1977 were marked by violence in Baluchistan and the North West Frontier, which led to the banning of the National Awami party and the declaration of a state of emergency. In the 1977 elections the People's Party won a large majority in parliament but the opposition parties who had fought the election together, accused the government of electoral rigging and called for the ending of the state of emergency. Civil disorder followed and in July 1977 a military coup deposed Mr Bhutto and reintroduced martial law. General Zia ul-Haq, the Chief Martial Law Administrator, lifted the state of emergency in September 1977 in preparation for new elections. However, these were postponed pending the trial of Mr Bhutto, who was hanged in 1979. Elections were to be held in November 1979, but were postponed again.

Political Development

Though politics do have a recognisably left/right spectrum (albeit within an Islamic framework), the factor of regionalism is also important. There are considerable social, economic and linguistic differences between the four provinces, and also a difference of weight (Frontier and Baluchistan being sparsely populated and less developed than the other two). In 1973 a new constitution was unanimously agreed which set up a federal system of government, and at the same time separated the positions of head of state and chief executive (President and Prime Minister respectively). The Pakistan-controlled part of Kashmir is still separately administered pending what Pakistan hopes will be a final settlement of the issue and there are federally-administered tribal areas. The federal constitution allowed for a bicameral parliament made up of a 210-seat National Assembly elected every five years, and a 600-seat Senate which could not be dissolved. There were also provincial assemblies. Since 1977 the constitution has been in abeyance pending elections; all the legislatures have been dissolved and government is by a four-man Council including, and headed by, the Chief Martial Law Administrator. Since January 1978 it has been assisted by an Advisory Council.

International Relations

The most obvious feature of Pakistan's foreign relations since independence has been its bad relations with India; the two full scale, if short, wars in 1965 and 1971 have been the flashpoints in a long story of major differences. One of the roots of this has been the feeling in Pakistan that the whole of Kashmir, as a Muslim majority area, should have gone to Pakistan in 1947. One of the practical effects of bad relations with India, a much larger and more populous country, has been to cause Pakistan to devote a high proportion of its resources to the armed forces. In February 1978 talks were held with the aim of improving Indo-Pakistani relations, and possibly arranging for future economic cooperation.

Among the effects of the 1971 war and the coming to power of the People's Party was Pakistan's withdrawal from the Commonwealth in January 1972. This had in fact been a plank in the People's Party election manifesto in 1970, although the immediate cause of the step was stated to be recognition of Bangladesh as an independent country by Britain and some other Commonwealth countries. The wish has been expressed for good bilateral relations with Britain and these are currently cordial.

Generally, the effects of the separation of Bangladesh have been to make Pakistan a more Middle Eastern orientated country and in many ways it may truly be regarded as the most eastern of the Muslim countries of the Middle East. Relations with Iran were particularly close and Iran under the Shah (along with other Middle Eastern countries) was an important source of economic aid. Relations with Afghanistan tend to be uneasy, with fears of Afghan support for separatist tendencies within Pakistan demanding an independent Pukhtunistan and Baluchistan.

The avowed aims of Pakistan foreign policy is to remain on good terms with all the great powers. However, relations with the Soviet Union, which has supported India and Afghanistan, have been mixed in recent years. Relations with China are good but those with the United States are uneasy.

5 THE ECONOMY

Agriculture

Agriculture is the mainstay of the economy, employing 56% of the labour force, and contributing 35% of GDP. The main crops are wheat, sugar, rice, maize, cotton and tobacco. Pakistan is fortunate in that being self-sufficient in food she has avoided the grinding poverty of certain other Asian countries. Of the commodity crops, cotton is the most important and, with rice, accounts for over 50% of export earnings. The government is presently attempting to overcome a recent decline in cotton yields by supporting cotton growing and making pesticides widely available. In January 1977 land reforms were introduced, so that no-one may now own more than 100 acres of irrigated land or 200 acres unirrigated. Waste land or state-owned land not used for public purposes has been handed over to landless peasants, or those who own less than the acreage allowed. Illiteracy (80%) remains the main obstacle to modern agriculture.

Natural Resources

Pakistan produces no more than 12% of its oil requirements and is dependent on Middle Eastern resources. Fortunately 70% of its energy requirements are met from non-oil sources as there are large deposits of natural gas and coal (470 million tons). Thanks also to ample hydroelectric power from imaginative dam projects electricity can be produced comparatively cheaply from the country's own resources. There is considerable potential for developing mining, with no less than 47 different kinds of minerals having been discovered. There is an estimated 400 million tons of iron ore, with extensive deposits of copper and some gold.

Industry

In 1947 little industrial development had taken place in what is now Pakistan, the bulk of such development having been in other parts of British India. Ever since independence efforts have been made to build up an industrial sector with some success, particularly in the development of the cotton textile industry; cotton (raw and yarn), cotton manufactures, carpets and rugs are now amongst the chief exports of the country. Though only 10% of the population is employed in the industrial sector, various other industries have been developed in recent years. These include surgical appliances, sports goods, leather goods, paper, paints and varnishes, and engineering goods including switch gear, transformers, cables and wires. Heavy industry is becoming increasingly important, with chemicals, rubber, fertilisers, vehicle assembly and machine tools; a steel mill is also being built. The textile industry has been adversely affected in recent years by restrictions from developed countries, low investment and world recession and, at present, the industrial sector is under pressure. Most major industries (except sugar and textiles) are nationalised, but some plants have been denationalised since 1977. There is at present very little investment in industry.

Economic Situation

Economic planning was only taken seriously after Ayub Khan became President in 1958 and took over the Planning Commission as part of his own secretariat. Thereafter the Planning Commission became involved in the continuous planning process of drawing up development plans both annually and for the five-year periods of the Second and Third Development Plans (1961-65 and 1966-70). Until 1968, when Ayub Khan was overthrown, Pakistan's growth rate was 5.5%, making it amongst the fastest growing developing countries in Asia. Later, however, various

PAKISTAN - STRUCTURE OF THE

| Age in years | 5 | 6 | 7 | 8 | 9 | 10 | 11 | 12 |

| 1 | 2 | 3 | 4 | 5 | 6 | 7 | 8 | 9 | 10 |
Primary   Middle   High

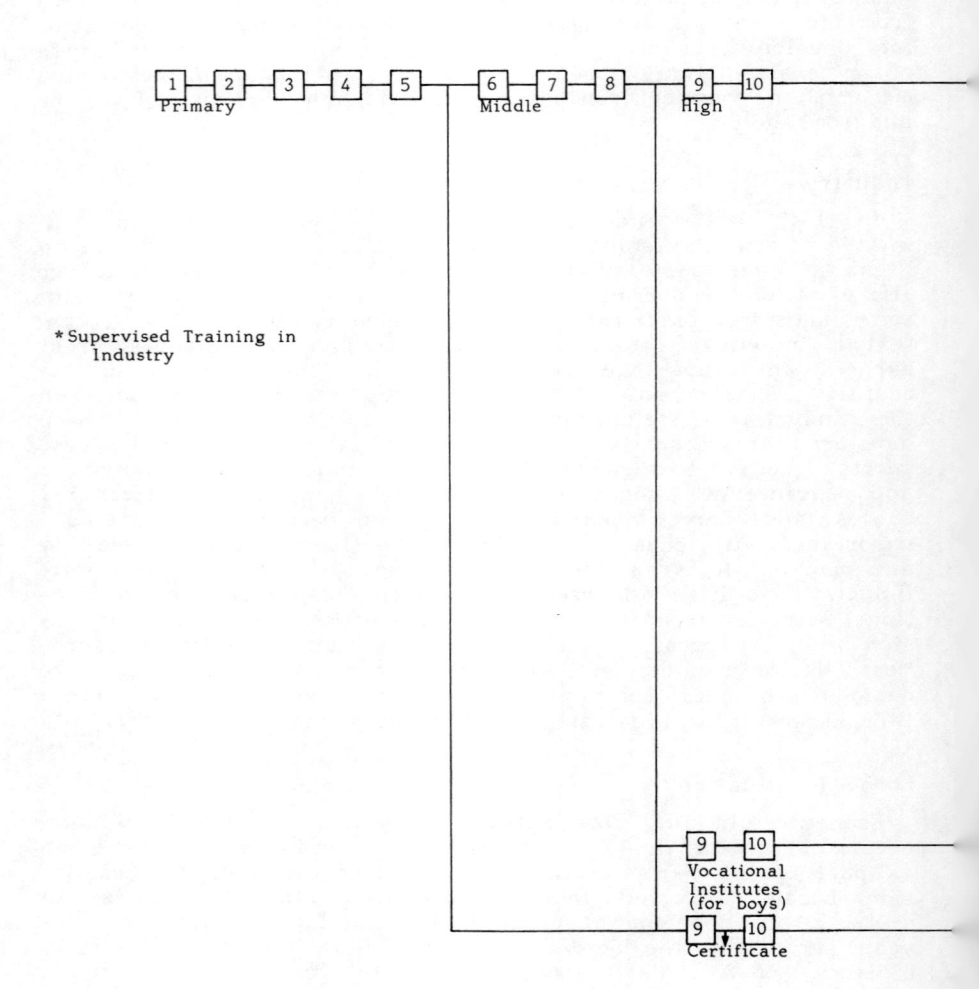

*Supervised Training in Industry

| 9 | 10 |
Vocational Institutes (for boys)

| 9 | 10 |
Certificate

EDUCATIONAL SYSTEM

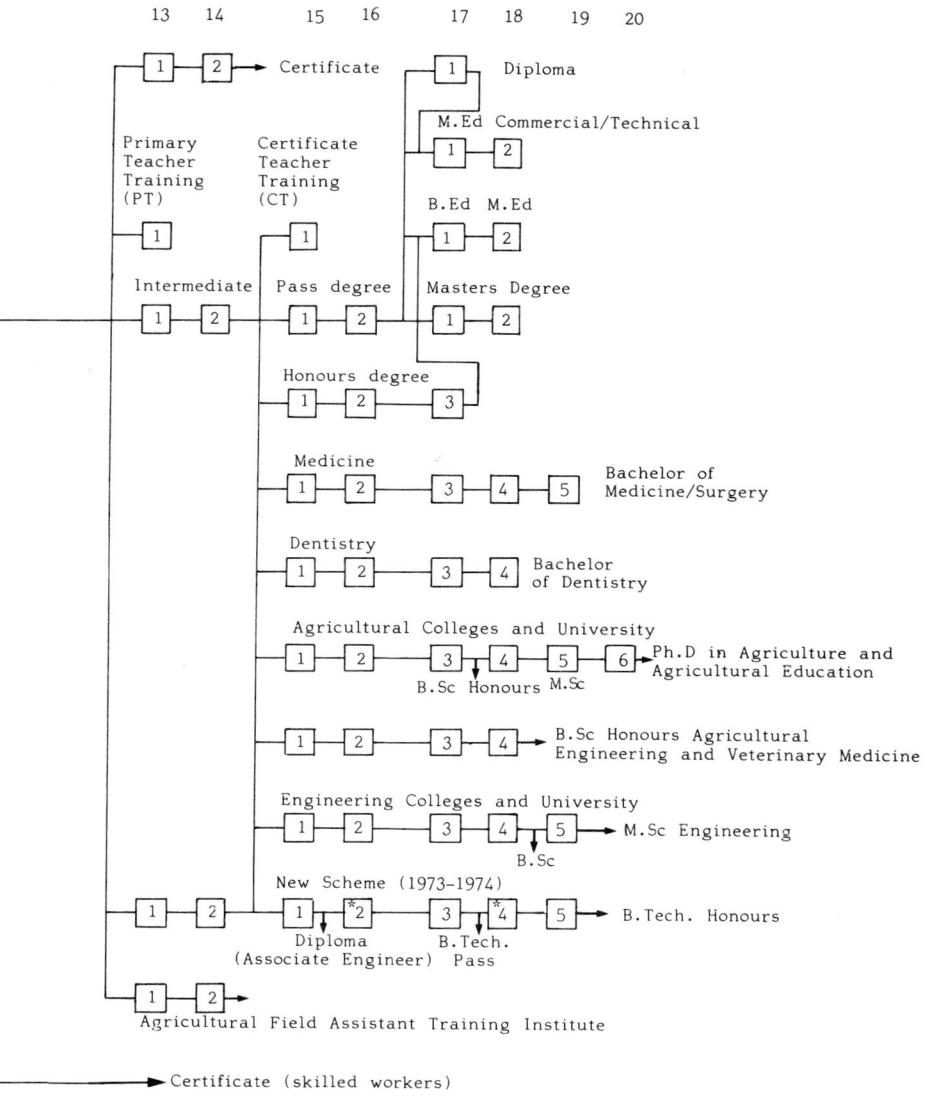

```
              13    14    15    16    17    18    19    20

              ┌─1─┬─2─┐→ Certificate  ┌─1─┐  Diploma
              │   │   │                └───┘
              │   │   │         M.Ed Commercial/Technical
              │   │   │         ┌─1─┬─2─┐
              │ Primary         └───┴───┘
              │ Teacher    Certificate
              │ Training   Teacher
              │ (PT)       Training
              │            (CT)       B.Ed   M.Ed
              ┌─1─┐        ┌─1─┐      ┌─1─┬─2─┐
              └───┘        └───┘      └───┴───┘
              Intermediate  Pass degree   Masters Degree
              ┌─1─┬─2─┐    ┌─1─┬─2─┐    ┌─1─┬─2─┐
              └───┴───┘    └───┴───┘    └───┴───┘
                                  Honours degree
                                  ┌─1─┬─2─┬─3─┐
                                  └───┴───┴───┘
                                  Medicine                          Bachelor of
                                  ┌─1─┬─2─┬─3─┬─4─┬─5─┐             Medicine/Surgery
                                  Dentistry                   Bachelor
                                  ┌─1─┬─2─┬─3─┬─4─┐           of Dentistry
                                  Agricultural Colleges and University
                                  ┌─1─┬─2─┬─3─┬─4─┬─5─┬─6─┐→ Ph.D in Agriculture and
                                          B.Sc Honours M.Sc           Agricultural Education
                                  ┌─1─┬─2─┬─3─┬─4─┐ → B.Sc Honours Agricultural
                                                       Engineering and Veterinary Medicine
                                  Engineering Colleges and University
                                  ┌─1─┬─2─┬─3─┬─4─┬─5─┐ → M.Sc Engineering
                                              B.Sc
                                  New Scheme (1973-1974)
              ┌─1─┬─2─┐          ┌─1─┬*2─┬─3─┬*4─┬─5─┐ → B.Tech. Honours
                                    Diploma    B.Tech.
                                    (Associate Engineer) Pass
              ┌─1─┬─2─┐→
              Agricultural Field Assistant Training Institute

  ────────────→ Certificate (skilled workers)

  (for women)
  ──────┬──┐ → Vocational Trades
  Diploma
```

weaknesses and strains became apparent, investment fell behind plan requirements, the growing gap between rich and poor widened and two years of war and civil turmoil led to a growth rate of 1.5% less than the population increase. Published figures also show that 60% of central government recurrent expenditure goes on defence. In 1972/73 this represented US$6 per capita which is a heavy commitment for a country whose total GNP per capita is only US$100. However, though weakened by the Bangladesh war, Pakistan did achieve a growth of 7% to 8% per annum in the early 1970s with a favourable balance of payments. But since then political unrest has affected the economy, with strikes, loss of production, price rises and inflation. The per capita income remains low and Pakistan is heavily dependent on overseas aid. The Five Year Plan 1978-83 places most emphasis on the production of basic foodstuffs and improvement of the rural infrastructure, and also calls for more investment in industry, but it has been inevitably and seriously disrupted by political uncertainty.

6 THE EDUCATION SYSTEM

Note: Each of the four provinces and Azad Kashmir has its own education administration. There is also a federal Ministry of Education in the capital Islamabad. Anyone interested in recent developments in detail would need to consult the education departments in the provincial capitals: Quetta, Peshawar, Lahore and Karachi.

Summary

There is no public pre-primary education. The primary cycle is a five year course starting at age 5 (Grade I) and continuing to about age 10 (Grade V). Then comes the five-year secondary stage up to Grade X offered at high schools. However, many pupils go to middle schools which only go up to Grade VIII. The matriculation examination is taken at Grade X and the intermediate (a higher secondary stage examination, but often taken in an intermediate college rather than school) at Grade XII.

The 1978 policy proposed that secondary and higher secondary/intermediate institutions would be merged into secondary schools covering Grades IX-XII.

Academic Year

The academic year for schools generally starts on 1 April, and runs to the following March, with a two-month summer vacation in June to August, a winter break during the last two weeks of December and a spring vacation during the last week of March; but it is constantly being disrupted by the political process.

Pre-Primary

Pre-primary education, which includes both kindergarten and nursery schools, remains entirely under private control. Schools are privately managed and are financed through fees and donations. The majority are in urban areas but detailed information about numbers and enrolments are unobtainable. For the foreseeable future there are no government plans to extend its involvement at this level, but the demand among enlightened parents is high, especially for English medium schooling.

Elementary

Elementary education is sub-divided into two levels: primary (Grades I-V) and middle or junior high (Grades VI-VIII). It normally begins at the age of 5 and for the majority of children continues for five years up to the age of 10 (Grade V) although in theory it should proceed to age 13 (Grade VIII). There are two main types of primary school: those run by provincial governments, those run by local bodies and mission schools. In all but a few special English medium schools the medium of instruction is Urdu. Most private schools were nationalised in October 1972 and were taken over by the provincial governments of Sind and Punjab. In North West Frontier Province, however, private schools were nationalised in the 1950s. In both rural and urban areas the majority of schools tend to be single sex institutions. One- and two-teacher schools predominate in rural areas. In 1979-80 there were 59,615 primary schools with an enrolment of 6.6 million pupils.

The medium of instruction at elementary level is the mother tongue. If this is not Urdu, then Urdu is introduced in Grade III. The syllabus includes: mother tongue, Pakistani/social studies, first foreign language (introduced in Grade III), mathematics, basic science, health and physical education, Islamiyat and arts; (in Sind, Sindhi is also compulsory). At middle level these subjects continue with the addition of English (13% of study time), agro-technical subjects (20% of study time) and Arabic or Persian as alternatives to arts. Hitherto promotion from one grade to another has depended upon annual examinations, usually of the essay type. The new policy, however, is to introduce automatic promotion from grade to grade. This will eventually be extended to grade VII/IX, but at the moment a special promotion examination is held at the end of grade V. However, this may soon disappear and be replaced by teacher's evaluation.

The aims of primary education have been outlined in the curriculum for primary schools as follows:

(i) to develop the moral, physical and mental aspects of a child's personality

(ii) to equip a child, according to his abilities and aptitudes, with the basic knowledge and skills necessary for an individual as well as for a citizen, and which

	should also be useful for further education
(iii)	to awaken in the child a sense of civic responsibilities and patriotism
(iv)	to lay in the child the foundation of desirable attitudes, including habits of industry, personal integrity, curiosity and healthy physical activity
(v)	to develop international understanding and a spirit of universal brotherhood
(vi)	to inculcate a scientific attitude.

Great stress is laid throughout on the ideologies of Islam and Pakistan.

The National Education Policy of 1978 led to government recognition and support for Mosque Schools, Mohalia Schools (where an elder lady of the village teaches girls in her home) and Madrassahs (Religious Institutions). Children in these schools will study the government curricula as well as religious instruction.

Secondary

Secondary education has traditionally been divided into two cycles - Grades IX and X being housed in secondary high schools and Grades XI and XII in higher secondary or intermediate colleges. The secondary high schools provided a general academic curriculum while the intermediate level offered courses in arts, sciences and technical education. Schools have either been 'all through' institutions or have been separated after Grade X. Recent trends, however, have been to combine general, agro-technical and commercial courses into a single comprehensive type school. This is part of a policy of developing educational courses more directly related to the local environment and employment possibilities, though there is a long way to go before this becomes the norm. In 1980 52% of students in higher secondary schools were enrolled in arts subjects; 43% in sciences and 5% in vocational streams. The aim is that 30% are in each of the arts, science and technical occupational streams. The assumption is that pupils leaving school after their matriculation or intermediate examination should be able to get a job as a trained middle level technician or worker.

Curriculum

This switch in emphasis has meant that not only are all-purpose schools and laboratory/workshops being built but also that curriculum changes are envisaged. There is a scheme for the integration of science courses (mathematics, physics, chemistry and biology). So far the change has only taken place at intermediate level, but the intention is to introduce integrated science courses further down the scale. It is hoped that ultimately students will be better prepared for a wider choice of course at the higher or professional levels of education but a shortage of teachers, particularly biology teachers, is bound to hold things back.

Technical, commercial and vocational courses are being formulated with local requirements of industry, trade and commerce in mind, and some aspects of these courses will be compulsory for those taking general courses. Amongst the courses to be offered in the vocational/technical fields are: electronics; auto-engineering; plumbing; household electrical appliances; dairy farming; poultry farming; vegetable farming; sericulture; crop and livestock production; shorthand and typing; insurance and estate broking; clearing, forwarding and shipping practices; home management; cooking and baking; first aid and home nursing; food production and presentation. Since education is to be introduced as an elective subject at secondary, intermediate and higher education levels it is hoped that a major part of the training of vocational teachers will take place in general secondary schools.

Agro-technical education has been introduced as a compulsory component in Grades VI-X and is being given 20-25% of total teaching time. The following elements are included in agro-technical education: industrial arts; agriculture; home economics (for girls), commerce; and general vocational subjects.

Examinations

The Secondary School Certificate Examination is taken at the end of Grade X. It is an external examination. Pupils are examined in nine subjects: Urdu, English, Pakistani studies, Islamiyat, a vocational subject, and either four science subjects or four general subjects (including general science and general mathematics or home economics). Promotion to Grade XI is based on this examination. The Secondary School Certificate is sometimes called the 'Matriculation Certificate'. At intermediate/higher secondary level the terminal examination consists of papers in Urdu and English with either four science subjects or four subjects from a social sciences/general group.

Private Schools

In the past the highest standards of secondary education have been offered in private or missionary institutions. Schools like Aitchison College Lahore, Karachi Grammar School, Abbotabad Public School, Lawrence College and the cadet colleges, conceived of by Ayub Khan as breeding grounds for the armed forces, still exist and still aim at high academic standards, but they are no longer accepted by the government as bastions of privilege. The policy is to make the facilities offered by these institutions available to a wider section of the community through scholarships and grants rather than abolishing them altogether. In fact, nationalisation has not yet been extended to cover all these schools since the more expensive English medium schools were exempted in 1972 provided they filled 20% of their places with scholarship pupils from poor backgrounds. Moreover there are still a number of non-nationalised English medium schools in the missionary sector, though it is misleading to talk of them as mission schools since the great majority of staff and pupils are Pakistani Muslims (e.g. the Cathedral School in Lahore, an Anglican foundation, has a Christian Pakistani Principal but overwhelmingly Muslim pupils and staff).

Higher

There are now 11 general universities with a total enrolment of 18,712 in 1978-80. There are also five specialist universities: two agricultural universities and three universities of engineering and technology with a total enrolment of 11,350 in 1979-80. In 1977 almost 40% of higher education students were following courses in Humanities or Law but this proportion has been declining in recent years.

Courses

Degree courses may be followed at a variety of institutes all of which are controlled by a university, at least in terms of their curricula, syllabi and standards. These are:

(i) university departments

(ii) institutes under the direct control of the university but with separate boards of governors

(iii) constituent colleges - combinations of university departments. Each unit is directed by an administrative head, known as the principal. They are under the full financial and academic control of the university

(iv) affiliated or degree colleges.

The university is only concerned with maintaining standards, providing syllabi and ensuring adequate facilities. Teams of inspectors visit the colleges from time to time. Affiliated colleges normally only provide courses of study for pass degrees. Pass degree courses last for two years (engineering is a four-year course and medicine a five-year course). Honours degree courses are for three years. The Ministry of Education has proposed that pass degree courses should be extended to three years. Degrees are awarded in three classes - first, second and third. Applications for MA/MSc courses are submitted to the head of department who selects graduates on the basis of merit. University instruction is at present normally in English but may be in Urdu, though by 1990 English medium education will have been phased out.

Research Centres

A University Grants Commission modelled on the British UGC was heen created to coordinate programmes and develop facilities without undue wastage and duplication. It is designed to act as a buffer between the government and university administrations as well as be the main disburser of government funds. It is also responsible for designating certain universities as area study centres. These centres will undertake research and advanced studies in areas of special interest to Pakistan. Similarly, Pakistan study centres have been set up in different regional universities. Their responsibility is to undertake research and teaching in the regional languages and literature of Pakistan. In order to oversee research into the language, literature and culture of Pakistan as a whole a National Institute of Pakistan Studies has been established at Islamabad University.

Centres of Excellence

An extension of this concept of specialisation has been the creation of a number of centres of excellence/national institutes. In order to improve standards in certain fields and to produce higher level expertise to help exploit the country's resources, specialist departments and institutes have been designated centres of excellence. Once chosen the centre is expected to draw up a development plan to be submitted to the Ministry. If the plan is approved the institute is allocated a proportion of the funds available for the centres of excellence. Many of these centres have already established links with overseas agencies (e.g. Ford, Rockefeller, the British Council) for recruitment of personnel. Admission to the centres is for gifted students from all over the country according to a formula stipulated by the Ministry. This aims to allocate a certain proportion of places to the various provinces and regions.

The seven centres which have been established are in Marine Biology (University of Karachi), Analytical Chemistry (Sind), Solid State Physics (Punjab), Minerology (Baluchistan), Geology (Peshawar), Water Resources Engineering (University of Technology, Jahore) and Physical Chemistry (Peshawar).

Scholarships/Fellowships

In order to prevent the drift from academic life to highly remunerative administrative posts the government has instituted a number of national professorships and research fellowships to attract outstanding scholars and scientists. In addition academic interchange at both staff and student level is greatly encouraged and over 100 scholars and teachers go overseas annually on various scholarships and fellowships. Several scholarship schemes are also available for undergraduate and post-graduate students. These include British Council Scholarships, Central Overseas Training Awards, Merit Scholarships and Cultural Scholarships.

Higher Technical and Vocational

Mention has already been made of the switch in emphasis towards vocational and technical courses at secondary and higher secondary level. In addition over 24 polytechnics have been created, specialising in trade and technician courses. Selected polytechnics also offer condensed one-year courses leading to a BSc (Technology) degree. These institutions are either financed and administered by the central or provincial governments or they are constituent colleges of the universities. They were first established during the 1960s in conjunction with the Ford Foundation and aimed to produce technicians to fill intermediate positions in industry or government service. Most courses offered were three-year diploma courses.

According to the 1972-80 Education Policy, polytechnics are to be converted into technical colleges and while certificate and diploma courses are expected to continue, students who complete a three-year diploma course will be encouraged to undertake industrial training for two years before being enrolled for an additional one-year's course leading to a B Tech degree. In order to facilitate this link between industry in both the public and private sectors and courses at the technical colleges special legislation will have to be enacted. In addition to traditional technical courses new programmes related to new areas of technology will be introduced. Included amongst these are: electronics and instrument technology; textile, cotton and wool technology, para-medical technology; leather technology; timber technology; plastic and rubber technology; gas and petroleum technology; development economics etc.

Concern is also being shown for consolidating and raising standards in the professions - agriculture and animal husbandry, engineering, medicine and education. In order to lay down minimum standards and to maintain uniformity of courses and examinations professional councils have been established in agriculture, engineering and law along the lines of the Pakistan Medical Council. It is expected that councils in other professions will be established.

Teacher Education

Teacher training is carried out in different institutions according to the level required. Primary teachers normally have a matriculation qualification and undergo a two-year course at one of the 55 teacher training schools. Those who wish to teach at middle or secondary level take a course at one of the 12 teacher training colleges. Those who wish to teach at secondary or higher secondary level require a degree qualification and take a one-year post-graduate course in a university department. There are a few specialist institutions: e.g. two physical training colleges, one training college for teachers of the deaf, one technical teacher training college and one vocational training institute. A small amount of teacher training in education is given at the two institutes of education and research (Lahore and Sind) where higher degrees are obtained.

In order to overcome a teacher shortage the Ministry has proposed that education shall be introduced as a subject in secondary and higher secondary schools, intermediate colleges and universities so that teachers will be trained during the course of their normal studies and will be ready to enter the profession without a long post-school training. Whether or not this proposition is feasible remains to be seen. On the other hand it does introduce a degree of flexibility since students can proceed to further education or different areas of teacher specialisation.

In-Service

A small number of in-service training establishments exist, such as the Education Extension Centre in Lahore, and expansion of training facilities, both initial and in-service, is planned. The 1978 policy proposed that all teachers should undergo an in-service training course at least once every five years.

Non-Formal and Adult

The government is committed to the eradication of illiteracy and has begun a massive literacy programme. It has set up free centres in village halls and factories, farms and schools, community centres and union council halls and it is prepared to make use of new technologies, and non-conventional methods to instil basic literacy. It is planned to open 276,000 centres throughout the country and to provide training to more than 11 million illiterates by the 1980s. (Up to the present, only a very small number of these centres have begun to function.) Staffing of the literacy centres is undertaken by social workers, teachers, volunteers and by members of the National Literacy Corps (cf the Iranian National Literacy Corps). The NLC is part of the National Service Corps, young people who do a year of compulsory social service rather than military service between the ages of 17 and 23. In time it is expected that the National Service Corps will incorporate a sizeable element of military training.

Initially the emphasis in adult education will be upon literacy but eventually it is hoped to expand the scheme to cover continuing life long education. Although priority in the courses is to be given to factory workers, farmers, workers engaged to special projects and adolescents, the ideal is to expand the programme to cover subjects like nutrition, health and hygiene, home economics, child care, embroidery and poultry keeping and to expand the clientele. By the 1980s it is planned to establish 500 factory schools, 3,500 farm schools, 5,000 special centres for women and 300 out-of-school youth centres. The 1978 policy proposed that 1,000 village workshop schools be established by 1983 to cater for young boys who dropped out of primary school: but only 50 workshops had been set up by the end of 1980.

Educational Technology

The most innovative element in the non-formal education field is the People's Open University, modelled on the British OU. The University has its headquarters in Islamabad but has regional centres throughout the country and aims to provide courses for people who cannot leave their homes or undertake full time study. Initially the People's University intends to concentrate on teacher training, intermediate and degree examinations and general literacy training for literacy workers, welfare workers and others concerned with innovation and change. The main instructional methods to be employed by the People's University are: correspondence, radio broadcasting, television, and workshops and queston/answer sessions in regional centres. These, however, are only indicative of a new commitment to the use of instructional technology. The Education Policy (1972-80) makes provision for the development of educational television and radio broadcasting services, the production of audio-visual materials, the distribution of 100,000 TV sets and 150,000 ratio sets, and the promotion of all forms of mass media to develop changing attitudes. Consequently a new Audio-Visual Education Section has been created and placed under the direct control of the Education Policy Implementation Unit of the Ministry of Education. The AVE Section is concentrating initially on teacher education as teachers are rightly seen as key figures in the introduction of new methods and technology.

7 EDUCATIONAL ADMINISTRATION

Centralised Powers

The administration of education is shared, unevenly, between the provinces and the central government. The powers of the central government were strengthened by a provision in the 1973 Constitution which gave powers to legislate over curricula, standards and policy. Ultimate control of the policy framework rests with the central government. The central government, by use of special powers, had already in 1972 carried out the nationalisation of most of what had up till then been a large private (including missionary) sector of education at school and college level. The only exceptions were a small number of the more expensive English medium schools. Martial law regulations have centralised matters much more firmly.

Regional Powers

The provinces, however, play an important part in educational provision and each province has its own Ministry of Education. They have very great powers in implementation according to local needs. Detailed administrative control of the system within a province is vested in directorates of education, with divisional and district inspectorates responsible to them. District inspectors are executive officers for a district and also members

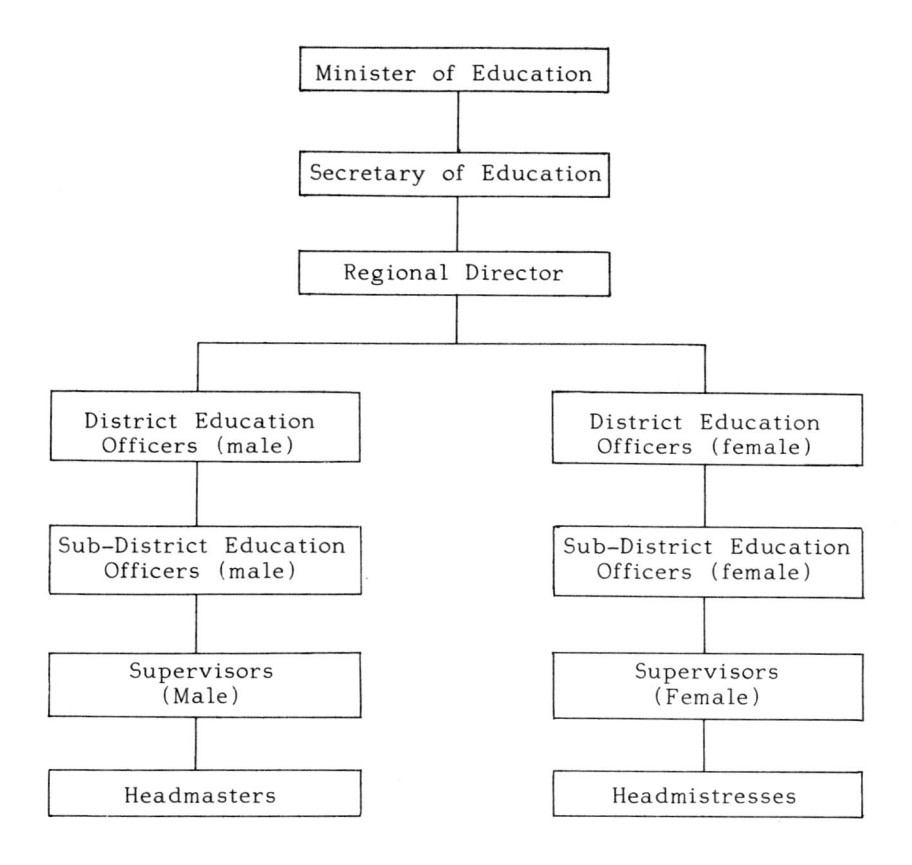

```
                    ┌─────────────────────┐
                    │ Minister of Education│
                    └──────────┬──────────┘
                    ┌──────────┴──────────┐
                    │ Secretary of Education│
                    └──────────┬──────────┘
                    ┌──────────┴──────────┐
                    │  Regional Director  │
                    └──────────┬──────────┘
              ┌────────────────┴────────────────┐
    ┌─────────┴─────────┐             ┌─────────┴─────────┐
    │ District Education│             │ District Education│
    │  Officers (male)  │             │ Officers (female) │
    └─────────┬─────────┘             └─────────┬─────────┘
    ┌─────────┴─────────┐             ┌─────────┴─────────┐
    │Sub-District Education│          │Sub-District Education│
    │  Officers (male)  │             │ Officers (female) │
    └─────────┬─────────┘             └─────────┬─────────┘
    ┌─────────┴─────────┐             ┌─────────┴─────────┐
    │    Supervisors    │             │    Supervisors    │
    │      (Male)       │             │     (Female)      │
    └─────────┬─────────┘             └─────────┬─────────┘
    ┌─────────┴─────────┐             ┌─────────┴─────────┐
    │    Headmasters    │             │   Headmistresses  │
    └───────────────────┘             └───────────────────┘
```

REGIONAL EDUCATIONAL ADMINISTRATION

322

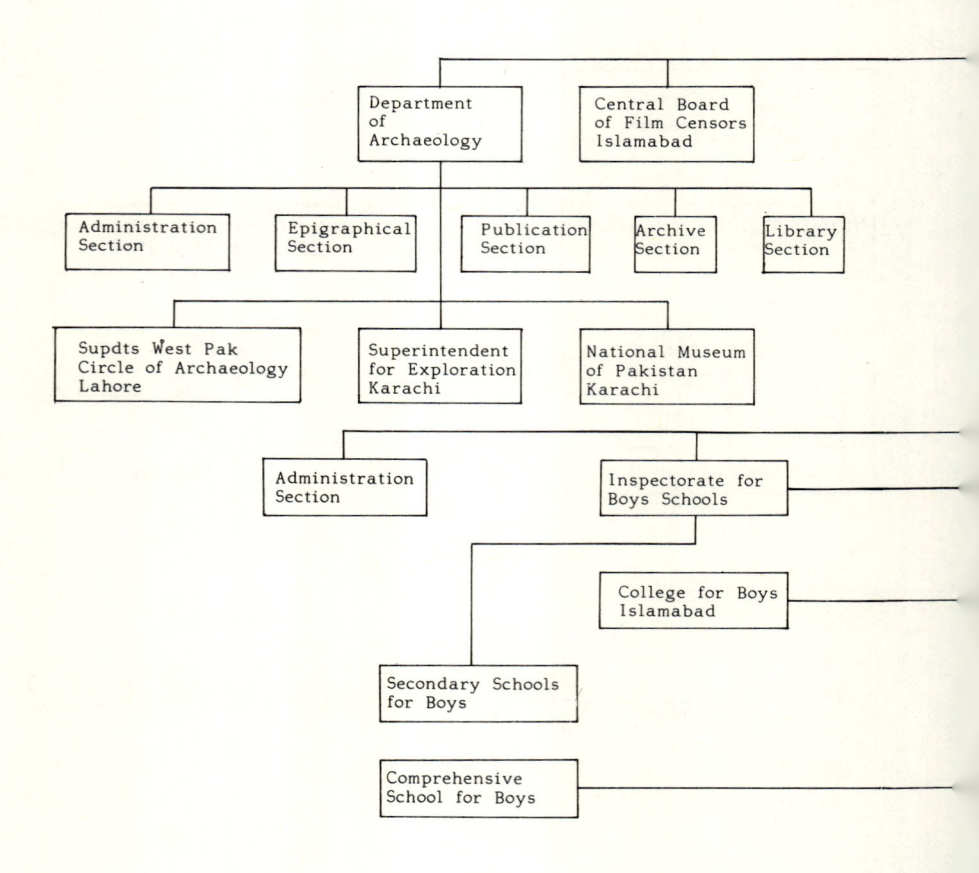

ORGANISATION OF

- Department of Archaeology
  - Administration Section
  - Epigraphical Section
  - Publication Section
  - Archive Section
  - Library Section
  - Supdts West Pak Circle of Archaeology Lahore
  - Superintendent for Exploration Karachi
  - National Museum of Pakistan Karachi
- Central Board of Film Censors Islamabad

- Administration Section
- Inspectorate for Boys Schools
  - College for Boys Islamabad
  - Secondary Schools for Boys
  - Comprehensive School for Boys

PAKISTAN
THE EDUCATION DIVISION

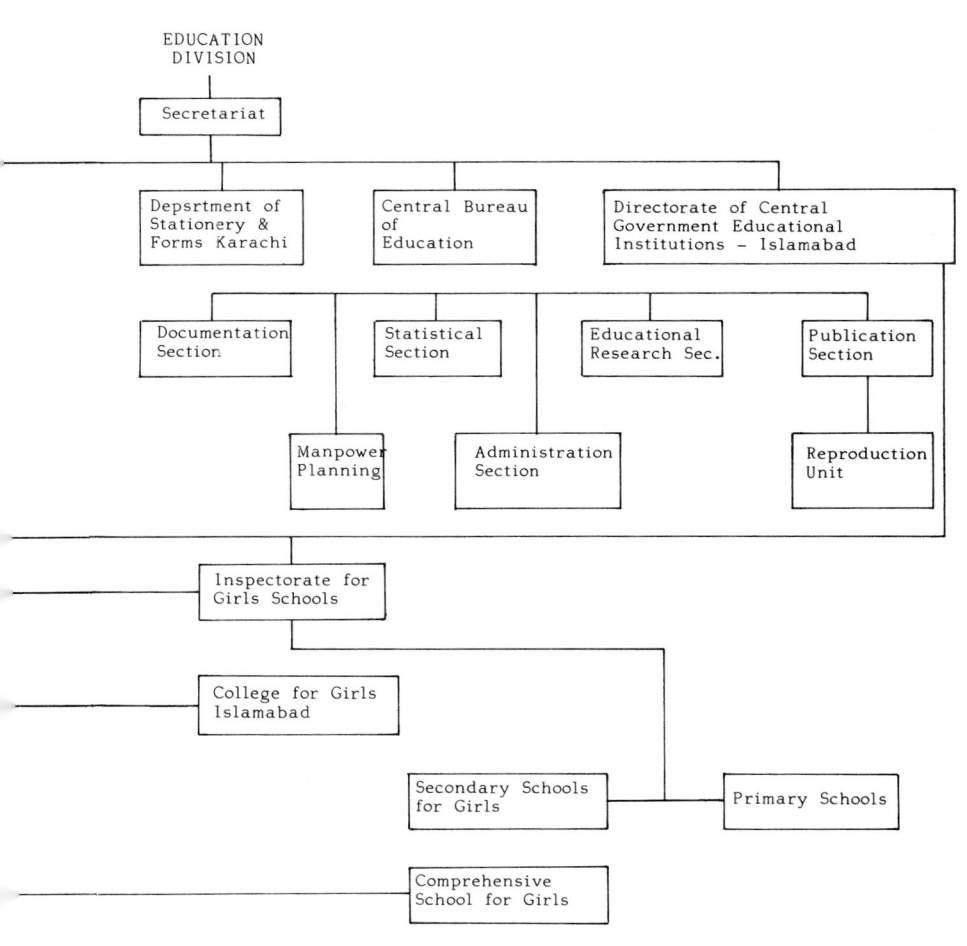

```
EDUCATION
DIVISION
  │
[Secretariat]
  ├─────────────────────┬──────────────────┬──────────────────────┐
  │                     │                  │                      │
[Department of    [Central Bureau    [Directorate of Central
 Stationery &      of Education]      Government Educational
 Forms Karachi]                       Institutions - Islamabad]
                                              │
        ┌──────────────┬──────────────┬──────────────┐
        │              │              │              │
  [Documentation  [Statistical   [Educational   [Publication
   Section]        Section]       Research Sec.] Section]
        │              │                             │
                  [Manpower      [Administration  [Reproduction
                   Planning]      Section]         Unit]

[Inspectorate for
 Girls Schools]
  │
[College for Girls
 Islamabad]
  │
[Secondary Schools ───── Primary Schools]
 for Girls]
  │
[Comprehensive
 School for Girls]
```

of the provincial education department. However, they also have special responsibilities for supervising examinations, inspecting staff and planning expansion. Boys' and girls' schools have parallel supervisory systems. The actual administrative burden is very severe, given the number of schools involved.

Examinations and Textbooks

Examinations at matriculation and intermediate level are carried out by separate examination boards, known as boards of intermediate and secondary education. A large and populous province like the Punjab has several boards. The boards are provincial government bodies and the chairmen are normally men experienced in education. Textbooks at school level are controlled and published by provincial textbook boards, responsible to the provincial governments, which exercise a theoretical monopoly, though in practice some English medium schools use certain non-board publications.

National Literacy Corps

The National Literacy Corps is an integral part of the educational organisation of the country and is under the overall coordination of the Ministry of Education. But whereas the Ministry is responsible for planning, policy and inter-provincial coordination, the provincial educational administrations are responsible for administering the scheme.

Universities

Universities are in a separate category; they have developed along the lines of British universities, and are corporate autonomous bodies. Degree colleges, even though affiliated to universities for examination purposes, are part of the government education structure and their staff are government servants but universities, which control degree and post-graduate examinations and are directly responsible for most honours degree and post-graduate teaching, are legally separate bodies and are not under direct government control. Such power as central and provincial governments have over universities comes, as in many other countries, from the power of the purse.

The Chancellor of Islamabad University is ex officio the President of the Republic: the chancellors of the other universities are ex officio the governors of the provinces. The overall administrative responsibility for the university lies with the vice-chancellor who is assisted by a registrar, a treasurer and a controller of examinations. The syndicate is the supreme authority on academic, disciplinary and financial matters: the academic council assists and advises on all academic matters.

8 EDUCATIONAL FINANCE

Sources of Funds

The financing of education in Pakistan is a complicated subject. Considerable funds still come from private persons, as education is so far only free up to Grade VIII apart from the fact that not all schools have yet been nationalised. Most public expenditure on education appears in the estimates of the provincial governments, as the considerable central government expenditure on education appears in budget estimates only as grants-in-aid and miscellaneous expenditure. University income is mainly derived from annual grants made by the central or provincial governments through their education departments - the ratio of the grant to the total budget varies but, in general, is more than half the total income. Until 1978 more funds for universities have come from provincial, rather than central, government except in the case of Islamabad University in the capital territory. From 1978 all universities have been financed from Federal funds. A separate University Grants Commission was set up in 1973 to be the channel for allocation of central government funds to universities.

Education Budget

As a percentage of GNP expenditure on education has been very low and was 2.0% in 1979, a figure which official Pakistan government publications freely admit was one of the lowest in the world. The aim of the government is that by the 1980s total expenditure on education will represent about 4% of the Gross National Product, and reach the recommended UNESCO level for developing countries. The government also plans to mobilise community support in both cash and kind. The total government expenditure on education in 1979-80 was 3,776 million rupees representing about 5% of all government expenditure.

Allocation of Funds

The percentage of the education budget allocated to the various levels in 1979 is shown below:

Primary	40.0
Secondary	32.2
Higher	16.5
General & Miscellaneous	11.3
TOTAL	100.0

The tendency is for expenditure on primary education and professional colleges, including teacher training colleges, to increase at a greater rate than other education sectors.

Overseas Aid

Overseas aid in education is, like other kinds of overseas aid, strictly under central government control but in practice there is very close consultation between the central and provincial governments over the application of such aid, a factor which can lead to delays in implementing such assistance but which ensures cooperation between the centre and the provinces. Coordination is carried out by the Economic Affairs Division. UNICEF is active at primary level, particularly in Sind Province. World Bank money has recently been allocated to a wide-ranging primary education project.

9 DEVELOPMENT AND PLANNING OF THE EDUCATION SYSTEM

Origins

The modern history of education in Pakistan begins with the British occupation in the 1840s. During the British period a modern education framework was built up, although for long comparatively few Muslims took full advantage of it as there was resistance to modern western education. Then this situation changed, partly because of the efforts of Sir Syed Ahmed Khan who was responsible for the founding of a college at Aligarh, which subsequently became Aligarh Muslim University, in Uttar Pradesh in India in the 1880s. Aligarh has a considerable intellectual influence over the Muslim intelligentsia and many of the older generation of academics in Pakistan in the 1970s attended this university, now in India, as young men. Its influence in acting as a synthesis between traditional Islam and modern knowledge was very considerable and in some ways the pattern set by Aligarh has been the model for the aims of the education system of independent Pakistan.

Educational Objectives

The aim is to develop an education system which will provide the necessary skills and knowledge to enable the country to fulfil its role in the modern world while retaining the cultural traditions of Islam. The position is summarised in one of the objectives of the education policy of the Bhutto government, the relevant extract reading as follows: "designing curricula relevant to the Nation's social and economic needs compatible with our basic ideology". Within this very wide framework there have in fact been certain antitheses and tensions, e.g. between traditional (i.e. Islamic) and modern sectors of education, between urban and rural, between education for boys and girls (below college level coeducation is very much the exception) and between the more and the less economically privileged. The 1979 policy shifted the emphasis more decisively to the maintenance and development of an Islamic society and values.

Planning Institutions

Planning is a function of central or provincial governments. In so far as it is more than a mere annual budgetary exercise of deciding how much money should go into the provincial or central budget for educational purposes, long term planning is a function of either provincial government planning departments or the central government planning commission. Starting from fairly modest beginnings the Central Planning commission has gradually become a key body in the process of economic decision-making. It was a useful instrument in the hands of army officers and top civil servants during the 1950s and early 1960s. Now any major schemes involving either provincial or central government funds require relevant planning commission clearance. An example is the scheme to develop centres of excellence in universities, financed by the central government, which requires the approval of the Central Planning Commission, itself a branch of the central government.

Current Trends

The main features of educational development in Pakistan in recent years, apart from general increase in numbers and expansion of the system at all levels, have been reformist in tendency. The advent of the Bhutto régime in Pakistan meant in education, as in other spheres, a policy of reform, with a greater degree of State intervention at all stages. The New Educational Policy of 1970, which included East Pakistan, was obviously inappropriate and the objectives of a new policy were set out in the policy document *Education Policy 1972-1980* which laid down a programme of educational reform at all levels. This had two main aims. The first was to maximise education so that its benefits could be made available to all sections of the population and educational privilege curtailed. The second was that there should be large scale reform of methods to make education more effective. Objectives were summarised as follows:

(i) to preserve, promote and practise the basic ideology of Pakistan and, to make it a code of individual and national life

(ii) to build up 'national cohesion' through the conscious use of the educational process

(iii) to develop individuals capable of facing up to objective truth and of adapting to technical and social change

(iv) to encourage youth to participate in programmes of social and environmental reform; to inculcate a sense of dignity of labour

(v) to eradicate illiteracy as quickly as possible through universal elementary education and a programme of adult education

(vi) to equalise access to education for the physically and mentally handicapped and for those from poor and backward areas

(vii) to reform the curricula so that there is a shift in emphasis 'from general education to a more purposeful agro-technical education'

(viii) to integrate general and technical education thereby simplifying transfer from one course to another

(ix) to provide academic freedom and institutional autonomy

(x) to involve parents, teachers, students and the community at large in educational affairs

(xi) to promote the welfare, dignity and sense of responsibility of both teachers and students.

Education was to be provided free up to grade VIII from 1972 onwards and for Grades IX and X from 1973 onwards. It was also anticipated that five years of primary education would become universal for boys from 1979 and girls from 1984 and that eight years of universal education would be available for boys by 1982 and for girls by 1987. These targets were reaffirmed in 1978.

There has been an attempt to develop certain subjects much more rapidly than others with the general aim of moving to a more scientifically orientated system. This reflects an understanding on the part of senior education officials that the key to improvement lies in the improvement in the quality of the teachers themselves and with this in mind efforts have been devoted to teacher training, including in-service training. A National Institute of Education, with a programme of comprehensive retraining in methods has been established in Islamabad. Initially it is concentrating on courses for training of primary teachers. Attempts have also been made to reduce the examination system by cutting out examinations for class to class promotion and moving to an internal assessment procedure. There are moves to improve the inspectorate, and strengthen its advisory as opposed to administrative role. The use of the mass media for education is being developed and the Open University has been set up which will devote considerable resources in the earlier stages to teacher training. There is undoubtedly a readiness to benefit from the experience of other countries in the development of their education systems and to encourage greater exchange of ideas.

The government of General Zia issued a new National Education Policy in 1978. Previous objectives to achieve equal opportunities, to develop the capacities of individuals and relate education to economic and technological needs have been restated. The major innovation in the document was to re-emphasise the Islamic character of Pakistan and the importance of the education system in promoting this ideal. The first four aims of the 1978 policy were:

(i) to foster in the hearts and minds of the people of Pakistan in general and the students in particular a deep and abiding loyalty to Islam and Pakistan and a living consciousness of their spiritual ideological identity thereby strengthening unity of the outlook of the people of Pakistan on the basis of justice and fair play

(ii) to create awareness in every student that he, as a member of the Pakistan nation, is also a part of the universal Muslim Ummah and that it is expected of him to make a contribution towards the welfare of fellow Muslims inhabiting the globe on the one hand and to help spread the message of Islam throughout the world on the other

(iii) to produce citizens who are fully conversant with the Pakistan Movement, its ideological foundations, history and culture so that they feel proud of their heritage and display firm faith in the future of the country as an Islamic State

(iv) to develop and inculcate in accordance with the Quran and Sunnah, the character, conduct and motivation expected of a true Muslim.

The means to achieve these aims were stated in the strategies of the policy:

(i) highest priority will be assigned to the revision of curricula with a view to reorganising the entire content around Islamic thought and giving education an ideological orientation so that Islamic Ideology permeates the thinking of the younger generation and helps them with the necessary conviction and ability to refashion society according to Islamic tenets

(ii) presently the two systems of education namely the traditional 'Madrassah and Darul Uloom' and 'modern school, college and university' are engaged in the dissemination of knowledge in their own way without any meaningful dialogue between the two resulting in a lopsided development of human personality in Pakistan. However, there are desirable features in both and the possibility of their fusion into an integrated national system of education will be explored.

The policy did reaffirm aims to expand provision which had not been realised. It was decided that all boys of five years old would be enrolled in school by 1982 and all girls by 1987. However, the most recent thrust of educational policy represents a move away from a relatively secular approach to education to a thorough going assertion of the importance of Islamic values.

This is seen in the 1978 proposals to support Islamic primary level schools, to make Islamiyat a compulsory subject in secondary education, to develop Arabic teaching at all levels, to revise curricula and textbooks in line with Islamic values and to expand Islamic studies at higher education level. There are conscious and deliberate efforts to reverse the movement towards secularism which occurred in the 1960s and 1970s.

PAKISTAN – THE EDUCATIONAL PYRAMID 1979-1980

MALE	Grade	FEMALE	TOTALS
24,645	Higher Education	8,427	83,062
99,300	XII	39,197	138,497
124,125	XI	47,037	171,163
191,246	Grade X	86,234	277,480
265,817	Grade IX	101,913	367,730
358,955	Grade VIII	141,110	500,065
411,690	Grade VII	172,468	584,158
510,806	Grade VI	195,986	706,792
652,201	Grade V	205,958	858,159
798,742	Grade IV	257,448	1,056,196
830,435	Grade III	291,774	1,122,209
1,074,680	Grade II	377,590	1,452,270
1,528,845	Grade I	583,548	2,112,393

331

PAKISTAN BASIC STATISTICS

Population Growth
(excluding Kashmir)

1965	1970	1975	1977	1979
50,190,000	60,607,000	70,260,000	74,866,000	79,838,000

Schools, Teachers & Pupils 1971-72 and 1979-80

	Schools	Teachers	Pupils
Primary (Grades I-V)			
1971-72	45,845	105,697	4,223,967
1979-80	59,615	147,000	6,601,227
Middle (Grades VI-VIII)			
1971-72	4,110	36,049	963,072
1979-80	5,779	52,993	1,791,015
Higher (Grades IX-X)			
1971-72	2,247	37,884	731,100
1979-80	3,898	59,876	1,290,420
Intermediate (Grades XI-XIII)			
1971-72	140	1,689	137,934
1979-80	197	2,408	185,000

Rates of Participation in Education 1970 & 1978

(Gross enrolment percentages = Enrolments divided by total population aged 5-9 [primary] aged 10-16 [secondary] and aged 20-24 [higher].)

	Primary	Secondary	Higher
1970	44	14	2.5
(female)	24	6	1.1
1978	54	16	2.2
(female)	30	8	1.2

Pupil Teacher Ratio (Primary)
1970, 1975 & 1978

1970	1975	1978
41	40	42

Numbers of Pupils in General Secondary Education,
Vocational Secondary and Teacher Training
(at Secondary Education Level)

	General Secondary	Vocational Secondary	Teacher Training
1970	1,428,194	21,573	12,877
1978	2,120,729	28,966	5,171

Distribution of Higher Education Students by Subject Area 1977

	Number of Students	% Female
Education & Teacher Training	6,184	52.9
Humanities & Religion	47,027	47.9
Law	11,091	1.8
Commerce & Business	12,735	5.2
Home Economics	2,365	100.0
Natural Science	20,992	23.2
Medicine & Health Services	22,291	24.2
Engineering	18,508	0.7
Agriculture	6,658	2.3

Expenditure on Education 1970 & 1971

		Expenditure (rupees)	As % of Gross National Product	As % of Government Expenditure
1970	Total	789,907	1.7	4.2
	Recurrent	480,370	1.0	3.6 (of Total Recurrent)
1979	Total	4,153,000	2.0	1.6
	Recurrent	3,225,500	5.1	5.5 (of Total Recurrent)

Distribution of Public Expenditure by Level of Education 1970 & 1978 (%)

	Primary	Secondary	Higher	Not Distributed
1970	39.7%	32.5%	16.4%	11.4%
1978	40.0%	32.2%	16.5%	11.3%

Basic Economic & Social Data

Gross National Product per capita 1979 – US$ 260

Average annual growth of GNP per capita 1960–1979 – 2.9%

Life expectancy at birth 1979 – 52 years

Percentage of the population of working age:
(15–64) 1960 – 52%
1979 – 51%

Percentage of the labour force employed in:

Agriculture
1960   61%
1979   57%

Industry
1960   18%
1979   20%

Services
1960   21%
1979   23%

Peninsular Malaysia

CONTENTS

1	Geography	338
2	Population	339
3	Society and Culture	341
4	History and Politics	344
5	The Economy	348
6	The Education System	355
7	Educational Administration	370
8	Educational Finance	377
9	Development and Planning of the Education System	379

Malaysia has important similarities with the countries of the Indian sub-continent to the West, particularly those related to economic structure, cultural diversity and a colonial legacy. But she also shares common characteristics, especially rates of economic growth and the specific nature of her cultural pluralism, with the South East Asia crescent of countries stretching to the east as far as Japan. The education system of Malaysia can be illuminated by comparison both with the countries which are her Western neighbours and those which lie to the north and east.

Like India, Pakistan, Sri Lanka, Bangladesh and Burma to the west and north, Malaysia is a primary producing country of several ethnic, linguistic and religious groups which was part of the British Empire. Her economy traditionally was based on the production and export of rubber and tin. These products are still important though they have been supplemented by the development of palm oil, forestry and petroleum. The work force is still engaged mainly in unskilled and rural based occupations. Malaysia's level of ecnmic development still classifies her as an underdeveloped country and the majority of her population is still rural. Her educational priorities still are similar to those of her Western neighbours – the achievement of universal primary education, the improvement in the quality of primary schooling, expansion of the proportion of the population that gains access to secondary education and the realignment of the character of education to allow diversification of the economy.

Also like her neighbours to the north west, Malaysia inherited an education system at the time of political independence which reflected the aims of the British colonial administration. Secondary and higher education had a literary/academic and British orientation which was not entirely compatible with new economic and political objectives. The English educational ethos is still influential especially at higher levels of education. English is still used as a medium at these higher levels though it is being phased out while the examination system reflects English patterns even though English-examination agencies are losing formal influence.

Again, like the other former British colonies to the north and west, Malaysia is a multi-cultural society. There are major ethnic divisions between Malays, Chinese and Indians and each group has associated linguistic and religious affiliations which intensify the divisions of Malaysian society. Cultural divisions have perhaps a greater importance in Malaysia than in these other countries because of the relative size of the competing groups. Malays form a bare majority while the Chinese constitute over a third of the population. The particular cultural characteristics of the Chinese and their socio-economic position tend to link Malaysia more to her Eastern neighbours than to those of Asian countries to the west. The communal relations issue is central in Malaysian politics and Malaysian education.

In other ways Malaysia is closer to her Eastern neighbours and has become more so over the last 20 years. Her level of economic development categorises her as a middle income country like Singapore, Thailand, the Philippines, Hong Kong and Taiwan rather than as a low income country like Pakistan, India, Bangladesh, Sri Lanka and Burma. Like the former group of countries (and unlike most of the latter), Malaysia experienced high rates of economic growth in the 1970s and a significant development of the industrial, urban sector.

These economic changes have given a greater impetus in Malaysia to the expansion of secondary and higher education and to the reorientation of education to technical training imperatives. They have meant also that Malaysia is still able to expand educational provision. Different strategies also can be allied to problems of cultural pluralism when greater educational provision for the less economically privileged groups remains a major policy option in an economy where employment opportunities for the trained and educated are still expanding.

Note: Unless otherwise stated, this Profile deals only with Peninsular Malaysia. Separate Profiles are issued for Sabah and Sarawak.

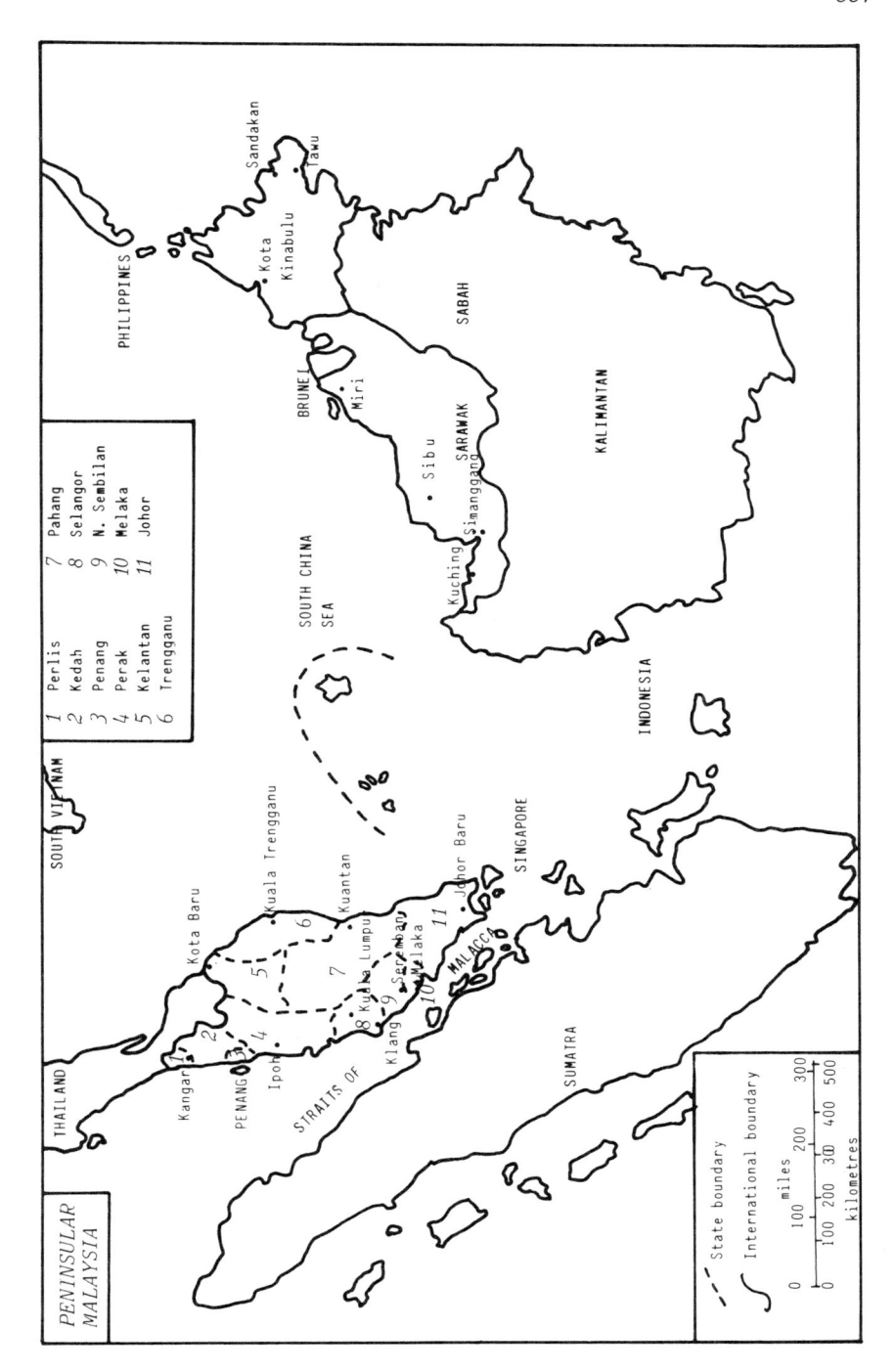

PENINSULAR MALAYSIA

1	Perlis	7	Pahang
2	Kedah	8	Selangor
3	Penang	9	N. Sembilan
4	Perak	10	Melaka
5	Kelantan	11	Johor
6	Trengganu		

1 GEOGRAPHY

Topography

The most striking feature of the political geography of Malaysia is the division of the federation into two halves – Peninsular Malaysia to the west and Sabah and Sarawak to the east – by 400 miles of the South China Sea. The total land area is 130,000 square miles or 332,800 sq km (about the size of the British Isles). Of this, Peninsular Malaysia occupies 52,000 square miles (about the size of England) and Sabah and Sarawak occupy 30,000 and 48,000 square miles respectively. A chain of mountains rising to 7,000 feet called the Main Range runs down the centre of Peninsular Malaysia through the states of Perak, Kelantan and Pahang, forming a barrier to communication between the east and west coasts. Rivers flow from the Main Range to both coasts, but the largest, the Sungei Kelantan and the Sungei Pahang, are on the east coast. The west coast comprises an alluvial plain, 600 miles long and up to 30 miles wide, fringed by mangrove swamps. This alluvial soil is fertile and contains extensive tin deposits. The major towns, industries and agricultural plantations are to be found on the west coast. The east coast consists of low sandy beaches, is less fertile and lightly populated. Most of the central part of the Peninsula is covered by tropical rain forest: huge trees with a canopy at 150 feet.

Climate

The climate is tropical with average temperatures around 80°F (26°C), high humidity and high rainfall. The rainfall in most places is over 100 inches (2,540 mm) per year, rising to 150 inches (3,810 mm) per year in the hills. The South West Monsoon from May to September is fairly mild but the North East Monsoon from November to February causes hazardous sea conditions and frequent flooding on the east coast and in Sabah and Sarawak, usually in January.

Communications

The main road arteries run up the west coast and the east coast and are connected by a road from Kuala Lumpur to Kuantan over the Main Range. These highways are being improved and a new road across the Main Range linking Penang and Kota Bharu should be completed in the early 1980s. A system of buses and shared taxis provides barely adequate public transport: car ownership is becoming increasingly common and over 60,000 new care are registered annually. A railway runs up the west coast from Singapore through Kuala Lumpur and Penang to the Thai border and another line branches to Kota Bharu. Some new rolling stock has been acquired but the system is outdated and in need of substantial imvestment if it is to compete with road and air travel on main routes. There are frequent internal flights to all major towns by the national carrier MAS. The most important routes are Penang

-Kuala Lumpur-Singapore and Kuala Lumpur-Singapore-Kuching-Kota Kinabalu. MAS retains a monopoly of flights to Sabah and Sarawak; several carriers operate to Europe, Australia and the Far East. For many years Malaysia relied on the port facilities of Singapore to which there are road and rail links, but the ports of Penang and Kelang have been refurbished, a new port opened in 1977 in Johore and another is under construction near Kuantan. The Straits of Malacca, between Peninsular Malaysia and Sumatra, are a vital shipping route between Europe and the Far East for heavy tanker and container traffic. There is a good internal post and STD telephone service, except between Peninsular Malaysia and Sabah/Sarawak, where operator delays can be several hours. International calls to Europe and Australia can normally be obtained within minutes.

2 POPULATION
Growth

The total population of Malaysia recorded in the 1980 Census was 13,435,588 of which 85% live in Peninsular Malaysia. The growth rate is about 2.6% per annum. The long term aim of the National Planning Board - part of the Prime Minister's Department - is to reduce the growth rate of 2% per annum over the 20-year period from 1966-1985, which it seems likely to achieve. The family planning programme began in urban areas but has been progressively extended into the rural health service. Over 30 government hospitals and numerous rural health centres now offer a family planning service. There has been no coercion; family planning has been projected as responsible parenthood at a time of increasing prosperity and declining infant mortality. But despite the success of family planning, 42% of the population is aged under 15, a figure which will fall only a few percent over the next ten years. This age structure means that on average every four persons of working age support three dependants with a consequent high demand for social services. This is further exemplified by comparing the size of the labour force - 4.8 million - with the total number of primary and secondary school students - 3.0 million (1978 figures).

Groups

Malaysia is a multi-racial community, and in Peninsular Malaysia the population consists of three main races: Malays (53%); Chinese (35%); and Indians (11%). The other 1% is a mixture of other groups. The term *bumiputra* has been coined to describe the Malays and other indigenous people.

Malays

The Malays are a Mongoloid people thought to have migrated from south west China at least 5,000 years ago, displacing the original aboriginal population (which still numbers over

60,000) into the central mountains. Their numbers have been increased by nineteenth and twentieth century migrations from Sumatra and Celebes. They are traditionally an agricultural and fishing people living in *kampongs* (small villages) and over 80% of them still live in settlements of less than 10,000 people. During the colonial period the Malays retained a considerable degree of political power and enjoyed preponderance in administration, the army and the police. Since independence, the Malays have used their political power to advance in other fields of activity.

Chinese

Although a small Chinese settlement is known to have existed in Melaka in the sixteenth century, the large influx of merchants and agriculturalists from the south east provinces of Kwangtung and Fukien began with the British capture of Penang in 1786 and the founding of Singapore in 1829. Tin mining in Perak was a major attraction; the Chinese mining community exceeded 50,000 as early as 1880 and Chinese immigration continued rapidly until controls were established in 1929. The Chinese still enjoy the major share of private wealth. This wealth and their urban base has enabled them until recently to enjoy superior education facilities and thus to dominate the professions as well as commerce.

Indians

Most of the Indians are descended from those brought from south India by the British in the late nineteenth and early twentieth centuries to man the rubber plantations and the railways. The majority are still employed in unskilled or semi-skilled jobs. Other significant groups are the Sikhs and Jaffna Tamils who served as policemen and executive officers respectively in the colonial government. Certain trades – such as the retail of textiles and books – are largely manned by Indians and their contribution to the medical and legal professions has been disproportionately high.

Distribution

The population density is much higher in west Malaysia (200 per square mile) than Sabah (25 per square mile) and Sarawak (23 per square mile). In Peninsular Malaysia, west coast states comprise only 40% of the mainland area but contain 70% of the population. The largest towns are all in the west; the Federal Territory of Kuala Lumpur (about 1 million), Georgetown on Penang Island and Ipoh (both about 300,000). The extent of urbanisation is increasing.

Slightly over half of the urban population is Chinese; the figures for 1975 were 56% Chinese, 30% Malay and 13% Indian, but a small though significant growth of the proportions of Malays and Indians has occurred since then, a result of the increasing involvement of Malays in industry and other urban employment. A more striking way of looking at the distribution is to say that one Chinese in two lives in a town, compared with one Indian in three and one Malay in six. In keeping with the greater urbanisation on the west coast, the proportion of Chinese is very much higher there than on the east coast. The east coast states are predominantly Malay; in Trengganu and Kelantan, Malays comprise 93% and 95% respectively of the population.

Immigration

Since independence in 1957, immigration has been strictly controlled. During the past 15 years, however, over 100,000 Muslim refugees from the south Philippines and a smaller number of Indonesian Muslims have come to Sabah and are still being assimilated. The Malaysian government understandably took a much tougher line with Vietnamese 'boat people' many of whom were ethnic Chinese.

3 SOCIETY AND CULTURE

Attitudes and Aspirations

The cultural and religious integrity of the three main racial groups is protected by the constitution and has been honoured. Religious and cultural differences are a strong barrier to intermarriage; the population will always be divided into three distinct racial groups and the formation of an identifiable Malaysian culture, incorporating elements from the various traditions will take generations.

Malays

Accounts written by Chinese and European travellers from the fifteenth century onwards portrayed a rural people whose animist culture had been overlaid by Hinduism and subsequently Islam, ruled by a hereditary sultan with an elaborate court and a passion for intrigue. This caricature was little affected by British indirect rule in the late nineteenth and early twentieth centuries. The culture was based on the *kampong* (village) and mutual help. Families were large, not wealthy, but well provided with the essentials of life, and they cooperated closely in *kampong* agriculture and fishing. Islam fostered a strong sense of brotherhood and belief in the life to come but reinforced the hierarchical structure in which the sultans functioned also as religious leaders. For the 80% of the Malay population who live in rural areas, much of this remains true today, but the government is urging the Malay community to become more competitive in education, business and professional life, which implies a more materialistic set of values and increasing urbanisation. Part of the price paid is an increasing problem of unemployment and drug abuse among drop-outs from urban schools who are reluctant to return to *kampong* life, but these problems are on a small scale compared with the horrors of urbanisation in some other parts of the world. Moreover, urban Malays have a strong tradition of returning to the family *kampong* at festival times, at least once a year, which helps to prevent estrangement between the urban and rural communities.

Chinese

The Chinese are traditionally an urban community monopolising commerce, mining and other entrepreneurial activities. Family and racial loyalties are very strong. Education is valued as a wise investment in the next generation and families spare no expense for their children. Before World War II, most of the overseas Chinese regarded themselves as temporary residents in south east Asia and transmitted a proportion of their earnings to China. This is no longer the case and the majority are Malaysian citizens, although about half a million have not yet been granted this status.

Indians

The Tamils lack the political power of the Malays and financial power of the Chinese. Many still live on rubber estates with large families and low incomes and in towns Indian labourers also suffer from a low standard of living. Those Indians and Ceylonese who have succeeded in gaining entry to the professions - notably law and medicine - constitute an urban elite and seem the most westernised section of the population. Many Malaysian Indians still have connections with India through relatives and arranged marriages with Indian brides, or see India as a place offering good opportunities for higher education.

Inter-Communal Relations and Government Policy

At independence in 1957, the constitution made provision for Malays to enjoy special rights and privileges. Traditional preferment in the army, police and public service continued after independence but selection for higher education remained meritocratic and the number of Malays entering the professions and commerce was small. An economic disparity was thus reflected in an educational disparity. Malay resentment against the more affluent Chinese became greater than the government realised and boiled over in riots and bloodshed on 13 May 1969. The government formulated a New Economic Policy (NEP) to enhance the economic status of the Malays; preferment in the public service became more marked, the major share of places in VIth forms and universities was allocated to the Malays and, most recently, firms of any size have been forced by legislation to employ a proportion of Malays. The Malays feel they are justified in making up for lost time since independence whereas the Chinese feel that the Malays are now advancing too fast, that their preferment is in excess of their share of the population and that what they, the Chinese, have fairly earned by honest effort is being unfairly taken from them. Their unease is exacerbated by the lack of precise targets for the economic rehabilitation of the Malays - the only official figure is that they should have a 30% share of equity by 1990. Characteristically, the Chinese have been unable to organise a united opposition to the NEP, individuals seeking instead to find a way round the policy by emigrating or sending their children or their capital overseas. This approach, while avoiding direct confrontation with the Malays, does encourage the accusation often levelled by Malay politicians that the Chinese are not sufficiently loyal to Malaysia to make sacrifices for the good of the nation as a whole. The Indians similarly resent the NEP; they have neither the wealth to circumvent it nor the political power to oppose it.

Chinese political leaders of the Malaysian Chinese Association (MCA) have traditionally been from the richest sections of society and prepared to cooperate with Malay politicians to preserve the interests of the *towkay* (businessmen) class, but in the 1978 election the majority of Chinese voted for the opposition Chinese party (DAP), thereby showing their dissatisfaction with this approach. Among the Malays, many of the benefits of the NEP have accrued to a relatively small urban group, whose conspicuous spending is resented by the rural Malays, in whose name the NEP was formulated but whose economic progress has been relatively slight. As an attempt to defuse growing resentment from the poor of all races, the government announced its primary objective for the 1965-70 economic plan as the elmination of poverty regardless of race, although the provisions of the NEP (pro-Malay in practice) continue to operate.

Language

Bahasa Malaysia (Malay) was introduced in 1967 as the sole national language, although English remains an official language in the courts and elsewhere. Government communications and parliament now operate entirely in Bahasa Malaysia. The process of converting to the use of Bahasa Malaysia as the medium of instruction will be completed in the school system by 1984 in Peninsular Malaysia and at university level by 1985, although Chinese and Tamil schooling is still available at primary level.

The National Language Policy has also tended to be a source of racial conflict, with the Malays seeing it as a proper step towards nation building while the non-Malays see it as an attempt to restrict their access to the international world of education and commerce. A measure of resentment has been the escalating enrolment in Chinese medium primary schools, and the increasing number of wealthy Chinese parents sending their children for English medium schooling overseas. Many high ranking and westernised Malays also educate their children overseas. After the 1969 riots, the imposition of tough sedition laws and the inauguration of the NEP, it was illegal to question the language policy. Gradually, however, the pendulum has begun to swing, with Malay politicians realising that a good standard of English might be in the long term interest. Within the last year measures to halt the decline in English have been actively considered by politicians, who nevertheless continue to stress the importance of maintaining the status of Bahasa Malaysia for purposes of national unity.

Religion

Islam is the official religion. All Malays are Muslim but the many sects of Christianity, Buddhism, Taoism, Hinduism and Sikhism in the non-Malay communities are allowed to worship freely and enjoy their religious restivals. They are, however, banned by law from proselytising amongst the Malays. Islam is seen as the strongest single uniting factor among the Malays and a powerful bulwark against communism. Overt observance of its rituals (most obviously the embargo on pork eating and the Ramadan fast) is enforced through para-legal means by the religious police and *syariah* courts. Non-Muslims must embrace Islam if they wish to marry Muslims. But Islam was not a major formative influence on the education system, and the legal system is based on English Common Law, not on Islamic Law, though there is increasing discussion in some circles about the desirability of the latter system.

Since the mid-1970s, various evangelist groups have gained adherents among young Malays, particularly in institutions of higher education both in Malaysia and overseas. Long robes for men and head coverings (rather like a nun's habit) for women are now common sights in the capital and elsewhere. Adherents of the more extreme groups reject material values and demand a return to fundamental interpretations of Islam. The government is doing its best to restrain them by promoting the more moderate *dakwah* (missionary) organisations and by point out that there is little basis in Islam for some of the more extreme interpretations. The most distressing event has been the desecration of Indian temples by some *dakwah* extremists who do not admit the religious tolerance enshrined in the constitution.

4 HISTORY AND POLITICS
Colonial Era

The first colonial power was Portugal which captured Malacca, a maritime state controlling the Straits of Malacca, in 1511 and remained until displaced by the Dutch in 1641. The British occupied Penang in 1786 and Singapore in 1819, persuading various sultans to cede their territories in exchange for financial support. The Dutch ceded Malacca to Britain in 1824. The importance of these three outposts to Britain was that they commanded trade routes between India and the Far East. Initially the British administration was under the control of Calcutta, and for 50 years there was no attempt to interfere in the Malayan hinterland. However, feuds between rival sultans and gang warfare among the increasing numbers of Chinese immigrant tin miners eventually caused the British to intervene on the mainland and in 1874 the Sultan of Perak was persuaded to accept a British resident. This system of residents extended to other states and in 1896 a federation was set up comprising Selangor, Negri Sembilan, Perak and Pahang. The power of the sultans was reduced but their positions were safeguarded. Several states accepted residents later and were ruled on an individual basis without joining the federation. These states of Kedah, Perlis, Johore, Trengganu and Kelantan retained a more Malay character. Under British rule the country prospered and the flow of Chinese and Indians increased until they became virtually as numerous as the Malays.

The chaotic system of administration - with the Straits Settlements (Singapore, Penang and Malacca), the federated states and the unfederated states all being ruled separately - continued until the Japanese invaded Malaya in 1941. The Japanese attempted with some success to cooperate with the Malays and to respect their political system and the authority of the sultans, but they were very harsh on the Chinese, many of whom were driven to become subsistence farmers on the hungle fringe. The Chinese formed a resistance movement, the MPAJA (Malayan People's Anti-Japanese Army) which was inspired by the Malayan Communist Party (MCP) and subsequently opposed the British attempt to re-establish their colonial status at the end of the war. A state of emergency lasted from 1948 until 1960 when the guerilla tactics of the MCP were finally defeated by the British policy of re-settling the squatter Chinese in 'new villages' (many of which are now prosperous settlements) thereby restricting the supply of food available to the terrorists.

Formation of Malaysia

The British attempted to centralise and nationalise the administration of Malaya after World War Two prior to granting independence. They proposed a Malayan union in which state powers would be vestigial and all residents of all races would become citizens. The inauguration of the Malayan union awoke a political consciousness among the Malays. Dato Onn Jaafar, the father of the present Prime Minister, founded the United Malay National Organisation (UMNO) in 1946 and fought successfully for a federal structure, safeguarding the power of the sultans and the partial autonomy of the states and limiting citizenship rights for non-Malays. These proposals were accepted by the British and the Malayan union was superseded by the federation in 1948. In 1949, the Chinese formed the Malayan Chinese Association (MCA) which was a welfare association designed to safeguard the communal and professional interests: it became a political party in 1951. In 1953 an alliance of the Malay UMNO, the Chinese MCA and the Indian MIC (Malayan Indians' Congress) was formed. Tunku Abdul Rahman became Chief Minister in 1955 and independence was granted in 1957.

The status of Singapore was a problem. It achieved internal self-government in 1959 and Lee Kuan Yew's Peoples' Action Party (PAP) favoured re-unification with Malaya. Malaya also favoured union as a way of restraining any communist infiltration in Singapore but was reluctant to allow a Chinese majority, which the inclusion of Singapore would imply. The solution adopted was to incorporate the states of Sabah and Sarawak, which had become British colonies after the war. This was agreed after a test of public opinion conducted in Sabah and Sarawak in 1961 by the Cobbold Commission, which found in favour of the creation of Malaysia but suggested guarantees for Sabah and Sarawak on the issues of language, immigration, and freedom of religion. Brunei declined to join the new federation. The Philippines and Indonesia were hostile to the formation of Malaysia and insisted on a UN enquiry in Sabah and Sarawak which found in favour of Malaysia. The Philippines pursued an ancient claim to Sabah based on a claim by the Sultan of Sulu, and Indonesia adopted a policy of *konfrontasi* which included armed incursions into Sabah and Sarawak and abortive landings on the Peninsula. Meanwhile the relationship between Kuala Lumpur and Singapore became strained when the PAP became involved in mainland politics during the 1964 elections by campaigning for Lee Kuan Yew's 'Malaysian Malaysia' idea. A rift developed beween the PAP and the alliance and eventually Singapore was expelled from the federation in August 1965; objections from Sabah and Sarawak were over-ruled. Confrontation finally ended in 1966 when both Indonesia and the Philippines recognised Malaysia.

Structure of Government

There are two houses of parliament. The more powerful is the lower house known as the House of Representatives or *Dewan Rakyat*. There are 154 seats: 114 for Peninsular Malaysia, 16 for Sabah and 24 for Sarawak. Elections are held at least every five years. Policy is decided by the Prime Minister and his cabinet, comprising ministers drawn from the various parties of the ruling coalition which is called the National Front *(Barisan Nasional)*. The upper house – the Senate or *Dewan Negara* – has 58 members, 32 of whom are appointed by the King to represent various groups and interests and 26 of whom represent the 13 states (2 members are selected by the legislative assemblies of each state). The Senate may delay but may not veto legislation made by the *Dewan Rakyat*. The King or *Yang diPertuan Agong* is a constitutional monarch elected by the nine sultans of the Malay states from among their number. He rules for a five-year period.

Of the 13 states, nine have sultans as hereditary rulers and the other four (Penang, Melaka, Sabah and Sarawak) have governors appointed by the King. There is a legislative assembly in each state, to which elections are normally held concurrently with federal elections. Each legislative assembly appoints a chief minister from among its members. The state legislative assemblies have authority over Muslim law, land matters including forestry and mining, agriculture, fisheries etc. and partial control of social welfare matters including scholarships within the state. All other matters are reserved for the federal parliament.

Recent Political Developments

The elections of May 1969 formed a watershed in Malaysian politics. The opposition won 37 of the 113 seats announced, with elections in Sabah and Sarawak to follow. The MCA won only 13 seats compared to 25 in 1964 due to Chinese voters switching to the DAP (Democratic Action Party, an offshoot of the PAP). The opposition line-up was: DAP 13; Parti Islam 12; Gerakan 8; People's Progressive Party 4. Riots broke out on 13 May with attacks on Chinese property; a state of emergency was declared, parliament was suspended and a National Operations Council was set up to rule under the leadership of Tun Razak, the Deputy Premier. The Malay backlash was a defeat for the laissez-faire policies of Tunku Abdul Rahman who was eclipsed and soon resigned. The NOC ruled for two years. It imposed a sedition act banning public discussion of various issues and a vigorous campaign to advance the economic status of the Malay race was formulated in the Second Malaysia Plan (1971-75). Parliament was recalled in 1971 and the alliance strengthened its position by persuading most parties to join the government, leaving the DAP as the only effective opposition. In the 1974 elections the alliance consolidated its position. The opposition was reduced to 10, including 9 DAP candidates. By 1978, a rift had developed between the Parti Islam, which held the majority of seats in Kelantan, and UMNO. In the 1978 elections the opposition consisted of the Parti Islam, which lost much support in Kelantan and elsewhere, and the DAP which again won Chinese votes at the expense of the MCA, showing Chinese disillusionment with the alliance policies. Out of 152 seats, the DAP won 16 and Parti Islam 5, although the opposition polled 45% of the votes cast. It was estimated that in urban areas 65% to 70% of the Chinese population had voted for the opposition.

International Relations

When confrontation with Indonesia ended in 1966, British and other commonwealth troops largely withdrew from Malaysia. In 1968, Britain announced that all British troops in south east Asia would be withdrawn by 1971; a five-power defence agreement was drawn up between Malaysia, Singapore, Britain, Australia and New Zealand which retained a token force in the region and contained a commitment to consult on defence problems in the event of external aggression. Communism is still suppressed internally; the MCP is banned and operates a guerilla campaign mainly along the Thai border and in the mountainous interior. There are said to be about 2,000 guerillas operating and since 1977 Thailand has allowed Malaysian forces to pursue them on to Thai soil. Along the Sarawak/Indonesian border an effective joint command has operated for some years. The security situation is thought to be under control.

Malaysia is understandably moving towards a policy of non-alignment. She has cultivated much stronger political ties with Singapore, Thailand and the Philippines through the Association of South East Asian Nations (ASEAN). ASEAN disavows any intention of becoming a military alliance but aims by common diplomacy to establish a 'Zone of Peace, Freedom and Neutrality' within the region free of superpower influence. Malaysia established diplomatic relations with Hanoi in 1973 and with Peking in 1979 and her policy is to attempt to maintain a balance between these powers and thereby neutralise their effects in the region. Relations with Hanoi have been clouded by the Vietnamese invasion of Kampuchea (ASEAN countries still recognise the Pol Pot regime) and the 1979 influx of 'boat people', mainly ethnic Chinese, from Vietnam. But Malaysia is also suspicious of Chinese intentions: China continues to supply 'moral support' for the MCP guerillas and Malaysia fears any influence from China dividing the loyalties of the four million Malaysian Chinese.

Malaysia has also been developing closer ties with fellow Islamic nations and has benefited from Arab loans and investment in the 1970s. She supports the Palestinian stance in the Middle East, wholeheartedly condemned the Soviet invasion of Afghanistan and - in the interests of Islamic solidarity - has issued no condemnation of the Iranian action in taking American diplomats as hostages.

5 THE ECONOMY

Note: Statistics refer to 1978 unless otherwise stated. The exchange rate is about M$5 = £1.

Economic Situation

For a developing country, still dependent on the production of primary products, Malaysia has one of the most stable and rapidly growing economies. The emphasis is on free enterprise, but there is considerable government direction and involvement; about two thirds of the investment capital is derived from private sources and one third from government funds. The GNP per capita had grown from M$680 at independence (1957) to M$3,184 (US$1,455) by the end of 1979. The average monthly income of a worker is in the range M$200-300 per month; 30% earn more than this and 33% less. The average figure for Kuala Lumpur is about twice the national average, whereas it is about half in the poorest east coast states. This is a much smaller geographical spread of income than is usual in developing countries. There is a wide gap in earnings between professionals (where salaries compare with those in the UK) and unskilled workers, smallholders and fishermen; even so, almost everyone is involved in monetary dealings and there is no crippling poverty and little malnutrition. The rate of real income growth is about 9% per annum.

Governmental direction of development proceeds by a series of five-year plans; the Third Malaysia Plan (1976-80) aimed at the 'elimination of poverty' and the 'restructuring of society' so that employment in the various sectors will reflect the racial composition of the country – in other words, improving the economic position of the Malays who comprise the bulk of the poorly paid agricultural work force. This restructuring requires a rapid rate of growth which is actually being achieved; the growth for 1976-78 was 8.7% per annum in real terms.

Trade

Exports amount to over half the GDP and raw materials – notably rubber, tin, palm oil, timber and crude oil – account for 73% of exports. The economy is therefore vulnerable to fluctuating commodity prices and world recession. Nevertheless, Malaysia's balance of trade has been consistently in her favour and her reserves are equivalent to seven months' imports. The pattern of trade is shown overleaf.

As can be seen from the diagram, in 1978 the surplus on merchandise was M$3 billion. In 1979, however, exports increased in value by 39% to M$26.5 billion and imports by 29% to M$20 billion, producing a record merchandise surplus of M$6.5 billion. The deficit on invisibles was M$4.3 billion leaving a surplus of M$2.2 billion on current account. After taking into account short and long term capital flows, the overall balance of payments was in surplus by nearly M$1.8 billion.

Major Economic Sectors

Agriculture

Agriculture accounts for 25% of GDP and 45% of total exports – mainly to the EEC, Japan and the USA. Rubber is the major crop, accounting for 21% of exports, but the acreage under rubber has been steadily declining as oil palm, a more profitable crop, is replanted in old rubber plantations. Palm oil now accounts for 10% of exports. The rate of timber exploitation has increased in the 1970s and logs now comprise 14% of exports. There is little replanting of forests, for much of the cleared land is used for plantation crops, and there is concern among conservationists that all lowland forest will have been cleared in about ten years at the present rate of exploitation. Malaysia is not quite self-sufficient in rice, the staple diet, despite the introduction of double cropping and the expansion of irrigation schemes. Periods of drought in recent years are partly to blame for this.

The government is making extensive efforts to aid the agricultural sector not only because of the importance of agricultural exports but also because 44% of the work force are employed in agriculture and over half of these are estimated to have incomes too low to meet all their basic needs. More than two thirds of the agricultural work force are Malays. The main

EXPORTS

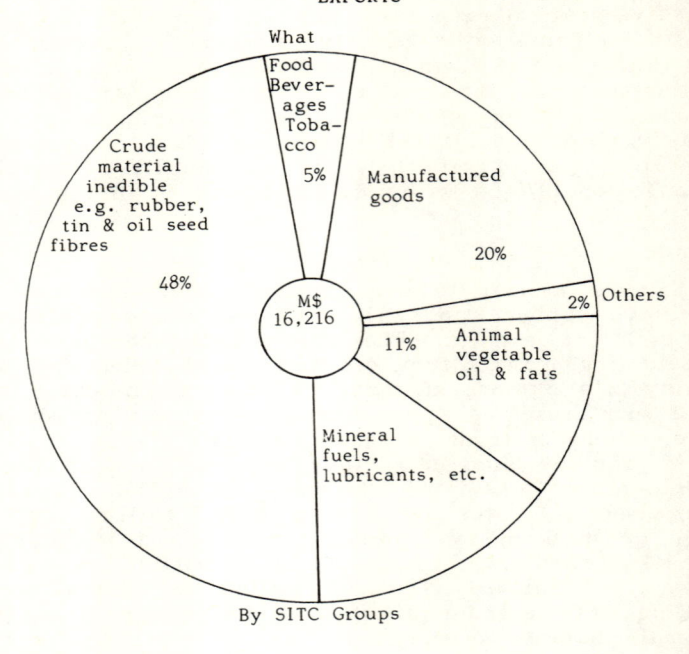

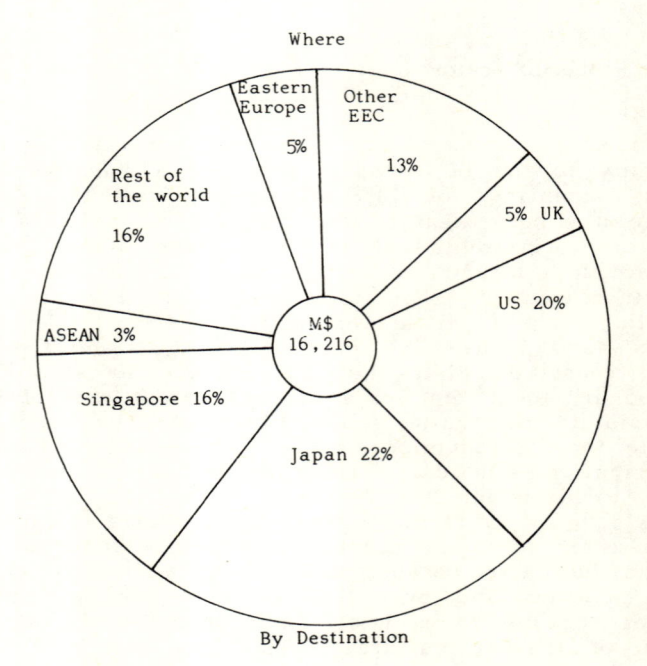

What

- Food Beverages Tobacco 5%
- Manufactured goods 20%
- Others 2%
- Animal vegetable oil & fats 11%
- Mineral fuels, lubricants, etc.
- Crude material inedible e.g. rubber, tin & oil seed fibres 48%

M$ 16,216

By SITC Groups

Where

- Eastern Europe 5%
- Other EEC 13%
- UK 5%
- US 20%
- Japan 22%
- Singapore 16%
- ASEAN 3%
- Rest of the world 16%

M$ 16,216

By Destination

IMPORTS

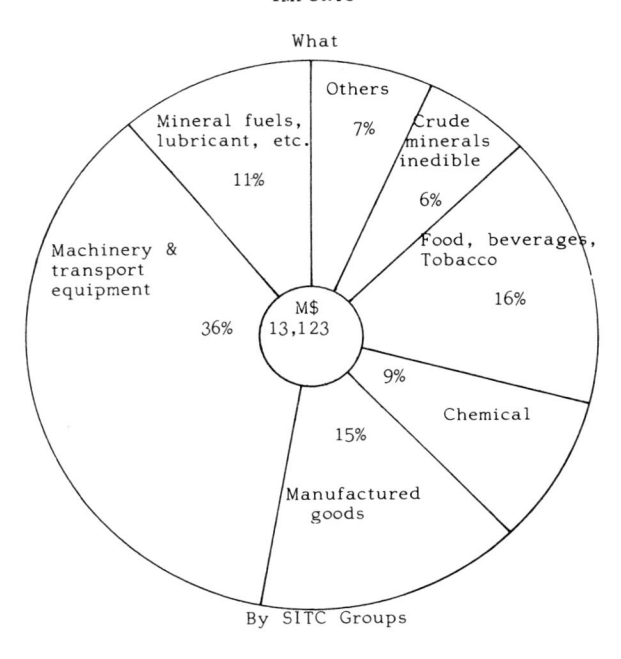

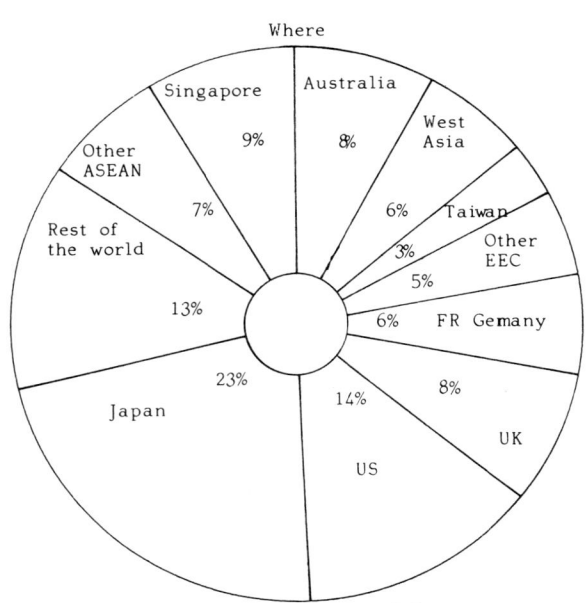

What

- Others: 7%
- Crude minerals inedible: 6%
- Food, beverages, Tobacco: 16%
- Chemical: 9%
- Manufactured goods: 15%
- Machinery & transport equipment: 36%
- Mineral fuels, lubricant, etc.: 11%

M$ 13,123

By SITC Groups

Where

- Australia: 8%
- West Asia: 6%
- Taiwan: 3%
- Other EEC: 5%
- FR Germany: 6%
- UK: 8%
- US: 14%
- Japan: 23%
- Rest of the world: 13%
- Other ASEAN: 7%
- Singapore: 9%

By Major Countries of Origin

efforts have been made in situ through drainage and irrigation schemes, double cropping of rice, assistance with replanting for rubber smallholders and stock improvement through the research efforts of MARDI and the Rubber Research Institute. The other approach is land develoment; FELDA (the Federal Land Development Agency) and other bodies will open and settle 1 million acres of virgin land from 1976 onwards. No comprehensive plan exists for agriculture but the government intends to announce one shortly; measures have been announced to prevent the supplanting of rubber by oil palm and more profitable crops such as cocoa will probably be more extensively tried. Diversification will make the agricultural sector less vulnerable to fluctuation in the world demand for raw materials.

Mining

Mining accounts for 5% of GDP and 26% of exports; crude oil has overtaken tin as the major export in this sector. Production of tin will continue to decline as mines are worked out, but the high world prices should maintain the value of earnings for some years. The exploitation of petroleum was impeded by the government's attempt to introduce legislation to gain voting rights in the oil companies in excess of their shareholdings. This attempt has been abandoned and a successful agreement has been concluded between Petronas (the government oil agency), and the major companies. The production of oil from offshore drilling, mainly in Sabah and Sarawak but increasingly in Trengganu, has more than doubled in the period 1975-78 to 230,000 barrels per day, compared with a domestic consumption of 130,000 barrels per day. Domestic consumption is expected to rise so that Malaysia would require to import oil by 1985. Vast quantities of natural gas associated with the petroleum deposits, hitherto largely flared and wasted, are increasingly being exploited commercially. Investment by the oil companies accounts for 12% of private investment but generates few employment opportunities.

Manufacturing

This is the fastest growing sector, expanding at 14% per annum and accounting for 19% of GDP and 20% of exports, mainly to ASEAN, the EC and the USA. This is an impressive growth from less than 10% of GDP at independence (1957). The main industries are textiles, electrical and electronic machinery, wood and rubber products and transport equipment. As yet, little of the manufacturing is downstream activity related to the major commodity exports, but this could be a profitable trend in future. The manufacturing sector is capable of rapid employment generation and the government intends that Malays should be weaned away from lower paid jobs in agriculture into the higher paid manufacturing sector. The Industrial Coordination Act of 1976 requires medium size and large firms to employ a work force reflecting the racial composition of the population. This Act is thought to have reduced non-oil private investment and hindered local companies from expansion, but the government has given assurances that the Act will not be too rapidly or rigidly enforced.

Employment and Manpower Planning

The rate of unemployment is about 6%, though it is slightly lower than that for Chinese and higher for Indians. The figure for the 15-19 age group is as high as 17% in urban areas, reflecting the migration of youth to towns in search of employment. Employment opportunities are growing faster than the population and projections show a rate of unemployment below 4% by 1990. There is little graduate unemployment as yet, but there are signs that arts graduates are finding it difficult to get the jobs they would like.

There is evidence of a drift of Malays away from agriculture and into other sectors of the economy; they have increased their representation by 5% since 1975 in professional, technical, managerial and sales jobs, although they comprise less than one third in most of these categories and are generally in the lower paid jobs. The creation of a commercial sector among the Malays is a slow process. The incomes of all races have benefited from the growth of the economy and there is little evidence that Malays, most of whom are in rural areas, have caught up much in earning power relative to the other races. Figures for the median incomes are as follows (at current prices):

M$ per household per month

	1970	1973	1976
Malay	120	163	229
Chinese	268	343	482
Indian	194	277	359
All	166	227	304
Urban	265	342	494
Rural	139	184	262

Although agriculture is by far the largest employer of labour, the rapid growth of manufacturing will exacerbate the present shortage of high and middle level manpower in the scientific and technical fields. A considerable expansion of higher education was therefore planned for 1976-80, increasing the output of graduates from 3,300 to 4,300 and diploma holders from 2,300 to 3,600 per annum. There will be an even larger expansion in the output of semi-skilled workers from 8,600 to 13,800. By 1980, Malays will comprise the largest racial group in all these categories of people trained within Malaysia.

Regional Development and Communications

Special consideration was given in the Third Malaysia Plan to development assistance for the poorest states - Kedah and Perlis, Sabah and Sarawak, and the east coast states. Some, such as Pahang, Sabah and Trengganu are responding with a growth in their per capita income of more than 10% per annum but others such as Kelantan and Kedah are still lagging badly. Irrigation schemes are improving the standard of living of the agricultural communities in these poor states, but land development schemes have made little improvement to incomes so far.

Ownership of Assets

It is the government's target that through natural growth by 1990 the ownership of equity should be: Malays 30%, non-Malays 40% and foreign 30%. The figures for 1971 were: Malays 4%, non-Malays 34%, foreign 62% and for 1978: Malays 10%, non-Malays 44%, foreign 46%. There has been a rapid growth of equity and the wealthier non-Malay community has taken more advantage of this than the Malays. Most Malay holdings are through trusts reserved for them and individual holdings are still minute. It is apparent that the earning power of the Malays needs to be improved substantially if the target of 30% of equity is to be reached by 1990.

Investment and External Assistance

Total investment is currently about M$10 billion and represents about 25% of GDP. About two thirds of this money is private investment, although it is suspected that some of it is disguised government investment. The government encourages foreign investment by granting 'pioneer status' to new companies, which allows tax holidays of up to 10 years, but also requires a partial Malay ownership and payroll. National savings are running at the very high figure of over 31% of GNP (1979). In 1978, government revenue was M$8.5 billion, about half of which came from export duties and corporation tax relating to the major commodities. Current expenditure was M$8.1 billion and development expenditure M$3.4 billion. This left a deficit of M$3 billion to be found by borrowing. By 1979, the national debt had reached M$21 billion of which M$16 billion was financed by domestic borrowing (mainly government securities purchased by provident funds and other institutional investors) and M$5 billion by external borrowing from the World Bank, Asian Development Bank, bilateral sources such as Arab loans and Yen credits and the international markets. The public sector is growing rapidly and public development expenditure during 1975-80 is expected to be M$25 billion. Malaysia's external debt service ratio (interest payments as a percentage of exports) is about 2.5%. This is one of the lowest figures in the region. Malaysia has never defaulted on loan agreements and has no difficulty in obtaining external loans. Aid in the form of technical assistance, mainly from Colombo Plan sources, is valued at the small sum of M$60 million per year.

Prospects for the Early 1980s

Exports are expected to grow at a satisfactory rate, though the exceptional 40% growth during 1979 is unlikely to be repeated. More stimulus is likely to come from growth of the domestic economy and the overall growth rate should be maintained. The balance of payments is likely to remain favourable. Perhaps the most difficult problem, apart from the continuing problem of helping the Malay community raise their incomes and equity holdings, will be to prevent inflation rising due to pressures from higher import prices.

6 THE EDUCATION SYSTEM

The Ministry of Education is charged with the provision of schooling and further education. Children are entitled to nine years of free but non-compulsory education from the age of 6. English is being progressively phased out as a medium of instruction throughout the education system and replaced by Malay, a process which will be complete at VIth form level by the early 1980s. Primary education will continue to be available in Chinese and Tamil.

Academic Year

The school year runs from January to November, but the various universities and other further education establishments have different academic years which usually start around May (the interval allows for the marking of public examinations and the selection of pupils for further and higher education). In schools where two shifts are operating, children attend morning school for half the year and afternoon school for the other half.

Pre-Primary

There is no government system of pre-primary education, but the number of private kindergartens is increasing especially in the towns. The estimate for 1979 was 828 schools and 87,000 pupils. There seems to be no plan for introducing government kindergartens, but one Islamic organisation, PERKIM, has expressed an intention of establishing such schools.

Primary

Children enter primary school at age 6. There are six years of primary schooling, known as Standards 1 to 6. Although schooling is not compulsory, over 95% of children start school at Standard 1 and over 90% reach Standard 6; 93% of children aged 6-11 are in school. The enrolment in primary schools in 1980 was 2,006,748. There is automatic promotion from Standard 1 up to Form III i.e. for the first nine years of schooling, although national assessment tests are held in Standards 3 and 5, to measure pupils' attainment in the hope that their weak points can be identified and rectified. Although schooling is free, textbooks cost about M$20-30 per year and transport in urban areas can cost M$25 per month. A textbook loan scheme started in 1975 to help pupils whose parents earn less than M$500 per month.

English as a medium of instruction was finally phased out of primary schools in 1975. The former English medium schools have converted to Malay medium, but Chinese (Mandarin) and Tamil medium schools remain. It is interesting to note that whereas in 1971, 78% of Chinese children went to Chinese medium schools and 53% of Tamil children to Tamil medium schools, these figures had become 87% and 49% by 1978, which seems to show that a greater proportion of Chinese are selecting Chinese medium schooling now that the English medium option has been removed. If we look at all the races combined, about 65% of children are educated in Malay, 30% in Chinese and 5% in Tamil at primary level.

A national syllabus lays down what shall be taught in each subject. A recent analysis has shown that about 50% of time is devoted to communicative subjects (languages and mathematics), 20% to environmental subjects (history, geography, civics and science) and the remainder to physical education, religious education, arts, music, health science and co-curricular activities. The time spent on language is not surprising; students in Malay medium schools study English from Standard 1 and those in Chinese or Tamil schools study Malay from Standard 1 and English from Standard 3 and thus have to study three languages at age 8.

Secondary

Secondary education is divided into the following stages which take a total of 7-8 years:

(i)   a 'Remove' class for children who attended Chinese or Tamil medium primary schools, to prepare them for studying in Malay

(ii) lower secondary (forms I to III)

(iii) upper secondary (Forms IV and V)

(iv) VIth form (Lower and Upper VI).

Formerly English was the main medium of instruction but it has been progressively replaced by Malay. From the beginning of 1979, all arts subjects were taught in Malay throughout the school including the VIth form. Science VIth forms were converted entirely to Malay by January 1982. Tuition is free in Malay medium classes, but textbooks are not (apart from the loan scheme).

Education at secondary level has shown an enormous expansion since 1964, when a selection examination held at Standard 6 in primary school was abolished. For example, in 1963/64, 42% of Standard 6 pupils passed this examination and entered secondary school - an intake of 63,519. This figure jumped to 160,792 after the abolition of the examination in 1964/65 and by 1978 it had grown to 214,187, which represents over 85% of pupils in Standard 6. The total enrolment at secondary level including VIth forms was 1,084,833 in 1980. The vast majority of secondary schools are day schools, but some have residential hostels attached for rural children. There are 12 historically prestigious residential schools for selected Malays (such as Malay College, Kuala Kangsar) and a further 11 residential schools have been built, one in each state, which take about 90% Malays. In addition, MARA has built five junior science colleges for Malays and another five are planned. These new residential schools emphasise science from Form IV onwards.

Lower Secondary

Students from Chinese or Tamil medium primary schools must spend on year in a Remove class before beginning secondary education in Malay medium. There is no secondary education available in Tamil, but there are about 40 private (fee paying) Chinese medium secondary schools which a minority of Chinese students attend. The age at which children start lower secondary education is therefore 12 or 13. The main subjects taught in lower secondary school are Bahasa Malaysia, English, history, geography, civics, mathematics, integrated science (based on the Scottish syllabus). In addition, students study one vocational 'elective subject', either commerce, agricultural science, home economics, or industrial arts. Syllabi are formulated in great detail by the Ministry of Education and textbooks are chosen from approved lists. The three-year course leads to the *Sijil Rendah Pelajaran* (SRP), a literal translation of the former English medium Lower School Certificate. The SRP examinations, run by the Federal Examinations Syndicate, are mainly objective tests marked by computer and are the means of selection for upper secondary education.

There were 778,312 pupils in lower secondary education in 1980.

Upper Secondary

Candidates with the best SRP results are offered places in academic IVth forms and others are given places in vocational schools run by the Ministry of Education. Of those pupils completing lower secondary schools in 1980, 59.9% were selected for upper secondary education. No school fees are charged. The rest seek vocational education from other government or private institutions or else look for jobs. The academic IVth form is divided into science and arts streams, though there is a common core of subjects including Malay and English. In the past, Malays have shunned science, so nowadays they

358

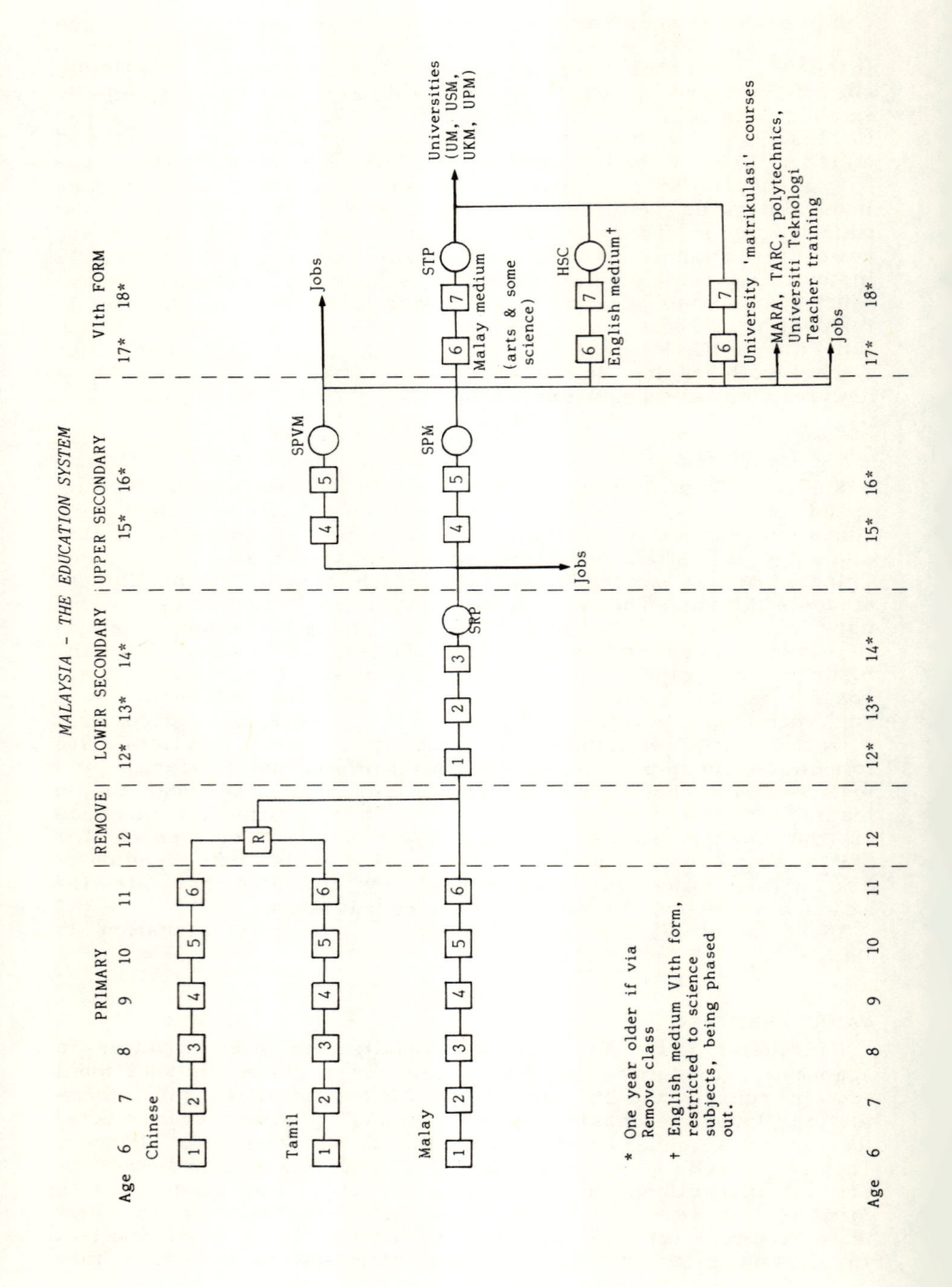

MALAYSIA - THE EDUCATION SYSTEM

Age	PRIMARY	REMOVE	LOWER SECONDARY	UPPER SECONDARY	VIth FORM
	6 7 8 9 10 11	12	12* 13* 14*	15* 16*	17* 18*

Chinese: 1–2–3–4–5–6
Tamil: 1–2–3–4–5–6
 → R (Remove class)
Malay: 1–2–3–4–5–6

Lower Secondary: 1–2–3 → SRP → Jobs

Upper Secondary track 1: 4–5 → SPVM ○ → Jobs
Upper Secondary track 2: 4–5 → SPM ○

VIth Form:
- 6–7 → STP ○ Malay medium (arts & some science) → Universities (UM, USM, UKM, UPM)
- 6–7 → HSC ○ English medium† →
- 6–7 → University 'matrikulasi' courses → MARA, TARC, polytechnics, Universiti Teknologi, Teacher training → Jobs

| Age | 6 7 8 9 10 11 | 12 | 12* 13* 14* | 15* 16* | 17* 18* |

* One year older if via Remove class
† English medium VIth form, restricted to science subjects, being phased out.

are strongly encouraged to enter the science stream if the SRP results are good. In the science stream, biology, physics, chemistry, mathematics and additional mathematics are offered as separate subjects; in the arts stream general science is studied. Science syllabi are based on the English Nuffield ones.

In 1980 94% of pupils were in academic schools, 2% in technical schools and 4% in vocational schools.

For all subjects, syllabi prescribed by the Ministry of Education lead to the *Sijil Pelajaran Malaysia* (SPM) which is the Malay-medium successor to the Malaysian Certificate of Education (MCE). This examination is set and marked by the Federal Examinations Syndicate with some cooperation from the Cambridge Local Examinations Syndicate; it enjoys widespread international recognition. The certificate is greaded overall (Grades 1, 2 or 3) and individual subjects are graded 1 to 9; grade 6 and above is called a 'credit' and is equivalent to an 'O' level pass; grades 7 and 8 are called a 'pass' but are below 'O' level pass standard. A pass in Bahasa Malaysia is a requirement for passing the examination as a whole; a credit in Bahasa Malaysia is required for entry to tertiary education. For those who fail or do badly in SPM, it is possible to sit the examination the following year as a private candidate; there are numerous private schools offering facilities for students who wish to repeat the examination.

VIth Forms

The MCE examination represents a major hurdle and from 1971 to 1980 only about 13% of Form V students were admitted to Form VI. Fees are M$15 per month, but most Malay students receive government scholarships which cover the fees. In 1980, the total size of the VIth form was 27,461 but there were a further 13,000 students studying full or part time in private schools for 'A' levels or HSC. Students take four subjects, either sciences or arts, plus a general paper. All VIth forms are now conducted in Malay. The final examination is known as Higher School Certificate (HSC) or, in the Malay version, *Sijil Tinggi Persekolahan* (STP). It is conducted jointly by the Malaysian Examinations Syndicate and the Cambridge Local Examinations Syndicate. Cambridge sets the papers, which are translated where necessary into Malay, and accepts responsibility for the standard of the subjects examined in English; the Malaysian universities accept responsibility for the standard of the subjects examined in Malay. This transitional arrangement has led to the continuing international recognition of the HSC/STP, but it ended with the 1981 examination. A Malaysian Examinations Council was set up to run the STP from 1982 onwards.

Technical and Vocational

There are at present nine technical schools, which are normal secondary schools except that additional subjects such as technical drawing are offered and examined at MCE/SPM. These schools are run by the Technical and Vocational Division of the Ministry of Education. The same division also runs 29 vocational schools with a total enrolment in 1978 of 11,050, which represents 4.6% of students who take SRP. These vocational schools provide a two-year course of upper secondary education (Forms IV and V) leading to the *Sijil Pelajaran Vokesyenal Malaysia* (SPVM = Vocational Education Certificate). Students may choose one of the following options: woodwork and building construction; fitting and machining; sheet metalwork and welding; air conditioning and refrigeration; electrical installation and maintenance; radio, television and electronics servicing; motor maintenance; commerce; agriculture; home science. It is compulsory to take science, mathematics, Bahasa Malaysia and English as well as the vocational subjects and the SPVM examination is of the same standard as MCE/SPM. In the past vocational schools took students with poor LCE/SRP results, but now that 'white collar unemployment' threatens students who leave school with MCE/SPM, the popularity of vocational schools, which do offer better employment prospects to Form V leavers, is growing among the more able students. The schools offer vocational education rather than skill training: students with good results in the SPVM can continue their studies at a polytechnic. The vocational schools and the SPVM have been converted to Malay medium.

MARA

This is an organisation set up to advance *bumiputras* professionally and economically. It has established nine training institutes with a total enrolment of 2,300. They offer a two-year course in similar subjects to the government vocational schools, except that the skill training component is somewhat higher and the academic component lower. A certificate is awarded on completion of the course. The Ministry of Culture, Youth and Sports runs a similar school. Other agencies offer more specialised training: the Ministry of Agriculture has six vocational schools offering a three-year post-LCE/SPM course to about 700 students; there are options in agricultural extension, husbandry, plantation crops, mechanisation etc. The Ministry of Labour runs two industrial training institutes (ITIs) offering skill training courses to students who are usually sponsored by local industries: periods of study alternate with periods in industry and a qualification similar to the City and Guilds is awarded by the NITTCB (National Industrial Trades Training Certificate Board). The annual output from these two institutes is about 900. The Ministry of Health offers paramedical training and many public bodies such as the National Electricity Board, Telecommunications Department, Post Office etc. have their own training schools for new recruits. Large firms and banks also conduct formal in-house training. The idea of apprenticeship is also widespread among small Chinese firms, such as motor repair shops.

The recent Cabinet Review Report on Education stressed the need for greater opportunities for vocational education. Prior to the publication of the report, plans for another 24 vocational schools and three ITIs during the period 1980-85 were announced. Meanwhile there has been a proliferation of private technical and commercial institutes offering full and part time courses for City and Guilds, LCC and other similar examinations. The 1978 enrolment in such institutes was over 37,000. They are of very variable quality and the Ministry of Education intends to tighten the system of licensing and inspection.

Higher

There are five unversities. For direct admission to degree courses in all except Universiti Teknologi (q.v.) the minimum requirements are passes in two subjects at principal level in the HSC/STP examination (i.e. 'A' level) or a pass in one subject at principal level and two at subsidiary level (i.e. one 'A' level and two 'O' level passes on three 'A' level papers). A credit in Malay at MCE/SRP is compulsory. There are also various faculty requirements. A quota system operates whereby approximately two thirds of the places are allocated to *bumiputra* students. Most universities also offer pre-university or *matrikulasi* courses for *bumiputras* as an alternative means of entry. The overall balance between science and technology courses and arts courses in 60/40 in favour of the former. A clearing house similar to UCCA has been set up to enable students to be considered by all the universities; it also controls admission to matriculation courses and to the MARA Institute of Technology. Fees are low - about £150 per year - and most Malay students are given state or federal scholarships. Most first degree courses take four years (six for medicine). It is planned that all teaching in the universities should be in Malay medium by 1985; meanwhile the proportion of teaching in Malay varies from one university to another and also from subject to subject.

University of Malaya (UM)

Formerly a university college allied to a similar institution in Singapore, the university was established in its present form in 1961 and is the oldest in Malaysia. There are eight faculties: arts and social sciences, science, economics and administration, education, law, engineering, medicine, dentistry. The medium of instruction is mostly Malay in years 1 and 2, but English still predominates in years 3 and 4, especially in the science and technical courses. The university has, with British assistance, prepared a course to improve the reading skills in English of Malay medium pupils and leads the other Malaysian universities in remedial measures of this kind. UM degrees enjoy worldwide recognition, including the medical degree which entitles medical graduates to full registration with the British GMC. The enrolment at UM has been static for the past few years and stands at about 8,200 of whom about 48% are Malays. The majority of students enter with HSC qualifications but there is a basic sciences course for *bumiputras* with MCE or poor BSC/STP results as an alternative method of entry to science, engineering, medicine and dentistry degree courses. The style of teaching is patterned on the old British model; a three-term year; an examination for an ordinary degree after three years and a fourth year for honours.

UM offers a wider range of post-graduate courses than the other universities. There are master's courses in economics, public adminsitration, education, engineering, and various medical disciplines; the medical faculty also teaches for some British and Australian medical post-graduate qualifications. There is a similar range of post-graduate diploma courses, the largest of which is in education which trains about 800 students per year. Although a number of PhDs are awarded, there is relatively little research done at the university and no large research groups comprising staff and PhD students which are so characteristic of British universities. A centre for advanced studies is being set up to encourage the development of inter-disciplinary research activities, but it is too early to say whether it will succeed in boosting research activity at the university.

Universiti Sains Malaysia (USM)

This university, which has a strong science bias, was established in Penang in 1969. The enrolment was 3,300 in 1978. Intake is mainly via HSC/STP but a *matrikulasi* course is run at the residential science schools in Penang and Kedah as an alternative route for Malays, who comprise about 53% of the enrolment. The university operates a two-semester year and the American system of 'credits'. There are schools of biological sciences, chemical sciences, physics, mathematics, applied science, pharmaceutical sciences, housing building and planning, humanities, and comparative social sciences. There is also a centre for educational studies which supplies the education component for a four-year degree course in science/ humanities with education. There is a small number of master's courses and there is a handful of PhD students. The university has recently set up Malaysia's third medical school.

A unique feature of USM is the off-campus programme, begun in 1971 and coordinated by the centre for educational studies. The current enrolment is around 900. Students study on their own with the aid of materials supplied by the university, but the appropriate books from USM's library stock are available in various public libraries and there are science centres which coordinate the programme in each state. Students take from three to five years to complete the first part of their degree course, after which they must attend full time at USM for the final year of study.

Universiti Kebangsaan Malaysia (UKM)

This university (the name means National University) was established in temporary buildings in Kuala Lumpur in 1970 to provide higher education in Malay for students graduating from Malay medium schools. All faculties except science and medicine have moved to a new campus at Bangi, 20 miles away. All classes were conducted in Malay from the outset and the student population is over 90% Malay. The intake is mainly from matriculation courses run in local VIth forms rather than via HSC. The 1978 enrolment was 4,300. There are faculties of economics and management, Islamic studies, social science and humanities (including education), science, medicine (which uses the General Hospital, Kuala Lumpur for clinical teaching) and an institute of Malay language, literature and culture. Many of the students take general rather than honours degrees and some general arts graduates have faced difficulties in gaining suitable employment. The medical faculty, founded in 1973, has not applied for GMC recognition, but the first batch of 40 students graduating in 1979 satisfied British and other external examiners; however, the intake has expanded to about 150 and students have been accepted with qualifications as low as one grade E at HSC. A branch campus in Sabah is being expanded and will soon offer full degree programmes in some subjects.

Universiti Pertanian Malaysia (UPM)

The Agricultural University, founded in 1971, is based on a merger of the former Serdang Agricultural College and the faculty of agriculture at Universiti Malaya. The site at Serdang is 14 miles from Kuala Lumpur. There are seven faculties: agriculture, agricultural engineering, resource economics, and agribusiness and educational services which offer only degree courses, and forestry, veterinary medicine, and science which offer both four-year degree and three-year diploma courses. A two-semester system has been adopted. The intake is nearly 90% Malay and most of the teaching is done in Malay. The entrance requirement for degree courses is HSC/STP ('A' level) whereas the diploma courses start from MCE/SPM ('O' level). The enrolments for 1978 were 1,769 (diploma) and 1,405 (degree).

Universiti Teknologi Malaysia (UTM)

The University of Technology was formed in 1972 by upgrading the Kuala Lumpur Technical College. This college offered three-year post-MCE diploma programmes which continue to be the major activity at the university; the 1978 enrolment was 2,459 (diploma) and 817 (degree). The enrolment is nearly 90% Malay and nearly all courses are conducted in Malay. Admission is at MCE/SPM level and students are accepted for five-year degree or three-year diploma courses depending on their grades. In some subjects the degree and diploma students follow the same syllabus for the first two or three years, whereas in others the courses are distinct from the outset. There are five faculties: built environment (architecture - a six-year degree course - and quantity surveying), civil engineering, electrical engineering, mechanical engineering (which also offers a degree in petroleum engineering), and surveying (land surveying and property management). There is also a centre for science studies, which offers degrees and diplomas in science with education, and a centre for humanities which offers service courses. There are plans to move the university to a new site at Sekudai near Johore Bahru by the mid-1980s.

Further

As mentioned above, two universities, UPM and UTM, run large numbers of post-MCE/SPM diploma courses. The other major futher education institutions are MARA Institute of Technology, which is exclusively for *bumiputras*, and the semi-private Tunku Abdul Rahman College, the student body of which is almost entirely Chinese. Both of these run courses at approximately OND and HND level as well as a number of professional courses at degree level, although neither college is empowered to award degrees. There are two polytechnics running courses at OND level and a further five are planned during the 1980s. There are also a large number of private institutions offering certificate and diploma courses (usually externally examined by a British body such as City and Guilds).

Institiut Teknologi MARA (ITM)

The MARA Institute of Technology was set up in 1965 as part of the attempt to introduce more Malays into the world of business and commerce; admission is restricted to *bumiputras* Most courses have been taught in English. In 1982, however, the medium of instruction changed to Malay. The main campus is at Shah Alam, about 15 miles from Kuala Lumpur, but four branch campuses have been established in the states of Perlis, Trengganu, Sabah and Sarawak offering the initial years of a number of diploma courses. The 1978 enrolment was 6,986.

There are 12 schools: engineering, accountancy, law and administration, hotel and catering management, business and management, applied science, architecture planning and surveying, art and design, mathematics and computing, secretarial science, library science, mass communication. These schools offer courses in a wide variety of subjects most of which require MCE/SPM for admission and lead to an internally assessed diploma after three years. A number of advanced diplomas are offered for students who do well in their diploma courses and these advanced diplomas are regarded by the government and the local professional bodies as equivalent to first degrees. Although these advanced diplomas are offered in civil, electrical, electronic and mechanical engineering, architecture, town planning and quantity surveying - and others are mooted - the government has firmly resisted attempts by ITM students to press for university status for the institute. A range of courses for external professional examinations such as the British ACA, ICMA and ICSA examinations in accountancy and administration are also offered by ITM to students with HSC/STP. The school of library science, besides offering a three-year diploma for students with HSC/STP runs the only post-graduate diploma course in librarianship in Malaysia.

Tunku Abdul Rahman College (TARC)

This institution was founded as a pre-university college in 1968 and is funded from private sources (mainly the Malaysian Chinese Association) and the government on a 50/50 basis. It is housed in a new campus at Setapak, 5 miles from Kuala Lumpur, and a branch campus is planned in Johore. The 1978 enrolment is 3,800, the vast majority of whom are Chinese; the college is open to all races but necessarily charges relatively high fees and selects strictly on academic merit.

The largest school is pre-university studies with some 2,500 students preparing for HSC/STP examinations in arts and sciences. There are other schools: business studies which offers three-year post-HSC/STP diploma courses in accounting and management, during which students all take the British ACA, ICSA or ICMA examinations; arts and sciences which offers three-year diploma courses (students used to sit the London external BSc concurrently with the diploma, and though this is no longer possible a similar arrangement with an American university is planned); technology which runs two-year post-MCE/SPM certificate courses of approximately OND standard in building, electronics, materials science and automotive technology, and three-year post-BSC/STP diploma courses of approximately degree standard in the same subjects (British examinations such as the Institute of Building and CEI are taken concurrently with the diploma); and extra-mural studies which offers short courses in languages, etc., to members of the general public. TARC diplomas are not recognised by the Malaysian government (although the British qualifications taken with the diploma are recognised) but TARC graduates are much in demand in the private sector. TARC acts as a sort of Chinese MARA and to some extent alleviates the problems faced by those Chinese students unable to find places in Malaysian VIth forms and universities and who cannot afford to study overseas.

Polytechnics

Ungku Omar Politeknik in Ipoh was established in 1968 with UNESCO and World Bank assistance and is run by the Technical and Vocational Education Division of the Ministry of Education. The polytechnic offers two-year post-MCE/SPM/SPVM certificate courses (roughly equivalent to OND) in various branches of civil, electrical and mechanical engineering and commerce and a three-year diploma in accountancy. A working attachment of six months forms part of the course. New courses have started in marine engineering (five years including two years sea training and practical experience, a venture heavily supported by the Japanese) and secretarial science. The medium of instruction is in the process of conversion from English to Malay. The 1978 enrolment was 1,487 and was expected to reach 1,800 by 1980. A second polytechnic at Kuantan is housed in temporary buildings; the 1978 enrolment was 342 but the institution should expand rapidly in the 1980s when permanent premises are ready. There are plans to build five more polytechnics in the next decade.

Teacher Training

The Malaysian system for training teachers largely follows the old British model; the majority of teachers are non-graduates and are trained in colleges, whereas the training of graduate teachers is confined to universities.

Graduate

Universiti Malaya and Universiti Kebangsaan both offer nine-month diplomas of education to graduates of their own and other universities to train as specialist teachers of one or more subjects. The output for 1979 is UM 650 and UKM 320. All five universities also offer four-year BEd programmes in a restricted range of subjects: the total output for 1979 is around 300. These teachers are mainly trained to teach Forms IV, V and VI and are little used in the lower forms of secondary schools. There is one other type of course run by Universiti Pertanian and Universiti Teknologi to produce non-graduate science teachers by means of a three-year course for students with MCE/SPM ('O' level). These teachers are intended to teach in the lower and middle forms of secondary schools.

Teacher Training Colleges

There are 19 TTCs in Peninsular Malaysia and three each in Sabah and Sarawak. The facilities are steadily being improved; most colleges have microteaching studios and the construction of language laboratories is planned. The colleges offer a two-year course to students with MCE/SPM and currently produce about 5,500 teachers per year in the Peninsula and another 1,200 in Sabah and Sarawak. The minimum standard for entry is three credits at SPM, including Bahasa Malaysia, but many candidates have four or five credits. In 1978 there were over 65,000 applicants for only 5,530 places. There is a strong bias in favour of Malay candidates who are thought to be allocated for about 80% of places. All trainees are on government scholarships and are bonded for five years. The period of training was extended from two years to three in 1981. At the same time, the minimum entry requirement is likely to be raised to five credits at SPM.

The two-year course begins in May each year. The language of instruction is Bahasa Malaysia. In the first year all students follow a broadly based course which concentrates on 'middle childhood' - i.e. Standard 4 to Form I. In their second year the trainees specialise in either 'early childhood' (Standards 1 to 3) or 'early adolescence' (Forms I to III) allowing an area of specialisation. The academic content of the courses concentrates on topics in the relevant school syllabus in order to improve the depth of the teachers' knowledge and does not include materials from 'A' level courses. The courses of study are:

(i) professional education courses: education, audio-visual education, library utilisation and management, civics, religious education

(ii) language proficiency courses (Malay and English)

(iii) school subject courses (primary school subjects) for the 'early childhood' group and subject specialisation for the 'early adolescence' group

(iv) co-curricular activities

(v) practical teaching.

The final examination is set by the Teacher Training Division; there are boards of examiners for each subject comprising training college lecturers.

The organisation of teaching practice has been recently revised. Trainees do three weeks practice in the first term of their second year and three months at the end of their course at the school to which they are due to be posted. This should eliminate the problem of starting the academic year in January with trainee teachers who are likely to be reposted to other schools in April, but it will unfortunately prevent college lecturers from supervising their own trainees in many cases.

Specialist Courses

Some teacher training colleges have particular specialisations within the normal two-year course - e.g. home science in Johore Baru and mathematics and science in Penang. In addition, institutions in Kuala Lumpur run specialist in-service courses for trained teachers. The Specialist Teachers' Training College runs one-year courses in arts and crafts, music, home science, physical education, audio-visual education, librarianship, vocational guidance, commercial subjects and the teaching of the blind and deaf. The Language Institute runs three-month courses for teachers of English. Universiti Malaya has recently started a one-year TESL course for non-graduate experienced teachers and a one-year certificate course in educational technology. A programme ran for several years to improve the Bahasa Malaysia of teachers who were trained in English medium; this process is considered complete in the Peninsula.

Adult and Non-Formal

Apart from on-the-job training adult education is not highly developed in Malaysia. The Ministry of Education runs centres where school drop-outs can catch up on the secondary schooling they have missed: in 1978 there were 106 such centres with 13,894 students. This total, which has been falling for many years, is equivalent to only one third of the number of students who are enrolled in private commercial and technical colleges. There are also adult literacy classes and classes in 'national solidarity' run by various government bodies. A more imaginative approach is provided by the trade unions; large unions have their own education committees which run weekend and other courses in law, economics and related subjects. The trade unions have recently established a workers' institute of technology in Kelang (about 20 miles from Kuala Lumpur) to offer more opportunities for vocational training to adults. The Women's Institutes offer valuable courses in home economics and child care; for girls in rural areas married in their teens this represents the only form of continuing education available. The role of adult education in tackling the problems of rural youths who migrate to urban areas is as yet unexplored; there is little guidance on the use of leisure, no 'liberal education' courses, few hobby clubs apart from sports, public library development has been slow and television contains little of educational value. Perhaps the increasiong problems of urban migration may eventually stimulate more interest in the potential scope of adult education, which has so far been the Cinderella of the Malaysian system.

Management Training

Various bodies provide in-service training in management and supervision, notably the National Productivity Centre (NPC) and the Malaysian Institute of Management (MIM) both situated in Kuala Lumpur. About 3,000 participants attend short courses annually. The National Institute of Public Administration (INTAN) runs a wide range of in-service training courses in Kuala Lumpur for administrators and managers in the public sector, including a nine-month diploma in public administration. The current capacity is about 2,000 people per year, but this will increase when three branch campuses are built in the 1980s in other parts of the country with World Bank assistance.

Research

It has been mentioned that Malaysian universities are primarily undergraduate teaching institutions and there are few research groups, although a number of academics are active on individual projects. There are, however, a number of bodies outside the education system undertaking large scale research programmes of international renown, including the Institute for Medical Research, MARDI (Malaysian Agricultural Research and Development Corporation) and the RRI (Rubber Research Institute). The RRI has a budget of over £5 million, raised through a levy on rubber producers with which it conducts fundamental and applied research into the production, properties and uses of rubber.

Regional Institutions: RECSAM

The South-East Asian Ministers of Education Organisation (SEAMEO), a body funded by the UN, has established various training establishments in member countries, such as RELC (Regional English Language Centre) in Singapore and TROPMED in Indonesia. Malaysia provides facilities for RECSAM (the Regional Centre for Science and Mathematics Education) in Penang, which was established in 1970. The director is Malaysian and the staff are on secondment from SEAMEO countries, the United States, Britain, Australia and New Zealand. As Vietnam, Laos and Cambodia no longer participate actively in SEAMEO the remaining countries are the constituent countries of ASEAN: Malaysia, Singapore, Thailand, Indonesia and the Philippines. RECSAM provides a range of training courses, usually lasting ten weeks, in various aspects of science and mathematics education and curriculum development, to which member countries send 'key personnel' as participants. There are an average of 15 courses and a total of 180 participants per year. Consultants from Malaysian, British and other universities are often invited to teach on certain courses. In addition to the courses, there are two continuing education research projects at RECSAM. Planning and budgeting is done on a quinquennial basis by the governing board.

Overseas Study

The majority of Malaysians who study overseas are privately-financed non-Malays, mainly Chinese, whose access to VIth form and university education in Malaysia is limited by the application of quotas. The number studying in the various countries in 1978 was approximately 16,900 in Britain, 6,000 in Australia, 6,000 in India, 1,000 in the US and smaller numbers in Canada and New Zealand. Australia has been many students' first choice because tuition was free and a loophole in immigration rules has allowed over 80% to remain and gain permanent residence. Britain has been popular because fees were modest and British qualifications, particularly in professional fields, enjoy full recognition in Malaysia. India is remarkably cheap and many Malaysian Indians study there, though only a minority of Indian universities are recognised by the Malaysian government. The pattern is expected to change during the 1980s: Australia has increased fees and closed the immigration loophole; Britain has put up fees to 'full cost' levels. The United States and Canada are beginning to receive more applications. The greatest demand in all countries has been for degree and professional courses in subjects such as medicine, dentistry, law and accounting. The effect of the conversion of the Malaysian school system to Malay medium has been to induce a greater proportion of parents to send their children overseas for 'A' levels, pre-university courses, and even to boarding schools in Britain, Canada and Australia.

Besides the private students, there are about 6,000 Malays studying overseas, nearly all on scholarships from government or quasi-government bodies; over 500 a year have been sent to Britain since the early 1970s to do 'A' levels followed by degree courses. The official figures for 1978 are that 28,268 Malaysians were studying overseas, of whom 22,385 were non-Malay and 5,883 Malay. Out of this total, 17,513 were doing degree or similar courses, which compares with a total enrolment of 18,064 in Malaysian universities. While it is true that 64% of the students in local universities are Malay, a very different picture emerges if one adds the students in overseas universities; the ratio is then Malays 45%; Chinese 47%; Indians 8%. The Malaysian government understandably takes students studying overseas into account for manpower planning purposes and often cites the large number of non-Malays studying overseas in support of its own policy of limiting their admission to Malaysian universities.

7 EDUCATIONAL ADMINISTRATION

The System

Partly as a legacy from the past, but nowadays as a conscious attempt to build a nation out of the diverse races, languages and religions, the Malaysian system of education is highly centralised. The uniformity of curricula, syllabi, timetabling and examinations has already been described. The administrative structure consists of three tiers; the federal ministry, the state education offices and the individual schools and colleges. Ultimate responsibility rests with the Minister of Education, who is a member of the cabinet and who is assisted by two deputy ministers and a political secretary. The ministry contains two types of officials: officers of the Malaysian civil service, who are subject to transfer to other ministries, and officers of the education service, who are liable to be transferred between schools, colleges and the various professional posts in the ministry at federal and state level. The chief civil servant is the secretary-general, who is directly responsible to the minister. The head of the professional divisions is the director-general, who is assisted by two deputies. The secretary-general also has two deputies who are responsible for the various administrative divisions.

Each state education office is headed by a director of education who is responsible for administering the schools in his state. His staff includes education officers, school and subject organisers and executive staff. The headteachers of primary schools and principals of secondary schools report to the state education officer. The principals of teacher training colleges report to the Teacher Training Division of the ministry and the principals of vocational and technical schools and polytechnics report to the Technical and Vocational Education Division.

Ministry of Education

The Ministry of Education is divided into 18 divisions, the names and functions of which are as follows:

(i) *Educational Planning and Research Division (EPRD)*
Long and short range planning; devising alternative strategies for policy makers; monitoring development and performance; data collection and analysis

(ii) *Schools Division*
Administration of schools, including organisation, supervision, professional support, finance and the posting of teachers

(iii) *Teacher Training Division*
Pre-service training of non-graduate teachers; in-service training programmes

(iv) *Curriculum Development Centre (CDC)*
Curriculum evaluation and revision for primary and secondary schools. The CDC is divided into different sections dealing with separate subjects at separate levels, but projects on population education, compensatory education and an integrated primary curriculum are also being carried out

(v) *Examinations Syndicate*
Administration of the following national examinations; Standard 3 and Standard 5 tests, SRP and with the Cambridge Local Examinations Syndicate, SPM and STP/HSC

(vi) *School Inspectorate*
Inspection of schools and advice to teachers and head-teachers on professional matters

(vii) *Technical and Vocational Education Division*
Running of vocational schools, technical schools, polytechnics and the technical teachers' college; curriculum development in technical and vocational courses

(viii) *Educational Media Service*
Planning, production and evaluation of educational TV and radio programmes for schools; provision of audio-visual materials for schools; training teachers in use of the media

(ix) *Finance and Accounts Division*
Financial planning, administration and control

(x) *Development and Supply Division*
Planning and implementation of five-year development programmes; supply of equipment to schools; implementation of projects involving foreign loans (e.g. World Bank, Asian Development Bank)

(xi) *Higher Education Division*
Secretariat to Committee of Vice-Chancellors; coordination of university development and finance; coordination

ADMINISTRATIVE STRUCTURE -

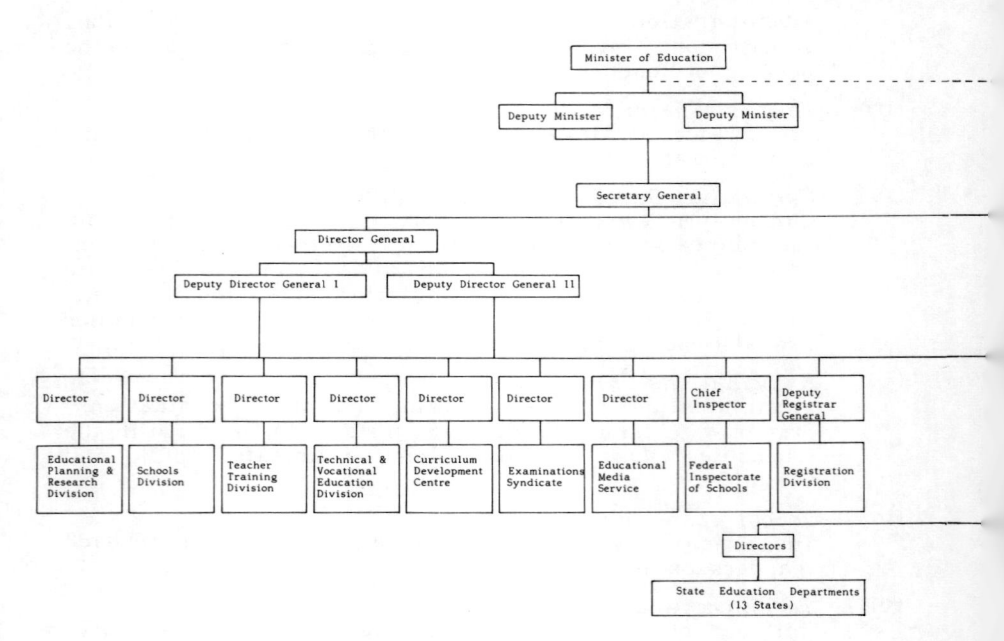

```
                          ┌─────────────────────┐
                          │ Minister of Education│
                          └─────────────────────┘
                        ┌─────────┴─────────┐
                ┌───────────────┐   ┌───────────────┐
                │ Deputy Minister│   │ Deputy Minister│
                └───────────────┘   └───────────────┘
                          │
                ┌─────────────────┐
                │ Secretary General│
                └─────────────────┘
                          │
                ┌─────────────────┐
                │ Director General │
                └─────────────────┘
              ┌───────────┴────────────┐
    ┌──────────────────────┐  ┌──────────────────────┐
    │Deputy Director General I│  │Deputy Director General II│
    └──────────────────────┘  └──────────────────────┘
```

Director	Director	Director	Director	Director	Director	Director	Chief Inspector	Deputy Registrar General
Educational Planning & Research Division	Schools Division	Teacher Training Division	Technical & Vocational Education Division	Curriculum Development Centre	Examinations Syndicate	Educational Media Service	Federal Inspectorate of Schools	Registration Division

Directors

State Education Departments (13 States)

MINISTRY OF EDUCATION

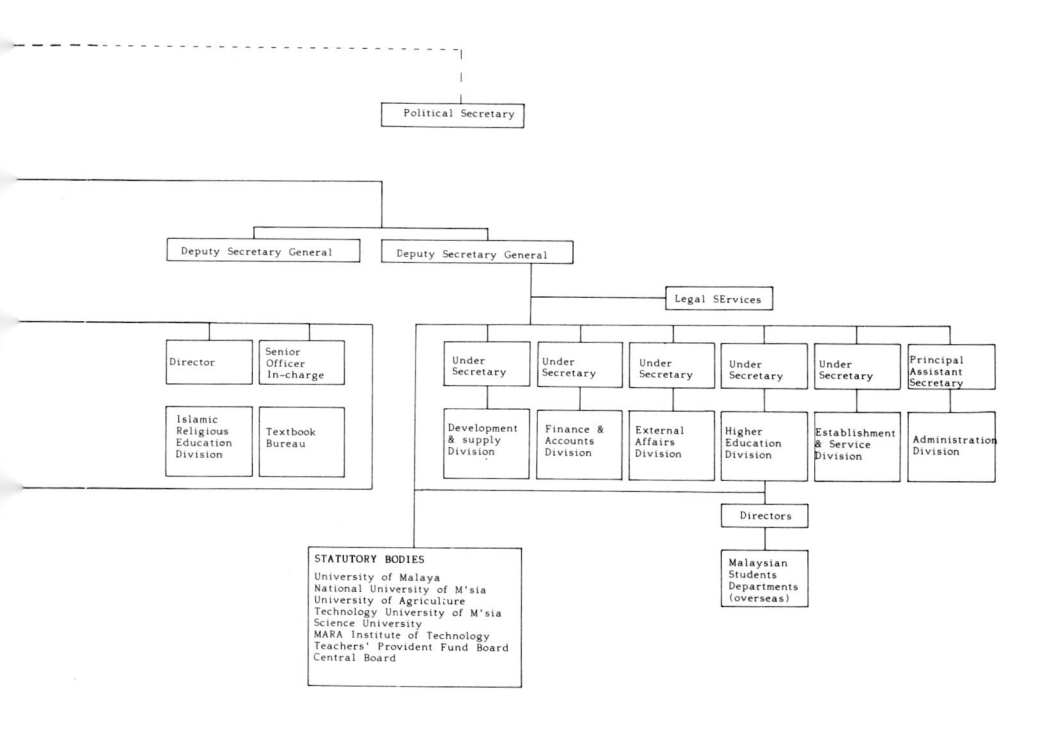

Organizational Chart

- Political Secretary
  - Deputy Secretary General
    - Director
      - Islamic Religious Education Division
    - Senior Officer In-charge
      - Textbook Bureau
  - Deputy Secretary General
    - Legal SErvices
    - Under Secretary
      - Development & supply Division
    - Under Secretary
      - Finance & Accounts Division
    - Under Secretary
      - External Affairs Division
    - Under Secretary
      - Higher Education Division
        - Directors
          - Malaysian Students Departments (overseas)
    - Under Secretary
      - Establishment & Service Division
    - Principal Assistant Secretary
      - Administration Division

STATUTORY BODIES
University of Malaya
National University of M'sia
University of Agriculture
Technology University of M'sia
Science University
MARA Institute of Technology
Teachers' Provident Fund Board
Central Board

of admissions to universities and matriculation courses; registration of students studying overseas

(xii) *Islamic Education Division*
The teaching of Islam in schools

(xiii) *Service and Establishments Division*
Appointment, conditions of service, promotion for all officers in the ministry (in cooperation with the Public Services Department, Public Service Commission and Treasury)

(xiv) *Foreign Affairs Division*
Liaison with UNESCO, SEAMEO and Commonwealth agencies

(xv) *Scholarships and Training Division*
Adminstration of scholarships for schools and higher education within Malaysia; processing of scholarships offered by Commonwealth or other governments; awarding of federal scholarships for overseas study; administering schemes for further training of ministry officers at local and foreign universities

(xvi) *Registry of Schools and Teachers*
Keeping records of teachers; registering both government and private schools

(xvii) *Textbook Bureau*
Evaluation and production of textbooks for schools; running the textbook loan scheme

(xviii) *Administration Division*
Liaison with other ministries; answering parliamentary questions; provision of physical facilities for the ministry.

The ministry has spawned a number of high level policy committees in recent years in an attempt to coordinate the work of the various divisions.

(i) *Education Planning Committee*
Established in 1971. Takes the most important decisions on policy. Chaired by the Minister of Education and comprises both deputy ministers, the secretary-general and his two deputies and the director-general plus his two deputies. The director of the Educational Planning and Research Division (EPRD) is secretary to the committee

(ii) *Central Curriculum Committee*
Set up in 1967. Responsible for curriculum policy and implementation. The director-general is chairman and the committee consists of his two deputies and the directors of the other divisions concerned. The Curriculum Development Centre (CDC) is the secretariat

(iii) *Finance Committee*
Set up in 1967. Responsible for curriculum policy and implementation. The director-general is chairman and the committee consists of his two deputies and the directors of the other divisions concerned. The Curriculum Development Centre (CDC) is the secretariat

(iv) *Development Committee*
Established in 1976. Chaired by the secretary-general and contains senior officials from the Ministry of Education and the Public Works Department. The Development and Supplies Division is the secretariat. The committee oversees the building programme and related matters.

States Education Offices

As outlined above, the State Education Officer and his staff are responsible for administering, through the headteachers and principals, the schools in each state. The staff include school organisers, one or more of whom is responsible for supervising each type of school: e.g. Tamil primary schools, Chinese primary schools and Malay primary schools; similarly there are organisers for secondary schools. The main function of these organisers is to ensure that the provisions of the 1961 Act are being carried out; that each school has an appropriate number of qualified teachers, the necessary space, furniture, equipment and books, class sizes within acceptable limits; that needy students obtain financial aid; that examinations are properly conducted and so on. There are also subject organisers, e.g. for Malay, English, science, etc. who supervise the teaching of individual subjects mostly in secondary but also in primary schools. They have confusing designations; the senior language organiser is the 'State Language Officer' and the senior science organiser is the 'State Science Supervisor'. They complement the efforts of the school organisers and also give professional advice where necessary to teachers. There are a number of other officers responsible for vocational guidance, school libraries and examinations; a state media officer acts as a link between the schools and the Educational Media Service.

School Inspection

Although school inspectors are attached to the state education offices, they report to the federal inspectorate, not to the state education officer. The inspectors specialise in various subjects and conduct full inspections, day inspections and subject inspections. The aim is to inspect each school annually but the staff is insufficient to do this. Reports are prepared at three levels: matters within the control of the headteacher are reported to him; the state education officer receives a report on matters he can control; and any matters of wider significance are reported to the minister via the director-general.

Schools and Colleges

The highly centralised system places most headteachers and principals in the role of full time administrators. Headteachers are responsible for administering the dictates of the 1961 Act and carrying out the instructions of the ministry; they have very little say in curriculum matters which are spelt out in great detail by the CDC. They are mainly concerned with keeping their schools in good repair and supply, financial administration, student discipline, and the deployment of staff. Many problems are referred upwards to the state education office and hence to the Ministry of Education.

Universities

The administration of higher education is less centralised and only partly controlled by the Ministry of Education. The main role of the ministry is coordination. A Higher Education Council comprising the five vice-chancellors, the Minister of Education and his senior officials, and a secretariat which is the Higher Education Division, attempts to ensure a certain uniformity of practice and to prevent excessive duplication in courses and facilities.

Each university has a three-tier system of administration. The lowest tier, but that with the most effective power, is the University Council. In Universiti Malaya this comprises 16 members, most of whom are from government departments and only three - the vice-chancellor and two members of staff - from within the university. The chairman is apointed by the Minister of Education. Two committees decide most of the business: a financial committee, chaired by the Treasury representative, and a working committee, which controls staff matters. Ninety percent of the university's funds derive from the federal government and it is through the University Council that the government exercises administrative control. The middle tier is the Senate which consists entirely of academic staff and is responsible for academic matters. In Universiti Malaya it numbers about 100. The highest tier is the Court, an enormous forum of over 200, which includes all members of the Council, Senate, 30 representatives from the professions and industries and numerous other appointees. It meets annually to discuss a report presented by the university administration. Initiatives proposed by the Court are referred to the Council and Senate for study.

Under the 1971 Universities Act, the vice-chancellor enjoys considerable autonomy. (For example, each university has been able to tackle the implementation of teaching in Malay at its own pace.) In most universities there are three deputy vice-chancellors. One is in charge of staff matters and a second in charge of finance, both subject to the constraints laid down by the Council. The third, appointed by the Minister of Education, is responsible for student discipline. Disciplinary legislation introduced in 1975 requires students to obtain permissionsion before establishing any society, raising funds, or holding meetings; student demonstrations are banned. Though the university is a statutory body, university teachers are bound by a restrictive code of practice similar to that for civil servants. This prevents them from engaging in political activities or from publishing or making statements on matters relating to confidential information or university policy.

8 EDUCATIONAL FINANCE

Sources of Finance

The federal government is responsible for providing both the recurrent and the capital development expenditure on education; state authorities are not required to contribute. Most schools are owned by the government but the system inherited schools which are privately owned by missions, Chinese associations, etc., the former are fully assisted both in recurrent and capital expenditure, the latter receive recurrent assistance and in some instances capital grants. There is a small minority of completely private schools which receive no government assistance. Schools do not charge tuition fees except in VIth forms but parents have to find up to M$200 per annum per child for miscellaneous expenditure on sports, uniforms, textbooks and transport. Scholarships to offset this are available for a proportion of needy students and there is the textbook loan scheme. In teacher training colleges instruction and board are free and trainees receive an allowance. Other colleges including universities charge modest fees; a wide range of scholarships are available, especially for Malay students.

Analysis of Expenditure

The recurrent and capital expenditure on education for recent years is as follows (M$ million):

Year	Recurrent	Capital	Total	% of Total Government Spending
1976	1,259	218	1,437	18
1979	1,942	422	2,364	17
1980	2,053	522	2,575	12

In 1980 the distribution of current expenditure by sector was as follows (in comparison with 1978):

	1978 (%)	1980 (%)
General Administration	2.8	3.5
Primary and Secondary Education	69.5	70.0
Technical and Vocational Education	1.7	1.6
Teacher Training	4.0	4.0
Higher Education	14.7	12.7
Overseas Students	6.2	7.1
Examinations	0.6	0.4
Other	0.5	0.6

Capital Development expenditure is planned on a quinquennial basis. In the Third Malaysia Plan, the education and training sector has been given a vote of M$2,146 million for the period 1976-80, which represents about 10% of the capital expenditure on all sectors. A rough breakdown of this sum according to spending agency is:

	M$ million
Ministry of Education	
Peninsular Malaysia	1,359
Sabah	220
Sarawak	237
Other agencies (MARA, Ministry of Labour, etc.)	330
	2,146

A more detailed breakdown for the Peninsula is:

	M$ million
Primary education	262.7
Secondary education	262.6
Vocational and technical	23.7
Higher technical	22.7
Universities and colleges	592.5
Teacher training	92.7
Others	102.0
	1,358.9

The expansion of facilities for schooling is the major item and rural areas, especially Sabah and Sarawak, have been given priority. But the rapid expansion of the universities has also consumed a large portion of the capital fund.

Aid to Education

As Malaysia became more affluent during the 1970s, donor countries steadily reduced their bilateral aid. British aid for the early 1980s is less than £1 million per year and is largely devoted to the provision of about 20 experts and about 50 scholarships per year. Other Commonwealth and West European countries provide smaller aid programmes whereas aid from the Communist bloc countries is rarely taken up. The relative unimportance of bilateral aid may be seen by comparing the total number of British-sponsored Malaysian students in Britain - about 100 - with the total of 5,000 Malaysian sponsored and 11,000 privately financed Malaysian students in Britain. The subsidy of Malaysian students in Britain was the major source of British aid to Malaysia in the 1970s, a fact which has only come to light now that the subsidy has been withdrawn.

The main donors of multilateral aid, in the form of soft loans, are the World Bank (IBRD) and the Asian Development Bank. Projects in the educational field which have been partly World Bank financed include the construction of a large number of primary and secondary schools, Kuantan Polytechnic, four pilot teachers' resource centres in four rural states and three industrial training institutes. In the 1980s it is likely that the World Bank will be involved in constructing more industrial training institutes whereas the ADB may finance the construction of up to five new polytechnics.

9 DEVELOPMENT AND PLANNING OF THE EDUCATION SYSTEM

Historical Development

In the nineteenth century little attention was paid to education. In the Straits Settlements (Penang, Malacca, Singapore and Labuan) and the federated states (Selangor, Perak, Pahang and Negri Sembilan) four to six years of elementary education were provided for the Malays on the assumption that they would continue in their traditional occupations as farmers and fishermen. Even more modest facilities were provided in the non-federated states (Johore, Kedah, Perlis, Kelantan and Trengganu).

Until 1920 there was no provision for Chinese and Tamil medium education in view of the immigrant status of these groups. The Chinese community therefore organised its own schools (engaging teachers from China) and provided a 12-year programme. However, since the medium of instruction was Chinese, the products of the schools were confined to employment within their own racial group. This underlined and perpetuated the dichotomy between indigenous Malays and immigrant Chinese and led to Chinese schools becoming cradles of social and political unrest, with the result that legislation was introduced in 1920 to establish registration and control of these schools. Under the Labour Code of 1912 small per capita grants were provided by the administration in the federated Malay states to stimulate growth of Indian vernacular education in order to stabilise the Indian labour force by perpetuating Indian values and way of life. In general, however, facilities were poor and the rate of drop-out from the limited four-year system was high. English medium education was pioneered by the Christian missions, the first school being started by the Anglicans in Penang in 1816, followed by the Roman Catholics and Methodists. The aim of these schools was to inculcate western traditions and Christian concepts of morality. They constituted a valuable source of manpower for the junior administrative service and the British-owned commercial houses and were consequently given generous aid by the British administration in addition to strong local community support. Unhappily for the future development of the country they served almost exclusively the urban, immigrant population, since more than 70% of the Malays, living in rural areas and economically disadvantaged, could not aspire to English medium education.

With the signing of the Federation of Malay Agreement, enshrining the specialist privileges of the Malays, the Malay community pressed for educational reform. Following the opposition of the Chinese to a proposal to abolish their schools a compromise was reached whereby English and Malay were taught in Chinese schools while all vernacular schools were given state aid until enough national schools could be established. The Razak Report of 1956 proposed that Malay should become the medium of instruction, but that the other languages and cultures should be preserved. However, conditions during the Emergency placed constraints upon the rapid implementation of such proposals for educational development which had to await the more favourable political climate following independence.

Education Act 1961

The Razak Report (1956) was enacted by the Education Ordinance of 1957. This was reviewed in 1960 by the Rhaman Talib Report, the recommendations of which formed the basis of the Education Act of 1961, which is still in force. The main developments which derived from this comprehensive Act were: universal free primary education (achieved in 1961); automatic promotion up to the ninth year, i.e. Form III (achieved in 1965); centralised control of primary education; the expansion of teacher training; the introduction of Bahasa Malaysia as the medium of instruction in progressive stages (started in primary schools in 1961 and to be completed in secondary schools by 1982).

Education Policy

The Education Act 1961 defined the fundamental principle of the education system as follows: "the education policy of the Federation . . . is to establish a national system of education which will satisfy the needs of the nation and promote its cultural, social, economic and political development . . . and for the progressive development of an education system in which the national language is the main medium of instruction".

The continuing objectives of educational policy at school level are:

(i) to provide a minimum of nine years' general education to all who wish to attend

(ii) to preserve and sustain the languages and cultures of each community

(iii) to unite the various races and create a national identity.

It is apparent that there is some conflict between objectives (ii) and (iii) which requires a compromise in implementation; for example parents can choose Malay, Chinese or Tamil medium when their children attend primary school (ii), whereas secondary schooling is only available in Malay (iii). The policy for higher education is formulated along racial lines consistent with the New Economic Policy. Manpower plans aim towards 30% Malay participation in the professions, business and industry by 1990. This means that during the 1980s at least Malays will continue to receive preferential access to higher education and probably to VIth forms.

Educational development plans are drawn up as part of national five-year development plans, one example of which is the Third Malaysia Plan (TMP) 1976-80, which outlines the implementation of the New Economic Policy. The objectives of the education and training programmes under the TMP are (as quoted by the Ministry at a UNESCO conference in 1979):

(i) Consolidation of the education system to promote national integration and unity through:

(a) the phased implementation of the national language as the main medium of instruction in schools

(b) closing the gap in educational opportunities among regions and races

(c) the eventual integration of the education system of Sabah and Sarawak with the national system

(ii) Orientation and expansion of the education and training programme towards meeting the manpower needs of the country through:

(a) improved coordination of these programmes

- (b) a sharper definition of their objectives and methods
- (c) expansion in areas of critical manpower needs

(iii) Improvement of the quality of education and increased effectiveness for nation building through:
- (a) reduction in wastage rates
- (b) more intensive evaluation
- (c) improvements of curricula, teaching methods, and teacher/pupil ratios

(iv) Improvement of the research, planning and implementation capability to meet the above objectives.

Besides the 1961 Act and the various five-year plans, there have been a number of other reports and reviews which have affected policy. In 1967 the Aziz Commission examined the teaching service. By its implementation all teachers became government employees controlled by a central board and the different categories and salary scales of teachers were greatly reduced in number. In 1973 the Murad Report investigated the problem of school drop-outs. The report recommended amongst other things greater expenditure on schooling, the introduction of compensatory education, particularly in rural areas, and the amalgamation of small schools into larger educational complexes. Some of these recommendations were reiterated in the recent Cabinet Review of Education.

Cabinet Review of Education

A cabinet committee was set up in 1974 to review educational policy and implementation. Its report was published in November 1979. The report is likely to be accepted in its entirety and implemented during the early 1980s. The major recommendations are as follows:

(i) the primary curriculum, which is overcrowded and academic in style, should be revised to concentrate on the 3Rs

(ii) a criterion-referenced test should replace the existing Standard 3 and 5 tests; remedial teaching should be based on the results of this test. (This will require more trained teachers, teaching aids and smaller classes)

(iii) as soon as resources allow, all children should receive 11 rather than the present nine years of education - i.e. automatic promotion up to Form V

(iv) the overall grading of LCE/SRP and MCE/SPM certificates should be abolished, but subject grades retained

(v) the division into arts and science streams in Form IV should be abolished and a general curriculum followed up to Form V

(vi) more vocational schools should be built and their curricula revised to include more practical training. (In fact the number of vocational schools will double from 24 to 48 and five new polytechnics will be built during the Fourth Malaysian Plan period 1981-85. In the longer term, when the period of schooling is extended to 11 years, probably half the students in Forms IV and V will attend vocational schools)

(vii) the period of basic teacher training should be extended from two to three years (this started in 1981)

(viii) the position of English as a second language is reaffirmed; more TESL teachers should be trained. English resource centres should be set up in the states; the lower primary English curriculum should be made more informal

(ix) the construction of new schools and classrooms should be accelerated to remove the need for morning and afternoon sessions. Multi-class schools should be amalgamated or provided with more teachers. More hostels should be built

(x) the provision of libraries in schools, particularly primary schools, is inadequate. All schools should have a library and an adequate library grant. Teachers should be better trained in librarianship

(xi) the provision of special education for the deaf, blind and mentally handicapped should be improved.

Implementation: The Immediate Future

The 1980s should see the implementation of many of the cabinet committee's recommendations, except that the provision of two extra years of schooling for all may need to be deferred. Whilst the recommendations foreshadow a big expansion in vocational education and teacher training and a substantial revision of curricula, the main objectives of education and the highly centralised structure of the education system are unchanged.

The Fourth Malaysia Plan, 1981, contained a section on education and training prepared by the Educational Planning and Research Division of the ministry. Implementation will be reviewed when the mid-term review of the Plan is published in 1983/84. One aspect which was not pursued in depth by the cabinet committee is that of manpower planning. The Prime Minister's Department has set up a team to review this aspect; their recommendations will have implications for technical and higher education.

384

PYRAMID OF ENROLMENTS 1978 - MALAYSIA

University
Age 19/20
to 23/24   22,297

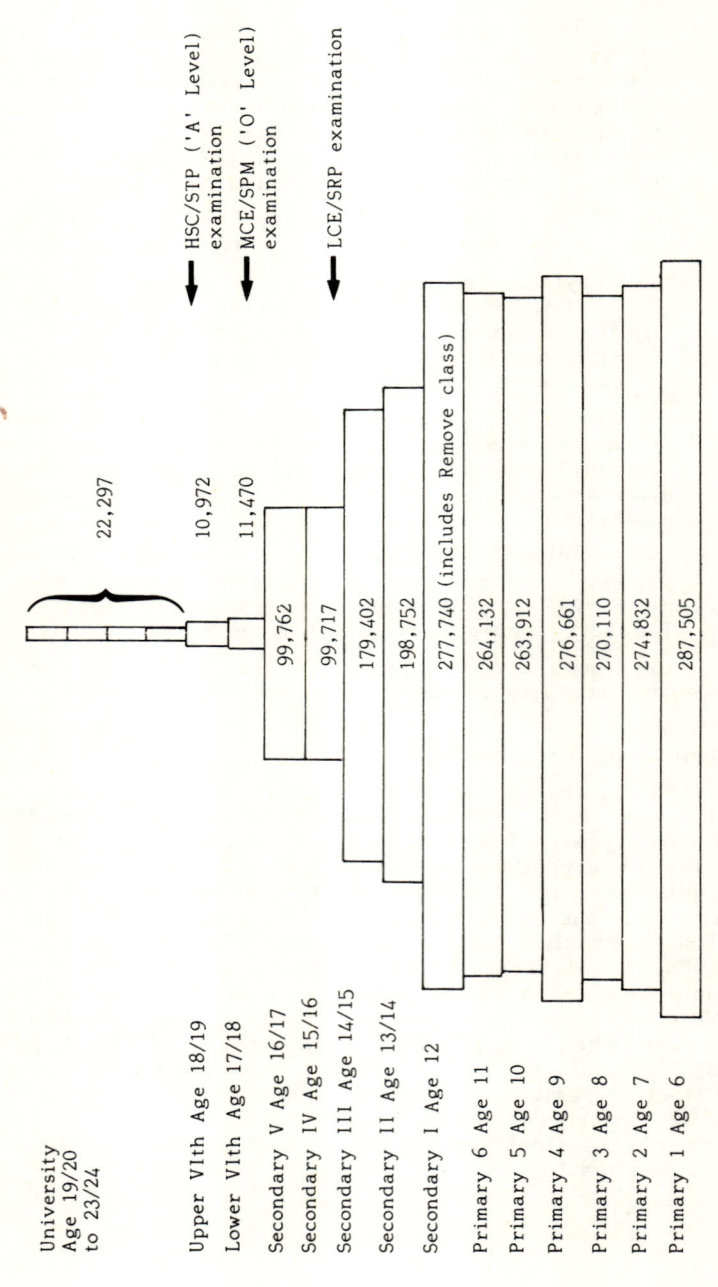

Upper VIth Age 18/19   10,972
Lower VIth Age 17/18   11,470   ← HSC/STP ('A' Level) examination
Secondary V Age 16/17   99,762   ← MCE/SPM ('O' Level) examination
Secondary IV Age 15/16   99,717   ← LCE/SRP examination
Secondary III Age 14/15   179,402
Secondary II Age 13/14   198,752
Secondary I Age 12   277,740 (includes Remove class)
Primary 6 Age 11   264,132
Primary 5 Age 10   263,912
Primary 4 Age 9   276,661
Primary 3 Age 8   270,110
Primary 2 Age 7   274,832
Primary 1 Age 6   287,505

Note: There is no significant difference in male/female enrolment below university level, where it is 2:1

Source: Letter from Ministry of Education, April 1980

PENINSULAR MALAYSIA BASIC EDUCATIONAL STATISTICS

Population

1970	1975	1980 (census)
10,391,000	11,918,000	13,435,588

% literacy 1970

Total	Male	Female
59.5	72.2	45.1

Enrolment Ratios

Primary = total no. of pupils divided by no. in age group 6-11
Secondary = total no. of pupils divided by no. in age group 12-18
Higher = total no. of pupils divided by no. in age group 20-24

		Primary	Secondary	Higher
1970	Total	91%	35%	1.7%
	Male	95%	40%	2.4%
	Female	87%	29%	0.9%
1980	Total	93	52	3.0*
	Male	95	54	3.9*
	Female	92	51	2.0*

*1978

Enrolments 1970 and 1980

	1970	1980
Primary	1,421,469	2,006,748
Lower Secondary	378,535	778,312
Upper Secondary (academic)	84,925	262,272
Upper Secondary (vocational and technical)	4,981	16,785
Fifth Form	10,619	27,461
Teacher Training	2,558	13,188
College	3,830	17,861*
University	9,494	18,064*

*1978

Schools and Teachers 1970 and 1980

	Primary Schools	Teachers	Secondary Schools	Teachers
1970	4,443	45,307	807	21,128
1980	4,341	61,332	884*	42,690

Pupil:Teacher Ratio in Primary Schools 1970 and 1980

1970	1980
32	27

Higher Education Students by Field of Study 1978

	Total	% Female
Education and Teacher Training	882	53%
Humanities and Religion	669	39%
Law	894	44%
Social and Behavioural Sciences	8,409	42%
Commerce and Business	4,745	42%
Natural Science	9,253	34%
Mathematics	297	49%
Medicine and Related Subjects	1,335	30%
Engineering	6,224	11%
Architecture	1,433	27%
Agriculture	1,736	13%
Other	1,955	59%

Educational Expenditure as a Percentage of Total Government Spending

1976	1980
18	12

Current Educational Expenditure by Sector 1980

Primary and Secondary Education	Higher	Other
70%	19.8%	10.2%

Basic Social and Economic Data

GNP per capita 1979 US$1,370

GNP per capita Annual Rate of Growth 1960-1979 4.0%

Life expectancy at birth 1979 - 68

Proportion of the labour force employed in:

Agriculture	1960	63%
	1979	51%
Industry	1960	12%
	1979	16%
Services	1960	25%
	1979	33%

Current Teachers' Salary Scales

(i) College Trained with LCE (Form III)
M$265 x 20 - 305/325 x 20 - 445/495 x 24 - 645 x 30 - 735

(ii) College Trained with MCE ('O' level)
M$405 x 30 - 465/495 x 50 - 705/765 x 40 - 1,045

(iii) College Trained with STP ('A' level)
M$525 x 40 - 605/645 x 40 - 965/1045 x 40 - 1,205

(iv) Diploma UTM/UPM with science education
M$ 685 x 40 - 765/805 x 40 - 1,045/1,125 x 40 - 1,285 x 60 - 1,405

(v) Pass Degree with Dip.Ed.
M$805 x 60 - 925/1,045 x 60 - 1,285/1,405 x 60 - 1,705 x 100 - 2,005

(vi) Honours Degree with Dip.Ed.
M$925 x 60 - 1,045/1,165 x 60 - 1,405/1,525 x 60 - 1,705 x 100 - 2,205

(Source: Letter from Ministry of Education, April 1980)

Sabah

CONTENTS

1 Geography 390
2 Population 392
3 Society and Culture 393
4 History and Politics 394
5 The Economy 396
6 The Education System 398
7 Educational Administration 406
8 Educational Finance 407
9 Development and Planning of
 the Education System 413

1 GEOGRAPHY

Topography

Sabah (formerly North Borneo), situated within 4° - 7° north of the equator, occupies the north eastern tip of the island of Borneo, of which it forms about a one twelfth part. To the west of its heavily indented coastline lies the South China Sea and to the east the Sulu and Celebes Sea. The State of Sarawak, which is also part of the Federation of Malaysia, adjoins it on the south west and Indonesian Borneo (Kalimantan) on the south east. The total area of the State of Sabah is 29,388 square miles (75,233 square kilometres) - roughly the size of Ireland. The long and jagged coastline of 900 miles (1,449 kilometres) is formed mainly of alluvial flats with many creeks and swamps, and some fine harbours. Between the west coast and the Crocker Range (an impressive mountain range which runs parallel to the coast) there is an extensive and relatively heavily populated plain. It is here that the bulk of the population lives. Further inland there is a productive valley at Tenom, fertile plains at Tambunan and Ranau, and a wide area of grazing land at Keningau. A larger plain, mainly undeveloped, occurs at Sook. Elsewhere the land is largely mountainous, densely forested, and dissected by numerous rivers which are important as they are often the only means of communication with the interior from the east. This is particularly true of the vast areas in the centre of the country which have so far been little developed. The whole country is dominated by the rugged Mount Kinabalu, 13,455 feet (4,101 metres), the highest point in South East Asia. It is often visible from places a good 100 miles (161 kilometres) distant.

Climate

The climate is reasonably healthy and seldom oppressively hot, except right on the coast. It is, of course, tropical, but there is sufficient rainfall to moderate the temperature, and the nights can be cool with temperatures in the region of 72°F (22°C). On the coast, the day temperatures vary between 76°F (23°C) in the early morning and 90°F (32°C) in the afternoon. Annual rainfall varies from 60 to 120 inches depending on the locality. The difference in regional rainfall characteristics and the seasonal variations are caused by the prevailing winds. the north east monsoon begins in October or early November and lasts until March or April and the south east monsoon prevails from the beginning of May until August. Between the monsoons there are periods of indeterminate winds lasting about six weeks. The highest rainfall is in the south west in Beaufort and Labuan and the lowest and most evenly distributed rainfall is in the interior in Tenom, Keningau and Tambunan and Tawau. On the west coast the wet season occurs during the south west monsoon and during the intermediate period, while on the east coast the heaviest rainfall is during the north east monsoon. The typhoon belt passes just north of Sabah - thus giving Sabah the name 'land below

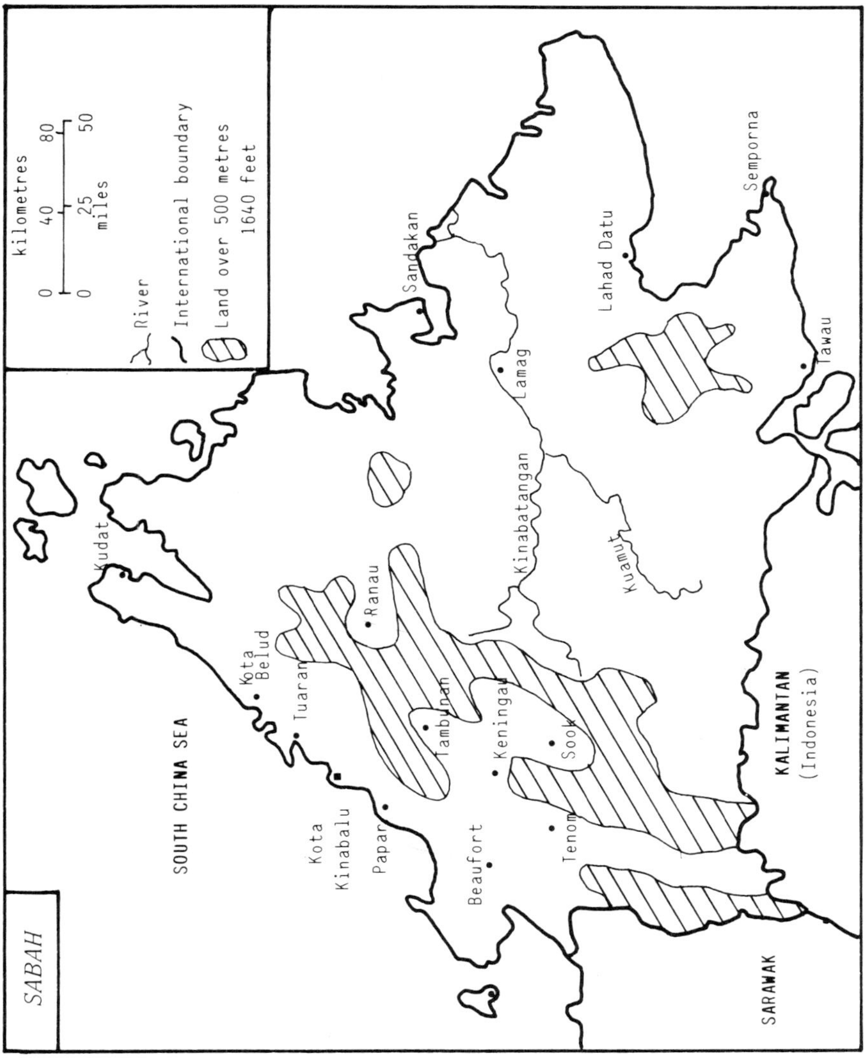
SABAH
kilometres
0
40
80
0
25
50
miles
River
International boundary
Land over 500 metres
1640 feet
SOUTH CHINA SEA
Kudat
Kota
Belud
Tuaran
Kota
Kinabalu
Papar
Beaufort
Tenom
Keningau
Sook
Tambunan
Ranau
Kinabatangan
Lamag
Sandakan
Lahad Datu
Semporna
Tawau
Kuamut
KALIMANTAN
(Indonesia)
SARAWAK

the wind'. Although typhoons are unknown, severe rainstorms accompanied by high winds are not infrequent.

Communications

There is a reasonably good road network on the west coast, linking the capital Kota Kinabalu with the town of Kudat about 82 miles north and Beaufort about 60 miles to the south. Inland there is a road over the Crocker Range to Tambunan, Keningau and Tenom, which lie south east whilst the trans-national highway from Kota Kinabalu to Sandakan, the thriving port on the east coast, has now been completed. Sandakan and two other ports on the east coast, Lahad Datu and Tawau, also have their own small networks of road. Under the Third Malaysia Plan (ended in 1980) a number of new roads were built, particularly one linking the main towns on the east coast and another running south from Papar to Beaufort. Other roads are also being improved. A railway 96 miles in length runs southward from Kota Kinabalu to Beaufort and then inland to Tenom through the spectacular Padas Gorge. Frequent air services are provided by MAS to the bigger towns by Fokker Friendships, and less frequently to small airstrips in the interior by Islanders and Skyvans. There are also daily air services to Brunei, Sarawak, Singapore, Kuala Lumpur and Penang, and flights several times a week to Kota Baru, Hong Kong, Manila, Zamboanga City, Taipei and Seoul. There are at present no direct flights from Kota Kinabalu to Indonesia although there is an infrequent service by a Bali Air Islander from Tawau. Singapore is 1,000 miles by air, Kuala Lumpur 1,200 miles, Hong Kong 1,200 miles, Manila 600 miles and Darwin (Northern Australia) 1,500 miles from Kota Kinabalu. The Philippines sea-border comes within a few miles of the north and east coast of Sabah.

2 POPULATION

Growth

The 1970 census gave a population of 653,500. The estimated population in 1980 was 863,000 giving a growth of 32.1% in ten years. The total school enrolment in 1978 was 189,777 from a total population in the 5 to 14 age group of approximately 225,000 ankd in the 15 to 19 age group of approximately 100,000. Birth control is encouraged through the Sabah Family Planning Association, and large families of 10 or 12 children are becoming less common, but it was estimated in 1977 that 56.6% of the total population was below the age of 20 and improved medical facilities, better living conditions and lower infant mortality are all tending to increase population growth.

Groups

Despite the relatively small size of its population, Sabah contains many diverse communities. The largest are the *Kadazans*, a largely rural, farming people, predominantly

Christian and Catholic, who made up about 26% of the population in 1975 and who are located mainly on the West Coast and Interior Divisions. The second largest group are the *Chinese* who made up about 19% of the population in 1975 and are spread all over the State, although tending to be concentrated in the major towns and engaged in commerce. They are mostly descended from immigrants from south China over the last 100 years and speak a variety of Chinese dialects, although Hakka predominates. Apart from the Kadazans the *Bajus* are the biggest indigenous group, forming 11% of the population in 1975. They live mainly on the coasts, around Kota Belud in the west and Tawau-Semporna in the east, engaging in fishing, farming and cattle rearing. They are predominantly Muslim. Other indigenous groups are the *Muruts* (4%), who live in the interior and who have until recently existed mainly by hunting and shifting cultivation, and small numbers of *Brunei Malays* and *Kedayans*. Other races (Indonesians, Filipinos, Peninsular Malays, Indians and Eurasians) accounted for some 15% of the 1975 population, and the proportion has probably increased further since then, with the continued arrival of refugees from the Moro uprising in the southern Philippines, and an influx of Indonesian labour to work on plantations and construction projects. Europeans, including Americans and Australians/New Zealanders, formed less than 0.3% of the population in 1975.

3 SOCIETY AND CULTURE

Education and Culture

The rural communities are not particularly interested in secondary education beyond Form V level, but the populations of the towns are becoming increasingly aware that higher education is a necessary pre-requisite for social and economic advancement. All communities, but more particularly the Chinese and Indians, are therefore becoming extremely anxious to further the education of their children, and there is great pressure on places in the senior forms. As a result, many children are sent overseas for school studies, to Singapore, Britain, Canada, Australia and New Zealand.

There is a very strong movement to support national and State culture, as is evidenced by the existence of a separate Ministry of Culture, Youth and Sports in the State government. This ministry controls the Sabah Museum, the Sahab State Archives and the Sabah State Library and supports research into the cultures of the various ethnic groups, and the recording of their folk stories, legends, traditional music and dances. A State cultural dance group exists and gives frequent performances. Traditional cultural gatherings such as the Kadazan Harvest Festival celebrations and various sorts of *tamus* (traditionally truce-trade periods between warring groups, but now largely market day festivals) are also officially encouraged and the various festivals of non-indigenous groups, such as Chinese New Year and Christmas, are officially tolerated and enthusiastically celebrated.

Language

Bahasa Malaysia (Malay) is now the official national language with English as the second language, and the only language other than Malay which is taught in all schools, although some of the private (Chinese) schools teach Mandarin as well. The process of changeover from English to Bahasa Malaysia as the medium of instructions was completed up to the end of secondary school at VIth form level by the beginning of 1982.

Religion

Islam is the official religion of Sabah and around 40% of the population are reckoned to be Muslims. Mass conversions still occur, indicating that the proportion of Muslims is increasing, but these are not so frequent, nor so large in scale, as was the case during the Tun Mustapha era. Religious toleration is a feature of the present régime and Christianity is the second most common religion, 24% of the population belonging to one or another of the various sects. A considerable number of the Chinese are Buddhists and there are also Hindu and Sikh temples in the major towns. Animism is still practised by some of the remoter peoples of the interior.

4 HISTORY AND POLITICS

Development

After the first chronicled European contact with Borneo made by Magellan's ship in 1521 with the Sultan of Brunei, the various European attempts to colonise Borneo in the seventeenth and eighteenth centuries failed. At the end of the eighteenth century, Alexander Dalrymple secured on behalf of the East India Company a cession of land from the Sultan of Sulu which extended down to Kimanis to include the major part of the west coast of what is now Sabah. Until then, the area had been in the hands of the Sultan of Brunei and the Sultan of Sulu, the border varying according to their relative strengths. In an effort to subdue the pirates who were looting the very profitable trade routes between Singapore, Sulu and China, Britain secured in 1846 the island of Labuan, now part of Sabah, to be used as a naval base. Various adventurers including Americans, Australians, Scots, with Spain and Holland looking on in the background, then tried to acquire land rights, but it was not until 1881 that the international rivalry was settled. For land granted by the Sultan of Brunei, an administration was set up in 1881 by the granting of a charter by Gladstone to the British North Borneo Company. This gradually extended its domain over the years, and the charter company was to remain responsible for the administration of the country which was then called 'British North Borneo' until after World War Two, when it was taken over by the Colonial Office in 1946.

Federation

Under the Colonial Office, North Borneo was administered as a separate territory, but when Malayan independence was being considered, Tungku Abdul Rahman received formal support for his Malayan plan of expanding the federation to include Singapore and the Borneo territories of North Borneo, Brunei and Sarawak. The response in Singapore was favourable, Brunei never got off the ground, North Borneo and Sarawak had to be dealt with separately. Initially, the Malayan project was viewed with suspicion in North Borneo as a possible Malay takeover plan, and after a meeting with political leaders held in Jesselton in 1961, the Governor of North Borneo advised that closer relations should be established between the Bornean territories themselves before they could join the federation. Soon afterwards, there was a meeting of the Malayan/Bornean group of the Commonwealth Parliamentary Association and the opposition of the Bornean leaders began to relax. The result was the appointment of an Anglo-Malayan Commission under Lord Cobbold, a former Governor of the Bank, to find out the wishes of the Borneans. After a two-month tour of the territory, the Commission in 1962 reported unanimously in favour of amalgamation. Tungku Abdul Rahman and Mr Macmillan signed an agreement that the transfer of British North Borneo should be carried out by 31 August 1963, when a new federal state of Malaysia was to come into being.

Government and Politics

Although Sabah is part of Federal Malaysia, local state politics assume a far greater importance for the average Sabahan than do federal politics, a characteristic which stems from the state's independent existence prior to 1963, and from the '20 points' or 'freedoms', which Sabah retained when it acceded to Malaysia. Many of these 20 points no longer apply, but the State still retains control over immigration from Peninsular Malaysia and Sarawak, so that travel documents are required by all Malaysians who enter or leave the State, and considerable control is still exercised over the raising of revenue from sources such as road tax, export levies, etc.

Until 1975 the political affairs of the State were dominated by the Sabah Alliance, which was officially a coalition of several parties including the Sahab Chinese Association (SCA) and the Sabah Indian Congress (SIC) but which was in reality dominated by the third partner, the United Sabah National Organisation (USNO) led by Tun Mustapha. Unfortunately, the state of emergency which was declared throughout Malaysia in 1969 following racial disturbances in the Peninsula enabled Tun Mustapha to assume various powers, including detention without trial, which were not revoked when the emergency was lifted. However, in July 1975 reports of excesses in expenditures, widespread corruption in the granting of timer concessions and, above all, rumours that he was contemplating secession from Malaysia brought about a reaction which took the form of the resignation of a group of political leaders from the

Sabah Alliance and the formation of a new political party *Bersatu Rakyat Jelata Sabah* (BERJAYA). Within weeks of being founded it gained considerable political and moral strength when Tun Fuad Stephens (formerly Datuk Donald Stephens, the State's first Chief Minister and a much respected leader) resigned his position as *Yang Dipertua Negri* (State Governor, or Head of State) to become its leader. It rapidly became clear that Tun Mustapha had lost the support of the federal government and that this support had been transferred to BERJAYA. Eventually Tun Mustapha was forced to step down as Chief Minister and, in a general election which was called in early 1976, the Alliance was heavily defeated and USNO greatly weakened by subsequent defections. BERJAYA has remained in power ever since. Datuk Harris bin Mohd Salleh, the leader of the original 1975 revolt from the Sabah Alliance, became the new Chief Minister after Tun Fuad's death in an air crash in 1976, in which three other ministers and several senior civil servants were also killed and he has, in the period since then, made a remarkably good job of constructing a new administration. BERJAYA was founded as a multi-racial party, and contains representatives of all the State's major religions. There are still, however, a number of factional opposition parties, including the rump of USNO. But Sabah does not have, and never has had, the Communist insurgency problems which have affected Sarawak and Peninsular Malaysia.

International Relations

International relations remain officially a federal matter and are therefore controlled by Kuala Lumpur. Relations with Indonesia and Brunei are cordial, but there is still considerable tension in the relations with the Philippines, despite verbal assurances by President Marcos that Filipino territorial claims to large parts of Sabah have been dropped. There are frequent cases of piracy in the Sulu Sea area, some of which are alleged by the Sabah government to be the work of the Philippines army, leading to counter claims by the Philippines that Sabah is aiding the Moro insurgents in southern Philippines by giving military training to refugees from this area. This Sabah strongly denies.

5 THE ECONOMY

Development

Economic development in Sabah is based, as in the rest of Malaysia, on the principles of the New Economic Policy (NEP) with some modifications due to the specific economic conditions encountered in Sabah. The two main objectives of the NEP are the eradication of poverty and the correcting of the economic imbalance between the traditionally trade-orientated races (specifically the Chinese) and the *bumiputras* (literally 'sons of the soil') who have until recently existed by subsistence farming, labouring and unskilled jobs of various kinds. Under the recent Third Malaysia Plan, the major aim was the raising of productivity and income in the agricultural sector, coupled with numerous incentives (including soft loans and positive discrimination in the award of contracts) to encourage *bumiputras* to branch out into trade, manufacturing, service industries, etc. Nevertheless, Sabah remains a firmly capitalist state, with a virtually free market economy. Exchange controls are virtually non-existent and there is almost a boom town atmosphere about the major urban centres which is in marked contrast to the simple life of the rural *kampongs* (villages), although signs of increasing wealth are to be seen even there, with shiny, new expensive cars to be found parked alongside traditional wooden stilt houses.

Under the Third Malaysia Plan the improvement of the infrastructure of the State did receive major attention in the form of the construction of new roads and bridges, and the improvement of harbour facilities. This emphasis is likely to continue during the Fourth Malaysia Plan now in force, and will also include major developments such as hydroelectric power scheme in the Padas Gorge, the preliminary work for which has already started. Under the British aid programme to Malaysia, a Sabah Regional Planning Study is being made by a team of British development consultants, who were due to complete their work in 1980. The Sabah Development Plan, for which this is part of the preparation, is being designed to guide development up to the year 2000.

Economic Situation

The economy of the country is basically agrarian, though there are attempts at small scale light industrial development, and the development of mineral resources, particularly the oil and gas fields around Labuan, are assuming a rapidly increasing importance. Strenuous efforts are being made to diversify the agricultural economy, and large areas of land (mainly logged-out timber land) are being made available for the intensive cultivation of crops such as oil palm, cocoa, coffee and tea. Efforts are also being made to make the State at least self-sufficient in rice production, and improved communications are also likely to lead to an expansion of vegetable growing activity in the high lands around Mount Kinabalu, possibly resulting in the export of both fresh and preserved vegetables. There is already a considerable export trade in sea food (particularly prawns) from Sandakan, but timber exports (mainly of raw logs) remain the single most important revenue earner. Rubber production has declined due to a shortage of labour, and many estates have been allowed to revert to nature, or have been felled to make way for more lucrative and easily managed crops. Future developments are likely to concentrate initially on resource-based (particularly timber-based) industry, initially to produce materials such as plywood, chipboard and hardboard for local consumption, but eventually to produce all of these, and other products such as wood pulp or paper, for export. Food self-sufficiency is also a major target, and the search continues for further mineral resources. Limestone, asbestos, chromite, coal, silica, lead, zinc and silver are all known to exist in more or less economically extractable quantities, and large deposits of low grade copper ore are already being exploited in the Ranau area.

Up-to-date figures for GNP etc., are difficult to come by, but it is now generally accepted that Sabah has the highest per capita income of any state in the Federation except Selangor, and is likely to overtake even that state within the next three to four years. The State now regularly runs a large surplus on its balance of trade, this being some M$2 billion in 1979. Foreign investment is encouraged, especially in joint venture projects, and where the investment introduces new technology. Foreign aid to Sabah is insignificant except in the form of various World Bank loans for infrastructure projects, and various bilateral and multilateral agreements entered into at federal level. The major constraint on development is a shortage of labour, coupled occasionally with shortages of materials (e.g. cement) due to the high dependence on imports.

6 THE EDUCATION SYSTEM

Academic Year

The academic year starts in January and consists of three terms. There are short holidays of two weeks each in April and July and a long holiday of approximately eight weeks from mid-November to early January. All schools work a five-day week, although compulsory extra classes on Saturday mornings are sometimes imposed if a school takes holidays additional to those officially permitted (e.g. for particular religious festivals).

Pre-Primary

Currently most pre-school education is run in the form of kindergartens by private organisations, although in 1977 there were 13 kindergartens run by the Sabah Islamic Council (MUIS) and the State government, in association with the Sabah Foundation, currently has plans to open a network of kindergartens throughout the State. The Sabah Foundation is also establishing a kindergarten for its own headquarters staff in Kota Kinbalu. There were 57 kindergartens registered with the Department of Education in 1979, catering for 8,245 pupils. This is an apparent fall in numbers of institutions since 1977 when there were 88, the difference being accounted for by the absence of all but one MUIS kindergarten from the 1979 list.

All kindergartens must be registered with the Education Department, and are subject to inspection by the School Inspectorate. The medium of instruction may be Malay, English or Chinese, but the majority of those registered teach in Chinese, the actual figures being:

```
Chinese medium    38
English medium    16
Malay medium       3
```

A book entitled 'Guidebook for Kindergartens in Malaysia' issued by the Ministry of Education in Kuala Lumpur has been used as the basis for curricula in some kindergartens. Others use materials and methods developed by the particular institution, or imported from the USA, Europe or Australia. Somewhat surprisingly, there are several kindergartens which claim dates of foundation in the 1920s, the earliest being the SDK Sin Hwa in Tawau dating from 1922.

Primary

Primary education is free but not compulsory. It is offered in the media of Chinese and Bahasa Malaysia, English medium primary education having been phased out in 1975 except in the special case of the Kinabalu International School, the intake to which is restricted to non-Malaysian children. Most primary schools now teach in Bahasa Malaysia, although all are supposed to teach English as a second language. In 1979 there were 823 primary schools, 633 of them government operated, 179 voluntary aided and 11 private, with some 134,300 pupils.

The primary course lasts six years, and the official starting age is 6+. Promotion is automatic from standard 1 to standard 6. The standard 6 examination was abolished in 1978, allowing automatic promotion up to Form III of secondary school. The rate of transition from primary to secondary schools is now about 81%.

There is a common curriculum for all schools in Malaysia, and the present position is as set out in the 1979 Cabinet Committee Report on Education which (paraphrased in translation) states:

> "The division of time at present in primary schools is approximately: 51% communication subjects (languages and mathematics); 21% environmental subjects (civics, history, geography, science); 20% arts and co-curricular subjects; 8% Islamic studies. Basic skills – the 3Rs – should be taught as well as subjects designed to achieve individual development, physical and emotional, and to instil ethical values. As well as learning the basic skills, children should be introduced to ways of learning which will enable them to reason subsequently."

Secondary

Secondary education up to Form III level is free but not compulsory. Beyond Form III it is neither free nor compulsory. All education up to Form V level is in Bahasa Malaysia, English medium education having been progressively phased out since 1976. For pupils from Chinese medium primary schools there

SABAH - EDUCATIONAL

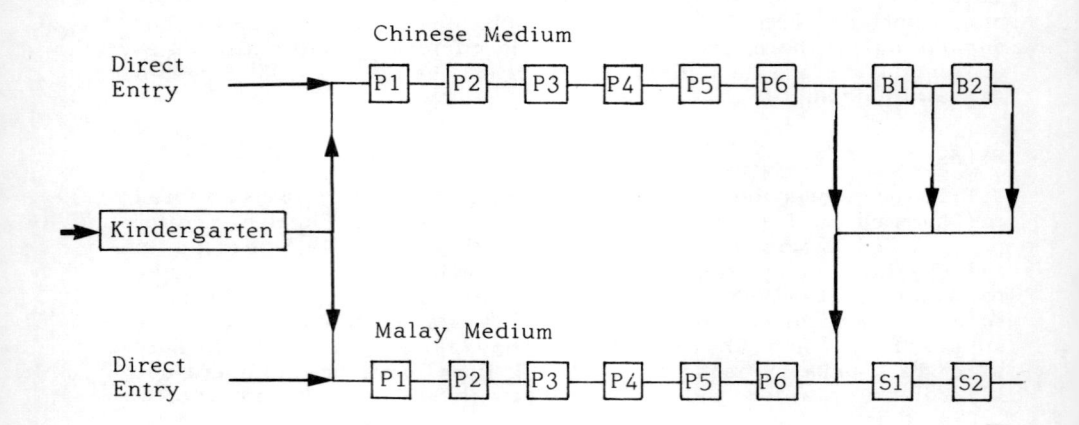

KEY

B Bridge
L Lower
P Primary
R Remove
S Secondary
T Teacher Training
U Upper
V Vocational
* In Peninsular Malaysia or Sabah + Peninsula

FLOW DIAGRAM 1979

Employment, Further Education or Overseas Education

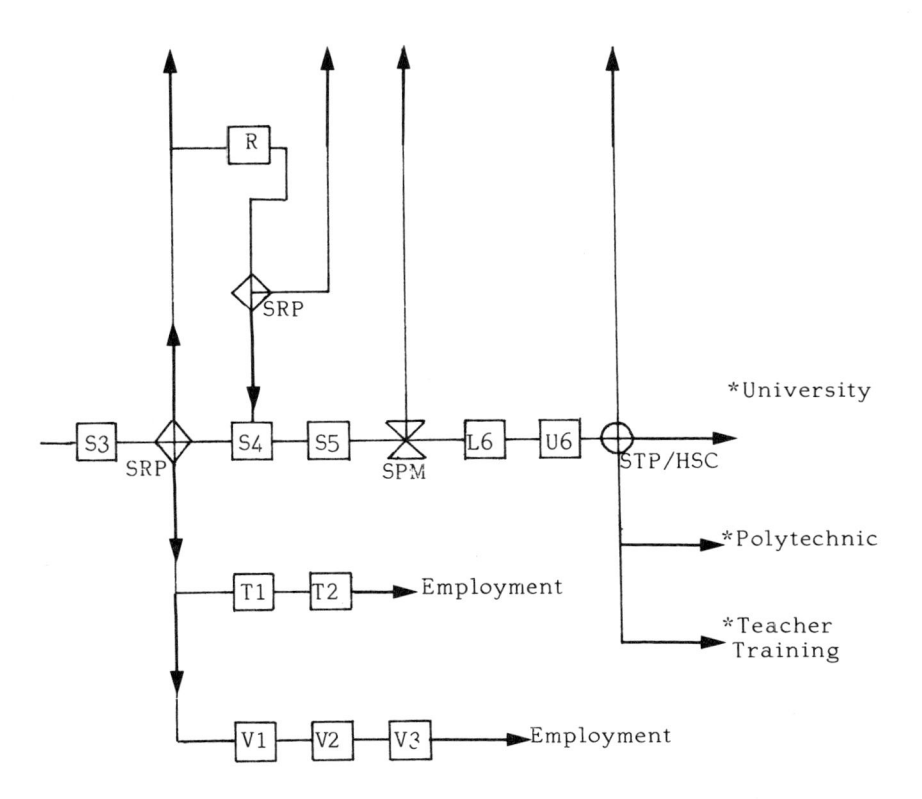

```
                  ┌───┐
                  │ R │
                  └───┘
                    │
                  ◇
                  SRP

──[S3]──◇──[S4]──[S5]──⋈──[L6]──[U6]──⊕────────→ *University
         SRP            SPM                STP/HSC
         │
         │                                        →  *Polytechnic
         ├──[T1]─[T2]──→ Employment
         │                                        →  *Teacher
         │                                             Training
         └──[V1]─[V2]─[V3]──→ Employment
```

is a one-year bridge class between primary and secondary education; this offers additional language classes and can be extended into a two-year course for those pupils with special language difficulties. In 1979 there were 100 secondary schools in Sabah, 49 of them government operated, 37 voluntary aided and 14 private. These schools catered for some 61,600 pupils but of the 100 schools only six had VIth forms. Of the remainder 54 were IVth and Vth form schools and 40 IIIrd form or 'middle' schools.

The lower secondary course is divided into two cycles: a three-year lower cycle (Forms I - III) leading to the Malay-medium SRP examination (the English medium Lower Certificate of Education examination was phased out in 1977) and a two-year upper cycle (Forms IV & V) comprising those pupils whose results in the SRP examination are good enough to qualify them for entry to the limited number of places. The upper cycle leads to the Malay medium SPM examination (the English medium Malaysian Certificate of Education having now also been phased out) and successful candidates may then proceed to the VIth form to study for the STP/Higher School Certificate. VIth form studies before 1982 were in both Malay and English medium, but changed over entirely to Bahasa Malaysia in 1982. The Remove class, which served the same purpose as the bridge class, but for pupils transferring from Chinese to English medium at Form III level, has now been abolished, except as a second chance mechanism for SRP.

As with primary schools, the curricula for secondary schools are standard throughout Malaysia. Students sitting for SPM must take Malay, English and a third compulsory subject chosen from geography, history or Malaysian studies. Pupils are placed in arts, science or technical streams at Form IV level. As far as specific subjects are concerned, religious education is compulsory only for Muslim pupils, non-Muslims being given lessons in their mother tongue instead. All pupils study Malaysian history but may opt for Commonwealth history at SPM instead of south east Asian history. Modern mathematics has been taught in all schools since 1978, having originally been introduced on trial in 1970. Likewise integrated science, originally introduced on trial in 1969, has been taught in all schools since 1975. Separate sciences are studied by the science streams in Forms IV and V, and general science by the arts stream. Civics, taught as 'local affairs' in the first four years of primary school, is taught as a subject in its own right throughout the lower secondary course. Chinese language (Mandarin) may be taught in any school if more than 15 parents request it. At VIth form level, pupils are streamed into arts or sciences, and in general study only those subjects which they will offer at STP/HSC level to fulfil university entry requirements.

Technical and Vocational

In 1980 there were two technical/vocational institutions operated by the Department of Education. These were the

Vocational School, Likas, Kota Kinabalu and the Vocational School, Sandakan. However, a further three technical and vocational schools were under construction as part of the Third Malaysia Plan.

The Vocational School, Likas, offers courses in electrical work, motor mechanics, heavy plant fitting, building construction and carpentry, fitting, turning and machining, radio and television servicing, and welding and sheet metal work. The Vocational School, Sandakan, offers the same seven courses and also a commercial course. In all cases the courses last three years post-SRP. Also under the Third Malaysia Plan, a technical/vocational stream is being introduced into certain of the larger government secondary schools at Form IV and V level. Properly equipped workshops for woodwork and metalwork (including turning and machining) are being provided, as are rooms for teaching needlework and cookery, which can be offered as separate subjects at SPM level (at lower secondary level they are taught together as home science). In 1977, 19 government and 15 aided schools offered home science courses and the number is increasing.

A vocational school is operated by the Agriculture Department at Timbang Menggaris, north of Kota Belud. This also offers three-year courses post-SRP, in subjects such as animal husbandry, agricultural economics, agricultural mechanics, agricultural extension work and home economics (for girls). Like the vocational school at Likas, it was built with Colombo Plan funds in the early 1970s by the New Zealand government.

A further technical/vocational institution is the Industrial Training Centre on Labuan Island. This is being funded by the Federal Ministry of Labour and Manpower (estimated cost M$7 million. Apprenticeship courses and both preliminary and advanced competency courses in general mechanics, general machinery, cold storage and refrigeration, carpentry, woodwork, masonry, plumbing, architectural drafting and mechanical drafting are offered, with places for 300 trainees.

Teacher Training

There are at present three teacher training colleges in Sabah: Gaya College in Kota Kinabalu, Kent College in Tuaran and the Sandakan Teacher Training College. A fourth college is under construction at Keningau under the Third Malaysia Plan. Of the three colleges which already exist, Kent College trains teachers for the primary level only, Sandakan TTC trains teachers for both primary and lower secondary levels, and Gaya College trains teachers for lower secondary level only. In all cases courses are two years in duration. Upper secondary teachers are trained at teacher training colleges in the Peninsula. The entry requirement for primary teacher training in SRP, and for lower secondary teacher training SPM.

Other teacher training activity includes vacation courses for untrained teachers who cannot attend full time teacher training. This started in 1977 and is carried out at all three teacher training colleges. There is also a programme, partly funded by UNICEF, for the academic improvement of teachers without SRP/LCE qualifications which is carried out at 14 centres (usually secondary schools) throughout Sabah. Classes are run at weekends and are open to trained and untrained teachers who have served for four years or more. The programme started in 1971 and each cycle lasts one year. In-service training courses in, for example, the teaching of modern mathematics or integrated science are run by specialist sections of the Education Department such as the Mathematics and Science Centre. There is also a six-month Bahasa Malaysia language training course which is run at Kent college and retrains existing English or Chinese medium teachers to teach in Bahasa Malaysia. Approximately 180 teachers a year have attended this course since it started in 1975. Smaller numbers had already been trained at previous courses run at either Gaya or Kent colleges since 1971.

Higher

There is as yet no fully fledged university in Sabah, although both the MARA Institute of Technology (ITM) and the University Kebangsaan Malaysia (UKM) have branch campuses in Kota Kinabalu, and there is a proposal for the establishment on Labuan Island of an ASEAN (Association of South East Asian Nations) university for which Datuk Harris has donated 500 acres of land. Both the MARA Institute and the UKM are being provided with permanent campuses near Kota Kinabalu by the state government although both are still in temporary accommodation at the time of writing.

The UKM branch campus was originally set up in 1974 at Kinarut, about 20 miles from Kota Kinabalu on a 24-acre site provided by Yayasan Sabah (the Sabah Foundation) but was moved in 1979 to a secondary school campus at Bukit Padang in Kota Kinabalu. The permanent campus at Kuala Menggatal will have an area of 909 acres and development work is already proceeding. At present there are only about 100 students, but the development programme (in two stages) envisages about 2,500 students by the year 1990. Courses will be developed which have particular relevance to the exploitation of natural resources. Until the move from Kinarut to the present temporary campus, students could do only preliminary and first year degree level courses in science and horticulture in Sabah. Students at other levels and in other subjects had to travel to the Peninsula for study. From the 1979 science intake, however, the entire degree course is carried out in Sabah. A similar development programme for arts courses will be carried out between 1981 and 1984. The federal government has provided an initial allocation of M$10 million for Phase 1 of the development.

The MARA Institute is also being provided with a campus at Kuala Menggatal, of 750 acres in this instance, and development work has already started using a M$5 million launching grant provided by Yayasan Sabah. In the meantime, there are some 340 students (1979 figure) studying on pre-university and first year courses at the temporary Yayasan Sabah/ITM campus in Kota Kinabalu.

Non-Formal and Adult

Further education classes were first started in Sabah in 1967 and their main purpose is to provide an opportunity of further education to those who were, for one reason or another, unable to pursue their education in school to a sufficiently high level. Particular attention is being given to courses for those who are too young to start work and to under-qualified primary school teachers. Classes range in level from Primary 6 to Form VI and students are prepared to take the SRP, SPM and STP/HSC examinations. The number of classes and students varies from year to year, but in 1976 (the latest year for which figures are available) there were 99 classes and 2,900 students, atracting M$145,000 in federal government grants. Further education classes are also assuming an increasingly important role in providing Bahasa Malaysia tuition to the general public as the use of the national language is progressively emphasised both in government and commerce.

Educational Media

An audio-visual aids section of the Department of Education has been in existence since 1966, but it did not assume its present importance in the education programme until educational radio and educational television programmes were started in 1975 and 1976 respectively. The Educational Media Service (EMS), as it is now known, is responsible for supporting the efforts of other sections of the department in improving the quality of teaching and improving the standard of education, in rural schools especially, by broadcasting programmes for both teachers and pupils. The EMS is also responsible for training teachers in the use of audio-visual aids, and in the use and evaluation of radio and TV programmes. There are 6 regional centres where these courses are carried out and 2,000 teachers had been trained by the end of 1977. It is also heavily involved in English language teaching through responsibility for the production and distribution of the SELM materials, and also through its involvement with the proposed installation of language laboratories for ELT in the three teacher training colleges.

Under the Third Malaysia Plan the construction of a permanent studio complex for the EMS has been started to enable it to produce its own programmes for both radio and television. At present programmes produced in Kuala Lumpur are used, mostly in unmodified form, and a number of BBC ELT radio programmes are also being used. Also under the Third Malaysia Plan radio/cassette recorders have been distributed to all schools. Plans to distribute television receivers to all schools have, however, been frustrated by the problems of power supply, remoteness from servicing facilities and, in the case of certain island schools on the east coast, the refusal of school principals to accept the sets in the belief that they represent too much of an attraction to pirates. Nevertheless, many schools do now have TV sets, operated from small petrol generators where mains electricity does not exist.

7 EDUCATIONAL ADMINISTRATION
Education Department

Education is the responsibility of the Federal Ministry of Education of which the Sabah Education Department forms a part. The Director of Education is a federal officer, responsible to the Minister and is normally seconded from Peninsular Malaysia on a two- or three-year contract. (The Chief Minister's Department nevertheless maintains a strong interest in education and is particularly concerned with improving the lot of the native Sabahans.) The Director of Education is advised by a Board of Education and local education committees. Administratively Sabah is divided into five regions: West Coast (South) and Labuan, West Coast (North), Sandakan, Tawau and Interior. Each region is administered by an education officer with at least three supervisors (one each for English medium, Malay and Chinese education), one organiser of PE and one supervisor of mathematics and science. Each district (the smallest unit) also has a schools supervisor. There is a central inspectorate which consists of eight inspectors and two officers from the Education Department. An additional two officers are responsible for kindergarten inspection. The inspectorate reports on operations to the Director of Education, but is directly responsible to the Malaysian Chief Inspector of Schools in Kuala Lumpur.

Boards and Committees

The Sabah Board of Education advises the government, drawing up major guidelines and proposing policies. It also acts as a coordinating body. It was established early in the history of Sabahan education and its members represent government agencies, communities and school boards of management throughout the State. The local education committees each cover one or two administrative districts. Their members are drawn from school management committees, school principals and representatives of local communities and the chairman of each committee is a prominent local dignitary; the secretary is the district officer and the regional education officer or district supervisor attends meetings in an advisory capacity. The local education committees advise the Director of Education and the Board on the administration and management of education and the welfare of pupils, and also make proposals for the establishment and development of school projects.

Educational Provision

The major provider of primary and secondary schools is now the government (74% of schools in 1979), the proportion of government schools having increased steadily due to new construction and the taking over of local village committee schools. These committees provided what were known as 'native voluntary schools', usually in remote areas. The last such schools were taken over by the department in 1976. The Churches also manage schools (subject to government inspection) and local committees (usually of Chinese business men) have some institutions. There are also a few estate schools left, run by estate managements for the children of their employees. Most of these schools are government-aided, but there are a number of purely private Chinese schools and about a dozen primary schools run by the Seventh Day Adventist Church which refuse to accept government funds for religious reasons.

8 EDUCATIONAL FINANCE

Education Budget

Total expenditure on education in 1978 was M$121,797,000 approximately, representing an increase of some 12% over 1977 and 350% since 1970. Of the 1978 budget 24.3% was spent on development and 75.7% on recurrent expenditure, compared with 10.5% and 89.5% respectively in 1970. In the Third Malaysia Plan (1976 to 1980) M$197 million was allocated to development expenditure on education in Sabah, sub-divided as follows:

	(M$1,000)
Government primary schools	56,116
Government secondary schools	113,293
Technical education	16,540
Teacher training	4,900
Capital grants to aided primary schools	135
Capital grants to aided secondary schools	220
Educational Media Service	3,796

Sources of Funds

As already stated, primary education is almost entirely paid for by central government as is secondary education (except for for the revenue from fees and a proportion of the money for capital costs in aided schools which comes from the resources of the mission or other supporting agency). Scholarships have been financed by a number of agencies, including the British Council, UNICEF, the Liberation Education Trust and the British, Australian and New Zealand governments under the Colombo Plan. However, at the present time the two most important sources of scholarship funds are the Sabah Foundation and the Native Scholarships scheme.

ORGANISATION OF SABAH DEPARTMENT

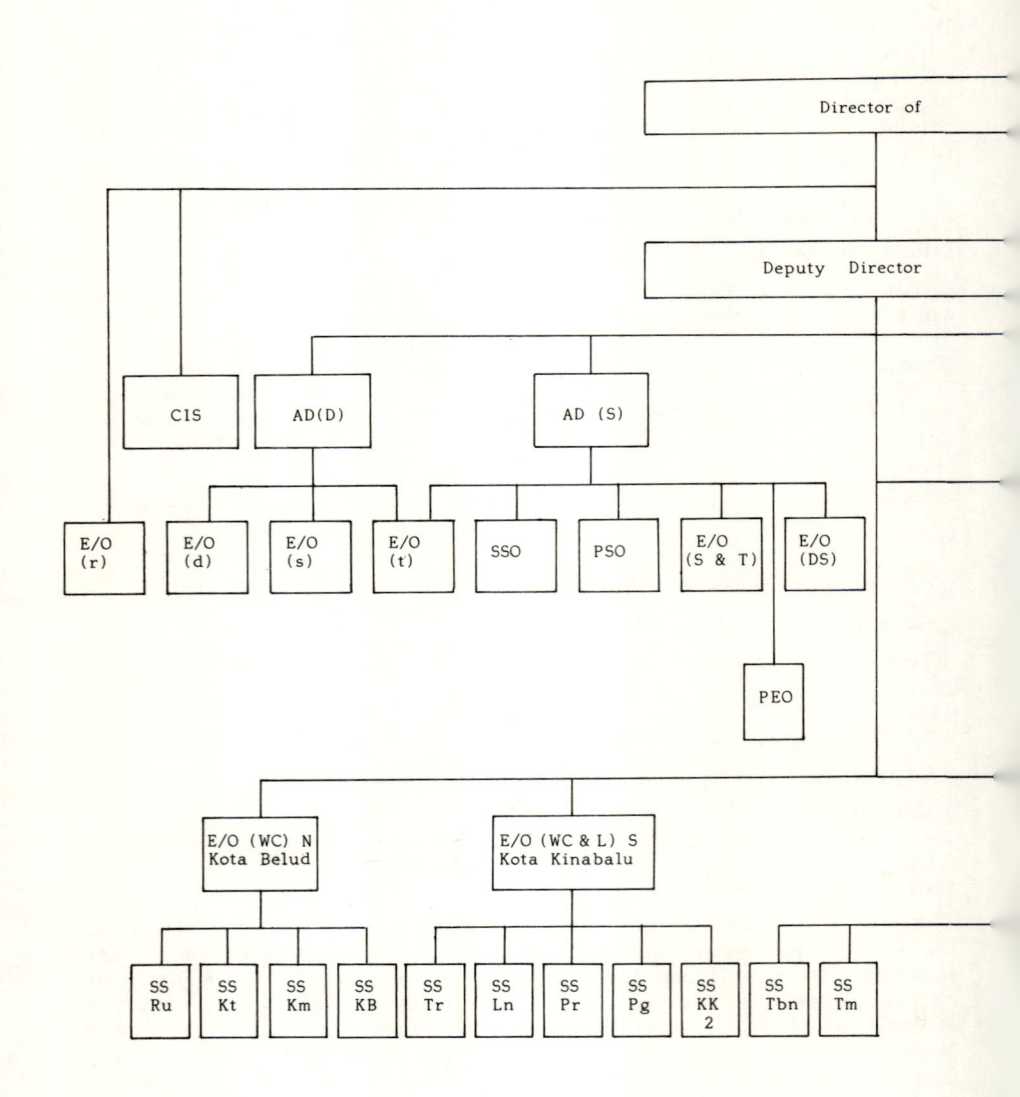

```
                                    ┌─────────────┐
                                    │ Director of │
                                    └──────┬──────┘
                                           │
                                    ┌──────┴──────────┐
                                    │ Deputy Director │
                                    └──────┬──────────┘
                                           │
        ┌──────────┬────────────────┬──────┴──────┐
     ┌──┴──┐   ┌──┴──┐          ┌───┴───┐
     │ CIS │   │AD(D)│          │ AD(S) │
     └──┬──┘   └──┬──┘          └───┬───┘
        │         │                 │
   ┌────┤   ┌─────┼─────┬─────┐  ┌──┼────┬──────┬──────┐
┌──┴─┐ ┌┴──┐ ┌┴──┐ ┌┴──┐ ┌┴──┐ ┌┴──┐ ┌─┴─┐ ┌───┴───┐ ┌┴───┐
│E/O │ │E/O│ │E/O│ │E/O│ │SSO│ │PSO│ │E/O│ │ E/O   │ │E/O │
│(r) │ │(d)│ │(s)│ │(t)│ └───┘ └───┘ │(S&T)│ │(DS) │
└────┘ └───┘ └───┘ └───┘                  └───┘ └───────┘
                                                      │
                                                   ┌──┴──┐
                                                   │ PEO │
                                                   └─────┘
```

E/O (WC) N Kota Belud	E/O (WC & L) S Kota Kinabalu	
SS Ru, SS Kt, SS Km, SS KB	SS Tr, SS Ln, SS Pr, SS Pg, SS KK 2	SS Tbn, SS Tm

OF EDUCATION 1979

```
┌─────────────────┐
│   Education     │
└─────────────────┘


┌─────────────────┐
│   of Education  │
└─────────────────┘
```

| AD (A) | AD (TT) | AD (EMS) |

| E/O (L & R) | AO | ES | E/O (TB) | E/O (MS) | A/C | ETVO | ERO |

| AA (S) | AA (A) | SEO (G) | SEO (E) | SAO (G) | SAO (A) | SAO (A&T) | ECO | ISCO | TTC | AVO |

| E/O (1) Keningau | E/O (S) Sandakan | E/O (T) Tawau |

| SS KP | SS Bft | SS Spg | SS Kgu | SS Nbn | SS Bln | SS Ktg | SS Skn | SS Ld | SS Spa | SS Twu |

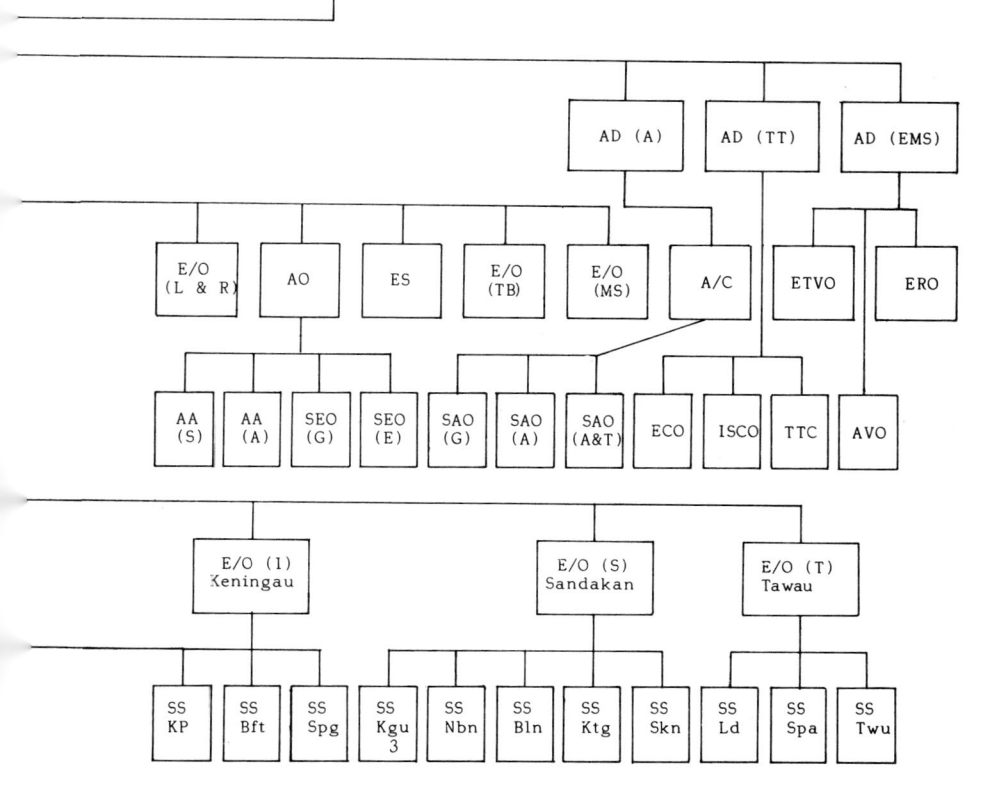

Key to Organisation Chart 1979

CIS	=	Chief Inspector of Schools
AD(D)	=	Assistant Director of Education (Development)
AD(S)	=	Assistant Director of Education (Schools)
AD(A)	=	Assistant Director of Education (Accounts)
AD(TT)	=	Assistant Director of Education (Teacher Training)
AD(EMS)	=	Head of Education Media Services
E/O(R)	=	Education Officer (Registration)
E/O(D)	=	Education Officer (Development)
E/O(S)	=	Education Officer (Statistics)
E/O (T)	=	Education Officer (Technical Education)
SSO	=	Secondary Schools Organiser
PSO	=	Primary Schools Organiser
E/O(S & T)	=	Education Officer (Scholarships & Training)
E/O(DS)	=	Education Officer (Domestic Science)
E/O(L & R)	=	Education Officer (Language & Religion)
A/O	=	Administrative Officer
ES	=	Examination Secretary
E/O(TB)	=	Education Officer (Textbooks)
E/O(MS)	=	Education Officer (Mathematics & Science)
A/C	=	Accounts Officer
ETVO	=	Educational TV Organiser
ERO	=	Educational Radio Organiser
PEO	=	Physical Education Officer
AA(S)	=	Administrative Assistant (Services)
AA(A)	=	Administrative Assistant (Appointment)
SEO(G)	=	Senior Education Officer (General)
SEO(E)	=	Senior Education Officer (Establishment)
SAO(G)	=	Senior Accounts Officer (General)
SAO(A)	=	Senior Accounts Officer (Audit)
SAO(A & T)	=	Senior Accounts Officer (Accounts and Tenders)
SS Twu	=	Tawau Schools Supervisor, English Language, Educational Media Services, Physical Education Officer, Accounts Officer
ECO	=	Examination & Curriculum Organiser
ISCO	=	In Service Courses Organiser
TTC	=	Teacher Training College
AVO	=	Audio-Visual Organiser
E/O(WC) N KB	=	Education Officer (West Coast) North, Kota Belud
E/O(WC & L) S KK	=	Education Officer (West Coast & Labuan) South, Kota Kinabalu
E/O(I) Kgu	=	Education Officer (interior) Keningau
E/O(S) Skn	=	Education Officer (Sandakan) Sandakan
E/O(T) Twu	=	Education Officer (Tawau) Tawau
SS Ru	=	Ranau Schools Supervisor
SS Kt	=	Kudat Schools Supervisor

SS KM	=	Kota Marudu Schools Supervisor
SS KB 1	=	Kota Belud Schools Supervisor, English Language, Educational Media Services, Physical Education Officer, Mathematics & Science, Accounts Officer
SS Tr	=	Tuaran Schools Supervisor
SS Ln	=	Labuan Schools Supervisor
SS Pr	=	Papar Schools Supervisor
SS Pg	=	Penampang Schools Supervisor
SS KK 2	=	Kota Kinabalu Schools Supervisor, English Language, Educational Media Services, Physical Education Officer, Mathematics & Science, Accounts Officer
SS Tbn	=	Tambunan Schools Supervisor
SS Tm	=	Tenom Schools Supervisor
SS KP	=	Kuala Penyu Schools Supervisor
SS Bft	=	Beaufort Schools Supervisor
SS Spg	=	Sipitang Schools Supervisor
SS Kgu 3	=	Keningau Schools Supervisor, English Language, Educational Media Services, Physical Education Officer, Mathematics and Science, Accounts Officer
SS Nbn	=	Nabawan Schools Supervisor
SS Bln	=	Beluran Schools Supervisor
SS Ktg	=	Kinabatangan Schools Supervisor
SS Skn	=	Sandakan Schools Supervisor, English Language, Educational Media Services, Physical Education Officer, Mathematics and Science, Accounts Officer
SS LD	=	Lahad Datu Schools Supervisor
SS Spa	=	Semporna Schools Supervisor

The Sabah foundation is a semi-government organisation funded by the exploitation of a 3,330 square mile timber concession. Founded in 1966, by 1978 it had awarded 15,443 scholarships for secondary education within Malaysia, of which 1,977 were for study in the Peninsula. Also, 273 scholarships had been awarded for diploma and degree level studies within Malaysia and 60 for similar studies outside Malaysia. In the 1979/80 academic year the Foundation is wholly or partly funding 209 students at various institutions in Britain. The Foundation is also funding the provision of hostels for secondary schools in rural areas and has ambitious plans to provide free school milk, orange juice, uniforms and footwear for all primary and secondary school children in Sabah. In 1978 the Foundation was spending not less than M$6 million per annum on its education programmes.

The Native Scholarships scheme started in 1962 with the awarding of 635 scholarships to *bumiputras*, at a total cost of M$240,000 divided between the State and federal governments. State government involvement ceased in 1973 but the scheme has continued to expand, the total allocation in 1977 being M$5,985 million. Scholarships range in value from M$510 per annum for Forms I and II to M$710 per annum for Upper VI. Native scholarship holders are also exempted from the payment of fees and get an annual grant of M$50 or M$80, depending on distance, for transport fees, if they are not boarding pupils. By 1976 the total number of native scholarship holders was 27,324.

Government grants to schools come in various forms:

(i)   grants for salaries (less revenue from fees)
(ii)   grants for equipment and clerical assistance
(iii)   grants for remission of fees for poor students
(iv)   capitation grants for books, operating costs etc.
(v)   development grants for buildings.

Aid from External Agencies

Other than loans from the World Bank, external aid to education in Sabah is negligible. UNICEF is partly funding some in-service training .programmes, and the Van Leer Foundation has agreed to provide financial assistance for a programme of teacher training and curriculum development designed to improve teaching in the small rural primary schools. Various volunteer agencies (but not now VSO) provide teachers for subjects where there is a shortage of local teachers. The British Council is assisting with English language teaching.

The World Bank, under the fourth World Bank Loan for Education, is financing 27 new primary schools, 1,082 new primary classrooms and 540 staff quarters at a cost of some M$45.6 million. It has also been involved in the financing of secondary schools, technical vocational schools and teacher training colleges, as well as the educational television service.

9 DEVELOPMENT AND PLANNING OF THE EDUCATION SYSTEM

Development

Before 1881 there is no record of education in Sabah, though it is likely that there were traditional Koranic schools, and it is known that there was a Roman Catholic mission school on the island of Labuan. In 1883 two primary schools were opened by Roman Catholic missionaries - one in Sandakan and the other in Inobong, about 10 miles from Jesselton. By 1900 there were seven mission primary schools and in 1909 the Education Department was set up to supervise them. By 1911 there were 13 English medium primary schools and 8 Chinese medium offering a six-year course. In 1915 the first government school was opened in Jesselton, to train the sons of chiefs and prepare them for active participation in their country's affairs. The first Malay medium primary schools opened in the early 1920s, and by 1930 there were 4,749 pupils receiving education. Between 1940 and 1945 education was seriously disrupted by the Japanese occupation. During Sabah's postwar period as a Crown Colony a five-year development plan was drawn up emphasising primary education for all, and beginning vocational training. In 1952 the Kent college teacher training institution was opened, in a decade which also saw the setting up of the first education councils, and the first government secondary school. By independence another teacher training college had been opened, and the total number of those being educated had reached 70,000.

Since independence, the picture has been one of steady growth in all sections of educational provision, but especially in primary education, with an increasing emphasis on the use of Bahasa Malaysia as the medium of instruction. The staffs of schools have also been progressively Malaysianised and there are now relatively few expatriate teachers except at upper secondary level. Increasing wealth is enabling larger sums to be spent on education, including money for the development of school libraries and a mobile library service, free textbooks for primary school children and better supplies of science and other equipment for all schools.

Educational Objectives

The official objectives under the Third Malaysia Plan were as follows:

(i) to provide a place in school for every child of primary school age

- (ii) to extend facilities for secondary education, especially in the rural areas, in order to bring about a better degree of balance in educational opportunities and standards between the rural and urban areas
- (iii) to improve the quality of education in primary and secondary schools and to develop Bahasa Malaysia as the main medium of instruction in primary and secondary schools
- (iv) to extent facilities for teacher training to cope with the expansion of primary and secondary education, especially facilities for the training of teachers in Bahasa Malaysia.

These official objectives are by no means easy to implement and must inevitably be long term. They are, in fact, almost identical to the stated objectives of the Second Malaysia Plan (1971-75).

THE EDUCATIONAL PYRAMID - 1980

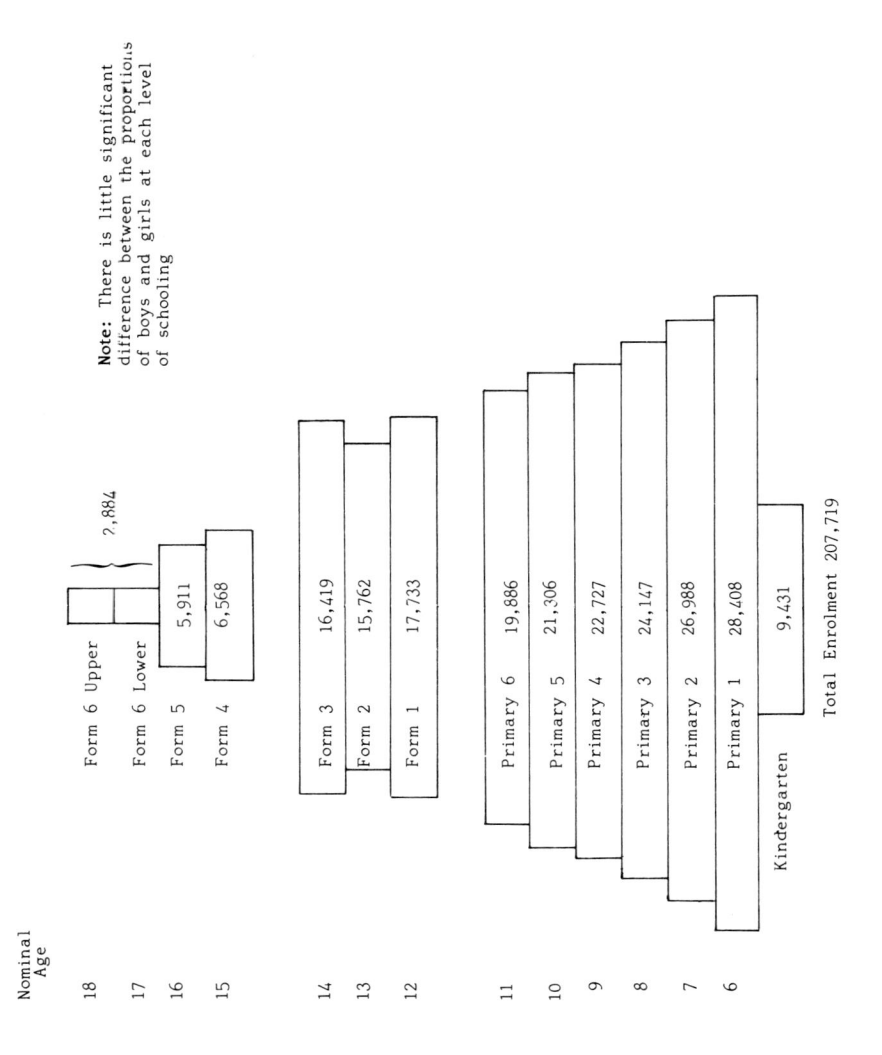

Nominal Age		
18	Form 6 Upper	2,884
17	Form 6 Lower	
16	Form 5	5,911
15	Form 4	6,568
14	Form 3	16,419
13	Form 2	15,762
12	Form 1	17,733
11	Primary 6	19,886
10	Primary 5	21,306
9	Primary 4	22,727
8	Primary 3	24,147
7	Primary 2	26,988
6	Primary 1	28,408
	Kindergarten	9,431

Total Enrolment 207,719

Note: There is little significant difference between the proportions of boys and girls at each level of schooling

SABAH BASIC EDUCATIONAL STATISTICS

Number of Schools (a)

As at 30 September	Total	Primary	Secondary	Technical & Vocational
1969	752	666	84	2
1970	782	695	85	2
1971	806	711	93	2
1972	828	726	100	2
1973	861	759	100	2
1974	865(b)	775	88(b)	2
1975	873	780	91	2
1976	899	803	94	2
1977	909	811	96	2
1978	917	818	97	2
1979	923	823	100	2

Source: Department of Education

(a) Government maintained, Government aided and private schools.

(b) From 1974 onwards, Government Secondary Schools with both English and Malay streams are now considered as single schools and not counted twice as in the past.

Number of Schools, Pupils, Teachers by Management, Medium and Level 1978

Level & Medium of Instruction	Total	Schools Government	Native Voluntary	Mission	Others	Private	Pupils	Teachers Trained & Untrained
KINDERGARTEN	55	–	–	–	–	55	7,957	202
Bahasa Malaysia	3	–	–	–	–	3	269	11
English/ Bahasa Malaysia	14	–	–	–	–	14	1,594	46
Chinese/English	38	–	–	–	–	38	6,094	145
PRIMARY	818	628	19	71	89	11	131,690	5,360
Bahasa Malaysia	726	625	19	57	14	11	107,113	4,520
Chinese	92	3	–	14	75	–	24,577	840
SECONDARY	97	46	–	33	4	14	58,087	2,296
Bahasa Malaysia	88	46	–	33	3	5	54,662	2,161
Chinese/Bahasa Malaysia	9	–	–	–	–	9	3,425	135

Source: Department of Education

Vocational Education

Year	Total Schools	Total Instructors	Total Trainees	Intake to Year I	Intake to Year II	Intake to Year III	Total Graduated
1971	2	24	246	101	87	58	72
1973	2	28	273	141	70	62	76
1974	2	30	285	83	119	83	73
1975	2	33	297	82	96	119	119
1976	2	35	300	115	89	96	118
1977	2	68	303	120	103	80	118
1978	2	51	399	184	122	93	97

Teacher Training

Year	Total Colleges	Total Lectures	Total Trainees Primary	Total Trainees Secondary	Year I Primary	Year I Secondary	Year II Primary	Year II Secondary	Year III Primary	Year III Secondary	Total Graduated Primary	Total Graduated Secondary
1972	2	60	384	183	163	90	149	93	72	–	129	92
1973	2	66	381	202	125	114	163	88	93	–	192	85
1974	3	67	419	260	234	149	120	111	65	–	149	111
1975	3	78	419	165	213	77	206	88	–	–	234	149
1976	3	89	480	276	206	185	274	91	–	–	214	147
1977	3	88	473	338	201	189	272	149	–	–	271	150
1978	3	89	550	343	350	154	200	189	–	–	200	189

419

Sabah Expenditure on Education
1969-1978

Year	Recurrent Expenditure M$	Development Expenditure M$
1969	21,633,684	3,331,880
1970	24,286,461	2,838,033
1971	25,871,118	4,433,512
1972	30,440,768	8,780,160
1973	40,864,523	6,809,703
1974	84,649,206	8,749,434
1975	89,205,794	15,426,521
1976	85,977,120	17,053,327
1977	85,840,799.57	22,914,810.65
1978	92,221,310.00	29,575,955.47

Sarawak

CONTENTS

1 Geography 422
2 Population 424
3 Society and Culture 427
4 History and Politics 428
5 The Economy 431
6 The Education System 434
7 Educational Administration 440
8 Educational Finance 442
9 Development and Planning of
 the Education System 443

1 GEOGRAPHY

Topography

Sarawak covers approximately 123,000 sq km (48,050 square miles) and occupies most of the north western coastal part of the island of Borneo. It lies just north of the equator between latitudes 0°50' and 5° North and longitudes 109°36' and 115°40' East. The 720 km coastline is washed by the South China Sea. In the north it abuts on the Malaysian State of Sabah and the British Protectorate of Brunei but the greater part of its land boundary is with the Indonesian province of Kalimantan, which comprises more than two thirds of the total area of Borneo.

Sarawak may be divided into three broad topographic units: an alluvial swampy coastal plain, further inland a belt of undulating country, and finally the sharply rising mountainous interior. The coastal plain varies in width from less than one kilometre to over 150 km (100 miles). In the south west it is broken in places by isolated mountains. The boundary with Indonesia follows the watershed of a long and irregular mountain range forming part of the spine of Borneo. The highest mountain in Sarawak is Murud at 2,420 metres (7,950 feet). It is a land of rivers and streams. All the main rivers rise close to the Indonesian border and flow westwards or north westwards to the South China Sea. In the interior the rivers flow swiftly, often through deep gorges and over dangerous rapids. When they emerge onto the broad flat coastal plain they meander sluggishly and divide into numerous tributaries. The Rajang is the longest river at 560 km (350 miles); of lesser length are the Baram, Limbang, Saribas, Lupar and Sadong.

Climate

The climate is characterised by heavy rainfall, uniformly high temperatures and high relative humidity. The north east monsoon brings tropical rains from October to February. Owing to the high incidence of cloud, temperatures rarely exceed 36.5°C (97.7°F) with very little variation throughout the year; temperatures are generally lower in the mountainous interior than on the coastal plain. The mean relative humidity over the year is about 85%. The mean annual rainfall throughout the State is over 2,500 mm (100 inches) and most of the area receives 3,000-4,000 mm (120-160 inches) per year.

Communications

The main means of communication are by river and by air, there being as yet no integrated road network. A trunk road linking the state from north west to north east is still incomplete between Sibu and Bintulu. All towns are located on rivers which provide the link in most places between the interior and the coast. The coastal waters are very shallow and the existence of bars at most river mouths hinders the development of ports. Apart from Kuching the provincial ports

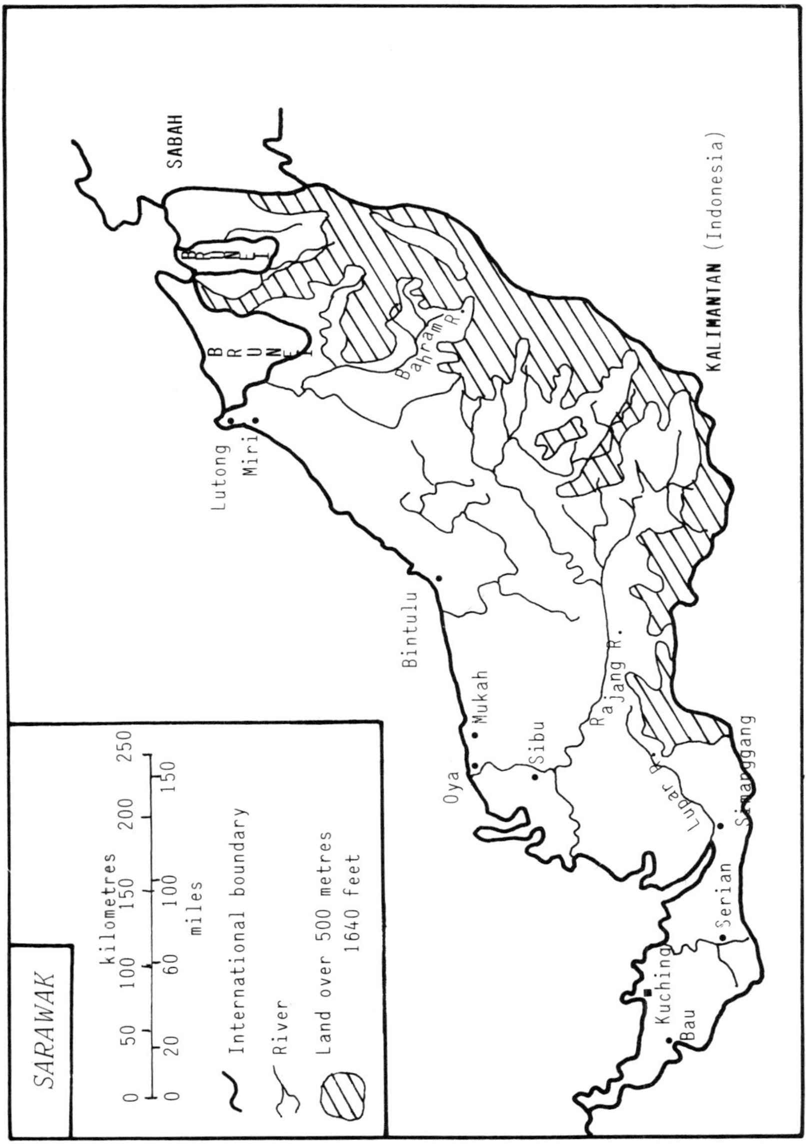

are Sibu, Bintulu and Miri. River transport is by shallow draft launch, outboard motorcraft and hand propelled boats. Certain inland areas are completely isolated from modernising influences. There are rural air services operated by the Malaysian Airlines System to some ten small towns and rural settlements. Sarawak's principal lines of communication with the outside world lie through Singapore or Malaysia since the State is not in a central position in relation to world shipping or air routes. Kuching is some 730 km (456 miles) from Singapore and 1000 km (625 miles) from Kuala Lumpur. There is a road link with Brunei but none with Sarawak's other neighbours. There are daily air services to Singapore, Kuala Lumpur and Kota Kinabalu in Sabah, thrice weekly to Brunei and weekly to Pontianak in Kalimantan.

2 POPULATION

Growth

The first enumeration in 1939 showed a population of 490,585. The population has increased rapidly since 1947, and in 1960 the figure had risen to 744,529. At the census of 1970 the total figure was 976,269 and the 1977 population was estimated to be in excess of 1,100,000. According to the 1970 census 461 persons out of every 1,000 persons in the country were under 15 years old. The growth rate of the population is between 2.5% and 2.6% per year in spite of birth control and family planning, both of which are actively encouraged by the government.

Distribution

Sarawak is sparsely populated (about 22 people per square mile) and the population is unevenly distributed, the heaviest concentrations occurring on the coastal plains and valleys of the west where in some places the pressure on land has become acute. Very few people live in the hilly interior of the eastern half of the State where large areas are practically uninhabited except for scattered bands of nomads. This small population is largely the result of poor soils. The genuinely nomadic elements of the population are small and confined to the dense forests of the north east but even they are gradually being settled in semi-permanent camps.

The populations of the main towns, according to the 1970 census were: Kuching 63,535; Sibu 50,635; Miri 35,762. More accurate figures for today might be 120,000 for the Greater Kuching Area and 80,000 for Sibu. Except for Kuching and Bau the towns have grown up only in the last 100 years as a combination of government station and market centre. More recently the growth of the oil industry has affected the development of Miri and Lutong. A future population growth point is Bintulu which is likely to turn into a main town by 1990. Although there have been many phases in the history of settlement, only the last and current phase has had a great impact on the landscape. Major changes in population and settlement patterns have occurred only very recently. During the last 30 years they have resulted in modifications of the traditional coastal and interior settlement patterns. Rural-urban migration has been marked in the three principal towns since 1947 and is beginning to become a problem. The expansion of commerce, of the oil and rubber trade and of small scale industries continues to attract increasing numbers of indigenous migrants from rural areas.

Groups

Ethnically the population is very mixed. The 1970 census showed the following distribution by community:

Ethnic Origin	Total	%
Iban (Sea Dayak)	303,461	31.1
Land Dayak	83,612	8.5
Malay	181,426	18.6
Melanau	53,379	5.5
Other Indigenous	50,696	5.2
Chinese	293,949	30.1
Other Non-Indigenous	9,746	1.0
	976,269	100.0

Under the category of 'other indigenous' are included Kayans, Kenyahs, Kelabits, Muruts, Punans, Penans, Bisaya, Kedayans, Bajau, and Suloh. 'Other non-indigenous' includes Indians, Indonesians and Europeans. In this document the term 'Dayak' is used to cover all indigenous races other than Malays and Melanaus. Borneo did not attract many immigrants and was passed by when more fertile neighbours such as Java were being populated. The various Sarawak peoples arrived at different times from Celebes, Sumatra and Malaya: the most recent immigrants are the Chinese who arrived during the past 100 years.

Ibans (Sea Dayaks)

Ibans are largely rice cultivators, the majority of them practising shifting cultivation of dry *padi* in hilly areas some 80 to 160 km from the coast. They are spread widely throughout rural Sarawak, but are to be found concentrated in large numbers along the Batang Lupar and the Rajang rivers. Their characteristic system is still the longhouse, which is a federation of families, a method of living originally contrived for purposes of defence.

Land Dayaks (or Bidayuhs)

Land Dayaks are almost entirely restricted to an area within a radius of about 95 km inland from Kuching. They are an unaggressive people who suffered much in past centuries from depredations by the warlike Ibans. Like the Ibans they are primarily shifting cultivators of hill *padi*. Originally longhouse dwellers, they are tending to change to individual houses.

Malays

Malays are essentially a coastal and a riverine people. Their settlements consist of individual houses built on stilts, usually close to the water's edge. Kuching District is the principal Malay stronghold, also the coastal areas of the south west. They engage in a variety of occupations including fishing, boat building, farming and gardening. Many are employed in government services. They are exclusively a Muslim community.

Melanaus

Melanaus are principally concentrated in the low lying plains in the area of Oya and Mukah, in the centre of the Sarawak coastline. They have long been famous as sago producers. In most recent years they have found employment in the timber industry and rubber planting. Ethnically they provide a link between the Malays and the Dayaks. Their physical appearance is such that they are frequently mistaken for Malays. The community includes both Muslims and Christians.

Other Indigenous

These peoples are to be found for the most part in the north east part of the state, principally in the interior. Many of them still live in longhouses though some have, under missionary influences, adopted individual houses and others are still nomadic. The economy of their settlement is on the whole similar to that of the Ibans.

Chinese

The Chinese are now the second largest community in Sarawak. The migration from the mainland is believed to have started early in the nineteenth century, there being no evidence of earlier permanent settlements. During the past 35 years the Chinese population has more than doubled, a process in which immigration has played a negligible part. The Sarawak Chinese are originally mostly from the maritime provinces of south east China and fall into at least seven major dialect groupings with an overall preponderance of Hakkas, Hokkiens and Foochows. The Chinese tend to concentrate in and around towns especially in the area of Kuching, Sibu and Miri. They are principally traders and merchants, though large numbers can also be found in lowland rural areas cultivating the more remunerative cash crops, in particular rubber and pepper. They have achieved higher educational standards than the other racial elements in the State.

3 SOCIETY AND CULTURE

Social Patterns

Society has tended to be plural rather than homogenetic. The various races not only differ widely in character but also are at different stages of social evolution. The Malays range from the simple fisherman or farmer to the blue-blooded aristocrat but all have the common bond of Islam. The Dayaks may be primitve nomads, settled longhouse dwellers or westernised members of urban communities, some of them adhering to their old pagan animistic beliefs, while others have embraced Christianity with different degrees of conviction. The Chinese community embraces Teochew and Hokkien merchants, Hakka miners and farmers and Foochow timber tycoons, to name but a few elements. The Chinese tend to retain their customs, values and languages and they provide the intellectual cream of the population. Rising indigenous nationalism and the urge to protect their interests in the face of policies designed to favour the indigenous peoples have drawn them into the political arena from which they had previously held aloof.

Among the younger generation the town dwelling Malays are most open to the impact of Western civilisation. The Dayaks are less so, but are abandoning their traditional hairstyles, body tattoos and earrings; the Chinese tend to dress soberly and unostentatiously. Among the Chinese and the Malays the family still exists as a strong influence, though to a lesser degree among the latter. In recent years drug dependence has become a serious problem particularly among the children of newly affluent urban families. Young people from the rural areas who drift to the towns often turn to petty crime and prostitution.

On the new national Malaysian scene, the Malays, although a minority group, are in the political ascendancy. Further the Malays have a greater consciousness of ethnic unity and regional political entity than the other indigenous races, whose lives have been confined to the longhouse or village community. At present the various races live in a harmony, which a policy based on the over-riding interests of any one group could quickly disrupt. The present government policy is to provide every incentive and encouragement for the advancement of the indigenous races in the fields of education, public life and commerce.

Language

All groups of the population have at least one distinctive language. Malay is widely understood for ordinary day to day purposes. The adoption of Bahasa Malaysia as the first language of the State, in line with the rest of Malaysia, presents difficulties and will take several years to achieve. The present policy is to introduce Bahasa Malaysia as the main medium of instruction in the schools, to give every assistance for its study, and to use it on all official and ceremonial occasions. However, by and large English is still the main working language in Sarawak.

Religion

There is no State religion in Sarawak and the Constitution guarantees religious freedom. According to the 1970 census 25.88% of the population was Muslim, 19.31% Christian, 8.6% Buddhist, 16.59% no religion and 29.62% other religions (mainly animists). However, these figures are not very reliable as, for security reasons, full census returns were not completed in respect of almost 10% of the population. A truer estimate might be about 24% Muslims, 20% Christian and 10% Buddhists. (Buddhism is strong among the Chinese community throughout Sarawak.)

Islam reached Sarawak in the mid-fifteenth century. Though the Muslim faith took hold among the people of the coastal plains, the indigenous peoples of the interior continued their pagan animistic practices. The Muslim community today consists principally of the Malays together with some of the Melanaus and Kedayans. Proselytising of Muslims is forbidden.

The first Anglican Mission led by Francis McDougall reached Sarawak in 1848 and immediately began medical and educational work which has continued ever since. The influence of the Anglican Church has been strongest among the Ibans of the first and second divisions, the Land Dayaks and the Chinese in the Kuching area. Towards the end of the nineteenth century Roman Catholic missions started to set up churches and schools and they have been particularly successful in the Kuching area, along the Rajang river and in Miri and along the Baram river. The American Methodists established a strong foothold among the Foochow Chinese in Sibu and the Lower Rajang area. The Borneo Evangelical Mission from Australia has been active among the indigenous peoples of the north east. The last comers were the Seventh Day Adventists who started a few schools in the inter-war years.

4 HISTORY AND POLITICS

Early Settlement

The excavations at the Niah Caves have revealed traces of the earliest recorded human civilisation in Asia dating back to BC 40,000 to 50,000. There is at present no conclusive evidence as to the inhabitants of Borneo in prehistoric times. The indigenous peoples of today are probably descendants of dolichocephalic Indonesian migrants, who arrived from the Asian mainland and first settled on the coast. Successive waves of immigrants followed and gradually displaced the earlier settlers, pushing them into the interior. There are traces of both Indian and Chinese settlements in the vicinity of Kuching and elsewhere, but there is no indication of systematic migration and occupation from India and China.

Brooke Rule

The history of Sarawak as an integral state begins with the landing in 1839 of James Brooke. At the time Sarawak was the southern province of the Brunei Sultanate. The oppression of the Sultan's viceroy had goaded the Malays and Land Dayaks into revolt and the Sultan had sent his uncle, the Rajah Muda Hashim, to pacify the country. James Brooke departed after a short stay and returned in 1840 to find the fighting still in progress. At the request of the Rajah Muda Hashim, he interceded in the dispute and in return for suppressing the revolt was rewarded for his services by being installed in September 1841 as Rajah of the territory from Cape Datu to the Samarahan River. Further territory was acquired from Brunei in 1953 and 1861. In 1864 Britain recognised Sarawak as an independent state. James Brooke was succeeded as Rajah by his nephew Charles Brooke in 1868. During the latter's reign, which lasted until 1917, large additions were made to the Sarawak Raj. With the transfer of Lawas in 1905 it extended to its present boundaries. Sarawak was accorded British protection in 1888. It remained the personal domain of the Brookes until 1941 when the third Rajah, Sir Charles Vyner Brooke, introduced a new constitution which abrogated his absolute powers. Before the end of 1941 Sarawak was occupied by the Japanese army for nearly four years. The third Rajah resumed administration in 1946, but he decided that for the sake of Sarawak's economic future it would be best for her to come under the British Crown. Sarawak became a Crown Colony on 1 July 1946.

British Rule

There was considerable opposition to cession from many Malays and the anti-cession movement reached its climax with the murder of the second governor, Mr Duncan Stewart, in December 1949. After this act of violence all overt opposition to cession ceased. The economic development of Sarawak proceeded rapidly and limited political development was encouraged. By 1962 there were six political parties and a democratic system of local government had been established. In 1962 a commission, under the chairmanship of Lord Cobbold, visited North Borneo and Sarawak and recommended that it would be in the best interests of the two territories for them to obtain their independence as member states of the Federation of Malaysia. An intergovernmental committee was established to consider the terms of federation and it recommended a number of constitutional safeguards including reserved rights on immigration, education and distribution of legislative powers, the official use of the English language and protection of the special position of the indigenous races. These recommendations were agreed to by all the governments concerned. In 1963 the Constitution of

Sarawak was amended to provide for a representational government in the *Council Negri* to prepare for independence and a system of indirect representation through electoral colleges was established. On 16 September 1963 Sarawak obtained independence as a state within the Federation of Malaysia.

Independence

The early years of independence from 1963 to 1966 were marked by confrontation with Indonesia and continuing British influence, with British forces in day-to-day control of security and British officials in key government positions. Confrontation came to an end in August 1966 and following a minor constitutional crisis in September a new State Government took office with the strong backing of the federal government. British influence waned with the departure of key government officials and the grip of the federal government in Sarawak began to strengthen.

In May 1969, after communal riots in Kuala Lumpur, the central government suspended the Constitution and invoked emergency powers in both East and West Malaysia and for more than a year Sarawak was ruled by a State Operations Committee. The first general elections since independence were held in 1970 and after much bargaining between political parties an alliance party took power under the leadership of Datuk Abdul Rahman Ya'kub, a Muslim Melanau. However, one important political party, the Sarawak National Party (SNAP), representing Dayak and Chinese interests, remained in opposition. From 1971 onwards a serious security situation developed with considerable anti-government activity by communist terrorists. This was exacerbated by the worsening economic situation due a slump in timber prices. However, in March 1974 the security situation improved dramatically after a general amnesty was declared (called Operation Sri Aman). The Alliance government was returned to power in 1974 and in late 1976 SNAP joined the government. Federal elections in 1978 and State elections in 1979 resulted in overwhelming wins for the government coalition (now re-named the *Barisan Nasional* or National Front). Since 1974 the economic position of Sarawak and the security situation have steadily improved. The State government policy aims as far as possible at integration with federal policies.

System of Government

Sarawak is ruled by the *Yang Dipertua Negri* (Governor), who is appointed for a five-year term by the *Agung* (King) of Malaysia. Sarawak is represented in the Malaysian *Dewan Rakyat* (House of Representatives) in Kuala Lumpur by 24 elected members. The *Dewan Undangan Negri* (State Council) consists of 48 elected members. Members of both houses are elected for a period of five years by direct majority vote in constituencies. The State Cabinet consists of not more than nine ministers, including the Chief Minister. State subjects are communications, public works, agriculture, forestry, local government, welfare, land and native law and immigration. For purposes of administration Sarawak is divided into seven divisions, each in the charge of a resident. Each division is divided into districts in the charge of a district officer. There is also a local government system of municipal and district councils and a system of paid community leaders.

Political Situation

Unlike Peninsular Malaysia the major political parties in Sarawak are multi-racial in character, each one representing at least two community groups. The oldest political party is the Sarawak United People's Party (SUPP) which is mainly supported by Chinese but has some Dayak members. The party currently holds 11 seats in the State Assembly. The Sarawak National Party (SNAP) is mainly supported by Dayaks but has some Chinese and a few Malay members. This party, which was in opposition continuously from 1966 to 1976, currently has 16 seats in the State Assembly. The *Parti Pesaka Bumiputra Bersatu* (PBB) was formed by merger of two parties and has Malay and Dayak membership. It currently has 18 seats in the State Assembly. These three parties together form the *Barisan Nasional* (National Front) coalition government at State level and are part of the larger coalition of parties forming the federal *Barisan Nasional* government. The Chief Minister, Datuk Patinggi Tan Sri Haji Abdul Rahman Ya'kub, is from the PBB. The major opposition parties are *Parti Rakyat Jati Sarawak* (PAJAR) (Malays and Dayaks), the Sarawak People's Organisation (SAPO) (Chinese and Dayaks) and the Democratic Action Party (DAP) which is supported mainly by Chinese. None of the opposition parties have a single seat in the State Assembly but SAPO has one seat in the federal House of Representatives. Independents hold three seats in the State Assembly.

There is general support for the National Front government in Sarawak and, with the exception of some DAP and independent candidates, opposition candidates polled few votes in the last State elections. The major political issues exploited by the opposition parties are inequality of opportunity, particularly of Chinese vis-à-vis indigenous people, and Sarawak's claim to a greater share of the revenue from her oil. Although there is still some residual mistrust of Peninsular Malaysia there is no significant separatist feeling.

5 THE ECONOMY

General

Sarawak's economy is part of the economy of Malaysia as a whole. Malaysia has a mixed economy which is regulated by a series of five year plans. The Second and Third Malaysia Plans were based on the New Economic Policy which was formulated in the aftermath of racial disturbances in 1969. The Policy has two prongs. The first prong is to reduce substantially the incidence of poverty by 1990 by the implementation of policies and programmes directly geared towards the needs of the poor. The second prong of the policy aims to restructure Malaysia society so that the identification of race with economic function and geographical location is reduced and eventually eliminated. The objective is to achieve by 1990 50% employment and 30% participation in the national wealth by Malays and other indigenous people of Malaysia (collectively known as *bumiputras* or 'princes of the soil'). This is pursued through policies in employment, investment, business opportunities and education which actively favour Malays and other indigenous people over non-indigenous people (mainly Chinese).

Agriculture

The economy of Sarawak is still mainly agricultural. The rural economies subsist mainly on rice, but because of poor soil and inefficient farming methods the total production of both wet and dry *padi* is insufficient to meet the needs of the poulation. In 1977 about 38% of Sarawak's rice requirement was imported. Sarawak is a major world exporter of pepper. Rubber is still an important export industry and palm oil has developed strongly in recent years. Other crops are mainly for domestic consumption.

Natural Resources

Sarawak is rich in natural resources. Of the minerals, oil, gold and antimony, bauxite, mercury, phosphate and coal have been worked in various periods of her history. There are other minerals including dolomite, fireclay and glass sand which have never been worked. Recently deposits of quality coking coal and natural gas have been found in commercial quantities. Petroleum is the most important mineral resource in Sarawak. In 1977 annual production was more than 40 million barrels. The entire rights for exploitation of oil and natural gas have been vested in the National Petroleum Company, Petronas, to which Sarawak Shell is the principal contractor.

The other major natural resource is timber. Three quarters of the land area of Sarawak is covered by natural forests and one third of this area has been designated 'Permanent Forest'. The rate of exploitation of forests has been much slower than in Peninsular Malaysia and Sabah and with careful control the reserves of timber should be maintained almost indefinitely. A major problem is shifting cultivation. It has been estimated that for every log exported another is burned by shifting cultivators.

Manufacturing

Manufacturing industry forms a very small part of Sarawak's economy. Timber processing is on the increase and it is estimated that there are now about 260 factories including sawmills and factories for mouldings, dowels, plywood, flooring and furniture making. Factories for manufacturing oxygen and other industrial gases, cement and assembling cars and trucks mainly for East Malaysian consumption, have opened recently. In addition the following types of goods are produced for local consumption: alcoholic and non-alcoholic beverages; textiles; metal containers; canned food; pottery; wood and steel ships; and plastics.

Trade

The trade and commerce of Sarawak centres on the collection of primary products for export and the local distribution of imported consumer and capital goods. The economy is heavily dependent on the export trade and is highly vulnerable to fluctuations in the prices of the major export commodities in the world market. In 1977 the export value of various products was:

	M$000
Agricultural products	266,500
Timber	342,955
Petroluem & products	1,423,253
Other goods	120,540
TOTAL	2,153,248

Economic Development

The economic position of Sarawak is healthy with a growth rate of 8.2% in 1977 and 7.5% in 1978 and a perennial balance of trade surplus. The main thrust of development in Sarawak is towards exploiting the State's natural resources and building up a manufacturing economy. The major growth in the future will take place in and around Bintulu during the 1980s and 1990s. A deep water port is under construction at Tanjong Kidurong, near Bintulu, which will serve a new liquified natural gas plant to be built there. An urea and ammonia plant under ASEAN will also be sited at Bintulu and negotiations have been taking place with Reynolds Aluminium International for the establishment of an aluminium plant there. Bintulu is also the site for a projected new university. To meet the demand for cheap electricity for developments in Bintulu and Peninsular Malaysia a feasibility survey is being undertaken for a hydroelectric project on the Rajang river above the Pelagus rapids. The main problem in implementing these devlopments is the shortage of labour, particularly skilled labour, in the State and it is likely that large numbers of immigrant workers will be required. This will undoubtedly cause social problems in the future.

Rural Development

The problem of rural development in Sarawak is an intractable one. rural communities are so widely scattered and sparsely populated that the provision of intra-structural and extension services is extremely difficult and expensive. Great strides have been made in providing health and education services and there are now schools and clinics in the remotest places. However, they have not been matched by other services and agricultural development schemes have not affected the majority of the rural poor. The traditional economies are stagnant and many rural communities face serious malnutrition as a result of exhaustion of the soil and scarcity of fish and game. Rural-urban migration is accelerating and the trend in many areas is towards depopulation. It remains to be seen whether the projects for building roads, for agricultural schemes and for agricultural extension and training which are in progress or planned to begin within the next five years can reverse this trend and provide a measure of prosperity for the mass of the rural population.

6 THE EDUCATION SYSTEM

Academic Year

The school year begins in January. There are two holidays of 2 weeks each in April and July and a long holiday from early November to early January.

Management of Schools

The principal agencies providing education in Sarawak are the federal government, Chinese committees, Christian missions and private committees. The majority of schools run by the Chinese committees and Christian missions are government aided and are virtually controlled by the Education Department. At primary level in 1977 there were 1,204 government and aided schools and ten private schools. At secondary level there were 78 government and aided schools and 40 unaided schools. The unaided secondary schools included 13 schools offering Chinese medium education and 27 mission and private committee schools offering English medium education to drop-outs from the government system.

Medium of Instruction

Up to January 1977 the majority of primary and secondary schools in Sarawak were using English and Chinese as the medium of instruction. There were a few Bahasa Malaysia medium primary schools and some Bahasa Malaysia medium classes in secondary schools. With the extension of the 1961 Education Act to Warawak in 1976 the main medium of instruction is changing from English to Bahasa Malaysia in stages. The first stage was the conversion of Primary 1 in 1977 and the process will be complete when the Upper VIth Form changes to Bahasa

Malaysia medium in 1989. Chinese medium primary and secondary schools are not affected. In 1977 the numbers of students studying in each medium were as follows:

	Primary	Secondary
Bahasa Malaysia	61,597	13,292
English	74,464	55,834
Chinese	50,243	2,261

Pre-Primary

The government does not provide pre-primary education in Sarawak. Such pre-primary schools as exist in the larger towns are established primarily through self-help. This private provision expanded in the 1970s so that 10,481 pupils were enrolled in 1979 compared to 4,907 in 1970.

Primary

The primary course lasts six years and is divided into four years of lower primary (Primary 1-4) and two of upper primary (Primary 4-6). The starting age is normally 6+ but in many rural schools an alternate-year entry system is operated and many children are 7+ on admission. Primary education is free but not compulsory. In many rural primary schools boarding facilities are provided for children who cannot attend as day pupils. Enrolments have increased from 94,773 in 1960 to 202,054 in 1979 and primary education occupies about two thirds of the teaching force. Many primary schools are extremely remote and to reach them takes days of hard travelling.

A national syllabus lays down what is taught in each subject. The usual subjects are taught, including science in the upper classes where suitably qualified teachers are available. The curriculum contains no rural emphasis because it is essentially uniform for all schools. English and Bahasa Malaysia are compulsory languages in all schools whatever the medium of instruction.

Promotion in primary schools is automatic. In Primary 1-4 schools conduct their own examinations. On completion of Primary 5 there is a national assessment examination designed to measure the pupils' attainment so that remedial action can be taken as required; (unlike Peninsular Malaysia there is no Primary 3 assessment examination). There is automatic promotion from Primary 1 to Secondary Form III. Textbooks in Chinese medium schools and English medium classes are chosen from a recommended list but the textbooks used in Bahasa Malaysia medium classes are all published by the Ministry of Education.

THE SCHOOL SYSTEM OF SARAWAK - 1977

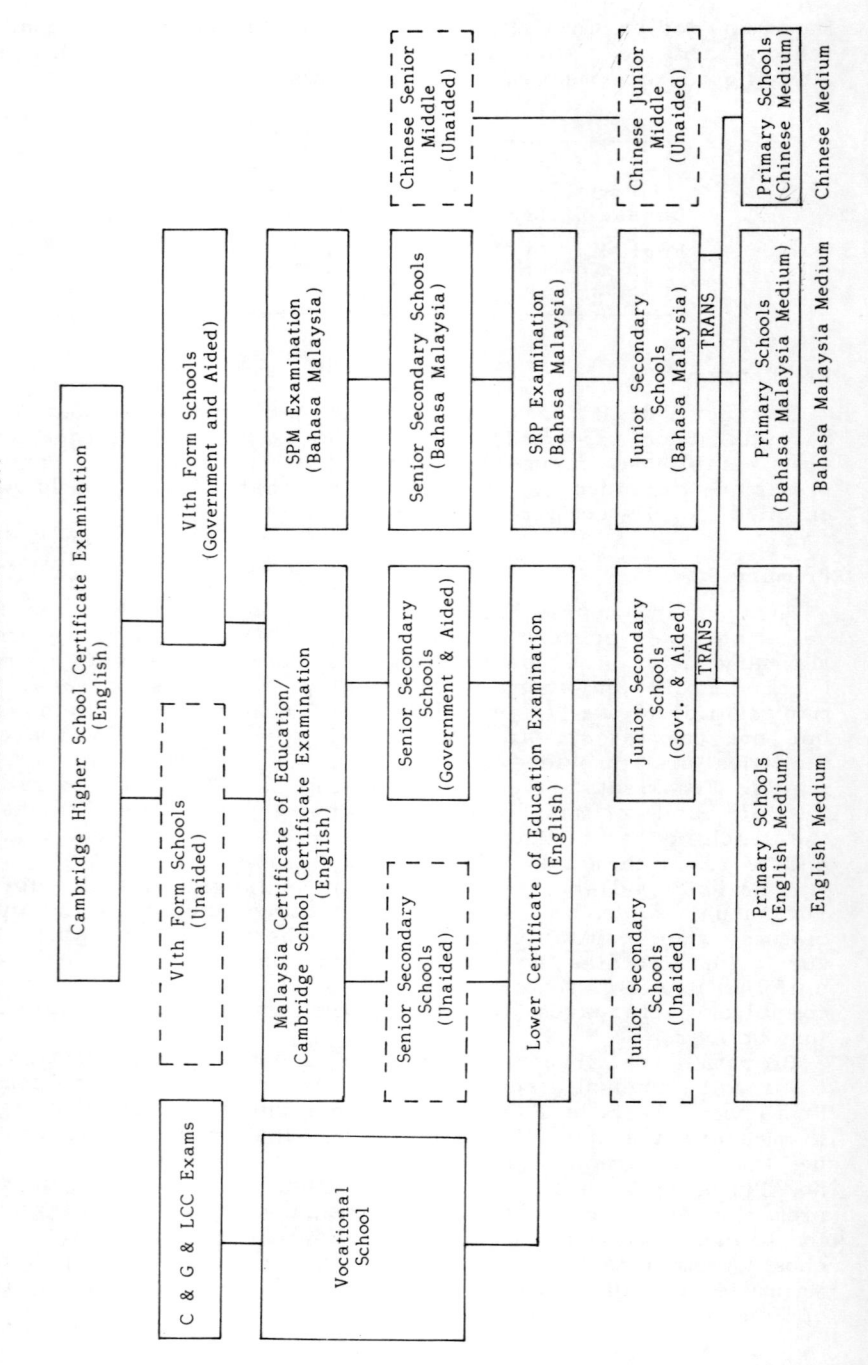

Secondary

Secondary education in English and Bahasa Malaysia medium schools is divided into three stages:

Junior Secondary (Forms I-III)
Senior Secondary (Forms IV-V)
Lower and Upper VIth Forms

making a total of seven years in all. Transition classes provide an additional year for primary students admitted to government and aided secondary schools using a different medium (i.e. Chinese to English, Chinese to Bahasa Malaysia or English to Bahasa Malaysia). Chinese secondary schools are often described as 'middle' schools. The junior secondary course lasts three years, comprising junior middle 1-3. the senior course lasts three years and comprises senior middle 1-3. The government provides only English and Bahasa medium secondary education and all Chinese medium schools are run by private committees. Enrolment in secondary schools increased from 9,266 in 1960 to 89,374 in 1979, and secondary education occupies about one third of the teaching force. All rural secondary schools provide boarding facilities and, in most, boarders form the greater part of the school population. The average size of secondary schools in 1977 was 886.

Junior Secondary

At the junior secondary level the government and aided schools are organised on comprehensive lines. The curriculum is academic but there are optional practical subjects including agricultural science, domestic science and industrial arts. The three-year course leads to the Lower Certificate of Education (LCE) or its Bahasa Malaysia medium equivalent *Sijil Rendah Pelajaran* (SRP) taken at the end of Form III. These examinations are organised by the Federal Examinations Syndicate. For the time being English medium students are not required to pass Bahasa Malaysia in order to obtain an LCE certificate but a pass in English is compulsory. Bahasa Malaysia medium students must pass both English and Bahasa Malaysia. All students must pass in mathematics and either history or geography. In 1985 all students will sit for the Bahasa Malaysia medium SRP examination.

Senior Secondary

Senior secondary education is selective. In 1976/77 the percentage of students proceeding from Form III to Form IV was 64.8%. As a general rule students with the best grades are encouraged to go into science classes, the others into arts classes. The best *bumiputra* students are sent to junior science colleges of which there are now two, in Kuching and Miri. Up to 1978 most English medium students completing Form V sat for the Senior Cambridge School Certificate but with effect from 1979 all students sit for the Malaysian Certificate of Education (MCE) or its Bahasa Malaysia medium equivalent, the *Sijil Pelajaran Malaysia* (SPM). Both the examinations are conducted by the Federal Examinations Syndicate (in cooperation with the Cambridge Local Examinations Syndicate). The majority of papers are now set and marked by the Malaysian authorities. In Sarawak English medium students must pass in English to obtain a certificate but they are exempted until 1983 from the requirement to pass the Bahasa Malaysia paper. Bahasa Malaysia medium students must pass Bahasa Malaysia to obtain a certificate but a pass in English is not compulsory. English medium students in Sarawak may take either the Cambridge English Language paper (the 121 syllabus) or the MCE English Language paper (the 122 syllabus). The majority of schools are still preparing students for the Cambridge paper. To obtain a Cambridge School Certificate, however, a student must sit for the Cambridge English Language paper as an *additional* paper, i.e. irrespective of whether he has sat the paper for his MCE Certificate. In 1987 all students will sit for the Bahasa Malaysia medium SPM examination.

VIth Form

Admission to VIth forms is highly selective and is decided on the results of the MCE/SPM, though a proportion of places are reserved for *bumiputras.* Some *bumiputra* students are sent to Peninsular Malaysia for pre-university courses. After two years pupils sit for the Cambridge Higher School Certificate (HSC). The papers set for the Malay medium version, the *Sijil Tinggi Persekolahan* (STP), are translated directly from the HSC and the examination is still conducted by Cambridge. However, it is likely that the Federal Examinations Syndicate will take over this examination in the near future.

Technical and Vocational

There are vocational schools in Kuching, Sibu and Kiri which provide two-year courses in preparation for the *Sijil Pelajaran Vokesyenal Malaysia* (Malaysian Vocational Education Certificate) in various craft subjects. Before the SPVM was introduced in 1978 students took a three-year course following the City and Guilds of London Institute syllabus. There are also one-year full time courses in shorthand, typewriting and book-keeping. The entry qualification is completion of junior secondary education. The total student enrolment in the three schools in 1979 was 793. The Miri Vocational School was, in 1980, converted into a centre for crash courses in various skills needed for the construction of the deep water port and other developments at Bintulu. The vocational school in Sibu offers full time courses of three months duration for local and coastal mates and masters. There is also provision for vocational subjects in the curriculum of the secondary schools; the subjects offered are commerce, industrial arts, home economics and agricultural science. There is no government provision in Sarawak for vocational and technical education beyond the level represented by the vocational schools and students wishing to further their technical education must go abroad or to Peninsular Malaysia. There is, however, one private technical college which opened its doors in 1979. There are also a few private schools offering commercial subjects.

Teacher Training

A two-year residential course for the training of teachers is available at three teachers' colleges: Batu Lintang Teachers' College in Kuching, Rajang Teachers' College, Binatang and Sarawak Teachers' College, Sibu. A fourth college to be located in Miri was expected to open in 1982 or 1983. The minimum entry qualification for teacher training is an MCE certificate. Although the colleges follow the integrated teacher training syllabus prescribed by the federal Ministry of Education which is designed to provide training for both the primary and the lower secondary age range, in practice Batu Lintang Teachers' College concentrates on training teachers for the junior secondary level and the other two colleges cater for the primary level. Rajang and Sarawak Teachers' Colleges are Bahasa Malaysia medium but Batu Lintang still had an English medium stream until the end of 1981. No training courses are available in Sarawak for graduate teachers. Students sent to Malaysian or to overseas universities for training as teachers take a diploma in education at their universities after obtaining their degree. In 1977 there were 1,325 teachers in training in Sarawak.

Higher

There is no university in Sarawak. However, there is a branch campus of the Universiti Pertanian Malaysia (University of Agriculture) near Kuching which prepares students for diplomas in agriculture, forestry etc. and for the first year of degree courses. There are plans to establish a permanent campus of the univeristy in Bintulu during the 1980s which will provide degree and diploma courses in mathematics, natural sciences, agriculture, forestry, fisheries and other applied sciences, and social sciences and humanities. There is also a branch campus of the MARA Institute of Technology for first year students only. A permanent campus is planned for Bako, near Kuching. The majority of students who wish to pursue higher education must do so in Peninsular Malaysia or abroad. There is a limited number of scholarships available from federal and State government sources.

Non-Formal and Adult

The Sarawak Council for Further Education provides instruction through night schools in 15 centres. The principal subjects taught are Bahasa Malaysia, English and typing. Adult literacy and vocational classes are conducted by the State Adult Education Department under the wing of the Ministry of

Agriculture and Rural Development. The Department of Agriculture also organises 13-week courses for young farmers at three centres in Sarawak.

Educational Broadcasting

Educational broadcasting is provided by the Education Media Service of the Ministry of Education using facilities provided by Radio Television Malaysia. All educational television programmes are made in Peninsular Malaysia but EMS Sarawak is responsible for its own educational radio programmes. Schools are provided with radios and every secondary school in a television receiving area is provided with a television set. The current priority is broadcasting for primary schools. There are two technical cooperation officers from Britain working in the field of educational radio, in radio production and utilisation and evaluation respectively.

7 EDUCATIONAL ADMINISTRATION

Education Department

Primary and secondary education in Sarawak is administered by the Ministry of Education through the State Director of Education. There is a Federal Assistant Minister of Education with responsibility for Sabah and Sarawak. The Department of Education has its Head Office in Kuching, seven divisional officers in charge of an education office in each of the seven divisions and district offices in each district. The administration of education is highly centralised and syllabi, curricula and examinations are controlled by the central Ministry. However, the Director of Education in Sarawak has greater responsibility than his counterparts in Peninsular Malaysia in that he directly controls all aspects of educational administration in the State.

Inspection

The inspection of primary and secondary schools is the responsibility of the School Inspectorate. There are three zones, i.e. Zone 1 based in Kuching (covering the first and second divisions), Zone 2 based in Sibu (covering the third, sixth and seventh divisions) and Zone 3 based in Miri (covering the fourth and fifth divisions). The Chief Inspector and all secondary school inspectors are based in Kuching, Sibu and Miri. The school inspectors are responsible for advising the Director of Education on all aspects of the administration of schools and reporting on individual teachers. They also assist with in-service courses in various subject areas.

441

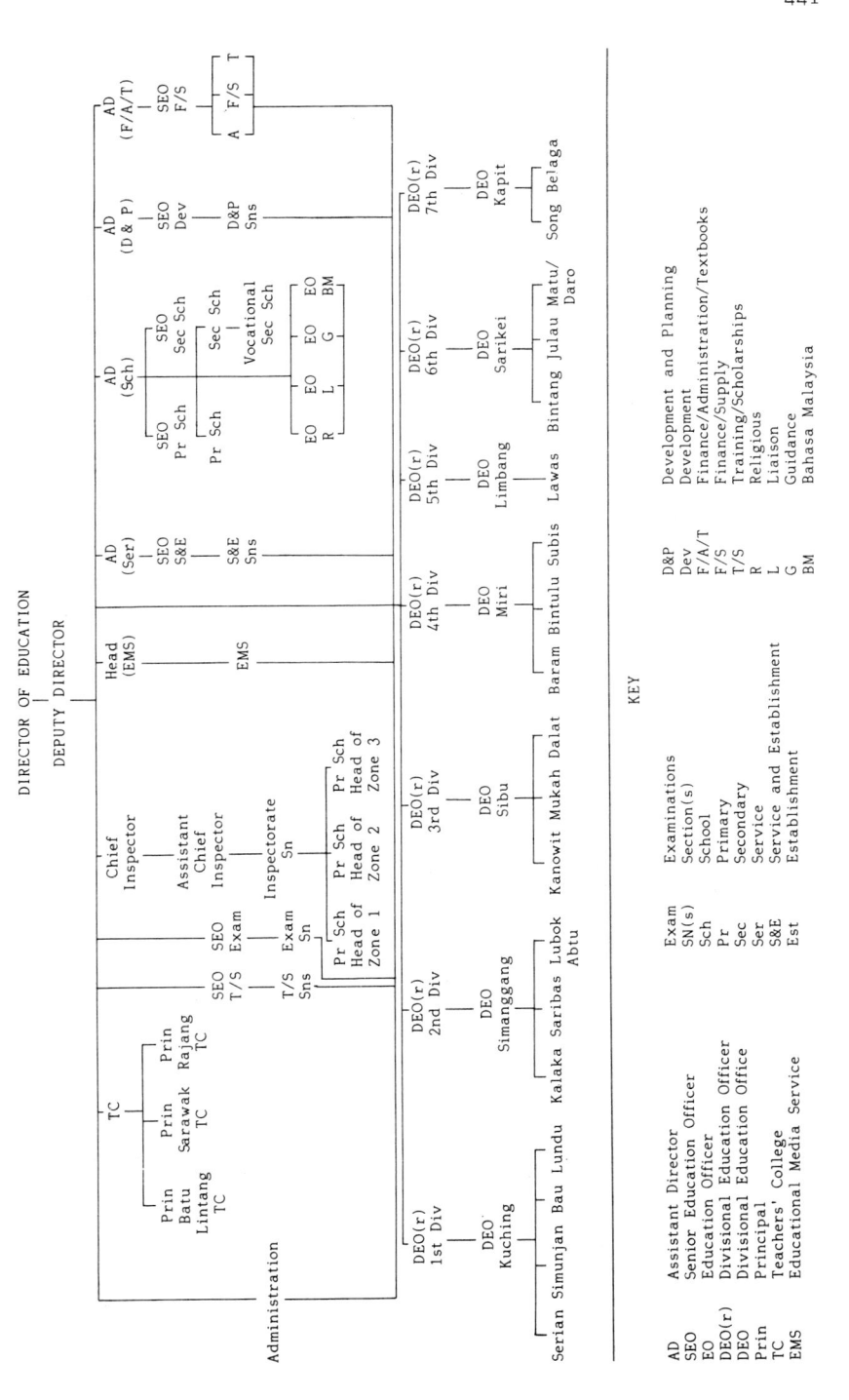

ORGANISATION OF THE EDUCATION DEPARTMENT 1979

DIRECTOR OF EDUCATION
DEPUTY DIRECTOR

Administration

	Chief Inspector	Head (EMS)	AD (Ser)	AD (Sch)	AD (D & P)	AD (F/A/T)
TC	Assistant Chief Inspector	EMS	SEO S&E	SEO Pr Sch	SEO Dev	SEO F/S
Prin Batu Lintang TC	Inspectorate Sn		S&E Sns	Pr Sch	D&P Sns	A F/S T
Prin Sarawak TC	Pr Sch Head of Zone 1			SEO Sec Sch		
Prin Rajang TC	Pr Sch Head of Zone 2			Sec Sch		
SEO T/S	Pr Sch Head of Zone 3			Vocational Sec Sch		
SEO Exam				EO R	EO L	EO G	EO BM
T/S Sns						
Exam Sn						

DEO(r) 1st Div	DEO(r) 2nd Div	DEO(r) 3rd Div	DEO(r) 4th Div	DEO(r) 5th Div	DEO(r) 6th Div	DEO(r) 7th Div
DEO Kuching	DEO Simanggang	DEO Sibu	DEO Miri	DEO Limbang	DEO Sarikei	DEO Kapit
Serian Simunjan Bau Lundu	Kalaka Saribas Lubok Abtu	Kanowit Mukah Dalat	Baram Bintulu Subis	Lawas	Bintang Julau Matu/ Daro	Song Belaga

KEY

AD	Assistant Director	Exam	Examinations
SEO	Senior Education Officer	SN(s)	Section(s)
EO	Education Officer	Sch	School
DEO(r)	Divisional Education Officer	Pr	Primary
DEO	Divisional Education Office	Sec	Secondary
Prin	Principal	Ser	Service
TC	Teachers' College	S&E	Service and Establishment
EMS	Educational Media Service	Est	Establishment

D&P	Development and Planning
Dev	Development
F/A/T	Finance/Administration/Textbooks
F/S	Finance/Supply
T/S	Training/Scholarships
R	Religious
L	Liaison
G	Guidance
BM	Bahasa Malaysia

8 EDUCATIONAL FINANCE

Education Budget

Education is financed by the federal government. The total recurrent expenditure on education in Sarawak in 1977 was M$100,861,000. The average unit costs for providing education in government and aided educational institutions at various levels in 1977 were as follows:

	M$
Primary Schools	265.12
Secondary Schools	552.25
Vocational Schools	1,148,80
Teachers' Colleges	3,369.06

School Fees and Books

All government and aided secondary schools charge school fees at rates regulated by government. The new Bahasa Malaysia medium classes in government and aided secondary schools are exempted from payment of tuition fees. English medium classes in government and aided secondary schools pay fees prescribed by the government but there is provision for remission of fees in cases of need. Private schools charge fees considerably higher than those prescribed for government and aided secondary schools. Textbooks are not free for all pupils (even at primary level) but the majority 86% in the State (in 1977) receive free books through the Ministry of Education Textbooks on Loan Scheme.

Aid for External Agencies

Aid from external agencies is comparatively insignificant. The major aid agency is the World Bank which is currently providing loans for building primary and secondary schools, a new teachers' college in Miri and training awards. Aid in the form of assistance with in-service training and overseas awards is provided by UNESCO, ODA and the British Council. A few overseas training awards are provided by other countries. Volunteer teachers in secondary and vocational schools come from Britain, Japan, Germany, Australia, New Zealand and Canada.

9 DEVELOPMENT AND PLANNING OF THE EDUCATION SYSTEM
Brooke Rule

There is no evidence of the existence of any kind of formal education in Sarawak prior to 1880, though there would certainly have been a few Koranic schools providing religious training for young boys of the more important Malay families. During Brooke rule education was provided by Christian missions, by the government and by Chinese school boards. The first mission school was established in 1848, the first government Malay school in 1883 and the first Chinese school in 1892. In line with their primary objective of preserving existing cultural patterns, the Brookes encouraged the growth of different types of school to meet the needs of the Malay, Dayak and Chinese communities, providing instruction for each in their own language medium.

The Anglican and Roman Catholic missions started schools in the main centres of population in the nineteenth century. These schools used English as the language of instruction and followed a limited academic curriculum with a predominantly Western background to the subjects studied. Most of these schools had secondary forms. The American Methodist Mission, the Seventh Day Adventist Mission and the Borneo Evangelical Mission from Australia set up schools early in the present century. Mission schools were financed mainly by fees and government subventions. There was no system of training teachers.

Towards the end of the nineteenth century the Brooke administration began to set up schools to cater for the Malay section of the population, providing a primary course in the Malay language. No fees were charged. A few teachers were trained in Malaya. And in response to the increased demand at the beginning of the present century for Chinese education in Sarawak, a large number of independent Chinese schools managed by local committees came into being. They were financed by fees and local collections. The curriculum and textbooks followed closely the pattern of mainland China, from where the greater part of the teaching staff was drawn.

The Education Department was first created in 1924 but was closed down during the depression of the early 1930s and did not reopen until 1939. In 1930 the first candidates from Sarawak sat for the Senior Cambridge Examination. In 1939 a small college was opened for the training of teachers for government Malay schools, 25 new government Malay schools and two Dayak schools were opened and plans were made for the provision by the government of secondary education in English. As a result of the Japanese occupation mission schools and many Chineses schools were closed but most of the government Malay schools continued to function.

British Rule

In 1946 the mission and Chinese schools were reopened and the Education Department was reconstituted. The colonial government decided in 1948 that local authorities should assume general responsibility for primary education in their areas, expenditure being financed almost entirely by government grants, and in consequence many new schools were started.

After 1946 there was an increasing demand for education from the Dayak population. The colonial government, the resources of which were severely limited, encouraged self-help methods particularly in respect of the construction and maintenance of schools. The Dayaks accepted this policy and organised the building of many schools. They accepted the need for payment of fees and for boarding facilities for children from distant villages. Feelings of racial pride made the Dayaks unwilling to use the Malay language in their schools; they were also opposed to the use of native languages beyond what was absolutely necessary, on the grounds that this would delay the progress and development of their people. The maximum use of English was insisted on. In 1948 a teacher training centre was opened at Batu Lintang, Kuching, to provide teachers for the new Dayak schools and for Malay schools by means of a two-year course of instruction.

The colonial era was a period of transition from the laissez-faire policy of Brooke rule to a policy of control and planning in the whole field of education. The principal aims of the Education Department were to provide universal, free and compulsory education at the primary level, to overcome the wide disparity in educational level between the indigenous races and the Chinese, and to bring the then existing different school systems into a national system.

Independence

When Sarawak became a State within the Federation of Malaysia in September 1963 education became a federal responsibility subject to an agreement between the governments concerned that the existing policy and administration of schools should continue undisturbed and that the Director of Education should carry out his duties in consultation with the State government, until that government decided otherwise. During the first ten years of independence the pace of educational development was much accelerated, though integration with the federal system of education proceeded only gradually. Free primary education was introduced in 1966 and in 1973 the Education Department took over the administration of primary schools from the local authorities. Secondary education, which until 1971 was restricted to about 30% of primary school leavers, was open to all by 1975 and the common entrance examination at the end of the primary course was abolished. A State education service with terms and conditions of service comparable to the civil service was set up in 1973.

Sarawak was slow in following Peninsular Malaysia and Sabah in introducing Bahasa Malaysia as the main medium of instruction in schools. However, on 1 January 1976 the 1961 Education Act was extended to Sarawak with the concurrence of the State government. This in effect meant that the State government accepted the objectives of the national system of education, including the introduction of Bahasa Malaysia as the main medium of instruction in the schools. This began to be implemented in January 1977 when Bahasa Malaysia became the medium of instruction in Class 1 of all English medium primary schools. The mass re-training of teachers for the new medium began in 1976 and will continue into the 1980s. With the extension of the Act other differences between the system of education in Peninsular Malaysia and Sarawak have begun to disappear and the federal government's control of educational policy and administration is virtually complete. The remaining differences are due to the late adoption by Sarawak of the National Language Policy, the physical separation of Sarawak from Peninsular Malaysia and historical factors.

Aims and Objectives

The government objectives for education are well summarised by the following quotation from the Third Malaysia Plan:

> "The education and training system has a multi-faceted role to play in a creation of a society based on the principals of the *Rukun Negara* (National Principles) and the realisation of the objectives of the New Economic Policy. The over-riding objective is national integration and unity. Bahasa Malaysia will continue to be implemented as a main medium of instruction to strengthen the basis for national integration and unity among the people of Malaysia, while the use of English will be extended as a strong second language. Policies and programmes for education and training will be geared to enable all Malaysians to participate more fully in the process of national development. To attain this objective, education and training will be oriented to meet the skilled manpower needs of the nation and to provide greater opportunity for education among those in the lower income groups and regions in the country.. . . The education and training system of Sabah and Sarawak will be progressively integrated with the national system."

Planning

The authority for planning is the federal Ministry of Education. Educational planning is included in the five-year plans. The Director of Education is responsible for submitting development plans for Sarawak to the central Ministry. The university sector of education is also planned by the Ministry of Education.

Current Trends

As already noted, the federal Ministry's control of education in Sarawak is now complete and there is no separate State education policy. Sarawak has lagged behind Peninsular Malaysia not only in its late adoption of the national language as the medium of instruction but also in educational provision, and much of the thrust of development is aimed at narrowing this gap. The technical and vocational education sector is seen as being particularly important and this is likely to be considerably expanded over the next few years. There is a recognised need for higher educational facilities within Sarawak and the permanent campuses of the Agricultural University and the MARA Institute of Technology which are planned for the 1980s should go a long way towards meeting this need.

Much effort is being expanded on re-training teachers for Bahasa Malaysia medium and this is currently a high priority. There is a recognition of the fact that the standard of English will go down unless the teaching of English is improved but so far few steps have been taken in this direction.

There is also recognition of the serious problems caused by unrestricted entry into secondary schools, including organisational problems and the teaching and management of children of wide ability and interest range. Seminars have been organised with the assistance of tutors from Britain to identify the problems and devise methods of overcoming them.

EXTRACT FROM THE REPORT OF THE INTER-GOVERNMENTAL COMMITTEE ON MALAYSIA, 1962

17 Certain aspects of religious education have been dealt with under the head "Religion". In addition:

   (a)   Although Education (item 13(a) of the Federal List in the Ninth Schedule) will be a Federal subject, the present policy and system of administration of education in North Borneo and Sarawak (including the present Ordinances) be undisturbed and remain under the control of the Government of the State until that Government otherwise agrees. In particular:

      (i)   the present policy in the Borneo States regarding the use of English should continue;

      (ii)   knowledge of the Malay language should not be required as a qualification for any educational opportunity until such time as the State Government considers that sufficient provision has been made to teach Malay in all schools in the State;

      (iii)   there should be no application to the Borneo States of any Federal requirements regarding religious education;

      (iv)   state provisions for the special position of the indigenous peoples should continue to apply;

(v) the Directors of Education in the Borneo States who would be officers serving in Federal posts and responsible to the Federal Ministry of Education through the Ministry of Education, should carry out much the same duties as they do at present in consultation with the State Government concerned;

(vi) to enable local wishes to be fully consulted and taken into account as far as possible, the Directors of Education of the Borneo States should continue to be advised by the respective existing Boards of Education and the local Education Committees; and

(vii) in the case of Sarawak the local authorities should continue to be used as agents for primary education; and

(b) When expansion of higher education facilities was being considered by the Malaysian Government the requirements of the Borneo States should be given special consideration and the desirability of locating some of the institutions in the Borneo States should be borne in mind.

448

SARAWAK - EDUCATIONAL PYRAMID 1977

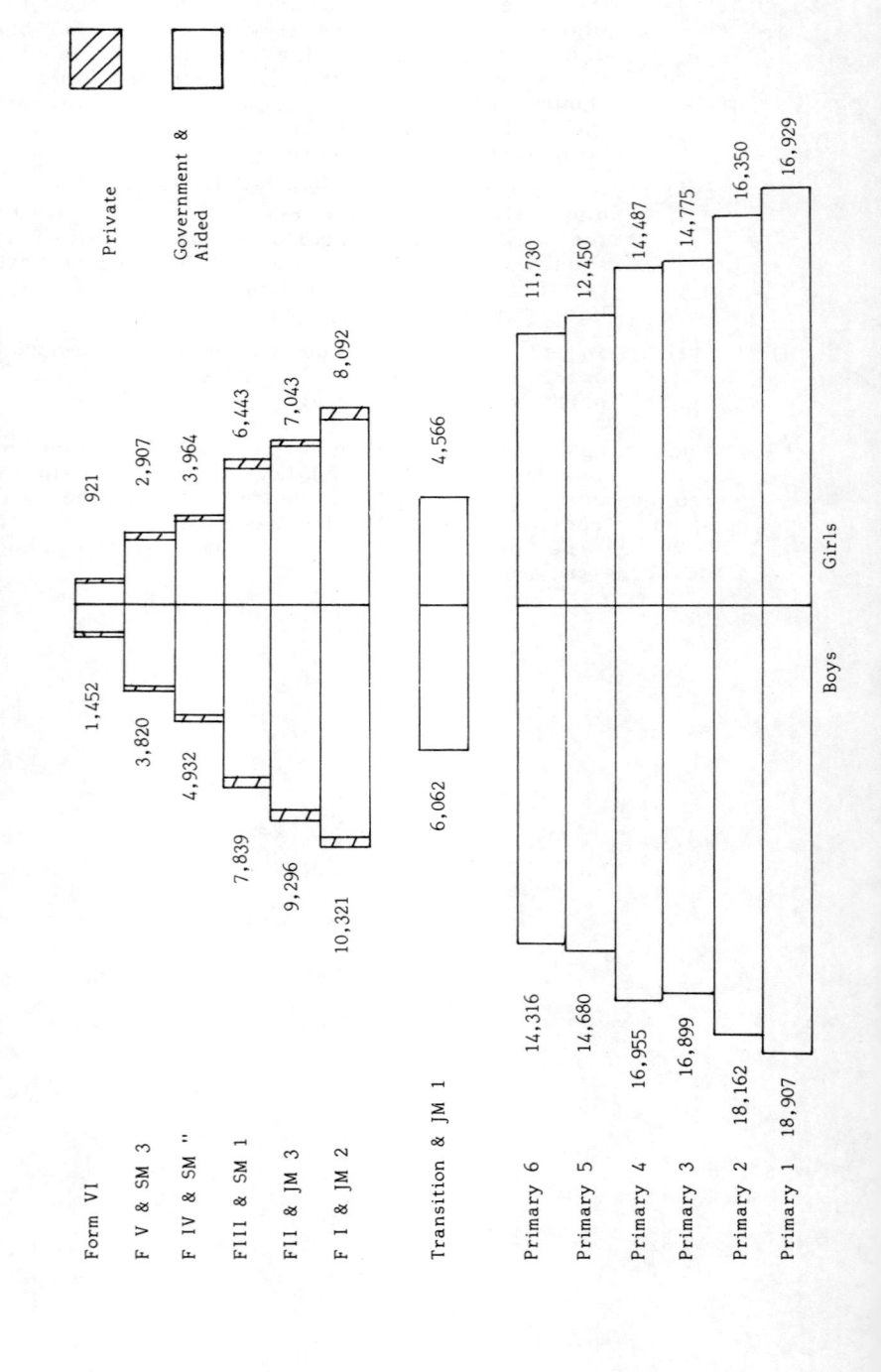

Private

Government & Aided

	Boys	Girls
Form VI	1,452	921
F V & SM 3	3,820	2,907
F IV & SM "	4,932	3,964
FIII & SM 1	7,839	6,443
FII & JM 3	9,296	7,043
F I & JM 2	10,321	8,092
Transition & JM 1	6,062	4,566
Primary 6	14,316	11,730
Primary 5	14,680	12,450
Primary 4	16,955	14,487
Primary 3	16,899	14,775
Primary 2	18,162	16,350
Primary 1	18,907	16,929

SARAWAK BASIC EDUCATIONAL STATISTICS
Enrolments in the Education System – 1977

Primary

	Male	Female	Total
Grade 1	18,907	16,929	35,836
Grade 2	18,162	16,350	34,512
Grade 3	16,899	14,775	31,674
Grade 4	16,955	14,487	31,442
Grade 5	14,680	12,450	27,130
Grade 6	14,316	11,730	26,046
Total	99,919	86,721	186,640

Secondary

	Male	Female	Total
Transition & JM	6,063	4,566	20,628
Form I & JM2	10,321	8,092	18,413
Form II & JM3	9,296	7,043	16,339
Form III & SM1	7,839	6,443	14,282
Form IV & SM2	4,932	3,964	8,896
Form V & SM3	3,820	2,907	6,727
Form VI Lower	854	521	1,375
Form VI Upper	598	400	998
Total	43,722	33,936	77,658

Vocational (secondary)

	Male	Female	Total
1st Year	168	–	168
2nd Year	119	–	119
3rd Year	57	–	57
1 year course	–	113	113
Total	344	113	457

Teacher Training (Secondary

	Male	Female	Total
1st year primary	262	209	471
2nd year primary	154	215	369
Total primary	416	424	840
1st year junior secondary	113	129	242
2nd year junior secondary	139	104	243
Total junior secondary	252	233	485
GRAND TOTAL	668	657	1,325

Public Examination Success Rates

Sarawak Junior and Lower Certificate of Education (English medium) (inc. unaided & private)

Year	No. of Candidates	Passes	Percentage Pass
1966	4,944	2,643	53.45
1970	5,785	3,794	65.58
1975	9,995	6,975	69.78
1976	13,001	9,548	66.64
1977	14,327	5,834	40.72
1978	14,933	7,001	46.88

Note: In 1977 the Sarawak Junior Examination was replaced by the Lower Certificate of Education.

Cambridge School Certificate (inc. private candidates)

1966	1,371	796	58.06
1970	3,894	2,238	57.47
1975	5,621	3,223	57.34
1976	5,987	3,291	54.97
1977	6,560	3,387	51.63
1978	8,000	3,296	41.20

Higher School Certificate (inc. private candidates)

Year	No. of Candidates	Passes	Percentage Pass
1966	168	112	66.67
1970	460	217	47.17
1975	1,441	422	29.29
1976	1,691	481	28.44
1977	1,973	547	27.72
1978	2,159	487	22.56

Total Public Recurrent Expenditure

Total recurrent expenditure figures for Sarawak are not available. For the total public recurrent expenditure for Malaysia please refer to the Education Profile for Peninsular Malaysia.

Percentage of GNP Spent on Education

Figures not available.

Total Population

1960 (census)	744,529
1970 (census)	976,269
1977 (estimate)	1,173,756

Percengage of Population in Each Age Group

	%
0 - 14	46.1
15 - 29	24.6
30 - 44	14.8
45 - 59	9.5
60 - 74	4.2
75+	0.8
	100.0

Number of Schools, Enrolments and Teachers

Primary

Year	No. of Schools	Enrolment	No. of Teachers Trained	No. of Teachers Untrained	Student-Staff Ratio
1950	Not available	37,670	Not available	Not available	—
1960	850	94,773	947	2,075	31:1
1970	1,220	144,007	2,671	1,733	32:1
1975	1,238	173,927	4,110	996	34:1
1977	1,254	186,640	4,218	1,398	33:1

Secondary

1950	Not available	1,753	Not available	Not available	—
1960	40	9,266	143	239	24:1
1970	112	35,459	562	862	25:1
1975	116	61,342	1,316	1,000	26:1
1977	118	77,658	1,834	1,104	26:1

Teacher Training

1960	1	306	Not available	Not available	—
1970	3	374	55	—	7:1
1975	3	879	79	—	11:1
1977	3	1,325	107	—	12:1

Number of Schools, Enrolments and Teachers (contd.)

Vocational

Year	No. of Schools	Enrolment	No. of Teachers Trained	No. of Teachers Untrained	Student-Staff Ratio
1970	2	209	Not available	Not available	–
1975	2	310	Not available	Not available	–
1977	2	457	41		11:1

Total Development Expenditure on Education 1977 (in M$000)

		% of total
Secondary Schools	20,472,762	62.9
Primary Schools	7,530,034	23.2
Teacher Training	3,502,450	10.8
Schools Broadcasting	31,846	0.1
Technical and Vocational Education	839,193	2.6
Loan to School Managements	100,000	0.3
Television Education	775	0.0
Education Offices	46,876	0.1
Total	32,523,936	100.0

Total Public Recurrent Expenditure on Education (in M$000)

	1965	%	1970	%	1975	%	1976	%	1977	%
Primary	11,703	65.7	18,028	65.8	41,841	56.2	44,975	52.7	49,393	49.0
Secondary	3,747	21.1	6,794	24.8	26,090	35.0	31,949	37.4	40,845	40.5
Teacher Training	774	4.3	1,094	4.0	2,421	3.2	3,313	3.9	4,464	4.4
Vocational Education	149	0.8	190	0.7	374	0.5	433	0.5	525	0.5
Other(including educational broadcasting)	78	0.4	41	0.2	263	0.4	407	0.5	994	1.0
Administration	1,348	7.6	1,231	4.5	3,502	4.7	4,270	5.0	4,640	4.6
	17,799	99.9	27,378	100.0	74,491	100.0	85,347	100.0	100,861	100.0

Singapore

CONTENTS

1 Geography	456
2 Population	458
3 Society and Culture	458
4 History and Politics	459
5 The Economy	461
6 The Education System	462
7 Educational Administration	468
8 Educational Finance	470
9 Development and Planning of the Education System	470

Singapore shares with its neighbours to the north and east - Malaysia, Thailand, the Philippines, Hong Kong, Japan - a relative economic prosperity and rapid economic growth in the 1970s. As in many countries of the south east Asian region, Singapore's society is culturally diverse and there are tensions between traditional values and the changes brought by social and economic modernisation. Again, as in Malaysia but also in the countries of the Indian sub-continent, the capacity of the education system to respond both to demands for economic and social change and to traditional attitudes is affected by a strong British colonial legacy.

Yet Singapore is in several ways, quite different from these other countries. Its population is relatively small but concentrated in a very small land area. It is a city state without a significant rural or agricultural sector. Singapore achieved a rate of economic growth and a degree of industrial development in the 1960s and 1970s which was unparalleled by any other south east Asian country. Its GNP per capita is second only to that of Japan in Asia and puts Singapore near the top of the league of middle income countries.

These economic conditions have meant that the education system in Singapore is not faced with quite the same issues as in other Asian countries; where it is, the outcomes often have been a little different. Universal primary education has been attained and the major quantitative aim of the Singapore government is to achieve mass lower secondary schooling. The demands of an industrialising economy have meant that technical and vocational education is relatively well developed. The cultural divisions between the Chinese majority and the Malay and Tamil minorities have been expressed in the education system by separate language schools or streams. But the pressures of a modern industrial economy have meant that the cultural identity of all three groups finds less and less expression in educational practice as English medium, schooling increasingly predominates.

The colonial educational legacy, however, has changed less and perhaps has been strengthened by the development of an economy in which an international language and international culture became more important. Institutional links with British educational institutes – universities for post-graduate study, British school examination boards, British expatriate teachers and educational materials – remain strong.

While the Singapore education system has not suffered from the difficulties of diversifying from English academic traditions of education which have affected some other from British colonies in Asia, the English traditions of early selection of students in the primary and secondary schools still persist and may create conflicts with popular demand for greater equality of opportunity. Similarly the English character of education in Singapore puts obstacles in the way of education being used to foster a strong and distinctive national identity.

1 GEOGRAPHY

Topography

The island of Singapore lies off the southern tip of the Malay peninsula to which it is connected by a Causeway. In area and shape it is similar to the Isle of Wight covering 225 square miles. At its widest point the island is 20 miles across; the maximum north to south measurement is 14 miles. For the most part the island is low lying, and much of the present land area consists of former swamp reclaimed from the sea or made habitable by drainage.

Climate

Situated some 70 miles from the equator, Singapore has a tropical climate with no clearly defined seasons. Annual rainfall is about 95 inches and the temperature rarely falls below 70°F or rises above 92°F. Humidity is high almost throughout the year.

Communications

By virtue of its position at the narrowest point of the Malacca Straits, Singapore has become the communications centre of South East Asia, and its port is the fourth busiest in the world.

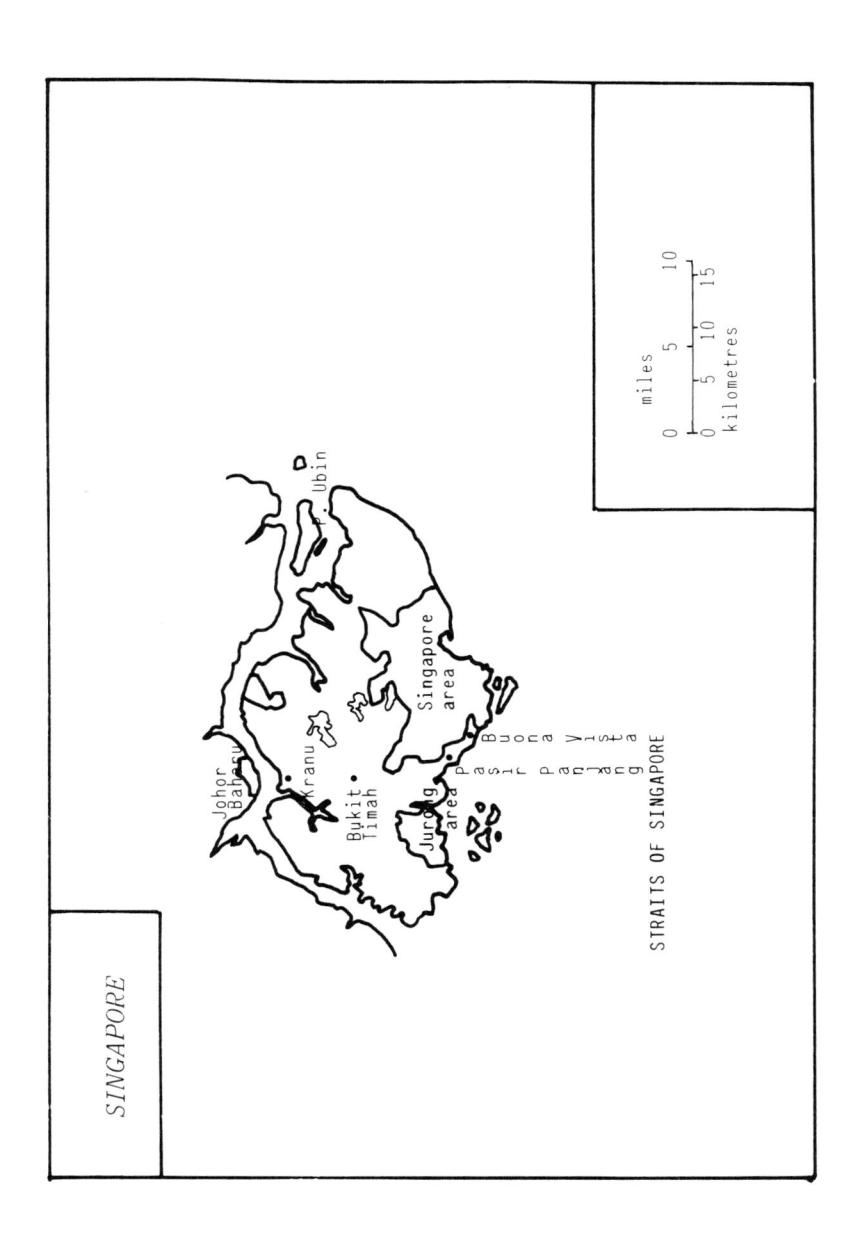

SINGAPORE

Johor Bahru
P. Ubin
Kranji
Bukit Timah
Singapore area
Jurong area
Pasir Panjang
Buona Vista
STRAITS OF SINGAPORE

miles 0 5 10
kilometres 0 5 10 15

Facilities for refuelling and repairing ships are unrivalled in South East Asia and the shipbuilding industry in Singapore, though relatively new, is enjoying a period of rapid expansion. Singapore has one international airport (Paya Lebar) and three subsidiary airfields, and there is a road/rail link with Malaysia over the Causeway. The road network is of a high standard and its further development is the subject of ambitious plans although there are problems due to traffic congestion and inadequate public transport services.

2 POPULATION
Growth

In 1979 the population was estimated at almost 3.4 million of whom 76% were of Chinese race, 15% were Malays, 7% were of Indian origin and 2% were Europeans, Eurasians and others. The annual rate of population increase was 1.0% in 1977-78. This compares with 2.8% per year in the early 1960s. The government has vigorously pursued a policy of population control through family planning and uses propaganda and financial disincentives to discourage families of more than two children.

Distribution

The population is concentrated in the city and in massive public housing developments on the fringes of the city area. There are further housing developments in the north of the island and in the west, at Jurong. This, together with the growth of industries outside the city, encourages a more even distribution of the population but with a population density of 9,500 per square mile the vast majority of people continue to live in an urban environment.

Language

The official languages in Singapore are Chinese, English, Malay and Tamil. Several dialects of Chinese are spoken and English is the language in which most government and much commercial business is conducted.

3 SOCIETY AND CULTURE
Social Patterns

Because of the low incidence of inter-marriage and the barriers of language and three main racial groups - Chinese, Indian, and Malay - have preserved their distinctive cultural and social identities. Among the Chinese majority there are further linguistic and cultural divisions arising from the different Chinese provinces from which they originate. However, the greatest division among the Chinese is between the products of Chinese language schools and English language schools and between those who espouse traditional Chinese values and those who find a more congenial tradition in Europe or America.

In general the English educated and western oriented have enjoyed greater job opportunities and economic mobility, and tend to favour modern and progressive ideas. The Chinese educated form a stronger cultural unit but find their career opportunities more limited; they also tend towards puritanical views on western habits and exercise a generally conservative influence.

The Malays are in general ill-adapted to the competitive urban life of modern Singapore and therefore enjoy relatively little economic power. Much of the small rural population consists of Malays, who also tend to occupy the more menial jobs in industry and commerce. Many of the best educated and most able Malays have undoubtedly preferred to make their own careers in Malaysia rather than Singapore.

Periodic communal violence was a feature of Singapore in the 1950s and early 1960s. There has been no recent case of such violence (though in 1969 a dangerous situation arising from events in Malaysia was only narrowly prevented from spreading to Singapore) and there appears to be little likelihood of a recurrence partly because of full employment and increasing prosperity and partly because of the efficiency of internal security arrangements.

Education is potentially an emotive issue for the various social groups particularly if it should seem that any particular language or culture is being suppressed. The policy of bilingualism whereby two languages (one being English) are used as media of instruction in the schools, is intended to blur the distinction between the different language streams, so making future dissent on the subject less likely. However, the importance attached to education in the Chinese medium by those who find their values in the Chinese cultural tradition should not be underestimated. Local prejudices on such matters as long hair and 'permissiveness' indicate how much the views of this group can affect national policies.

Religion

Although all the major religions of the world are represented in Singapore, the State is basically secular and a high degree of religious tolerance is apparent in all fields. A number of schools began as religious foundations or mission schools: these have mostly been assimilated into the State system, although some, especially the Roman Catholic schools retain their religious character.

4 HISTORY AND POLITICS

Development

Before the nineteenth century Singapore appears intermittently as a settlement and port of call in dispute between the rulers of Java and Siam for its strategic position. When in 1819 Sir Stamford Raffles took possession of the island for the East India Company he found little more than a fishing village set in jungle and mangrove swamps. His belief in its potential set in jungle and mangrove swamps. His belief in its potential as a trading centre was, however, amply justified. In 1826 Singapore became part of the Straits Settlements and by the end of the century it has developed into the main sea port and commercial *entrepôt* of South East Asia.

Independence

Occupied by the Japanese from 1942-45, Singapore became after the war a separate colony and in 1958 a self-governing state within the Commonwealth. In 1963 Singapore joined the newly formed State of Malaysia but two years later, in August 1965, separated from Malaysia as a result of political differences and became for the first time an independent sovereign nation.

Although the transition from colony to independent republic was not effected without some sharp differences of opinion, the colonial era, from which modern Singapore was created, has left no sense of bitterness and relations with Britain have continued to be close and friendly.

Politics

The People's Action Party (PAP) led by the dominating personality of Mr Lee Kuan Yew has been in power since 1959. Since 1968 the PAP has held all the seats in parliament.

The government's policies have been guided by pragmatism rather than ideology and the highest priority has been given to economic development. Its success in promoting the country's prosperity has secured the support of the great majority of the population and there is no reason to suppose that a change of government will take place in the foreseeable future as long as this prosperity is maintained. The two greatest dangers facing Singapore in the past were communalism and communism. Communalism, arising from the dissatisfaction of the Malays in Singapore, has become less important with the increasing prosperity of the country and the lapse of time since Singapore's separation from Malaysia. Improvements in Singapore's relations with Malaysia over the last two years have also diminished the danger of communal troubles. The danger of communism, very real in the late 1950s and early 1960s, has virtually disappeared as a result of full employment, rising standards of living and strong measures against left wing leaders. However, the government has continued to pursue a stringent anti-communist policy.

Although Singapore has a parliamentary system based on the British model, it has its own characteristics and a different mode of government. Ideas come almost exclusively from the top while parliament is called upon to ratify rather than to debate decisions taken at ministerial level. The distinction between the official and the political level is not as clear cut as in Britain and quite minor decisions may be taken by ministers. One effect of this is that the government is in a good position to direct all aspects of government to a desired end. Thus, for example, the close relationship between the government and the National Trade Union Congress has enabled the government to maintain a high degree of labour discipline while restraining the growth of wages in the interests of encouraging foreign investment.

International Relations

Singapore is a member of the British Commonwealth and has been an active participant in its organisation. Close relations with Britain have been diversified particularly as the British presence in the Far East has declined and as Singapore has become a major economic and financial centre in South East Asia. Good relations have been developed with neighbouring countries, and despite an anti-communist internal policy, with China.

5 THE ECONOMY

Economic Situation

Since attaining full independence in 1965 Singapore has set a fast pace of economic development. Excellent communications with the rest of the world, established port facilities and good internal communications all helped to give the Republic a head start. Since 1970 annual growth has been high and per capita GNP at US$3,295 in 1978 was second only to Japan in Asia. Political stability, a relatively high level of education, low labour costs and a disciplined work force combined with the government's determination to foster economic growth and encourage foreign investment have provided the incentives for a massive influx of foreign capital. Formerly dependent on the *entrepôt* trade for most of its commerce, Singapore has become a substantial centre for manufactures of all kinds and the leading financial centre in South East Asia. Tourism also developed in the 1970s.

The government has maintained close control over the development of the economy, and investment projects have been carefully selected. In recent years this has involved a swing away from labour-intensive to capital-intensive industries. Singapore, notorious in the 1950s and early 1960s for its high rate of unemployment, is now short of labour and is obliged to allow a substantial influx of non-skilled workers from Malaysia and Indonesia. The social problems caused by these immigrant workers and the uncertain future for any country whose livelihood depends on low wages have encouraged the government to place the emphasis on high technology capital-intensive industries. The clearest case of this is the petroleum industry. Singapore is the world's third largest centre for oil refining and the industry is the largest in Singapore, yet only some 2,000 people are directly employed by the oil companies here.

Industry

Singapore is very conscious of the need to produce a skilled work force to satisfy the demands of its general economic policies. With this in mind strong emphasis is placed on vocational training and technical education. The Singapore Armed Forces (national service is compulsory) are regarded as one source of technically trained personnel. A section of the Ministry of Labour (the National Productivity Board) is exclusively concerned with training for industry and the upgrading of technical and management skills.

Singapore has no useful mineral deposits or other valuable physical resources. It is dependent on Malaysia for its supplies of water which are drawn from reservoirs in Johore and carried to Singapore by pipeline.

6 THE EDUCATION SYSTEM

Objectives

Over the past decade education in Singapore has evolved two primary objectives. These are, first, to contribute to the building of a cohesive multi-racial society. Before independence Singapore was in the words of Mr Lee Kuan Yew: "A conglomeration of migrants, each one for himself". Its transient population of Chinese, Malays, Indians and others came in the hope of making a little more money than was possible in their home countries, and had little interest or motivation besides. Through education it is intended to fashion national consciousness and a national identity. Secondly, education is a means to develop Singapore's only natural resource - its people - by providing the know-how and skills necessary for modernisation and the furthering of its progress as an independent commercial and industrial city state.

Within the context of these major objectives, the stated aims of education are as follows:

(i) to provide at least ten years' schooling to every child from the age of 6. Primary education is free for children of Singapore citizens, and thereafter assistance for those who need it is given in the form of bursaries, remission of fees and loan of textbooks

(ii) to establish the principle of bilingualism throughout the system. Education in the schools is available in the four official languages, Chinese, English, Malay and Tamil. Parents are free to choose the medium of instruction, but pupils are increasingly being required to study a certain range of subjects and reach an adequate degree of proficiency in a second language. Either the language of instruction or the second language must be English

(iii) to emphasise at all stages the importance of science and mathematics and technical training in relation to the Republic's manpower and development needs

(iv) to inculcate attitudes of social discipline and responsibility, racial harmony and loyalty to the Republic. To this end there is a heavy emphasis on extra-curricular activities, especially through organisations such as the National Cadet Corps, Police Cadet Corps, Red Cross Society, Scouts and Guides.

Planning

In education as in other sectors planning is highly centralised and can readily adapt to changing priorities. During the early 1960s the need was to have enough schools, and teachers, trained or untrained, to meet the rapid expansion of the educational system. In 1968, following the announcement of the run-down of the British Services, the efforts of the Ministry of Education's Planning Unit were concentrated on re-tooling the system to produce technically qualified manpower for industrial development. In 1972 the Unit was expanded into the Planning and Development Section, concerned to make recommendations for additional schools to service the high density new towns now under construction.

Following a reorganisation in 1973 three main divisions were created in the Ministry with responsibility for Schools, Services and Development. The Development Division has taken over the planning function and is expected to work in conjunction with the Institute of Education. These administrative changes have hardly affected the actual process of planning, which continues to be directed by a small group of senior officials. Currently the emphasis is on raising the quality of education by means of curriculum reform, better amenities and improved teaching methods.

Pre-School Education

Until 1978 pre-school education was provided by private organisations (churches and private individuals) and by the People's Association. Since 1978 there has been an expansion of government provision - so that enrolments rose from 4,883 in 1975 to 11,529 in 1979. Almost 40% of pupils were in government schools in 1979 and almost half the five year olds in the country were receiving pre-school education.

Primary Education

There are six grades of primary education for children aged 6 and above. There is practically universal enrolment and equality between girls and boys. There are four types of school based on the language of instruction that is used - English, Chinese, Malay and Tamil. Parents are free to choose the kind of school to which they send their children. There have always been far fewer pupils in the Malay and Tamil schools compared to English and Chinese but in the course of the 1970s many Chinese parents began to send their children to English rather than Chinese schools because of the economic advantages of a knowledge of English and because the medium of the Chinese schools - Mandarin - was often quite different from the Chinese dialects used at home.

The distribution of primary pupils in the various language schools and the growing popularity of English schools are indicated by the following figures:

Year	English	Chinese	Malay	Tamil
1970	62.5	31.7	5.4	0.3
1979	83.4	16.2	0.3	0.02

In all schools, however, English is taught as part of an official bilingual policy.

Primary schools can also be divided between government schools, government aided schools and unaided private schools. Enrolments in government schools have been increasing while those in other types are declining so that there were only 87 pupils in unaided schools in 1980 and only 26% of pupils were in aided primary schools in 1980 compared to 36% in 1970.

Primary school pupils follow a common course for three years when they concentrate on learning of languages. In the fourth, fifth and sixth grades, there are three streams - the Normal Bilingual Stream, the Extended Bilingual Stream and the Monolingual Stream. In the Normal Stream are pupils who are expected to pass the Primary School Leaving Examination after six years of primary school. In the Extended Bilingual Stream, pupils study two languages, but take seven or eight years to complete the course. Monolingual stream pupils study only one language.

Pupils are allocated to stream according to ability and potential with the Normal Stream containing the most able and the Monolingual Stream the least able pupils. Pupils are assessed regularly to allow lateral movement between streams.

The curriculum consists of three blocks - the English language block in which Mathematics and Science are taught (43% of the time); the mother tongue block including civics, history, geography, art and crafts (43% of the time) and a third block of physical education, music, etc. (14% of the time).

The Primary School Leaving Examination consists of tests in two languages, mathematics and science. About 55%-60% pass and are admitted to secondary schools. Others stay on to repeat the examination.

There is a shortage of schools so that a double shift system is used with one set of pupils and teachers using the school in the morning and another in the afternoon.

Secondary Education

Secondary education is divided into two stages – the four-year course leading to the Singapore-Cambridge GCE 'O' level examination followed by a two-year course culminating in the 'A' level examination. All six years are provided in some schools while others cover the four-year first stage only. There are nine Junior Colleges covering only the 'A' level course. There are both government and aided schools at each level. As in primary schools, the double shift system is common.

Again as in primary schools, there are different classes and streams according to language, and to the ability of the students. In 1980 76% of secondary students were in English streams, 23% in Chinese classes, 0.6% in Malay groups and 9.06% (107 pupils) in Tamil streams. The equivalent proportions in 1970 were 62% English, 32% Chinese, 6% Malay and 0.2% Tamil. The three ability streams are the Special Course, the Express Course and the Normal Course. The top 10% of pupils (on the basis of primary school examination) are placed in the Special Course. They are expected to complete 'O' level course in four years and to study English and their mother tongue as first languages. The Express Course contains about 45% of students who are expected to gain at least three passes after four years in 'O' level but who study English as a first language and their mother tongue as a second language.

The Normal Course contains the 45% or so of pupils who study for a lower level examination – the Certificate of Secondary Education after four years and perhaps take 'O' level after a fifth year. They are not expected to qualify for the second stage two-year course. They concentrate on English and study their mother tongue at a lower level.

There is lateral movement between streams. Some unsuccessful students are channelled into Vocational and Industrial Training Bound courses during the secondary school course.

The curriculum of the secondary school course includes English, the second language, mathematics, science, literature, history, geography, art and craft, music, PE, civics, current affairs, and moral education. In the latter two years English, the second language, science and mathematics are core subjects while students choose options from the other subjects.

In the pre-university course students take three 'A' level subjects together with a general course and a second language course. The same academic subjects are offered as in the secondary school together with economics and computer science. The most able students complete the 'A' level course in two years in Junior Colleges while the others take the course in three years in a secondary school.

Vocational Education

Vocational training is provided by nine vocational institutes set up in 1967/68 as part of Singapore's policy of rapid industrialisation. Student intake continues to rise steeply. Each institute specialises in craft/artisan/apprentice level courses in its own sector of the metal, building, electrical and motor vehicle trades and the manual and applied arts. For secondary school leavers one- or two-year programmes of general as well as technical education lead to the Trade Certificate; there are also six-month artisan courses designed to provide primary school leavers with a basic industrial skill. The vocational institutes, formerly controlled by the Technical Education Department of the Ministry of Education, are now the responsibility of the Industrial Training Board, a semi-autonomous body established in 1973 to involve the industrial sector more directly in training.

A Hotel and Catering Training Centre is run in association with a fully operational commercial hotel.

Higher Education

The university and the other tertiary institutions are statutory bodies and therefore autonomous although the Ministry of Education is represented on their governing boards and is concerned to supervise and coordinate their policies. The medium of instruction in institutions of higher education is now English.

Admissions are based on the results of the Singapore-Cambridge GCE 'O' and 'A' level examinations. Total enrolments in higher education (excluding teacher training) rose from 7,000 in 1962 to nearly 15,000 in 1972. A substantial proportion of students in higher education are not Singaporeans, e.g. 38% of students at the University of Singapore are from Malaysia or other countries of the region.

The National University of Singapore operates generally on the British pattern and offers the usual range of subject options: since 1968 its priorities have been directed by the Vice-Chancellor, Dr Toh Chin Chye, firmly towards the subject areas of the curriculum contributing directly to economic and industrial development. Nanyang University, which was intended originally to cater for the products of Chinese medium secondary schools by conducting courses entirely in Mandarin, was amalgamated with the National University in 1980.

Technical training at technician diploma level is provided by three institutions with a current combined student intake three times greater than in 1960. The Singapore Polytechnic was the first to be established and has always used English as its medium of instruction. Ngee Ann Technical College originally used only Mandarin but switched to English in 1971, as did the Nanyang Technological Institute. Ngee Ann now awards joint diplomas with the Polytechnic of Central London. The Singapore Technical Institute was set up in 1969 and is administered by the Industrial Training Board, its diplomas being of equal status to those of the Polytechnic and Ngee Ann Technical College.

Concerned to establish itself as a 'brain resource centre' for South East Asia, the Republic hosts various regional bodies such as the South East Asia Ministgers of Education Organisation (SEAMEO) Regional English Language Centre, the Regional Institute for Higher Education, the Institute of South East Asian

Studies and CEPTA.

Teacher Training

It is intended that all teachers should be professionally qualified, but although much progress has been made still roughly one primary teacher in ten is untrained.

The former Teacher Training College has been primarily responsible for teacher education. The Institute prepared graduates for professional diplomas and post-graduate degrees of the University of Singapore, arranged in-service courses and undertook the retraining of arts teachers to enable them to teach technical subjects.

In 1973 the TTC was reorganised as a statutory body and renamed the Institute of Education. The Institute offers a one-year Diploma course for graduates and a two-year Certificate course for secondary school leavers with GCE 'A' level subjects. It has absorbed the Research Unit of the Ministry of Education and operates a local research programme. Post-graduate students continue to be prepared for higher degrees of the University of Singapore.

Non-Formal Education

Adult Education Board

Since it was formed in 1960 the AEB has tended increasingly to underpin the formal education system, i.e. by running courses to prepare drop-outs at primary level for employment or further training in the vocational institutes, secondary and pre-university level evening classes, and courses for those having difficulty with the second language. Other courses are concerned with self-improving practical or commercial subjects as well as with recreation and leisure activities.

The People's Association

Since 1960 the People's Association, a statutory body funded by the Ministry of Culture, has sought to provide a means of two-way communication between the people and the government, and to encourage mass participation in recreational, cultural and vocational activities. This it does in 184 Community Centres throughout the Republic. The great majority of those using the Centres are from the Chinese-educated and lower income groups and efforts are being made to broaden the membership by improving the quality of Centre programmes and amenities. The Association makes a significant contribution to the regular and well-orchestrated national campaigns, e.g. for Family Planning or against Crime and Pollution or to Keep Singapore Clean.

Department of Extra-Mural Studies, University of Singapore

The University has since 1964 organised programmes of study to enable adults to further their adult education in subjects appropriate to University sponsorship, e.g. economics and business administration, science and technology, and law. The majority of students participate in order to improve on their graduate or secondary school qualifications, and very few have only a primary or lower secondary school background.

National Service

All male Singaporeans are at age 18 subject to a 30-month period of National Service in the armed services or police, during which time they are offered language courses and other learning opportunities as well as education in citizenship and nation building.

ETV and the Educational Media Service

Established in 1966, the ETC service is part of the Ministry of Education and is located in the Institute of Education. Its policy is decided by a broad based advisory committee answerable to the Minister of Education together with specialist sub-committees which determine the nature and content of a wide range of teaching support programmes used throughout the school system.

The ETC service has recently merged with the Audio-Visual Inspectorate of the Ministry to create the Singapore Educational Media Service. Increasing attention is being given to the range of instructional materials produced to support the ETV programmes, e.g. teachers' notes, charts, tapes, transparencies and multi-media kits. There is an instructional materials library mainly concerned with distributing films to schools, and it is planned to create a number of resource centres where teachers can make their own teaching materials.

7 EDUCATIONAL ADMINISTRATION

Overall responsibility rests with the Minister for Education, assisted by a Minister of State and a Parliamentary Secretary. The Industrial Training Board, on which sit representatives of business and industry, has charge of institutions concerned with industrial training and apprenticeship. The training and utilisation of scientific and technical manpower at professional level come within the portfolio of the Minister of Science and Technology, who since 1968 has also been Vice-Chancellor of the University of Singapore.

All government and government aided schools are under the control of the Ministry of Education. Government schools are established, financed and managed by the Ministry. Government aided schools were first established by religious missions and other bodies and are administered by school management boards: the control exercised by the Ministry over these schools extends

ADMINISTRATIVE CHART

```
                                    Cabinet
                                       |
                         Minister for Education
                         Minister of State
                         Parliamentary Secretary
                                       |
                              Ministry of Education ─────────── Industrial Training Board
                                       |                                (Director)
        ┌──────────────┬───────────────┼───────────────┐                    |
   Schools Division  Services Division  Development Division        Technical education
   (Deputy Director) (Deputy Director)  (Deputy Director)           Vocational training
        |                  |                  |                     Trade teaching
   Primary Schools    Examinations       Planning & Statistics      Apprenticeship &
   Secondary Schools  ETV & Media        Curriculum development     in-plant training
   School organisations Guidance/Counselling Textbooks                      |
   Administration &   Special education  School libraries           ┌──────┴──────┐
   Inspection         Private schools    Publications         Vocational      STI
                                                              institutions    Hotel/Catering
                                                                              Training School

   Kindergartens    Primary    Secondary    Junior      Centralised
   Private Schools  schools    schools      colleges    workshops


   ┌──────────────────────────────────────────────────────────────────────────┐
   │ University of │ Nanyang    │ Institute of │ Adult Education │ Polytechnic │ Ngee Ann        │
   │ Singapore     │ University │ Education    │ Board           │             │ Technical College│
   └──────────────────────────────────────────────────────────────────────────┘


   ▭ = Statutory bodies
```

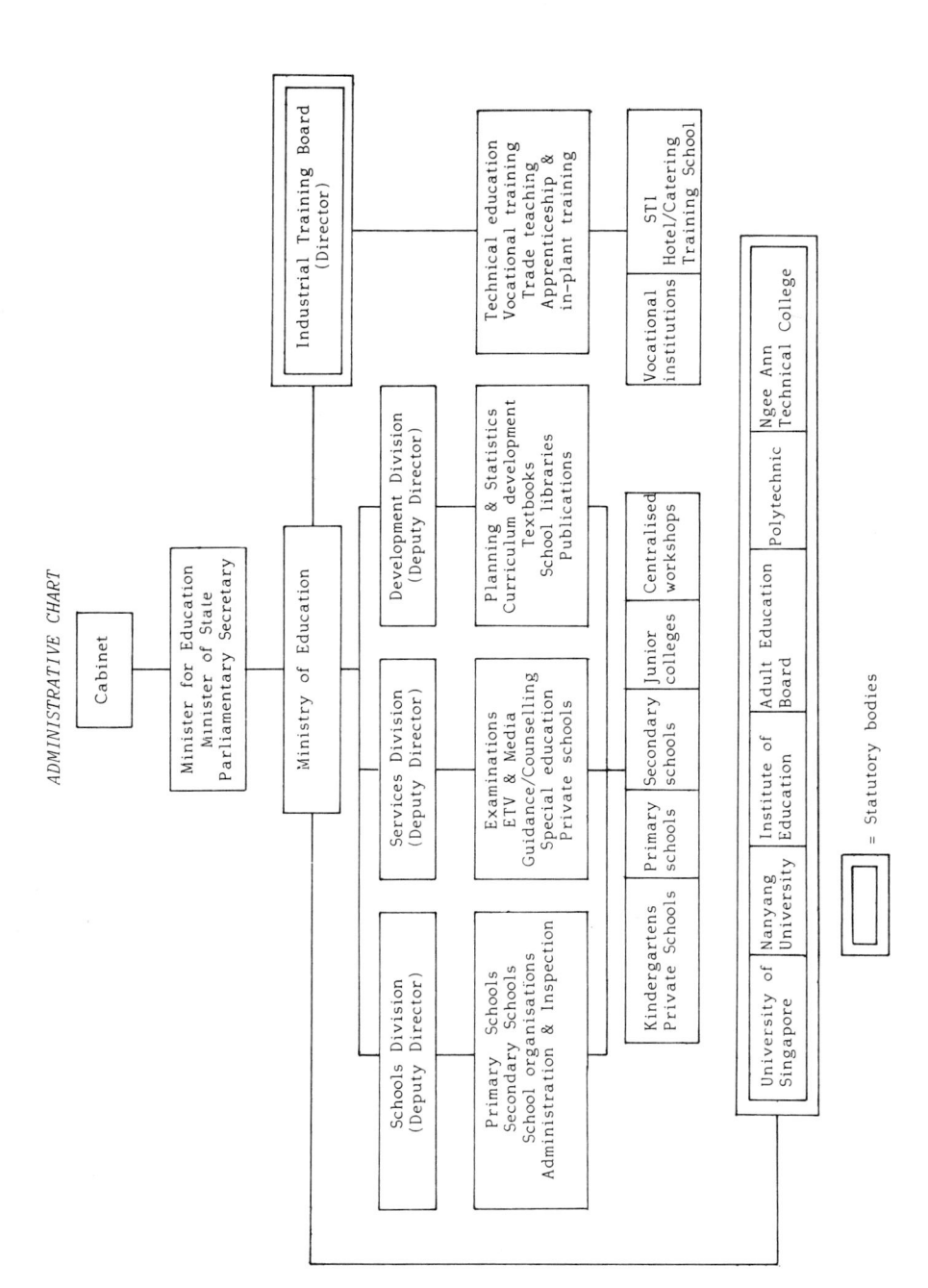

469

from approving the appointment of teachers to overall supervision of all aspects of the schools' activities. The staff of government aided schools are not full government employees although their salaries are based on those of the government schools. Curricula for government and government aided schools are prescribed by the Ministry, and common syllabi are followed as far as possible in the four language streams.

General supervision is exercised by Inspectors responsible for implementing the policies of the three divisions of the Ministry, and for the teaching of technical subjects and workshop practice in schools. Industrial training in the vocational institutes is supervised by superintendents of the Industrial Training Board.

8 EDUCATIONAL FINANCE

Formerly the biggest item in the national budget, education now takes second place after Defence. Expenditure on education has risen steadily since 1960 but expressed as a percentage of total government expenditure has shown a downward trend from 24.3% in 1964 to 11.7% in 1970, and to 7.5% in 1978. Voluntary contributions from private sources, though encouraged, are relatively small. The proportions of the educational budget spent at the primary, secondary and tertiary levels were in 1962 64%, 20% and 16%; in 1978 39%, 37% and 15%. In recent years the emphasis has been increasingly on technical and vocational education.

Government aided schools receive grants of up to 50% for development costs and a per capita grant for recurrent costs based on pupil enrolment. The universities and other tertiary institutions receive block grants annually from the Ministry of Education to finance capital development as well as recurrent costs.

9 DEVELOPMENT AND PLANNING OF THE EDUCATION SYSTEM

The government prides itself on its pragmatic approach to education as to other matters and there is no great gulf between theory and practice in the education system. Singapore has had considerable success in achieving the aims defined earlier. It is well on the way to a basic ten years of schooling for all; determined efforts are being made towards bilingualism: curricula have been revised and teachers re-trained to emphasise education for economic development, and there are clear indications of progress in the direction of social integration and national awareness.

However, the pace of change has brought its problems. The crucial importance of educational qualifications in terms of job opportunity results in a relentless dedication to passing achievement-oriented examinations and a growing competition especially for entry to pre-university classes and tertiary institutions The policy of bilingualism is an ambitious one (most children entering Primary 1 know neither English nor Mandarin) and is putting the whole system under strain. Mass transfers of teachers within schools and language streams will be necessary for its implementation, as will the adequate provision of suitable teaching materials and some fusion of the differing educational styles of the Chinese and English sections: Chinese medium schools have traditionally been more authoritarian than English medium schools. It remains to be seen, for example, how far the most child centred approach of the Ministry's Primary Pilot Project which involves the planned integration of English language, mathematics and science (and to which British Council and CEDO staff have contributed) will take root in the Chinese medium schools.

These achievements have, moreover, been made possible by a degree of centralised direction and control, motivated by political and cultural as well as educational considerations, which lies heavily across the system. Principals and teachers have little say in professional policy; changes and initiatives start at the top rather than in the classroom, and at tertiary level student admissions and activities are subject to close surveillance. Teachers' associations and student unions are restricted in their role and effectively anaesthetised. All this has its effect on the morale of the teaching profession, which is not attracting top quality recruits. The development of professionalism has been retarded and there is a constant need to retrain and upgrade teachers to maintain academic standards. The government is conscious of these weaknesses and the recent restructuring of the Education Service and revision of salaries are aimed at improving current opportunities and the status of teachers.

Internal Efficiency

The internal problems of the educational system may be summarised as follows:

(i) too much centralised and bureaucratic control and direction

(ii) excessive dominance of the system by formal examinations

(iii) consequent apathy of principals and teachers and stress on conformity rather than independence and initiative

(iv) shortages of trained and graduate teachers especially those with the right language qualifications and teachers of technical subjects

(v) strains resulting from the demands of bilingualism, crowded curricula and a heavy burden of semi-official 'extra-curricular' activities.

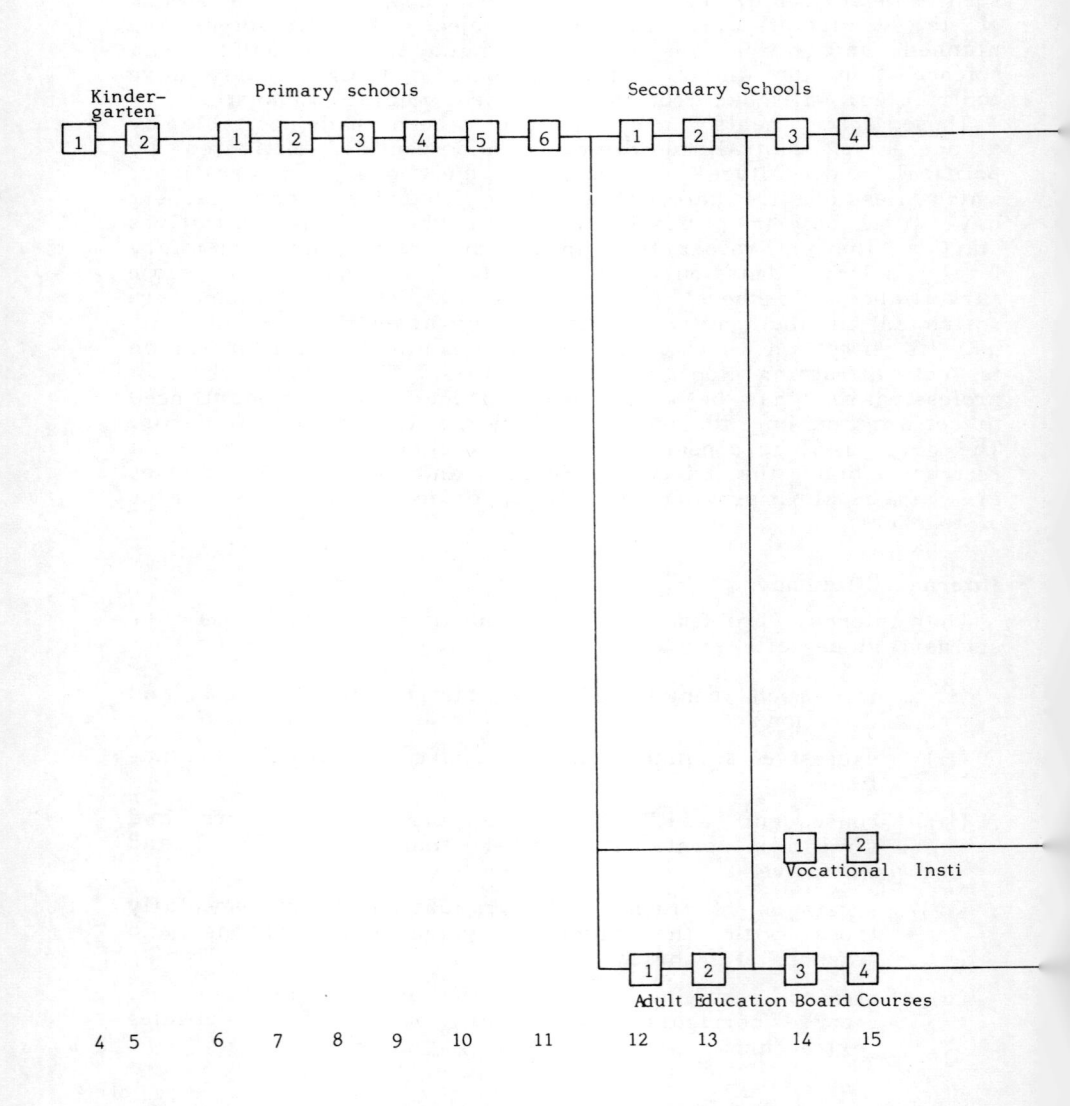

THE EDUCATIONAL SYSTEM

Kinder-garten	Primary schools	Secondary Schools

| 1 | 2 | | 1 | 2 | 3 | 4 | 5 | 6 | | 1 | 2 | | 3 | 4 |

| 1 | 2 |
Vocational Insti

| 1 | 2 | | 3 | 4 |
Adult Education Board Courses

4   5   6   7   8   9   10   11   12   13   14   15

OF SINGAPORE

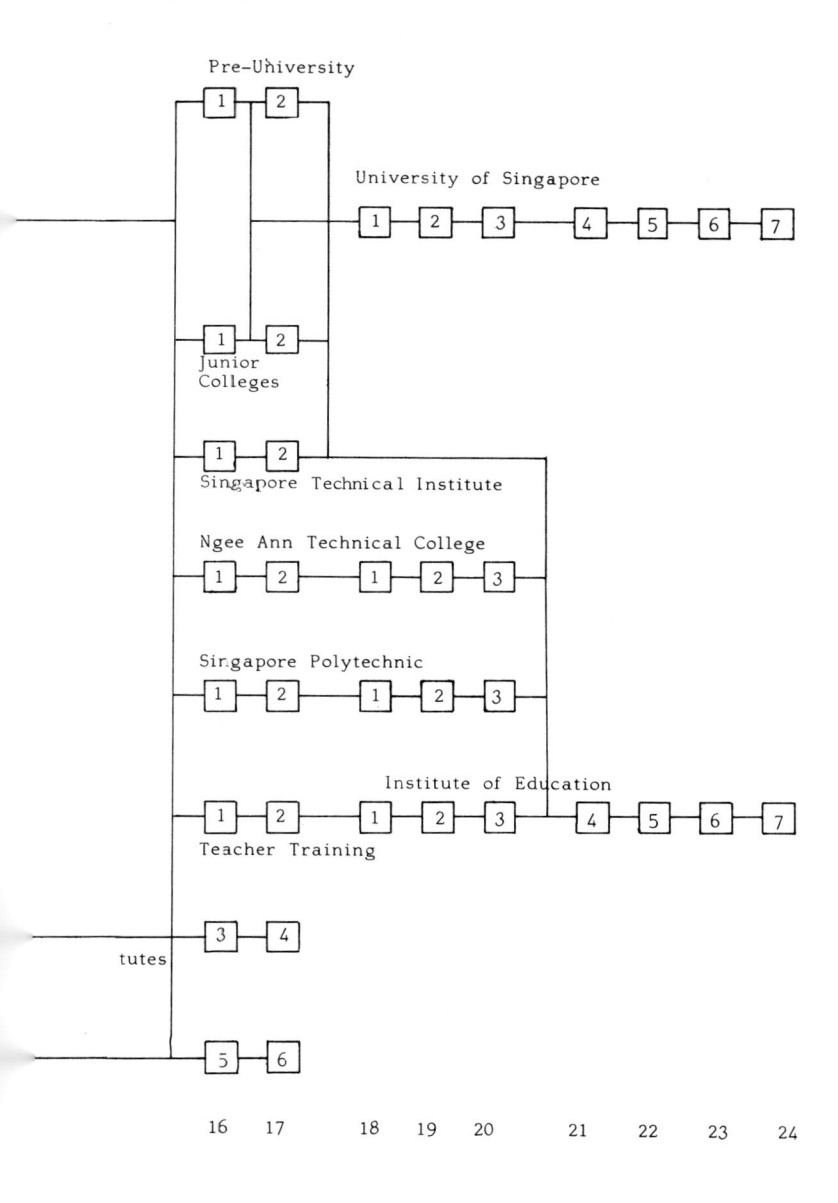

Pre-University
1 — 2

University of Singapore
1 — 2 — 3 — 4 — 5 — 6 — 7

1 — 2
Junior Colleges

1 — 2
Singapore Technical Institute

Ngee Ann Technical College
1 — 2 — 1 — 2 — 3

Singapore Polytechnic
1 — 2 — 1 — 2 — 3

Institute of Education
1 — 2 — 1 — 2 — 3 — 4 — 5 — 6 — 7
Teacher Training

tutes
3 — 4

5 — 6

16 17 18 19 20 21 22 23 24

External Relevance

The spectre of unemployable school leaver or arts graduate has been well and truly laid in Singapore. The reorientation of the education system has undoubtedly contributed to high growth rates and full employment. There are, however, signs of over-reaction and the imbalance resulting from relative neglect of the arts and the humanist subjects gives cause for concern.

Trends and Possibilities

Due to a stabilising of population growth the rapid expansion of the education system up to and during the 1960s has levelled off. Since 1968 there has been a decrease in enrolments and relatively less overall public spending on education. However, expnsion in secondary and tertiary education continues apace especially at levels and in institutions concerned with scientific, technical and industrial training, and in the University of Singapore.

A system which allows parents to choose the medium of instruction for their children will come under strain when one of the languages acquires greater prestige and commercial value than the others. the shift towards English has created the need for educational reorganisation.

The Ministry's policy of bilingualism is partly a reaction to the logistic stresses and strains created by this trend towards English and partly the result of fears of over-exposure to Western cultural influences. The Ministry is therefore concerned to emphasise the importance of mother tongue (the 'cultural' language) as well as English (the 'working' language). Nevertheless three out of the four papers in the Primary School Leaving Examination are examined in English, whatever the nominal medium of instruction of the school.

Although the trend towards English may be temporarily slowed by the policy of bilingualism, the fact is that English is increasingly recognised as the language of international communication and of leadership in government and commerce, and this appears likely to ensure its continued dominance. There are current indications of declilning standards in both English and Chinese in the schools, and fears that it may be more difficult than the authorities realise to establish either as an effective lingua franca are growing. Should it succeed, however, bilingualism will make education in Singapore at once more homogeneous and more likely to achieve its wider aims.

SINGAPORE BASIC EDUCATIONAL STATISTICS

Population	
1970	1979
2,070,000	2,363,000

Enrolment Ratios 1970 and 1979

Primary = Enrolments divided by the population aged 6-11
Secondary = Enrolments divided by the population aged 12-17
Higher = enrolments divided by the population aged 18-24

	Primary	Secondary	Higher
1970	105	46	6.8
1979	107	59	8.8*

* 1978

Institutions, Teachers and Students 1970 & 1980

	1970	1980
Pre-primary		
Schools	48	121*
Teachers	200	558
Pupils	4,822	11,529
Primary		
Schools	427	342
Teachers	12,248	11,267
Pupils	363,518	296,608
Secondary		
Schools	125†	144
Teachers	6,550	8,019
Pupils	145,740	170,316
Technical & Vocational (excluding higher)		
Institutes	12†	17
Teachers	–	912
Students	2,879†	12,543
Higher		
Institutions	7†	4
Teachers	1,070†	1,947
Students	12,970†	22,511

* 1979   † 1969

Higher Education Students by Field of Study 1978

	Students	% female
Education and Teacher Training	5,472	72
Humanities	2,056	60
Law	414	53
Commerce and Business	2,597	47
Natural Science	1,520	47
Medicine and Related Fields	846	45
Engineering	9,827	16
Architecture	965	41
Other	417	6

Government Educational Expenditure 1970 and 1978

Year	As a % of Total Government Spending	As a % of GNP
1970	11.7	3.1
1978	7.5	2.5

Government Educational Expenditure by Level of Education

Year	Primary	Secondary	Higher	Other
1970	44.2%	33.5%	14.7%	7.6%
1978	38.5%	36.7%	14.7%	20.0%

Basic Social and Economic Data

Gross National Product per capita 1979 - US$3,830
Annual Growth of GNP per capita 1960-79 - 7.4%
Life expectancy 1979 - 71 years
Proportion of the labour force employed in:

Agriculture		
	1960	8%
	1979	2%
Industry		
	1960	23%
	1979	38%
Services		
	1960	69%
	1979	60%

Sri Lanka

CONTENTS

1	Geography	480
2	Population	482
3	Society and Culture	484
4	History and Politics	486
5	The Economy	488
6	The Education System	489
7	Educational Administration	501
8	Educational Finance	503
9	Development and Planning of the Education System	503

Sri Lanka has a degree of educational provision which is highly developed – almost over-developed – in relation to the economic conditions which prevail and in comparison with the other countries of the Indian sub-continent. Universal primary education has almost been achieved whle over half the appropriate age group is in secondary schooling. Only at university level does Sri Lankan provision fall to about the norm of other countries at similar levels of economic development.

Some of the political instability which has characterised Sri Lanka in the last ten years or more can be attributed to this high level of educational provision. there is chronic unemployment or under-employment among secondary school and university graduates which has fed political unrest. The communal conflict between the majority Jinhalese and the Tamils who form 20% of the population is inflamed further by the relatively high level of education among the Tamils which has given them access to more highly regarded and lucrative posts.

Yet the comparatively high level of educational provision in Sri Lanka in many ways enriches the country and its society. It may be linked to strong popular demand for education which in turn can be related to the economic, zonal and religious structures of the nation. There is less resistance to education, especially of women, than in the Moslem states to the North. The prevalence of wage earning occupations in the tea and rubber plantations since the nineteenth century have created positive attitudes to education.

However, there are problems and conflicts in the education system and in its relationship with the under society. The quality of primary education is affected by the large number of untrained teachers and the small size of many schools. Secondary schooling to a large extent follows the British colonial model with an emphasis on literary and academic education. Students with this type of background increasingly find it difficult to get appropriate employment when clerical and administrative occupations in an agricultural and commercial economy have not expanded as rapidly as the provision of education.

There are major problems in the relationship between the education system - even if it is reformed - to give greater emphasis to technical studies as the Sri Lankan government has attempted. The per capita income is low. The economy is based on agriculture, especially the export of tea and rubber. The rate of economic growth has been low in comparison with may other Third World countries. There are likely to be great difficulties in absorbing and using educated people effectively in such an economic structure.

1 GEOGRAPHY

Topography

Originally named Ceylon, the island was renamed Sri Lanka when it became a republic in May 1972. Its area is 25,332 square miles (64,750 sq km) approximately half the size of England. Its greatest width is 140 miles (224 km) and length north to south 270 miles (432 km). It is separated from India by 30 miles of the Palk Straits, which are so shallow that ships cannot pass round the north of the island. While the greater part of the country is low lying and flat, the high central massif in the south west is the main feature of the island's physical structure and the dominating factor in climate and fertility. In many places the plateau rises steeply in magnificent escarpments with a few peaks over 7,000 feet (2,100 metres). The country is relatively well watered by short and steep rivers.

Climate

The climate is essentially tropical, but equitable. It varies from the warmth of the plains where temperatures change little throughout the year (average 27°C) to the temperate atmosphere of the hills. As in most countries lying close to the equator, the seasons are not well defined (there is no winter) and the length of the days is almost equal throughout the year. The island lies in the path of two monsoons: the south west monsoon (May to September) which brings heavy rains, and the north east monsoon (November to January) which is irregular and liable to fail. The southwest quadrant of the island is known

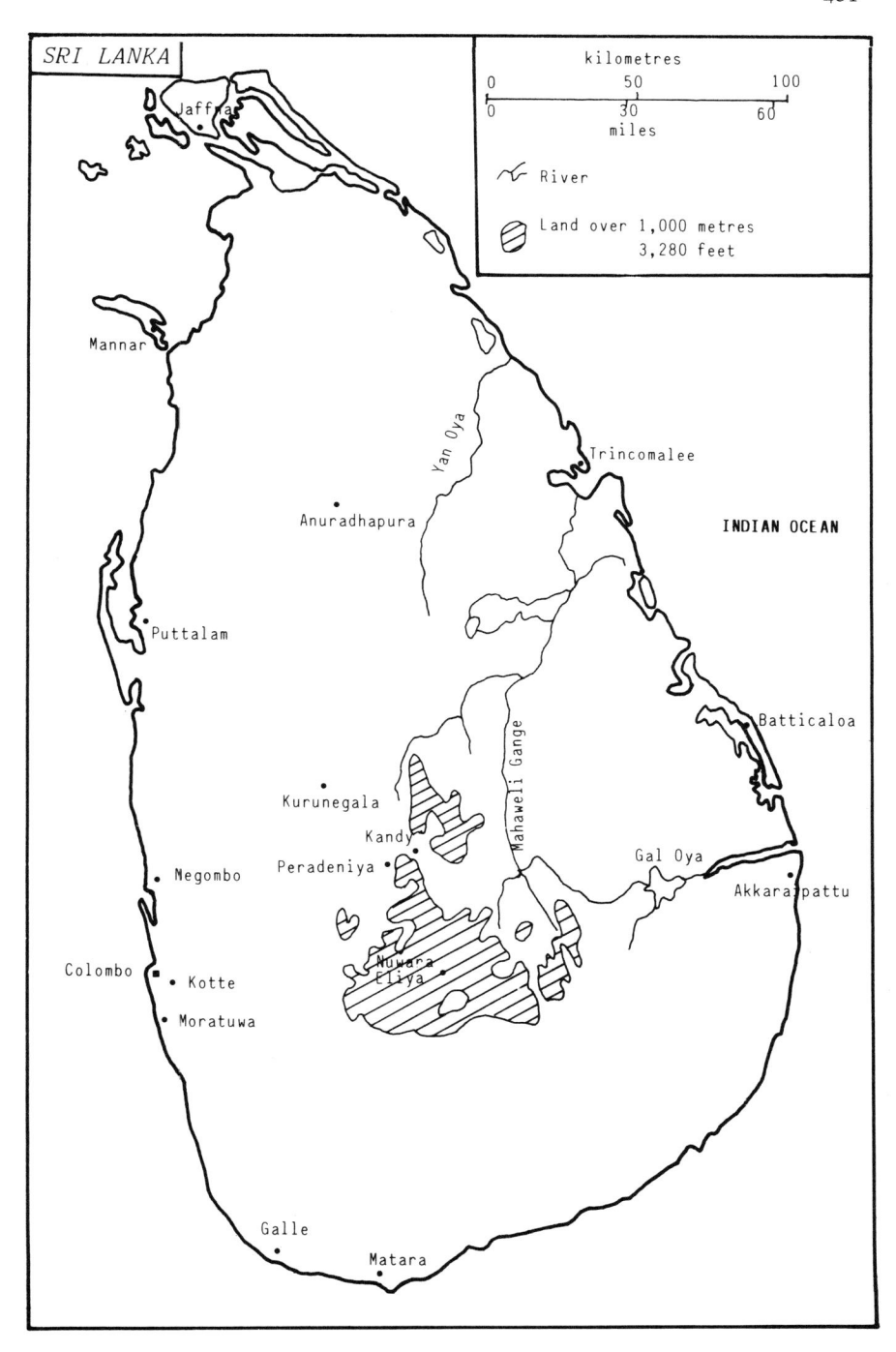

SRI LANKA

as the 'wet zone', and in it conditions are most favourable to agriculture. In other sectors of the island there is a very marked dry season during the south west monsoon, some variable inter-monsoonal rain and a heavy concentration of rainfall during the north east monsoon. Three quarters of the country lies in this 'dry zone' where the soil is poor and rainfall erratic. Only about a quarter of the acreage under cultivation is in the dry zone.

Communications

Central Sri Lanka is hilly and thickly wooded but communications are relatively highly developed with a network of tarred roads, a railway that connects the important towns (937 miles of track) and a well developed motor bus service. The north and several places on the east coast can be reached by air transport. Air Ceylon also runs a number of international services. The port of Colombo is one of the most important in the East.

2 POPULATION
Growth

The population has almost doubled in the last quarter of a century and the 1971 census showed that it had then reached 12.7 million. The 1981 census recorded a population of 14.6 million. Recent trends indicate a decline in the birth rate. Between 1960 and 1970 population grew by 2.4% per annum. Between 1970 and 1979 the rate had fallen to 1.7% per year.

Distribution

About 73% of the population lived in the rural areas and worked as peasant farmers or on the plantations in 1980. The remaining 4 million live in cities and towns. The greatest concentration is along the western seaboard where five of the eight principal towns with a population of over 50,000 each are situated. Of those by far the largest is the Colombo/Dehiwela/Mt Lavinia/Moratuwa/Kotte complex which can be regarded as Greater Colombo and which has a total population of about 1 million, of which Colombo accounts for around 635,000. Outside the Colombo complex, Jaffna in the northern Tamil area is the second largest town over 100,000, followed by Kandy in the central hill area with a little less than 100,000.

Groups

Sri Lanka nationals as a whole are known as 'Ceylonese' and include two principal language groups: the Sinhalese and the Tamils. Groups not defined by language are the Muslims and the 'Burghers'. The number of Europeans in Sri Lanka has dwindled in recent years, to a few hundred (mainly attached to foreign or international missions).

Sinhalese

About 72% of the total population are Sinhalese, who are of two main types: low country Sinhalese who inhabit the plains and have been affected by 400 years of European impact; and the Kandyans from the hills and dry zone jungles who have been so affected for only 150 years. (Their differences are rapidly disappearing, but the population census still distinguishes between the two groups.)

Tamils

They are of South Indian origin and speak Tamil, a Dravidian language used over wide areas of South India. They account for approximately 20% of the population and are divided into 'Ceylon' Tamils and 'Indian' Tamils. The former represent 11.1% of the population and have been resident in the island for over 2,000 years. They are mainly concentrated in thje north and east. The majority are peasants, but as a result of their long tradition of setting a high premium on education, the Tamils have provided a relatively large number of able men and women in all aspects of the professional and business life of the country. Their demand for parity of status for Tamil with Sinhala as the official language of the country has caused communal antagonism between the Tamils and Sinhalese for many years, but the language problem is an expression of more deep seated economic and education fears. In 1976 a Tamil Separatist Party was formed. The Indian Tamils, descendants of the labourers brought to the island by the British in the nineteenth century to work on the tea and rubber plantations, account for 9.4% (1.2 million) of the population. The citizenship of the Indian Tamils was for long a subject of dispute between India and Sri Lanka. An agreement was reached between the two countries in 1964 on repatriation of the Indial Tamils to India, but implementation has been slow and the number so far repatriated annually falls well below the target figures set by the agreement.

Muslims

The Muslims comprise an important minority – about 7% of the population. They are composed of three groups: 'Ceylon' Moors, 'Indian' Moors, and Malays. By far the largest of these are the Ceylon Moors, descendants of Arab traders who have lived in the island for about 900 years. The Indian Moors are more recent inhabitants, their Arab ancestors having spent several centuries on the Indian sub-continent. The Malays are the descendants of Muslim traders from the East rather than of Arabs. The Muslims speak the language of the people they live among – English, Sinhala or Tamil. Many are agriculturalists, but they are also prominent in business and dominate the gem trade.

Burghers

Most of these are descendants of Europeans who served under the Dutch East India Company and their mother tongue is English. In British times they formed an important class from which were drawn many professional men and government administrators. Since independence and the withdrawal of British protection and patronage, the community has lost its privileged position and more than half of the post-war population of 100,000 have migrated, mainly to Australia and Britain.

3 SOCIETY AND CULTURE

Social Patterns

Before the first European colonisers arrived the structure of the society was in broad terms comparatively straightforward: it was based on the village as the social unit and the family as the biological unit. Both had their roots in the cultivation of paddy and were regulated by kinship and feudalism, customs, religious beliefs, cults, ceremonies, and by forms of caste distinction. Western ideas brought by the colonisers and the rise of commerce and trade, the spread of education, the opening of the island by a network of modern communications, the general impact of industrial technology and the growth of urban centres, have made the structure more complex and sophisticated.

Today the island's society is stratified in a number of distinct layers: at the top are the westernised elite, composed of the old land-owning aristocracy, the 'new rich' who benefited from the economic opportunities opened up by the British and a middle class drawn mainly from the professions. (Potential barriers of language and religion are cut across by virtue of the elite's common background of English education, values and ideals which give its members a large degree of homogeneith.) There is a predominantly peasant small farmer class accounting for almost 70% of the population though this excludes the Tamil estate workers who have pursued their customs and beliefs within the boundaries of the estate, married within their own communal group and have not merged with the Sinhalese neighbouring villagers. There is also a small but growing industrial and mercantile class.

Village and Family

Although these factors have influenced village social patterns the village - and the family - still remain the fundamental pillars of the national social structure. Village life is remarkably similar throughout the island. Its preservation and continuity are largely dependent on the labours of the women rather than the men. The tradition of family ties and loyalty is strong. Among all groups kinship is recognised in all lines and through all ranks and is most discernible in the kin-nepotism which is a built-in part of the social mores. In recent years, however, new factors have appeared which may well have profound consequences on family and - to a lesser degree - on village life. The introduction of the indigenous languages *(swabasha)* as the language of instruction in schools and the implementation of new laws imposing a ceiling on property and land ownership must eventually reduce the influence of the western elite class, and the introduction of compulsory English and science in all schools from an early age will provide greater opportunities for the village child to reach higher education, the professions and white collar jobs which would mean an escape from village life with a consequent weakening of village ties.

Caste

One often hears that caste is no longer very important and is disappearing, but its concept and strictures retain remarkable potency, although it has lost much of the rigidity and shades of distinction found in the Indian system. In the controlling of village government, marriage and ritual status, caste is still an active force and has great bearing on appointments, marriages etc. throughout the island at all levels of the social structure. Caste groups in many parts of the island tend also to emerge as powerful voting factions during elections. The most striking feature is the numerical strength of the highest caste (the *govigama*, originally the farmers and tillers of the land) who form more than half of the Sinhalese population. The strict observances connected with caste tend to be forgotten in social intercourse (though in private life much of the detail is still observed) and city life affords the best escape from the stigmas attached to caste inferiority in village and rural areas.

Religion

Sri Lanka, its people, culture and customs can only be understood in the light of its Buddhist tradition. For more than 12 centuries Buddhism has shaped character and thought patterns. Today about 68% of the population is Buddhist (representing most of the Sinhalese) but the proportion rises to 76% if non-national Tamils are excluded. About 80% of Buddhists live in rural areas. Until a few years ago the Buddhist calendar, based on the phases of the moon, was in use and even today the full moon day is a public holiday. Many habits, customs and beliefs are influenced by Buddhist philosophy and astrologers and Buddhist monks are brought in for numerous aspects of daily life (e.g. births, marriages, journeying, building a house). Sri Lanka is the seat of the practically uniform orthodox doctrine of *Theravada* Buddhism.

The majority of the Tamil population is Hindu. Muslims form 7% of the population. The propagation of Christianity, first attempted by the Portuguese and Dutch from the sixteenth century onwards, grew stronger in the last decade of the nineteenth century under British rule and west some way to undermine the status of Buddhism. There are now just under one million Christians (including the Burghers) and these form an influential minority, but the rise of militant nationalism has helped weaken their position and led to a revival of Buddhism.

4 HISTORY AND POLITICS
First Colonisation

When the Portuguese arrived in the sixteenth century they found an effete and decadent society ravaged by disease, poverty, war and internal dissention. This was what remained of a civilisation which had flourished from the first century BC to the thirteenth century AD, had built great cities such as Anuradhapura and Polonnaruwa, had evolved a gigantic and intricate system of reservoirs, dams, sluices and canals to irrigate the dry northern plains for rice cultivation, and which had experienced a great spiritual and cultural renaissance through the spread of Buddhism. Portuguese rule extended mainly over the maritime provinces but by the middle of the seventeenth century it had been displaced by the rule of the Dutch who dominated Ceylonese trade for over a century before they too were displaced by the British. The most lasting Dutch legacy was a Roman Dutch Law, a vigorous Burgher community and a network of canals.

British Rule

The breach between the British and the Dutch during the Napoleonic wars led to the acquisition of the Dutch colonies and settlements in the East and in 1796 the British gained control over the ports of the maritime provinces of Ceylon. The newly acquired territory was at first administered as part of India, but in 1802 the island came to be ruled as a crown colony by a governor appointed from London. Thirteen years later the Sinhalese ceded the rest of the country to the British and the last of the Kandyan kings was deported to India. Under the British crown colony system, new laws were introduced and by slow degrees Sinhalese were admitted to responsible positions in the administration. Coffee and tea plantations were opened, roads and railways built, and communications between provinces made easier. With the development of trade, commerce and industry began to flourish and the European way of life and thought considerably influenced the middle class.

Political Development

As the national movement gathered momentum, there was a demand for a more rapid expansion of the democratic system and in 1931 constitutional reforms created a State Council under a system of adult franchise. In 1948 Ceylon was granted independence as a member of the Commonwealth to be ruled by a parliamentary system on the British model with a House of Representatives elected by adult franchise and a Senate (later abolished). A new constitution was introduced by the United Front government in 1972, declaring Sri Lanka (Ceylon) a republic within the Commonwealth. The House of Representatives was renamed the National State Assembly and the Governor-General was replaced by the President of the Republic. There is a multi-party parliamentary system with a viable opposition of both left and right groups. Government is centralised with most power lying in the hands of ministers, though major families also have influence.

Political Situation

The increase in population, inflation, the scramble for State employment, and the determination of the party in power to remain in power, have in thje past made for political instability and tension marked by eruptions of violence. Within the last 20 years, Sri Lanka has seen communal violence in a most savage form in 1956 and the assassination of a prime minister, Mr S W D Bandaranaike, in 1959. There were two reported attempted coups in the 1960s, one an abortive rising by senior army and police personnel in 1962. In 1971 there was a bloody insurrection from the left involving many young people, a main cause being frustration at lack of employment opportunities. After this a state of emergency was declared.

A United Front government took power in 1970 but during the course of its seven-year rule lost its Trotskyist and Communist elements leaving the Dri Lanka Freedom Party (a social democratic party led by Mrs Bandaranaike) in sole power. This government pursued a policy of nationalisation and land reform. Educational reforms aimed at making the system more relevant to the country's economy were introduced. The final years of SLFP rule were characterised by accusations from the Opposition of corruption, nepotism and inefficiency. In the elections of July 1977 (postponed from 1976) the United National Party led by Mr J R Jayawardene, had a landslide victory giving it 139 out of 168 seats in the National State Assembly. The second largest party in parliament is now the Tamil United Liberation Front (17 seats) which pursues a mainly separatist policy. The SLFP has been reduced to seven seats. The new government took power with many promises of honesty and efficiency but was immediately plunged into a renewed spate of communal violence of serious proportions.

Since 1979 there has been continuing political and social unrest indicated by strikes and demonstrations and actions by Tamil extremists. This was worsened by a severe economic crisis in 1980-81.

International Relations

Sri Lanka follows a non-aligned foreign policy, her chief initiative in international affairs being the idea of a zone of peace in the Indian Ocean. She draws aid from both West and East and despite the fact that the former government's internal policies have seemed to bring her closer to the USSR and China (the latter having been particularly generous in providing food and other aid) her non-alignment is a genuine stance. She hosted the Fifth Non Alignment Summit Conference in Colombo in August 1976 and is therefore Chairman of the Movement for the next three years. Sri Lanka is an active member of the Commonwealth and has both set up an office in Brussels and signed a Commercial Cooperation Agreement with the EEC (May 1975).

5 THE ECONOMY

Agriculture

Agriculture is the principal economic activity and 27% taken together with forestry, hunting and fishing accounted for about 27% of GNP in 1979. In the fertile southwestern 'wet zone' the three principal crops that account for about 80% of the country's total exports are grown: coconut along the coast and broadening inland north of Colombo, rubber on the ridges inland, and tea above the 3,000 feet contour, although there is also some low country tea. Rice is the major domestic crop. Sri Lanka is one of the world's leading producers of natural rubber and in 1975 accounted for 4.5% of total world production. Nevertheless, tea remains the mainstay in foreign exchange earnings and accounts for some 48% of total exports. In 1975 tea exports by volume maintained traditional levels. In 1976 the volume dropped significantly but was compensated for by higher prices. However, competition increased from newer tea producers such as Kenya and Tanzania who with the advantage of more recently planted and higher yielding clones have tended to achieve significantly higher prices than Ceylonese exporters. The five-year plan 1972-1976 aimed to achieve self-sufficiency in essential foodstuffs, but adverse climatic conditions hampered efforts to achieve increased domestic food production, particularly of rice and sugar. The resulting gap had to be covered by various types of external assistance, some but by no means all on concessionary terms.

Industry

Sri Lanka has had few natural resources to stimulate industry. A wide variety of precious and semi-precious stones are mined including sapphires, rubies, zircons, garnets and beryls and there is some graphite and iron ore, though the contribution of mining to GNP is small. But it seems certain that there are commercially exploitable quantities of oil offshore. Manufacturing industry is a relatively small sector of the economy. The principal industries are food processing, textiles, tobacco products, chemicals, cement and petroleum refining. Machinery and metal products are increasing in importance. The five-year plan aimed at expanding the industrial sector with the development of export-oriented and labour intensive industries.

Foreign Currency

Sri Lanka is heavily dependent on foreign aid to finance the trade deficit as well as help development projects. The largest donor is the USA, with FDR, China, Japan and Britain providing large contributions. Britain fell from first to second position in trade in the mid-1970s both as a market for Sri Lankan tea (after Pakistan) and a source of imports (after China). China is now the major trading partner (exchanging rice for rubber in large quantities). Britain took 7.9% of Sri Lanka's exports in 1975 and was the second largest importer of Sri Lankan goods.

Economic Situation

Despite annual growth rates of 3.9% in real terms between 1970 and 1979, the main problem facing the managers of the Sri Lanka economy has been the increasing disparity between the rates of increase of prices of imports (especially of petroleum derivative products) and of the prices of the traditional exports, namely tea, rubber and coconut products. To illustrate this widening gap it should be remembered that using 1967 as the base year, the terms of trade in 1961 wre 136 whereas in 1975 the corresponding figure was 46.

The continued increase of the labour force combined with the lack of economic growth has meant that unemployment and under-employment remain serious problems. The tenuous nature of the base data available makes it difficult to arrive at precise conclusions but it is widely recognised that unemployment certainly amounts to over 20% of the available labour force.

Future Trends

There is reasonably good evidence of a downturn in the population growth rate. Given some success in future years, with agricultural diversification and productivity programmes, there is some basis for envisaging a point where the Sri Lanka economy could begin to break out of the vicious circle of its dependence upon external capital and other resources to meet total requirements. These requirements are swollen by the continuing need to provide consumption expenditure on food imports, food subsidies and extensive welfare programmes, notably in the health and social services.

6 THE EDUCATION SYSTEM

Academic Year

The theoretical academic year lasts from January to December throughout the whole system. There are three terms of three months each with a month's holiday in between and examinations in December. However, recent political disturbances together with the imposition of the new educational reforms have put the academic year into a state of disarray and the commencement and continuation of classes is to a large extent dependent on the political situation at any given time.

The Structure of Schooling

There have been two major changes in the structure of schooling in the 1970s. Up to 1972 children entered eight-year primary schools at the age of 5. This was followed by four years' secondary schooling (in two stages) which led on to higher education. In order to widen access to secondary schooling in response to popular demand, a three-tier system was introduced in 1972. Children entered five-year primary schools at the age of 6. These led to four-year junior secondary schools. The pre-higher education stage was provided for in two-year Senior Secondary schools.

In 1978 the primary course was extended to six years and the junior secondary school to five years. The 5 + 4 + 2 system was replaced by a 6 + 5 + 2 structure. The purpose of the reform is to prepare those pupils who leave at the end of the primary or junior secondary phases to enter employment or vocational training more smoothly.

In 1980 a policy was introduced of grouping the 9,794 schools into 1,000 clusters. This was to increase efficiency of schools - 2,000 of which had enrolments of less than 100 - to allow sharing facilities like science laboratories which were in short supply and to associate non-formal education centres which formed school institutions.

Throughout the school system, the medium of instruction is Sinhala or Tamil. Until a few years ago some schools had an English stream but there have more or less disappeared.

Pre-Primary

This is voluntary and entirely private. There are about 200 schools mainly in urban centres.

Primary

The State is obliged to provide schooling to all who seek to enter primary schools though education is not compulsory (apart from old plantation schools which were set up for the children of tea estate workers).

The curriculum has been reformed and is built around 11 themes which aim to teach basic skills of language and number through the medium of practical activities and environmental studies. The objective is to prepare children for a useful role in the local community. However mathematics and (more recently) English have been introduced in the upper grades.

Enrolment for Grades 1-5 was 1.98 million in 1979 which covered 98% of the age group.

Junior Secondary

There is now a common curriculum of ten compulsory subjects which include science and English. Technical and pre-vocational studies occupy 20% of curriculum time. This curriculum replaced a system of streaming pupils into arts or science areas which operated until the mid-1970s.

The first public examination is held at the end of the junior secondary school course when pupils sit the General Certificate of Education (Ordinary level) examination. This is similar to the old English School certificate which it replaced. For the award of the certificate, passes in six subjects are required including in the compulsory subjects first language (Sinhala or Tamil) and mathematics. The other subjects include English, science, social studies, religion, aesthetic studies, technical subjects and health and physical education.

Satisfactory passes in 'O' level are required to enter senior secondary school. Many pupils repeat the final grade of junior secondary school to achieve this result.

Senior Secondary

The senior secondary course is still of two years duration and leads to the Sri Lanka GCE advanced level. Four subjects are taken. A large number of subjects is available but choices must fall within one of five areas – physical sciences, biological sciences, social studies, humanities and commerce.

The secondary programme comprises a specialist curriculum designed exclusively to cater for the needs of those entering university. However, about 30,000 to 40,000 pupils sat the GCE 'A' level examination annually in recent years, of whom only 3,500 gained a university place. (In crude terms, of a student cohort of 100 entering school at Grade I, only one entered university after 12 to 14 years of education.) Most of the remainder became unemployed – as there was only a restricted number of other openings where the subjects which pupils had studied were relevant.

Schools

Government

In 1980 there were 9,794 government schools. The *vidyalayas* provide educational facilities up to Grade V but also in a large number of cases up to Grade IX. The *madhya maha vidyalayas* and the *maha vidyalayas* provide classes leading to the National Certificates. The majority of *vidyalayas*, catering to the needs of the local community, are quite small whereas the *maha vidyalayas* tend to be much larger with an average of 500 pupils. The total enrolment in government schools in 1979 was 3.14 million pupils. The teaching cadre in 1979 was 120,000.

PRIMARY | JUNIOR SECONDARY

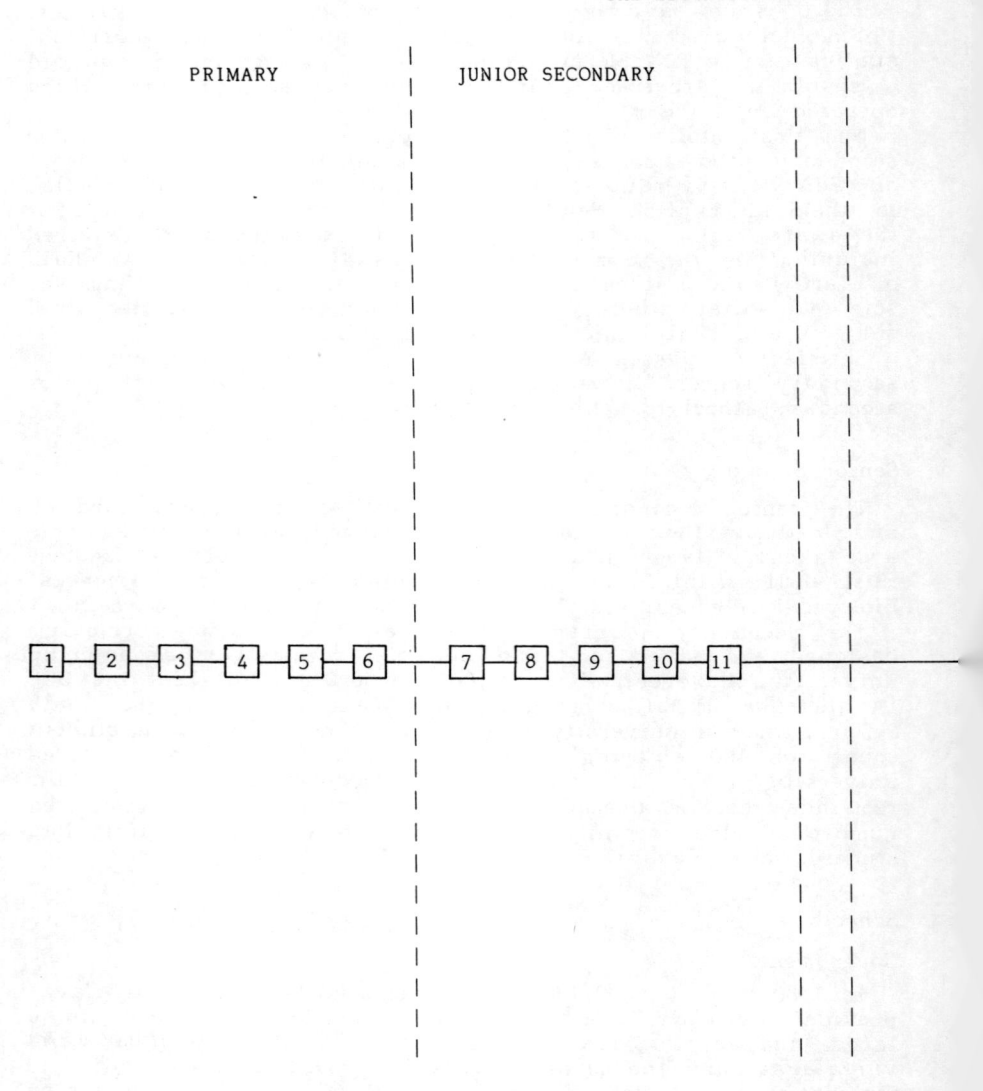

|1|–|2|–|3|–|4|–|5|–|6| |7|–|8|–|9|–|10|–|11|

OF SRI LANKA

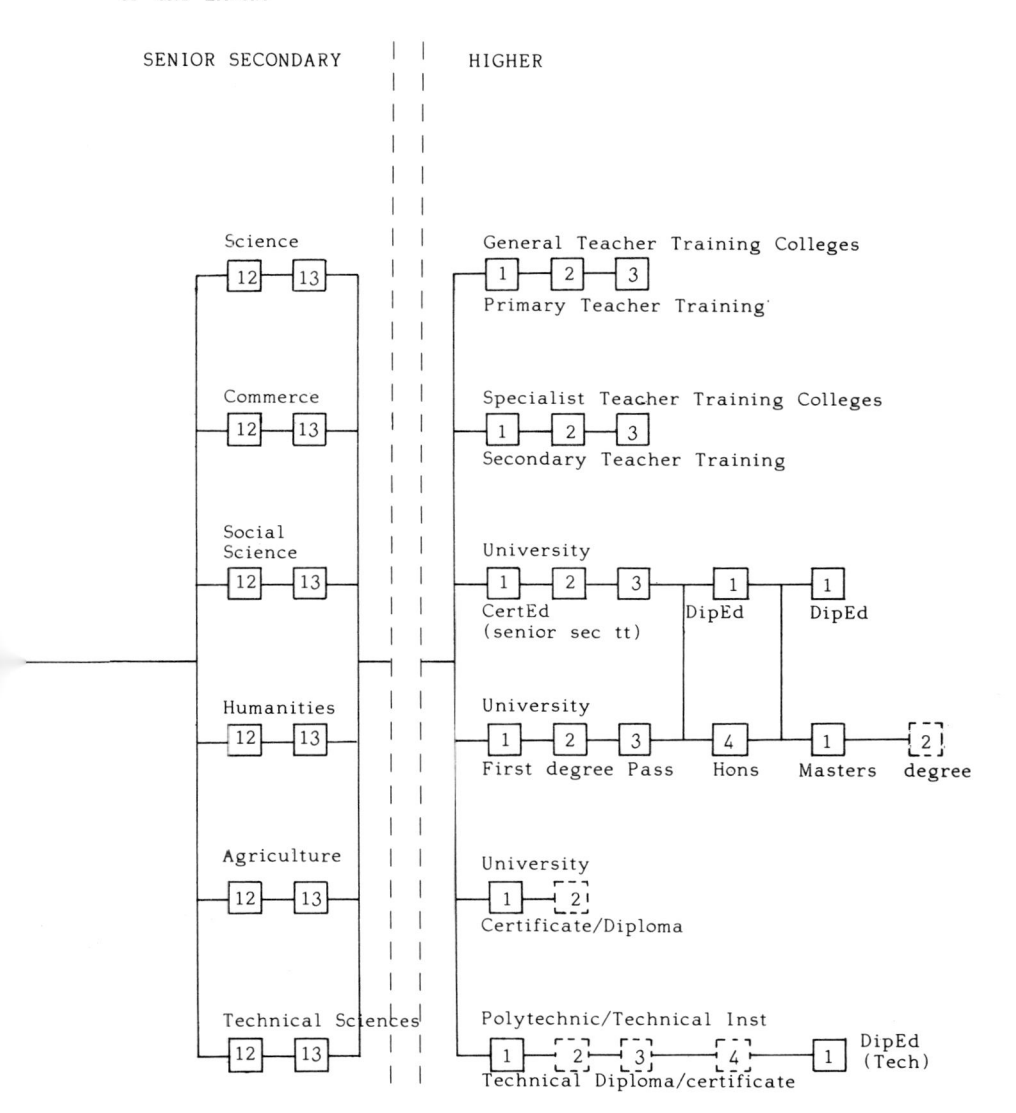

SENIOR SECONDARY | HIGHER

Science
[12]—[13]

General Teacher Training Colleges
[1]—[2]—[3]
Primary Teacher Training

Commerce
[12]—[13]

Specialist Teacher Training Colleges
[1]—[2]—[3]
Secondary Teacher Training

Social Science
[12]—[13]

University
[1]—[2]—[3]   [1]   [1]
CertEd   DipEd   DipEd
(senior sec tt)

Humanities
[12]—[13]

University
[1]—[2]—[3]—[4]—[1]—[2]
First degree Pass Hons Masters degree

Agriculture
[12]—[13]

University
[1]—[2]
Certificate/Diploma

Technical Sciences
[12]—[13]

Polytechnic/Technical Inst
[1]—[2]—[3]—[4]—[1] DipEd (Tech)
Technical Diploma/certificate

17   18   19   20   21   22   23

Private

Private schools account for less than 2% of the country's total enrolment. In their heyday, when they were known as assisted schools, they numbered over 3,000. Most of the assisted schools were associated with one religious denomination or another and bore a resemblance, *mutatis mutandis*, to the English public school. When a government ordinance in 1947 abolished fees in government and assisted schools, the latter were given the option of entering the free education scheme or remaining outside the scheme unaided. Out of 3,079 assisted schools in 1945, only 115 remained outside the free education scheme. They were divided into two categories: denominational schools which received a grant-in-aid from government and which accordingly were not permitted to levy fees; and private schools which levied fees but received no government assistance. The first type came to be known as 'non-fee-levying assisted schools', and the second 'fee-levying private schools'. The Assisted Schools and Training Collegves Act of 1960 gave the option to non-fee-levying assisted denominational schools to enter the free education scheme and become State schools or remain outside but unaided by government. Only 32 schools chose the latter option and are now known as non-fee-levying schools. With 13 fee-levying schools there were 45 private schools functioning in 1975.

Private schools are not entirely independent. They must be registered with the Ministry of Education and are inspected and approved by its supervisory staff, whilst the pupils must take the State examinations and follow the State policy governing education. These schools still undoubtedly play an important role in Sri Lanka (though their future is uncertain) and are still regarded as producing some of the best education and training; the number of applicants for entry is considerable and far outnumbers the places available.

Other

There were about 770 estate schools in 1975 and practically all are located on the tea and rubber estates. They provide education for the children of the Indian Tamils working on the estates only up to Grade V (i.e. 10+ years) under the old system. they are maintained by the estates' management, but receive financial assistance from the government which recently declared its intention to take them over completely. There are also 289 *pirivenas* (Buddhist seminaries) which similarly provide very elementary education.

From 1979 plantation schools began to be taken over by government. After 1980 non-fee-levying private schools received government aid while the *pirivenas* were also aided from this time.

Technical and Vocational

The main areas covered by technical and vocational education are engineering and allied fields, commerce and business studies, and agriculture. Development plans for technical education envisage close cooperation between those responsible for pre-vocational courses at secondary level and those responsible for technical/vocational programmes, as it is intended to introduce short courses into the latter, which will be designed to train pupils to take up productive work in their home areas.

Since the reforms were initiated in 1972 the number of technical institutes has risen from 11 to 20, 8 of which have been upgraded to senior technical institutes (described as polytechnics) with the introduction of new courses, for example in business studies and specialised branches of engineering. The minimum age for admission to technical institutes is 17. There are diploma and certificate courses lasting for 1-4 years from craft to higher technician level. Entry qualifications range from the unsuccessful completion of the eighth year of education to the successful completion of the Higher National Certificate of Education or GCE 'A' level. Technician level courses in engineering and allied fields are conducted in the polytechnics and a few of the junior technical institutes while craft level career courses are conducted mainly at the junior technical institutes. Commercial and business study courses leading to a diploma are centred in the polytechnics, while those leading to a certificate are provided in both senior and junior institutes.

Higher

Until recently there was only one university - the University of Sri Lanka. It was established by the University of Ceylon Act of 1972 and comprises six campuses - Peradeniya, Colombo, Vidyodaya and Vidyalankara (all formerly separate universities), Katubedde (which prior to 1972 was the Ceylon College of Technology), and Jaffna (opened October 1974). Four campuses are situated within a radio of nine miles from the centre of Colombo; Peradeniya, near Kandy, is about 68 miles from Colombo; Jaffna is about 240 miles from Colombo. The intention behind integration of the campuses into a single university was to encourage an integrated approach to the planning of higher education in terms of national needs and resources and to avoid costly duplication. From the beginning of the academic year 1972, a relocation of some faculties and departments was put into effect, by way of 'rationalising' the availability of study facilities. Facilities were expanded overall by the creation of the new campus at Jaffna. The United National Party's election manifesto favoured the break up of the five campuses into three universities: Colombo, Peradeniya and Jaffna, although this is still subject to discussion.

An Open University was established in 1980 and also the University Colleges at Ruhnne and Batticaloa were set up between 1972 and 1981.

Organisation

The university is financed solely from central government funds. The executive body is the Board of Governors whose members include among others, the Vice-Chancellor, the Secretaries of the Ministries of Education, Planning and Finance, and the Presidents of campuses. All academic matters are controlled by the University Senate. Each campus has a President and a Campus Board, the Chairman of which is the President. The Board is responsible for the internal administration of the campus, subject to the directions of the Board of Governors.

Entrance

Entrance to university has traditionally been by way of the GCE 'A' level examination. University entrance requirements arising from the introduction of the HNCE examination have still to be defined. The authorities have contemplated the possibility of setting up a one-year pre-university course. Competition for university places is severe. The complex system of adjusting the examination marks of candidates for university entrance to improve the prospects of those from the poorer areas, became a major cause of grievance to the Tamil community, since it led in effect to discrimination against Tamils. It has now been abolished by the United National Party government.

Courses

University courses cover the full spectrum of higher studies but within the context of educational reform new disciplines and courses related to job opportunities and national needs have been introduced. Admissions to science and science-based courses have been instituted in selected subjects.

Languages

The position on use of English and the vernacular languages at the university is complex and tends to vary from campus to campus. Some courses are in English only: for example architecture and applied science honours degree courses at Kattubedde Campus; some science honours courses (i.e. the third and fourth years) in physics, chemistry, botany and zoology. Some specialist courses are in English but only from the second year: for example, medical, dental and veterinary science, agricultural science and engineering. All lectures in years 1, 2 and 3 of the arts faculties are (with the exception of the honours English course) in Sinhala or Tamil. General science courses may be conducted in Sinhala, Tamil or English but at two campuses are in Sinhala only. Each campus has a special English course for new entrants (in principle about 8 hours a week in the first year, but less insome cases). This tuition is only moderately effective. Proposals have been made to establish a pre-university course in English and if the full one-year pre-university course were to be established English would certainly be included in the curriculum.

Enrolment

In 1978 there were 17,485 students in all higher education institutions.

Teacher Training

The minimum qualification for teaching has been GCE 'O' level passes in four subjects. The would-be teacher serves a probationary period of up to two years in a school before becoming eligible to apply for entry to a teacher training college. Thus institutional courses for trainee teachers are almost all of an 'in-service' type in that those enrolling are teachers already in service, although many in fact could be categorised as pre-service courses. Teachers who have had no education at a teacher training college can sit for a Ministry of Education examination after a specified number of years in service and qualify as certified teachers, but as the government has placed high priority on teacher training and college intakes have been expanded, the number of teachers with this qualification should decrease.

Teacher training courses offered are of three main types:

(i) courses of one year duration conducted in the university's Department of Education (at Colombo) for graduate teachers leading to a post-graduate Diploma in Education (a specialised Diploma in Education in the teaching of educationally sub-normal children was introduced in 1976 and about 20 graduates a year follow a course in the teaching of blind children)

(ii) courses of two years duration conducted in teacher training colleges for teachers specialising in English, science, mathematics, agriculture, etc. Teachers qualifying in these courses are designated 'secondary trained teachers'

(iii) courses at one of the 25 teacher training colleges specialising in primary education. These courses were extended from two years' to three years' duration in 1978.

In addition to the above there are BEd and MAEd courses, although there are seldom more than ten teachers studying for the master's course at one time. A three-year correspondence course (with additional short residential units) was introduced for untrained non-graduate teachers below the age of 45 to help overcome the backlog of untrained teachers. This course is now being phased out. There is a university certificate course, consisting of part of a degree programme with some study of educational subjects, intended to train teachers for Grades X and XI; this course represents the only *non-graduate, pre-service* training offered.

Technical

A technical teacher training centre was established in 1972 to provide a one-year full time day course for teachers at the technical institutes. Although the Ministry of Agriculture provides courses in agriculture and agricultural engineering at technician and craft level, it is the responsibility of the Ministry of Education to train the teacher educators to meet the needs of the agricultural schools run by the Ministry of Agriculture. There is only one specialist agricultural teacher training college (Kuliyapitiya) but courses are also provided in a number of the other teacher training colleges and the technical colleges.

In-Service

The ministry has introduced a programme for the establishment of a number of field study centres, to provide seminars and other in-service tuition for primary/secondary school science teachers and for teacher-trainers. A residential centre at Peradeniya was established at the end of 1976. An existing field centre at Thondaimannar is to be upgraded and incorporated in the programme, and proposals for the establishment of a centre at Matara seem to be well advanced.

However, there are very large numbers of untrained teachers. In 1979 23,000 were recruited partly to cope with the expansion of primary education and partly to teach the science and vocational subjects which became compulsory in junior secondary schools. Distance education techniques are being developed to train these teachers.

Special

Surveys are carried out annually through the medium of the health authorities and the government agent in each district. So far 16 out of 26 districts have been surveyed over the past few years. The island-wide estimate extrapolated from these surveys is that there are about 4,000 children suffering from visual handicaps, 22,000 from deafness (partial or complete) and 100,000 mentally retarded children, classed as slow learners. Of these 1,000 to 1,500 are at present being provided for in the educational programmes.

Special education has hitherto concentrated on the needs of the blind and deaf children, but is now additionally being related to the problems of the slow learner. At present there are 13 residential schools for the blind and deaf, catering for 355 blind children and 830 children with impaired hearing.

There is also one residential school for physically handicapped and one for mentally handicapped children. The integrated programme, which involves the operation of special units in normal schools, has 450 children with impaired hearing and in addition programmes are beginning in Kalutara, Colombo North and Matale for the teaching of slow learners.

Non-Formal and Adult

Non-formal and adult education is still at an early stage of evolution but in recent years a number of developments have taken place. In March 1971 a workers' continuing education course was introduced on the Colombo campus of the university and extended to the Peradeniya campus in May 1973. In July 1976 a new post of Director of Non-Formal Education was established in the Ministry of Education. The initial intention is that this department should exercise a coordinating role in respect of the various ministries which administer relevant programmes. Earlier a community *(Janatha)* Education Unit was set up with a view to introducing community education as a component of teacher training courses. The aim is to produce teachers to work closely with the local community. A ministerial committee has been appointed to consider the reorganisation of rural development work and a National Youth Service has been established to coordinate youth programmes.

In general non-formal education in Sri Lanka relates to community and agricultural development at village level. there is little need for literacy work as the literacy rate is high. Ignoring children in the age group 0-4, the percentage of literate people in the community is approximately 84%. For persons between the ages of 10 and 74 the average literacy rate is 76.5% (men 84% and women 67.8%). The programmes offered may be roughly classified into youth work, technical training and rural development activities. Government-sponsored youth schemes include: agricultural projects designed for youth settlement, practical farm schools, young farmers' clubs, and programmes of the Department of Small Industries. There are also non-government organisations involved in youth work, notably *Sarvodaya*, a Buddhist movement which runs youth farms and youth leadership courses. Technical programmes are offered at vocational training centres and through the National Apprenticeship Scheme. The major religious institutions are also responsible for a number of vocational training programmes. Rural development work is organised by the Rural Development Department which offers on-the-job training through its network of rural development officers and residential courses for officials of local groups. District Development councils sponsor projects at village level and the Farmer Education and Training Programme offers short localised courses to working farmers. A voluntary women's organisation, the *Lanka Mahila Samiti*, has local branches and runs model training centres. In addition the National Library Services Board is expanding its work in rural areas by means of a book box loan scheme, seminars for librarians, etc.

Distance Learning

In May 1977 the recently established Technical Education Extension Services Unit together with the Technical Education Curriculum Development Unit were merged to become the Sri Lanka Institute of Distance Education (SLIDE). The Institute offers at the moment three groups of courses:

(i) diploma courses in mathematics, science and management. The first two of these aim to upgrade teachers who completed their formal education on leaving school so that they are qualified to teach their specialities at a more advanced school level. The diploma course in management is also for people who have completed secondary education, and aims to give training to managers of small enterprises, including farms, and middle management in larger enterprises

(ii) a new series of three-year certificate courses in engineering subjects. These are for people already in employment and will replace the present promotion tests based upon the City and Guilds examinations

(iii) lower level courses of practical application — in subjects such as poultry farming — will also be offered.

It is the present intention of the Ministry of Education that the three diploma courses will mark the highest educational level at which the Institute will offer courses although there has recently been opened an Open University type institution. The courses are based upon correspondence with periodical face-to-face tuition. External candidates of the University of Sri Lanka work through a separate organisation called the External Services Agency.

Educational Broadcasting

Plans for a school broadcasting service in Sri Lanka were made initially in 1971 with the aim of giving support to curriculum changes at primary and junior secondary levels. Since then the Educational Broadcasting Service has continued to expand its activities in close collaboration with the Curriculum Development Centre which provides advice on current educational directions and concepts. At present educational broadcasting is conducted entirely by radio though the new Ministry of Education has expressed keenness to introduce an educational television service. There are approximately 1,350 medium wave radio sets (given by UNICEF) at registered listening schools, and also sets presented by the Ministry of Education. Approximately 650 schools make use of educational broadcasts each term.

7 EDUCATIONAL ADMINISTRATION

In 1978 the Ministry of Education was divided into the Ministry of Education with responsibility for schools and the Ministry of Higher Education. In 1979 a separate Ministry of Education Services was given responsibility for buildings, books and materials though its financial provision comes under the Ministry of Education. Matters concerning the recruitment of teachers and educational personnel, their promotion and disciplinary control were placed under the Public Science Commission in 1979.

Centralised Control

Education is highly centralised and its administration is vested in the Ministry of Education. For schools and colleges, the ministry prescribes the curricula and syllabi to be followed, the textbooks to be used and issues directives as to methods of instruction. It also conducts examinations. It is directly responsible for the recruitment of teachers, their training, conditions of service, and postings. Officials of the ministry exercise control over educational broadcasting through membership of the Joint Committee on Educational Broadcasting (with officials of SLBC) and through consultation and collaboration on the various programme series. However, in the past the relationship between these two organisations has not always been entirely satisfactory. The Minister of Higher Education is Pro-Chancellor of the University and since the University Act of 1972 has had considerable control over University decision-making.

Examinations

The examinations conducted by the Department of Examinations fall into six broad categories: school examinations; examinations pertaining to students in the teaching profession; technical examinations; recruitment examinations; proficiency, efficiency bar and miscellaneous examinations; and foreign examinations. Some are relatively small affairs but the school examinations ae a major operation.

Publications

The Department of Educational Publications provides textbooks for schools and the university. It ensures the publication of textbooks on science, mathematics, social studies and pre-vocational studies, as well as teachers' handbooks and other curricular material. The books used in higher education in the indigenous languages are mainly translations of originals in English recommended by the university.

Ministry Organisation

The Minister of Education is appointed by the President and is a member of the cabinet. In addition to the Minister and the Deputy Minister and his parliamentary and private secretaries, there is a permanent staff headed by the Secretary for Education, who is also Director-General of Education and is responsible for advising the Minister on policy and for formulating plans for development. He is assisted by three Deputy Director-Generals of Education, each responsible for one of the following areas:

- (a) school organisation (implementation of the school programme, staff supervision, building and equipment)
- (b) curriculum development and teacher education
- (c) planning.

The Secretary/DG and the DDGs are assisted by Directors of Education (attached to the ministry office) in charge of special areas which include English, teacher training, science and mathematics education, non-formal education, technical education, etc. (A unit dealing with special education has recently been set up. Its brief includes surveys, educational programmes and teacher training.) Establishment matters are administered by a Senior Assistant Secretary with assistants in charge of specific subjects including foreign aid awards. Financial matters are under the charge of a Chief Accountant responsible for preparation and submission of estimates and for obtaining the necessary provision for maintenance and development of the education system. The ministry has its own school buildings section, under a director assisted by schools works engineers and architects responsible for the building, maintenance and repair of all government schools.

Regional Responsibilities

Since 1960 administration and management authority has to a large degree been delegated to Regional Directors of Education in charge of the 15 regions into which the island is divided. The larger regions are sub-divided into educational districts, which number 25 in all. A Regional Director's staff includes Chief Education Officers, Education Administrators and Circuit Education Officers in charge of particular subjects, e.g. science, English, handicrafts, aesthetic studies; and Master Teachers in science and English have been appointed to each region. A Regional Director is responsible for the schools in his area but not technical institutes, which remain under ministry control. He oversees the construction, maintenance and repair of school buildings; supervises the work of the teachers and arranges for recruitment, postings and transfers within his Directorate.

8 EDUCATIONAL FINANCE

Government Budget

With the exception of the private schools and the estate schools, the education system including higher education is financed by government through the Ministry of Education and has been since 1945. In that year the government instituted the principle of free education and tuition fees were abolished in almost all schools and colleges, in return for which the government undertook to meet the costs of their teachers' salaries and running expenses. Educational broadcasting is basically financed by SLBC in the way of staff, programme transmitters and other overheads. The ministry helps in the financing of publications. The proportion of actual government expenditure which is devoted to education has varied over recent years. In 1978 Rs934 million were spent in education representing 5.9% of government expenditure and 2.2% of GNP. Both proportions have fallen since 1970.

Students' Contribution

In the private sector, students are required to provide their own uniforms, textbooks and stationery and to pay a facilities and service fee to meet the cost of library books and equipment for extra-curricular activities. The government gives a limited amount of aid to promising students in the form of scholarships to cover maintenance, books and clothing.

Foreign Aid

Foreign aid accounted for about 2% of financial input into education. The major programmes between 1978 and 1980 were UNICEF support for a Small Schools Development Programme; Swedish International Development Agencies support for science, technical and agricultural education as well as non-formal and distance education, and French support for non-formal education. UNESCO played a major role in the development of engineering courses at the University in the early 1970s while the USA contributed to the development of University level agriculture studies.

9 DEVELOPMENT AND PLANNING OF THE EDUCATION SYSTEM

Origins

following the introduction of Buddhism, an indigenous system of education was founded by the establishment of village schools, temple schools and *pirivenas*. The village and temple schools represented the primary and post-primary stages of the system, providing general education for the Buddhist laity, whilst the *pirivenas* made provision for higher education for both layment and clergy. (Two *pirivenas*, Vidyodaya and Vidyalankara, have been raised to university status as campuses of the university.) Curricula in all these were geared to the

Buddhist religion and so Pali and Sanskrit – the languages of the Buddhist canon – had an important place. Secular instruction was very limited. Christianity came with the Portuguese and with it the rise of a Catholic population. The need for Christian instruction led to the introduction of a 'Western' system of education, supported by missionaries who organised parish schools and colleges and whose primary objective was to promote their religion. The Dutch, on establishing their rule in the mid-seventeenth century, organised a system of village and parish schools to provide instruction in reading, writing and religion; they made attendance compulsory up to the age of 15 and, unlike the Portuguese, took sole responsibility for education. But the number touched by education remained a small fraction of the population.

British Period

The British administration required for its political stability and for the advancement of commercial interests a nucleus of native loyalists to be employed in the middle grades of the government service and commercial establishments. It further developed education, English and Christianisation being considered to be the essential basis for its purposes. The missionaries collaborated wholeheartedly in the promotion of education, which resulted in the evolution of a school system having two separate components; a small wealthy high grade group of schools giving English medium instruction and a wider network of less well endowed schools giving instruction in the vernacular. Further, in terms of management and control there was a clear dichotomy, schools being either government or private. This led to serious inequalities in the allocation of funds from government ot the different types of schools and in the opportunities for higher education and employment for pupils graduating from the English medium and vernacular schools. In 1869 the government defined its responsibilities by establishing a Department of Public Instruction (later the Department of Education). Thereafter a series of legislative measures made the system more functionally adequate for community needs. The operative law for the present system of education was embodied in the Education Act of 1939.

After 1939

From 1939 onwards and particularly after World War II, the changes that occurred in Sri Lanka were not confined to constitutional ones. The social and economic structure too underwent significant changes. The school system in many respects was static and increasingly out of gear with the development needs of the time. Legislation enacted by 1947 and 1951 aimed at democratisation of education by providing equality of educational opportunity. The measures included: adoption of the mother tongue of the pupils as medium of instruction; provision of free tuition in government schools, technical institutes and at university level; extension of State management to most schools; establishment of 66 *madhya maha vidyalayas* or central schools providing facilities for study to GCE 'A' level in both arts and science subjects; and introduction of scholarships for entry to the central schools.

Introduction of Planning

Planning only came to be recognised as a special and separate function of the Ministry of Education in 1968, when planning duties were for the first time assigned to a senior official. However, the ministry had in 1962 completed an analysis of educational costs in Ceylon and a few years earlier work had commenced on curriculum development in secondary school science. At the same time plans were drawn up for programmes aiming at the rapid expansion of science teaching facilities for GCE 'O' and 'A' levels. The school system had been unable to cope with the increasing demand for science graduates and secondary school leavers with a science-based education. Firstly, there was the shortage of science teachers and of laboratory facilities in the senior schools. Secondly, there was a scarcity of university science lecturers which inhibited the output of science graduates who could have taught in schools. Thirdly, the switch over after 1956 of the medium of teaching from English to the national languages meant that the techer force in this specialised area was limited to those able to teach science in the latter medium. These science programmes, financed and implemented through the ministry's budget, were the first decisive and practical examples of planning in education in Sri Lanka. In March 1971 a separate unit for educational planning was set up so that the full cycle of planning, organisation, administration, management and evaluation and review of plans were undertaken by the same team.

Five Year Plan

The first overall and comprehensive plan was produced by the planning unit in November 1971. Called 'Medium Term Plan for the Development of Education 1973-1977', it diagnosed the limitations of education in the country as an over-emphasis on academic-type curricula which were framed to cater for the needs of that small minority of the output of the educational system who competed for the limited number of jobs available as doctors, engineers, administrators or teachers. The plan defined the main objective of the curricular changes to be inaugurated from 1972 at the integration of the academic and vocational aspects of education in the general school system. It sought "to equip students with a good general education together with a basic familiarity with one or more vocational opportunities available to them". Detailed objectives of the five year plan were defined as:

- (i) realignment of the curriculum to ensure that education, including general education, formed an integral part of the national programme of development (emphasis on pre-vocational studies, science teaching, teaching of English)
- (ii) improvement of quality and effectiveness by reducing the number of examination repeaters and dropouts while maintaining standards
- (iii) improvement of provision and standards of teacher education and the quality of administrative and management personnel
- (iv) consolidation and extension of the work of the past decade in curriculum development, examination reforms, etc.
- (v) provision of a greater degree of equality of educational opportunity for poor urban and rural children.

Other Developments

New developments proposed or being implemented may be summarised as follows:

- (i) the government has contemplated (but not so far implemented) the setting up of a number of '12-year colleges' in secondary schools in major centres to give a pre-university course for students who have taken the GCE 'A' level. This would be a means of bridging the gap which threatens to exist between the probable achievements of the school system and the current expectations of the university which has been pressing for such a preparatory course
- (ii) community education projects are being introduced into the programmes of teacher training colleges and should be a component of all courses from 1977
- (iii) the provision of correspondence courses will be increased from 1978 to include diploma courses in engineering, agriculture and food science; and further and adult education seem likely to be given increased consideration
- (iv) the government may revive plans for a period of compulsory national service for school leavers and pre-university (the plans were set aside in 1975 primarily for financial reasons)
- (v) strengthening of the authority of the university administration will have to be put in hand, through the medium of amendments to the Higher Education Act, which was in part repealed by the University of Ceylon Act of 1972
- (vi) the government will have to face the implementation of its intention to bring the estate schools into the

national system; (depending upon the degree of integration envisaged, there will be a more or less significant financial involvement: at present 51% of the school age children on the estates receive primary education only and 39% no schooling at all)

(vii) a development of potential importance is the setting up of a Science Education Research Unit under the auspices of the national Science Council, to encourage such research at school and university level.

APPENDIX

NON-FORMAL AND RURAL DEVELOPMENT EDUCATION

Activity in non-formal education is fragmented between various agencies, government and private, and in general relates to community and agricultural development at village level. There would seem to be a need for a more comprehensive programme and for closer coordination and integration at the national level. In relation to this it is encouraging that the government has recently set up three organisations with a coordinating role: the Directorate of Non-Formal Education in the ministry; a ministerial committee for rural development work and the National Youth Service.

Youth Work

Youth settlement schemes (41) have been developed since 1965 as agricultural projects designed specially for the settlement of youth (girls as well as boys in some cases) and involve approximately 2,800 young people (though a number of schemes have neglected training aspects).

Practical Farm Schools (19) are intended to provide training in agricultural practices to young men and women wishing to engage in agriculture, after leaving school, on their own lands or lands reallocated to them by government; (but most students became applicants for government employment, e.g. in the Department of Agriculture); most of these schools have now been taken over by the education authorities to serve as training institutions for agricultural teachers in schools.

Young Farmers Clubs of which there are 3,000 with a registered membership of about 100,000, train youths aged 15 to 25 in various aspects of agriculture, farm management and marketing (but only about 40% of these clubs are functioning effectively).

The Department of Small Industries offers programmes mainly designed for young people of 15 to 24 in the rural sector. Annually about 10,000 school leavers are enrolled in textile production societies as apprentices for on-the-job training in handloom or powerloom weaving. The department runs approximately 250 workshops and training centres in a wide range of trades and crafts which include net weaving, pulp and rag toys, reed products, rattan and coir products, gem cutting and pottery. The training period is approximately 6 months. Training of longer duration and higher levels of instruction is given in 68 industrial schools managed by the department and 95 institutions in the private sector which are assisted by the government.

Sarvodaya (Lanka Jatika Sarvodaya Shramadana Sangamaya) is a private organisation active in about 400 villages. It was founded in 1958 with the aim of involving youth in rural development work. The impulse of the movement is found in the moral and religious principals, basically Buddhist, which form its core. It generally seeks to initiate a communal project such as a village road, which can activate a community project at the village level, but it also runs an educational institute to train youth in leadership, and a number of youth farms to assist young people to find gainful employment. At Tanamalwile in the Moneragala region it has established a project which combines a practical farm school with a number of farm enterprises designed to develop or demonstrate suitable patterns of diversified agriculture in the region.

Technical Training

Vocational training centres (two in Colombo and one at Marawila) are run by the Department of Labour (Vocational Training Branch, Employment Division) together with over 200 mobile centres operating throughout the country. At the former 450 trainee craftsmen are trained annually, courses being provided in radio servicing and repairs, electrical wiring, welding, fitting, etc.; the mobile centres offer courses of about six months' duration to groups of about 15 trainees per centre, in a variety of mechanical skills, masonry, carpentry, etc.

The National Apprenticeship Scheme was started in 1971 and organises courses in 16 different trades, available to about 600 youths over 16 years with 'O' level or equivalent.

The Sri Lanka Technical Institute, a private institution run by the de la Salle brothers, is at Ragama. The Institute takes in orphaned or deprived boys at the age of 16 and gives them training until age 21. The facilities include a mechanical engineering workshop, a woodwork shop, and an agricultural wing.

Rural Development

The Rural Development Department, set up in 1948, operates through a network of 230 Rural Development Officers, each llooking after several villages, and through over 5,000 voluntary Rural Development Societies in the villages (but the estates sector has not been included in such development). From 1970 the department has received substantial aid from the Konrad Adenauer Foundation, mainly in the field of training. The department has been able to establish ten provincial residential centres (to which the chief officials of each Rural Development Society come for a week's training in community development matters) and a central, also residential, Rural Development Training and Research Centre in Colombo (at which Rural Development Officers and public officials at the village level receive a month's training).

The Farmer Education and Training Programme organised by the Department of Agriculture is directed principally at the adult farming population. These courses are each of one day's duration and are organised around one or two practical farming programmes of immediate concern to the farmers of a given locality.

District Development Councils were established in 1971 by the Regional Development Division of the Ministry of Planning and Economic Affairs. Each Council covers the area served by the local government authority – the village or town council. They are intended to motivate the rural population to organise the planning and implementation of development at the village level. The projects, mainly organised as cooperative centures are designed to provide subsidiary food crops, minor irrigation works, diversification of small industries, etc., and to create employment for unemployed local youth.

The *Lanka Mahila Samiti* is a nationwide voluntary organisation for women which is said to have over 2,000 branches and promotes homecraft, mothercraft, cottage industries, agricultural pursuits, social hygiene, etc. The emphasis is on the 15 to 25 age group. There are 24 model centres throughout the island, with a trained supervisory worker at each centre.

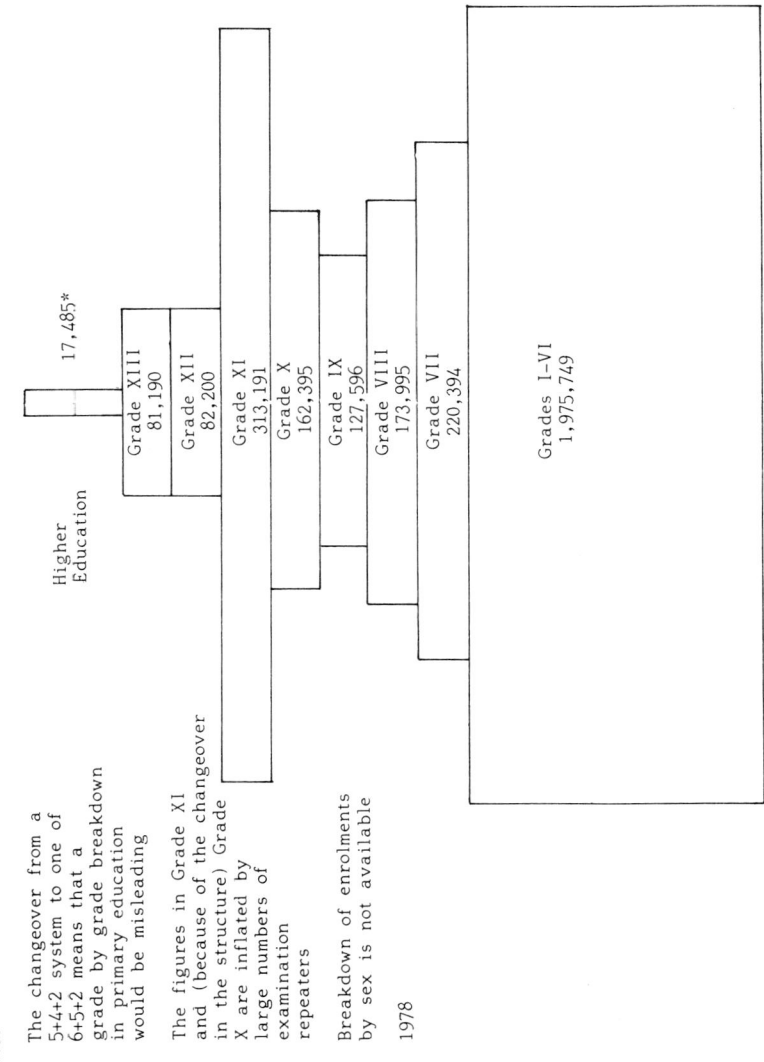

EDUCATIONAL PYRAMID 1979 - SRI LANKA

Higher Education 17,485*

Grade XIII	81,190
Grade XII	82,200
Grade XI	313,191
Grade X	162,395
Grade IX	127,596
Grade VIII	173,995
Grade VII	220,394
Grades I-VI	1,975,749

Notes

1 The changeover from a 5+4+2 system to one of 6+5+2 means that a grade by grade breakdown in primary education would be misleading

2 The figures in Grade XI and (because of the changeover in the structure) Grade X are inflated by large numbers of examination repeaters

3 Breakdown of enrolments by sex is not available

* 1978

Population

1970	1975	1979
12,516,000	13,514,000	14,741,000

Literacy (%) among adults 1971

Total	Male	Female
77.6%	86.0%	69.5%

Enrolment Ratios 1979

Primary = enrolment divided by the total population aged 5-10
Secondary = enrolment divided by the total population aged 11-17
Higher = enrolment divided by the total population aged 20-24

	Total	Male	Female
Primary	98.0%	–	–
Secondary	53.0%	63.0%	41.0%
Higher*	1.3%	1.6.	0.9%

Schools, Teachers and Pupils 1978 and 1979

	Schools	Teachers	Pupils
Primary	8,712*	60,835*	1,975,749
Secondary	–	58,755*	1,159,967

* 1978

Pupil Teacher Ratio in Primary Schools 1978 = 32

Percentages Repeating Grades 1979

Grade	1	2	3	4	5	6	7	8	9	10	11	12	13
	5	18	12	14	14	10	28	7	9	4	19	4	15

Higher Education Students by Field of Study 1978

	Total	% Female
Education and Teacher Training	10,881	61
Humanities and Religion	29,420	32
Law	9,682	13
Social and Behavioural Sciences	2,598	27
Commerce and Business	6,632	31
Natural Science	10,389	23
Medicine and Related Subjects	17,248	30
Engineering	19,473	13
Agriculture	5,075	17
Other	774	33

Expenditure on Education

Year	As a % of the Budget	As a % of GNP
1970	13.6	4.0
1980	7.0	2.2*

* 1978

Basic Social and Economic Data

Gross National Product per capita 1979 – US$230
Annual Growth of GNP per capita 1960-79 – 2.2%
Life expectancy at birth 1979 – 66 years
Average annual growth of population 1960-70 – 2.4%
Average annual growth of population 1970-79 – 1.7%
Percentage of the Working Population in

	Agriculture	1960	56%
		1979	54%
	Industry	1960	14%
		1979	14%
	Services	1960	30%
		1979	32%

Thailand

CONTENTS

1 Geography	516
2 Population	518
3 Society and Culture	519
4 History and Politics	521
5 The Economy	523
6 The Education System	525
7 Educational Administration	539
8 Educational Finance	544
9 Development and Planning of the Education System	545

Thailand, like several other countries of South East Asia, experienced considerable economic growth in the 1970s. But she is still a relatively poor country with a predominantly rural population mainly engaged in agriculture. Traditional values – associated especially with Buddhism – prevail despite modernising forces. Yet Thailand's educational response to the conflict between strong traditions and powerful elements of change have not been constrained by the same European colonial legacy which has affected many other Asian countries.

Economic growth in Thailand has allowed for educational expansion. Primary education is widely – almost universally available – while almost half the appropriate age group is in lower secondary schools. Upper secondary and higher education are well developed for a low income country. But there are constraints on the further expansion of post-primary education which are related not only to availability of government resources but also to the capacity of a mainly rural, agricultural, peasant society to absorb very large numbers of educated people. Thailand's economic development should not obscure the fact that her per capita income, while three times – or more – that of India, Pakistan, Vietnam or Cambodia is less than half that of Malaysia or that nearly 80% of the labour force is engaged in agriculture.

Thailand has faced fewer of the strains of religious and linguistic divisions which have affected many other Asian countries. The overwhelmingly Buddhist culture is tolerant of potentially conflicting intrusions while the Thai language predominates in both daily use and in education. But the secularist and Western nature of education is alien in some respects from traditional Buddhist conservatism and creates some social divisions.

Education in Thailand is free from direct colonial influences. The modern education system is the product of Thai initiative in the late nineteenth and early twentieth centuries. Western models were imported and grafted onto traditional Thai educational borrowing. The structure of the school system – both historical and contemporary – has been perhaps closer to that of France than of any other major Western country. The present day curriculum and system of assessment – and the comprehensive nature of the higher education system – is closest to practice in the United States of America.

These borrowings are not necessarily dysfunctional. The school structure, curriculum models and examination procedures allow for a high degree of diversity and flexibility. But there are still problems of relationship between a largely imported and alien education system and a traditional Thai society and culture.

1 GEOGRAPHY

Topography

Thailand covers an area of some 514,000 sq km (198,000 square miles) – almost the size of France. It is surrounded to the west and north west by Burma, to the north and north east by Laos, and to the east and south east by Cambodia. Southern Thailand consists of a long peninsula bounded on the west by the Indian Ocean and on the east by the South China Sea and the Gulf of Thailand, while to the extreme south lies Malaysia.

There are five natural regions. The central plain, with a third of the population and with the capital, Bangkok, is the political and economic hub of the country. Made up of flat alluvial lands watered by the floods of the Chao Phya River and its tributaries, it is frequently referred to as the Rice Bowl of Thailand (sometimes of Asia). The north and west are mountainous and are noted for their teak forests, soya beans and opium poppies. Numerous hill tribes live in the area. The densely-wooded southern peninsula abounds in tin, rubber, coconut and date palms. By far the poorest region of the country is the Korat Plateau of the north-east, where irrigation is inadequate and the soil is poor. Apart from rice subsistence farming it produces kenaf and silk, and some cattle ranches have been established.

Climate

The climate is essentially tropical, although north and east of Bangkok it can be described as savanna. In most of the

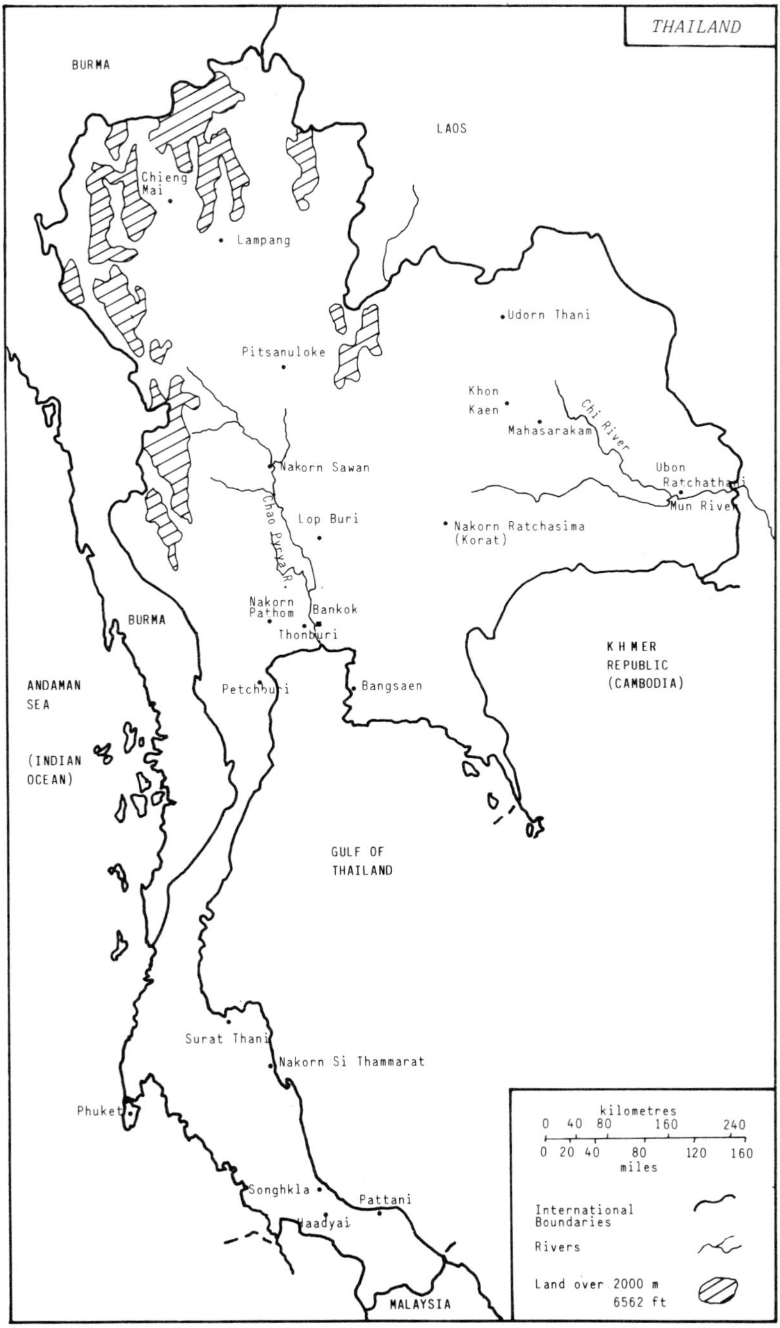
THAILAND
BURMA
LAOS
Chieng Mai
Lampang
Udorn Thani
Pitsanuloke
Khon Kaen
Mahasarakam
Chi River
Nakorn Sawan
Ubon Ratchathani
Mun River
Chao Pyrya R.
Lop Buri
Nakorn Ratchasima (Korat)
Nakorn Pathom
Bankok
Thonburi
BURMA
KHMER REPUBLIC (CAMBODIA)
ANDAMAN SEA
Petchburi
Bangsaen
(INDIAN OCEAN)
GULF OF THAILAND
Surat Thani
Nakorn Si Thammarat
Phuket
kilometres
0 40 80 160 240
0 20 40 80 120 160
miles
Songhkla
Pattani
Haadyai
International Boundaries
Rivers
Land over 2000 m 6562 ft
MALAYSIA

country there are distinct seasons: the wet season (May to November), cool season (November to February) and hot season (February to May). The average annual rainfall in Bangkok is 130 cm (55 inches) and the annual mean temperature is 28°C (82°F) though during the day in the hot season the temperature can rise to 41°C (106°F). There is relatively high humidity.

Communications

There are road and rail connections between all major centres. Good metalled roads connect Bangkok with the main regional centres and there is a growing network of secondary roads which are also metalled. Travel within the rural areas, however, still depends on laterite roads and, in the remoter areas, footpaths. The major rail connections are from Bangkok north to Chiengmai, through the south to Malaysia, and through the north east to the Mekong River, which forms the border with Laos. But much local travel and country-wide transport still depends on the country's extensive network of canals and rivers. Bangkok is an important port.

2 POPULATION

Growth

The first census in Thailand was taken in 1911, when the population was 8.3 million. At the census in 1970, the population was enumerated at 34.4 million, although after adjustment for under-enumeration, it was estimated to be about 36 million. The estimate at the end of 1980 was 46,961,338. The annual rate of natural increased decreased from about 3.1% in 1964/65 to about 2.8% in 1974/75 and to 2.4% average between 1970 and 1979. In 1970 about 45% of the population was under 15 years of age and about 25% was in the age group of 15-29 years. In that year a National Family Planning Programme was officially established with the objective of reducing the population growth rate to about 2.5% by the end of 1976.

Distribution

The average density is 80 per sq km (172 per square mile), but density is as high as 280 per sq km in certain parts of central Thailand. Despite considerable immigration to the towns, more than 80% of the population still live in villages and work as peasant farmers. Traditionally most of the farmers owned their own land, but lately landlords have acquired considerable holdings and the government has initiated a Land Reformation Plan. But, although the country is predominantly rural, it is dominated by one large urban centre, Bankok metropolis, which, with its smaller twin city Thonburi (part of the same conurbation) had a poulation of 5,153,902 in 1980. It is the capital, main port and main commercial and industrial centre of the country. The estimates annual growth rate of the population in Bangkok between 1970-80 is about 4.1% and for the whole kingdom 2.4%. Chiengmai, in the north, Thailand's only other city, has an urban population of approximately 150,000 and only five other towns have populations of over 25,000.

Groups

Although 80% of the population of Thailand is made up of Thais, there are numerous other ethnic groups within the country. The hill tribes - the Miao, Yao, Liso, Karen, Lahu - have settled over a long period, and today number about 250,000. Others were in occupation of lands at the time of boundary changes (e.g. Khmers, Mons, Malays). Today there are about 200,000 Khmers, 100,000 Mons and 700,000 Malays. Yet others have settled as immigrants (e.g. Chinese, Indians, Europeans).

Chinese

The Chinese are by far the largest group after the Thais, and number about 3 million. Originally welcomed by the Thai monarchs from the seventeenth to the late nineteenth centuries, they were assimilated into Thai society within one or two generations and added an important cultural and economic dimension to the nation. With the growth of Thai and Chinese nationalism in the earlier part of this century their presence became less welcome, since apart from retaining their own culture and individuality they dominated the economic life of the nation. A series of measures were taken by the Thai authorities during the 1930s, 1940s and 1950s to ensure Chinese assimilation, and although relations are now generally harmonious there still tend to be underlying tensions. The Chinese in Thailand are concentrated largely in the towns. Only about 300,000 are Thai nationals.

Others

The Indians and Pakistanis, who number about 60,000, have a much shorter history of residence in Thailand. They tend to be connected with the textile trade, money lending and a few other traditional occupations and live mostly in the Bangkok area or in the south. The Vietnamese, who also number about 60,000 are more recent immigrants, many of them being refugees from the Vietnamese war. These the government aims eventually to repatriate. They have mostly settled in the north east. Europeans, who number several thousand, tend to be a transient population. They mainly live in and around Bangkok.

3 SOCIETY AND CULTURE

Urban v Rural Society

Within Thai society there are great differences between the modernising, urban, class-structured sector, and the conservative, rural peasant sector of farmers whose culture and mode of life have for centuries revolved around the cultivation of rice. Rural society is remarkably similar in pattern from one village community to another. Veneration is held for the aged, those with religious merit (i.e. the local abbot and monks) and those with education. Hence teachers in rural areas are still highly respected. Since education in the past was for conformity to the existing system, there was little conflict between the generations, but also, little social change. Urban society, mainly concentrated in Bangkok, is highly structures and royal rank and official position in the civil service still carry the highest prestige. But wealth, education and personal connections are increasingly facilitating social mobility. The industrial labour force evinces some collective organisation in the establishment of a few labour unions. Whereas teachers are highly regarded in rural areas, they are little more than lowly paid employees in the city. The urban population is becoming increasingly Westernised and out of touch with the style and problems of life in the country.

Family Structure

The extended family was the traditional social unit, with arranged marriages; and even in the towns many houses still include accommodation for the elderly and for the wife's family. But with modernisation the tendency is for the nuclear family to become the basic social unit, with arranged marriages becoming the exception rather than the rule. Similarly, monogamy is fast becoming the norm, though polygamy remains tolerated. Women are emancipated and work alongside men, andin the cities many women have influential posts in business, the professions and government service.

Religion

Thailand is a Buddhist country. Buddism was introduced in the third century BC and took firm hold from the sixth century AD. As much as 94% of the population profess to be followers of Buddhism and in spite of the educational and technological advances religion is still today, as it was in the past, the keystone of Thai culture. An amorphous mass of customs, attitudes, and animist traditions etc. affect the daily life and actions of the majority of people, and one cannot travel far without seeing a group of monks in their saffron coloured robes or the rooflines of some of the country's 24,000 *wats* (temples). Even in sophisticated circles, very many people like to consult an astrologer and have the monks perform a religious ceremony before taking any major decision. This is even more true among the peasant families. In the villages the local *wat* is the centre of community life. It may be a community centre, a dispensary, hospital, warehouse or social shelter, or the village primary school. It is still commonly accepted that a young man should become a monk for at least a few months of his life. Individual monks are referred to as *bikkhus*. Collectively they are known as the *Sangha*. The total membership of the *Sangha* is about 170,000 in addition to 85,000 novices and 120,000 temple boys - a sizeable proportion of the possible working population. The *Sangha* is presided over by the Supreme Patriarch who is appointed by the King.

Buddhism is remarkably tolerant of other religions and for this reason alone there are few converts to other religions. There are about 700,000 Muslims, the largest religious minority in the country, most of whom are ethnically Malay and are concentrated in peninsular Thailand. Christians (Thai, Chinese and Vietnamese converts) number only 150,000, though the work of Christian missions in fostering education has been considerable.

Language

Since Thai policy has for long been to encourage assimilation into Thai society, and since some of the ethnic minority groups have cultural affinities elsewhere (e.g. the Malay to Malaysia, the Lao to Laos), the education system is used to create a sense of national loyalty to Thailand. Language policy is an important instrument in this. Apart from distinct alien languages - Chinese, Malay, English - Thai is the predominant language, and the central Thai dialect is recognised as the lingua franca. Thai is the medium of instruction in all schools (except for a few in the north for hill tribe children). English is not widely used, though some knowledge of it is held generally to be desirable and it is unofficially recognised as the major second language. It is an elective subject in the schools at all levels.

4 HISTORY AND POLITICS

Before 1918

The earliest record of the Thais is in sixth century Chinese annals, in which they are mentioned as living in south west China. By the seventh century they had already begun their southward migration, and in 1238 established what was to be the first important centre of Thai power and the cradle of modern Thai civilisation at Sukothai (today little more than a series of magnificent ruins). Sukothai's position declined within a century and was replaced by that of Ayudhya which became the capital of the Thai empire from the mid-fourteenth century until its destruction by the Burmese, after a long series of wars, in 1767. The Thais recovered remarkably quickly under the inspired leadership of a half-Chinese general, Taksin, who moved the capital to Thonburi; but it was the first kings of the present Chakri dynasty who consolidated the position. Two great nineteenth century kings, Mongkut (1851-1868) and Chulalongkorn (1968-1910) initiated wide-ranging programmes of reform and modernisation, using expertise from all Western sources. But, although some territory was ceded to both Britain and France, bu astute diplomacy Thailand retained her independence when the rest of south east Asia succumbed to colonial rule. By siding with the Allies in World War I Thailand was recognised on equal terms at the Treaty of Versailles.

Political Development

In 1932, a revolution led by officers and intellectuals ended the absolute monarchy and promulgated the first constitution. The 1930s saw the decline of parliamentary democracy and the growth of military power and nationalism. After World War Two (in which Thailand sided with Japan) there was a succession of civilian governments who attempted to restore democracy. But by 1948 military rule had been reimposed and despite attempted coups continued until 1957. Again attempts were made to restore parliamentary democracy but decisive action was hampered by pressure groups, and in 1958 military rule was again imposed. But the régime of FM Sarit Thanarat commanded wide support, carried out numerous reforms, attacked corruption, gave the King a greater role in public life and introduced an interim constitution. This government continued under the leadership of FM Thanom Kittikachorn after the death of FM Sarit. In 1968 a new constitution was introduced, and in 1969 elections were held (11 years after the last) which returned FM Thanom's party and government to power. But the government felt unacceptably constrained by the misuse of parliament by pressure groups, and on the pretext that internal security was threatened by Communist subversion, in November 1971 FM Thanom dissolved parliament, abrogated the constitution and restored martial law. Resistance grew and in October 1973 the government was driven out by student demonstrations which attracted vast popular support. At the height of the civil disorder the King played a vital role in easing out the ruling military dynasty and installing a civilian government.

The new government was led by Professor Sanya Dharmasakdi (a former university rector and President of the Supreme Court). It had been specially charged with introducing a permanent constitution and preparing for elections, and to this end the King called a National Convention which elected a 299-member Constituent Assembly to draft the constitution; this was approved in October 1974. Elections were held in 1975 to elect the 300-member lower house (the 100-member upper house was to be appointed by the King). No less than 44 parties contested the elections and 22 won seats. This fractionalism in parliament made stable government difficult and in October 1976 there was yet another military coup and the National Assembly was dissolved, martial law being declared. In October 1977 this government was overthrown in a bloodless coup led by the same military leaders who brought it to power. They set up a 23-man Revolutionary Council, abolished the oppressive 1976 constitution (the eleventh since 1932) and promised a return to democracy. Elections were held in April 1979 after the new constitution was drafted by the appointed National Legislative Council.

Regional Government

The country is divided into 71 provinces including Greater Bangkok *(Changwad)*, each of which is administered by a Provincial Governor, appointed by the Minister of the Interior. The Minister also appoints District Officers, who administer sub-divisions of the provinces. The larger towns govern themselves through municipal councils, while the villages elect their own headmen.

Internal Relations

At various distant periods in her history Thailand has been involved in major and protracted wars with Burma and Cambodia. Although this history still has resonance, Thailand's current foreign policy is based on the ideal of regional cooperation, which is realised through the Association of South East Asian Nations (ASEAN) and the South East Asian Ministers of Education organisation (SEAMEO). Her closest regional allies are Malaysia and the Philippines. Communist subversion in the border areas of the north and north east receives some support from Communist forces in Indo-China, and made Thailand a natural ally of the USA in the Cold War and Vietnam (during which bombing was launched from US air bases in Thailand). Thailand joined SEATO in 1954, and the Alliance's HQ were in Bangkok. However, since 1975 Thailand has attempted to forge closer relations with her communist neighbours and is following a policy of close diplomatic interest with the Khmer Republic (Cambodia) and Vietnam. Relations with Laos are complicated by Laotian political dependence on Vietnam (which Thailand would prefer kept at a distance) and economic dependence on Thailand itself. Border insurgency remains a problem and tensions exist with Laos and the Khmer Republic. Under successive military régimes Thailand followed the USA in having no official contact with China, but since 1975 diplomatic relations have also been established with the People's Republic.

5 THE ECONOMY

Agriculture

The Thai economy is based primarily on agriculture, products of which account for some 70% of the country's exports. Rice, which is the principal source of foreign exchange, accounts for about 17% of the total revenue from exports. Tapaioca is now an increasingly important export crop also. About 75% of the population earn their living on the land of which only about 34% is cultivated. However, the relative importance of agriculture in the economy is gradually declining; its share of the Gross Domestic Product had fallen from 43% in 1951 to a level of 20% in 1979. Traditionally most of the farmers owned their own land, but lately landlords have acquired considerable holdings, the return of which to the farmers is currently a hot political issue.

Industry

Since 1960 the share of the industrial sector in GDP has been steadily increasing and is now about 20%. However, local production still falls far short of the demand for manufactured goods which constitute more than half of the total imports. There is a long tradition of liberal free trade in Thailand and this is reflected in the fact that the industries which have been established since industrialisation really got under way are largely in the hands of private enterprise. Most of the 40,000 registered factories in Thailand are small undertakings but there is also an impressive range of medium and large concerns including two oil refineries, several iron and steel mills, integrated textile mills, ten vehicle assembly plants and tyre factories. About 8% of the labour force is employed in industry.

Natural Resources

There is a small mining sector which contributes about 2% of GNP and about 85% of mineral production is tin. However, there are also deposits of wolfram, scheelite, antimony, coal, copper, gold, iron, lead, manganese, silver, zinc and precious stones. Thailand is one of the world's leading producers of rubber (386,000 tonnes in 1976/77). There are also large resources of natural gas, enough to supply the country's needs for about 20 years, and exploration is being made for offshore oil. Ten offshore concessions in the Gulf of Thailand have been granted to foreign oil companies, including one British.

Trade

The principal countries from which Thailand imports are (in order) Japan, the USA, Saudi Arabia, the Federal Republic of Germany, Qatar, Britain, Singapore, Taiwan, Australia and other EEC countries. Her principal export markets are in Japan, the USA, south east Asia and the EEC. Principal exports are rice, teak, rubber, maize, kenaf (a jute substitute) and silk; and principal imports are manufactured goods, machinery, chemicals and fuels.

Economic Situation

Few developing countries can match Thailand's record of economic growth over the past decade. The GDP increased at an average annual rate of 7.7% between 1970 and 1979. Three five-year development plans went a long way to establishing the infrastructure necessary for further development. They were geared largely to the development of the industrial sector, but the Fourth Development plan (1977-81) was pledged to the expansion of rural incomes and employment, with rural development and agricultural diversification programmes, to reduce dependence on a few staple crops. Industrial development was to be geared towards agriculture-based export-oriented and labour intensive industries. After major setbacks in 1975 the growth rate in 1978 was 8.7% and the Plan aimed to sustain this, at the same time limiting inflation to 6% and population growth to 2.1%.

6 THE EDUCATION SYSTEM
Reform

In accordance with the 1960 Education Act there are, in Thailand, four levels of education, viz. kindergarten, elementary, secondary and higher. These categories still pertain but a considerable restructuring of the education system took place after 1978.

A system of lower primary, upper primary, lower secondary and upper secondary education (4:3:3:2/3) was replaced by one of primary, lower secondary and upper secondary (6:3:3).

Academic Year

The academic year, which lasts from mid-May to mid-March, in all government schools at all levels, was divided into two semesters (mid-May to mid-October and mid-November to mid-March. In 1978 this had the effect of increasing the number of working days per year from 180 to 220, in effect allowing the previous seven years of primary education to be taught in 6. Schools teach either a five- or six-day week. In private schools with elementary sections only, a three-term system is still allowed to operate (i.e mid-May to late August, early September to early December, and mid-December to mid-March). However, where private schools develop a secondary section, the two-semester system is applied throughout the school.

Kindergarten

Kindergarten education until recently was largely provided by the private sector and is voluntary. There is no stipulated period for such instruction. Whereas formerly there were three grades, with children entering at the age of 4 and going on to elementary schools at age 7, it is increasingly becoming the practice for children to begin formal schooling at the age of 6. The number of children enrolled in 1979 was 336,364, of whom 146,984 (44%) were in government schools.

Elementary *(Prathom Suksa)*

Before 1978 elementary education was divided into two cycles of four and three years. Since then a unified six-year course has been introduced. Education is compulsory by law between the ages of 6 and 12.

There are both public and private primary schools though less than 8% of all pupils are in private institutions. Up to 1980 only a minority of schools were controlled directly by the Ministry of Education while the majority were the responsibility of the Local Administration Department of the Ministry of the Interior. So in 1978, 2% of pupils in public primary

THE STRUCTURE OF THE REFORMED

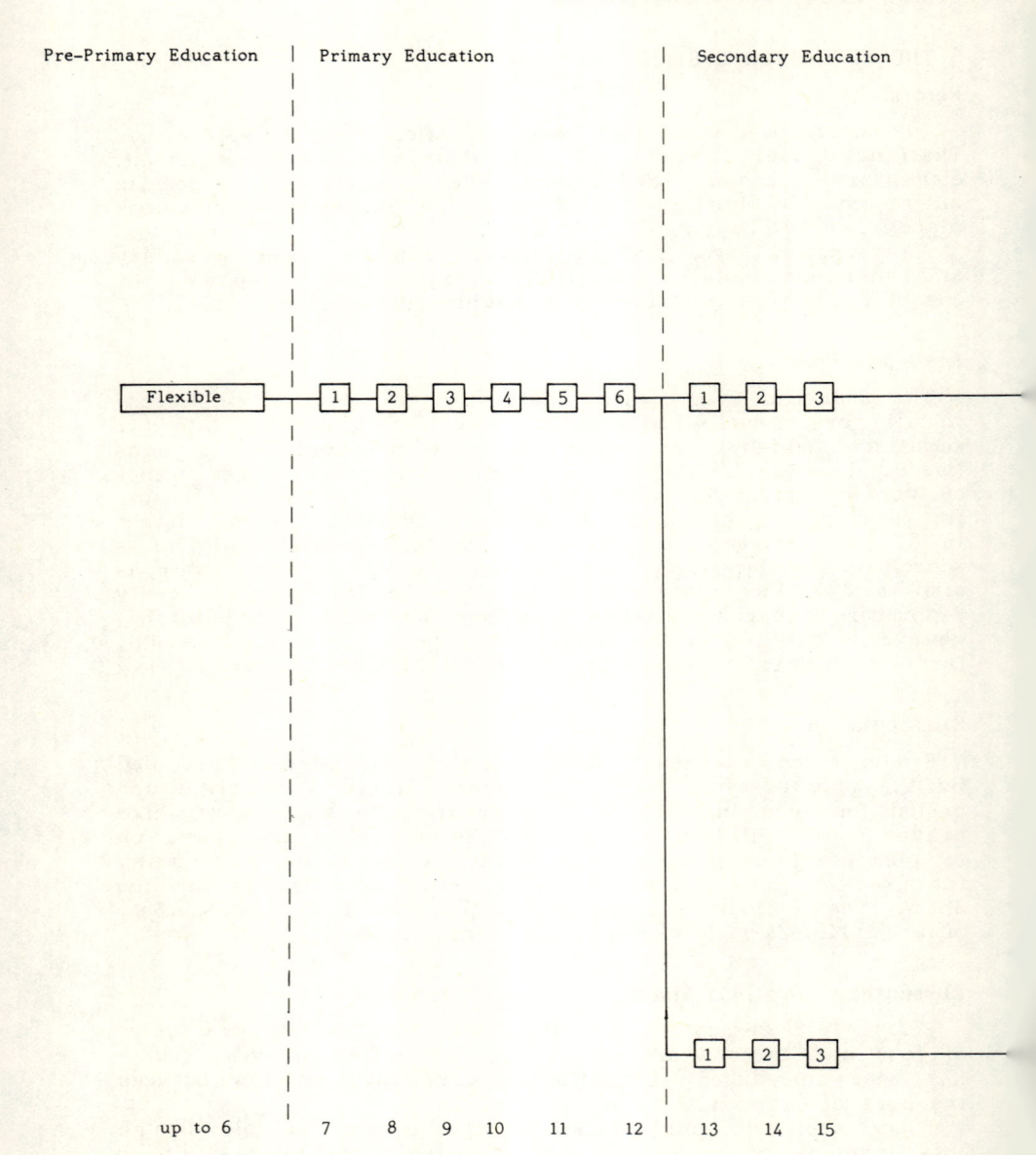

Pre-Primary Education | Primary Education | Secondary Education

Flexible — 1 — 2 — 3 — 4 — 5 — 6 | 1 — 2 — 3

1 — 2 — 3

up to 6 | 7 8 9 10 11 12 | 13 14 15

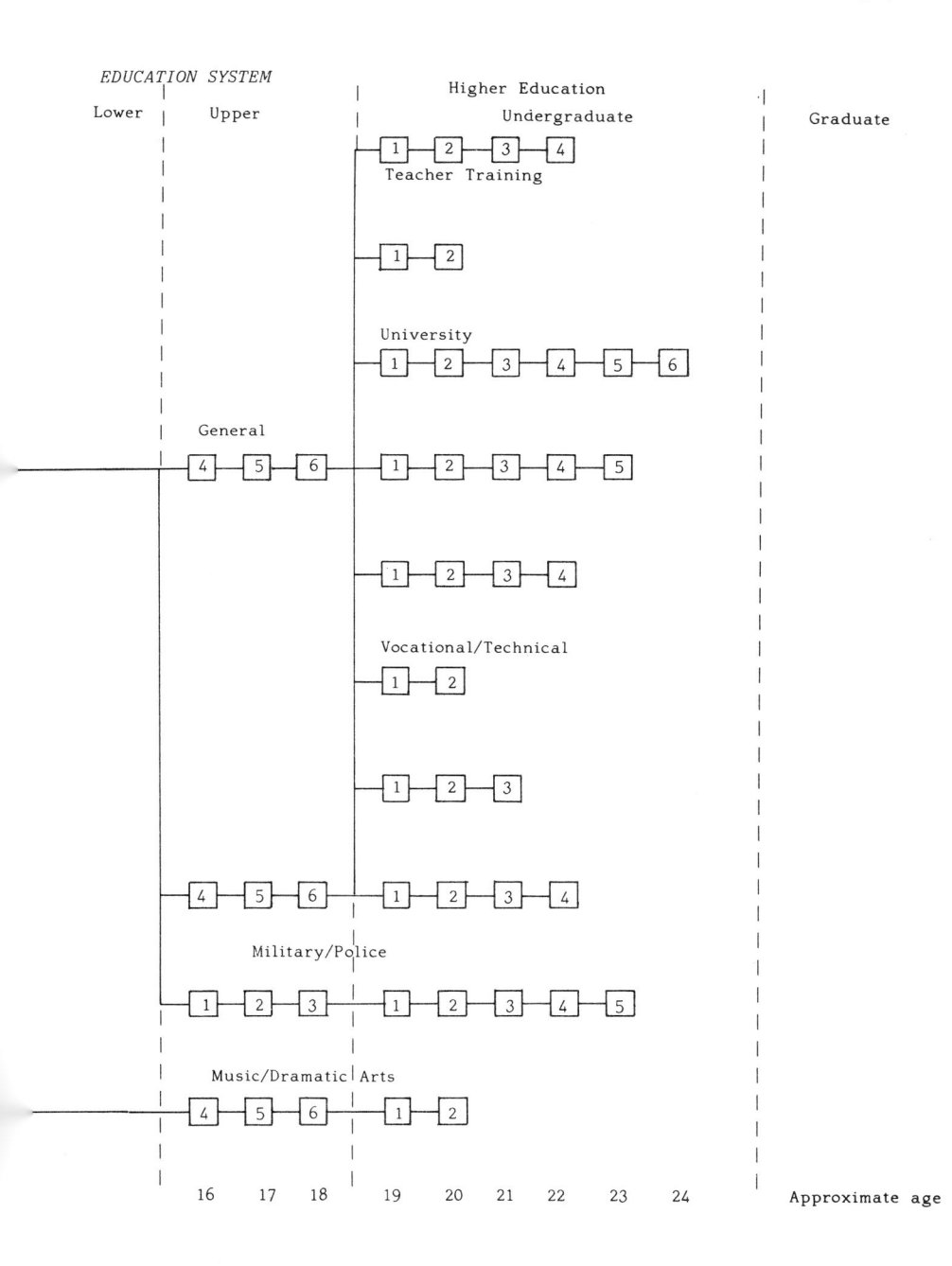

EDUCATION SYSTEM

| Lower | Upper | Higher Education | | Graduate |

Undergraduate

| 1 | 2 | 3 | 4 |

Teacher Training

| 1 | 2 |

University

| 1 | 2 | 3 | 4 | 5 | 6 |

General

| 4 | 5 | 6 | | 1 | 2 | 3 | 4 | 5 |

| 1 | 2 | 3 | 4 |

Vocational/Technical

| 1 | 2 |

| 1 | 2 | 3 |

| 4 | 5 | 6 | | 1 | 2 | 3 | 4 |

Military/Police

| 1 | 2 | 3 | | 1 | 2 | 3 | 4 | 5 |

Music/Dramatic Arts

| 4 | 5 | 6 | | 1 | 2 |

16 17 18   19 20 21 22 23 24   Approximate age

schools were in institutions administered by the Ministry of Education, 91% were in schools run by the Local Administration Department and 7% were in municipal schools. Since 1980 all public primary schools have been transferred to the Ministry of Education.

In the unified six-year primary curriculum, developed in 1977, subjects are grouped into four areas, namely basic skills, character development, life experience and work orientation. A large part of the curriculum in the life experience and work orientation areas varies with local conditions. In terms of the contents of the primary school curriculum, basic skills include the Thai language and mathematics; character development includes moral education, physical education, fine arts, musical values and special activities aimed at enhancing the quality of life; life experience includes social studies, science and hygiene (to be taught in an integrated fashion rather than as separate subjects); work preparation includes such subjects as agriculture, crafts and trades. Foreign languages are not compulsory in the primary school, but may be offered as electives in grades 5 and 6. Government guidelines for curricula and syllabi are followed in all schools, government or private.

Examinations are administered by local authorities at the end of Grade VI. Internal examinations which determine student promotion are held at the end of grades 2 and 4.

Secondary *(Mathayom Suksa)*

There are three types of secondary school: academic, vocational and comprehensive, and the same kind of gradual transformation from existing curricula designed for specific purposes, whether academic or vocational, towards a more comprehensive type of education is taking place within the secondary sector. Until 1965, all the academic stream schools concentrated on academic subjects, while practical vocational training was left to secondary vocational schools. In 1966 it was decided that this would not satisfy the country's needs for trained middle level manpower. Rather, the academic secondary schools should be transformed into comprehensive schools using a combined academic/vocational syllabus. All three types of schools exist, and varying curricula are followed. Not all schools have yet developed all the grades necessary to complete the secondary curriculum, but in due course the final pattern should emerge (see chart). At secondary level the possibility of vocationalisation will be realised through the implementation of a curriculum which will consist of compulsory core subjects, optional areas and more specialised elective subjects. There still remains a distinction between general and vocational schools. The division of secondary education into two cycles, each of three years makes it possible for specialised vocational education to take place in the second of these cycles. Secondary education, then, aims at providing students with general knowledge and skills useful for earning a living, enabling them to continue their studies at a higher level if they so desire.

Lower Cycle

The content breakdown of what might be termed a comprehensive syllabus at lower secondary level (grades 7-9) is as follows (periods per week):

	Grade 7 Compulsory	Grade 7 Elective (up to)	Grade 8 Compulsory	Grade 8 Elective (up to)	Grade 9 Compulsory	Grade 9 Elective (up to)
1 Language						
Thai	4	–	4	2	4	–
Foreign	–	6	–	6	–	8
2 Science–Maths						
Science	4	–	4	–	4	–
Mathematics	4	–	4	–	–	6
3 Social Studies	5	–	5	–	5	4
4 Personality Development						
Physical Education	3	2	3	2	3	4
Art Education	2	2	2	4	–	6
Activities	3–5	–	2–5	–	3–5	–
5 Work & Occupation	4	6	4	6	4	12
Total	35		35		36	

Upper Cycle

For grades 10-12 in 1978 (a transitional stage) the total semester credits required are approximately 150.

Compulsory subjects (approximately 50 semester credits)

	Approx. Credits
Thai language	18
Social Studies	18
Science	9
Physical Education	5
Sub-total	50

Elective subjects (approximately 100 semester credits)

Thai language	up to	24
Social Studies	up to	24
Sciences	up to	66
Mathematics	up to	36
Vocational subjects	up to	84
Physical Education	up to	18
English	up to	60
Second foreign language	up to	24
Art Education	up to	18
Other subjects	up to	12
Special activities	up to	6
Sub-total	up to	100
Grand total	150 semester credits	

Vocational

The secondary vocational school curriculum for grades 10-12 produced in 1978, is designed to offer training in professional subjects and technical skills. The aim is to supply manpower needed for the development of the national economy, particularly in the fields of agriculture, industry, commerce and home economics. Whereas for the comprehensive type of school the vocational subjects are intended to be occupationally orientated, for this type of school skill training is to be offered. There are general subjects, all compulsory, worth 45 semester credits. For the occupational subjects, 55 subjects are compulsory and 40 credits elective.

Private Schools

The private sector plays an important and significant role at all levels of education, except in teacher training. Whereas, in 1977, there were about 2.5 million students in the formal school system at all levels in Ministry of Education schools, and a further 6 million under other authorities, almost 1.25 million children were receiving education in the private sector. With increasing government provision of places, however, the private sector share of enrolments is expected to continue to fall. The main types of private school are Chinese, Muslim and Thai, but a handful of schools operate for the European, Japanese and American children of foreign business and diplomatic parents. Some religious schools operate in the Muslim south.

Technical and Vocational

In addition to the secondary schools offering vocational courses there are several other types of training, particularly at post-secondary level. Many of them may be classed under the heading of non-formal or adult education, but within the formal system the following pattern is found.

In addition to general education courses of an academic type, provision is made under the aegis of the Department of Vocational Education for instruction to be given in areas of specialisation, such as trade and industry, commerce, home economics, fine arts and crafts, agriculture; and for there to be several levels of teacher training matching these specialisations. Schools, colleges, polytechnics and universities provide a wide variety of short and long term courses to cater for varying vocational needs by means of day courses. Additionally, by means of evening classes, many of the same institutions cater for adults who are either seeking to gain or improve qualifications to enhance their earning power, or attempting non-formally to complete their grade-school qualifications so as to reach a take off point from which to qualify for entry to the adult education opportunities offered, or who wish to participate in life long education schemes, to which government is increasingly turning its attention.

In 1974 an Institute of Vocational Technology was created with the status of a department within the Ministry of Education. Originally it aimed to provide two year courses for graduates of vocational colleges, leading to a Bachelor degree in technology, the fields to be covered being vocational teacher training, engineering, business, home economics, fine arts and agriculture, using the campuses and staff of nine existing colleges, with the prospect of there being a central campus in Bangkok, to control and oversee activities. This has now become the Institute of Technical and Vocational Education (ITVE) and includes the provision of general trades teaching courses up to diploma level (i.e. technician training). Its headquarters (a technical teacher training college) is at Thawet, Bangkok and courses are run at 10 technical institutes, 4 business institutes, 4 home economics colleges and 10 agricultural colleges.

Stemming from the agricultural element provided in the primary and secondary curricula, vocational agricultural schools (of which there were 22 in 1978, in addition to 6 agricultural colleges running secondary level courses) lead on to 13 vocational agricultural colleges where post-secondary courses lead to a higher certificate *(diploâm)* in agriculture. Two institutes of agricultural technology at Bang Pra and Mae Jo offer two-year degree courses in agricultural technology. Four universities, Kasetsart, Chulalongkorn, Khon Kaen and Chiengmai offer several further specialisations, including veterinary science, forestry, fisheries, soil and food science and so on.

Higher

For those students who have completed grade 1 or its equivalent in the school system there are 14 State higher educational institutions and 10 private colleges, all now under the jurisdiction of the Office of State Universities.

The State higher educational institutions in the capital are as follows:

> Chulalongkorn University
> Thammasat University
> Mahidol University
> Kasetsart University
> Silpakorn University
> The National Institute of Development Administration
> The Asian Institute of Technology
> King Mongkut's Institute of Technology
> Srinakharinwirot University (3 branches)

All of these are sited in or near the Bangkok-Thonburi area. Chulalongkorn is the oldest, largest and most famous of the Thai universities, having been founded in 1917. Other universities followed, developing from training schools or colleges established by various ministries (Thammasat being originally the law school of the Ministry of Justice: Kahidol becoming a university from within the Ministry of Public Health: Kasetsart being founded by amalgamating the School of Agriculture and the School of Forestry within the Ministry of Agriculture) but they have developed other faculties over the years. In addition, three regional universities, Chieng Mai in the north, Khon Kaen in the north east and Prince of Songkhla in the south have been established within the last decade. Four further branches of Srinakharinwirot University (the former College of Education) have been opened at

Mahasarakam, Pitsanuloke, Bangsaen and Songkhla. More recently, in addition to the establishment in 1982 of Ramkhamhaeng University (an open access university admitting all qualified applicants) a new open university(entitled Sukothai Thammathirat University) was established in 1978.

In 1975 the Chiang Mai College of Agriculture (Mae Jo), formerly under the Department of Vocational Education, Ministry of Education, was reorganised and upgraded as the Institute of Agricultural Technology and came under the jurisdiction of the Office of State Universities. In the same year the Teachers' Training College Act was promulgated giving degree-granting status to 17 teachers' training colleges under the supervision of the Ministry of Education, while the Institute of Technology and Vocational Education Act was announced, combining 28 technical colleges as one institute preparing vocational teachers both at a level below that of a degree and at bachelor's degree level. There are also Army, Air Force, Navy and Police Academies, while a considerable number of Thais are studying full time overseas for first or second degrees.

In 1979 there were 388,791 undergraduate students in universities and 9,400 post-graduates. Ramkhamhaeng University had the most students (307,000) followed by Srinakharinwirot (23,936), Chulalongkorn (16,296), Thammosat (10,859), Kasetsat (8,850) and Chiang Mai (8,563).

University teaching is closer in appearance to the system followed in the United States than to that in Britain, and a credit system is used. Examinations are held at the end of each semester and a 60% pass mark is required to continue and to graduate. All courses are conducted in Thai but English at tertiary level, while not a compulsory subject, has an important place among general foundation subjects in the first and second years of study: of an obligatory 30 credits in general education subjects (out of a total of 240 qualifying for the award of a degree), 6 are awarded to language courses. Because comparatively few technical books have been translated into Thai (though considerable efforts are being made to change this situation) attention is paid to improving students's knowledge of English in the first years of their courses so that they may use it as a library language at the upper levels of their studies.

The period 1964-74 was the most important decade in university history, witnessing the foundation of the regional universities and the upgrading of other institutions to university status. Since then efforts have been made to coordinate programmes offered within universities so as to meet social needs. The introduction of a nationwide credit system was initiated in 1957 and while still not wholly accepted, may be quoted as an example of educational innovation over a long period of time leading to standardisation. Curriculum development, along the lines of the development of interdisciplinary programmes within universities seeks to enhance flexibility and responsiveness to local and national social needs.

Teacher Training

Teacher training has been offered at the secondary and higher education levels, providing teachers for primary and secondary education. The whole question of teachers' qualification is complex and altogether there are 38 ways to become a teacher in general education and 9 ways to become a vocational school instructor. Though in recent years teacher training has been the fastest growing sector of the education system, a slow down is gradually coming into effect.

The number of students in training fell from 130,959 in 1976 to 88,690 in 1978. There has also been an upgrading of the level of training. In 1976, 72,267 students were preparing for the Teachers' Certificate in secondary level institutions (55%) while in 1978 the number had fallen to 23,830 (27%). The largest proportion of students in 1978 were taking the Diploma in post-secondary institutions (68%) though only small proportions were following degree courses in university level education (0.2% in 1976 and 5% in 1978).

By 1982 the secondary level certificate was phased out and all teachers now are offered either post-secondary or degree level studies. The general upgrading trend towards producing academically better qualified teachers has developed since 1974, and by 1978 some 3,000 teachers with a BEd degree had graduated from the teachers' colleges. Though the Department of Vocational Education, the Department of Physical Education, the Department of Fine Arts and the faculties of education at seven universities all train some specialised teachers, the vast majority are produced by the Teacher Training Department and the Srinakharinwirot University (formerly the College of Education). The latter has 7 branches (4 of them outside Bangkok). It offers bachelor degrees in arts and science as well as education. Of the 36 TTCs, 25 now offer BEd courses, but the majority of these in a limited range of major subjects only. Thus students wishing to major in, say, English may not be able to do so at the college where they did their Education Certificate.

Six basic types of pre-service training are given:

(i) a two-year course after grade 10 or a one-year course after grade 12 leading to a Lower Certificate (this has now been phased out)

(ii) a two-year course after the Lower Certificate or grade 12 leading to a Higher Certificate

(iii) a four-year course after the Lower Certificate or after grade 12 leading to a BEd degree

(iv) a two-year course after the Higher Certificate leading to a BEd degree

(v) a two-year course after the BEd leading to an MEd degree (at Srinakharinwirot University only)

(vi) a one-year course after BEd leading to a Higher Certificate for Specialised Teaching (also at SNU only).

The Lower Certificate qualifies a teacher for work in elementary schools, the Higher Certificate or Diploma for work in lower secondary schools, and a degree for work in upper secondary schools, though in theory teachers with the higher qualifications may also teach in the lower levels. Courses are organised on the credit system. The curriculum at the Lower Certificate level has to provide not only teaching methods and practice but also an education equal to that of grades 11 and 12 in ordinary secondary schools. Thus almost 60% of the periods are devoted to general education. At the higher level more time is given to major, minor and elective subjects.

Rural Development

In a large number of Thailand's rural communities the teacher may well be the only educated outsider, and if these communities are to develop along the desired path it is necessary for the teacher not only to be effective in the classroom, but also an agent of change in the community at large. In recent years the curriculum has given added emphasis to rural and community development subjects.

Non-Formal

As stated in the National Educational Policy of the National Education Scheme 1977, the significance of non-formal education is underlined as follows:

> "The State shall endeavour to step up and promote various kinds of out-of-school education in order to make available life-long education to all, especially to those who missed initial formal schooling."

The Adult Education Division of the Ministry of Education is among the most important agencies carrying out several out-of-school activities which are intended to complement general schooling by a transferred credit system and to provide opportunities for educational and vocational advancement for the disadvantaged. Apart from the Ministry of Education, several other government and private agencies run adult education and training courses (such as the Department of Labour) the central coordination system being at present under the National Committee on Non-Formal Education.

The first official schemes started in 1940 and there are now a large number of out-of-school programmes emanating from four different ministries. Considerable efforts have been made to improve non-formal and second-chance education, with varying success, though high growth rates, particularly in respect of the literacy campaign, seem to have been achieved. programmes emanating from the Ministry of Education may be listed as follows:

(i) the Functional Literacy Programme
(ii) the School Equivalency Programme

(iii) the Village Newspaper Reading Centres Project
(iv) the Radio and Television Programme
(v) the Interest Group Programme
(vi) the Mobile Vocational Training Programme
(vii) the Private Special Vocational Schools Programme
(viii) the Polytechnic Schools Programme.

The Ministry of Agriculture and Cooperatives operates

(i) the Training of Young Farmers Scheme
(ii) the Training of Advisers to Young Farmers Scheme.

The Ministry of the Interior operates:

(i) Youth Training Centres
(ii) Youth Training in Sensitive Areas
(iii) Village Development Committee Training.

The Ministry of Industry, through various UNDP/ILO assisted projects, such as the National Institute for Skill Development, the Management Development and Productivity Centre and the Small Industries Service Institute, operates a variety of training courses for adults, related to industry. The list of activities is by no means exhaustive.

Functional Literacy

This programme is taught through evening classes. Beginning in 1970, it had by 1975 an enrolment of 17,807 adult learners. Figures for 1977 are given as 18,362 and for 1978 as 21,320.

School Equivalency

General adult education provides an opportunity for those who need grade level equivalency certificates for employment purposes and is therefore known as the School Equivalency Programme. Instruction is provided at five levels which have equivalences in the school system as follows:

Level 1 = primary grades 1 & 2
Level 2 = primary grades 3 & 4
Level 3 = primary grades 5 & 6 (+7)
Level 4 = lower secondary level (M1-3)
Level 5 = upper secondary level (M4-6)

These 'second chance' evening classes are also mainly carried out in **regular** schools. In 1974, 687 schools participated, **holding 3,000** or more classes, with enrolments as follows:

Levels 1 & 2 -   6,090
Level 3   - 58,998
Levels 4 & 5 - 53,675

By 1977 total enrolment was quoted as 132,566 and for 1978, 132,955.

Village Newspaper Reading Centres

This project was set up in 1972 to provide the community with news and information, to promote literacy skills and to prevent relapse into illiteracy. It had 3,929 centres functioning in 1978, with expectations that 5,094 would be in operation in 1979. Eventually it is planned that there will be 8,400 such centres functioning in Thailand. Information is further propagated through the use of wall newspapers. In a fortnightly edition of 50,000 copies matters concerning general education are distributed throughout the country, while a monthly edition of 20,000 copies focuses on family planning and population problems.

Radio and Television

While in 1974 a comparatively limited use was being made of the mass media in non-formal education, there has been a considerable expansion since then, particularly in the use of radio. Since 71% of households in Thailand have radio sets, radio has an advantage over other mass media. Television has been recognised as an effective tool of education and the Centre for Educational Technology and the Department of General Education, in cooperation with existing radio and television stations, are beginning to develop programmes. At present, for radio purposes, five 30-minute programmes of general education are broadcast weekly by the Adult Education Division but the number of listeners they reach is not known.

In 1974 it was recommended that the provision of educational advancement opportunities should be focused on areas where school facilities were still in shortfall. These were identified at grades 5 and 6 of the primary sector (Level 3 in the Equivalency Project) in some of the most disadvantaged regions, where also a form of accelerated lower secondary schooling (level 4) was required. Accordingly a Radio Correspondence Project was set up. The project pilot phase began in 1976, though it came effectively into operation in 1977, and will by 1984 involve the General Education Programme at Levels 3 and 4, interest group subjects and functional literacy courses. Courses given at present are of two main kinds:

(i) academic level 3
(ii) interest group courses

(level 4-13 started in 1980).

Academic courses are broadly equivalent to the 'in-school and 'second-chance' courses at these levels, but are 'group study' orientated. The Interest Group Programme was organised to provide training on request to any group on any subject arranged by the Adult Education Division. The topics for study are based on the problems, needs and interests of the people so that what is studied can provide the knowledge and experience necessary to help them and their community. Interest group subjects are determined by needs assessment surveys. They may cover any topic from family law to family planning, but initially they are focused on agricultural and health topics mainly. Courses may be of unequal duration, though generally last between 5 and 30 hours of sessional group meetings. Learners are supplied with self-instruction manuals. Radio programmes (for both academic and interest group subjects) are broadcast and relate to the contents of each session. All programmes are produced in the regional centres to give them relevance to local conditions or customs. At present each regional centre uses the Public Relations Department and other local transmitters. When the projected second educational transmission network is operating, radio correspondence will have 20 hours of air time each week.

Student enrolment for level 3 in 1979 was 1,684 and for interest groups 2,250. For 1980 the numbers for levels 3/4 were estimated at 5,250 and for interest groups 6,100; and for 1981 estimates are: for levels 3/4 - 7,200, for interest groups - 6,650. By 1984, with the inclusion of functional literacy courses, it is estimated that there will be 119,340 students taking courses.

Libraries

In addition to functional literacy, reading centres and radio programmes, there is a modest system of public libraries which was initiated in 1948 through provincial authorities and in 1974 this consisted of 330 libraries, with an estimated readership of 204,780. More up to date figures are not to hand.

Vocational

In terms of vocational advancement and skill training, the Mobile Vocational Training Programme augments the adult vocational schools' evening class programme which started in 1949. The latter offers short courses in auto-mechanics, radio repairing and farm machinery. Mobile adult vocational units began in 1950, offering three-week courses in agriculture, dressmaking and mechanics. Mobile Trade Training Schools started in 1960 under the Department of Vocational Education and were transferred in 1973 to the Division of Adult Education. These offer a wide range of courses of a maximum duration of 300 hours. Of these 32 were operating in 1979 and 11 more became operational in 1980. Some of them are attached to life long education centres, 24 of which are being established, under an IBRD project, to coordinate adult education programmes at provincial level.

The ten polytechnics offer short courses of about $3\frac{1}{2}$ months duration in several trades ranging from auto-mechanics to typewriting, while the National Institute for Skill Development, created in 1969 under the Department of Labour, runs pre-employment, upgrading instructor/foreman, on-the-job and other training courses and is the only training institution to have some direct link with industry. It consists of a national centre in Bangkok and five regional centres in Ratchaburi, Chon Buri, Lampang, Wat Thatung and Khon Kaen. A sixth regional centre is (with assistance from German aid sources) being constructed at Songkhla. By 1976 some 16,363 trainees had received instruction, of whom some 10,000 had graduated. The Ministry of Defence, through its military technical school, provides training in several industrial trades, while other governmental and para-governmental agencies such as the Railway Engineering School, the Post and Telegraph School and the Electrician Training Centre, the Prison Department, and certain municipalities, operate pre-service and in-service training courses for employees. Many thousands more young people learn their trades on the job.

Agricultural

For agriculture, courses in practical agriculture are run by the Ministry of Education; the Ministry of Agriculture and Cooperatives provides agricultural extension services, while the Ministry of the Interior provides support for socio-economic development of the rural population. Universities run rural development projects mainly for villagers. Additionally, non-governmental agencies assist at this level.

7 EDUCATIONAL ADMINISTRATION

Ministerial Responsibility

The educational administration of Thailand up to 1980 was unusual in that education was carried out by four ministries. The Ministry of Education was responsible for all secondary education, a small portion of primary education, and most of teacher training and vocational/technical training, which overlap into post-secondary education. The Ministry of the Interior supervised most primary education administered by local authorities (*Changwad* administrative organisations and municipalities). The Office of University Affairs, with ministry status, supervised government universities and private colleges, and the Office of the National Education Commission, under the Office of the Prime Minister, was the long term policy and planning body for all levels of education. In addition, a few other ministries carried out non-formal education and specialised education for specific groups of people, such as the military academies of the Ministry of Defence. The objectives, responsibilities, administrative systems, and implementation of education vary greatly for different types of institution.

In 1980, however, the Ministry of Education assumed total responsibility for primary education. The Local Administration Department of the Ministry of Interior lost its educational responsibilities.

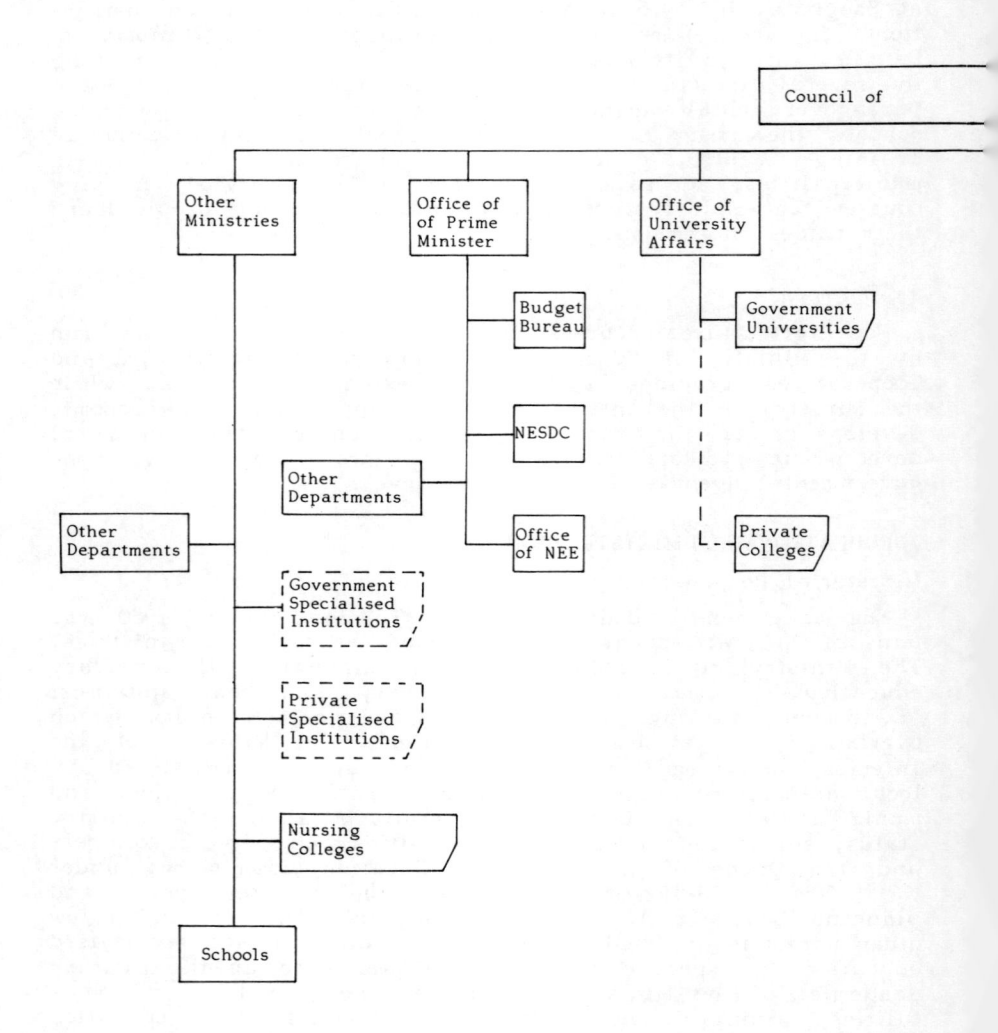

ORGANISATION OF

```
                                                    ┌──────────────┐
                                                    │ Council of   │
                                                    └──────┬───────┘
        ┌───────────────────────┬───────────────────────┤
  ┌─────┴─────┐         ┌───────┴───────┐       ┌───────┴───────┐
  │ Other     │         │ Office of     │       │ Office of     │
  │ Ministries│         │ of Prime      │       │ University    │
  │           │         │ Minister      │       │ Affairs       │
  └─────┬─────┘         └───────┬───────┘       └───────┬───────┘
        │                       │                       │
        │                       ├──┐                    ├──┐
        │                       │  │ Budget Bureau      │  │ Government Universities
        │                       │                       │
        │                       ├──┐                    │
        │                       │  │ NESDC              │ (dashed)
        │             ┌─────────┤                       │
        │             │ Other   │                       │
        │             │ Depts   ├──┐                    │
        │             └─────────┘  │ Office of NEE      ├──┐
  ┌─────┴─────┐                                         │  │ Private Colleges
  │ Other     │
  │ Departments│
  └─────┬─────┘
        ├── (Government Specialised Institutions) [dashed]
        │
        ├── (Private Specialised Institutions) [dashed]
        │
        ├── Nursing Colleges
        │
  ┌─────┴─────┐
  │ Schools   │
  └───────────┘
```

EDUCATION IN THAILAND

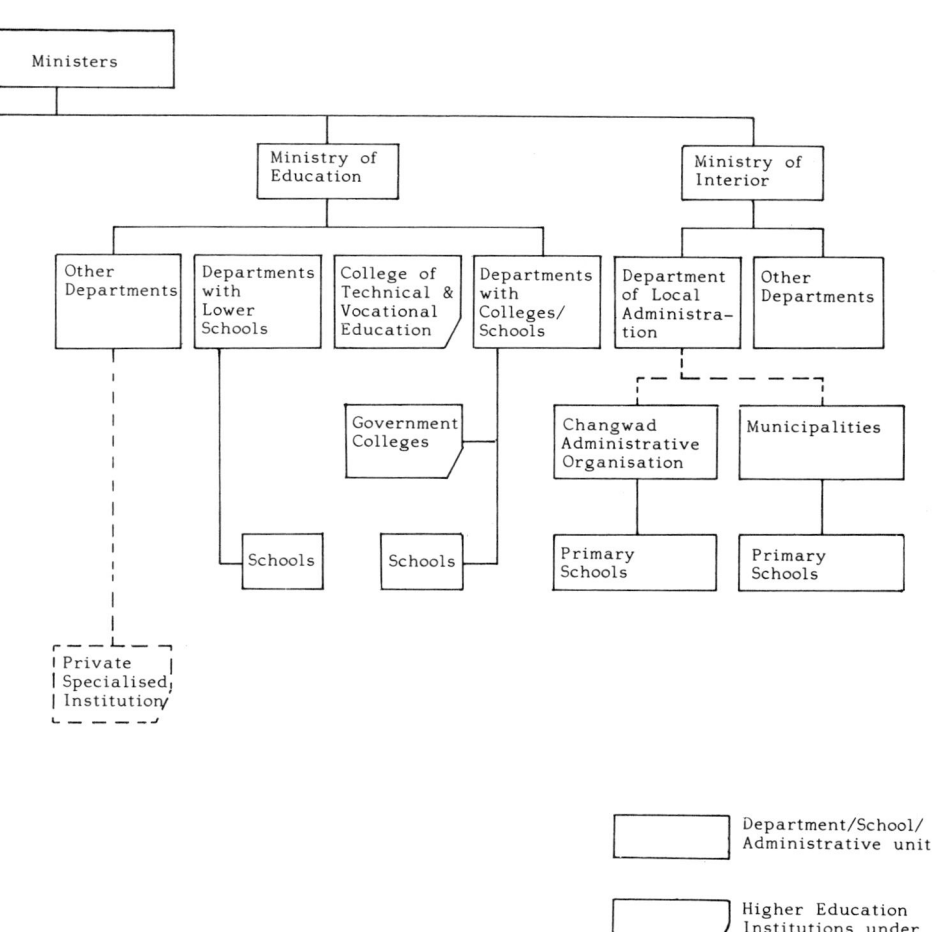

	Department/School/ Administrative unit
	Higher Education Institutions under Central Planning
	Higher Education Institutions not under Central Planning
NESDC	National Economic & Social Development Commission
NEC	National Education Commission

Office of the Prime Minister

Within the Prime Minister's Office there are some organisations concerned solely with administering education, and various organisations part of whose functions are related to the educational system. The National Economic and Social Development Commission (NESDC), the Budget Bureau and the Civil Service Commission (since all teachers are civil servants) are examples of the latter. The National Education Commission (NEC) is the most important of the former. The NEC is responsible for the overall coordination of planning, for ensuring that the activities in different parts of the edcational system are consistent with one another and for carrying out educational research of general interest. It has to report to the Cabinet on serious educational problems (suggesting solutions), and recommends on reorganisation of the education system and on the development of new policies etc.

Ministry of the Interior

Public administration in Thailand is carried out at three levels, central, regional and local. These interact in an attempt to provide sensitivity to identified national and local needs and flexibility for their coordination. In the field of education an example of this is that in 1963 authority for most public primary schooling in municipal areas was transferred from the Ministry of Education to the municipalities themselves, while in 1966 responsibility for most of the remaining schools in the public primary system at local level passed to a Department of Local Administration within the Ministry of the Interior. The Ministry of Education, however, resumed control in 1980.

Ministry of Education

This Ministry, however, remained and remains responsible for the pedagogical aspects of primary education - textbook production, curriculum development, primary school teacher training and the supervision of instruction. The Ministry was always responsible for all types of secondary education, academic, vocational or comprehensive and for teacher training. Post-secondary programmes at government colleges (which include the College of Technology and Vocational Education with its 28 campuses, 32 vocational and technical colleges, three commercial colleges, 13 agricultural colleges, 36 teacher training colleges, seven physical education colleges, 1 dramatic arts college and 1 fine arts college) are also its responsibility. The private sector runs several types of schools which are supervised by the office of the Private Education Commission which has the status of a department within the Ministry of Education. The ten private colleges come under the office of University Affairs.

Office of University Affairs

This office was established in 1972 and is responsible for the administration of government universities. While the Budget Bureau has considerable influence over university budgeting, and long range planning falls to consideration by the office of the National Education Commission, the OUA handles broad policies and regulations, setting the standard of curricula and university personnal administration, among other matters. It is responsible for programme accreditation and standards, approving curriculum development and change and keeping a check on Bachelor's degree programmes. For higher degrees a special committee makes recommendations to the office.

Regional and Local Level

Below the central (national) bodies described above, lie three sub-levels of administration exercised through the Regional Education Office, the Provincial Education Office and the District Education Office. Demarcation lines between their functions are not, however, rigid. Overall responsibility for both regional and local administration rests with the Office of the Under Secretary at the Ministry of Education. The Ministry of Education carried out the regionalisation project for educational development and educational administration outside Bangkok in 1958, in order generally to improve the quantity and quality of education in the rural areas. The partial transfer and decentralisation of responsibility for elementary school pupils was completed in 1966 in order to promote *local* interest and initiative throughout the country for expansion and improvement at this level of education.

The country, then, has 71 provinces *(Changwad)*, grouped into 12 regions *(Khets)*. Each region is headed by a Regional Education Officer who, while having no 'direct line' administrative responsibilities, serves as a general supervisory and in-service training agent for the Ministry of Education. In each regional office there are 9 or 10 elementary supervisors and a few secondary supervisors. Each of the 71 *Changwads* has a *Changwad* Education Officer appointed by the Ministry, but as he is responsible for all education in his particular province he also serves the local authority. Under him are several District *(Amphur)* Education Officers, responsible for helping day-to-day operation at schools in their districts but, again, appointed by the Ministry. In municipal urban areas elementary schools are run by the municipal authorities who raise much of their own educational revenue, employ teachers directly, and operate their schools with a fair degree of autonomy, though they use the Ministry-recommended curricula and textbooks. The administrative chain of responsibility from village teacher and headmaster to Minister thus runs from village of *Amphur*, to *Changwad* to the Provincial Governor, who consults the Regional Education Officer in matters affecting the overall policy.

8 EDUCATIONAL FINANCE

Sources of Funds

With the exception of the fee paying private schools and the upper classes in secondary schools both recurrent and capital costs for education are met from the national budget. Local and municipal schools are expected to be maintained by the communities they serve but obtain some financial help from the Ministry. About 50% of the total construction costs of elementary schools go on labour and it was hoped that in the rural areas community participation in constructing new buildings would increase until, by 1980, 5.8% of total expenditure on elementary education could be saved. Overall the government meets about 90% of educational costs. Only 6.5% of this expenditure comes from fees paid by students. Another 2% or less comes from gifts and properties.

School Fees

In private schools, fees can be as much as 1,200 baht or more per annum at secondary level (40 baht = £1 approx.). At upper secondary level in public secondary schools they are 500 baht against an average total cost per pupil (at 1977 figures) of 2,000 baht at secondary general schools and 5,000 baht at secondary vocational schools. The lower the fee a private school charges, the higher the number of teachers whose salaries are subsidised by the government, so there is, even in the private sector, an incentive to charge low fees.

Education Budget

The educational budget grew rapidly both in absolute and proportionalo terms in the early 1970s. In 1970 17.3% of government spending and 3.5% of GNP went on education. These proportions rose to 21% and 3.9% in 1976. Since then the relative growth has slowed down to 19.3% of total government spending and 3.2% of GNP in 1979. The emphasis in expenditure is still on primary schooling which received 60% of educational funds in 1978 (53.5% in 1970) compared to 20.8% on secondary schools (19.5% in 1970) and 11.5% higher education (13.8% in 1970).

Overseas Aid

Mention should be made here of two foreign funded projects, the UNDP/UNESCO Institute for the Promotion of the Teaching of Science, and the IBRD's National Curriculum Development Centre which began operations in mid-1974.

9 DEVELOPMENT AND PLANNING OF THE EDUCATION SYSTEM

Origins

The strong link between the King and the priesthood has had a powerful influence on educational development throughout the country. For 600 years, from the thirteenth to the middle of the nineteenth century, education in Thailand remained virtually unchanged. It was based on monastic schools situated in the Buddhist temples and concentrated on teaching boys reading, writing and religion. It was a training for life and concentrated on character training designed to fit into the religious ideals of the country. Although actual vocational teaching might have been taught in the monasteries it was generally undertaken elsewhere - under parental or craftsman's guidance. Nevertheless all that was taught in the schools had a meaning and significance, and the knowledge and culture gained by the pupils was a help and guide to them in later life. When King Chulalongkorn (1968-1910) decided to introduce a more Western-type of schooling it was natural that he should not only incorporate the monks into his scheme but should use the *wats* as sites for village schools. Today 50% of the country's primary schools are still in local *wats*, though the monks no longer act as government teachers.

Development

King Chulalongkorn's modernisation was a response to and a protection against imperialistic pressures from the colonial powers in surrounding countries. He felt that if Thailand was successfully to resist colonisation not only was a trained and educated elite cadre of government officials (mostly of royal blood) necessary but also a general modernisation of the education system was essential. As a result, and despite the fact that Thailans was (and is) a Buddhist country and had (and still has) a mainly peasant economy, a Western protestant, urban, materialistic type school system was grafted on to the existing system without any prior attempt being made clearly to define its objectives, both internal and external, or to study carefully whether the stated and hidden objectives of the system were consistent with the overall social and cultural goals or even mutually consistent. By 1921 the government of the day felt sufficiently convinced of the rightness of this policy to introduce a Compulsory Education Act and between 1921 and 1932 compulsory primary education was gradually extended to cover, in theory, 80% of the country. During the 1930s attempts were made to extend education further in the belief that democracy was only possible if the electorate were educated and in an attempt to foster a growing sense of nationalism.

Aims and Objectives

Three main types of objectives can be discerned in the various policy documents outlining a National Education Plan (1895, 1951, 1960, 1971, 1977 and 1981). Firstly there are those relating to academic theories of child development and which read like lists of objectives developed by liberal Western educators of the day, but bear little relation to the realities of Thai society. The third type of objective relates education to other social, cultural and economic goals. For example, 'secondary and higher education institutions should produce the skilled manpower needed for the country's development'. This type of objective, which no longer assumes education to be an end in itself but a means to a further end, has occupied a larger place in the last decade since Thailand has become more concerned with 'development' per se.

The objectives of the National Scheme for Education of 1960 are couched in highly generalised terms. Though worthy in themselves they are much concerned with citizenship, acquisition or moral and cultural values and the inculcation of a democratic outlook. By the time the second Five-Year Plan went into operation in 1966, the emphasis on objectives had changed to a concern for economic development and social equality, together with a recognition that the tools of education (improved curricula, textbooks, buildings, teacher training) needed improvement in order to upgrade standards of performance. The objectives of the third Five-Year Plan (1971), though following the trends of the previous ones, were even more specific, concerned with improving both the efficiency of the system (with regard, for example, to reducing repeater, drop out and failure rates) and with expansion of facilities in various fields (medicine, technology, and teacher education) so as to meet the country's future manpower requirements.

The detailed objectives of educational development during the fifth Five-Year Plan (1982-1986) are as follow:

(i) to integrate all aspects of the education system - formal and non-formal, with economic and social development

(ii) to improve the quality of education - through curriculum development, in-service teacher training and improved supervision

(iii) to improve the efficiency of administration

(iv) to promote educational equity especially among less priviledged groups in rural areas

(v) to encourage the private sector to participate more in educational provision especially at higher education level

(vi) to provide pre-primary schooling for 35% of 4-5 year olds by 1986

(vii) to provide 43% of 12-14 year olds and 31% of 15-17 year olds with secondary education by 1986.

Thus, over a decade or so, the overall objectives have moved from a theoretical child centred orientation towards greater emphasis on development, problem solving and other national and social goals. The government attaches considerable importance to the expansion of secondary education. Not only does it consider such education a necessary part of general education for those who have to live and work in the modern sector of the economy, but also it is realised that secondary education supplies the intake needed by higher educational institutions if they are to produce the high and middle level manpower required for economic and social development. Further, the rural areas is again specifically a concern, as is the idea of education being a 'life long' process and the linking of education with an improvement in the quality of life.

Planning Institutions

It was not until 1963 that an office with special responsibility for all aspects of educational planning was established in the Ministry of Education. This new division, the Educational Planning Office (EPO) began a revision of the Six-Year Plan, carried out research relevant to future plans, and began collecting and analysing the statistics needed for its function. Responsibility for preparing the education part of the Third Plan was divided among the National Economic and Social Development Board, the National Education Council and the Educational Planning Office.

Planning

The first Six-Year National Economic Development Plan was produced in 1961 and covered two phases, 1961-63 and 1964-66. Before this, in 1958, a Regional Education Development Plan including higher education (REDPHE) had been produced. The main aim of REDPHE was to increase educational opportunities outside Bangkok and the central regions where all higher and most secondary education facilities were sited. The section of the NED Plan (1961-66) dealing with education was based closely on the REDPHE plan, not yet fully implemented by 1961, and the National Scheme for Education. It listed four main aims: to improve and expand lower elementary education with a gradual increase of compulsory schooling from 4-7 years; to produce sufficient qualified teachers, especially in vocational education; to expand university education and provide courses more relevant to manpower needs; and to increase the supply of trained teachers. During the period of the plan, enrolment in the first grade of primary schooling increased from 4 million (approximately) to 4.8 million but most of the increase took place in the Bangkok/Thonburi area, and of the 11.6 million baht expended over the six-year period a good deal went to establish two new universities.

Second Plan

In the second Five-Year Plan which was completed in 1971, the most important emphasis was on the quantitative expansion of secondary, technical, professional and teacher education in order to provide both the middle and high level manpower needed for economic development. It is claimed that the effort made was so successful that manpower shortages in most fields were eliminated during the Plan period. Certainly more funds were released and expenditure over the second Five-Year Plan (1967-71) almost doubled (from 11,600 million baht to 20,050 million baht) even though the second Plan period was a year shorter. In total, including all public and private educational expenditure a figure of around 4% of GDP was being spent directly on education by 1971 and over 18% of the national budget was devoted to this sector. Enrolment at primary level had grown from 4 million to over 5.5 million, and had more than doubled (to 550,000) at secondary level. Both vocational and teacher training enrolments had shown similar dramatic increases and university entrants had increased by about 40%. Enrolments at the regional universities increased very rapidly with Khon Kaen enjoying a 35% pa growth and Chiengmai a 31% p.a. (cf. Thammasat 2.6% p.a. over 1966-71).

Third Plan

The third Five-Year Educational Plan was an integral part of the National Five-Year Plan for Economic and Social Development and it went into operation on 1 October 1971 finishng on 30 September 1976. More work went into the preparation of the third Plan than into any previous one. Very careful evaluation of past expansion, bottlenecks, and problems was made before any policies, targets or objectives were formulated. In-service courses were held for the regional and local educational staff to help them identify their problems and to prepare annual operational plans over the five-year period involved. By localising the research and setting specific and attainable local targets it was hoped to avoid setting unrealistic overall objectives.

In the third Plan economic and social aspects were emphasised and, since manpower shortages had been largely overcome by the previous Plan, stress was placed on improvement in the quality and effectiveness of all levels of education. Expansion of upper elementary education, particularly in the rural areas, was aimed at, and for the first time in Thailand the introduction of life long education was seen as a major objective of the educational System. The planned increase in enrolments for most types of education was about the same as for the second Five-Year Plan except for vocational training and teacher training. The reduction in growth in these two sectors was due to increasing emphasis on non-formal vocational education and a return to normal teacher training levels after the crash programme expansion of earlier years. The percentage increase in enrolments during the third Five-Year Plan period was estimated as follows:

Grade	% increase in enrolments 1971-76
1 - 4	19.2
5 - 7	67.3
8 - 10 (Academic)	66.6
11 - 12 (Academic)	72.1
11 - 13 (Vocational)	27.9
Teacher Training (full time)	67.4
Higher Education	40.8
Adult and non-formal education	158.8

In universities the greatest growth was expected in medicine (13.9% p.a.), with engineering, education, and the natural sciences increasing faster than the overall average rate. Enrolments in law and social sciences were expected to decline. Again, the fastest growth was expected in the regional universities, with Songkhla the pacemaker at an average 36.5% p.a. up to 1976.

Fourth Plan

The emphasis on development of educational policies which serve national and social goals allied to a more professional approach to planning, identification of specific problems through evaluation of previous plans and reorganisation of educational and administrative structures so as to achieve more efficiently and cost-effectively the stated goals, was exhibited even more clearly in the fourth National Economic and Social Development Plan (1977-1981), which has just been implemented. Economic recession in the latter half of the third Plan period did, despite efforts to provide in greater degree educational opportunities leading to better job prospects, result in problems associated with slow economic recovery: income disparities, unemployment, basic resource depletion and environmental deterioration. It is increasingly coming to be realised that education must not be viewed as an autonomous system but as one closely related to the economic and social structures of society and that for educational reform to be successful, other systems should be changed as well. How effectively this works out in practice must remain to be seen, and the overall effectiveness of the Plan will depend on developing economic, political and social factors which it is impossible to predict. However, the two main educational priorities of the Plan remain the equalisation of educational opportunities and the revising of the administration and planning mechanisms. The development approach now being adopted is one of decentralisation of the social services, complementing national development efforts in other fields which aim at reducing existing economic and social gaps. The channelling of social services such as educational facilities, sanitation, social welfare, food and nutrition to the rural areas will, it is expected, contribute positively to achieving the objectives of a more equitable income distribution, alleviating unemployment problems and reducing the rate of population expansion. As a background to this government realises that planning is a continuous process and as preconditions for the effective implementation of various key development policies and programmes closer links are required between national planning, budgeting, the management of the civil service and the improvement of project preparation and implementation capabilities of the key operating agencies during the period of the Plan.

The following policies and guidelines on educational development were to be applied during the fourth Plan period:

(i) the system of educational administration modified so that there is more autonomy in policy matters concerning education in the central, regional and local areas

(ii) the education system also modified, so that it becomes more closely related to the nation's economic and social development. This should be done by linking the education system to local conditions, by creating greater flexibility in the education administration, by forging a link between in-school and out-of-school education and by providing educational facilities in line with the needs of the labour market

(iii) the quality of every level and type of education improved regardless of whether it is urban or rural education, or whether it is public or private education. This was to be done by giving proportionally more attention to the areas or institutions coping with low quality education

(iv) the contents and process of learning in each level and type of education modified to suit the actual conditions in each region and to meet the social, cultural, political and economic needs of the region and the nation. This was to be done by concurrently teaching both theoretical and practical subjects, by revising the curricula and process of learning into a combination that contains moral and spiritual wisdom along with other materialistic subjects, and by cultivating the belief in the democratic system with the King as the Head of State and the respect and affection for the institutions of the Nation, the Religion and the King

(v) the system of training teachers and educational personnel improved to produce teachers with the right quality and in the quantity required by the economy and provide those with vocational training with proper support in terms of welfare and well being

(vi) the provision of educational facilities by private educational institutions promoted with respect to academic and other work in line with national policies, programmes and identity concerning educational organisation. The government was to increase efforts to provide compulsory education on a nationwide basis and allow private participation within the limits to be specified by the government

(vii) the scope of out-of-school education expanded to cover a variety of fields to meet the interests, needs and demands of the majority of the population

(viii) efforts made to provide more equal opportunities in access to education. Compulsory education to be provided by the government in every region of the country within as short a time as possible. As for non-compulsory education, the government should encourage private institutions to participate to help create more equal opportunities in education in accordance with economic conditions and local circumstances.

Fifth Plan

The fifth Plan (1982-1986) which was published in 1981 represented to retrenchment in some ways from previous plans. There was concern for the financial difficulties which government would face in responding to rising demand especially for secondary and higher education and a determination that the efficiency and quality of the system should be improved.

While quantitative targets of expansion were restated, especially at pre-primary level and there was a stated objective of providing for the less privileged, the main emphasis was a qualitative improvement with relatively unchanging provision of resources.

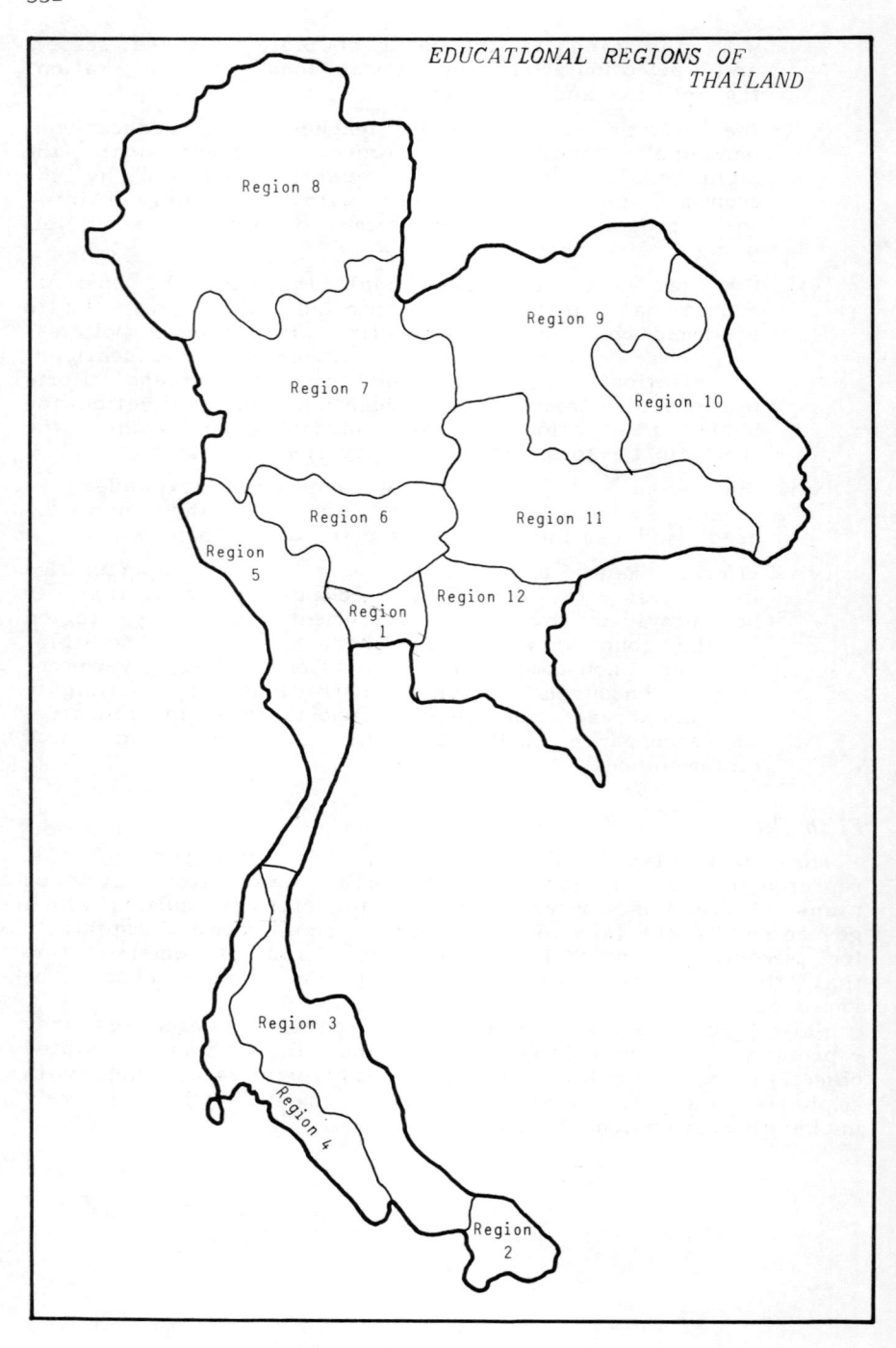

EDUCATIONAL REGIONS OF THAILAND

THAILAND BASIC EDUCATIONAL DATA

Population	
1970	1980
36,370,000	46,961,338

Enrolment Ratios

Primary = Enrolments as a percentage of the population aged 7-13
Secondary = Enrolments as a percentage of the population 14-18
Higher = Enrolments as a percentage of the population ages 20-24

Year	Primary	Secondary	Higher
1970	81%	17%	3.3%
1978	82%*	29%	6.5%

*1977

Institutions, Teachers and Students 1970 and 1979

Pre-Primary			
Year	Schools	Teachers	Pupils
1970	395	2,857	134,355
1979	–	–	336,364

Primary			
1970	–	162,512	5,634,782
1979	–	–	7,272,289

Secondary			
1970	–	44,756	695,023
1979	–	–	1,529,564

Higher Education Students by Field of Study 1977

Education and Teacher Training	38,949
Humanities	11,234
Law	46,019
Social and Behavioural Science	40,421
Commerce and Business	41,236
Natural Science	8,536
Mathematics and Computer Science	1,853
Medicine and Related Fields	9,749
Engineering	10,255
Agriculture	4,610

Government Expenditure on Education

Year	As a % of total government spending	As a % of GNP
1970	17.3%	3.5%
1980	20.4%	3.2%*

*1979

Government Expenditure on Education by Level

Year	Pre-Primary	Primary	Secondary	Higher	Other
1970	0.5	53.5	19.5	13.7	12.7
1978	0.6	60.0	20.8	11.5	7.1

Basic Social and Economic Data

    Gross National Product per capita 1979 - US$590

Average annual growth of GNP per capita 1960-1979 - 4.6%

        Life expectancy 1979 - 62 years

    Proportion of the labour force engaged in:

Agriculture	
1960	84%
1979	77%

Industry	
1960	4%
1979	9%

Sciences	
1960	12%
1979	14%

SECTION B

Introduction

The Latin American countries, amid their differences, share certain common characteristics: a colonial experience, a strong religious tradition, the influence of European thought especially in the nineteenth and early twentieth centuries, and contemporaneously, influence from the USA. Just how to interpret these patterns of influence in their current intersection with the economic histories of the Latin American countries is a matter of considerable debate. Terms such as 'cultural domination', 'neo-colonialism' and 'economic dependency' occur frequently in discussions of the Latin American condition – not least in discussions among Latin Americans themselves.

The early colonial experience and the Catholic religious tradition produced a particular pattern in educational provision: not much elementary education but a clear elite tradition of literary and humanistic studies. The provision of schooling was not seen as a State responsibility until Latin America began in the mid and late nineteenth century to be influenced by European and, in particular, French ideas. French influences stretched back, for radicals, to the French revolution itself, and included as the century wore on an interest in positivism, encyclopaedist views of knowledge, and an acceptance of the virtues of centralised administrative control. Against these ideas, which included arguments for the State provision of education, was opposed a conservative vision of education as a matter for the family and the religious authorities.

The socio-economic context in which these ideas found a place in the late nineteenth and early twentieth centuries was, however, sharply different from Europe. Latin America before the 1930s was characterised by urbanism but not industrialisation. The Latin American city, with its professional bureaucratic and literate middle classes was well developed before World War One, and contained a high proportion of the national population, typically over one third. In contrast, rural areas remained fixed in a rather paternalist, even harsh, socio-economic and politically conservative pattern, with agriculture typically dominated by major landowners who also were, or were in strong alliance with, the political elites. In the inter-war period, these two groups moved into political conflict with middle class reformist and nationalist groups in growing alliance with the developing industrial unions and the emerging industrial bourgeoisie challenging the traditional ruling groups. In fact, however, industrialisation when it began to occur rapidly from the early thirties was as much a result of changes in the international industrial order as deliberate policy. With the Depression, and later World War Two, local industrial development occurred to supply domestic demand, in the relative absence of foreign competition.

These traditions, and the inter-war developments, have framed much of the contemporary conditions of Latin America, Latin American education, and debates about the intersection of socio-economic conditions and education. For example, from the 1950s international economic penetration of Latin America strengthened. At the same time, domestically, gaps between the city and the country, between the middle classes and the rural masses widened in access to and control of the distribution of economic and social resources. Typically it was in the 1950s and 1960s, secondary education rather than literacy education which expanded and was 'successful'. Economic policies stressed import substitution, orientation toward the external market of the wealthy sector of the domestic market, and increasing capital-intensive agriculture. The results included social and educational polarisation - considerable sectors of the population remain or have become marginalised under these processes of modernisation, and in education there has been a slow expansion of mass education and an explosion of higher education provision.

How to explain these socio-economic and educational developments has been a matter of considerable debate. The emerging terms of the Latin American debate offer a double critique.

First, an economic-historical analysis of the ways in which the natural resources of Latin America have been developed and used by colonialist and neo-colonialist powers, with a system of external (and capitalist) domination. In this process, local elites in particular Latin American countries have benefited, but not the majority of the population. Whilst the economic history of Brazil is perhaps the most dramatic example of these processes - a paradigm case - the case offered is a general one, and the argument is that the processes and structures of economic dependency are continuing. The second element in the critique is to emphasise the ways in which educational development framed in international influences has been inappropriate for Latin American conditions, has been unsuccessful in context, and based on theories about the relations between education and economics which are likely to compound economic dependency. Thus, for example, under attack with some regularity are educational policies in literacy and the universalisation of primary education, which were adopted in the early 1960s partly under UNESCO influence. In practice, the major improvements have been the quantitative expansion of secondary education, and an explosive expansion of tertiary education - rather than a marked reduction in illiteracy rates of the even provision (regionally and to minority groups) of primary education. Similarly under attack have been external influences in education, whether these were expressed through regional agencies such as the Alliance for Progress and its programmes of the 1960s, or through educational aid programmes which resulted in large numbers of able young people receiving education abroad. The modernisation theories which underpinned much of the development aspirations of the 1960s and the 1970s have also been criticised. In education, the emphasis on the development of 'human capital' - relatively well trained manpower drawn from the upper secondary and tertiary levels of the education system - has been interpreted as being ineffective in producing national development, compounding problems of regional and rural maldistribution of education, and as locating the Latin American economies more firmly within an international economic system over which and in which the Latin American countries have relatively little control.

The radical edge of the Latin American interpretations of their economic and educational condition is, then, strong, even bitter. Paradoxically it has been generated by persons who were either trained abroad or were influenced by European and Marxist modes of analysis; and the critique has been popularised by North American writers among others and diffused by publication in the international journals with metropolitan languages. Less surprisingly, perhaps, it has produced relatively few indigenous and original responses, with the notable exception of Paulo Freire's literacy programme which ran into problems of implementation.

Of course the differences among the Latin American countries are also considerable. Economically Peru, for example, is relatively poor. It missed the boom period of the 1960s and 1970s which other countries such as Brazil did not. Venezuela's economy like Mexico's until very recently has been expanding, based on natural reserves of oil, and Venezuela has the highest per capita income in Latin America. Argentina has been, for a long time, the most economically developed of the Latin American countries, with both a strong agricultural sector and a considerable industrial base. The Brazilian economy is potentially perhaps even stronger, and it demonstrated remarkable growth in the 1960s and early 1970s. However, Brazilian agriculture and problems of rural development are posing considerable difficulties, and it is not unusual to think of 'two (or more) Brazils' as a shorthand definition of the important differences between regions, and between cities and the countryside.

Culturally Brazil is an example of a Latin (more correctly a Luso-American) country in which an indigenous population of Indians was overborne by European culture, mixed in part with African negro influence. Some synthesis of these cultural elements seems to be emerging fairly successfully, to which should be added the absorption of other immigrant groups, especially Italians, Japanese and a small German minority. Peru is another country in which there was a major indigenous group before colonisation. Currently the population is split between Indian, mixed blood *(mestizos)* and persons of Spanish descent. The numerical minority of Europeans dominate culturally with the important language being Spanish. Veneuela and Colombia also have a high proportion of mestizos - about 60% of the population in each case. Similarly, those of European descent dominate the main economic and social structures, and dominate linguistically. In contrast in Argentina and Chile the indigenous Indian populations were relatively small and their cultural influence smaller. Both countries are characterised by the immigration of European groups other than Spaniards. All of the countries mentioned are pre-dominantly Roman Catholic in religion.

In education, amid the differences between countries, there are certain phenomena which recur fairly widely. Typically, the administration of education is centralised. In many of the Latin American countries, this has led to a recent reform pattern - a degree of decentralisation of administrative structure, usually by strengthening regional offices. In terms of the structures of schooling systems, the general pattern has tended from the 1960s to be of the 6-3-3 variety, but the secondary school systems have been dominated by European rather than North American assumptions about high status knowledge. Thus, the prestigious part of the secondary school system has been the academic (rather than vocational) sectors. In several of the Latin American countries an effort has been made to upgrade the status of vocational studies in the upper secondary school. The effort has not been universally successful. Higher education and the universities have undergone remarkable expansion, especially during the 1970s. Problems of the 'massification' of higher education are now being addressed, as are the choices of occupation (the traditional professions) which are implicit in the admission demands of students. Efforts are being made to alter faculty structures and to strengthen the study of scientific and technological subjects.

The actual efficiency of the educational system is, however, causing anxiety. Primary education in several of the countries is characterised by very high drop-out and repeater rates, and transition into secondary education is common only for half of the age group. There are, of course, also sharp regional differences within countries, and important differentials in educational success between children in towns and in the country, and among children of different racial groups. Where possible, middle class parents will frequently purchase private education for their children. The expansion of higher education has brought participation rates up to about 10% of the age cohort. However, there are difficulties emerging both with the size of class groups and over questions of the quality and qualifications of staff, as a consequence of rapid expansion. The strong tradition of academic autonomy in the universities has still survived fairly well, but it is under pressure in several of the Latin American countries from governments interested in either the modernisation of studies or universities as sources of political opposition.

At the time of writing, these issues of efficiency are unlikely to be solved. Educational systems on the continent are under pressure from the double forces of inflation and recession. They are unlikely to be allocated major increases in real resources. Temporarily, the pace of progress, which has been considerable since the 1950s – is likely to slow.

Argentina

CONTENTS

1 Geography 566
2 Population 569
3 History and Politics 570
4 Society and Culture 573
5 The Economy 575
6 The Education System 578
7 Educational Administration 587
8 Educational Finance 588
9 Development and Planning of
 the Education System 590

Argentina historically has been the most developed country in Latin America economically, culturally and in political influence. Economic stagnation and political instability over the last 20 years mean that this primacy has been challenged at least in terms of the economy and external influence by countries such as Brazil and to some extent Venezuela. Lack of economic development or of strong political initiatives have meant that there has not been a major expansion or change of direction in the education system in recent years.

Education in Argentina follows a classic Latin-American pattern. The administration is centralised. The structure and curriculum are similar to those found in the past in continental Western Europe. Primary schools have uniform curricula and the pupils must reach required standards to progress through the grades. Secondary education has remained academic though, as in other Latin-American countries, a division was made in the late 1960s between a first and second cycle and vocational sections were introduced in the upper secondary cycle. Higher education continued to be offered mainly in universities which provided largely courses preparing for the traditional professions. The autonomous democratic nature of universities, based on the Cordoba Reform of 1918, which influenced most of the rest of Latin America, has survived despite frequent and often damaging attacks.

The provision of education in Argentina historically has been fuller than in most other Latin-American countries but this lead has been reduced in recent years when there has been a lower rate of growth in Argentina. Over 90% of primary aged children are in school but still the disadvantaged groups do not have full education. Secondary education occupies about half the relevant age group though this proportion did not grow greatly in the 1970s. As in other Latin-America countries the number of higher education students expanded rapidly in the 1970s but the proportion of the age group enrolled in higher education institutions, while high by the standards of other areas of the world, was about par for Latin-America in the late 1970s despite Argentina's lead over the rest of the continent in the 1960s.

Without major economic development or political initiatives there is little sign of significant growth or change in educational provision and practices. As in the industrialised countries, with which Argentina shares many common characteristics, there has been educational retrenchment since the late 1970s.

1 GEOGRAPHY

Topography

Argentina is situated between latitude 22°S and 55°S and is 7,000 miles by sea from both the English Channel and New York. It has a total area of 2,791,310 sq km (1.08 million square miles). In size it is second only to Brazil in the whole of Latin America. It is five times the size of France and 12 times the size of Britain. In shape it is an inverted triangle tapering from the northern border (nearly 1,600 km long) to the south. Its length is about 3,500 km (2,200 miles) and in places it is 1,570 km (980 miles) wide. The coastline is about 5,000 km (2,500 miles). In addition Argentina claims a section of the Antarctic landmass and certain Antarctic and South Atlantic Islands including the Falkland Islands, a total area of 1,235,714 sq km.

Argentina may be divided into six regions:

(i) the *pampa* - a 518,000 sq km area of grassland with rich alluvial soil especially in the east, which extends from the *chaco* region in the north down to the Colorado river in the south and from the Atlantic coast to just east of the Andes

(ii) the *littoral* - (or Mesopotamia) - consisting of the west bank of the Paranà and the area between the Paranà and Uruguay rivers; characterised by swamps, scrub and rolling countryside

(iii) the north west - a rugged arid area consisting of mountains and bleak plateaux between 1,800 and 5,500 metres high (6,000 and 18,000 feet) with

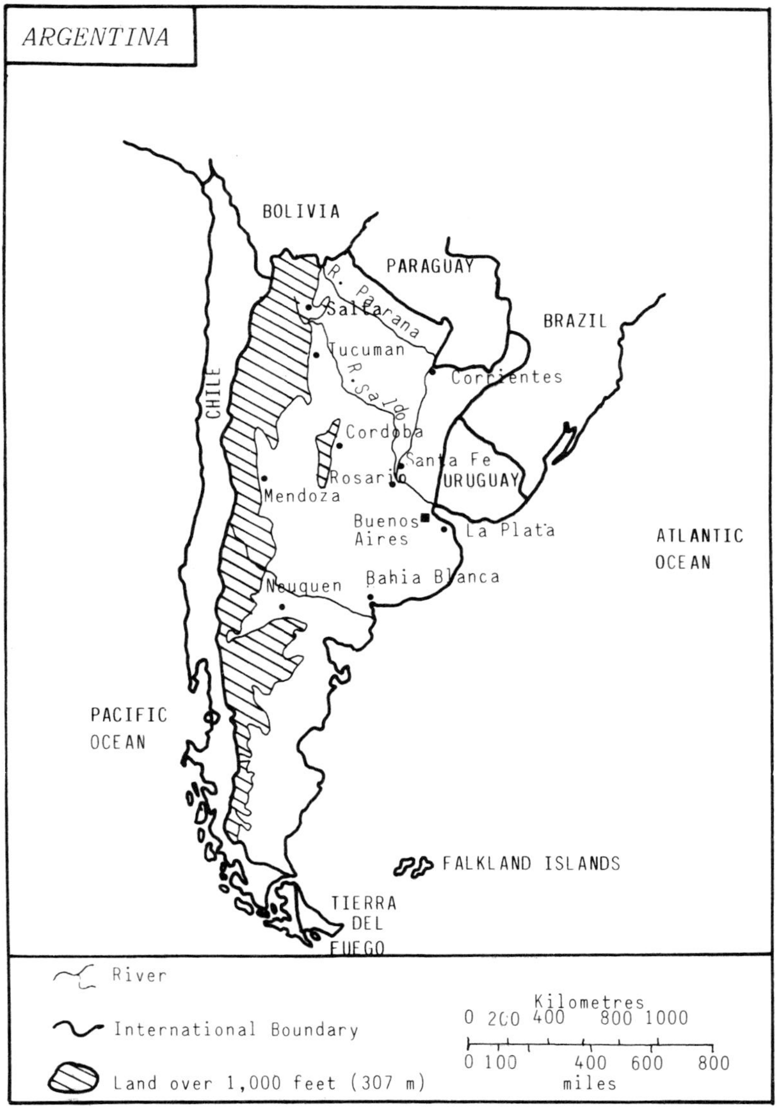
ARGENTINA
BOLIVIA
PARAGUAY
BRAZIL
CHILE
R. Parana
Salta
Tucuman
R. Saldo
Corrientes
Cordoba
Santa Fe
Rosario
URUGUAY
Mendoza
Buenos Aires
La Plata
ATLANTIC OCEAN
Neuquen
Bahia Blanca
PACIFIC OCEAN
FALKLAND ISLANDS
TIERRA DEL FUEGO
River
International Boundary
Land over 1,000 feet (307 m)
Kilometres
0 200 400 800 1000
0 100 400 600 800
miles

    agriculture practised in a few 'oasis' areas where soil and water supply is adequate

(iv) the *chaco* - an area of plains in the north of the country with wide meandering silted rivers and scrub woodlands

(v) Patagonia - the southern part of Argentina which covers a quarter of the territory but holds only 3% of the population. This is an area of plateaux, steppes and high winds - spectacular but treeless and unattractive to settlers except for the areas near the Atlantic and the Andean foothills

(vi) the Andean mountains - running from north to south in the west and forming the border with Chile.

Climate

  There is a wide range of climates in Argentina ranging from sub-tropical in the south to sub-Antarctic in Tierra del Fuego. The central zone has a temperate climate with rainfall evenly spaced throughout the year. In Buenos Aires from December to the end of February the heat can be oppressive - maximum temperatures 27°C (80°F) to 39°C (95°F) and humidity is high (about 70%). In the *pampa* rainfall varies from 100 cm (40 inches) in the south to an erratic 50 cm (20 inches) in the north. In the *chaco* the climate is extreme with summer temperatures over 105°F and in the north there are frosts all the year round with sparse rainfall (about 25 cm) most of which falls as snow. In Patagonia it can be cold with some snow in the winter months. The region is arid and only the western mountain slopes along the Chilean border have enough rain to allow forest growth.

Communications

  The period 1890-1910 was the great era of railway expansion. The system radiated from Buenos Aires and the port areas of the River Plate and Bahia Blanca, following the old colonial and Indian tracks, and no feeder lines or connecting links were provided for cross country communication. Road construction, when it developed, tended to follow the railways and with this competition the railways became less profitable. Neither system opened up the more isolated areas of the interior. Transport is therefore mainly concentrated in the east central provinces and communication with most of the southern region is feasible only by air. There is now about 39,807 km of railway track carrying 8% of freight and 15% of passenger traffic. Road development is slow and piecemeal, but at the .end of 1975 there was about 311,893 km of road (20% paved) including 137 km of motorway, carrying 80% of freight and 82% of passenger traffic. In December 1975 the Colon-Paysandu Bridge across the River Plate was opened, the first road link with Uruguay. The trans-Andean tunnel

'Cristo Redentor' is now being built at a height of 3,200 metres above sea level (length 3,254 km). River steamers operate on the Plate, Paraná, Paraguay and Uruguay rivers. Today there is an extensive network of internal air services through inter-provincial services have been abolished as they are considered uneconomic.

2 POPULATION

Growth

The population growth rate is low by Latin American standards (1.7% between 1970 and 1980) and the dramatic increases in population over the last century have been caused by immigration. However, President Péron aimed to double the population by the year 2000 - a figure subsequently amended to 35 million - and restrictions were imposed on the sale of contraceptives. The 1970 census total was 23,364,431 which included the 3,300 people in the Antarctic sector i.e. Falkland Islands, South Orkneys, South Georgia, South Sandwich Isles and "sovereign territories of Argentina in the Antarctic". The total population in 1980 was 27,862,771.

Distribution

The economic development of Argentina from the early days tended to concentrate immigration in the port towns (Rosario, Buenos Aires and later La Plata and Bahia Blanca). Industrial development again concentrated on the coastal areas so that the growth of the urban population continued as people moved in from the countryside looking for work. Now about two thirds of the population live in urban areas. The following table shows the developing pattern over the last 175 years:

Year	Total Population (in millions)	Urban % (in towns over 2,000)	Rural %
1800	0.5	25	75
1914	8.0	53	47
1947	16.0	63	37
1960	10.0	74	26
1970	23.5	75 (est.)	25 (est.)
1975	24.5	79	21
1980	27.8	81	18

Argentina, unlike Brazil, has only one city of over a million inhabitants which continues to attract the bulk of migrants (though Tucúman is nearing this figure). At present Buenos Aires has 3 million inhabitants but Greater Buenos Aires (including the suburbs) has a population of over 8 million (33% of the population). The four eastern provinces and Buenos Aires together hold 71% of the population in 20% of the country's area. In view of this distribution an overall density figure of 8.4 per sq km (21.75 per square mile) is meaningless. The density variation is more revealing, ranging from 17,061 per sq km in Buenos Aires to 0.16 per sq km in the southern province of Santa Cruz. The most densely populated province is Tucúman, the small sugar growing province in the north west (39.2 per sq km) followed by Buenos Aires province (24.2 per sq km) and Santa Fé which includes the city of Rosario (15.7 per sq km). Further development need not necessarily disturb this pattern. Patagonia has valuable deposits of oil and natural gas; but exploiting these will be a capital-intensive rather than a labour-intensive operation and so is unlikely to induce any large population movement.

Groups

The indigenous Indian population of Argentina was small in number. There were a few peaceful tribes in the north, and in the south a community of the tougher Araucanos who had come from Chile. By 1852 the Spanish settlers numbered some 1.2 million. Expansion to the south was resisted by the Indians until disease and the Indian War of 1878-83 virtually exterminated them. The Indian population has now disappeared, although in certain areas (particularly in the north along the Andes) Indian ancestry is evident. In these areas 50% of the population are *mestizos* (mixed blood) but in the country as a whole *mestizos* constitute only 2% of the population, and Argentina prides itself on being a 'white' European country. By 1930 the number of European immigrants had reached 6 million and following World War Two, in the short period between 1947 and 1951, nearly 630,000 more immigrants arrived. Since 1856 the largest of the immigrant groups has been the Italian and the next largest the Spanish. There are also substantial German, Dutch and British communities (probably the largest British community outside the Commonwealth). Around 1840 there was an African community in Buenos Aires but it has long since lost its identity.

3 HISTORY AND POLITICS

Origins

Jual de Solis made landings on the eastern seaboard in 1516 followed by Magellen in 1520, before be went south to enter the Pacific via Cape Horn. However, the first settlement of Buenos Aires failed and later in the century the Spaniards colonised Argentina from the west. Until 1776 Argentina was part of the Spanish vice-royalty based at Lima and all trade with Spain had to pass through Perú. In that year the vice-royalty of Rio de la Plata, based at Buenos Aires, was established to rule the eastern colonies, the littoral entered Atlantic trade and the long isolation of Buenos Aires was over. However, the two-stage development of the country gave rise to two sets of interests which have figures in Argentine history ever since, often in conflict. The population of the interior traditionally looked west and not to Buenos Aires.

The Nineteenth Century

There were aspirations towards independence from Spain but little was achieved until the two British attempts to capture the port of Buenos Aires in 1806 and 1807. These were instrumental in firmly uniting the population of Buenos Aires and in 1810, following Spain's demise at the hands of Napoleon, Argentina was able to set up its own national government. But this in effect was only a government for Buenos Aires and its immediate hinterland; the provinces were not taken into consideration and the split between the town and the interior was thereby perpetuated. The Tucúman Congress of 1816 declared Argentina's independence but the constitution approved by Congress in 1819 was rejected by the provinces. In 1853 a federal constitution was drawn up after a period of civil war and general unrest and in 1880, after a further short civil war, Buenos Aires ceased to be merely a provincial capital and became the federal capital of Argentina. The second half of the century saw spectacular development and political consolidation accompanied by large scale immigration. In 1912 an electoral code established universal male suffrage.

Since 1930

After World War One a process of decline began and 1930 saw the first military coup. It is a sad phenomenon that since 1930, despite great natural resources and a democratic past Argentina has slipped into a chronic political instability marked by numerous military revolts and abortive coups. The most significant figure to have emerged from Argentine politics in the last 40 years is Juan Domingo Perón, a colonel at the time of the 1943 military takeover, who as Secretary for Labour in the military government expanded the unions and mobilised the proletariat. He was briefly imprisoned by a counter-coup in 1945 but released to be elected president in February 1946. Despite social reforms and economic development, discontent and factionalism grew in the country and in 1955 he was overthrown by a 'Liberating Revolution' which led to a purge of his supporters (peronistas). In 1966 yet another military revolt overthrew the civilian administration but in 1973 the military government restored civilian rule. (In 1969 and 1970 there were popular rebellions in Córdoba and Tucúman based on the traditional hostility to Buenos Aires in the interior.)

In the elections of March 1973 the *Frente Justalicia de Liberación* obtained the largest majority in congress but in July President Campora resigned to allow the election of General Perón, who returned from 18 years exile in Spain. In the September elections he obtained 62% of the vote. Ten months later he was dead, and his widow, Maria Estela Perón, the vice-president, succeeded him. Senora Perón was unable to retain the support of the groups who had united behind her husband and an upsurge of violence followed. Her chief minister, Rega, was widely distrusted, labour unrest increased and assassination and kidnapping were rife, despite the imposition of a 'state of siege' (martial law) in November 1974 and the outlawing of left wing guerilla groups in September 1975. In that year over 700 people were killed by terrorists.

Present Government

In the face of corruption, incompetence and anarchy, on 24 March 1976 the army, led by its commander-in-chief Lt-General Jorge Rafael Videla, overthrew the president in a bloodless coup and installed a three-man *junta* made up of the heads of the armed services. Five days later General Videla was sworn in as president. The *junta* dissolved Congress and the provincial assemblies, dismissed all provincial governors and senior judges, suspended all political and trade union activity and removed all government officials from post. It declared its intention of restoring civil government once public order was achieved. Anti-guerilla offensives were mounted against various groups but in 1976 1,000 people were killed and widespread labour unrest continued, fostered by the government's anti-inflation policies.

Videla's Presidency ended in March 1981. After then a new military *junta* headed by General L F Galtieri took power. He resigned following the Falkland crisis of 1982 and the war with Britain.

Political Organisation

Argentina is a federal republic consisting of a federal distict (Buenos Aires), 22 provinces and the national territory of Tierra del Guego, Antarctica and the South Atlantic Islands. Each province has a provincial government headed by a governor. By the 1853 Constitution the division of powers is similar to that obtaining in the United States but allows the president a larger authority to intervene in provincial affairs and impose a state of siege. Government is by the executive president approved by a legislature and a separate judiciary. Under the 1853 Constitution the president was elected for six years, but in 1973 the term was reduced to four years. The president cannot be re-elected immediately. The National Congress is bi-cameral, consisting of a senate and a chamber of deputies. Elections are held for the president and his vice-presidential partner, governors and members of the national and provincial assemblies. At present the supreme national organ is the *Junta Militar* with executive power vested in the president. There are eight cabinet ministers (six military personnel). A commission has been established to advise the *junta* on legislative matters.

The army is, and has been since 1930, the major element in Argentine politics. Whoever rules in Argentina has been dependent at least on the passive acceptance of the military. National service is compulsory between the ages of 20 and 45 and involves either one year spent in the army or air force or 14 months in the navy. In 1976 the armed forces had a strength of 132,800 men.

International Relations

Argentina is a member of the UN and many of its specialised agencies. It is also a member of OAS (Organisation of American States), CTAL *(Confederacione de Trabajadores de America Latina)*, IDB (Inter-American Development Bank) and LAFTA (Latin-American Free Trade Association). It favours a stronger, more independent and more united Latin American position in inter-American affairs. President Perón's aim was to occupy a third position between capitalism and communism and he sought a leading role in the Third World. In pursuance of this aim Argentina's relations with other countries have tended to disregard the political complexions of their governments. New trade agreements have been reached with Cuba, despite OAS objections. Agreements have also been made with China, Poland and Czechoslovakia (though these moves started under the military president General Lanusse) and with the USSR, covering trade and technical cooperation. The River Plate boundaries with Uruguay have been agreed for the first time, and there are now large HEP projects on the Uruguay and Paraná rivers shared with Uruguay and Paraguay. Difficulties with Brazil have caused uneasiness in diplomatic circles but friendly relations have been reassumed with the rest of Argentina's neighbours, other American states and a host of trading nations.

The war with Britain in 1982 produced a change in Argentina's international position. Relations with the USA and Western Europe have deteriorated while Argentina's standing and support in Latin-America has improved, though traditional tensions remain.

4 SOCIETY AND CULTURE

Social Patterns

The historical development of Argentina, colonised from the west and lacking the gold and silver sought by the *conquistadores*, meant that the social traditions of *hidalgo* and noble, strong elsewhere in Latin America, did not strike roots in Argentina. The colonisers did not produce a ruling caste of the 'top 40 families' in Argentina as they did elsewhere. Instead there developed a society of adventurers and individualists; and with the River Plate excluded from trade by royal fiat, there grew up a tradition of illegal trade and smuggling, and a buccaneering spirit which still exists, nourished by the vast open spaces and opportunities for rapid advancement. Subsequent waves of immigration brought enterprising workers and middle men, looking for prosperity and prepared to work hard to get it. Generally the outlook is still strongly materialistic and sometimes ostentatiously so. It is a society, at least in Buenos Aires, where hard work and inititive can bring rewards, although the methods used in achieving them might not always meet with universal moral approval.

While the family tradition is strong, there is a considerable difference in values between the young and their elders. Women work and have rights. Divorce is not recognised, but separations are plentiful; divorces are, however, obtained in other countries and remarriages do take place. They are viewed tolerantly, though legally they are bigamous.

Cultural Traditions

Culturally Argentina presents anomalies. It is wholly Europeanised, having no indigenous culture comparable with, say, Mexico; yet it is excluded from Europe by distance and from Latin America by its very Europeanisation. The Spanish traditions in Argentina are obvious, particularly in the interior where townships have all the marks of Spanish origin - the *plaza* with the town hall *(cabildo)* on one side, the church or cathedral on the other, and the local or provincial government offices nearby. But the traditions of other national groups are strong and there are, particularly in Buenos Aires, communities that have not integrated into a single society that is purely and recognisably Argentine. They retain their languages of origin and even after generations their Spanish may be far from perfect. So, for example, the Italian influence is strong in the conurbations of the River Plate and in lower class city culture; a basically Italianised dialect *(lunfardo)* has developed. There are several local foreign language newspapers and five community hospitals - among the best in Buenos Aires.

Nevertheless, Argentina's cultural achievements (in the narrower sense) are high. It has produced scientific Nobel prizewinners like Houssay and Leloir and writers like Jorge Luis Borges. In Buenos Aires are theatres that can rival London, Paris and New York both in *avant garde* and traditional works. Its standards in opera and music generally are internationally respected: the Colon Theatre is regarded as among the four or five best in the world. These achievements rest on the foundations of a strong tradition of education and a high literacy rate (90%).

Religion

The country is predominantly Catholic (90% with 2% Protestant). Religious freedom was granted to Englishmen in 1825, and to all foreigners by the 1853 Constitution. Religion played, and still does, a more vital role in the interior than in the coastal conurbations of the Plate. The influence of the Catholic Church, however, was limited by legislation in the 1880s, especially in public school education from which it was eliminated in 1884. The Church on the whole is liberal, not obvious in its presence (one rarely sees a priest recognisable as such, in the streets) but it is still a considerable force in the personal lives of many people, particularly women. The Roman Catholic Church founded, and runs, over half the private schools at primary and secondary levels and 11 universities.

5 THE ECONOMY

Regional Variations

The coast is characterised by increasingly developed industrial activity and (until recently at least) full employment. The interior provinces are under-populated, poor and unable to develop themselves without federal grants. The interior has been starved of employment as development has always been concentrated in the coastal towns. As a result of railway development better and cheaper products from the USA and Europe killed many local home industries in the interior and led to a greater dependence on raw material production only. Some attempt is now being made to move industry away from the coast through tax concessions and incentives. But industrial development does not necessarily require labour-intensive processes and distance adds to costs, both in shipping raw materials from the ports and in returning manufactured goods for sale in urban centres. Despite a long Atlantic coastline there are as yet few deep water ports and the lack of cross connections between main railways and roads adds to the problems.

Economic Situation

Argentina's economy is based on great agricultural wealth and broad industrial activity protected by high tariff policies. It is one of the most highly developed countries in Latin America and should be in a strong economic position, but political instability has proved a constant strain on the economy which has been characterised by a slow rate of growth and rapid inflation. The major cause of inflation in 1975 was the large fiscal deficit (139 million pesos) which was mostly caused by massive salary increases (100% to 130%) combined with the accumulation of undeclared funds enabling widespread tax evasion. Inflation rose to an all time high of over 800% and the trade deficit was US$1,000 million. The peso was devalued 13 times between March and December. The government announced a six-month austerity programme with wage rises limited to 12% but in the face of labour unrest this ceiling was raised to 20%. At the time of the coup the total foreign debt had reached US$8,808 million, loans from international institutions were being withheld and all foreign investment had ceased.

In April 1976 the new government introduced a recovery programme based on free marked principles and with the reduction of the inflation rate as the main priority. The fiscal deficit was reduced by sacking 300,000 public employees, State companies were denationalised to reduce government expenditure and stimulate investment and production, tax reforms were instituted (including the introduction of wealth and capital gains taxes), the exchange market was liberalised, incentives were given to foreign investment and prices were left to market forces rather than government intervention. Salary increases were set nationally (15% across the board in June 1976) and a minimum monthly wage was fixed. The monthly inflation rate fell from 34.9% in April to 4.3% in July but a 2.6% drop in industrial production was predicted for 1976. In late 1976 the government was seeking loans from the IMF and international banks to meet debt obligations and a three-year economic plan was being drafted. The present official estimate of the inflation rate is 120% per annum. Whether this rate can be held in view of the dependence on imported raw materials, EEC import restrictions and an abnormally high note issue to cover government expenditure, must remain doubtful.

Further austerity measures were taken in 1980. But economic difficulties have persisted, especially since the 1982 war, and serious problems of international credit have intensified.

Agriculture

In the first decades of this century Argentina was one of the grain bowls of the world; today agriculture accounts for 14% of GDP (in 1976 US$ 1,840 per capita). Agricultural products, though they have not increased in quantity and may indeed have decreased, nevertheless have still gained in value because of world increases in the price of meat proteins and cereals. Main food crops and cereals with an annual output of 20 million tons made up of maize, wheat and grain (sorghum); fruit, sugar and wine are also produced. Livestock are reared on the *pampa* within a 600 km radius of Buenos Aires and meat for some time formed the basis of Argentina's exports. Latterly, however, the meat industry has suffered from domestic prices being held to an unprofitable minimum by the government and in 1974 the EEC (which had been taking 70% of Argentinian beef) banned beef imports to maintain domestic prices. Sixty million hectares (22% of Argentina's surface) is forested but only about 39 million carry exploitable timber and of this 10 million is suitable only for firewood.

Tax on farm products and their export has tended to discourage modernisation of agriculture and investment of capital in it, though the new government policy is to maximise farm products to finance industrial development. The land is fertile but undernourished, farms are too large for intensive agriculture and while the returns on capital and investment in farming are low compared to industry there is no incentive to further invest capital in improvements. But to low profit margins in farming must be added the consistent increase in land values, and where farms are very large a low profit margin does not preclude large financial returns on comparatively inefficient farming of land. At present a project is planned aiming at increasing arable and livestock output through mechanisation involving a loan of US$89 million from the International Development Bank.

Fisheries

Since 1967 Argentina has claimed sovereignty over the continental shelf which extends for 450 miles off Patagonia and which holds enormous reserves of fish. Elsewhere the fishing limit is 200 miles. There is a major project to develop fisheries though the industry has not yet reached its full potential; but it too has experienced export difficulties.

Natural Resources

The most important mineral deposits are iron ore, coal and oil (though over half Argentina's coal requirements still have to be imported). In general basic raw materials are either lacking or have not been consistently exploited by succeeding governments, with the exception of oil, which has developed to the point where 90% of Argentina's needs are met from local resources; hydroelectric power development plans, for example, have been so held up that there are periodic shortages of electricity which will continue until 1990. There are deposits of asbestos, kaolin, lead, manganese, tin, wolfram and zinc; gold, silver, copper and magnesium are found in the Andes. Uranium deposits also exist and Argentina has the world's most extensive resources of boron. Nevertheless, the development of a mining industry has been very slow. The Energy Plan (1974-85) aims to reduce Argentina's dependence on petroleum and its derivatives and to increase the use of hydroelectric power, solid fuel and nuclear power. By 1985 hydroelectric power should be providing 48% of total electricity requirements. At the same time attempts are being made to raise the level of petroleum production and offshore prospecting has begun (including the area of Is Malvinas).

Industry

Manufacturing industry now accounts for 31% of GDP. Partly because the industries that grew up between two world wars were based on import substitution most of the industrialisation was based on foreign raw materials processed or assembled locally. Basic industries were originally meat processing, meat packing and animal byproducts, but the country is now self-sufficient in practically all consumer goods, consumer durables, vehicles and machinery. There is a large and rapidly growing heavy industry including plastics, textiles, steel, engineering and chemicals fostered by the offeriong of inducements for the establishment and expansion of industrial activity. These inducements now apply only to locally established firms. Local industry is heavily protected and State organisations must favour Argentine companies by law. Investment in basic industries has levelled offsomewhat and in 1975 fell by 30%, but the steel and textile industries are still expanding.

Trade

Cereals are now the principal export (maize accounting for about half) and Argentina is one of the world's largest exporters of wine. Until the EEC beef ban agriculture provided 80% foreign exchange earnings and increased world prices and import restrictions had produced a healthy foreign trade surplus. Trade now accounts for about 15% of GDP. New markets for beef have been found in the USSR, Israel and Iraq and the export of industrial products is growing, (including cars, lorries, tractors and other heavy equipment) especially to the rest of Latin America.

6 THE EDUCATION SYSTEM

What follows describes the system as it is at present. There are plans, however, to modify it so that there will be six years of primary school, three of middle school and three of secondary school instead of the present seven of primary and five of secondary.

Academic Year

There is a five-day week and the academic year is divided into two semesters. It runs from mid-March to early December with a mid-year break in July. Most students at all levels are part time. In schools, pupils normally attend either from 8.00 to 12.00 noon or from 1.00 to 5.00 p.m.

Pre-Primary

Kindergarten education or nursery schooling for children between the ages of 3 and 6 is well developed in both State and private sectors, particularly the latter. It is estimated that approximately 12% of the age group is enrolled in kindergartens (369,082 children in 1975). State kindergartens which are free, tend to be mainly in urban areas where mothers are out at work. The private schools cater for the middle and upper classes who can afford to pay for this education from an early stage. About two thirds of the schools and 70% of the pupils at this level are in the three provinces Buenos Aires, Córdoba and Santa Fé and the federal capital.

Primary *(Ciclo Primario)*

Primary schooling lasts for seven years from the age of 6 and is free and compulsory. Failing the completion of the course, school attendance is compulsory up to the age of 14. Otherwise pupils can finish compulsory schooling at 12. About 93% of the age group is enrolled. Promotion is automatic from the first to the second grade as these are regarded as forming a single unit. Between the second and the seventh grades, pupils are promoted from one grade to the next on the basis of continuous assessment, together with an end-of-year evaluation.

The curriculum at primary level is still organised by subjects and includes mathematics, language, natural sciences, rudiments of technology, social sciences, visual arts, musical education, practical work, physical education, foreign language and optional activities. The school timetable covers 25 hours weekly in grades 1 to 5 and 30 hours weekly in grades 6 and 7.

Secondary *(Ciclo Secundario)*

Secondary education is not compulsory (only 45% of the age group is enrolled) and is free in State institutions. The course normally lasts five years (a three-year *ciclo básico;* and a two-year *ciclo superior*) but can last 6 or 7 years according to the type of programme followed: general, commercial, teacher training, technical, vocational, art, and social welfare. The *bachillerato* in its various forms is the secondary school leaving qualification. In a few institutions there is a longer course leading to the qualification *bachillerato especializado,* the additional year enabling pupils to study one area more intensively. The specialisations are letters, biological sciences, physics and mathematics, teacher training and, in rural areas, agriculture. Promotion from one grade to another is automatic for those pupils who have obtained an average assessment mark of 7 (out of 10) or over during the year; otherwise promotion is decided after subject examinations administered by boards of examiners that meet in December and March each year. In secondary schools the pupils are taught by subject teachers in periods of 40 to 45 minutes' duration. The timetable covers 6 to 8 hours daily, or 30 to 36 hours weekly. Pupils spend 200 days a year in school, including examination periods.

Although the great majority of pupils attend for only half a day, since 1968 a number of all-day schools have been set up on a pilot basis, particularly in the capital area. In a large proportion of these English is being taught

THE EDUCATION SYSTEM

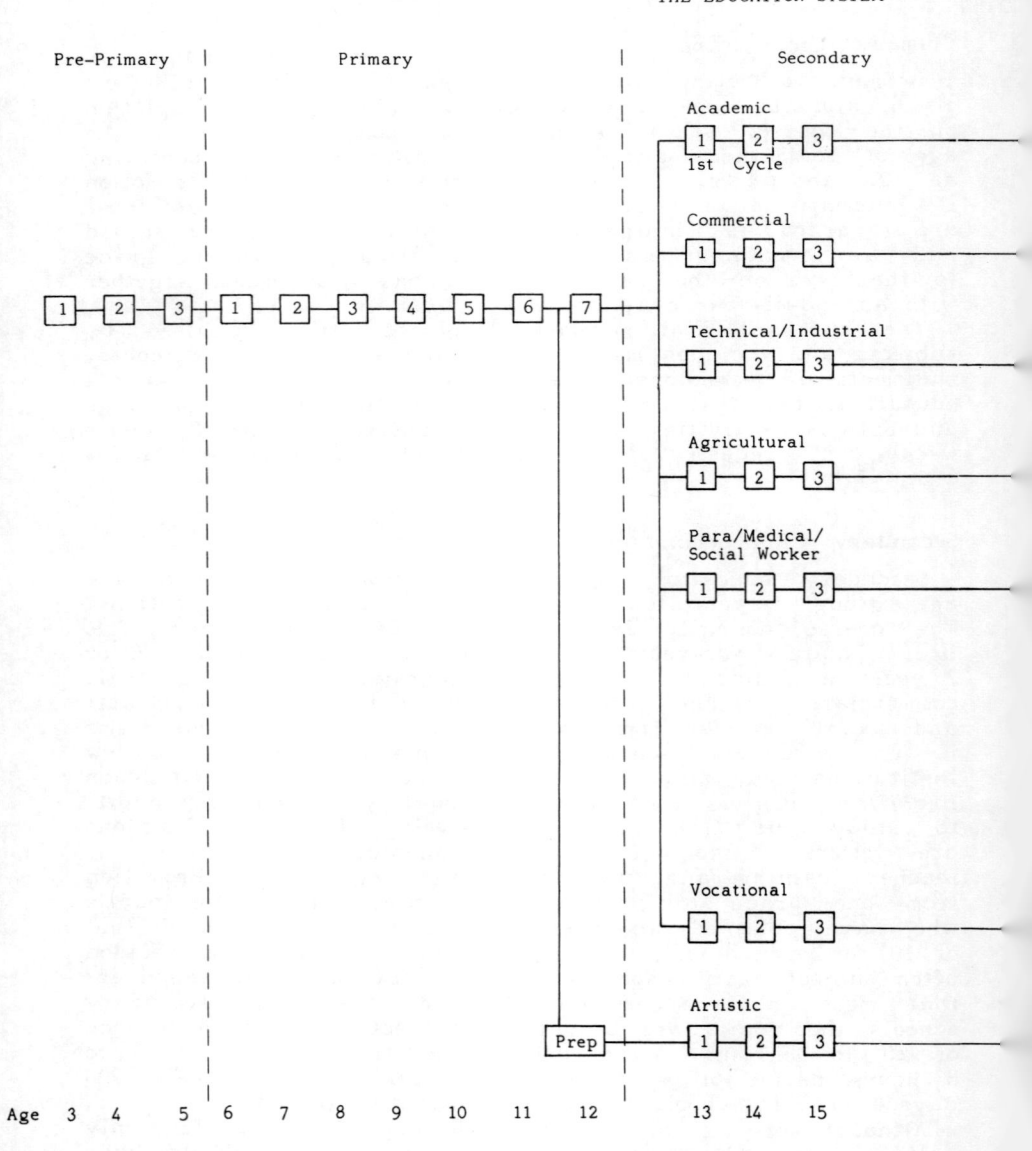

Pre-Primary | Primary | Secondary

Academic
- 1 — 2 — 3
- 1st Cycle

Commercial
- 1 — 2 — 3

Technical/Industrial
- 1 — 2 — 3

Agricultural
- 1 — 2 — 3

Para/Medical/Social Worker
- 1 — 2 — 3

Vocational
- 1 — 2 — 3

Artistic
- Prep — 1 — 2 — 3

Pre-Primary: 1 — 2 — 3
Primary: 1 — 2 — 3 — 4 — 5 — 6 — 7

Age 3 4 5 6 7 8 9 10 11 12 13 14 15

OF ARGENTINA

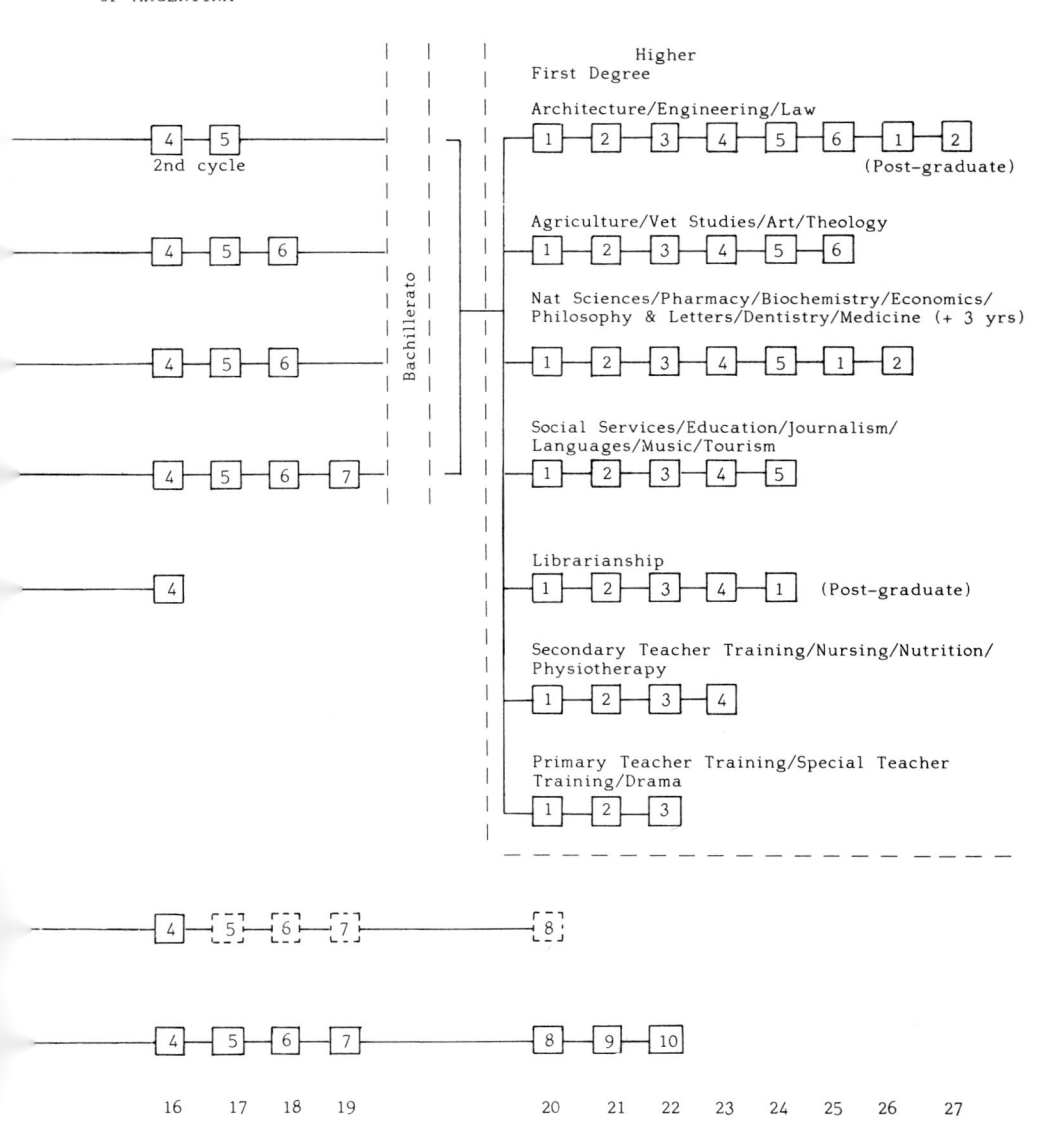

Higher
First Degree

Architecture/Engineering/Law
| 1 | 2 | 3 | 4 | 5 | 6 | 1 | 2 |
(Post-graduate)

2nd cycle

| 4 | 5 |

Bachillerato

| 4 | 5 | 6 |

Agriculture/Vet Studies/Art/Theology
| 1 | 2 | 3 | 4 | 5 | 6 |

| 4 | 5 | 6 |

Nat Sciences/Pharmacy/Biochemistry/Economics/
Philosophy & Letters/Dentistry/Medicine (+ 3 yrs)
| 1 | 2 | 3 | 4 | 5 | 1 | 2 |

| 4 | 5 | 6 | 7 |

Social Services/Education/Journalism/
Languages/Music/Tourism
| 1 | 2 | 3 | 4 | 5 |

| 4 |

Librarianship
| 1 | 2 | 3 | 4 | 1 | (Post-graduate)

Secondary Teacher Training/Nursing/Nutrition/
Physiotherapy
| 1 | 2 | 3 | 4 |

Primary Teacher Training/Special Teacher
Training/Drama
| 1 | 2 | 3 |

| 4 | [5] | [6] | [7] | [8] |

| 4 | 5 | 6 | 7 | 8 | 9 | 10 |

16 17 18 19   20 21 22 23 24 25 26 27

from the age of 8. Also, many private schools organise a full day's activities, often with the national *bachillerato* course in the morning and an English type education in the afternoon. In addition there are many private language institutions where parents pay for their children to receive lessons in a foreign language, particularly English.

Academic

The secondary schools with an academic bias, whose main aim is to prepare students for university entrance, are the national *colegios* or *liceos*. In 1978 492,117 pupils (34.2% of all studying at this level) were following academic courses. The course lasts five years. The aggregate number of hours per week spent on each subject in the *liceos* is as follows:

1st Cycle (3 years)

Spanish	14
Mathematics	14
History	12
Foreign language (French/English)	9
Geography	9
Physical Education	6
Biological Sciences	6
Democratic Education	6
Drawing	6
Music	6
Practical Activities	6
Physics/Chemistry (third year only)	2

2nd Cycle (2 years)

Mathematics	8
Foreign language (different from 1st cycle)	8
History	6
Literature	6
Chemistry	6
Physics	6
Philosophy	6
Biological Sciences	5
Geography	4
Physical Education	4
Civic Instruction	3
Democratic Education	2
Music	2

Commercial

State commercial school *(escuelas comerciales)* are well developed. Their programmes last six years and the basic cycle curriculum is similar to that of the academic schools, but in the second cycle 40% of the study time is devoted to commercial subjects as follows:

Accountancy	11
Technology of Trade	8
Mathematics	6
Foreign language	6
Stenography	5
Typing	4
Geography	4
Literature	3
Law	3
Commercial Law	3
Organisation of Trade and the Firm	3
Administrative Law and Fiscal Legislature	2
Political Economy	2
Physics	2
Hygiene and First Aid	2

Most students holding the commercial *bachillerato* ("Percto Mercantil") enter the economics faculties of universities. There are plans to revise the curriculum.

Technical

Many of these schools *(escuelas industriales)* are private institutions, some receiving support from local industry. Graduates of these schools are eligible to pursue higher studies; most doing so enter the university engineering faculties and higher technical institutes. The course, which lasts six years, has a higher proportion of specialised subjects than the commercial secondary course. Technical schools also tend to specialise in a particular area (e.g. mechanical or electrical engineering, civil engineering and building). A technical auxiliary's certificate may be obtained after the first cycle and a year's specialisation. Students who complete the six-year course successfully are awarded the title of 'Technician' in one special area. The fields include industrial management, aviation, mechanical or electrical engineering, automobile engineering, mining, naval construction.

There are also part time evening classes for adolescents and adults.

Vocational

Vocational education *(educación profesional)* is largely geared to girls who make up 85% of the enrolment. Courses last for one to 8 years, with 4 years as the norm, mostly concentrating on home economics, the clothing trade, and clerical work though some technical courses are offered. Graduates of these schools are not qualified to go on to higher studies.

Other

At secondary level students can also specialise in agriculture (seven-year course) at an agricultural secondary school or follow a para-medical course to qualify as a medical auxiliary. The para-medical courses are of a lower standard and last only three or four years. There are also four-year secondary courses for social workers and 'artistic' courses which involve a preparatory year and up to ten years' study. The total enrolment for non-academic secondary education in 1978 was 850,956 (66% of total secondary enrolment).

Higher

Education at the higher level is provided in universities and other higher institutions. At present the country has 61 national universities, of which 26 are private universities (mostly Catholic and fee-paying), and 8 provincial universities. In 1978 22.3% of the population aged 20-24 was in higher education. About 89% of these students are in the universities with 11% in higher education institutions (of which 8% are in teacher training). Of university students 85% attend the national universities and the largest (Buenos Aires) has over 200,000 enrolled. The total enrolment in higher education in 1978 was 477,725 of which 50% was female.

Until 1975 students had free entry to the faculty of their choice provided they had the *bachillerato* (the minimum entrance requirement), or obtained it before taking their first examination. In 1975 applicants were required to take an eliminatory entrance examination in some faculties and spend approximately three months studying basic subjects for their courses before actually starting degree work. In 1976, because of the large number of students who had not comleted their first year (in medicine, 2,000), the universities established quotas for the new entry (from 450 students for dentistry to 1,000 for science, for law, for economics, for medicine and for engineering). In 1977, the same procedure applied; prospective students were able to attend preparatory classes in the basic subjects and sat examinations in March for entry in April. Acceptance was dependent on the average marks obtained and on the number of places available.

University first degree courses vary in length from two to six years but most are of five years duration. The majority of students take six or more years to complete these courses (only about 30% obtain a degree in the specified time).

In practice a student does not move from one year of studies to the next after an end-of-year examination in several subjects, but each subject is taken individually at intervals. The student therefore has considerable control over the pace of his study. Most students (between 40% and 60%) attent university part time and have an outside job. Some degree courses lead to a professional title (e.g. *ingeniero, profesor*) others to the *licenciado*. In some fields a diploma may be taken after a few years and the *licenciado* is the second degree. In certain subjects a one- or two-year post-graduate course is available. The post-graduate degree *(doctorado)* is awarded on presentation of a thesis.

Professional courses outside the universities (e.g. paramedical studies, journalism, higher technician training, administration) are not extensively developed and account for only 3% of all students in higher education. Courses normally last two or three years. Most higher education outside universities is concerned with teacher training.

Teacher Training

Pre-Primary

There is a small number of institutions (both State and private) for the training of kindergarten teachers. The course lasts two years (two and a half years for students who have not followed the teacher training option at secondary school) and leads to the award of the *maestra jardinera* certificate.

Primary

Until 1970 primary teachers was trained in the secondary schools, following a two-year cycle after the *ciclo básico*. Primary teacher training now consists of the last two years of the secondary course followed by a two-year course at a higher teacher training institute and a one year practical period. Students must have completed their studies at the secondary level in some branch of the national school system and graduates from *all* branches of secondary education, including technical schools, are accepted. A minimum of 25 students is required for each course, and division into two shifts is authorised when the number of students exceeds 60. This new training is not designed to turn out a completely trained teacher, but one prepared to continue taking in-service training and refresher courses. The three basic aspects of the plan are: the 'modernity' of its approach; its 'flexibility' and the 'full time' system for practice teaching.

The curriculum comprises: 12 compulsory subjects, studied for one academic year each, divided into three basic groups, and five elective activities, of which the student is obliged to choose a minimum of two, each lasting for a four-month period. The compulsory subjects are: theory of education;

theory of learning; psychology of development; elements of philosophy; language and literature; mathematics; physics and chemistry; biology, social sciences; manual and aesthetic training; physical education; school organisation and administration. The elective activities include: a seminar on regional, social, economic and cultural problems; a seminar on contemporary problems in education; evaluation techniques; preparation of teaching material, and use of audio-visual aids and library techniques; speech and voice control. One of the distinctive features of the curriculum is the freedom left to the teachers to draw up detailed programmes in their respective subjects. This constitutes a radical change in the educational tradition of the country, although such freedom already existed in teacher training institutes at the third level.

Previously, in the curricula in force from 1942 to 1969, students in the normal schools were observers in the fourth year and took practice classes in their fifth year approximately once a week in the demonstration primary school attached to the normal school where they were studying. The new system makes one semester's full time teaching compulsory at some ordinary primary school in the area. During this teaching period, under the guidance of his teacher and the supervision of the principal of the establishment, the student will perform all the usual tasks of a primary school teacher.

Secondary

Secondary school teachers receive a four- or five-year training, at post-secondary level, the final qualification *(profesorado)* being the equivalent of a university degree. Some teacher training institutions *(profesorados)* are independent (whether national, provincial or private) and others are attached to universities in which case the teaching certificate is awarded after a one-year course taken after the first degree course. There is no block teaching practice; instead students spend about six hours a week on practical teaching throughout the course. The *profesorado* is awarded in particular specialisms including technical education.

Adult and Non-Formal

It is possible to take primary courses in adult literacy schools, in the armed forces and in prison, and secondary courses are available in the evenings (involving an extra year's study). One or two of the newly set up universities are beginning to cater for their local adult community ('second chance') needs: two-year *bachillerato* courses have been introduced for those over 20 and students over 25 are being accepted without formal qualifications. There is a national government scheme to reduce the rates of illiteracy and semi-literacy; (although the official illiteracy rate is 7% as much as 43% of the population has recently been classified as semi-literate). Life long education *(educación permanente)* is now becoming an important part of government forward education planning, and the government is looking to exploit TV and radio. A number of programmes are already being transmitted to educational institutions and the Ministry of Education has recently asked for a TV channel exclusively for educational use. A government working party is considering a countrywide policy for educational TV and a South American regional TV training centre has been opened in Buenos Aires. Financial help is provided for adult students to complete their studies through easy-term loans from the National Institute of Educational Credit (INCE).

7 EDUCATIONAL ADMINISTRATION

Centralised Control

The administrative structure is complex owing to simultaneous direction by various authorities at national, provincial, municipal and private levels. There are both national and provincial Ministries of Culture and Education (or equivalent institutions) under which come the agencies or departments which administer education at the various levels and supervise private education. The system was highly centralised and power lay very firmly in Buenos Aires, but from 1978 the administration of primary education was transferred to the provincial governments to the provincial governments with the central government retaining responsibility for planning and coordination, teacher training, research, methodology etc. Delegation of power and decentralisation is far from complete, but recently there has been evidence of a desire on the part of the government to involve teachers, parents and students in formulating plans for educational reform.

Organisation of the Ministry

In 1968, the internal organisation of the national Ministry of Education was revised. Recently, three posts at Secretary level and four at Under-Secretary level have been introduced to strengthen the infrastructure and define spheres of influence more clearly. The present structure is that within the Ministry there are three Secretaries of State for Culture, Education, and Science and Technology assisted by four Under-Secretaries. The Secretary of State for Education has two assistants – an Under-Secretary responsible for education and one for university affairs. In addition there is an Under-Secretary (General) responsible for administration, budget and educational development. In spite of these recent innovations, however, the network of agencies covering different aspects of education continues and decisions still tend to be made at the top.

University Administration

Central government control of the universities is strict. Funds for the national universities are allocated after consultation with the Council of Rectors of National Universities which is responsible for planning, coordination and the preparatin of university budgets. At present all national universities have been 'intervened': that is to say that the government has appointed an 'interventor' to take charge temporarily of the running of each university. The interventor is responsible directly to the government through the Ministry of Education. Prior to this the universities had been governed by the university assembly and a system of councils at various levels. Private universities have their own councils, but their statutes and teaching plans and programmes must be approved by the central Ministry, and they cannot receive any State subsidies.

8 EDUCATIONAL FINANCE

Education Budget

In the period 1955/65, between 1.4% and 1.9% of GNP was spent on education, but this has risen to approximately 2.7%. About two thirds of public educational expenditure is provided by central government and one third by provincial governments, although the latter is now increasing, especially at primary level. Central government also provides most of the public money for universities.

Like the national government, the provincial governments have decreed that all public education shall be free. Over half the provinces allocate between 20% and 30% of their budget to education, and most of them have set aside a permanent fund exclusively for education. The funds allocated to education at both national and provincial levels basically do no more than provide school buildings and pay the salaries of teachers. All equipment and materials have to be provided by the parents and by the cooperatives *(cooperadoras)*, groups set up by parents, teachers and people from commerce and industry in the area of each school.

Allocation of Funds

The percentage allocation of the Ministry of Education budget by level for 1978 was as follows:

Pre-Primary and Primary	40.1
Secondary	25.6
Tertiary	22.7
Other	1.9
Not by level	9.7
	100.0

ORGANISATION OF THE MINISTRY OF CULTURE AND EDUCATION

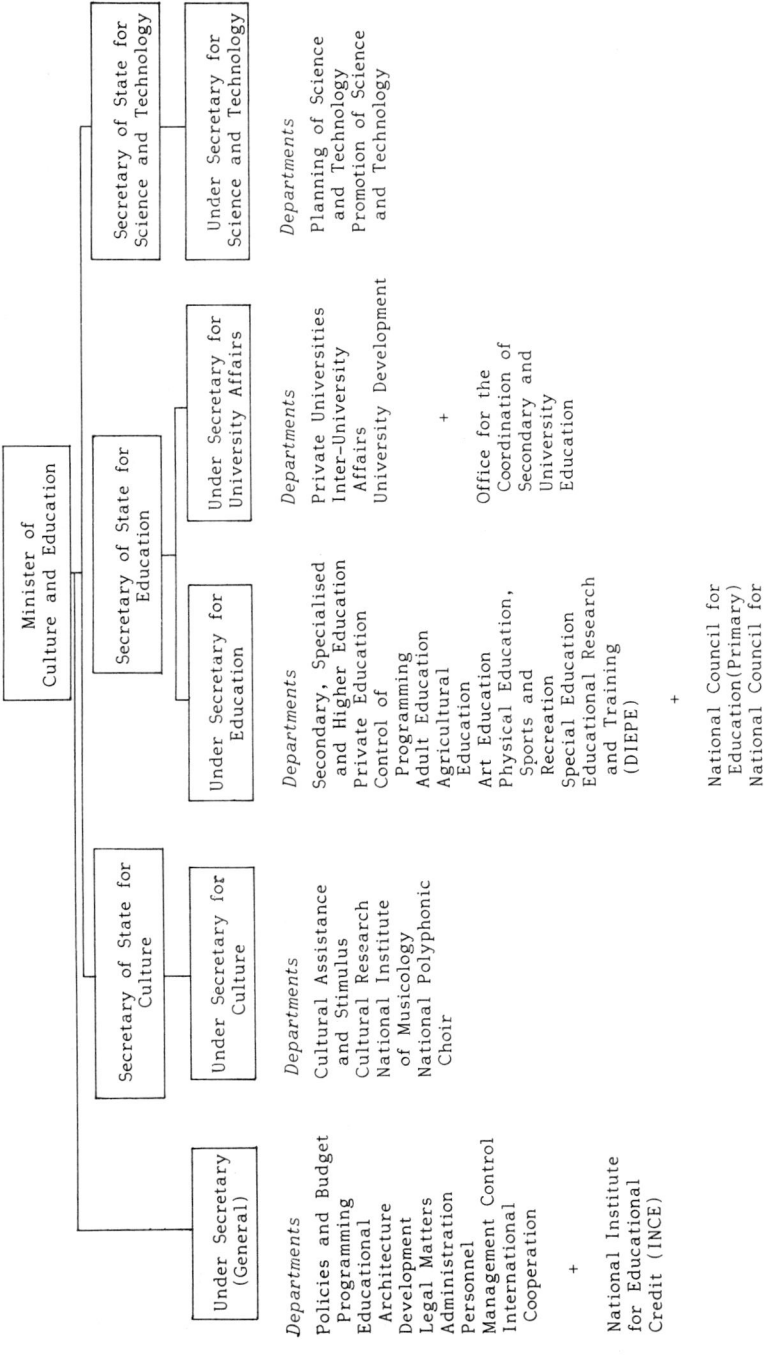

```
                        Minister of
                    Culture and Education
```

Under Secretary (General)

Departments
Policies and Budget
Programming
Educational Architecture
Development
Legal Matters
Administration
Personnel
Management Control
International Cooperation

+

National Institute for Educational Credit (INCE)

Secretary of State for Culture

Under Secretary for Culture

Departments
Cultural Assistance and Stimulus
Cultural Research
National Institute of Musicology
National Polyphonic Choir

Secretary of State for Education

Under Secretary for Education

Departments
Secondary, Specialised and Higher Education
Private Education
Control of Programming
Adult Education
Agricultural Education
Art Education
Physical Education, Sports and Recreation
Special Education
Educational Research and Training (DIEPE)

+

National Council for Education (Primary)
National Council for Technical Education
School Health Service

Under Secretary for University Affairs

Departments
Private Universities
Inter-University Affairs
University Development

+

Office for the Coordination of Secondary and University Education

Secretary of State for Science and Technology

Under Secretary for Science and Technology

Departments
Planning of Science and Technology
Promotion of Science and Technology

Financial Administration

The bulk of educational expenditure is made by the Ministry of Education. Some other ministries finance their own establishments but their share of the budget is small (about 5%). Each agency of the Ministry has its own budget fixed by parliament. The root of the problem is the existence of the diverse educational agencies. The national constitution makes no reference to the financing of education and the present system is the result of various laws passed at different periods in the past and revised at varying intervals. In 1965 the Permanent Education Fund was established, administered by the Ministry of Education for its own needs and also for the National Council for Education *(Consejo Nacional de Educación)* which administers primary schools, and the National Council for Technical Education *(Consejo Nacional de Educación Técnica)*. The universities are financed by the treasury through the universities departments in the Ministry of Education. National funds are used to subsidise private education through the payment of teachers' salaries.

9 DEVELOPMENT AND PLANNING OF THE EDUCATION SYSTEM
Origins

Until the middle of the nineteenth century, education had been in the hands of private organisations and individuals, particularly the Jesuits (until 1767, when they were expelled) and, of course, the Roman Catholic Church generally. Sarmiento (1811-1888), Argentina's first great educationalist, saw in the 1853 Constitution a way of using education and enlightened reforms to overcome the wretchedness and poverty particularly of the people of the interior and to bring about a unification of the country basing Argentina's future greatness on the foundation of schools and other institutions of learning. Sarmiento was particularly influenced by European ideas and as head of the Department of Schools from 1856 to 1861, had all the best texts translated into Spanish and introduced into schools foreign language teaching, music and singing. He also studied the North American education system when ambassador to that country in 1863. In 1868, as President of Argentina he created the primary school system and brought in North Americans to organise the 'normal schools' (based on the French *écoles normales*). He introduced school inspection, night school and the teaching of civics, physics and physical education. He raised the status of the teaching profession and secured independent government revenue for schools. After Sarmiento, almost three quarters of a century were to pass before education received such attention again.

Development

The Constitution of 1853 laid down that each province must provide primary education, that each individual has the right to education and that the National Congress must draw up plans for general and university instruction. In practice, many provinces were not able to provide primary education so that the government had to step in with subsidies, and even build its own schools, introducing the first of many complications which characterise Argentine education. Secondary schools did exist before 1853 but they were very few and catered for the privileged minority who wanted to enter the two existing universities of the time, in Córdoba (founded 1613) and Buenos Aires (1821). Later national colleges were set up (*liceos* for girls) to enable students to study in their home towns for university entry. These institutions gradually developed more general courses but still remained largely orientated towards the universities. By the end of the nineteenth century some industrial and art schools had been founded and with increasing demand from the new immigrant population of the time, primary education was made comulsory in 1884. Secondary education, however, was (and is) not; and this omission led to a stratified educational system closely linked to the country's socio-economic divisions. The primary school catered for the working classes handling the country's production of raw materials; the secondary school educated the middle class, the office workers and administrators; while the university was the stronghold of the upper classes, the land owners and subsequently, the big industrialists who control the country's economy.

Until about 1800 the education system was characterised by an academic encyclopaedism based on the French tradition. From about 1880 to 1920, positivism (a reaction against encyclopaedism) and a plea for a more practical and scientific education were being preached in universities and normal schools. Teaching began to be more practical and utilitarian and proposals were put forward for the establishment of intermediate schools to cover the period of early adolescence. World War One and its aftermath marked the defeat of the positivists who were criticised for being too humanistic. From then until the 1950s Argentine education reverted to its former emphasis on things of the spirit. Philosophy became important again; the scientific-biological aspects of teacher training courses virtually disappeared; experimentation practically ceased and the encyclopaedic tradition reasserted itself. The classical education replaced education for life, for industry and for independent work. The divorce between school and life was accentuated. the failure to set up the outward-looking intermediate school in 1916 is considered to be one of the biggest failures of national education in Argentina.

Subsequently stagnation set in, in spite of attempts from time to time to activate the system. With the advent of Perón in the 1940s education became of considerable political importance, being allied to a significant expansion in industry and urban population. In 1943 religious instruction had been made compulsory in all schools. In 1949 a new constitution was introduced, replacing the 1853 Constitution, and including significant references to education. The universities were required to introduce courses throughout all faculties for the "political education of students". Government approved textbooks designed to "exalt the sentiment of the Fatherland" were made compulsory for all schools. Teachers who were anti-Peronists were dismissed and replaced by Peronists, particularly in the universities, which were then first 'intervened' by the government. A scholarship system was introduced to help poor students, full time teaching by university staff was encouraged, university fees were abolished, and the social background of university students widened, and rectors of universities were appointed by the President for a period of three years. Five-Year Plans were introduced and the Second Plan laid down that "the ultimate aim of education is to bring about the moral, intellectual and physical development of the people of the basis of the National Peronist doctrine". After the fall of the Perón régime in 1955, the 1949 Constitution was abolished and the 1853 Constitution re-established. For the next 12 years education receded into the background until 1968, referred to as the "year of change in education".

Changes 1968-71

The principal structural changes in Argentine education proposed during the period running, roughly, from 1968 to 1971 included a number of modifications in the traditional system of educational stages or 'cycles' and plans for extending compulsory schooling to cover a nine-year period. The idea was that this period should be divided into two cycles; one of five years (primary school); and another of four years (intermediate school), during which an element of specialisation would be introduced. The secondary school course, in turn, would cover three years and would be both polytechnical (offering vocational training in a variety of fields) and multi-purpose or 'polyvalent' (i.e. leading to a certificate entitling its holder to enter any university). Important changes were also introduced into primary school organisation and teaching methods, one of the most fundamental being the adoption of what is called the 'curriculum theory' for the planning of school activities and the arrangement of syllabus contents. The reform programme was beginning to get under way in 1970 but was halted indefinitely early in 1971 with a change of President.

Curriculum Theory

In addition to various other temporary provisions, the "basic principles for the primary school curriculum" (cover the first, second and third years) were adopted on an experimental basis under a Ministerial Resolution of 2 October 1970. The 'basic principles' are now well accepted as part of the country's education system but implementation is slow. They are an attempt to replace the old-fashioned (programmes' - which, although sometimes of considerable academic merit, were mainly academic in character - by the curriculum-type scheme characteristic of a more up to date methodological approach. The fundamental idea of the educational philosophy underlying the curriculum theory adopted is that these principles should be regarded as guides on the basis of which each educational establishment, through the concerted efforts of its entire teaching staff, can work out the specific course of action to be followed during the year. Parents, members of the community and the pupils themselves are also invited to take part in this planning of the year's activities. Three fundamental aspects of the curriculum are stressed:

(i) individualisation, i.e. promoting the development of each pupil in accordance with his or her individual traits and characteristics

(ii) socialisation, i.e. integrating the above principle with the internationalisation of group standards

(iii) regionalisation, i.e. creating a national consciousness of the local conditions obtaining in each region of the country.

The content of the curriculum is dealt with at considerable length and schematic outlines are given for mathematics, languages, social sciences, natural sciences, music, plastic arts, physical education, and free activities. The schematic outlines are all constructed on the following pattern: specific objectives of the first cycle; general objectives common to all syllabi; content and patterns of activity; guidance for the teacher; basic information; methodological approach; attitude toward the pupil; principles of evaluation. Each outline concludes with a basic bibliography for the use of the teacher. Although changes of educational policy since 1971 did not cause the process of implementing these ideas formally to be annulled, they did nevertheless bring it to a temporary halt. It now seems that these principles may be taken up again: to what degree they will be implemented remains to be seen.

Planning Institutions

The legal bases of education in Argentina have their origins in various instruments including the national and provincial constitutions, laws, decrees and ministerial decisions. From 1966 onwards, the government has based its planning system on three organisations: the National Council for Development *(Consejo Nacional para de Desarollo)*, the National Security Council *(Consejo Nacional de Seguridad)*, and the National Council for Science and Technology *(Consejo Nacional de Ciencia y Tecnología)*. The main responsibility of these organisations is to formulate the lines of national policy in accordance with modern planning techniques. In March

1976, without disbanding the three planning institutions, the military government created a Ministry of Planning *(Ministirio de Planeamiento)* to formulate the National Plan which will provide the guidelines for future policy. In 1972, the Federal Council of Education was instituted with planning, coordinating and advisory functions. Its aim is to try to harmonise with the national education policy those aspects of national, provincial, municipal and private education which make joint action by the nation and the provinces difficult. The Federal Council consists of the Minister of Education and the provincial ministers.

Achievements and Aims

The National Plan for Development and Security 1971-75, in the section on education, refers to "the obsolescence of the education system which was directed initially towards literacy, to the transplanting of European culture and to the training of small groups of professionals and leaders according to the demands of the time; no reforms in depth were introduce which could have corrected the centralisation and rigidity of the system or aroused a critical spirit or developed creative attitudes". The main aim of recent reforms has been to break the straitjacket of formal education, to ease the transition between primary and secondary stages by creating an intermediate stage, and to reorganise education administration (with emphasis on delegation and decentralisation) and teacher training. The following is a list of major aims of the Ministry of Education

(i) to increase the number of children at the pre-primary stage

(ii) to provide more places at the primary stage so as to achieve 100% enrolment and to allow more children to attend for a full day

(iii) to reduce the school drop-out rate, particularly high in rural areas

(iv) to move towards compulsory schooling up to the age of 15 (either 7 years primary plus 3 secondary or 4 years primary, 4 intermediate and 2 secondary); a survey revealed that 90% of teachers are in favour of this

(v) to introduce more technical-vocational courses at tertiary level

(vi) to introduce transitional links between secondary schools and universities and reduce the emphasis on the academic, encyclopaedic *bachillerato* course

(vii) to eradicate illiteracy, particularly among adults; (only 0.4% of the population are attending primary courses for adults

(viii) to provide more opportunities for adults to follow courses at university and lower level, particularly those people who missed the opportunity when they were younger

(ix) to develop the use of TV and radio in education especially in *educación permanente*.

The priorities of government since 1978 have been:

(i) to reform secondary education so that it is more related to economic conditions and caters for a higher percentage of the age group

(ii) to increase the connection between secondary education and the world of work. Links are being established between secondary schools and industrial enterprises through "Dual Schools". Many technical options are funded at secondary level

(iii) to involve other national institutions in the finance and provision of education - including banks, the police, Air Force, trade unions and non-educational government ministries. Institutions run by these other agencies are called "Associated Schools".

PYRAMID OF ENROLMENTS - ARGENTINA
1978 (Primary) and 1978 (Secondary)

Age in Years

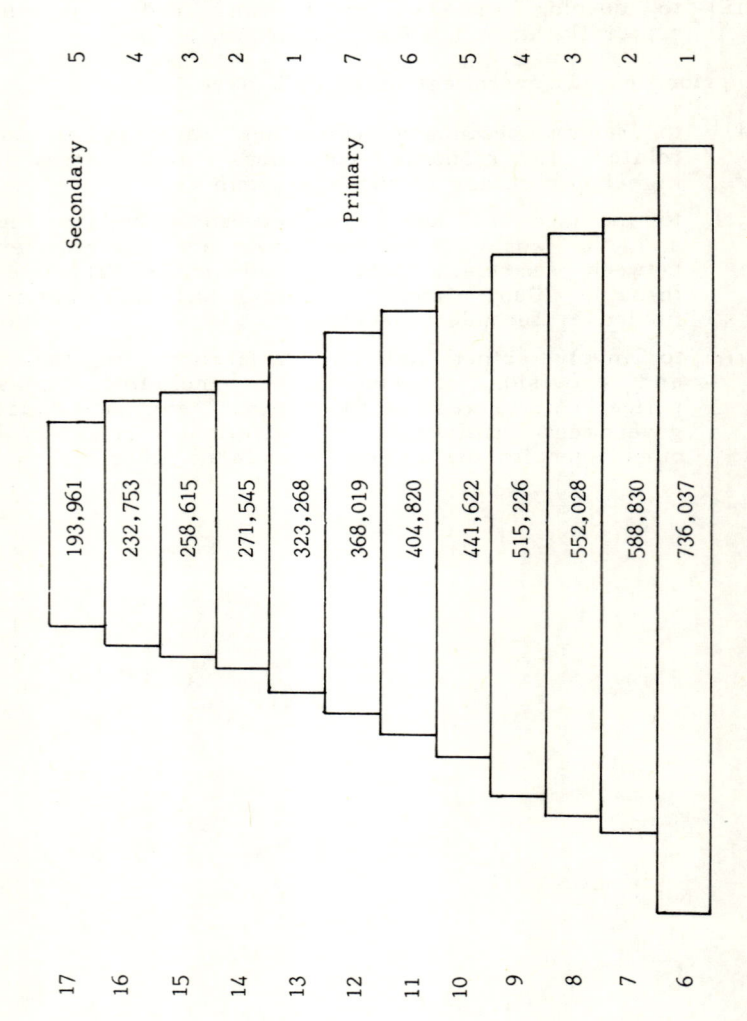

Age	Level	Grade	Enrolment
17	Secondary	5	193,961
16	Secondary	4	232,753
15	Secondary	3	258,615
14	Secondary	2	271,545
13	Secondary	1	323,268
12	Primary	7	368,019
11	Primary	6	404,820
10	Primary	5	441,622
9	Primary	4	515,226
8	Primary	3	552,028
7	Primary	2	588,830
6	Primary	1	736,037

Enrolment in Thousands

ARGENTINA BASIC STATISTICS

Population

1960	1970	1980
20,850,000	23,750,000	27,863,000

Enrolment Ratios

Primary = proportion of the age group 6-12 in primary schools
Secondary = proportion of the age group 13-17 in secondary schools
Higher = proportion of the age group 20-24 in higher education

Year	Primary	Secondary	Higher
1970	106	45	14.2
1978	110	56	21.9

Schools, Teachers and Pupils 1970 and 1977

	Schools	Teachers	Pupils
Pre-primary			
1970	3,808	11,639	223,251
1977	6,435	22,060	430,916
Primary			
1970	19,847	175,929	3,385,790
1977	20,590	199,384	3,680,185
Secondary			
1970	–	134,264	976,979
1977	–	173,041*	1,293,073*

* 1978

Pupil:Teacher Ratio Primary Schools

1970 19:1   **1977** 18:1

Higher Education Students by Field of Study 1978

	Students	% female
Education and Teacher Training	71,094	89
Humanities	29,284	77
Fine and Applied Arts	5,503	73
Law	55,761	48
Social and Behavioural Sciences	7,643	77
Commerce and Business	75,727	33
Natural Science	17,272	61
Medicine and Related Studies	81,652	57
Engineering	65,483	11
Architecture	32,259	43
Agriculture	27,885	26
Other	8,162	70

Expenditure on Education

Year	% of Total Government spending on education	% of GNP on education
1971	16.0%	3.3%
1978	10.9%	2.7%

Government current expenditure by level of education

Year	Primary	Secondary	Higher	Other
1970	29.0	30.3	21.0	16.2
1978	40.1	25.6	22.7	9.7

Basic Social and Economic Data

GNP per capita 1979 – US$2,230

Average annual growth of GNP per capita 1960–79 – 2.4%

Life expectancy 1979 – 70

Proportion of the labour force employed in:

Agriculture
1960	20%
1979	13%

Industry
1960	36%
1979	28%

Services
1960	44%
1979	59%

Brazil

CONTENTS

1 Geography	604
2 Population	604
3 Society and Culture	606
4 History and Politics	607
5 The Economy	608
6 The Education System	609
7 Educational Administration	614
8 Educational Finance	616
9 Development and Planning of the Education System	617

Brazil is a country as big as a continent. That is, its area is about the same as that of Europe including the European part of the Soviet Union. The population − estimated as over 120 million people − resides mainly along the Atlantic coast, where the major cities are concentrated with the obvious, famous and deliberate exception of Brasilia itself. Within this general pattern, the regional differences in Brazil are noteworthy. the most populous and prosperous States are Rio Grande do Sul, Sao Paulo, Rio de Janeiro and Minas Gerais. In contrast, the arid north east is seen by Brazilians as a region which is suffering severe problems of development, though it was once the most prosperous part of Brazil as the centre of the world's sugar industry. Many of the regions of Brazil have moved through this pattern of prosperity (e.g. the north with rubber, the south east and south with coffee), as the Brazilian economy has reacted to international demand for its raw materials − wood in the sixteenth century, sugar in the sixteenth and seventeenth centuries, gold and precious gems in the seventeenth century and coffee and rubber from the eighteenth century onwards. Thus until the 1930s the Brazilian economy was based on rural, primary production. From the 1930s onwards the economy has been under the stress of industrialisation coupled with rapid urbanisation. Most recently and especially in the decade 1964-1974, the Brazilian GNP grew at a rate approaching

10%, with relatively modest inflation (20%). After 1974 growth rates fell to about 5% and annual inflation was, on official figures, over 70% in 1979.

To adapt the education system to these demographic and economic pressures has proved difficult. Historically the influences of both European ideas and those of the Church have been strong. From the early 1930s, public debates about education were increasingly affected by the idea that education should be free, compulsory and provided by the State, an idea which took constitutional definition briefly in 1934. The resurgence of these principles in Brazil of the early 1950s was also linked with debates about centralisation and decentralisation of control of the system; the rights of the family to choose education for its children; and questions of the balance between the public and private proviison of education. The major reform of post-war Brazilian education was the Basic Law of 1961 which clarified the principles and structure of the national system. Further redefinitions were offered in 1968 (for higher education) and in 1971 (for primary and secondary education).

Despite the energy of the Brazilians in addressing their problems, the contemporary difficulties are considerable. Rural education, regional inequalities, illiteracy and high drop-out rates in the first level of the education system post one set of inter-linked issues. The demand for education and the remarkable expansion of higher education have produced stresses within the system, including at point of entry, the *vestibuler* , and have compounded the quality gap between private and public education - and emphasised also the gap between those groups which can afford to purchase education, and those which cannot. The supply of well qualified staff for higher education has attracted a great deal of energy (and money). Reorienting the schooling system towards work has been difficult - the long humanist tradition is proving difficult to break. Policies meant to introduce an element of 'professionalisation' - preparation for work - into the education of all have run into difficulties of implementation.

Just how far the Brazilians will get - and how quickly - in solving their educational problems is unclear. What is clearer is that they are producing excellent indigenous critical literature, and it seems possible that the solutions they will generate in the next few decades are increasingly likely to be indigenous also and based on a keen understanding of both Brazilian difficulties and the limitations of advice from abroad.

BRAZIL
VENEZUELA
GUYANA
SURINAME
FRENCH GUIANA
COLOMBIA
ATLANTIC OCEAN
Belem
Manoas
R. Amazon
Fortaleza
Recife
PERU
BOLIVIA
Brazilia
Belo Horizonte
PARAGUAY
Sao Paulo
Rio de Janeiro
SOUTH ATLANTIC OCEAN
ARGENTINA
Porto Alegre
URAGUAY
Rivers
Land over 1000 ft 308 m
International boundary
miles
0 200 400 600 800
0 200 600 800
kilometres

1 GEOGRAPHY

Topography

Brazil is the fifth largest country in the world, occupying half the land mass of outh merica and covering a surface area of 3¼ million square miles. It has abundant natural resources both mineral and agricultural yet it remains the 'land of tomorrow' since its riches lie scattered over an empty and still largely untouched interior. In recent years, successive governments have attempted to direct the attention of their countrymen to the wealth which lies in the interior of the country.

Climate

Although 90% of Brazil lies within the torrid zone, the climate is not exclusively tropical. Altitude, mountains, low river valleys and the sea all combine to provide a variety of climatic types which range from the heat and humidity of the Amazon rain forests to the parched scrub of the north eastern backlands and the cool rolling grasslands of Rio Grane do Sul. In view of these differences it is hardly surprising that the various regions of Brazil have developed distinct characteristics.

Communications

Lack of communications has always been a major obstacle to the development and unification of the country. Until recent times coastal sea routes and inland waterways were the only means of linking it scattered provinces. Now an extensive system of air transport fans deep into the interior and the development of Brasilia has stimulated a dramatic programme of road construction linking the capital with every corner of the country. Already Brazilians have accomplished miracles of highway engineering but problems of communications remain on a truly continental scale.

2 POPULATION

For 300 years Brazil was settled and populated by Portuguese, Negroes and Indians interbreeding in different proportions in different parts of the north and east, and each contributing and adapting their customs, foods, music and religions to the blandishments of the tropical environment. In the twentieth century they were joined by settlers from Southern and Eastern Europe and Japan who settled in the south to found small farms and supply much of the manpower for Brazil's early industrialisation. Brazil takes pride in the absence of overt racialism and in the mixed racial origins of its people. The 1950 census showed that 62% were considered 'white' (a very elastic classification since anyone attaining high status is classified as such despite actual physical appearance), 11% 'black' and 27% 'brown' but there were marked regional differences - the majority of 'whites' being in the south, the majority of 'blacks' in the east, etc.

The rate of population growth in Brazil is one of the highest in the world. Increasing steadily by 3% per annum the population passed the 120 million mark in 1980 and is expected to top 200 million by the end of the century. Brazilians view these figures complacently, confident that their untapped resources and empty interior will be able to support many times this number. Nevertheless, an expansion of this magnitude imposes considerable strain. It means, on the one hand, that health and education facilities must double in 30 years if even the present level is to be maintained; while, on the other, the non-productive proportion of the community is steadily rising. At present some 29.1% of the population is below the age of 15.

Population density in Brazil was in 1980 14.08 to the square kilometre, but statistics of this kind mean little. Settlement was originally concentrated on the coast and urbanisation and industrialisation in this century have reinforced this pattern. Today three quarters of all Brazilians live within a few hundred miles of the sea: the states from Rio de Janeiro southwards, for example, contain two thirds of the population while covering only 18% of the surface area, while the great inland zones of the Amazon basin cover 50% of the country but contain only 7% of the people. The Brazilian love for the coast makes it difficult to tempt them inland, and the south still acts as an irresistible magnet to the poor and, more significantly, the qualified.

The phenomenal growth of towns which is so typical of Lation American development has occurred in Brazil on an appropriately gigantic scale. In 1920, one quarter of Brazilians were town dwellers and totalled 7 million; by 1970 the proportion had increased to one half, but the number had gone up to 50 million. São Paulo with 8.5 million is now four times the size of Paris; Rio is larger than any American city except New York and Chicago; and the provincial capitals of Belem, Recife, Fortaleza, Belo Horizonte, Porto Alegre and Salvador are all topping the million mark.

But urban growth brings its problems. The cities stand as white concrete symbols of Brazil's spectacular expansion and self-confidence, but their outskirts are littered with shanty towns of poverty stricken migrants they cannot assimilate, their education, health and welfare services are being swamped by insatiable demand, and their public utilities are overstretched and liable to frequent breakdown. But in spite of these problems, urban and industrial growth have brought to a minority a life style similar to that of any other advanced country.

3 SOCIETY AND CULTURE

Regional differences, inequalities in development and a variety of human and geographical factors make the country a land of contrasts; but Brazil is undoubtedly one nation and beneath the diversity lies the unity of a people tied by the same culture, language, religion, institutions and ambitions. The basis of what is regarded as 'Brazilian culture' lies in the fusion of Portuguese, Negro and Indian influences. But their impact was not uniform: the trunk of 'Brazilial culture' was clearly European on to which the Negro and Indian elements were grafted. These strongly affect the national personality and way of life, but the laws, social structure, and institutions are plainly Iberian in form and origin. Industrial development, urban growth and immigration have modified many of the Latin traditions - the nuclear family is replacing the great family networks; women are less cloistered and employment is more common; and in São Paulo technical schooling is beginning to find social favour. On the other hand many traditional attitudes are still discernible - family loyalties provide security in an unstable world to the detriment of community consciousness; white collar employment retains its tremendous prestige; personal relationships and obligations are still paramount at all levels; and the humanistic tradition in education retains its hold.

The structure of Brazilian society at the end of the last century was a simple one. Rooted in a social and economic structure based on plantation agriculture there were, in Gilberto Freyre's classic phrase, only two classes, the 'masters' (the landowning families who dominated Brazilian life) and the 'slaves' (the illiterate and semi-nomadic share-croppers, cowboys and cane-cutters who lived in poverty and dependence). Urbanisation and industrial development revolutionised this simple pattern, and the main social feature of the twentieth century was the rapid emergence of a large middle class of bureaucrats and managers. But Brazilian development was marked by unique features which had their effect on education. Industry was capital intensive and caused little occupational change; similarly, the bulk of the new middle classes were employed in non-industrial sectors in the bureaucracy or in commerce; and because tariff protection made wages and profits high no challenge to traditional attitudes emerged from either workers or industrialists - who were in fact landowners diversifying their investments. As a result, the demand for technical schooling was considerably muted, and although the middle classes pressed vigorously for an expansion of secondary education, there was no demand for any change in its traditional orientation.

Religious Background

Ninety per cent of Brazilians are Catholics and the Church has always been a major force for national unity. Although influential, it has never been powerful as an institution and consequently has never stimulated anti-clericalism. The Church was legally separated from the State in 1890, and since that time it has become progressively more involved with social matters and with the welfare of the people as a whole. It has founded newspapers, trade unions, lay organisations for workers and youth, and has been active in education - in 1962, for example, a quarter of all university students were enrolled in Catholic institutions. Although the Church has its conservative wing, a notable feature of recent years has been the involvement of radical clergy and laymen in the social problems of the 'other Brazil' and their participation in literacy campaigns and community development projects which at times have verged on the edge of social protest.

4 HISTORY AND POLITICS

The 1967 Constitution defines Brazil as a Federal Republic of 23 States, 3 Territories and a Federal District (Brasilia). The central government consists of an executive headed by the President; a bicameral legislature chosen on a state basis by an electorate restricted to the literate; and a judiciary. This pattern is paralleled in the States and, at the lowest level of administration, the municipio. Many of the powers of the various entities are legally defined but there is a grey no-man's land of ambiguity and overlap.

The government machine in Brazil has traditionally been slow, buge and cumbrous with little hierarchy or coordination. Posts in the lower ranks are commonly regarded as occupational insurance and low salaries and part time working (a common feature among the professional classes) encourages neither job identification nor zeal. The bureaucratic jungle is so dense that the Brazilian character has developed traits aimed specifically at 'working' or evading the system. 'Jeito' (that is, the knack) is a much sought-after skill. In the past dynamic ministers have managed to galvanise their departments by sheer force of personality, but the general level of performance has been weak. The tradition of tying senior posts to the life of one administration also causes problems in that too frequently officials have been more interested in short-term projects aimed at publicity rather than less spectacular long term planning.

Brazil has had six constitutions and has experienced almost every form of government devised by man being successively a colony, an Empire (1822-1890) and oligarchic Republic, a Dictatorship (under Vargas until 1945), a Democratic Republic, a Parliamentary Democracy (1962-3) and a Military dictatorship. But in spite of this, there is little resemblance to the political turbulence popularly associated with Latin America: in Brazil there is a tradition of stability and non-violent change of government which reflects both the adaptability and the easy going tolerance of its people. Indeed, it could be said that in the past Brazilians were too tolerant and lacked the necessary ruthlessness to overcome their problems. Historically the focus of political and social power lay with the local landowners; politics at the centre were based on compromise and parties were founded not on specific policies but on loose alliances of family and regional interests. Consensus politics was the keynote of the system, and when in the early 1960s the left wing President Goulart attempted to introduce drastic reforms the result was economic and political chaos followed by military revolution of 1964. Since then Brazilian politics have undergone a profound change. The new government was dissatisfied with the uncontrolled fluctuations which had marked Brazil's fortunes and was convinced that the path to national progress lay in stability, planning and the application of technology and American style capitalism. In practice the result has been an enhancement in the power of the federal executive and a restriction of political expression; but the government's policies have produced unprecedented growth and its development plans have proved to be the most ambitious in the nation's history aimed at raising Brazil to the level of a 'developed' country by the year 2000. After 400 years of frustration and unfulfilled potential things have begun to happen in Brazil and the national mood is now largely one of buoyant self-confidence.

5 THE ECONOMY

Brazil's recent 'economic miracle' has been phenomenal (if unequal in its effects) by any standards. Originating in the 1930s in a policy of import substitution; expanding when the war removed European industrial competitors while increasing the price of Brazilian raw materials; and finally stimulated by the thrusting capitalistic policies of the military government which took over in the early 1960s – Brazilian industry is booming. The growth rate in 1972 was the highest in the world – over 11% – and the economy is said to be well into the 'take off' stage. Even in the world depression following the 1973 oil crisis, growth has not dropped below 3%. Foreign trade continues to increase and diversify making Brazil less vulnerable to fluctuations in commodity prices. In 1960, 90% of Brazil's exports were agricultural products (half being coffee); in 1972 this figure had fallen to 60% while exports of manufactured goods had risen to 27%.

Yet side by side with this prosperity lies the other Brazil – the neglected interior where poverty is measured in terms of malnutrition and illiteracy rather than in figures of per capita income. In the past it was thought that the wealth of the industrial sector would somehow percolate through to the rural areas: but this hope was disappointed. Now the government has declared that the 1975-79 Second National Development Plan will concentrate on the population as a whole and on developing traditionally neglected areas such as the north east (ironically, in colonial times, the most wealthy). But still the country can be seen as two regions – the south, modern, industrial and progressive, and the north, traditional, agricultural and backward. Since regional differences seem closely to reflect the rate of urbanisation, the gap is more properly describably as an urban-rural one.

6 THE EDUCATION SYSTEM
Objectives

For centuries Brazil was dominated culturally by Europe. Initially, it was the Jesuits who introduced education, and in the nineteenth century when Brazil sought a model for its cultural institutions it was to Europe, and particularly to France, that it looked. Thus the basic ingredient in Brazilian educational thought was the European tradition. It was essentially an elitist and humanistic tradition designed to cultivate the mind and provide an avenue to the 'noble' professions: secondary and higher education in Brazil were above all the mark of a gentleman. It was anti-technical and concerned with intellectual theorising rather than empirical investigation. It was reflected in concepts of 'authority' as to the purity of subject matter and as a result the system was rigidly centralised until 1961. It also manifested itself in encyclopaedic curricula, and emphasis on standards and in examinations designed to sift out the intellectually unworthy. Primary schools (being concerned with the 'instruction' and not the 'education' of the lower classes) were not included in this rationale, but they too reflected its style and attitudes.

In defining the objectives of education, governments expanded on this narrow educational view. Legislation variously defines them in terms of health, culture, nationalism, social integration and individual development - but in Latin fashion those were 'ideal' values unrelated to what was actually happening in the schools. But in the post-war years a new note was introduced. The transformations in Brazilian society had already produced an insatiable demand for education and to this was added a recognition that universal schooling was both a human right and a point of national pride. 'Democratisation' - that is the rapid expansion of facilities and a liberalising of the curriculum - became a national priority. In 1961 in the hope of introducing flexibility and relevance to local needs, the system was administratively decentralised. Some successes were achieved but the concepts underlying education were untouched and the measure had little effect on the working of the schools. The revolution of 1964 introduced an extra dimension. Planning and manpower needs became important; central control was reasserted and education became regarded as an investment which was expected to produce scientific research, technical skills and the developmental outlook which national progress required. And when the response seemed tardy, substantial reforms were introduced into the whole system.

Social status and level of education in Brazil are closely connected and a natural consequence of the rapid social mobility which has affected the country in recent years has been an accelerating educational demand. This has, however, expressed itself almost solely in quantitative terms and has reinforced rather than challenged the traditional features of the system. Thus, the time-honoured humanistic disciplines and academic institutions retain their hold and popularity in spite of the development-orientated policies of the government. There are signs of a change in favour of practical and technical studies, but attitudes of parents, students and traditional (i.e. non-scientific) educators are still far from at one with the aims of the authorities: the government hopes, however, that the atmosphere of development and technology which inspires the country at present will eventually produce a change in these attitudes.

Planning

The Basic Law of 1961 gave responsibility for educational planning to the respective State and Federal Councils of Education. It was, however, planning of a very limited nature, concerned with the allocation of funds and the establishment of generally accepted targets rather than with a detailed assessment of problems, resources and realities. Indeed, it was generally considered that the size of Brazil and the principle of decentralisation made real planning impossible. The revolution of 1964 changed this view: planning was to provide the blueprint for economic development and all fecets of national life (including education) were to play their parts. In 1967, the Ministry of Planning announced its ten-year development plan. The educational goals were general but clear: there was a need for greater efficiency, improved output, curricula more relevant for social change and economic progress, and the production of skills for the economy. Successive administrations most recently in the Second National Development Plan (1975-79) have reaffirmed these principles although words have sometimes failed to be translated into deeds, and specifically into the financial and human resources necessary for the successful implementation of the overall plans.

Administration

Administratively, education in Brazil has been decentralised since 1961. There are at present two levels of control:

(i) the States control primary and secondary education (whether the schools are run by private, municipal or State concerns) and discharge their responsibilities through two bodies, the State Councils of Education, controlling standards, examinations, primary curricula, optional/secondary subjects, expenditure and all other details of policy; and the State Secretariats of Education, providing administration and inspection

(ii) the Federal authorities have responsibility for higher education and for aiding financially and professionally other levels. These functions are performed by the Federal Council of Education (of 24 professional educators holding office for 6 years) with the Ministry of Education and Culture providing executive services.

By 1961, MEC had developed into a huge and complex bureaucracy with a stultifying influence over all aspects of the system, however minor. The Law removed many of its powers, but since its structure remained unchanged, MEC itself was left in considerable disarray. The policies of centralisation followed by governments after 1964, however, had their effect and in 1970 the Ministry was decisively reformed with the declared aim of achieving greater simplicity, greater efficiency, and greater coordination with other 'developmental' departments. The administrative responsibilities of the tates were untouched, but MEC's authority over planning, coordination and policy making were reaffirmed and sharpened.

The Basic Law of 1961 defined the structure of education. This framework remained in legal force for almost ten years and although some of its details have since been legally modified (notably by the 1968 law on higher education, and the 1971 reform of primary and secondary education) basically it still reflects the actual organisation of the system and the background against which present reforms must be viewed.

Pre-Primary Education

Pre-primary education is voluntary. Nursery schools may be established privately or through self-help. In 1978 944,583 pupils were taught in pre-primary education institutions.

Primary Education (1° grau)

Since 1971, eight years' education has been compulsory.

The language of instruction must be Portuguese. Curricula are decided by the states on the basis of criteria set by the Federal Council of Education.

Large businesses must provide schooling for employees' children or pay an educational levy.

Schools are open for $8\frac{1}{2}$ months per annum. The long vacation is in December-February and there is a break in July. Schools work a five-day week though Saturday working is common. The majority of schools work a 'shift system whereby the same facilities are used by two or even three 'shift' groups.

In 1978 21,473,100 children enrolled in primary schools; 87.5% of the schools are run by public authorities (federal, state and municipal) and 12.5% by private entities (though in prosperous urban areas this proportion may rise to over 20%).

Secondary Education (2° grau)

Secondary education is of three to four years' duration and not compulsory.

Curricula are decided by the states, etc., on the basis of criteria set by the Federal Council of Education. A basic core is common to all schools; following the 1971 Reform (Law 5692) it has become compulsory to include 'professionalisation' courses, though only a small minority of schools have yet done this.

There is no formal entry examination from 1° grau.

In 1978, 2,519,122 pupils were enrolled in 2° grau schools of which 46% were in private schools and 54% in public institutions.

First and second level education aim at the integral development of children and adolescents and their training/preparation for work.

Preparation for initiation to work, as an element of the integral training of the pupil, is compulsory in both first and second level education.

Initiation to work at the second level education may take the form of vocational training.

Vocational Training

Vocational training is also provided in the following ways:

(i) under the auspices of SENAI and SENAC – highly successful schemes run jointly by employers and government under the auspices of the Ministries of Industry and Commerce and Labour which offer apprenticeships and short term training for young employees in a nationwide network of special schools. The numbers enrolled have risen steadily from 40,000 in 1949

(ii) under emergency government training schemes launched in time of special need. Between 1964 and 1966, 72,000 workers were trained in this way

(iii) under an informal system of on-the-job training.

Teachers

Elementary teachers are trained in second level education. In 1972, of 765,000 1° grau teachers 69% had been trained. There are also emergency training programmes.

Secondary teachers are trained at university level in either the old amorphous faculties of philosophy or the new faculties of Education. In 1973, 67% of 2° grau teachers received some form of professional training.

Recent educational expansion has naturally affected the size of the teaching force which has risen from 100,000 in 1940 to 1,043,000 in 1975 (1° and 2° grau schools). It is now the largest professional group with 2.5% of the total work force.

Approximately 90% of primary and 45% of secondary teachers are women.

Higher Education

Higher education is a federal responsibility, though institutions are run by federal, state, religious and private entities. There are also large numbers of independent faculties offering specialised courses of undertaking research – often of the most advanced type. In 1980 there were 65 universities and 822 independent faculties enrolling a total of 1,311,799 students, 53% of whom were studying in private institutions.

University entrance is gained by an examination known as the *vestibular*. Recent moves to substitute a general examination have had little success.

Brazilian higher education has been undergoing continuous reform since 1961 and was the subject of radical reforms in 1968. The intention of this reform was to improve the quality and efficiency of the first degree course, particularly by reducing the independence and powers of individual faculties.

A significant recent innovation has been the establishment of a national plan for the development of post-graduate education, involving large scale expansion and improvement of courses and heavy investment in training, both in Brazil and overseas.

Non-Formal Education/Literacy

At federal level the major project in this field is MOBRAL (the Brazilian Literacy Movement). With the municipio as its basic unit and with the active cooperation of other entities from the army to the boy scouts, MOBRAL represents a coordinated attack by the government on the problem of illiteracy. The movement is financially well-endowed and has already inspired considerable enthusiasm among learners and teachers, most of the latter being amateurs. Its target to make 6 million people literate by 1974 at an annual rate of 1.5 million is said to have been achieved – but the Movement has been widely criticised for the methods it has used to reach this and has recently been the subject of a Senate investigation.

The Ministry of Education's Department of Supletivo (Compensatory) Education is responsible for organising a wide variety of courses mainly in general education, for the 15+ age group.

There are in addition numerous small schemes offering tuition through the post, radio or television for educational examinations and vocational courses. Catholic organisations (particularly the *Movimento de Educação de Base* or MEB) and dioceses also run a variety of literacy and community development projects in the interior often based on networks of radio schools.

7 EDUCATIONAL ADMINISTRATION

To a very real extent Brazil reflects an educational dichotomy. At one level it resembles any European country slowly adapting the practices of an elitist and humanistic past to the needs of a modern industrial present: while at another it is confronted with problems of illiteracy and rural poverty as acute as anywhere else in the Third World.

The rate at which the educational system has expanded in Brazil in recent years has been phenomenal. Between 1950 and 1974 places in primary schools increased from 6 million to 21.6 million; in secondary schools from 200,000 to 1.6 million; and in universities from 45,000 to 888,000. This naturally imposed a tremendous strain on the finances and fabric of the system and quality inevitably fell as resources were spread more thinly, shift systems were introduced and classes above the minimum cut back. But even so, with demand continuing to soar, the proportions enrolled only went up by a few percent while the actual numbers outside the system continued to increase. Similarly, the literacy rate rose encouragingly in the 30 years after 1940 from 44% to 67%, but the numbers of illiterates rose from 23 million to 33 million. In the Brazilian context too, there are problems in addition to those of cost and resources. In the rural areas, scattered population, wild terrain and population movements all conspire to keep enrolments down, while in the cities constant rural migration keeps demand perpetually ahead of supply. And everywhere, for a substantial part of the population, school no-attendance and drop-outs form part of a vicious circle of poverty and ignorance. Figures for the most recent 1° grau enrolments show that this state of affairs is continuing - 25-30% of pupils enrolling in the first year fail to enrol in the following year. In 1963, 70% of the age group enrolled in the first year of primary school, but only 17% completed the fourth year and only 7% the eighth year. The problem is therefore not restricted to a shortage of facilities but has wide economic and social ramifications.

In a country as diverse as Brazil such figures, serious though they are, tell only half the story. In education, as with everything else, there is a discrepancy between the amenities and prosperity of the towns and the impoverishment of the countryside. As the figures in the tables at the end of this chapter illustrate, the number of school places, the deployment of trained staff and the standard of equipment all reflect this basic fact. In the cities the commonest type of primary institution is the *grupo escolar* - attractively designed and picturesquely roofed in red tiles with fully trained staff and healthy pupils in blue and white uniforms with bulging satchels. At the other extreme are the crudely constructed and poorly equipped one-classroom schools of the interior with their ragged, under-nourished children and their solitary and generally untrained teacher. Secondary standards are naturally more

THE EDUCATIONAL SYSTEM OF BRAZIL 1978

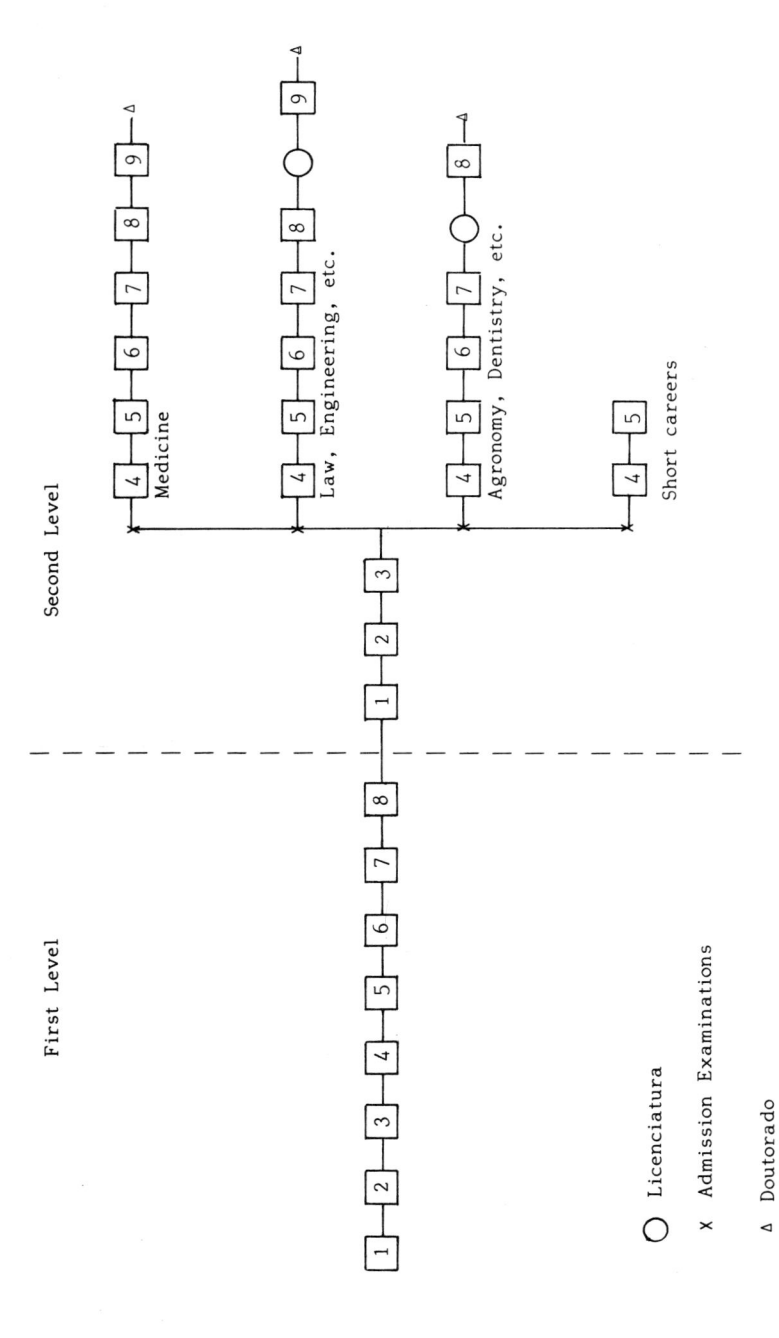

First Level | Second Level

Medicine
Law, Engineering, etc.
Agronomy, Dentistry, etc.
Short careers

○ Licenciatura
× Admission Examinations
△ Doutorado

uniform, but schools at this level are almost exclusively an urban phenomena.

Brazilian educationalists are aware of these shortages and inequalities; and they are also alive to the wastefulness of the system as measured in terms of drop-outs and repeaters. The rate of attrition in Brazilian education is among the highest in Latin America as shown by the figures given above. It is not difficult to find physical reasons for this in terms of untrained teachers, inadequate facilities, part time working, poor methodology and the shift system, but Brazilian planners argue that an additional reason lies in the concepts underlying the system. In spite of the legislative stress on socialisation and individual development they accuse educationalists of imposing excessive examination demands and unrealistic promotion criteria, and of following rigid and encyclopaedic curricula which encourage rote learning. In reality the harshness of the classroom picture created by these criticisms is considerably mollified by traditional Brazilian indulgence towards children, and in defence of the system it should be pointed out that these features were (and in some cases still are) typical of countries inheriting the European educational heritage – indeed in Brazil, as elsewhere, schools run on this basis by convinced and dedicated teachers can be highly effective in performing their allotted tasks. Local criticisms are therefore not just based on the style of the schools but on fundamental doubts as to whether their objectives, subject matter and methodology are in line with the needs of the modern world. The Reform of 1971 set out among other things to tackle this basic problem but there is as yet little sign that it has produced anything beyond superficial structural changes.

A structural problem which perplexed Brazilian educationalists throughout the 1960s was that of the poor 'articulation' between the levels of the system. Rocketing demand forced each to erect examination barriers and since these were based on the requirements of the new courses rather than what has been taught at the lower level, severe dislocations resulted. The worst of these was at university level where pressure was so great that the *vestibular* became a terrifying ordeal often held in huge sports stadia as the only premises large enough to hold the masses of candidates. The average success rate remained at around 40% but the number of *excedentes* (the surplus of candidates over places) has continued to climb to explosive proportions. Linked with the selectivity of the system was a second discussion point of the 1960s – 'democratisation'. In a situation where private education yields the best in examination results, and where private 'cramming' is a necessary ingredient to success at university entrance, it is hardly surprising that the upper and middle classes of society numerically dominate at both levels.

At a more qualitative level, Brazilian planners have been highly critical of the lack of 'relevance' of the products of the education system to their estimate of the needs of society. They point to the rote learning and verbal emphasis; the academic bias in secondary education; the dominance of the humanities in the universities; and the fact that rural education is widely regarded as an escape route to an urban office rather than as a preparation for work on the land. At first sight there seems good grounds for these complaints, but a broader view suggests that at school level they are exaggerated. There are certainly shortages at technician and technologist level but otherwise the education system seems to have served Brazil well: there is less 'qualified' unemployment than in most other developing countries to indicate that the wrong people are being produced and the economy has been able to absorb and use all comers.

At the university and sub-university levels, however, there are grounds for concern. While 61.2% of higher education students are studying humanities, letters and arts, only 38.8% are studying technological and agrarian sciences and health professions. Even those doctors and engineers who exist are seldom used to full capacity as there is a similar shortage of middle-level technical and professional support. The ratio of professional to technical is only 2:3 compared with 2:8 in most developed countries.

There are at the present time some 20 million Brazilians, mostly in the rural areas, who can neither read nor write. Successive governments have been conscious of the full implications of this statistic and more than a little embarrassed by it; economically, the link between illiteracy and under-development is appreciated; nationally, the fact that one third of the population neither benefits from nor contributes to the general prosperity is intolerable; and socially the mass of illiterates is a constant reminder of the gulf separating the 'two Brazils'. Official attempts to confront this problem in the past were spasmodic and the beneficial results they achieved were too frequently swamped by soaring demand. Unofficial attempts encountered other problems. Illiteracy and rural under-development were seen to be intimately mixed with problems of land holding and poverty and the result was that some agencies extended their activities beyond literacy into community development and sometimes further into social protest – an escalation which found no favour with the authorities. The present regime, however, is committed to education and national development and MOBRAL is regarded as the final solution to illiteracy. Its organisational framework, its work-orientated approach, its emphasis on follow-up action and the extent of government financial and political support demonstrate the soundness of some of its basic principles. On the other hand it is not tied in with any comprehensive development programme and it is unselective in its scope.

8 EDUCATIONAL FINANCE

The principles of Brazilian educational finance are simple: by law the states and municipios are obliged to spend at least 20% of their budgets on education, while the Federal

Government must reserve 12% to be allocated to the states in accordance with national plans. Figures (for 1974) give some idea of the overall proportions contributed i.e. the Federal Government provided 28%, the states 42%, private sources 23%, and the municipios 7%. No reliable figures are available to show the distribution of the total educational budget between the different stages of education. It is likely to be in the order of 45% for primary level, 25% for secondary level, 30% for tertiary level.

Given the responsibility of the states for the primary and secondary programmes, the resources of the individual states clearly determine the quality of educational provision. São Paulo for example, is able to spend almost as much on education as the rest of the country put together and is able to launch imaginative development schemes while poorer states are hardly able to cope with everyday problems.

Although education is identified as a priority area in the government's development plans, there is evidence of a lack of priority when it is considered alongside other developmentally important areas. Reliable figures are not available, but estimates presented to the senate in May 1976 suggest that the Ministry of Education's share of the national budget has fallen gradually from 9.74% in 1964 to 4.95% in 1974 and that as a percentage of GNP, expenditure on education has fallen over the past five years from 3.42% to 2.95%.

9 DEVELOPMENT AND PLANNING OF THE EDUCATION SYSTEM

In summary form, the problems which Brazilians detect in their education system can be listed as follows:

Internal Efficiency

(i) a serious shortage and unequal distribution of facilities

(ii) soaring demand outpacing supply

(iii) high drop-out, repeater and failure rates

(iv) lack of 'articulation' between levels of the system

(v) shortages of trained teachers at all levels: low salaries and part time working

(vi) encyclopaedic curricula

(vii) formalistic teaching methods

(viii) inappropriate educational aims and concepts.

External Relevance

(i) academic curricula and non-practical orientation

(ii) humanistic bias at higher levels resulting in shortages of technicians, doctors, scientists, etc. and probable over-production of lawyers and philosophers.

Trends and Possibilities

(i) the urban, progressive regions of Brazil with their European traditions and industrial bases have shown in recent years similar trends to those observable in Western Europe. The minimum length of schooling has become progressively longer. Curricula at the upper 1° grau level have become more uniform and there is a trend towards postponing specialisation until 2° grau cycle. At the upper levels there have also been clear signs of closer university involvement in developmental problems and a retreat from the 'ivory tower' image. Pressures too from the National Research Council (CNP) and MEC's department for top level training (CAPES) have also resulted in significant advances in the teaching of science and in the quantity and quality of advanced research. The foundation of the first faculties of education are also illustrative of a slight up-grading in the academic status of teacher training. At another level, a feature typical of the developing world can be detected - namely a phenomenal increase in demand and provision, matched by a fall in quality.

(ii) these underlying educational trends combined with the response of the government's technocrats and planners to the quantitative and qualitative problems of the system produced in the late 1960s a sweeping programme of reform. The extent and importance of these modifications can be appreciated by the following sumary. Some may be criticised, and some omissions may be noted, but overall the list presents an impressive catalogue of reform which in brazilian conditions only a single-minded and determined government could have achieved:

(a) *'Operation School'* launched in 1968 to mastermind the expansion of the primary system and the re-examination of curricul and criteria

(b) *The Reform Law of 1971* (Law 5692) - restructuring the school system into two levels, the *first* offering 'fundamental education' to all between the ages of 7 and 14; the *second* providing three or four years of secondary education of a type suitable for either university entrance or for the middle level manpower needs of the economy

(c) *University Reform* - following the lines of the recommendations of 1968, priority targets being:

- 'Operation Productivity, to improve administrative efficiency

- the concentration of university departments and faculties on to the same campus

(d) *Teachers* Accelerated training programmes for unqualified teachers. The establishment of university faculties of education. The encouragement of full time work (especially at university level) with improved salaries

(e) *Administration* The reform of both the structure and the 'spirit' of MEC. An expansion in educational expenditure and the creation of new sources of revenue. Expanded schemes for scholarships, etc.

(f) *Research and Development* An expansion of official educational research and dissemination facilities

(g) *Use of the Media* The Brazilian authorities, concerned that conventional educational methods cannot solve the country's problems, is anxious to give high level technology a vital role in their strategy. A number of cities now have ETV networks and a scheme is at present in operation in the north and north east of the country involving the use of an educational satellite which receives signals from the São Paula area and transmits them to 200,000 schools distributed throughout the target area. In 1975 plans were announced for extensive reorganisation and improvement of ER and ETV systems, within the new national broadcasting system (RADIOBRAS).

BRAZIL - PYRAMID OF ENROLMENTS

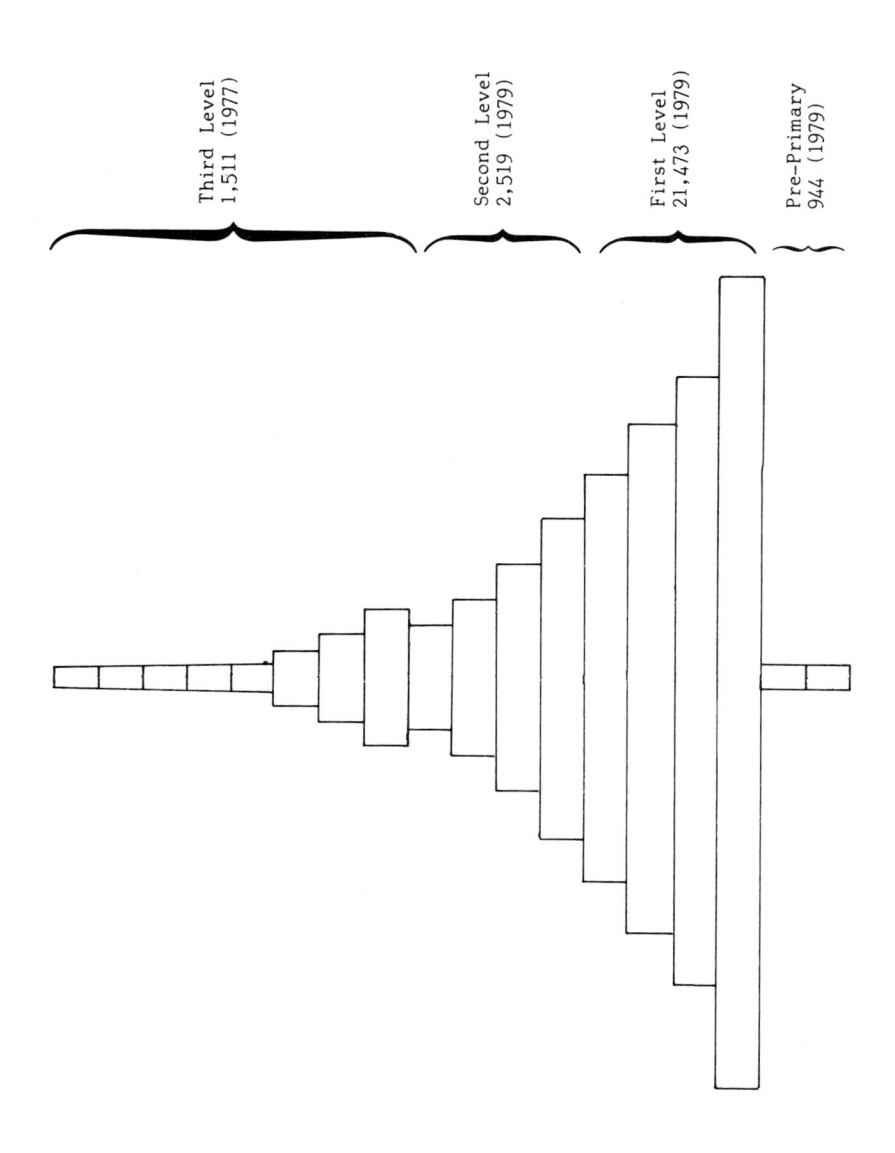

Third Level
1,511 (1977)

Second Level
2,519 (1979)

First Level
21,473 (1979)

Pre-Primary
944 (1979)

BRAZIL - ORGANIZATION OF

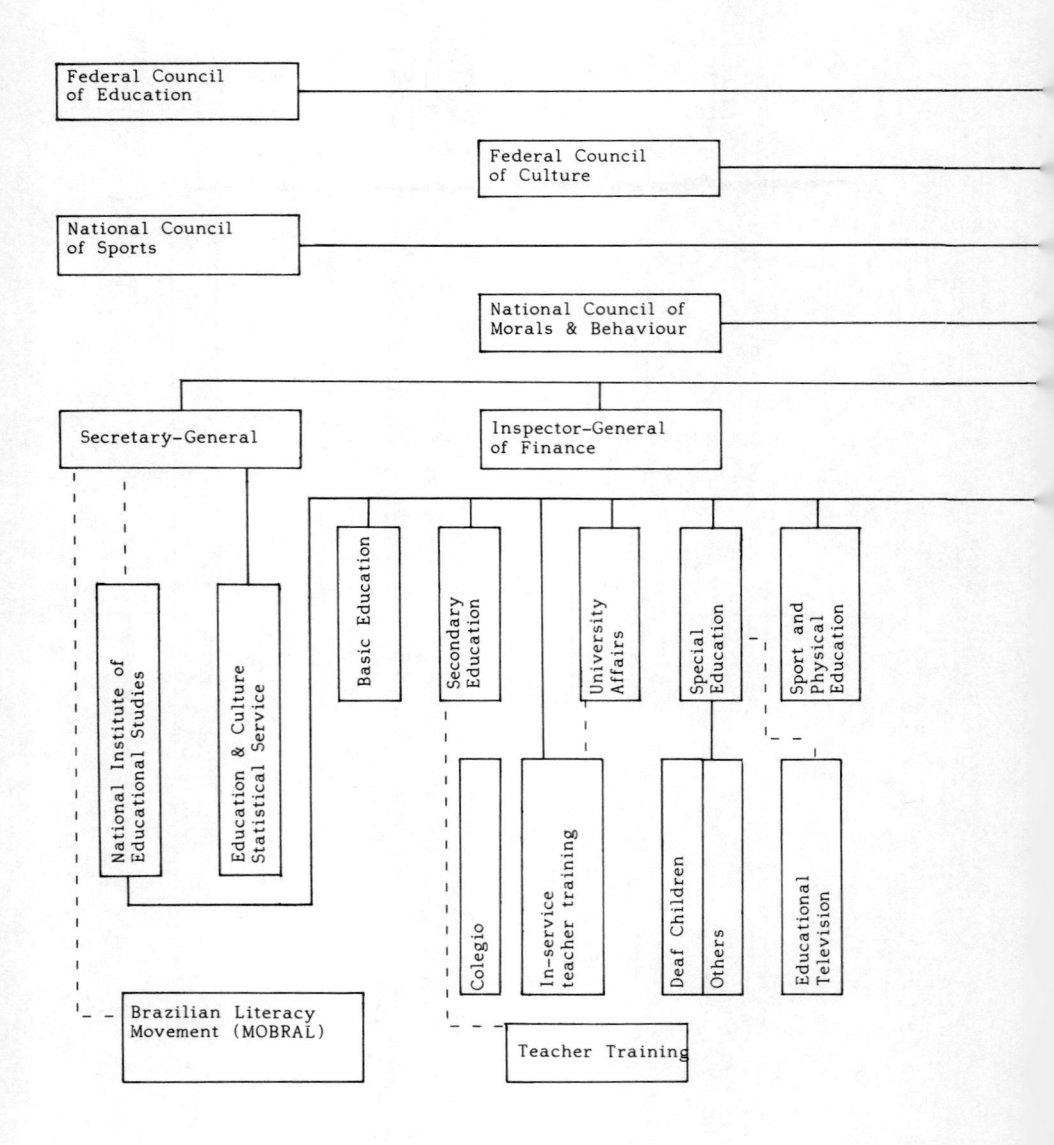

- Federal Council of Education
- Federal Council of Culture
- National Council of Sports
- National Council of Morals & Behaviour
- Secretary-General
- Inspector-General of Finance
- National Institute of Educational Studies
- Education & Culture Statistical Service
- Brazilian Literacy Movement (MOBRAL)
- Basic Education
- Secondary Education
  - Colegio
  - In-service teacher training
- University Affairs
- Special Education
  - Deaf Children
  - Others
- Sport and Physical Education
  - Educational Television
- Teacher Training

THE MINISTRY OF EDUCATION AND CULTURE

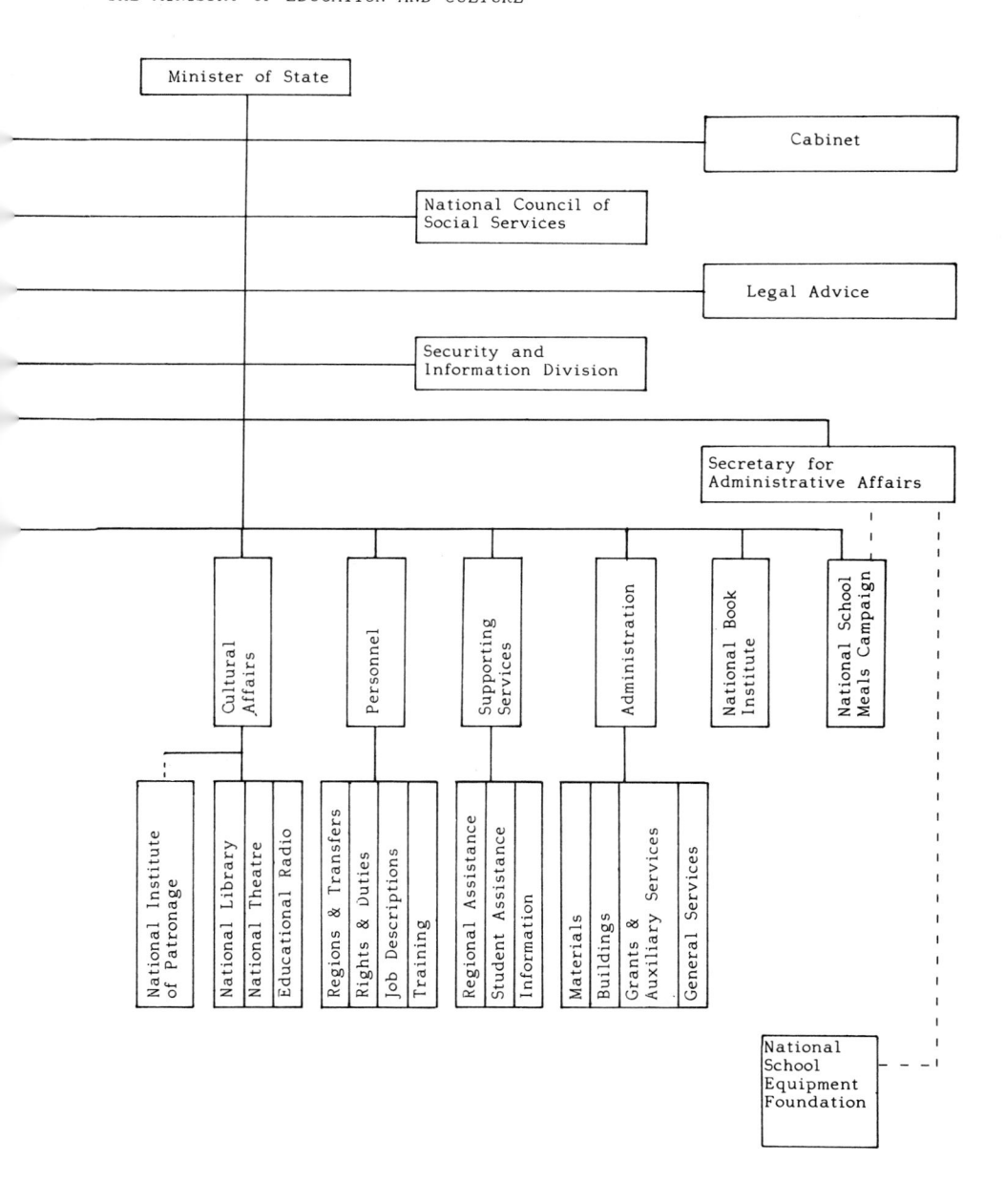

- Minister of State
  - Cabinet
  - National Council of Social Services
  - Legal Advice
  - Security and Information Division
  - Secretary for Administrative Affairs
    - Cultural Affairs
      - National Institute of Patronage
      - National Library
      - National Theatre
      - Educational Radio
    - Personnel
      - Regions & Transfers
      - Rights & Duties
      - Job Descriptions
      - Training
    - Supporting Services
      - Regional Assistance
      - Student Assistance
      - Information
    - Administration
      - Materials
      - Buildings
      - Grants & Auxiliary Services
      - General Services
    - National Book Institute
    - National School Meals Campaign
      - National School Equipment Foundation

623

BRAZIL BASIC EDUCATIONAL STATISTICS

Note: The uneven development of the country and the decentralised nature of the system make uniform statistics hard to obtain. Most of the following are drawn from the *Ministério de Educacao et Culture. Servico de Estatistica da Educacao e Cultura* and *Annuario Estatistico do Brasil 1972*.

Enrolments 1978

School Enrolments, 1978
(in thousands)

First level (Grades 1 to 8): 21,473
Second level (Grades 1 to 3): 2,519

Higher Education Enrolments, 1979

Enrolments on all courses: 1,311,799
Enrolments in universities: 613,192
Enrolments in isolated colleges: 698,607

Drop-outs, Repeaters, Wastage

The figures given for enrolments represent a static description of education and do not show the true rate of attrition in the system. This can be better appreciated by tracing the progress of the age group which began their primary schooling in 1963, i.e.

1º grau 1 1963	4,701,627
1º grau 5, 1967	777,354
2º grau 1 1971	503,132

The drop-out rate both during the year (14% Primary, 3% Secondary) and between years is high. The official rate from primary schools is as follows:

Primary 1-2	55%
Primary 1-3	68%
Primary 1-4	76%

Overall primary pass rate = 14,294,118 = 85%

Overall secondary pass rate = 1,774,160 = 92%

Repeaters – The impact of this is reflected in the number of repeaters in the various classes. Using the 1978 enrolment figures, the proportion of repeaters in first level is 19.4% and in second level, 7.2%. In 1978, 4.1 million first level pupils and 183,308 second level pupils were repeating.

The Expansion of the Education System

*Enrolments
(in thousands)*

	1964	1969	1974	1978
1° grau	11,670	15,013	19,286	21,473
2° grau	439	910	1,681	2,519
3° grau	142	348	–	1,311*

*1979

Number of Institutions

	1974	1978
1° grau	180,915	186,009
2° grau	10,885	30,631
Universities		65*
Indep. Faculties		822*

*1979

Higher Education Students 1979

Areas of Knowledge

Biological Sciences and Health professions	153,255
Technological Sciences	326,825
Agrarian Sciences	29,086
Humanities	696,070
Literature/Linguistics	81,741
Arts	24,822
TOTAL	1,311,799

Finance

% of GNP Allocated to Education

Year	1961	1963	1965	1967	1969	1971	1973
%	2.09	1.72	2,80	3.14	3.42	3.25	2.95

Sources of Funds 1974

Federal	State	Municipio	Total
22.7%	66.2%	11.1%	100.0%

Total Public Expediture on Education (000 Cruzeiros)

1965	1970	1974	1980
1,039,037	5,533,253	18,923,689	62,907,366

Federal Expenditure in Education 1978

First level	7.2%
Second level	8.7%
Higher Education	58.2%
'Supletivo' Education	4.5%
Special Education	0.4%
Physical Education	1.4%
Pupil Assistance	3.7%
Culture	2.2%
Administration	9.3%
Others	4.4%

These figures exclude state and municipal expenditure on education, as well as resources transfer from the Federal Government to the states, municipalities and federal district.

Salaries

Primary – the basic rate for a trained teacher for a 22½ hour week is 130% of the regional minimum wage (i.e. £20 per month in Rio/São Paulo)

Secondary – approximately £35 per month + £15 for a teaching diploma in addition to a degree.

Urban/Rural Distinctions

Distribution of Qualified Primary Teachers (1964 Census)

	Rural	Urban	Average
South	44%	85%	69%
North east	7%	55%	36%
Brazil	27%	72%	56%

Proportion of Age Group Enrolled in Primary School (1964 Census)

	Rural	Urban	Average
South	54%	84%	72%
North East	39%	79%	54%
Brazil	52%	82%	66%

Population Growth

1960	1965	1970	1972	1973	1980
69,730	81,010	93,390	98,854	101,700	121,113

Regional Variations

	North and Central West	North east	East	South
Per capita income – 1970 (US$)	$230	$179	$367	$552
% of national income	2%	9%	36%	50%
% of population	9%	21%	34%	37%
% of age group enrolled in primary school (1964)	72%	54%	66%	72%
% of primary teachers qualified	39%	36%	60%	69%
% of total secondary places	7%	16%	77%	
University students (% of age gorup) 1965	1.4%	1.1%	2.7%	3%
% literate	–	44%	64%	84%

Chile

CONTENTS

1 Geography 630
2 Population 632
3 Society and Culture 633
4 History and Politics 634
5 The Economy 635
6 The Education System 639
7 Educational Administration 645
8 Educational Finance 647
9 Development and Planning of
  the Education System 648

Chile's education system in structure has much in common with other Latin American countries. In terms of development since 1969 there have been stark changes, some of which have been reflected elsewhere in the sub-continent but rarely with such emphasis or abruptness. Under the Allende regime up to 1971 there were ambitious attempts to expand provision and opportunities for the poorest sections of society. Since 1971 the military government has been at the forefront of the movement to reduce the proportional importance of higher education and to make educational consumers pay for education received above the basic level.

The Chilean primary school is similar to that of other Latin American countries in curriculum and procedures by which pupils progress through the grades. It differs from many other South American countries in the all compulsory education is provided in a seven-year elementary course without a separate lower secondary stage. Secondary education is divided into the traditional academic and teacher trianing sectors together with more recent technical and vocational branches. Higher education is provided in universities which concentrate on preparation for the traditional professions.

The quantitative provision is also similar to that of other Latin American countries. Primary schooling is compulsory by law and universal elementary education is near to attainment. But the poorest groups of society both in big cities and in remote rural areas do not enjoy complete primary schooling. About half the relevant age group is in secondary schools and about 10% in universities which again is similar to the position of most other South American countries.

Chile differs from other Latin American states in the rather stringent means taken by the government since 1975 to achieve the educational objectives to which other governments also subscribe. The emphasis on efficiency at primary and secondary level has led to the charging of fees in state schools so that consumers pay for educational improvements. The devolution of control of primary schools to municipalities can be seen to be consistent with the decentralisation movement which has widespread support in Latin America but it also is a means of relieving central government of educational responsibilities. The stress on vocational education at higher levels has been accompanied by attacks on the autonomy and the resources of the traditional universities.

Chilean education between 1969 and 1971 was guided by a governmental insistence that expanded state provision should be a means of equalising opportunities at governmental expense. Since 1971 the education system has been affected by a market forces philosophy which has informed overall government policy.

1 GEOGRAPHY

Topography

The Republic of Chile is on the west side of south America, bounded by Peru at the northern tip, Bolivia to the north east, Argentina to the east and the Pacific Ocean to the west. Chile is approximately 4,200 km (2,600 miles) in length and varies between 80 and 240 km in width (50 to 150 miles); it covers an area of 742,000 sq km, about 70% of which is uninhabitable because of mountain and desert terrain.

Climate

The climate varies tremendously due to the fact that altitude ranges from sea level to 7,200 metres (24,000 feet) and that Chile extends from latitude 18°S to 56°S. There are six main climatic regions.

(i) Desert Chile in the north is one of the driest regions in the world (rain is scarcely known). This area includes the most important deposits of copper and nitrates

(ii) Mediterranean Chile in the centre is the main industrial area, based at the capital of Santiago. It has long, hot dry summers with cool winters and 38-50 cm (15-20 inches) of rain per year

(iii) Forest Chile in the south, with its timber, coal and allied industries has a climate similar to Britain's

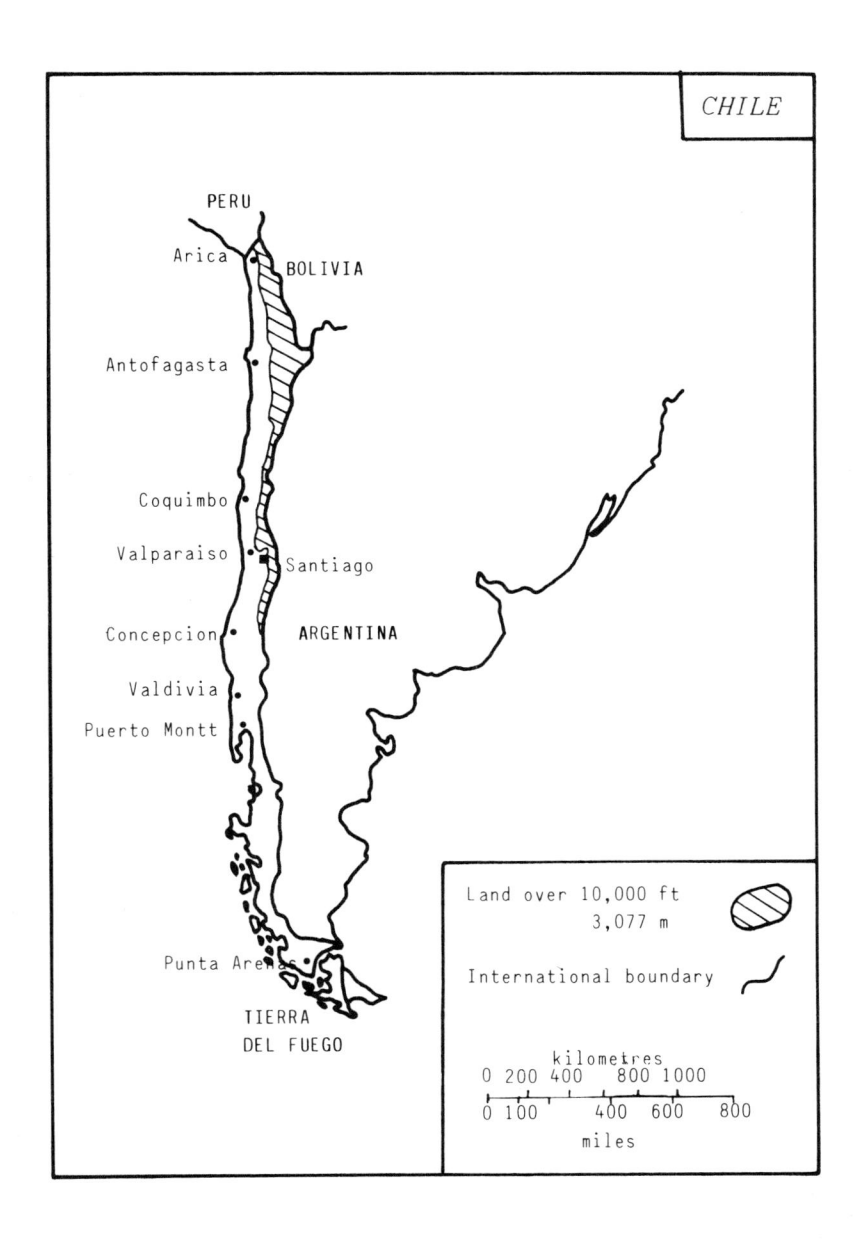

(iv) Atlantic Chile across the Andean watershed in Patagonia and Tierra del Fuego, has a cold climate with very strong winds, and was previously famed for its sheep; it is now being explored for oil and natural gas

(v) the last two regions comprise the Chilean Pacific Islands, which include the Juan Fernandez archipelago and Easter Island, and Chilean Antarctica, where the Chilean claim overlaps those of Britain and Argentina.

Communications

The ribbon-like shape of Chile makes communications very difficult. The country is isolated by its enormous natural barriers: the great Atacama desert and the mountain range of the Andes form a continuous wall to the east; the Pacific Ocean borders Chile to the west and stormy Cape Horn to the south. Distances are immense and while the Panamerican highway runs from Arica (on the Peruvian border) to Puerto Montt (in Forest Chile), communications with places in the remaining 1,600 km of southern Chile are limited to sea or air, unless one chooses to drive through Argentinian Patagonia. The Chilean railway network runs from Pisagua in the desert to Puerto Montt where the archipelago begins, and outside rail links are very limited. Virtually all air and sea links have hitherto been with Europe and the Americas, but the recent establishment of an air route over the Pacific to Australia via Fiji and Tahiti may open up more contacts with Australisia and East Asia.

2 POPULATION

Growth and Distribution

Chile's poulation in 1980 was estimated at 11.1 million and the annual growth rate between 1970 and 1979 was 1.7%, comparatively low by Latin American standards. Birth control is widely practised with the tacit approval of the government. In 1980, 80% of Chile's population lived in the urban areas such as Santiago (3.6 million), Valparaíso-Viña (0.7 million), Antofagasta (0.2 million), and Concepción (0.2 million).

Groups

Unlike neighbouring countries there are few pure Indians (not more than 300,000) though many Chileans have some Indian blood. Although colonised originally by the Spaniards, Chile has attracted large numbers of other European immigrants including Germans, Britons and Yugoslavs. On the first settlement these groups tended to stay together, the Germans in the southern regions of Forest Chile, the British in the ports of Valparaíso and Antofagasta and the Yugoslavs in the Magallanes area. Intermarriage is normal and there are no ethnic/racial groups, apart from a few Aymara speakers in the north and the Mapuche Indians in the south, whom the government wishes to see gradually integrated into the national community.

3 SOCIETY AND CULTURE

Influences

Neighbouring countries have had little effect on Chilean society or development; the influence has rather been from the settlers from North America or Europe.

Language

The basis of Chilean society and culture is Spanish. Castilian is spoken by all Chileans and is the language of education except in a very few private schools. English is the first foreign language.

Religion

Chile is predominantly Roman Catholic though declining numbers attend Mass. The influence of the Roman Catholic Church is much less strong than in Spain and subjects such as sex and contraception which would be taboo in Spain are widely discussed in Chile. The Church has done important pioneer work in private education. A number of schools were originally staffed by priests or nuns but their numbers are declining. About 60% of the RC clergy are non-Chileans.

Family Groups

The basic pattern of society remains family-orientated with few unmarried Chileans living away from home. Attachments are formed early and many girls marry in their teens, although most women continue to work after marriage. Families are large by European standards and six or eight children per family is not unusual.

Social Classes

For a Third World country, Chile has a large middle class accounting for some 30% of the population. But an estimated 21% of the population live in extreme poverty (almost 2 million people). The percentages of urban and rural poor are given as 67.8 and 32.2 respectively. However, as 80% of Chileans live in towns, there are proportionately more extremely poor people in rural areas. The Allende 'democratic Marxist' régime attempted to narrow this socio-economic gap.

Position of Women

Over 60% of marriages are common law only. Divorce is not recognised in Chilean law and annulment is expensive though quite frequent in middle class circles. There is little imbalance between the sexes in the education system and in 1977 42% of higher education students were women.

4 HISTORY AND POLITICS

Colonial Rule

Chile was conquered by the Spaniards in the sixteenth century and remained a Spanish colony until 1810. Colonial Chile was essentially isolated and backward with a reputation as the poorest of the Spanish colonies. Three hundred years of Spanish rule gave Chile a unifying language and religion and a system of education which still shows Spanish influence.

Independence

In 1810 the first independent government was formed and a successful war of independence ensured. Independence was, however, followed by a period of dictatorship and turbulence and it was not until 1830 that a political constitution was drawn up, which provided a base for the later emergence of parliamentary government. In the nineteenth century Chile experienced a variety of governmental methods and was governed by a series of autocratic presidents. In the latter half of the century the country was involved in revolutions and counter-revolutions. The War of the Pacific against Bolivia and Peru (1879-84) ended in a military victory for Chile but gave rise to a yet unresolved sequel of territorial disputes.

The Twentieth Century

The period up to 1918 was characterised by parliamentary rule and a succession of weak presidents. The twentieth century brought great economic and social change to Chile and the decline of the nitrate industry in the 1920s and the later worldwide depression brought Chile to the brink of economic chaos. In 1925 a new constitution was drawn up defining the republic as a 'unitary state' a continuing feature of a centralised nation. The new constitution provided for a strong executive, a labour code, social security, the separation of Church and State and the popular election of presidents who have decisive power in government. The first seven years of this implementation, however, did not see the establishment of a stable, constitutional government and Chile experienced a range of governments from a military junta to a socialist republic. Eventually the armed forces demanded that the government should be restored to those who, under the constitution, should administer it, and from 1932 to 1973 Chile maintained constitutional democratic government. Under the Christian Democrat government of President Frei (1964-70) a gradual programme of land redistribution was undertaken. This programme was greatly accelerated under Frei's successor, Salvador Allende.

Since 1970

The government of Popular Unity (1970-73) saw a rapid politicisation of all sectors of Chilean society and fluctuating economic fortunes. Industrial unrest and a deteriorating economic situation marked its final months, and in September 1973 President Allende was overthrown by a military coup in which he lost his life. Since then Chile has been governed by a four-man junta made up of the Army Commander-in-Chief, President Pinochet, and the heads of Navy, Air Force and Police. The 1925 constitution has been expressly superseded. A new constitution of 1980, approved by 'plebiscite', foresaw presidential elections in eight years. In the meantime Pinochet remains president.

The country is in a stage of siege with a nightly curfew and wide ranging powers of arrest and detention without trial to maintain internal security and ensure that the ban on all political activity remains effective. The Junta seeks to counter Marxism with its adopted ideology of 'geopolitics and national security', and courses on this are mandatory in some universities. The exodus of intellectuals and professionals from Chile, which had begun under Frei, increased markedly. The rights to assembly and strike action remain suspended.

International Relations

Chile's international isolation since 1973 has been increased by her withdrawal fromthe Andean Pact (Peru, Colombia, Ecuador, Venezuela and Boliva) in 1976, and plans for economic integration and educational cooperation with these countries have lapsed. Relations with Peru were increasingly strained as the centenary of the War of the Pacific (1979) occurred. Negotiations between the three countries over Bolivia's access to the sea are currently deadlocked. Chile is looking for a closer relationship with the military governments in the south and attends meetings of the River Plate basin countries (Brazil, Paraguay, Uruguay and Argentina) as an observer. Since 1980 relations with the USA have improved with the removal of sanctions. Relations with Argentina have become tenser.

5 THE ECONOMY

Pattern of the Economy

The mixed economy of Chile swung towards a greater degree of State ownership during the Allende régime, when all banks, many foreign companies and much agricultural land were nationalised. Since 1973 government policy has

THE EDUCATION SYSTEM

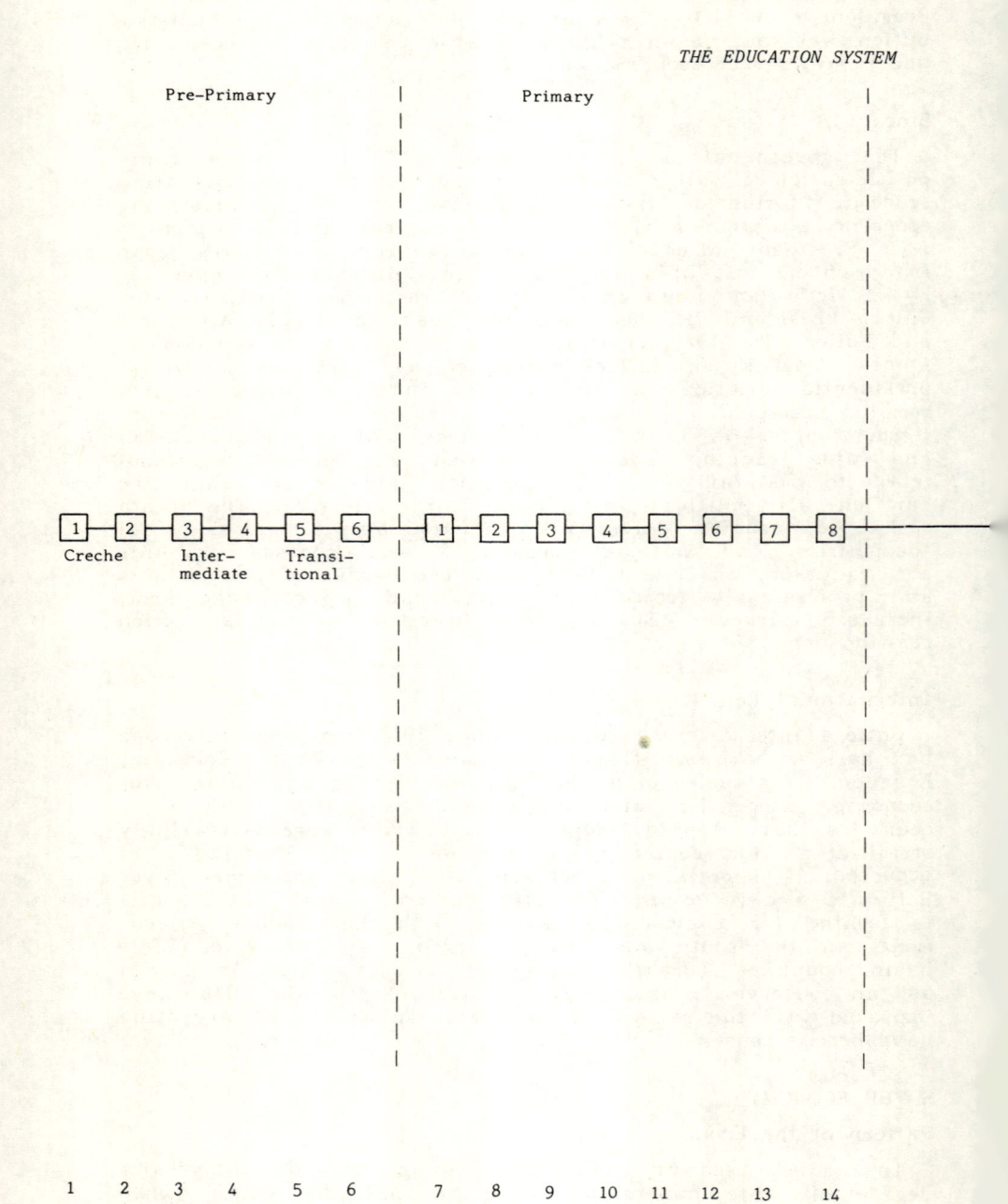

Pre-Primary | Primary |

| 1 — 2 — 3 — 4 — 5 — 6 | 1 — 2 — 3 — 4 — 5 — 6 — 7 — 8 |
Creche   Inter-   Transi-
        mediate   tional

1   2   3   4   5   6   7   8   9   10   11   12   13   14

OF CHILE

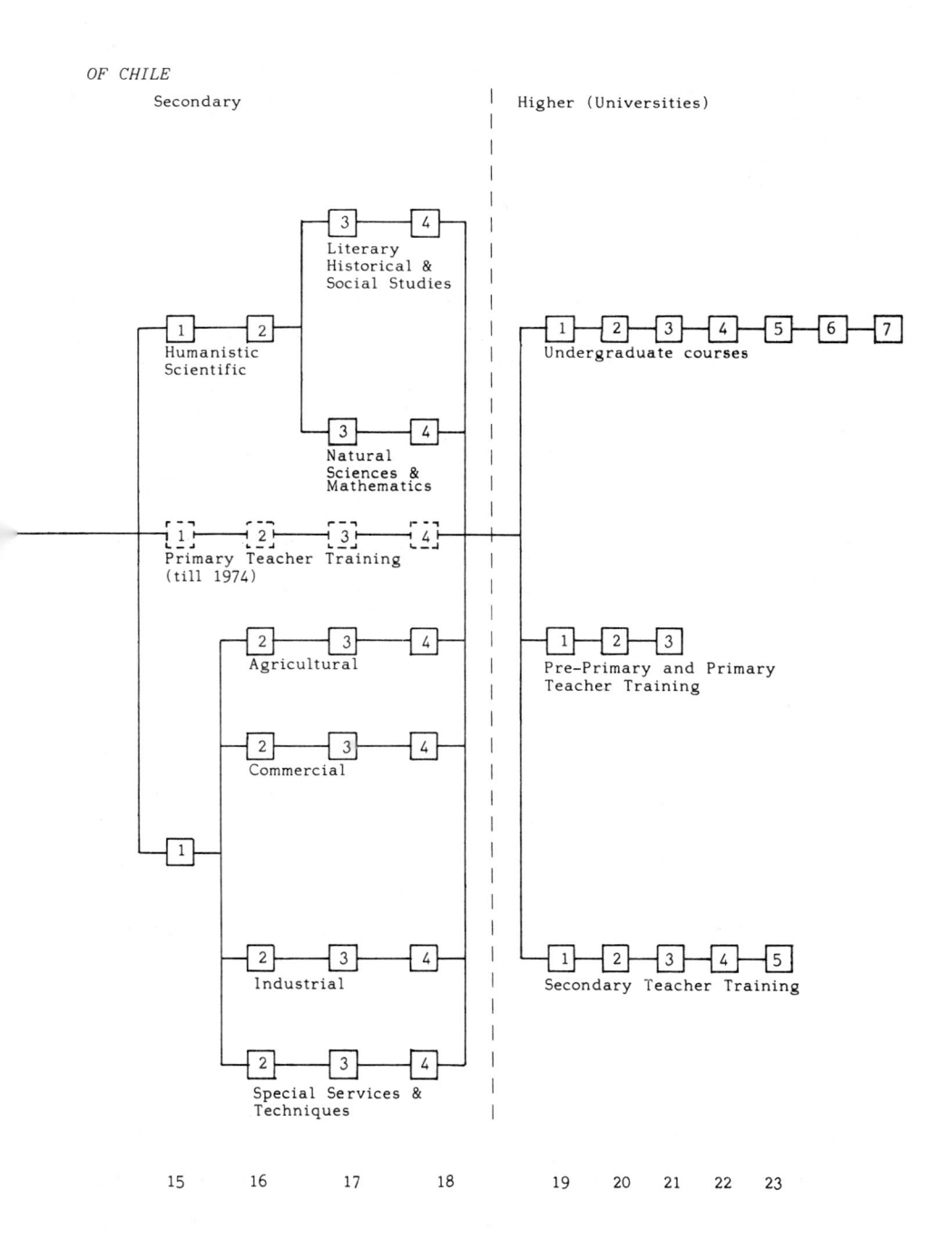

Secondary | Higher (Universities)

- Humanistic Scientific: 1 — 2
  - Literary Historical & Social Studies: 3 — 4
  - Natural Sciences & Mathematics: 3 — 4
- Primary Teacher Training (till 1974): 1 — 2 — 3 — 4
- Agricultural: 2 — 3 — 4
- Commercial: 2 — 3 — 4
- Industrial: 2 — 3 — 4
- Special Services & Techniques: 2 — 3 — 4

Undergraduate courses: 1 — 2 — 3 — 4 — 5 — 6 — 7

Pre-Primary and Primary Teacher Training: 1 — 2 — 3

Secondary Teacher Training: 1 — 2 — 3 — 4 — 5

15 16 17 18   19 20 21 22 23

been to sell State-owned companies and banks to private business with some important exceptions (coal, petroleum, the railways, the State bank) and to return expropriated land to its former owners. Import duties are being progressively reduced to accelerate progress towards a free market economy. The latter policy has resulted in a growing spate of bankruptcies in labour-intensive industries, and many allegations of 'dumping'.

Economic Situation

The Chilean economy suffered badly from inflation in the 1970s. Between 1970 and 1979 the annual average was 24.3%; a peak of 50.8% was reached in 1974 since when there has been some improvement. Since 1974 the imposition of the 'economic shock treatment' recommended by the ministers trained in Friedman/Chicago economics has resulted in a slow decline in the inflation rate but a sharp increase in unemployment, particularly in manufacturing and building. Chile's balance of payment depends heavily on the export of copper, and the slump in the price of copper has contributed to the critical economic situation. Unemployment is estimated at about 20% nationwide, but in certain urban areas is reported to approach 70%. Under-employment is common, and many companies on the brink of bankruptcy are reported to be hiring labour on a monthly basis only. The economic shock treatment has resulted in scarcity of money for industrial and agricultural credit, and interest rates on loans can be as high as 17% per month. There is little prospect of a rapid solution to the problems of stagnation, inflation and unemployment.

Emergency Programmes

There is a government emergency feeding programme which reaches a proportion of the children and nursing mothers most in need, although hampered by a good deal of bureaucracy. The churches and charities operate a wider-ranging emergency feeding programme. It is estimated that 70% of the population has suffered at some time from protein-calorie malnutrition. The government's public works programme affords work for approximately 200,000 people who would otherwise be unemployed, at a minimal wage of approximately £1 per day.

Agriculture

With its great area, varied climates and small population Chile should be almost self-sufficient in food production. Yet the 1976 crop of wheat (the chief source of protein in Chile) yielded an equivalent tonnate to that of 1931. Only 2% of all foreign investment in Chile goes to agricultire. Much of the land is still divided into small plots; there is a general lack of technical knowledge, and the horse, ox-team and wooden plough are still as common as the tractor. Chronic lack of credit has meant that many small holders have gone bankrupt and have sold their land back to the original owners. The producer has no guaranteed prices to help him plan, and cooperative ventures are actively discouraged. Many large landowners leave a high proportion of their acreage fallow. Attempts are being made to introduce agricultural extension services and to improve agricultural efficiency. Hard currency, which is at present being used for the import of essential foods, such as wheat, could then be spent on machinery and other goods necessary for development. The fisheries, though enjoying enormous potential, are even more under-developed than agriculture.

Natural Resources

Oil and natural gas deposits have been found in the south and the efficient exploitation of these could boost Chile's economy. There are coal deposits in Forest Chile, and radioactive minerals have been discovered in the Atacama Desert. Hydroelectric power is being developed, together with its spin-off in the form of irrgation schemes.

Trade

Most of Chile's exports go to the United States, Europe or Japan and there is comparatively little trade with adjacent countries. The government provides tax exemption to agricultural exporters and increasing amounts of fruit and protein foods are sold abroad. Chile has unilaterally decided to increase copper production by 15% over its allotted CIPEC quota.

Economic Aims

The aims of the Chilean government at present are:

(i) to increase the efficiency of agricultural production

(ii) to increase the export of copper

(iii) to export other goods, such as canned fruit, fish and wine

(iv) to develop natural resources

(v) to cancel the external debt

(vi) to control inflation.

6 THE EDUCATION SYSTEM

Academic Year

The academic year for all institutions runs from early March to early December. There is a break of some two weeks in July between the two semesters.

Pre-Primary *(Pre-Básica)*

Pre-primary schooling (or nursery education) has three stages - 'cradle room' from 0-2 years; median level (2-4); and transition level (from 4-6 years).

Pre-primary education caters for children up to the age of 6 and is not compulsory. Provision falls short of need but the 1980 figures show a 63% increase in provision over 1974. The overwhelming majority of schools are in urban areas (e.g. Santiago with 35% of the total population has 61% of the pre-primary State schools). The best of them are either private or sponsored by some State corporation or commercial institution for the children of their employees (18% of all provision in 1979). However, government gives subsidies to private schools. In general it can be said that only a fraction of the age group attend nursery schools and these are mainly from the upper socio-economic groups. In rural areas nursery schools are still virtually non-existent.

The organisation entrusted with the supervision of pre-primary education is the *Junta Nacional de Jardines Infantiles*, founded in 1970, which cooperates with the Ministry of Education and with other State and private institutions.

Since 1979 a National Board of Kindergartens has attempted to extend pre-primary education to poorer groups in conjunction with health and nutrition programmes.

Primary *(Educación Básica)*

Primary education covers the age range 6-13 or 14 is free (at State schools) and compulsory. An annual entrance fee of £4 is levied on each child, however, at both primary and secondary levels as a contribution to the upkeep of the school buildings. In 1980 2,320,408 pupils were enrolled - a drop of over 80,000 from the 1974 figure. This is due mainly to the economic depression but partly to a sharp decline in the birth rate during recent years. Of this total 427,716 were enrolled in private schools (mainly situated in urban centres). Thus about 18% of the age group was being educated privately.

The school curriculum is a fairly conventional one comprising reading and writing, mathematics, simple science, history, geography, social sciences, arts and crafts, music and physical education. A foreign language (either English or French) is introduced, at least in theory, at the beginning of the seventh grade. In a handful of prestigious private schools the foreign language tends to be introduced earlier. Some private schools have been granted 'experimental status' which allows all subjects apart from Spanish and Chilean history to be taught in a foreign language.

Examinations are devised internally within each school and marks are awarded on a scale of 7. Children who complete the full 8 grades of primary education receive a primary school leaving certificate.

More recently primary schooling has been divided into two cycles (4 then 3 years). In the second cycle it is urged that exploration activities and vocational orientation should come together in a more interdisciplinary approach.

Secondary (Educación Media)

In 1980 the secondary school population totalled 659,517 of which 149,194 (22.6%) were in private schools.

The secondary school system is divided into two categories: *humanistic-scientific* and *technico-professional:* the *humanistic-scientific* area offers two years of 'common course' studies, followed by two years of specialisation in literary, historical and social sciences or natural sciences and mathematics. The *technico-professional* area is intended to be less academic and more vocational. It is in turn subdivided into the following four categories:

(i)   industrial

(ii)   agricultural

(iii)   commercial

(iv)   special services and techniques.

Specialisation in one of these branches begins after a common year of general studies. Studies last four or five years depending on the specialisation.

The *liceos*, which provide humanistic-scientific education are much the more popular (attracting double the number of pupils). Within the *liceo*, mathematics, natural and social sciences enjoy greatest prestige, since success in these subjects leads on to university studies in medicine, engineering and economics, currently the most fashionable careers for middle-class children. In the technico-professional schools, commercial and industrial institutes greatly outnumber agricultural ones. The original intention was that those who completed these courses should move into industry, agriculture and commerce at the technician level, but in practice the majority aspire to the same university courses that form the objective of those in the humanistic-scientific secondary schools.

Students completing the four grades of secondary education are also awarded a school leaving certificate. These certificates are usually essential for obtaining 'white-collar' employment.

In 1980 it was proposed to transfer all technico-professional education to the private sector; thus government would withdraw from this area of education.

Vocational

While much university and secondary education is obviously vocational, there are also non-academic courses in various trades available to workers. The principal institution in this field is INACAP *(Instituto Nacional de Capacitación)* which until now has been largely funded from government sources. This offers a wide range of practical courses in areas such as motor mechanics, machine mending, building construction, mining, different aspects of agriculture and cottage industries, in 28 well equipped regional centres, each of which bases its courses on local manpower needs. Workers pay a very modest fee, and very modest prior academic qualifications are required (e.g. three years of primary education for many of the courses). Courses are normally arranged in three stages of approximately 400 hours each, designated as *formación*, *capacitación* and *especialización*, each lasting on average about four months. there are also many much shorter courses. Training is on a part time basis and most trainees are already in employment during the period in which they follow the courses. The courses are essentially practical and there are no formal examinations, successful completion of each stage being left to the instructor's judgement; but 100% attendance is required. In 1980 there were 13,500 workers in these programmes.

Similar types of courses are provided by certain university institutions, notably the *Instituto Tecnológico* of the University of Chile, Santiago, and the *Instituto Politécnico* of the Federico Santa Maria Technical University operating in Valparaiso with a branch in Talcahuano: but these are on a much smaller scale than INACAP.

Another large scale programme of this type is that provided by the *Departamento Universitario Obrera Campesino* (DUOC) of the Catholic University. DUOC was established in 1968, largely through pressure from the Christian Democrat party, and offers part time courses (mostly evening classes) in such subjects as electricity, computers, commerce, technical drawing, commercial art, sewing, dressmaking, health and education, under the slogan 'education is progress'. It also organises courses by request from *Centros de Madres* (Women's Institutes) and prisons.

Under the *Estatuto de Capitación y Empleo* (1976) employers are encouraged to facilitate job training for their employees and are entitled to deduct up to 1% from their tax declarations for this purpose.

Higher – Universities

In 1980 practically all higher education was provided by the universities, of which there were eight, as follows:

University	*Founded*	*Type*
University of Chile	1848	public
Catholic University of Chile	1888	Catholic
University of Concepción	1919	private
Catholic University of Valparaiso	1928	Catholic
Federico Santa María Technical University	1913	private
State Technical University	1947	public
Austral University, Valdivia	1954	private
University of the North	1958	Catholic

The two public universities are much the largest, each with numerous branches in provincial towns throughout the country. Standards and scope vary enormously between branches but in general the metropolitan branches are better financed and more dynamic than those in the provinces.

Courses

Under-graduate courses offered by the universities vary in length from two and a half years to seven years with a five-year degree course as the norm. The two technical universities concentrate on courses in science and technology but the State Technical University also offers degree courses in certain humanities including English. The remaining universities offer a wide spectrum of both academic and vocational courses, tending to emphasise those with immediate relevance to the economy of the region, e.g. mining technology in Antofagasta, forestry in Chillan and dairy farming in Valdivia. Post-graduate studies are offered mainly by the University of Chile and the Catholic University and vary from one-year diploma courses to doctorates requiring three years study. Specialisations in medicine are particularly well served in this respect.

Entrance

Entrance of undergraduate courses is based on a multiple-choice examination known as the *Prueba de Aptitud Académica* which is the only examination taken nationally and is valid for all universities in Chile. Each candidate is usually also required to take an additional *Prueba de Conocimientos Específicos* (Test of Specific Knowledge) in one of four areas: mathematics, natural sciences, social sciences, and arts. In addition to results in these examinations, the student's average marks obtained in secondary school are taken into account. The higher the candidate's score, the better the chances of being accepted for the university and course of his choice.

Fees

There has been a steep rise in fees for university studies, only partially offset by a limited number of bursaries for needy students. The social background of the student population is thus rapidly shifting upward and there are many drop-outs for financial reasons.

In 1980 and 1981 a number of proposals and decrees were issued which had the effect of restricting the autonomy of universities (including the closure of some universities) and limiting their enrolments and courses.

Teacher Training

From 1974-80 the responsibility of training teachers of pre-primary, primary and secondary levels was transferred entirely to the universities. Previously, the training of primary school teachers was carried out in the *Escuelas Normales* (Primary Teacher Training Colleges) and formed part of secondary education. Pre-primary and primary teachers in training are now required to take a three-year degree course at a university. Prospective secondary school teachers follow a five-year university course divided between education subjects and the subject specialism they have chosen to teach. Teachers receive a qualification which they refer to as a degree but it is equivalent rather to the UK Certificate of Education. From 1981, however, university control over primary teacher training has been modified.

In-Service

Efforts are being made to help unqualified and semi-qualified teachers obtain the full qualification by means of part time courses and there is increased activity in low cost schemes. In-service courses for different categories of State teacher have been offered since 1966. Since 1974 in-service training has been planned regionally with the appointment of *Equipos Tecnicos Regionales*, teams of experienced teachers who will take over responsibility for planning and conducting regional in-service training programmes.

Non-Formal

Many university branches maintain local radio stations with some educational content in their programmes but as they depend heavily on advertising revenue they are obliged to provide mostly popular fare in the form of news, sports, commentaries and pop music. The same problem affects Chilean television stations, although in recent years there have been attempts to provide television courses in such subjects as forest resources, economics, English and French. Interesting initiatives in the field of adult education have been taken in recent years by the *Universidad del Norte* in Africa; by the educational radio station *La Voz de la Costa*, based on Osorno, by the Protestant *Centro Audio-Visual Evangélico* (CAVE) operating in the Bío-Bío region, and by the Catholic *Centro de Investigación y Desarrollo de la Educación* (CIDE) in Quillota and San Felipe.

In the big cities, courses in subjects such as philosophy, art, history, electricity in the home or various handicrafts are offered periodically to members of the public by university extension departments or by cultural institutes maintained by the municipalities, while bi-national cultural institutes offer courses for learning foreign languages. In addition there is a great deal of informal education in the areas of child care, home economics, dressmaking and various handicrafts offered on a local basis by the *Centros de Madres*, which are widely distributed throughout both the poorer urban areas and the countryside.

Adult Literacy

According to the 1970 census 11.6% of the population was illiterate. The Ministry of Education and other organisations such as the *Instituto de Educación Rural* (IER) have mounted various literacy campaigns. In 1971, for example, a campaign was launched to reduce illiteracy by one third. By 1972 IER was maintaining 30 study centres throughout the country with the stated aim of 'improving the educational level of the rural population and enabling them to participate actively in the process of development'. A national literacy campaign began in 1979 aiming to reach 100,000 people.

7 EDUCATIONAL ADMINISTRATION

Central Control

The Ministry of Education is responsible for administering State and private schools and other institutes of further education. The Ministry also controls the budgets of the universities. Administration has traditionally been directed from the capital with regard to staff appointments and promotions in the State sector, textbooks, curricula, in-service training, libraries, archives and museums. A policy of decentralisation has been adopted and is being gradually applied.

Organisation

Within the ministry the Educational Planning Office and the *Superintendencia* are concerned with framing the rules and seeing that they are applied. The influence of the *Superintendencia* is considerable since all schools, public or private, are required to follow the curricula laid down by the ministry. Textbooks, syllabi, etc., are uniform for secondary schools throughout the country. The universities, however, are exempt from this type of control. The basic research on, and evaluation of innovations in methodology and curriculum reform are performed by the *Centro de Perfeccionamiento, Experimentación e Investigaciones Pedagógicas* (CPEIP) or Centre for Educational Research, Experiment and Training. The responsibility for in-service training *(perfeccionamiento)* also lies with the CPEIP.

Attempts to Decentralise

In 1968 a pilot scheme of regional educational offices was established with the object of decentralising the administration. But regional powers were limited and offices were still subject to the over-riding control of the ministry in

ADMINISTRATIVE ORGANISATION

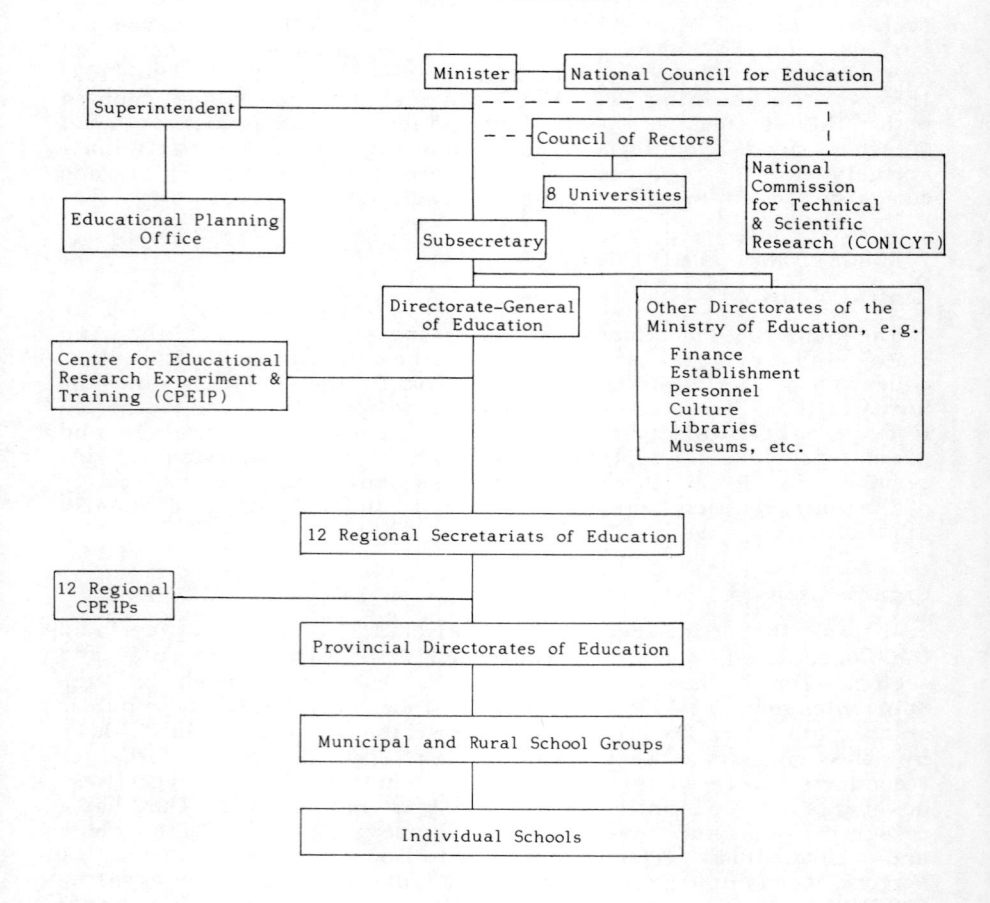

```
                              ┌─────────┬──────────────────────────────┐
                              │ Minister├──┤ National Council for Education │
  ┌────────────────┐          └────┬────┘  └──────────────────────────┘
  │ Superintendent ├───────────────┤─ ─ ─ ─ ─ ─ ─ ─ ─ ─ ─ ─ ─ ─ ─ ─ ┐
  └────────┬───────┘          ┌────┴────────────┐                   │
           │              ─ ─ ┤ Council of Rectors │               │
           │                  └────────┬────────┘   ┌──────────────┴────┐
  ┌────────┴───────┐              ┌────┴────────┐   │ National          │
  │ Educational    │              │ 8 Universities│ │ Commission        │
  │ Planning       │              └─────────────┘   │ for Technical     │
  │ Office         │         ┌─────────────┐        │ & Scientific      │
  └────────────────┘         │ Subsecretary│        │ Research (CONICYT)│
                             └──────┬──────┘        └───────────────────┘
                                    │
                         ┌──────────┴──────────┐  ┌──────────────────────┐
                         │ Directorate-General │  │ Other Directorates of│
                         │ of Education        │  │ the Ministry of      │
                         └──────────┬──────────┘  │ Education, e.g.      │
  ┌──────────────────────┐          │             │   Finance            │
  │ Centre for Educational│         │             │   Establishment      │
  │ Research Experiment & ├─────────┤             │   Personnel          │
  │ Training (CPEIP)      │         │             │   Culture            │
  └──────────────────────┘          │             │   Libraries          │
                                    │             │   Museums, etc.      │
                                    │             └──────────────────────┘
                        ┌───────────┴─────────────────────┐
                        │ 12 Regional Secretariats of Education │
                        └───────────┬─────────────────────┘
  ┌──────────────┐                  │
  │ 12 Regional  ├──────────────────┤
  │ CPE IPs      │                  │
  └──────────────┘      ┌───────────┴───────────────┐
                        │ Provincial Directorates of Education │
                        └───────────┬───────────────┘
                        ┌───────────┴───────────────┐
                        │ Municipal and Rural School Groups │
                        └───────────┬───────────────┘
                        ┌───────────┴───────────────┐
                        │      Individual Schools   │
                        └───────────────────────────┘
```

Note: — — — indicates autonomous bodies linked to the government through the Ministry of Education.

Santiago. Theoretically local committees in each region considered the particular educational requirements of their area and drew up plans accordingly. In practice all the main decisions were taken in Santiago. In 1974 the military government again declared its intention of decentralising the system and this is gradually taking place. Regional secretaries of the Ministry of Education were appointed. the regional education authorities have begun to exert much closer control and are now empowered to make modifications in the national syllabus at a regional level. Some interesting developments have resulted from this - for example the week-long projects *(semana para académica)* when schools are freed from the normal timetable to pursue a particular topic.

In 1974 the CPEIP began to implement the Ministry's policy of the decentralisation of education by drawing up agreements with universities in appropriate parts of the country for the in-service training of teachers on a regional basis at the proposed *Centros Regionales de Perfeccionamiento* (Regional In-Service Training Centres).

In 1980 a process of transfer began of control over basic (primary) and middle (secondary) schools to municipalities. This control extends over teachers.

University Administration

The universities are under military control. The government appoints university rectors and vice-rectors, and the previous system under which universities elected their senior officers has given way, under the nationwide ban on any type of election, to a system of centrally-appointed nominees. The ministry allocates university budgets. Matters of university coordination are controlled by the National Council of Rectors.

8 EDUCATIONAL FINANCE

Education Budget

In 1980, 17.1% of the national budget was destined for education. This amounted to about 3.2% of GNP. Most of the money comes from direct taxation but there are other minor sources such as 2% of the revenue from car licences paid via the municipalities, and a percentage of the taxes on copper. The Lottery of Concepción contributes towards the cost of the university in that town.

Allocation of Funds

The distribution between the various educational levels in 1980 was:

        Pre-school   5.08%
        Primary (Grades 1-8)   47.77%

Secondary (Grades 9-12) 18.91%
Normal (Primary teacher
  training) 0.77%
Higher (i.e. universities 27.42%

Until 1974 the cost of maintaining the universities was borne largely by the State, since even the private and the Catholic universities received huge subsidies. In 1974 approximately 49% of the education budget, amounting to 2% of the GNP, was being absorbed by the universities. This trend has now been arrested by rigorous pruning of university budgets and by the introduction of fees for students. The reductions in educational expenditure have hit the universities hardest, and the University of Chile had its budget trimmed by 14% in 1976.

Funding of Private Institutions

Private schools, if fee-paying, have to finance themselves from fees or investments, but non-fee-paying private schools, such as missionary schools, receive government assistance. Fees are fixed by the Ministry of Education and each private school has to seek ministry approval to raise fees, justifying the increase.

Future Trends

The trend for the immediate future, therefore, seems to be an increased share of the educational budget for primary and technical education, especially in those regions of Chile where under-development is most acute. However, the cost to parents of sending a child to school in the current economic crisis has risen.

9 DEVELOPMENT AND PLANNING OF THE EDUCATION SYSTEM
Origins

The first schools in Chile were founded by the Spaniards, and especially by religious orders such as the Jesuits, for the education of the sons of Spanish settlers. Education was therefore a replica of the European system with emphasis on the classics and learning by heart. The Spanish youths returned to Europe for higher education and so the aim was to prepare them for admission to European universities. There were no universities in Chile until the nineteenth century, when independence was achieved. Science was then introduced into the curriculum and at the end of that century President Balmaceda ordered the construction of primary, secondary and technical schools throughout the country. The first teacher training institute was established at the University of Chile, new methods were introduced and girls were admitted to schools for the first time. Education, until

1920, however, remained the privilege of the children of the well-to-do, who could afford the fees and did not need to rely on their children's earning power.

In 1920 a law was passed which aimed at giving, free of charge, six years of basic education to all children in Chile. The objective was not realised because there were insufficient schools and because education remained academic, unrelated to social and economic development, and therefore to the needs of the majority of the population.

Planning Institutions

The first plan for reform of the educational system appeared in 1928 but it was not until 1962 that an Educational Planning Office was set up. This now operates under the *Superintendencia de Educación* in consultation with ODEPLAN (the National Planning Office).

1965 Plan

In 1962 *La Comisión de Planeamiento Integral de la Educación* was set up to study the educational needs of Chile. In 1965 the recommendations of the commission began to be put into effect. Its aims were to modernise the system, to improve the training of teachers, to eliminate educational inequalities and to provide school buildings for the 200,000 children who were then not receiving any education. There were, undoubtedly, economic pressures behind this reform by the Christian Democrat government of President Frei, who argued that the development of Chile was dependent upon higher educational standards; and also, political pressures in that the Frei government wished to give Chile a democratic education system with equal opportunities for all.

Aims of Allende Régime

When President Allende assumed power in 1970, the government's chief educational aim became the creation of a socialist society. The pace of reform was accelerated in the following ways: by increasing by 78% the number of nursery school places available to working-class infants; by lowering the standard of university entrance to allow students without formal entrance requirements to be admitted; by offering free meals and lodging, loans and scholarships to students of working class origin; by expanding adult education places from 89,000 to 215,000 in order to combat illiteracy and provide technical training for labourers. It is necessary to add that adequate funds to provide for this expansion did not exist and that increasingly severe inflation and rising political tensions gradually produced a situation in which normal educational activities became practically impossible, especially in universities and secondary schools.

Aims of Military Government

There has been a plethora of statements of aims by the Junta since its accession to power on 11 September 1973. the most recent are as follows:

(i) primordial objective: to provide education for all citizens from kindergarten to adult

(ii) to build new schools and rehabilitate old ones

(iii) to implement a modular distance education plan for adults in the Santiago area

(iv) to re-structure technico/professional secondary education

(v) to develop in-prison education (two special schools for 14-18 year old delinquents were completed in 1976)

(vi) from 1978 to make secondary education fee-paying subject to a means test

(vii) to continue to provide free primary education

(viii) to enforce the collection of VAT on books and learning materials (this tax will provide funds for public libraries).

A summary of previous stated aims still being pursued reveals the following differences from the objectives of the two previous administrations:

(i) an increased emphasis on nationalism and the glories of nineteenth century Chilean military history

(ii) the disappearance of the various courses on civics and social science due to the ban on any type of political activity

(iii) the guarantees offered to private education, a sector frequently attacked under the Allende régime.

Plans for Underprivileged Areas

The University of Chile carried out a statistical analysis of the 1970 census in 1975 and produced a 'Map of Extreme Poverty'. This gave added impulse to the decision to switch educational resources into the public primary sector in general, and in particular the government promised to:

(i) build schools in remote and frontier areas hitherto inadequately covered or not at all

(ii) develop special programmes for use in areas with a substantial non-Spanish speaking minority, notably the Aymara speakers in the northern mountains, the Araucanians in Forest Chile, and the Pascuenses on Easter Island.

Plans for University Sector

Early in 1976 the Military Government announced its plans for rationalising the structure of university education. Four general principles were stated:

(i) university autonomy was defined as giving the universities freedom to decide all matters relating to teaching, research, administration and extension, provided decisions keep within the government's university policy and the law

university activities must be coordinated with the national development policy

each university should prepare its own plans and programmes aligned with national development needs

there must be inter-university coordination to avoid duplication and wasteful competition

Detailed objectives were stated as follows:

(i) to train specialists in accord with development needs

(ii) to create new two-year courses for the training of intermediate level technicians

(iii) to create new three-year general degrees so that those who do not wish to specialise further may leave university at this stage

(iv) to develop post-graduate teaching in order to diminish dependence on foreign science and technology

(v) to create universities of a functional and efficient size

(vi) to develop a system of curriculum renewal so as to avoid the perils of narrow specialisms or encyclopaedic requirements

(vii) to rationalise university activity on a regional basis so as to avoid duplication (this should result in the closure of several small branches and the amalgamation of others in certain towns).

Special attention is to be given to the needs of scientific and technological rsearch and it has been decided to set up a commission, subordinate to the Council of Rectors of universities, to set up programmes of medium and long term scientific development (corresponding to the National Research Council's general development plans) and to allocate research funds accordingly. To this end the government have promised to bring out a new basic university law and to redefine the responsibilities of the Council of Rectors.

Future Planning Strategy

The ten years from 1963 saw a general expansion in the educational system and a doubling of the university student population. During the Allende years the rapid politicisation of education caused convulsive upheavals particularly in the universities. Chile has produced a number of educational plans but one of the weaknesses of the system, which is as evident now as it always was, is that no plan has been given sufficient time to be implemented and evaluated before the next is introduced. The current slogan of 'continuous renovation' in education may well sustain the counterproductive state of flux and uncertainty within the education system.

CHILE BASIC EDUCATIONAL STATISTICS

Population

1960	1970	1979
7,683,000	9,720,000	10,917,000

Proportions of the Relevant Age Groups Enrolled at each Level of Education

Primary = Total enrolments divided by the numbers in the age group 6-13
Secondary = Total enrolments divided by the numbers in the age group 14-17
Higher = Total enrolments divided by the numbers in the age group 20-24.

	Primary	Secondary	Higher
1970	107	39	9.4
1979	118	55	11.9

Schools, Teachers, Pupils

	Schools	Teachers	Pupils
Pre-primary			
1970	1,092	–	60,360
1979	2,106*	3,388*	162,993
Primary			
1970	7,389	40,823	2,040,071
1979	8,210*	66,354	2,235,861
Secondary			
1970	–	–	302,064
1979	–	27,207	536,428

* 1978

Higher Education Students by Field of study 1978

Education and Teacher Training	37,338
Humanities	3,288
Fine and Applied Arts	4,882
Law	3,093
Social and Behavioural Sciences	16,138
Natural Science	4,911
Medicine and Related Studies	15,408
Engineering	38,572
Agriculture	6,578

Basic Social And Economic Data

GNP per capita 1979 - US$1,690

Average annual growth of GNP per capita 1960-79 - 1.2%

Life Expectancy 1979 - 67 years

Percentage of the labour force in:

Agriculture
1960   30
1969   20

Industry
1960   20
1979   20

Services
1960   50
1979   60

Colombia

CONTENTS

1 Geography
2 Population
3 Society and Culture
4 History and Politics
5 The Economy
6 The Education System
7 Educational Administration
8 Educational Finance
9 Development and Planning of
  the Education System

Colombia is typical of the group of countries which United Nations agencies have categorised as developing middle income states. The national income per capita is above that of the poorest countries and there has been a very healthy rate of economic growth in the 1970s, including the expansion of the manufacturing sector. Yet, as with several of these middle income countries the economy and population are still based on agriculture and the rural areas. There are many of the social problems associated with an under-developed country. Colombia has experienced expansion of economic activities and social services without yet escaping from the major social problems of a Third World country.

The Colombian education response to these economic developments and social conditions have not been very different from that of other Latin-American countries. Primary education provision has grown, and universal elementary schooling is near to achievement. But the character of primary schools has not changed radically. Schools are centrally controlled, teachers are trained at secondary level institutes and, despite proposals for curriculum reform, there has not been a major change in what is taught. Problems of improving the quality and of giving a new orientation to primary education still remain.

Economic growth has been associated with an expansion of demand for secondary schooling. The Colombian educational authorities have responded by attempting to diversify from the traditional pattern of academic secondary schools which prepare for university entrance. A basic lower secondary course has been introduced which gives more attention to vocational and technical subjects and which is intended to be terminal for most students. Upper secondary education has also acquired technical and vocational branches. But popular demand is still for academic secondary education and these pressures have been met in part by the growth of private secondary schools. An education leading to traditional professions via the universities is still the most highly valued.

The Colombian government is faced with a number of possibly conflicting educational priorities. There is a need to extend basic schooling to the substantial poorer group of society who have hitherto been deprived of full facilities. There is the need to meet popular demands for post-primary schooling and at the same time to deflect this demand to a more diversified range of courses consistent with the changing nature of the Colombian economy. Rates of economic expansion in the 1970s together with the survival of a democratic and efficient government made both aims possible but changes in economic or political conditions could undermine these achievements.

1 GEOGRAPHY

Topography and Climate

Colombia's land area is 1,126,400 sq km (440,000 square miles), roughly equivalent to the combined area of France, Spain and the Benelux countries. It is bounded in the north by the Caribbean and in the west by the Pacific. It shares land frontiers with Panama, Ecuador, Peru, Brazil and Venezuela. The dominant geographical feature of the country is provided by the three ranges of the Andes which cross the country from north to south, each having peaks which reach altitudes of over 5,000 metres (16,500 feet). Between the Cordilleras of the Andes flow the great rivers Magdalena and Cauca, joining together to flow into the Caribbean at Barranquilla. The principal effect is a wide variety of climates in which temperature is chiefly a matter of altitude. The following table illustrates the topography and climate of the country:

Altitude	Temperature	Extent	Denomination
From 0 to 1,000 m	Over 23°C	83% of total surface area	Hot
From 1,000 to 2,000 m	23°C to 17.5°C	9% of total surface area	Mediterranean
From 2,000 to 2,000 m	17.5°C to 12°C	6% of total surface area	Temperate
3,000 & over	Under 12°C	2% of total surface area	Páramo (inhospitable moorland)

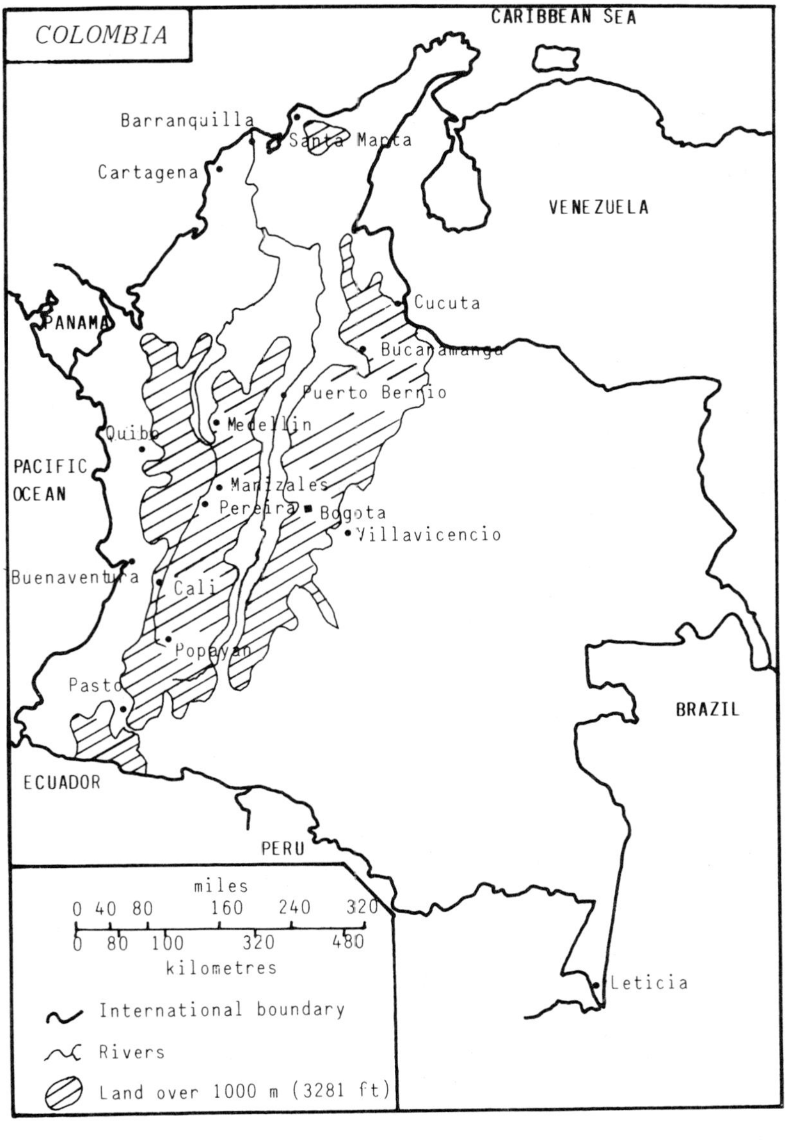
COLOMBIA
CARIBBEAN SEA
Barranquilla
Santa Marta
Cartagena
VENEZUELA
Cucuta
PANAMA
Bucaramanga
Puerto Berrio
Medellin
Quibdo
PACIFIC OCEAN
Manizales
Pereira
Bogota
Villavicencio
Buenaventura
Cali
Popayan
Pasto
BRAZIL
ECUADOR
PERU
miles
0 40 80 160 240 320
0 80 160 320 480
kilometres
Leticia
International boundary
Rivers
Land over 1000 m (3281 ft)

Statistics alone cannot do justice to the intricate and endless varieties of climate, terrain, economy and culture which Colombia contains - the tropical forests of the low lying areas, the fertile folds of the Andean foothills, home of Colombian coffee, the luscious pastures of the Sabana plateau, the endless varieties of mountain landscape reaching up to the level of permanent snow.

Communications

There are at least 18 cities in Colombia with over 100,000 inhabitants and all of these are linked by air. The road network between these cities is, however, inadequate and the engineering and economic problems involved in developing it are formidable. In the western jungles and in the vast eastern plains there are virtually no roads. The lack of adequate all-weather roads is a major factor retarding the economic and social development of the rural areas of Colombia. Of a total 53,200 km of road in 1978, 21,800 km were classified as major and the quality of these is being gradually improved. The Panamerican Highway runs through Colombia from Cucuta on the Venezuelan border via Bucaramanga-Bogotá-Cali - to Ipiales on the frontier of Ecuador. In 1979 plans were being made for a road link through the Darien Gap to connect Colombia with Central and North America. Colombia has 2,200 miles of broad and narrow gauge railway, but the railway system as a whole is in need of modernisation. In 1974, total passengers carried were 4.5 million, and freight 3 million tons. Telecommunications within and between cities are being constantly improved.

2 POPULATION

Growth

The last formal census was held in 1973, and more recent information comes from surveys based on samples and projections. The 1973 census indicated a total population of 22.5 million; the 1980 estimate was 27.3 million. The rate of population growth is a matter of considerable public interest, but there has been a significant decrease in the birth rate.

Between 1960-70 the annual rate of increase was 3.0%. This fell to 2.3% between 1970 and 1979. However, many of Colombia's social problems arise, and will continue for many years to arise, from the extreme pressure of population on available economic and financial resources.

Colombia has a Concordat with Rome which prevents any official birth control programme, though unofficial initiatives are not discouraged.

Distribution

The population is very unevenly distributed. Over 75% live in the Andean ranges and on the Caribbean coast.

A significant figure is the estimate that 42% of the population live in hot zones, 35% in temperate zones and 23% in cold zones. In 1980 it was estimated that 70% of the population was urban, compared to 48% in 1960. Nevertheless in common with other Latin American countries urban growth is explosive, but in contrast to some this growth is not concentrated on one or two cities but on a dozen or so regional centres. The largest city, the capital Bogotá, had a population of 4.3 million in 1980. Other large cities are Medellin (1.5 million), Cali (1.3 million), Barranquilla (0.9 million), Cartagena (0.5 million), Bucaramanga (0.4 million), and Cucuta (0.4 million).

Groups

The population is ethnically diverse, with a high proportion of people of mixed blood *(mestizos* and *mulatos)*. Estimates vary considerably: the following figures have been widely given for 1980:

Indians	1%
Negroes	5%
Zambos (Indian/Negro)	3%
Mestizos (Indian/White)	57%
Mulatos (Negro/White)	14%
Whites	20%

3 SOCIETY AND CULTURE

Differing Cultures

Like many developing countries Colombia faces considerable problems of nation-building. Ethnically, to the original interaction of Spanish conquistador with indigenous Indian have been added significant elements of negro and other immigrant groups. Ethnic differences have been further complicated by cultural, economic, social, linguistic and educational factors, while the geographical and communication features of the country have perpetuated a strong *'regionalismo'*. However, the modern State of Colombia, with such symbols of nationhood as a history of 'liberation', a constitution, public administration, armed forces, press, airlines, and cultural and sporting heroes, plays an increasing role in the minds of its citizens. Government policy sensibly encourages a measure of regional decentralisation wherever practicable.

Social Patterns

In social life the most important entity is the family to which each member owes a high allegiance. Family networks can be extensive, though combined with this Latin sense of family is a Latin individualism and respect for the individual as a person. Personal relations are valued highly and to transact any form of 'business' in an impersonal way runs counter to all Colombian values. The social structure of Colombia is closely linked with economic status, and presents a serious and generally recognised imbalance. There are affluent groups, deriving wealth from land, property, industry and commerce, enjoying easy access to the world outside Colombia. There are vast masses of the urban and rural poor, very often unemployed or under-employed, deprived of the basic essentials of food, housing, public services, and education. Between the extremes, an increasing middle class manages a somewhat uneasy existence with salaried employment either in the professions or in private or public institutions. Social movement between groups exists and is growing. Its further growth depends very largely on the growth of educational opportunity in the overcrowded cities and the rural areas.

Position of Women

Perhaps the most rapid social change – restricted so far to the upper and middle class – is the position of women. Many more girls are now being educated in secondary schools and universities than in the past and many more are to be found holding full time jobs. These educated women are demanding, and just beginning to get, more social freedom and respect in what has hitherto been a society under firm male rule.

Religion

Colombia is very much a Catholic country, though this is not to say that even a majority of Colombians are practising Catholics. But the influence of the Church, especially in the rural areas, and in education, is considerable and its rights are still protected by the Concordat with Rome. Although it is usually thought of as conservative, the Church is also committed to social development among the rural and urban poor. One of the most successful mass education projects, *Acción Cultural Popular*, with its own radio transmitters and organisational network, is a Catholic enterprise.

Language

There now remain no more than vestigial traces of any of the indigenous languages of Colombia and Spanish *(Castellano)* is strongly established as the national language, in which many Colombians feel great pride. Spanish is the invariable language of public life and of education, though there is increased recognition of the value of English as an auxiliary language (e.g. in commerce, tourism, and higher education at research level). Other European nations invest substantially in the promotion of their languages (French, German, Italian), but the predominant position of English is undoubted.

4 HISTORY AND POLITICS

Origins

Before the arrival of the Spanish conquistadores, areas of modern Colombia were inhabited by groups of Indian hunters or nomadic agriculturalists. More developed cultures, e.g. of the Chibchas, developed in the upper regions of the eastern Cordillera, and gave rise to the El Dorado legend. Other cultures e.g. the Tairona, Quimbaya, Sinu and Calima have been brought to light by archaeological research, and a selection of the artefacts are impressively displayed in the Banco de la República Gold Museum in Bogotá.

Colonial Period

The story of the 'conquest' of Latin America has often been told. Responding to the expansive spirit of the European Renaissance and driven by hopes of fantastic wealth, the Spanish conquerors with their superior weaponry and transport (on horseback) performed prodigies of penetration into the most inaccessible regions of the Andes, and their military rigour combined with proselytising zeal quickly led to the destruction of the indigenous cultures. Principal dates are:

    1502   Christopher Columbus first arrived off the coast
           of Colombia
    1525   Establishment of Spanish settlement at Santa Marta
    1533   Establishment of Spanish fortress at Cartagena
    1536   Jimenez de Quesada reached the area of Bogotá
    1538   The City of Santa fe de Bogotá founded.

Thereafter for almost three centuries Colombia was ruled under Spanish colonial administration. The El Dorado legend proved a disappointment, but the conquistadores and their descendants established a network of large land holdings in the most fertile areas of the country.

Independence

The colonial period ended in 1810 with the beginning of the wars of independence. These resulted partly from the spread of French and American revolutionary ideas, but also from the growing resentment of the Colombian-born settlers against the high handed behaviour of the Spanish colonial administrators, whose ranks they were not permitted to join. Under Simon Bólivar, the independent republic of La Gran Colombia was established in 1819, with Bogotá as its capital. This included what are now the territories of Panama, Ecuador and Venezuela, but did not prove to be a stable entity. After various secessions and realignments, the modern Republic of Colombia finally emerged in 1886. However, there was continual friction between the two rival oligarchies which called themselves Conservatives and Liberals, and which still survive to the present day as the two principal political parties. The Conservatives are traditionally associated with the agrarian interest, the Church and centralism, and the Liberals with cities, secularism and federalism but it is best to see them as two alternative ruling groups.

The Twentieth Century

The twentieth century began with the secession of Panama, a part of Colombia until 1903. The issue is not yet dead in Colombian hearts and minds, and is one of many factors in the attitude of the Colombians to the United States, which instigated the revolt leading to Panamanian independence. But the over-riding event of the twentieth century, from the shadow of which Colombia is still emerging, was the *'violencia'* of the 1950s. Starting with the assassination of Jorge Eliecer Gaitán, the first Colombian political leader who had organised substantial popular support for a programme of social reform, it led to murder and violence on a widespread scale throughout the country, and especially in rural areas. Liberals slaughtered Conservatives and vice versa in a conflict which left the country economically and politically shattered. A truce between the two parties was arranged in 1957 by which political and administrative power throughout the country was to be shared between them. The presidency alternated between them after 1958, but in 1974 the presidential election was open for the first time for 16 years, and not only to the traditional parties. The Liberals won both the presidential and general elections, with substantial majorities. In 1978, again a Liberal president, Dr Julio Cesar Turbay Ayala, was elected, with a programme for the maintenance of law and order, and general economic and social development. To give his régime an 'all party' character, various posts were given to Conservatives.

A significant feature of Colombian political life has been the failure to emerge so far of anything like a popular party: as a result it is not surprising that, although all men and women over 18 are enfranchised, the percentage of the electorate actually voting is very small (in 1978, 34%). Some 'subversive' opponents of the existing régime form guerilla groups which contribute their quota to the general insecurity of public life.

Government Organisation

Colombia is a unitary democratic republic headed by a President elected every four years. It is divided into 22 departments, four *intendencias*, four *comisarias* and the *Distrito Especial de Bogotá (DE)* (Special District of Bogota). The legislature consists of a 112-seat Senate and a 199-seat House of Representatives elected every four years. Each department also has its assemblies and municipal councils, elected every four years. The Executive consists of the President, and municipal mayors appointed by the governors.

Since 1958 these executive positions and all senior administrative posts in central and departmental government have been shared between supporters or members of the Conservative and Liberal parties. All senior posts are held by nominees of ministers.

International Relations

Colombia is a member of the United Nations, the Organisation of American States, the Latin American Association for Free Trade (ALALC), and the Andean Pact. Though close to the United States, in 1976 it became the first Latin American country to forgo US assistance, as the cultural/economic influence of ther USA on Colombian life is still generally resented. Since 1968 Colombia has been stabilising its relations with the Soviet Union and other countries of the communist bloc. However, relations with Cuba were broken in 1981.

Andean Pact

In 1969 the Agreement of Cartagena (subregional agreement) was signed by Chile, Colombia, Peru, Ecuador and Bolivia, and later by Venezuela in 1973 (the *Grupo Andino* – Andean Group), with the object of promoting the balanced and harmonious development of the member states of the Latin American Association for Free Trade, established by the Treaty of Montevideo 1960, and a continuous improvement in the standard of living of the inhabitants of the sub-region. Among measures discussed and agreed at subsequent meetings are the following:

(i) the harmonisation of economic and social policies of the different member countries by legislation where necessary

(ii) the collective planning and intensification of sub-regional industrialisation

(iii) the lowering of tariffs between member states with the aim of achieving a common tariff system

(iv) the planned acceleration of the development of the agricultural sector

(v) the canalisation of resources in and outside the sub-region to finance the investment necessary for the process of integration.

At a meeting of Presidents of the five nations in Cartagena in May 1979, further resolves were made to give renewed life to the Agreement.

Convenio Andres Bello

In 1970 the *Convenio Andres Bello* was signed between Colombia, Venezuela, Ecuador, Peru, Chile and Bolivia for cooperation in Education, science and culture. The five bases of the agreement are:

(i) the encouragement of good relations between the countries of the Andean region

(ii) the preservation of the cultural identity of their peoples within the framework of the Latin American heritage

(iii) the intensification of interchange of cultural riches between the countries

(iv) the joint development of their countries through education, science and culture

(v) the application of science and technology to raising the standard of living of the peoples of the region.

The Minisers of Education of the signatory countries meet regularly. The group has already agreed to recognise each others' primary and secondary systems. The group has also made a comparative study of the education systems of member countries.

5 THE ECONOMY
General

Substantial structural transformation has taken place and the country is now well advanced in the transition from a predominantly rural, agricultural and largely self-contained economy to an urban, industrial economy. The present Liberal government has expressed its intention to support industrial and agricultural expansion and to give priority to the oil and natural gas exploration programme. During the past decade Colombia has made excellent progress in export diversification and this has mitigated the effect of international coffee price fluctuation on internal expenditure. In 1959 coffee exports accounted for nearly 90% of foreign exchange earnings; by 1975 this proportion had dropped to 42% but the sharp increase in the international price of coffee in 1977 pushed the value of coffee exports back up to 63% of the total exports.

Agriculture

In spite of increasing industrialisation, some 28% of the total Colombian labour force is still employed in agriculture. In 1976 the agricultural sector contributed 26.2% of the gross national produce (GNP). Colombia produces about 15% of the world's coffee. Other important agricultural products are cotton, rice, potatoes, corn beans, sorghum, manioc (yucca), bananas, tobacco, barley, flowers, sugar cane, soya beans, cocoa, wheat, palm oil, timber and a great variety of tropical fruits. The country has rich and extensive pasture lands where cattle and sheep can be raised. The cattle population in 1977 was calculated at 25 million head although only 35% of the available land is currently being used; there is, therefore, much potential for expansion in this sector. By 1978 Colombia had become the third largest agricultural producer in Latin America, after Brazil and Mexico.

Industry

Colombia is now largely self-sufficient in consumer goods and exports of manufactured goods such as textiles, leather goods, footwear, rubber gloves, metal products, chemicals, pharmaceuticals and cement have been steadily increasing. There are three automobile assembly plants which were expected to produce 68,864 vehicles in 1978 and other plants assembling radios, television sets, sewing machines, refrigerators, washing machines, etc. from imported and locally manufactured components. Car tyres, batteries, glassware, chinaware and agricultural machinery are also manufactured and there is increasing local production of raw materials for industry. The iron and steel industry, though still small, is expanding.

Natural Resources

Electricity

Installed electrical capacity in 1977 totalled 3.9 million kw, of which over 70% was hydroelectric power. A capacity of 31.439 million kw is planned for the year 2000 mainly from hydroelectric sources. It is estimated that only 6% of hydroelectric potential has so far been tapped.

Oil and Gas

Although Colombia has oil deposits, a system of low internal domestic prices over the years discouraged exploration and in 1975 she became a net importer of oil. An intensive exploration programme has now been embarked upon and internal prices are gradually being increased. Recently discovered natural gas deposits in La Guajira are estimated to be capable of producing 400 million cubic feet daily for 20 yars. A gas duct to Baranquilla has been built and it is planned gradually to extend a gas network throughout the country.

Minerals

Colombia is the world's leading producer of emeralds, the eighth largest producer of gold and the ninth largest producer of platinum. There are large, and as yet largely unexploited, coal reserves, which are said to amount to 64% of known reserves in South America. However, plans for the exploitation of coal reserves in La Guajira and in central Colombia are being drawn up. The country is well endowed with non-metallic minerals (e.g. limestone, gypsum, clay, silica, sand, marble, salt) and large reserves of phosphate rock have been discovered. Lead, zinc and mercury are produced on a small scale. Mining has, however, hitherto played only a small role in the economy of the country and accounted for only 1% of GDP in 1976.

Trade

There has been steady improvement in the balance of trade.

Economic Situation

The Colombian economy is currently in a buoyant state. The effect of the substantial increase in the international coffee price has dominated the economic outlook of the country and has brought inflationary pressures. Inflation, measured by the average consumer price monthly index, rose to 30% in 1977 from its pre-1975 annual level of around 20%. The average annual rate between 1970 and 1979 was 21.5%. During the years 1960 to 1969 per capita income in Colombia grew at an average annual rate of 3% and reached approximately US$1,010 in 1979. The economy is thus developing rapidly and there is plenty of internal and external confidence about its future. The overall prospects are indeed more promising than they have been for many years. However, unemployment remains high, especially among the young, and there is little evidence yet of inherited wealth filtering down from the rich to the poor. In general, there is a good chance of sustained development if the government can control inflation and maintain balanced growth.

6 THE EDUCATION SYSTEM

Academic Year

For adaptation to climatic conditions there are two academic years in Colombia:

(i) Calendario B, in the southern departments of Valle, Cauca and Nariño, begins in September and continues until June

(ii) Calendario A, in the rest of the country, runs from February to November.

As in other American countries, the academic year is divided into two semesters.

Educational Reform

In 1975/76, under Minister of Education Hernando Duran Dussan, a major initiative was made to reform and rationalise the national education system. Principal measures introduced were:

> Law No.43 Of 1975, for the nationalisation of primary and secondary education
>
> Decree No.088 of 1976, for the restructuring of the education system and the reorganisation of the Ministry of National Education
>
> Decree No.102 of 1976, for the decentralisation of educational administration.

The structure of the new system envisaged in *'la reforma educativa'* is represented as follows:

Age							Years
	\multicolumn{6}{c|}{POST-SECONDARY}	5 to 2
	Intermediate Professional	Technological Training		University Training		Advanced Training	
17		\multicolumn{5}{c|}{Intermediate Professional Education}	2
16		Academic	Pedago-gical	Indus-trial	Commer-cial	Agri-cultural	Social Welfare	
15	BASIC	\multicolumn{5}{c|}{SECONDARY}	4
14							
13							
12							
11							
10		\multicolumn{5}{c|}{PRIMARY}	5
9							
8							
7							
6	\multicolumn{6}{c|}{PRE-PRIMARY}	

Public and Private Schools

The private sector represents a considerable part of the Colombian education system providing facilities at all levels from kindergarten onwards. As a condition of their licence to operate, private schools are required to offer some form of educational community service, e.g. to support a public school in a rural area or in an unprivileged urban area. In the private sector are to be found many secondary institutions of considerable academic and social repute, with varying types of educational tradition, e.g. in Bogota:

>Colegio Andino (German)
>Colegio Anglo-Colombiano (British)
>Colegio de la Salle (Catholic)
>Colegio de San Bartolomé de la Merced (Catholic)
>Colegio Nueva Granada (American)
>Colegio San Carlos (Franciscan)
>Gimnasio Moderno (Independent)
>Liceo Francés (French)
>Colegio CAFAM (Social Welfare Society)

Within the public sector some of the most notable institutions include:

>Colegio Nacional de San Bartolomé
>Instituto Pedagógico Nacional
>Externado Nacional Camilo Torres

Pre-Primary

The importance of this is widely recognised, both by those who are concerned about the early development of under-privileged children, as well as by professional families where both parents are working. Within the Ministry there is a Division for Pre-School and Special Education, though provision is at present restricted by economic factors. Most existing facilities exist in the larger towns and are provided by private organisations, but *Instituto Colombiano de Bienestar Familiar* (ICBF) (Colombian Institute of Family Welfare), another government agency, dependent on the Ministry of Health, is becoming active in this field. In 1979 there were 147,113 pupils in pre-primary education of whom 64% were in private institutions.

Primary

Primary education is by law compulsory, though in many areas sufficient schools still do not exist. It occupies five years (ages 7 to 12) and in public schools it is free. In 1979 the pupils enrolled in primary education totalled 4,337,607. Of these 85% were in public, and 15% in private schools. It was, however, recorded that the expansion of private primary schools was proceeding at a faster rate than public.

Attention was given in 1977/78 to reform and integration of the national primary curriculum, and curriculum development projects were initiated at various *Centros Pilotos Experimentales*, as a preliminary to their adoption on a national scale. A survey of the objectives of reformed primary education includes the following:

In the Area of Knowledge
- (i) the means of communication and personal expression
- (ii) the basic elements of quantitative thought
- (iii) the socio-cultural environment
- (iv) proficiency in practical skills for entering the world of work
- (v) the natural environment

In the Socio-Affective Area
- (i) attitudes of social cooperation
- (ii) a reflective attitude to contemporary life
- (iii) moral habits based on a sense of individual and social responsibility
- (iv) the development of creativity in work
- (v) development of aesthetic sense.

In the Psycho-Motor Area
- (i) motor development
- (ii) sensory development
- (iii) sensory-motor coordination
- (i) physical and sporting skills

A typical programme for primary education since 1971 is:

Areas	Hours per Week				
	1st	2nd	3rd	4th	5th
Religious and Moral training	3	3	3	3	3
Spanish	9	9	7	7	6
Social Studies	4	4	5	5	5
Mathematics	5	5	5	5	5
Natural Sciences	3	3	4	4	5
Aesthetic and Moral training	3	3	3	3	3
Physical Education	3	3	3	3	3
	30	30	30	30	30

Secondary

In 1974 provision for secondary education was made up as follows: private institutions 48%, public institutions 52%. A considerable number of secondary institutions continue to offer a traditional six-year course (ages 12 to 18, leading to the end of secondary *Bachillerato*, and geared very closely to university entrance. However, for some years within the secondary system, diversification has been encouraged, and various *modalidades* (specialisations) provided. These include commercial and industrial courses aimed to prepare for entry to work.

A typical programme of secondary education is given on the following page.

Reform

Within the Ministry of Education, working groups are designing the curriculum for the reformed secondary education. A proposal for the curriculum of *educación media vocacional* is as follows:

(i) Subjects in the Common Core:

Social Sciences
Language
Basic Sciences
Mathematics
Physical Education
Aesthetic Education
Vocational and Technical training

(ii) Specific 'Modalidades' (Specialisations)

Pure Science: Languages
Exact Sciences
Natural Sciences
Social & Economic Sciences

Applied Science Economics
Industrial
Agricultural
Community Development
Pedagogic
Physical Education & Recreation
Arts.

INEM and ITA

A notable innovation in the early 1970s was the establishment of *institutos nacionales de educación media* (INEM) – national institutions of middle education. These are large comprehensive secondary schools with a vocational bias provided and controlled by the Ministry's *División de Educación Media Vocacional*, in specially designed buildings with staff recruited under specially favourable contracts. They are important potential centres for curriculum development, and are provided more or less on the basis of one to each department, with two in the Special District of Bogota. Although their vocational character is important, they also provide a path to university education. The curriculum envisaged for the *colegios* INEM has been set out as follows:

Humanities

An extra foreign language
General sociology
Colombian sociology
Economics
Aesthetic education
Cultural history

Commercial

English
Typing
Shorthand
Book-keeping
Economics
Statistics
Commercial Organisation
Commercial practice
Data processing

Domestic Science, etc.

Home management
Dressmaking
Cooking
Hygiene
Child management
Recreation
Handicrafts
Country practice
Cosmetology
Nursing

Industrial/Technical

Building
Technical Drawing
Woodwork
Metal mechanics
Electricity

Agricultural

Cultivation and Animal husbandry

Parallel to the INEM a number of similar institutions with a specific agricultural bias have been established, known as *institutos técnicos agropecuarios* (ITA).

Examinations

Colombia has no public examination system and it is likely that standards of attainment vary considerably between one institution and another. At the moment children are examined at the end of each year of secondary studies and the final mark for the year is a computation of the examination mark (40%) and average marks for work during the year (60%). If a child fails in more than two subjects he has to repeat the year. Those who fail in one or two subjects have to study during the long holidays and take another examination. The examinations are internal but in the sixth year of the *Bachillerato* course the examination papers must be corrected by two teachers, the pupils' own teacher and another (usually a teacher from another school) delegated by the Ministry of Education.

Rural

Ever since the conclusion of *'la violencia'* in 1959, successive governments have been concerned with rural education, and a number of different programmes have been devised. Most of these are based on an integrative idea, for the coordinated provision in rural areas of primary, secondary and adult education, and of the extension activities of various government agencies. The best known is the programme of *concentraciones de desarrollo rural* (concentrations for rural development) which was initiated in 1971, and is a direct dependency of the Secretary-General of the Ministry of Education. Although the original project proposed 57 of these in all parts of the country, in 1977 the number in operation was 16, which it was claimed provided services to a total of 140,000 persons; within this figure, the provision of educational courses was as follows:

Primary level	42,000
Secondary (basic)	2,500
Adult	12,000

More recently plans for somewhat similar organisations capable of development under the administration of all local authorities have been described as *nucleos de desarrollo educativo* (nuclei of educational development), of which in fact both rural and urban models have been described. More formal programmes of agricultural secondary education have a long history and since 1969 courses in *enseñanza media agropecuaria* (agricultural middle education) have been provided at six *institutos técnicos agropecuarios* (ITA) and in ten of the INEM. In 1978 the following numbers of students were catered for:

ITA	3,116
INEM	2,000 (approx.)

Since 1978 pilot programmes for new types of primary schools in rural areas have been developed. Complete primary education is provided whereas before only two-year schools existed. This was intended to reduce wastage. These schools are intended to have new approaches to teaching with teachers using new methods and materials. Close relations with communities are developed giving parents a role in decisions. In 1981 650 of these new schools had been set up in 14 rural areas.

Indigenous

Interest has been developing in recent years in the educational problems of indigenous groups in Colombia. After an International Conference on Cultural Policy in Latin America and the Caribbean which culminated in the Bogota Declaration of January 1978, Decree No. 1142 of June 1978 established the right of indigenous communities to an education in accordance with the cultural identity of each. A current estimate is that there are some 300,000 members of distinct indigenous groups. The Colombian island of San Andres in the Caribbean presents its own special problems of bilingual eoducation. A new system of education is being developed in the eastern areas of the country where there are strong indigenous communities.

Technical

This is in the process of development at the prese time, but does not yet command high social prestige, so that the total number of students in technical education is very low compared with those taking traditional academic subjects.

Secondary

Technical secondary schools provide courses leading to the *Bachiller Técnico,* which after several years' approved experience in industry can be converted to the qualification of *Técnico Intermedio.* The INEMs are beginning to produce school leavers with some amount of technical training, in some cases to the level of *Bachiller Técnico.* However, SENA (the National Apprenticeship Service) is probably the major training organisation at this level. Its students, who are usually required to have completed at least four years of formal secondary education, are seconded from their industries for courses of between 18 months and three years. SENA is closely linked with the world of industry and commerce, and its courses are not orientated towards university education. Some industries are also known to run their own training schemes at apprentice level, but no exact information is available as to the extent of such schemes.

Post-Secondary

There are two types of institution offering technical education at this level. Universities (14 public and 10 private) are at present providing shorter vocational courses in addition to their regular first degree programmes. These courses last for up to three years and provide training for laboratory technicians, nurses and dental assistants, physiotherapists and managers, amongst others, as well as the various kinds of engineer. In addition there are a further 16 public and 14 private *institutos tecnológicos* (technological institutes) which provide courses leading to the qualifications of *Técnico de Alto Nivel* or *Tecnólogo*. Numbers of students registered in 1974 (latest year for which figures are available) were:

Area	Public	Private	Total
Administration & Economics	968	1,407	2,375
Agriculture	291	–	291
Fine Arts	425	114	539
Pure Sciences	406	161	567
Health Sciences	63	–	63
Social Sciences	173	296	469
Education & Humanities	1,024	715	1,739
TOTAL	3,350	2,693	6,043

Higher

Colombia provides a wide range of opportunities for higher education. The 1978 *Directoria de la Educación Superior* (Directory of Higher Education) lists a total of 125 approved institutions. About 45 of these are universities: some of them are of long standing (e.g. Pontificia Universidad Javeriana, 1622; Colegio Mayor de Nuestra Senora del Rosario, 1653; Universidad Nacional, 1825) with branches established in other cities; others are of more recent origin, and reflect the ambitions of various groups within the community to found their own universities. Other institutions are more specialised *centros, corporaciones, escuelas, fundaciones, institutos,* etc. founded for various types of professional training. In 1976, of every 100 students in higher education, 85 were in universities and 15 in 'other institutions'. The provision of higher education, as at other levels, is divided between public and private. The total numbers of students registered in the years 1972–76, according to official statistics, were as follows:

Year	No. of Students	Public Institutions	Private Institutions
1972	128,463	66,008	62,455
1973	149,435	70,748	78,687
1074	171,002	78,556	92,446
1975	195,689	95,580	100,109
1976	247,291	121,364	125,927

By 1979 the total number of students had risen to 274,893. Public universities include those financed by central and departmental governments, which keep fees to a low level; private universities are financed by donations, endowments and students' fees, which are usually much higher than in the public sector.

Entrance

University entrance is gained by examination and interview for which a prerequisite is the *Bachillerato*. A national university entrance examination is used by 30 universities and institutions although it is not obligatory.

Courses

A very wide range of courses is available at Colombian universities as a whole.

Most first degrees take four or five years to complete though a few courses are as short as three years and full medical qualifications take six to seven years. Many university courses are available for part time study, conducted principally at night, so that students can combine study with gainful occupation - in these cases, courses take eight or more years to complete. Degree structure is derived from the American pattern, in which students have to study a programme of unit courses, some compulsory (according to various prerequisites) and others elective: each course has a unit value and the total number of units required for graduation is prescribed in departmental regulations. Student performance on each course is indicated by a grade point on the scale 0.0 - 5.0, on which 3.0 is usually the minimum acceptable. At the end of the whole course, each student's grade points are averaged to show his general level of achievement.

Organisation

The administrative structure of the universities is both varied and complex. At the head is a Rector appointed by the President in the case of the national universities and by the Governor in the case of the departmental ones.

Rectors are usually, but not necessarily, academics. The organisational structure varies but as a general rule official universities have a *Consejo Superior* (Higher Council) which consists of representatives of the Ministry of Educastion, government, the Church, business and industry, students, teachers and professional organisations. The Rector reports to this *Consejo* though in practice the Rector has much authority. He is chairman of the Academic Council which consists of deans of faculties or divisions and representatives of students and lecturers. The *Consejo Superior* tends to delegate administrative powers such as budget preparation to the Academic Council. Deans of Faculties and Chairmen of Departments are either elected by faculty members or nominated by higher authorities. Within faculties responsibility for different academic areas is frequently delegated to 'coordinators'.

Teacher Training

Primary school teachers *(normalistas)* are trained in six-year *escuelas normales*, which have the status of secondary level institutions.

Secondary school teachers follow four-year courses in the pedagogic universities (Universidad Pedagógica Nacional, Bogota, and Universidad Pedagógica y Tecnológica, Tunja), or in various of the other universities, where responsibility for *'carreras'* in education is usually shared between Faculties of Education, which provide the education courses, and other specialist faculties, which teach the content courses. Special courses in physical, industrial, musical and religious education are also available and there are a few university level courses in pre-school and primary education. (See later for sample syllabi.)

In-Service

In-service teacher training is not well developed. The directorate within the Ministry which is responsible for in-service training has made some progress, initially with curriculum development at primary level, and retraining primary teachers in pilot courses at *centros experimentales pilotos* (pilot experimental centres). A national system of in-service teacher training was created by Decree in 1980.

Non-Formal and Adult

Despite increased expenditure on national education, a large proportion of the population lacks access to formal education or fails to complete it. In 1981, it was estimated that 19.1% of the population was totally illiterate, and another 55% had not completed primary education. Neglect of rural zones is also marked. It is not surprising therefore that much interest has centred on various projects for distance education, and other forms of non-formal education. A National Literacy Campaign began in 1980.

Ministry Activities

Since 1961, the Ministry of Education, acting now through the *División de Educación No-formal y de Adultos* (Division of Non-formal and Adult Education) has provided non-formal education by means of *equipos de educación fundamental* (fundamental education teams), each including an expert on agriculuture, on 'home and health' and on 'workshops'. Of these there are at present 30 in different parts of the country, with a total of 92 instructors, and in 1977 they provided courses for 15,788 adults.

Within the Ministry, there is also a *División de Medios de Educación a Distancia* (Division of Resources for Distance Education. The role of this division is to coordinate all developments in distance education in all areas up to university level. It is also developing plans for a distance teaching in-service training programme for primary school teachers which will include printed materials, audio-cassettes, tape-slide presentations and radio - as soon as resources can be assembled. There will be centres for educational technology in which all resources will be brought together. In 1977 a national committee for *'teleducación'* was established to plan, study, and advise the Minister in this field.

INRAVISION-FCP

This organisation, INRAVISION - *Fondo de Capacitación Popular* depends principally on the Ministry of Communications, and dates from 1967 (when it was first established as a direct dependency of the Presidency). It provides primary and secondary education by means of specially devised radio and television programmes, supported by *'telecentros'*. Courses are approved by the Ministry of Education, and lead to qualifications at primary or secondary level which have equal recognition to those obtained in the formal system. Students who have so far enrolled total:

                Primary   (1967-78)   79,500
                Secondary (1973-78)   101,670

These programmes are intended to appeal to members of the population of all ages who for various reasons have not been able to complete their formal education, and provide a fairly traditional curriculum, although by modern media. The use of the programmes is principally by urban students (79.3% - as opposed to rural, 10.9%, and 'others' 9.8%). At present the INRAVISION-FCP programmes are transmitted for about four hours daily on Cadena (Channel) 3. In 1978, under the outgoing Presidential régime, INRAVISION-FCP proposed a substantial programme to the Inter-American Development Bank for the improvement and extension of their services on a country-wide basis at a total cost of US$38 million, but support has not been confirmed by the new administration.

Open University Project (Proyecto Universidad Abierta)

Since 1974, on the model of the British Open University and with funds provided by IADB, the ancient Catholic Javeriana University has offered a programme of improvement for primary school teachers, using a simple mixed-media system, comprising written materials, television programmes (transmitted by INRAVISION) and group sessions. So far it is not clear that these courses lead to significant recognition by the Ministry of Education. The Project now has its own building with library and TV studio, and is seeking to develop its resources and its activities. It was planned that in the course of the recent (1974-79) project some 10,000 teachers would be 'improved'.

SENA

The National apprenticeship training organisation is an important agency of non-formal education. It originated in 1957 with assistance from UNDP and ILO, and is now an autonomous administration under the general supervision of the Ministry of Labour and Social Security. Its national headquarters are in Bogota, but there are 18 regional administrations. SENA provides 65 training centres in all parts of the couuntry, classified as follows:

Industrial	18
Commercial	14
Agricultural	16
Services	5
Arts & Crafts	1
Tecnicos Medios	3
Mixed	8
Marine Fishery	1

It also offers 62 *programas moviles* (mobile training programmes). SENA has more than 7,000 employees of whom 4,250 are instructors. Its educational philosophy includes attention to physical, recreational and cultural aspects of training, as well as the purely technical. SENA's budget is provided by a 2% tax levied on the payroll of all private industry, and 0.5% on national enterprises. The budget for 1978 amounted to US$64,000,000 which provided training for 793,000 workers, as well as various research activities.

Popular Action for Culture (Acción Cultural Popular)

ACPO is a historic and unique Colombian organisation which functions somewhat outside the official system. It originated in 1947, from the enthusiasm of Father Jose Joaquin Salcedo to provide basic education to the rural population by means of radio. Now, over 30 years later, ACPO has developed into a sophisticated organisation with its own administrative hierarchy and four broadcasting stations *('Radio*

Sutatenza¹⁾ capable of reaching 14 million of the population. It has a comprehensive philosophy of *educación fundamental integral* (EFI) in which the *'campesino'* (the peasant) is encouraged to learn in order to understand and improve the conditions of his existence: its courses provide training in literacy, numeracy, health, agriculture, economics and rural development; they have also an overt ethical and religious component. ACPO emphasises the inter-dependence of the technical and the inter-personal in distance education, and the broadcasts are supplemented by specially written booklets and '*campesino* libraries' (all printed by ACPO's own publishing company), by radiophonic schools in all parts of the country, by a national newspaper (*'El Campesino'*), and by a correspondence service with national headquarters. Instructors for the radiophonic schools are trained at three special *institutos campesinos*, which also offer courses to those who come for training from other Latin-American countries.

In the year 1978 ACPO claimed to have provided the following services:

Radiophonic schools	26,300
Students enrolled	91,200
Booklets sold	332,846
Library books	488,000
Copies of 'El Campesino'	1,650,733
Instructors trained	1,125
Letters answered	34,512
Hours of broadcasts:	
Medium wave	6,779
Short wave	3,915

Revenue is derived from ACPO's own services of broadcasting and publishing, which are provided on a commercial basis to the community at large. It also receives support from international philanthropic and aid sources, though, curiously, not from the Catholic Church in Colombia. At the present time ACPO faces fundamental questions about its future, especially in relation to changing circumstances, and is carrying out a major self-evaluation in collaboration with Florida State University, over a period of $2\frac{1}{2}$ years (1977-80).

7 EDUCATIONAL ADMINISTRATION

Public and Private Education

The object of the Ministry of Education is to provide a unified national system under full public control. However, because of the increasing demand for education at all levels, and the shortage of funds in the public sector, it is accepted that for some time to come a considerable part of national education will have to be provided by private educational establishments. All educational establishments are required to be registered with the Ministry of Education, and the

Minister is responsible for ensuring that adequate facilities are provided, and that schools are conducted in accordance with national policy. Private schools are not allowed to increase their fees without permission of the Ministry. Private schools throughout Colombia are represented by an *Asociación de Colegio Privados de Colombia*. In 1978 the Association announced a plan for 15,000 scholarships, to be awarded in collaboration with various commercial organisations.

Ministry of Education

The Ministry of Education is given overall responsibility not only for education in all its aspects, but also sport (e.g. the Olympic Committee, etc.) and culture (although in recent years COLCULTURA has campaigned - so far in vain - for independent Ministry status). The functions of the Ministry of Education are defined by law as the following:

(i) to establish the criteria and standards for the development of further education throughout the nation's territories

(ii) to undertake, in conjunction with the *Departamento Nacional de Planeación* (Department of National Planning), the planning of the development of educational and cultural services

(iii) to coordinate the execution of educational programmes with other sectors of the government, and with the authorities of the departments, the *Distrito Especial* (Special District) of Bogota, other agencies, and municipalities

(iv) to promote the expansion and improvement of education, science, culture and sport at all levels, either directly or through cooperation with other official or private organisations

(v) to exercise inspection over education both formal and non-formal, and over all manifestations (displays, exhibitions, books and media) which influence the cultural and moral level of the people.

The Ministry's main practical work consists in planning, control and inspection. In principle the Ministry lays down and controls all school curricula and syllabi, which are uniform for both private and public sectors. The Ministry does not undertake production of textbooks, and pupils throughout the country have to obtain what is required by particular schools and colleges from commercial sources. Generally speaking, the Ministry does not prescribe specific texts in any area of the curriculum.

Reorganisation

The intention of the reorganisation was to provide a unified system under central control; many formerly independent institutes and foundations were brought under Ministry jurisdiction. The outline structure of the Ministry is now as follows:

> Minister of Education
> Vice-Minister
> Secretary General

plus three special *oficinas* (offices) for:

(i) *Planeación* (planning)

(ii) *Jurídica* (Legal)

(iii) *Relaciones Internacionales* (International Relations).

plus three principal *direcciones generales* (general directorates) for:

(i) *Administración e Inspección* (Administration and Inspection)

(ii) *Servicios Administrativos* (Administrative Services)

(iii) *Capacitación y Perfeccionamiento Docente, Currículo y Medios Educativos* (Teacher Training, Curriculum Development and Educational Resources).

This last directorate-generalis responsible for all teacher training (including in-service) and occupies the building of the former *Centro Nacional de Perfeccionamiento* (CENAPER) built with an international grant in the early 1970s. It has also begun the process of explaining the educational reform and eliciting public cooperation by means of its monthly educational bulletin EDUCAR.

Independent institutes now responsible to the Minister of Education include the following:

ICFES	*Instituto Colombiano para el Fomento de la Educación Superior* (Colombian Institute for the Encouragement of Higher Education)
ICETEX	*Instituto Colombiano de Estudios en el Exterior* (Colombian Institute for Studies Abroad)
COLDEPORTES	*Instituto Colombiano del Deporte* (Colombian Institute for Sport)
COLCULTURA	*Instituto Colombiano de Cultura* (Colombian Institute for Culture)
COLCIENCIAS	*Instituto Colombiano de Ciencias* (Colombian Institute for Science)
ICCE	*Instituto Colombiano de Construcciones Escolares* (Colombian Institute for School Buildings).

DIVISIONS OF THE MINISTRY OF EDUCATION

1 Directorate of Administration and Inspection

   (a)   Division of Basic Primary Education
   (b)   Division of Basic Secondary Education
   (c)   Division of Middle Vocational Education
   (d)   Division of Intermediate Professional Education
   (e)   Division of Diversified Middle Education - INEM
   (f)   Division of Pre-School and Special Education
   (g)   Division for Development of Cooperative Institutions
   (h)   Division for Non-Formal and Adult Education

2 Directorate of Administrative Services

   (a)   Personnel Division
   (b)   Finance Division
   (c)   Division for Coordination of FER

3 Directorate of Training Curriculum and Resources

   (a)   Division of syllabus Design in Formal Education
   (b)   Division of Syllabus Design in Non-Formal Education
   (c)   Division of Printed and Audiovisual Materials
   (d)   Division of Resources for Distance Education
   (e)   Division of Educational Documentation and Information
   (f)   Division of Pilot Experimental Centres
   (g)   Division for Evaluation of Pupil Progress.

STRUCTURE OF THE MINISTRY OF NATIONAL EDUCATION

```
OFFICE OF THE MINISTER
│
├── 13 DEPARTMENTS ADMINISTERING FER
│
├── SECRETARY GENERAL
│       ├── OFFICE OF INTERNATIONAL RELATIONS
│       │       └── DIRECTORATE OF TEACHER TRAINING Curriculum-Resources ── 7 Divisions
│       ├── LEGAL DEPARTMENT
│       │       └── DIRECTORATE OF ADMINISTRATIVE SERVICES ── 3 Divisions
│       └── PLANNING OFFICE
│               └── DIRECTORATE OF ADMINISTRATION & INSPECTION ── 8 Divisions
│
├── VICE-MINISTER
│
└── 13 SPECIALISED INSTITUTES
```

Regional Responsibilities

In practice the implementation and financing of ministerial tasks is decentralised.

Under Law 43 of 1975, responsibility for the administration of primary and secondary education passed to the departments, *intendencias, comisarias* and the *Distrito Especial de Bogota*. The highest authority in the administration of education in a department is the Secretary of Education. This is a political appointment made by the Governor of the department and the holder changes with the government. The administration of education in the department is divided into districts each one run by an Education Officer answerable directly to the Secretary of Education. Under him is a team of supervisors whose task it is to visit the schools and institutes within their jurisdiction to see that the academic programme is adhered to and deal with requests and complaints.

8 EDUCATIONAL FINANCE

Sources of Funds

The sources of finance for education are the central government, the departments and other regional authorities, the municipalities, and the users of the private sector. Each of the local authorities maintains a *Fondo Educativo Regional* (Regional Education Fund) for the financing of local education, to which the central government contributes some 20% while the remainder has to be raised from local taxes. By law 10% of the national budget must be allocated to education. In 1980 this was over 20% but reduced to 18.9% in 1981. The total national budget for 1979, according to the *Proyecto de Presupuesto 1979*, was approximately 199,542 million pesos. The general distribution of this was:

	%	%
General Services		23.4
Economic Services		29.0
Cultural & Social Services of which:		44.8
Education	14.9	
Health	16.8	
Cultural	0.6	
Urban & Rural Development	8.5	
Insurance	4.0	
Unclassifiable (debt service etc.)		2.8

No figures are available for the value of the very substantial contribution to national education made by those who pay fees for private education.

Education Budget

The total education budget for 1979 was a figure of 20,005,484,000 pesos (comparative value - 80 pesos = £1 sterling approximately). The disbursement of this by administrative sectors was as follows (in thousands of pesos):

Official expenditure (Ministry etc.)	5,404,319
Administration	45,229
Direccion General de Administracion	92,314
Direccion General de Capacitacion	84,661
Direccion General de Servicios	57,674
FER Basic	8,363,379
FER Nationalisation	1,926,996
FER Additional Shifts	226,032
FER National Establishments	2,321,541
FER Cooperative Colleges	164,297
INEM and ITA	744,739
FER Sepcial Contracted Services	494,386
FER Special Services, not contracted	39,125
Centros Experimentales Pilotos	9,795
National Establishments	31,000
	20,005,487

The allocation by 'educational programmes' was as follows (in thousands of pesos):

General Administration	884,569	4.4%
Primary and Pre-Primary	8,213,504	41.1%
Secondary	4,034,362	20.2%
Intermediate	1,576,432	7.9%
Professional (including university)	4,562,000	22.8%
Non-formal	474,130	2.4%
Culture, etc.	206,800	1.0%
Food, nutrition	30,000	0.1%
International conferences, etc.	23,690	0.1%
	20,005,487	100.0%

International Aid

According to the 1977 Annual Report of the United Nations Development Programme (Colombia), in 1977 Colombia received total grants and loans of capital assistance, in all sectors of US$645,000. In the same period total grants for technical cooperation programmes totalled: US$46,243,700. This was made up from various sources in the following proportions:

Bilateral programmes	47%
UN System (other than UNDP)	14%
Foundations & Institutions	30%
UNDP	6%
Other multilateral organisations	3%
	100%

In the technical cooperation sphere, funds for projects in the education sector received a total of 26.7% of the total, e.g. US$12,367,000. this can be compared with the figures for 1976 of 9% (US$4,216,000), although it is pointed out that figures for various sectors fluctuate considerably from year to year.

An outline of specific educational projects of technical cooperation is as follows:

Source	Purpose	Value US$
UNDP/UNESCO	Planning & Administration	80,570
OAS (Organisation of American States)	Educational Technology & Teacher Training	587,700
Austria	University Studies	106,517
Belgium	University Studies	506,692
Canada	Technical Training (SENA) Furniture & Fisheries Rural Development	4,760,000
France	Teaching of French Technical Education	360,920
Federal Republic of Germany	Teacher Training Adult Education	4,682,8925
Netherlands	Non-formal Education	634,544
Switzerland	University Studies	25,000
USAID	Rural Development	139,000
US Peace Corps	Various Projects	197,000
Ford Foundation	Welfare & Ecology	25,000

9 DEVELOPMENT AND PLANNING OF THE EUDCATION SYSTEM

History

In the colonial era education was a matter of private initiative. What development there was resulted chiefly from the activities of the Catholic Church; when the Jesuits were expelled from Spanish America in 1767 they left behind them 141 educational establishments in Colombia. Inevitably the main subjects of study at the more advanced levels were theology, philosophy and law. There are long-established universities in Colombia whose raison d'être is still the degree courses which they offer in these subjects. In 1844, after Independence, basic aspects of education were clarified, new methods introduced and many pedagogical, teaching and administrative principles were established. In 1868, a Directory of Public Education was set up in each state to govern education in the different sections of the country. In 1903 important reforms in education were introduced, dividing it into elementary, secondary, professional, industrial and artistic education. In 1950 an elementary education system was created which discriminated against the rural sector in that it assigned only two years of study to rural schools and five to urban schools. This system was in force until 1963, when elementary education was standardised to five years; pre-schooling was deemed to be advisable but not compulsory. The latest changes are manifested in the Education Reform of 1976 described above.

Constitutional and Legal Bases

The Colombian education system is based on several articles of the National Constitution. The main provisions may be summarised as follows:

(i) freedom of teaching is guaranteed, but the State has supreme authority to inspect and supervise public and private centres of learning

(ii) elementary education is compulsory and free in government schools

(iii) the President of the Republic as Head of State and supreme administrative authority is in charge of regulating, directing and inspecting national public education, but he may delegate this function to the Ministry of Education and the governors of the departments

(iv) each person is free to choose his profession or trade but the government has power to regulate and supervise professional practice.

In addition to these constitutional provisions, there are many laws, decrees and resolutions whereby the government regulates the details of Colombian education.

Development Plans

Most régimes in their turn have proposed development plans. At present the Plan still guiding efforts in the education sector is embodied in the document *'PARA CERRAR LA BRECHA': Plan de Desarrollo Social, Económico y Regional* (TO CLOSE THE GAP: Plan for Social, Economic and Regional Development) and this comprehensive development plan contains four principal sections:

- (i) Macroeconomic Policy
- (ii) Sectoral Policies: Agricultural
  Industrial
  Export
  Regional & Urban Development
- (iii) Social Programmes: Food and Nutrition
  Health and Sanitation
  Social Services in Marginal Zones
  Education
  Physical Infrastructure
- (iv) Finance.

The 'gap' which needs to be closed is defined as existing:

- (i) between the country and the city
- (ii) between the rich and the poor districts
- (iii) between those who have access to the services for health and education, and those who are illiterate and under-nourished.

The Plan firmly embodies the view that none of these problems can be solved without an integrated approach.

The section of the Plan devoted to education begins with some basic objectives:

- (i) to convert into a reality the constitutional provision that primary education should be both free and compulsory
- (ii) to obtain for the education sector a level of 25% of national budget
- (iii) to increase the proportion of the education budget devoted to primary education to 60% of the total
- (iv) to redefine and modernise secondary education, providing especially diversification and vocational orientation which will enable the educational system to meet the various needs of national development.

These are followed by a diagnosis which attempts to analyse the admitted weaknesses of the existing system, characterised by high drop-out rates and poor quality. The principal problems are frankly stated as:

- (i) social and economic inequalities
- (ii) lack of basic and applied research, especially in socio-educational and curricula matters
- (iii) lack of coordination between formal and non-formal

programmes of education

(iv)   low academic and professional quality of teaching personnel

(v)   lack of attention to pre-school (0-7 years) education

(vi)   unequal distribution of services between urban and rural zones

(vii) deficient and inaccessible statistical information.

A principal conclusion drawn from the diagnosis is the need to plan not only for quantitative, but qualitative, improvement within the system. This can be achieved in the following ways:

(i)   in-service training of serving teachers

(ii)   mass production and distribution of teaching materials

(iii) adequate use of educational technology

(iv)   utilisation of the mass media both for the training of teachers and for basic instruction

(v)   increased participation by the community in direction and execution of the educational system

(vi)   progressive increase in the allocations to education from the national budget

(vii) coordination of the efforts of the education sector with other government programmes, such as those for food and nutrition, and for integrated rural development.

The Plan then proposes, with a good deal of shrewd and relevant amplification, an integrated educational structure based on the following levels:

> pre-escolar
> básica primaria
> básica secundaria
> media vocacional
> intermedia profesional
> superior
> no-formal e informal

These proposals, as we have already seen, were given legal effect by Law No. 088 of 1976, and at the present time public authorities are still in the process of trying to give substantial reality to the admirable concepts of *'Para Cerrar La Brecha'*.

In 1980, emphasis was placed (in Decree 030) on the expansion and reform of higher education. Higher education was to be open to all but to be directed to the needs of society. New professional specialisms were to be developed together with post-graduate studies.

Current Trends

Generally speaking, Colombians, with a variety of objectives, place high hopes in education. In response to the pressures of public demand, many private organisations – duly approved by the Ministry of Education – continue to come into the 'market'. In the public sector the Ministry continues to endeavour to expand the provision, to adapt curricula to national needs, and to improve the qualify of education. It is generally recognised that there are substantial obstacles in the way of achieving the ideal, in particular the scarcity of finance and resources, and also the prevalence of 'conservative' attitudes on the part of many teachers, students and members of the public. However, there is much evidence to show that slowly but surely Colombia is making a determined effort to improve its education system and to make a reasonable education available to all its citizens. The motto adopted by COLCULTURA is not without its relevance in many other parts of the educational system:

'TENEMOS MUCHO QUE HACER Y ESTAMOS HACIÉNDOLO'
(We have much to do, and we are doing it)

APPENDIX

TEACHER TRAINING SYLLABI

Outline Programme in Modern Languages for a Four-Year Carrera leading to the Licenciado en Lenguas Modernas, University of Los Andes, Bogota, 1978 (major-English; minor-French)

Note: 1 Credit = approximately 1 hour weekly for a semester.

Compulsory Courses (English)

English I	6 credits
English II	6 credits
Pre-composition	3 credits
Pronunciation	3 credits
Composition	3 credits
Conversation I	3 credits
Communication I	3 credits
Communication II	3 credits
Communication III	3 credits
Communication IV	3 credits
History and Theory	3 credits

Compulsory Courses (French)

French I	6 credits
French II	6 credits
Conversation & Phonetics	3 credits
Grammar & Composition and Syntasis	3 credits
French Literature	3 credits

Other Compulsory Courses

Techniques and Research	4 credits
Methodology	3 credits
Methodology II	3 credits
Teaching Design & Evaluation	3 credits
Pre-practice	3 credits
Practical Teaching I	6 credits
Practical Teaching II	6 credits
General Psychology	3 credits
Psychology & Learning	3 credits
Structure of French I	3 credits
Structure of French II	3 credits
Mathematics	4 credits
Humanities	6 credits

Elective Courses (Language)

Historical & Cultural Aspects of England and the USA I	3 credits
II	3 credits
III	3 credits
IV	3 credits
Short Stories in English I	3 credits
Short Stories in English II	3 credits
English Novel I	3 credits
English Novel II	3 credits
Drama and Poetry	3 credits
Advanced English	3 credits

Other Elective Courses

Mathematics II
Statistics
German
Social Studies
Technique of Study
Oral Expression
Written Expression

Total Credits	English (major)	54
	French (minor)	25
	Other compulsory courses	50
	Electives	17
		245

Outline syllabus for a Four-Year Training Course for a Teacher of Physics at the Universidad Nacional (Faculty of Sciences)

I Semester

Basic Physics I	8 hours a week
Algebra & Differential equations	5 hours a week
Chemistry	4 hours a week
Chemistry Lab	3 hours a week
Teaching Grounds	3 hours a week

II Semester

Basic Physics II	8 hours a week
Calculus I	5 hours a week
General Psychology	4 hours a week
Matricos and Vectors	5 hours a week

III Semester

Physics I	5 hours a week
Calculus II	5 hours a week
Statistics	5 hours a week
Psychology and Training	3 hours a week

IV Semester

Physics II	5 hours a week
Physics Lab I	4 hours a week
Calculus III	5 hours a week
Vector Analysis	3 hours a week
Administrative & Organisational Education	3 hours a week

V Semester

Physics III	5 hours a week
Physics Lab II	4 hours a week
Differential Equations	5 hours a week
Special Teaching I	4 hours a week

VI Semester

Modern Physics	5 hours a week
Physics Lab III	4 hours a week
Lineal Algebra	3 hours a week
Scientific Methodology	3 hours a week
Teaching Practice I	4 hours a week

VII Semester

Mechanics I	5 hours a week
Physics History	3 hours a week
Practical Physics	4 hours a week
Teaching Practice II	5 hours a week

VIII Semester

Circuits	3 hours a week
Thermodynamics	3 hours a week
Seminar (programmes & textbooks)	3 hours a week
Teaching Practice III	6 hours a week

THE EDUCATIONAL PYRAMID OF COLOMBIA 1979

HIGHER EDUCATION: 274,893

SECONDARY EDUCATION:
- Grade XI: 225,494
- Grade X: 187,912
- Grade IX: 263,077
- Grade VIII: 319,450
- Grade VII: 432,197

PRIMARY EDUCATION:
- Grade VI: 469,780
- Grade V: 477,137
- Grade IV: 563,889
- Grade III: 780,770
- Grade II: 997,650
- Grade I: 1,518,162

PRE-SCHOOL EDUCATION: 147,113

COLOMBIA BASIC EDUCATIONAL STATISTICS
Population

1960	1970	1980
15,397,000	20,530,000	27,300,000

Enrolment Ratios

Primary = Enrolments as a percentage of the total population aged 6-10
Secondary = Enrolments as a percentage of the total population aged 11-16
Higher = Enrolments as a percentage of the total population aged 20-24

Year	Primary	Secondary	Higher
1970	103%	24%	4.7%
1979	128%	46%	10.2%

Schools, Pupils and Teachers 1970 and 1979

	Schools	Pupils	Teachers
Primary			
1970	27,094	3,286,052	86,005
1979	35,102	4,337,607	139,277
Secondary			
1970	–	750,055	43,695
1979	–	1,879,118	85,938

Pupil Teacher Ratio Primary Schools

1970	1975	1979
38	32	31

Students in Higher Education by Field of Study 1977

	No. of Students	% female
Education and Teacher Training	43,616	57
Humanities	2,933	49
Fine and Applied Arts	11,078	37
Law	27,437	38
Social and Behavioural Science	11,258	77
Commerce and Business	64,910	33
Natural Science	6,702	56
Medicine and related fields	23,321	52
Engineering	36,291	12
Agriculture	9,931	11

Basic Social and Economic Data

    Gross National Product Per Capita 1979 - US$1010
Average annual growth of per capita GNP 1960-79 - 3.0%
        Life expectancy 1979 - 63
Percentage of the labour force employed in:

    Agriculture
      1960   51%
      1979   27%

    Industry
      1960   19%
      1979   21%

    Services
      1960   30%
      1979   52%

Proportion of the National Budget Allocated to Education and Proportion of the Education Budget Allocated to Higher Education (in 000 pesos)

Year	National Budget	Allocation to Education	% of National Budget	Allocation to Higher Education	% of Education Budget	% of National Budget
1966	7,719,600	955,656	12.3	218,314	22.8	2.8
1967	8,132,200	1,056,928	12.9	255,379	24.2	3.1
1968	11,011,400	1,379,283	12.5	319,803	23.2	2.9
1969	14,664,000	1,865,953	12.7	433,362	23.2	2.9
1970	18,237,600	2,485,916	13.6	559,134	22.5	3.1
1971	23,598,000	3,301,928	14.0	787,136	23.8	3.3
1972	24,457,200	4,098,870	16.7	1,075,163	26.2	4.4
1973	31,471,800	5,551,631	17.6	1,293,493	23.3	4.1
1974	44,146,400	6,541,642	14.8	1,460,701	22.3	3.3
1975	53,080,900	8,561,080	16.1	2,626,579	23.7	3.8
1976	59,982,700	10,439,146	17.4	2,371,694	22.7	3.9
1977	74,739,400	14,524,124	19.0	3,332,234	22.9	4.4
1978	86,580,619	16,233,162	18.7	3,060,450	18.8	3.5
1979	108,256,514	21,373,566	19.7	4,739,240	22.1	4.3

Cuba

CONTENTS

1 Geography 700
2 Population 702
3 Society and Culture 702
4 History and Politics 704
5 The Economy 706
6 The Education System 709
7 Educational Administration 716
8 Educational Finance 716
9 Development and Planning of
  the Education System 717

Cuba is a typical Latin American country which, since 1959, has reorganised its political, economic and social system on socialist lines consistent with an Eastern European interpretation of Marxism–Leninism. Understanding of Cuba should be based on appreciation both of the Latin American context and the plans for socialist reconstruction.

The Latin American elements are reflected in economic, social and cultural structures. Cuba has an agricultural rural economy based on the production and partly the export of sugar, tobacco and various foodstuffs together with the mineral extraction of nickel. It has a level of national income which ranks it as a middle-income country with a GNP per capita which is about average for Latin America. The society is made up of a large rural population and is racially divided. The culture is firmly Hispanic.

The socialist reconstruction is reflected in a governmental system in which the Communist Party plays a crucial role in every official agency: in State control of the economy and attempts at comprehensive economy planning; in the role of ideology in creating a mass socialist consciousness; and in the importance of education and social services in priorities for social improvement.

The educational system has Latin American origins which have many contemporary survivals. The structure of six–

year elementary schooling, three-year general lower secondary education and three-year upper secondary schooling and then university studies is very similar to that of other Latin American countries (and contrasts with the Soviet system of a ten-year school beginning at the age of 7. The core of the curriculum of general education would be recognisable in other Latin American areas. The university retains elements of the Latin American model. Education reforms since 1959 - dividing secondary education into two cycles, adding technical and vocational institutions at upper secondary level and dividing university faculties into departments often related to new economic and social priorities - are very similar to those proposed or adopted in other Latin American countries.

There are specifically socialist elements of Cuban education which have been introduced since 1959 which can be comprehended more fully in relation to practices in Eastern Europe. Political/ideological education - both in the curriculum and through extra-school organisations - is modelled on Soviet practice. Similarly the Soviet concept of polytechnical education, interpreted to mean work study programmes at each level of education and a strong emphasis on science in the curriculum, has been introduced. Technical and vocational studies at upper secondary and higher educational levels which are related to State-decided economic manpower requirements are also reminiscent of Soviet practice at least in the thoroughness of their implementation.

Quantitatively, Cuba's educational development since 1959 has been very impressive. Universal elementary education was achieved by 1970 and universal lower secondary schooling was almost complete by 1980. Higher proportions of the age group than was common in Latin America were enrolled in higher levels of education. Much adult education was also achieved. These quantitative attainments were gained through the high priority given to education in Cuba's socialist policy and in the high proportion of natioanl income devoted to education.

The result of this expansion has been that Cuba in recent years has faced educational issues similar to those of many industrial countries with which her level of education provision is comparable. Enrolments at primary and, more recently, at lower secondary level, have been static. More concern has been given to improving quality - in teacher training, curriculum reform and in attempts to monitor and improve pupil performance. In some ways Cuba, though an economically under-developed country, has a mature educational system.

1 GEOGRAPHY

Cuba consists of the Isla de Cuba stretching 1,250 km east to west and varying in width between 31 and 191 km with a total area of 105,007 sq km. There is also the Isla de Pinos (2,300 sq km) and some 1600 islets and cays. Cuba is at the westerly end of the Greater Antilles chain

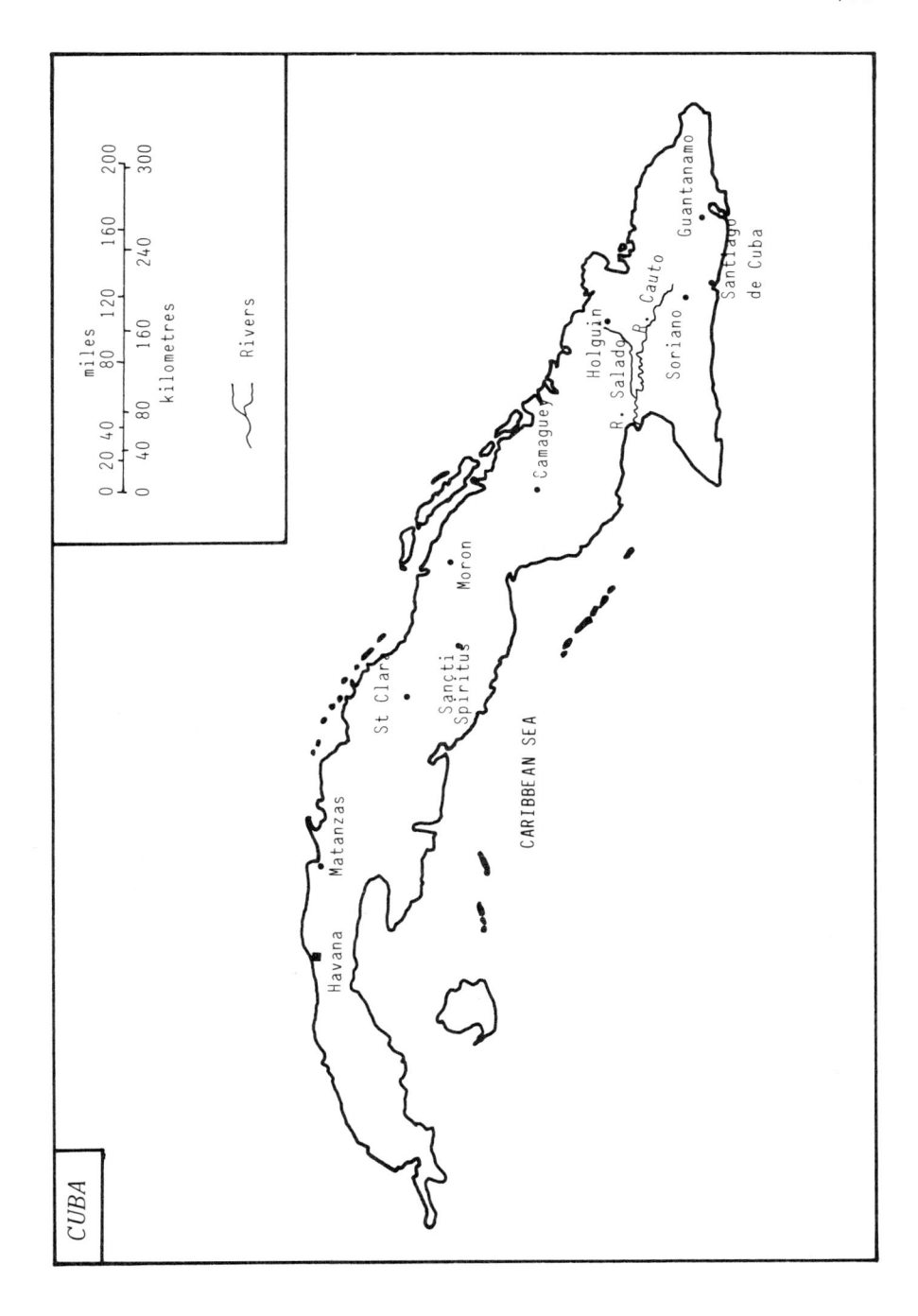

at the entrance to the Gulf of Mexico. Florida is 145 km to the north with Jamaica 140 km to the south, and Haiti 77 km to the south east and the Mexican Yucatan peninsula 210 km to the west.

Over half the Isla de Cuba is flat with gentle hills and wide fertile plains. The mountains of the Sierra Maestra in the south east contain the highest peak of the Caribbean - the Pico de Turquino (1,974 metres). The generally flat and undulating land allows for the production of crops, cattle ranching and tobacco.

Cuba's location just south of the Tropic of Cancer and its exposure to the trade winds gives her a pleasant, subtropical climate. The temperature varies between about 21°C and 27°C with a rainy season between May and October and a dry season between November and April. There are, however, frequent hurricanes.

The internal transportation system is well developed. In 1959, there were 10,104 km of road (5,896 metalled) which had grown to 29,543 km (12,427 metalled) by 1975. The Central Highway (1,145 km) is the backbone of the system and joins the principal towns and cities. There is a well developed system of State buses to carry passengers both in towns and in the countryside. There are 5,053 km of State, public service railways and over 9,000 km of industrial railways mainly serving the sugar mills. Internal air flights are scheduled between Havana, Varadero, Camaguey and Santiago de Cuba. External air services are provided by the Cuba National Airline, and those of the Soviet Union, Canada, Spain, Czechoslovakia, East Germany and Mexico.

2 POPULATION

The population in 1981 was 9,796,000. The rate of growth of population has slowed down from 2.0% per annum on average between 1960-70, to 1.4% between 1970-79 and 1.1% between 1979-80. The growth rate in the 1970s was lower than that of any other Latin American country, except Uruguay, and was little more than most of the industrial countries.

About 65% of the population was urban in 1980 - a proportion similar to those of Brazil, Mexico, Colombia and Peru though rater less than the percentage in Argentina and Chile. The major towns in 1979 were Havana (1,986,500 people), Santiago de Cuba (33,600), Camaguey (236,500), Holguin (164,800), Guantanamo (159,200), Santa Clara (154,200), Matanzas (100,600), Cienfuegos (93,000) and Bayamo (92,060). The overwhelming majority live on the Isla de Cuba with little more than 30,103 on the Isla de Pinos.

3 SOCIETY AND CULTURE

Any account of Cuban society and culture should consider the conditions prevailing before the revolution of 1959, the radical changes that occurred since then and the extent to which pre-revolutionary patterns still persist.

Pre-revolutionary Cuba was deeply divided on the bases of social class and race. There was a fairly high degree of linguistic and religious unity. Since 1959, government has attempted to reduce or remove social class and racial distinctions. There have been considerable achievements but some of the old divisions remain.

Before 1959 there were great social divisions between the mass of the population who were employed as labourers on sugar estates or cattle ranches or were peasant smallholders and the rich landowners and the urban elite. To some extent the acute social divisions corresponded to the racial distinctions of a society which consists of 37% European, 11% Negro and 51% mixed.

Since 1959 there has been a growth of the urban industrially based population - increasing from 22% of the labour force in 1960 to 31% in 1979. However, a high proportion of the population is still found in the countryside engaged in agricultural activities. Government policies have encouraged this, especially the Agrarian Reform Laws following the Revolution, which broke up some of the big estates and expanded peasant holdings as well as creating smallholder cooperatives. Substantial numbers of people are still engaged in unskilled work in sugar plantations which are now State-owned. Though economic growth has been higher since 1959 than in the whole of the period between 1900 and 1959 when real incomes were stagnant, there has not been much of a radical change in the material or occupational conditions of much of the population.

The main changes in the way of life of the rural population since 1959 have been in social services and social organisation. Free State health services have been widely provided and health provision is the best in Latin America. Over 90% of children are born in hospitals. Similarly educational provision has increased so that Cuba has the lowest rate of adult illiteracy and the highest level of participation in secondary education in Latin America.

Attempts to create a new socialist man have not been entirely successful, however, and many traditional attitudes associated with traditional rural society still persist. Equality, cooperation and self-reliance are the official aims of Cuban rural development. Some movement has occurred towards their realisation but there are still some traditional suspicion and hostility.

Cuba has had a rich cultural tradition. It was hispanic in origin and based on the unity given by a common language - Spanish - and common religion - Catholicism. Since 1959, Cuba has become officially an atheistic country but still a Catholic culture survives. The universal use of Spanish is also associated with the development of a particular Cuban development of the language, especially in vocabulary.

Cuban cultural achievements before the revolution in areas such as music were already considerable. Since 1959 there has been a great development - with government support - of the plastic arts, dance, the cinema and the theatre.

Conscious attempts to create a new culture have been accompanied by an artistic flowering seen in the development of art galleries and exhibitions and State theatre, ballet and cinema companies.

4 HISTORY AND POLITICS

Cuba became a Spanish possession on the visit of Christopher Columbus in 1492. Spanish rule was consolidated under the rule of Governor Diego Velazquez from 1511 when the three aboriginal Indian peoples – Siboneyes, Fainos, and Guarahatabeyes – were subdued. Spanish rule continued, except for a brief British occupation in 1762–63, until 1898. A plantation economy developed linked to Spain.

Opposition to control by metropolitan Spain developed in the nineteenth century especially from the locally born Spanish (crillos) and mixed peoples. Following sporadic outbursts of resistance, the 'Independence' or 'Ten Year War' broke out in 1868. Despite a nominal Spanish victory in 1897, resistance continued. In 1898 there was armed intervention from the USA on the behalf of the local resistance and in 1898 Spain formally relinquished sovereignty.

The USA considered Cuba to be of strategic interest and instead of handing over control to the Cubans, an American military government remained in power until 1902. A Cuban government under an elected President – Tomas Estrada Palma – assumed power in 1902. But American involvement continued. The Platt Amendment to the American Constitution authorised American military intervention in Cuba in the event of any threat to American security. This was accepted by the two countries by a treaty of 1903. Despite American assurances not to intervene in the internal affairs of the country, this did occur between 1906 and 1909 and between 1912 and 1917. Strong resentment in Cuba at American intervention led to the abrogation of the Platt Amendment in a treaty of 1934 but the USA retained a naval base at Guantanamo Bay.

In 1952, the elective presidency was undermined by a coup led by a former president Fulgencio Batista. He established a dictatorship and his period of rule from 1952–59 was marked by corruption and oppression. The economy was dominated by American interests and the rich Cuban upper classes.

Fidel Castro led an abortive attempt to take over an army barracks in Santiago in 1953 supported by students. On his release from exile on the Isla de Pinos, Castro from 1956 led revolutionary forces, with mass support, which overthrew the Batista in January 1959. Castro's government quickly introduced measures redistributing land from the large estates and nationalising large enterprises, many of which were American owned or funded.

The USA retaliated by banning the import of Cuban sugar in 1960, breaking diplomatic relations in 1961, and imposing a general embargo on trade and other relations. The American government also supported an abortive counter coup by

Cuban exiles in the USA which led to the Bay of Pigs fiasco of 1961.

Since then the Cuban government adopted a more thoroughly socialist programme and ideology. Close relations with the Soviet union and East European countries were fostered while Cuba supported revolutionary movements in other parts of Latin America as well as, in the 1970s, Africa. Relations with the USA continued to be very strained.

Government

Castro initially returned to the 1940 democratic Constitution which Batista had suppressed. Castro became Prime Minister. After the Bay of Pigs invasion, a Socialist Republic was proclaimed, and a one party state was established in 1961. This new form of government is regulated by the 1976 Constitution.

The Cuban government has a Party-Government-State structure. The head of the Party - Fidel Castro - is also President and Head of State. The parliamentary institution is the National Assembly of People's Power containing 481 deputies which is elected every five years. These deputies are elected from local Assemblies of People's Power which are chosen by popular suffrage. The National Assembly which is not in permanent session elects from its members a 31 member Council of State as a permanent standing body. On the recommendation of the President the National Assembly appoints a Council of Ministers which holds executive and administrative authority.

The Party, through the Assembly and the Council of State, exercises influence over the government headed by the Council of Ministers. There are also regional/provincial and municipal Assemblies exercising a similar function in relation to local and regional governments. Since 1976 there have been 14 provinces and 169 municipalities.

There are also a range of State enterprises controlled by government and supervised by the Party concerned with the nationalised areas of the economy.

Cuba's governmental structure is very similar to those of the countries of Eastern Europe. Government's influence extends very widely in Cuban life and alternative large private agencies do not exist. But the all pervading State system has the different elements of the party - the policy making and representative institution - and the government which has executive and administrative functions.

International Relations

Since 1961 Cuba's international relations have been dominated by unremitting hostility from the USA and close ties with the Soviet Union and Eastern European countries. American antipathy is expressed in an embargo at almost every level - diplomatic, economic and cultural - which has lasted since 1961. It was based initially on the nationalisation of American interests in Cuba in 1960 and the establishment of a socialist régime. When Cuba reacted to this by developing closer relations with the Soviet Union, including the placement of Soviet missiles on the island leading to the 1962 Cuban missile crisis, the hostility with the USA intensified. American antipathy is based on a long standing tradition that Cuba is an American sphere of influence and that no other major power should have political power in the Western hemisphere.

American hostility has been further reinforced by the Cuban policy of supporting revolutionary movements in Central and South America and the Caribbean. Since the mid-1970s Cuban troops have been sent to support radical political movements or governments in Africa - especially Angola and Ethiopia - which has also contributed to the lack of improvement of relations with the USA.

Since the early 1960s Cuba's relationship with the Soviet Union and Eastern European countries have been very close. The USSR is the major market for Cuban exports - especially sugar, tobacco and nickel. Cuba joined COMECON in 1972 which reinforced this economic dependence. Cuba has consistently supported the Soviet Union in world political issues.

Cuba's relationship with other Latin American and Caribbean countries is mixed. Right wing or military governments have been hostile and have not usually maintained any diplomatic contact - including the states of Central America, Argentina, Chile and Brazil. Cuba has given strong support to radical governments - as in Nicaragua or Grenada - while relationships with countries such as Colombia and Venezuela have varied between distant and cordial. Mexico on the other hand has consistently maintained relaxed relations with Cuba.

5 THE ECONOMY

Despite the introduction of a planned and State-controlled economy on the Eastern European model, Cuba's economic condition has many of the characteristics of a typical Third World country. In 1959, Cuba's economy was based on four primary products - sugar, tobacco, nickel, and beef cattle. Eighty per cent of foreign earnings came from sugar exports, mainly to the USA. Tobacco and nickel were also exported with little processing. There was single crop production in sugar and tobacco on large estates and inefficient cattle ranching. Since 1959 Cuba has remained a primarily export-orientated agricultural/mineral extraction economy. Sugar is still the major product - though exports are sent to Eastern Europe rather than the USA and sugar production has not expanded sufficiently nor have methods been sufficiently modernised to allow a transformation of the economy. Manufactured goods are still largely imported but from Eastern Europe.

Economic change has mainly been in the direction of diversifying agricultural production. Dairy cattle, poultry, citrus fruit and rice production have developed. Industry has also expanded, especially construction, but also mineral refining and consumer good production. But the export-orientated agricultural base of the Cuban economy has not been challenged.

Cuba's gross national product per capita – at US$1,410 in 1979 – was around the median for Latin America and Caribbean countries. There is neither the great poverty nor the movement towards a mass consumption society which typify the extremes of South America. Economic growth – at an average of 4% per capita per annum between 1960 and 1979 – has been higher than normal in the sub-continent but was not as great as that of, say, Colombia, Brazil or Mexico, and did not fulfill some of the hopes that were entertained for Cuba in the early 1960s.

Cuba's natural resources are considerable. The soil is fertile and the climate equable which aid the growing of tropical and sub-tropical agricultural products such as sugar, tobacco, citrus fruits, tropical fruits and coffee. In some areas, the grasslands are suitable for extensive stock breeding. Cuba has also important mineral reserves. The nickel reserves are the largest in the world while iron and cobalt also exist and there are some petroleum deposits. The natural wealth of the Caribbean and the many deep and sheltered bays of Cuba provide potential for a large fishing industry. The climate, the natural beauty of the island and the beaches could be the foundation for a considerable tourist industry.

These natural resources are either undeveloped or have been inefficiently exploited in the past. Sugar has been the major export and continues to be so. But efforts to increase production in the early 1970s – including drafting workers from other sectors – were unsuccessful. Cane cutting was unmechanised. Even in 1975 only 30% of sugar cane was cut mechanically. In the 1976-80 Five Year Plan great emphasis was placed on mechanising sugar production and improving plant selection, the use of fertilisers and on more irrigation. But despite plans to increase sugar production, Cuba's economic development was seen to depend on more than one crop, the world price and demand for which was unreliable.

The other major agricultural products in 1959 were tobacco and, for the internal market only, beef. Cattle ranges were very inefficient with low grade animals and disease. There have been attempts since then to diversify agricultural production. While beef production has not developed effectively, dairy and poultry produce – from farmers' cooperatives mainly – have been given greater emphasis. The aim has been to meet the internal market for a more protein rich diet. In these areas – as with citrus fruits and fishing – there was considerable development in the 1970s though still falling short of targets.

Agriculture – and especially sugar, was the leading priority of government in the 1960s. In the 1970s there was a shift of objectives towards industrialisation. The construction industry together with various light and consumer industries expanded in the 1960s and 1970s.

Construction was helped by the mechanisation of agriculture, industrial development and by the growth of public buildings - especially educational. Sugar industries grew in response to restriction of imports. These developments were similar to those of other middle income countries, though they were accentuated by the special conditions in Cuba.

There has also been a development of heavy industry. Partly this was associated with the development of nickel processing plants. But there was also a growth in the steel industry using local iron ore and nickel. Cuba has achieved a larger heavy industrial sector than is common in Latin America which was linked not only to the policies of government and to the local mineral resources, but also to the embargo on trade with North America and the distance from the main trading partners in Eastern Europe.

Cuba's external trade up to 1959 was overwhelmingly with the USA in terms of both imports and exports. After the American embargoes of the early 1960s, the Soviet Union became the dominant source of trade. There was a dependence particularly on fuel from the Soviet Union and massive balance of payments deficit with Eastern Europe accumulated. It was to reduce this deficit that the great emphasis was placed on increasing sugar production in the 1960s, since the other potential source of foreign exchange - nickel - required increased foreign technology for development. Though there has been no trade with the USA since 1961, commercial relations with other Western countries have continued. These contacts developed in the early 1970s when the world price and demand for sugar increased and the percentage of imports from the West increased from 17% to 41% in 1975. However, the fall in the price of sugar from 1976 reduced this trade dramatically and strengthened the economic dependence on Eastern Europe. Those relations were intensified by Cuba's membership of COMECON from 1972 and the provision of soft loans and credit by the Soviet Union.

Cuba in the 1960s was mainly an agricultural country relying on agricultural exports. The 1959 Revolution had not changed the basic economic structure. The main changes were that the large estates were nationalised, some land was redistributed to small farmers who began to work through cooperatives, there was some diversification and improvement of agricultural production and the main trading partner became the Soviet Union rather than the USA. But the pattern of traditional small farmer and large plantation production for a home market and export did not change. In the 1970s there was greater industrial development which was encouraged both by Cuba's siege economy and socialist planning. But further industry-based economic expansion is inhibited by the survival of a traditional agricultural sector and by the limited opportunities for markets and foreign technology which the American restrictions on trade have created.

6 THE EDUCATION SYSTEM

The Academic Year

The school year begins on 1 September and ends on 31 August. In elementary schools there are 40 weeks of classes broken down into four equal periods. In rural secondary schools the 40-week course is divided into two twenty-week semesters while in the urban secondary schools the 34-week course of two semesters (of 16 and 18 weeks) is supplemented by a period in which students carry out productive activities in rural areas.

The Structure of Education

There are two parallel education structures in Cuba. Regular education for children and young people takes place in pre-primary, elementary, basic secondary, upper secondary and higher education institutions. Adult education occurs in elementary, lower secondary and upper secondary level institutions and gives access to the regular system higher education facilities.

Compulsory education begins at the age of 6. It is preceded by Day Care Centres for children from birth to 4 years and by a one-year pre-primary grade in elementary schools. Elementary education has six grades for children of 6 years upwards. It is followed by a three-grade Basic Secondary school though pupils who have dropped out of elementary schools or are educationally retarded may attend two- or three-year polytechnical schools. Upper secondary level education occurs in three-year pre-university institutions, in four-year primary teacher training schools and two types of vocational institutions - three- or four-year polytechnical institutes and one- or two-year polytechnical schools. There is also a one-year polytechnical institute between upper secondary and higher education levels. Higher education occurs in University Centres and Higher Institutes.

Adult education has three levels - four-grade Worker Farmer schools at elementary level, four-grade Worker Farmer secondary schools and the six-grade Worker Farmer faculties covering upper secondary level education.

There are also special schools for the physically and mentally handicapped and extra-curricular education provided by a variety of State and mass organisations.

Pre-School Education

Day care centres, catering for children from the age of 45 days to 4 years, were set up in 1961 with two objectives. Firstly they were to help the early development and education of young children and secondly to enable more mothers to go to work or otherwise to take an active role in society.

By 1981 there were 832 day care centres with over 96,000 children. These constituted around 10% of the relevant age group so the institutions are still limited access and to some extent experimental institutions. However, the greater importance to be given to this sector was signalled by the decision in 1980 to transfer responsibility for day care centres from the Childhood Institute to the Ministry of Education. In 1981 also new curricula with a more formal institutional content were introduced so that their function was seen to prepare children for elementary schooling.

In addition to education of young children, the day care centres have parent education functions through lectures and parent committees to prepare parents to help their children more carefully.

Five-year olds are educated in the pre-school grade of elementary schools which are fully incorporated into primary education.

Elementary Education

The six-year elementary school is State controlled, coeducational and usually day-time, though there are some half-boarding schools in remote areas or for children with social difficulties. There are still some incomplete primary schools providing four grades in rural areas while in 1981 still only 27% of students had both morning and afternoon sessions in school.

Over 98% of children aged 6-12 have been in elementary schools since the mid-1970s though the actual enrolments have declined - with declining birth rates - since the late 1970s. total enrolment in elementary schools in 1981 was 1,592,000. The achievement of virtually universal primary education and the lack of pressure of expanding enrolments have meant that more attention has been given to improving the quality of primary education in recent years.

The primary school course is divided into two cycles covering Grades 1ო4 and 5-6. Since 1978 a system has been introduced whereby one teacher takes all subjects and moves up with the class until the end of the fourth Grade. The intention has been to reduce repetition and wastage and to improve the quality of preparation for upper primary education. Children are promoted automatically from Grades 1 to 2 but no child should enter Grade 3 unless he or she has reached an adequate standard, defined particularly as the ability to read and write. Thereafter, promotion through the grades is based on attainment and grade repetition occurs for those who do not reach the standard. This system is seen to be essential to improve the quality of education and its importance has been stressed by the President. However, promotion rates improved considerably in the early 1970s, and have been stabilised since 1975.

The curriculum aims of the first cycle are to provide a sound training in the mother tongue and mathematics, to develop the skills and habits necessary for independent work, to inculcate a love for study, to prepare pupils for learning the content of the curriculum of the second cycle. In the second cycle, there are separate syllabi for each

THE STRUCTURE OF THE EDUCATIONAL SYSTEM 1981

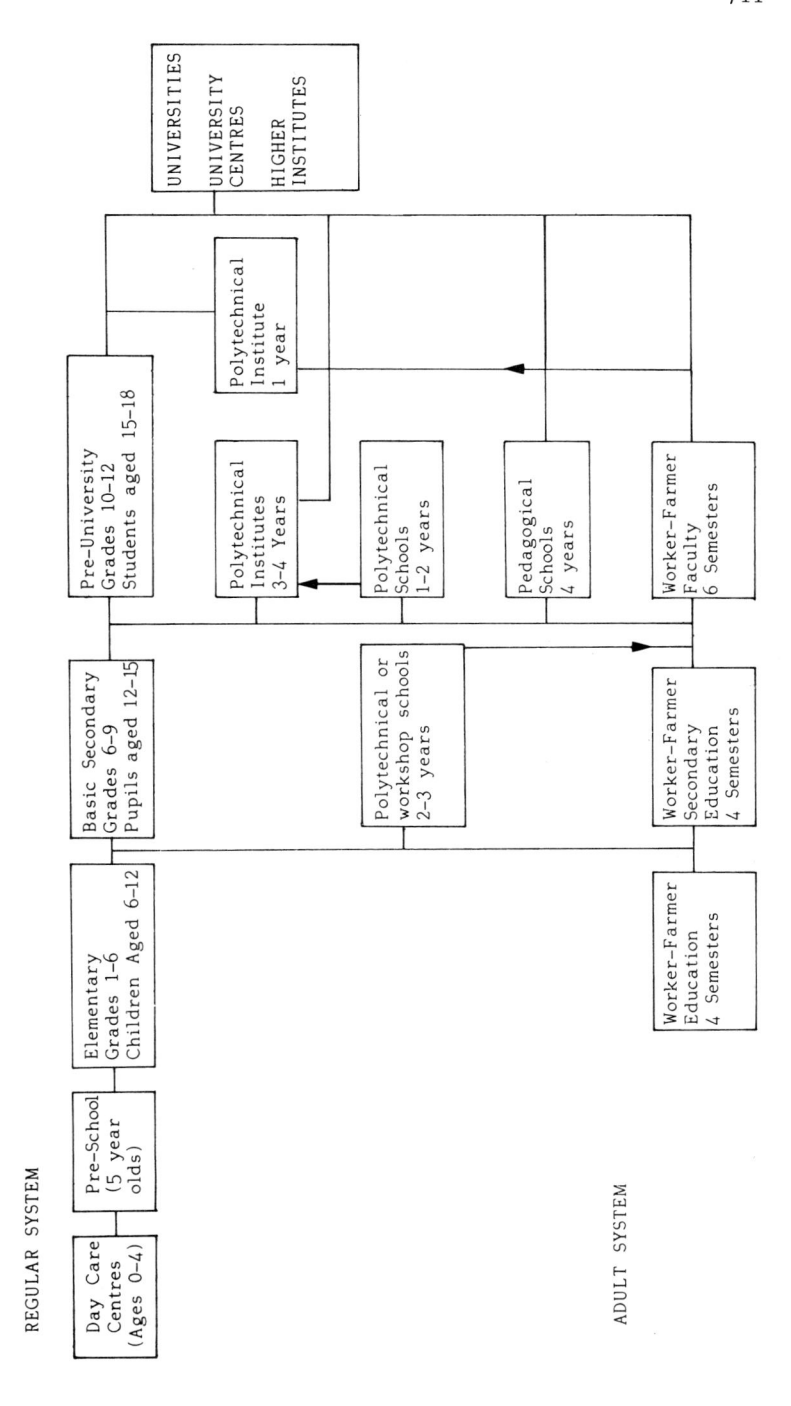

REGULAR SYSTEM

| Day Care Centres (Ages 0-4) | Pre-School (5 year olds) | Elementary Grades 1-6 Children Aged 6-12 | Basic Secondary Grades 6-9 Pupils aged 12-15 | Pre-University Grades 10-12 Students aged 15-18 | | UNIVERSITIES UNIVERSITY CENTRES HIGHER INSTITUTES |

- Polytechnical Institute 1 year
- Polytechnical Institutes 3-4 Years
- Polytechnical Schools 1-2 years
- Pedagogical Schools 4 years
- Polytechnical or workshop schools 2-3 years

ADULT SYSTEM

- Worker-Farmer Education 4 Semesters
- Worker-Farmer Secondary Education 4 Semesters
- Worker-Farmer Faculty 6 Semesters

subject. The main thrust of the primary school curriculum is similar to that prevailing traditionally in Western Europe which is consistent both with Cuba's Hispanic traditions and with more recent Eastern European influences.

Soviet influence is marked particularly in the place given to polytechnical and work study concepts. At elementary level this is expressed in the importance given to school gardens in which children are supposed to work in out of school hours during the whole school year. But it also receives expression in the label General Polytechnic and Labour Education which covers the whole period of schooling from the first to the twelfth grades and in the proportions decreed for each area of study during this period - that is 39.22% of time of science, 37.2% on humanities, 3.21% on aesthetic studies, 18.96% on workshop education and 1.29% on electives.

There are also out of school facilities for children of elementary school age. The José Martí Pioneers Organisation organises Pioneer Palaces in cities on the Soviet model for children up to the ninth grade and there are scientific-technical interest circles, often organised in the Pioneer Palaces giving vocational and professional guidance to elementary and secondary school pupils though in 1981 only about a third of pupils attended these courses.

Secondary Education

Three grades of basic secondary education are provided (7-9) followed by three of pre-university upper secondary school (Grades 10-12). There are also technical and vocational schools at upper secondary level - Workshop Schools of the Youth Movement which provide trade training as well as giving a general education to those aged 13-16 who dropped out of the elementary system or lagged behind in their work. Enrolments in these schools have been dropping in recent years as the proportion of the age group entering general secondary education has risen.

Entry to basic secondary education schooling, as with entry to upper secondary and higher education, is on the basis of passing tests taken at the end of the final grade of the preceding level. These tests are nationally controlled and administered by the Ministry of Education but the marks obtained are added to those achieved in regular internal tests. However, the overwhelming majority of sixth grade elementary pupils - about 97% - go on to lower secondary education. Overall 80% of 13-16 year olds were in school in 1981 though there were drop-outs particularly associated with early marriage in rural areas.

The great expansion of lower secondary education occurred in the mid-1970s following the earlier growth of primary education. Since 1980 enrolments have been static with 1,170,000 students in 1981. Given the obstacles to secondary education in traditional rural areas, lower secondary schooling is as near universal as is feasible.

The content, methods and organisation of lower secondary education do not differ greatly from upper elementary schooling. There is a distinction, however, between schools in towns and those in the countryside. The latter are often boarding schools and give a particular emphasis to work study programmes. Students (both lower and upper secondary) often supply the principal workforce for agricultural harvests – especially citrus fruits, tobacco and coffee. Urban lower and upper secondary school students spend 45 days each year on a 'school goes to the countryside' programme of agricultural work. Similarly the political and ideological training content of the curriculum - based on Marxism/Leninism - is stronger at lower and upper secondary levels of education.

Pre-university institutes provide general upper secondary education in Grades 10, 11 and 12. Entry is selective and based upon the student's academic record - both cumulative and in the ninth grade national tests and is an alternative to elementary school teacher training and other vocational and technical courses. About a third of all ninth grade leavers go on to pre-university institutes and most of the rest to the other types of institutions. Academic upper secondary education has not been allowed to achieve the numerical predominance in Cuba that it has in many other Latin American countries.

The curriculum of pre-university institutes is general and academic on the pattern of basic secondary education with the same additional work study, political education and cultural and physical education elements. Since 1981, however, technical-military training has been added to the curriculum of all senior secondary schools.

Vocational and Technical Education

The largest number of ninth grade leavers enter vocational and technical institutions. There are polytechnical schools which give a one- or two-year skilled worker training and polytechnical institutes which provide a four-year course to technician level. These latter institutions also give the full general education needed for entry to higher education institutions. There are also boarding vocational schools covering Grades 7-12 on the outskirts of provincial capitals to provide a general secondary education with a strong vocational bias for students who have obtained the highest marks in each province. In addition there are workshop schools at lower secondary level (see above) and one-year polytechnical institutes for pupils who have completed pre-university education.

Admission to vocational schools, as with pre-university institutes, occurs on the basis of the academic record of students in lower secondary education. Almost all Grade 9 leavers enter some form of general or vocational upper secondary education. Rather more students enter vocational courses than general courses and 48% of these vocational students in 1981 were women.

Adult Education

Adult education has had a central place in educational priorities since the 1959 revolution. A massive literacy scheme was launched in 1961 and this was followed by more formal and systematic adult education provision. The slogan has become 'Cuba is one giant school' and in 1981, one out of three inhabitants were in formal study programmes (one out of two if children under six are excluded).

Adult education institutions exist in parallel to the school system. There are Worker-Farmer education institutions providing elementary level education up to the sixth grade equivalent. These have four grades with each course lasting one semester of a school year. Between 1974-1980 this sector received priority under the slogan the 'Battle for the sixth grade'. This elementary provision is followed by Worker-Farmer secondary level in four grades equivalent to lower secondary education and preparing workers for entry to polytechnical institutes and schools. The priority from 1981-1986 is this level under the slogan the 'Battle for the ninth grade' where the intention is to raise the general educational attainment of the whole population to lower secondary level.

There is also the Worker-Farmer pre-university level in six grades which makes it possible for adults to enter higher education. There are in addition language schools providing foreign language courses for workers and special courses for cadres in political mass organisations and in marine fishing studies.

The curriculum of the Worker-Farmer institutes at all levels consists of almost 60% mathematics and natural science and over 40% humanities and social sciences.

There were 391,000 students in adult education courses in 1979-80 compared to 2,498,812 in equivalent elementary and general secondary (lower and higher) schools.

Teacher Education

The massive expansion of elementary school education in the 1960s and early 1970s was accomplished without trained or qualified teachers. Volunteers were used especially in remote areas. This brought problems of quality which have brought a great emphasis on pre-service and in-service teacher training. On the other hand most present-day senior educationists were volunteers in the 1960s and so there is considerable first hand experience of mass education among senior educationists.

There are two levels of teacher training. Elementary school teachers are prepared in upper secondary level teacher training schools. Students are selected after the ninth grade of basic secondary education and are given an education over four years which is equivalent to pre-university upper secondary courses together with pedagogical training. Day care centre teachers are also trained at these institutions.

Post-elementary teachers are trained in higher pedagogical

institutes which have four-year courses leading to a Licenciate degree. Students are selected from those who have completed Grade 12 of the Pre-university studies or equivalent levels in polytechnical institutes. There are three types of higher pedagogical institutes - those for teachers in general education, technical and vocational education and foreign languages.

There is considerable emphasis on in-service and upgrading teacher training courses organised by the Institute of Educational Improvement. From 1978 elementary and pre-school teachers could study part time for the Licenciate degrees in elementary education or pre-school pedagogy and psychology.

Higher Education

Higher education has expanded in the 1960s and 1970s in Cuba as in other Latin American countries. Universities were seen after the revolution of 1959 to have a key role in developing a new socialist man and in training the technical specialists need for rapid social and economic change.

Higher education before 1959 was dominated by the University of Havana, though there were other universities including some private institutions. The university was typically Latin American in its organisation into large traditional faculties, relative autonomy from government and the inclusion of students and teaching staff in university governing bodies. the universities were also centres of political opposition to régimes before 1959 including Castro's movement against Batista.

Universities were reorganised in a number of ways after 1959. The faculties were broken down into departments and schools from 1960 - on the American model adopted rather later in other Latin American countries. Many of the older smaller universities were closed down and university centres set up for each province - 39 in 1981. The number of students increased from 15,000 in 1959 to almost 200,000 in 1981. The demand for university education remained high and it had big priority in initial government plans.

Student selection was on the basis of Grade 12 academic achievement (including higher education entrance examinations) together with ideological/political records. Scholarships are provided for many students but courses (and student admissions) are related to more precise manpower requirements. The Soviet model of highly specialised technical courses has been adopted in preference to the older Latin American generalist tradition. Marxist/Leninist ideological courses and productive work activities are compulsory.

However, older traditions of relative university autonomy (despite government dictation of political, work study and manpower needs related courses and the abolition of life time staff tenure) have survived. Co-gobierno of students and teaching staff on the National Council of Universities survives.

The major change in recent years has been a shift towards

mature, adult and part time students. Students can enter from adult education institutions. In 1981 51% of all higher education students were studying part time whilst working including around 50,000 of the 200,000 students taking correspondence courses.

7 EDUCATIONAL ADMINISTRATION

The system of educational administration before the 1959 Revolution was highly centralised. Central agencies still retain considerable power but it has been modified by the establishment of Assemblies of People's Power since 1976 which have some influence at provincial and local level.

There are two central administrative institutions – the Ministry of Education and, since 1976, the Ministry of Higher Education responsible for all aspects of higher education. The Ministry of Education implements government educational policy. It works through provincial municipal education offices.

However, a 'double subordination' principle applies at provincial and municipal levels. The education offices are responsible to provincial and municipal popularly elected Assemblies of People's Power in administrative matters largely relating to the provision of education. They are responsible to the Ministry of Education in normative and methodological matters including general principles of education, teaching methods and curriculum content and the training of teachers.

There are specialised agencies under the aegis of the Ministry of Education responsible for particular sectors. The Permanent National Commission for the Revision of Curricula, Syllabi, and Textbooks of the Central Institute of Pedagogical Sciences convenes groups of scientists, pedagogics and teachers to draft syllabi which, after revision, are promulgated by the Ministry of Education. Similarly other national groups – including labour unions, the Party, and student unions – are consulted by the Ministry of Education on educational matters in broad terms.

National educational policy is formulated in national representative and executive institutions such as the National Assembly of People's Power, the Council of State and the Council of Ministers. The relationship between educational plans and those of other sectors is proposed in five-year national plans.

8 EDUCATIONAL FINANCE

Education is financed by central government. There is some foreign aid expressed particularly through the education of about 8,000 higher education students in Eastern Europe.

Cuba devotes a very high proportion of its national wealth to education. In 1976 over 32% of total government spending was deovted to education, in 1980 about 8% of the GNP. In 1978 4.7% of current educational expenditure was allocated to pre-primary education, 34.9% to primary, 37.7% to secondary and 12.1% to higher.

9 DEVELOPMENT AND PLANNING OF THE EDUCATION SYSTEM

The major change in the history of Cuban education came with the 1959 Revolution. However, since 1959 a number of changes in priorities can be discerned.

In the 1960s the major emphasis was on the expansion of mass education. This took two forms - there was a rapid growth of elementary schooling and the major development of elementary level adult education. The stress was on the mass of the population and particularly those groups especially in rural areas, adults and women who had hitherto had restricted access to education. In common with other policies, educational priorities focused on rural areas and on mass mobilisation.

There was less attention to quality as untrained teachers were recruited to maintain the impetus of the massive drive towards universal primary education. Educational standards were sacrificed to achieve rapid growth.

The provision of universal education was seen not only as an equalitarian movement based on the recognition of human rights. There was perceived also to be a need to create a mass socialist consciousness in a revolutionary society. Another element in the early changes, consistent with this intention, was the infusion of a strong ideological element in the content of education. Largely this was a socialist ethos based on Marxism/Leninism but there was also a strong view of a Cuban historical cultural heritage.

By the early 1970s, elementary education - both for children and adults - had become universal. The rate of expansion slowed down and stopped in line with the decline in population growth. Quantitative targets moved towards the achievement of universal lower secondary schooling. In the period 1981-85 as universal lower secondary schooling has been achieved so the emphasis has been seen to be on upper secondary schooling.

The main changes in educational trends since the mid-1970s have been qualitative rather than quantitative. There has been a stress on improving the quality of elementary teachers - seen in the emphasis on curriculum reform, improved in-service teacher training and an increase in the number of school inspectors. There has been an emphasis in policy documents on pupil attainments at primary level so that assessment procedures have been given careful attention and the system of grade promotions on the basis of pupil achievement has been intentionally retained.

This change is consistent with Soviet educational practice. Many other educational changes in the 1970s can be seen to have a Soviet origin and influence. The principle of polytechnical education - or work study - which is associated with the Soviet Union has permeated all levels of Cuban education. There is also an emphasis on highly technical courses at upper secondary and higher education level in line with State manpower requirements. Yet the Soviet influence does not mean that these changes are entirely foreign to Cuban tradition. Marxist/Leninist elements introduced in both the

Soviet Union and Cuba have been added to educational traditions which in both countries have a common continental European base.

These various changes and priorities can be seen in the list of objectives offered by the Cuban Ministry of Education in 1981:

(i) to strengthen the role of the school as a centre for the development of the multilateral and harmonious personality of children and young people

(ii) to constantly increase the quality of teaching and education

(iii) to continue the work to improve the efficiency of the National System of Education as to the achievement of optimum promotion rates and course retention

(iv) to raise the scientific and ideological preparation of the teaching staff

(v) to raise pre-school education to a qualitatively higher level and to extend its services considerably

(vi) to give specialised care to the greatest possible number of physically and mentally handicapped children and young people

(vii) to implement compulsory education up to the ninth grade

(viii) to pay more attention to the training of skilled workers and mid-level technicians to meet the present and future needs of domestic economy

(ix) to spare no effort to improve the quality and fulfilment of the curricula for higher education

(x) to raise the level of education of all workers. Having achieved the minimum sixth grade during the past five-year period, it is our aim to raise this level for all workers up to the ninth grade in the coming years.

CUBA BASIC EDUCATIONAL STATISTICS

Population

1970	1979
8,551,000	9,775,000

Enrolment Ratios

Primary = Enrolments as a proportion of the population aged 6-11
Secondary = Enrolments as a proportion of the population aged
    12-18 (1970) 12-17 (1979)
Higher = Enrolments as a proportion of the population aged 20-24

Year	Primary	Secondary	Higher
1970	121%	22%	3.7%
1979	112%	71%	19.2%

Schools, Teachers and Pupils

	Schools	Pupils	Teachers
Pre-School			
1970	–	134,258	4,037
1979	–	122,637	4,798
Elementary			
1970	15,190	1,530,376	56,555
1979	12,675	1,550,323	86,519
General Secondary			
1970	–	186,667	15,273
1979	–	825,852	61,930
Secondary (Technical & Vocational)			
1970	–	27,566	4,645
1979	–	214,615	16,163

	Students	Teachers
Secondary (Teacher Training)		
1970	21,008	–
1979		

Schools, Teachers & Pupils (contd.)

	Students	Teachers
Higher		
1970	–	–
1979	146,240*	10,736*
Adult		
1970	–	–
1979	391,990	24,201

*excluding correspondence courses (52,059 students)

Higher Education Students by Field of Study 1978

Education and Teacher Training	49,999
Humanities	3,298
Fine and Applied Arts	859
Law	3,320
Social and Behavioural Science	698
Commerce and Business	15,549
Mass Communication	1,572
Natural Science	4,846
Mathematics and Computer Science	1,352
Medicine and Related Fields	13,998
Engineering	8,528
Architecture and Town Planning	5,034
Trade, Craft and Industrial Programmes	9,020
Transport and Communications	1,938
Agriculture, Forestry and Fishing	13,003

Public Expenditure on Education

Year	As a % of Total Government Expenditure	As a % of GNP
1970	18.4%	4.2%
1976	32.4%	6.9%

Public Expenditure on Education by Level

Year	Pre-Primary	Primary	Secondary	Higher	Other
1974	3.3%	36.1%	37.4%	11.7%	11.6%
1978	4.7%	34.9%	37.7%	12.1%	10.7%

Basic Economic and Social Data

Gross National Product per capita 1979 - US$1,410
Average annual growth of GNP per capita 1960-1979 - 4.4%
Life expectancy 1979 - 72 years
Proportion of the labour force employed in:

           Agriculture
               1960   39%
               1979   24%

           Industry
               1960   22%
               1979   31%

           Services
               1960   39%
               1979   45%

Mexico

CONTENTS

1 Geography 724
2 Population 726
3 Society and Culture 726
4 History and Politics 727
5 The Economy 729
6 The Education System 734
7 Educational Administration 745
8 Educational Finance 746
9 Development and Planning of
   the Education System 747

Mexico experienced considerable economic growth in the 1970s, largely associated with the development of petroleum extraction though the growth of expenditure associated with this wealth overexpanded in the early 1980s and led to financial crisis. Mexican education also expanded during this boom especially at secondary and higher levels. Despite this quantitative growth, Mexican education still had structural distortions which inhibited its full orientation to new economic and social conditions.

The education system of Mexico has many similarities with those of other Latin American countries. The salient differences are that firstly several agencies play a major part in educational provision. There are both federal and State schools at each level, which can impair coordination, as well as a significant private sector. Secondly, while Mexico has attempted to diversify secondary schooling to provide more technical and vocational studies, like other Latin American countries, upper secondary schooling is to a large extent controlled by the autonomous universities which tends to reinforce its academic character. Thirdly, Mexico has a substantial Amerindian population. While the Mexican government has followed a policy of making Spanish language universally known and used and has given recognition to pre-colonial cultures, the achievement of universal education involves special cultural provision for Indian peoples.

Mexico has taken substantial steps towards the achievement of universal primary education, including special provision for disadvantaged groups. By 1980, the goal was in sight though economic difficulties have restrained the more ambitious projects. Secondary education expanded very considerably in the 1970s but still became available for less than half the relevant age group. The popular pressures for secondary schooling are likely to affect government education policies. Similarly, there has been a major growth in higher education in the 1970s, though again age participation rates have remained lower than in some other Latin American countries. The demand for higher education is also likely to grow and the institutional capacity of the old autonomous universities to absorb this and remain efficient will be further stretched.

1 GEOGRAPHY

Topography

Mexico lies between latitudes 16°N and 32°N and longitude 95° and 117°W. It is the third largest country in Latin America with a land area of 1,972,500 sq km (760,000 square miles). It is bounded to the north by a frontier of nearly 3,200 km (2,000 miles) with the United States of America, and to the south by frontiers with Guatemala and Belize. Mexico has 9,600 km (6,000 miles) of coastline on the Caribbean, the Gulf of Mexico and the Pacific.

A cross-section across Mexico would reveal two narrow low lying coastal plains, each with a high mountain range on its landward side. Between these ranges, the western and eastern Sierra Madre, there is a plateau at a height of between 1,500 and 2,400 metres (5,000 to 8,000 feet) which accounts for most of the total surface area. The country in general is rugged and apart from the tropical south the prevailing impression is one of aridity - 70% of the land surface is classed as arid or semi-arid.

Climate

Given the great variations in altitude it is not surprising that Mexico contains a wide variety of climatic conditions. Much of the north and west of the country is desert with little rainfall but in the central plateau on which Mexico City is situated the year is divided into a wet season lasting roughly from June until September and a dry season for the remaining months. At night the temperature seldom rises above 13°C (53°F) even in summer, and in winter there can be sharp frosts. The lowlands are hot and wet with an average temperature of 18°C (64°F).

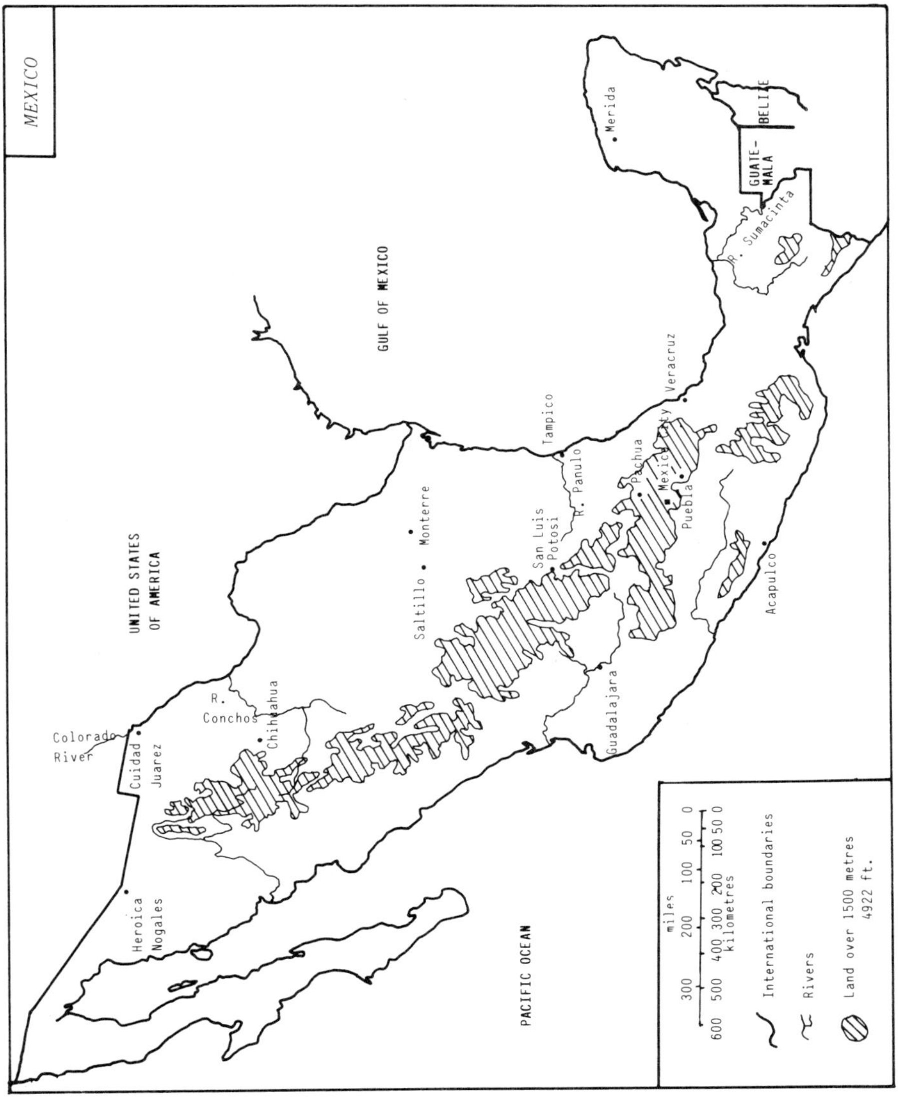
MEXICO
UNITED STATES OF AMERICA
GULF OF MEXICO
PACIFIC OCEAN
GUATE-MALA
BELIZE
Merida
R. Sumacinta
Veracruz
Tampico
R. Panulo
Pachua
Mexico City
Puebla
San Luis Potosi
Monterre
Saltillo
Acapulco
Guadalajara
R. Conchos
Chihuahua
Colorado River
Cuidad Juarez
Heroica Nogales
miles
300 200 100 50 0
600 500 400 300 200 100 50 0
kilometres
International boundaries
Rivers
Land over 1500 metres 4922 ft.

Communications

Land communications are improving rapidly. The road network (approximately 160,000 km - including three sections of the Pan-American Highway) connects all the main towns and road transport accounts for about 70% of all public passenger traffic and 60% of freighter traffic. About 40% of the road network is paved. However, substantial areas of the country are still unapproachable or difficult to approach by road and the terrain encourages air transport. Good services connect all towns of any size. A World Bank loan of £25 million has assisted airport development and there are now nearly 900 airports and landing fields, including 42 international airports. By contrast Mexico's 24,700 km rail system has grown little in recent years and has increasingly relied on government subsidies; uneconomic railway lines have been replaced by highways. Mexico has 36 ports handling about 30 million tons of cargo a year of which the largest are Veracruz, Tampico and Acapulco. The government has set up a port coordination commission to help modernise the ports.

2 POPULATION

Distribution

The urban population has grown from 30% of the total in 1940 to 67% in 1980. The largest cities - Mexico City, Guadalajara and Monterrey - are expanding at a rate of about 10% per year.

The drift of population to the towns is caused by the population explosion, a shortage of cultivable land and the hope of a higher standard of living. The population of Mexico City and its suburbs is now about 13.9 million while Guadalajara has an estimated population of 1.7 million and Monterrey 1.2 million.

Groups

Most Mexicans are of mixed Indian/European descent *(mestizos)*. Fifty-five per cent are in this category compared to 15% European and 29% Indian. Only 10%, however, use Indian languages.

The proportion of unassimilated Indians is declining. Indians generally tend to be among the poorest sections of society.

3 SOCIETY AND CULTURE

Social Patterns

Mexico is the home of machismo - the philosophy of the male ranging freely. Its counterpart - the family group consisting only of a mother and children - is common. However, marriage is much more stable in the middle classes, where family relationships are closer to the standard Western model, but the man still has far greater dominance and independence than in Britain. Mexico is characteristic of male dominated societies in that violence can erupt and guns are commonly carried. As one would expect the older generation of women generally lead circumscribed lives. This is changing, however; the number of women in employment is increasing rapidly and the younger Mexican woman is distinctly more emancipated than her mother, although her horizons are still limited by European standards.

One can discern a movement away from the old system of personal and family loyalties towards a system of institutional loyalties, but the senior Mexican still tends to have his own group of personal followers. Family ties stretch to considerably remoter degrees of kinship than in Britain. Mexicans have a courtesy, helpfulness and hospitality which astonish the British visitor but this is very real concern with personal relationships where the family is concerned or where there is a degree of personal self-interest is counterbalanced by some degree of indifference to general welfare. Duty towards one's neighbour in the Biblical sense does not generally exist in Mexico.

Religion

Mexico is a predominantly Catholic country (96% of the population are nominally Roman Catholic) and the bulk of the ordinary people have an ingrained Catholic attitude to life, even though it may often be overlaid by paganism, both ancient and modern. A century of bitter struggle between Church and State, culminating in severe persecutions during the early 1930s, stripped the Church of most of its temporal power. Religious education in schools is forbidden by law (though the ban is ignored in many private schools), and the wearing of vestments in public is prohibited. Nevertheless, the Catholic Church is not without influence, which it exerts mainly as a right wing political force. But the Church has no control over and little influence upon the shape of education.

Language

Spanish is the official language and official policy is to achieve universal knowledge of the language. About 15% do not have fluency in Spanish. The Indian languages spoken include Nahuatl, Otomi, Maya, Zapoteca, and Tarasea.

4 HISTORY AND POLITICS

Historical Development

Mexican history reaches back many thousands of years to the first of the major civilisations, the Olmec, which developed in the area of the Isthmus of Tehuantepec about

3500 BC. The Maya civilisation followed, mainly centred in the Yucatan Peninsula, and reached its peak in about 400 AD. Later civilisations emerged from the central area of the country known as the Valley of Mexico and these in their turn were displaced by the highly militant warrior culture of the Aztecs (or Mexica) who gave the country its name. But even at its highest point in the late fifteenth century the Aztec Empire only covered a small part of what is now Mexico. In 1519 the Aztec Empire was conquered by a small Spanish expeditionary force under Hernan Cortés and the Spaniards rapidly overran the surrounding areas. The conquered territory became the Kingdom of New Spain.

After 300 years of Spanish rule the Mexicans began their struggle for independence in 1810 and completed it in 1821 after a long guerilla campaign. The rest of the nineteenth century was unhappy, characterised by military coups and foreign intervention (like the ill-fated Hapsburg Empire of 1860 to 1867). It also saw the loss of half the national territory to the USA. A long period of dictatorship ended in the ferocious revolutionary war of 1910-1917, and the promulgation of the 1917 Constitution by which the country is still governed. However, modern Mexico really dates from the nationalisation of petroleum in 1938, and the industrial expansion of the following years under President General Manuel Avila Camacho. Since then in contrast to other Latin American countries Mexico has enjoyed a continuous period of stable government. This has been marked by a resurgence of interest and pride in the great Indian heritage of pre-colonial times.

Political Organisation

The written constitution of Mexico is very similar to that of the United States of America. Constitutionally the United Mexican States is a federal republic consisting of 31 states and the federal District of Mexico City. The executive is led by the President who is elected for six years and who appoints the cabinet. The legislature or National Congress consists of two houses - the Senate (with 64 members elected for six years - two from each state and the Federal District) and the Chamber of Deputies (with 245 members elected for 3 years). Each state has its own constitution, governor (elected for six years) and chamber of deputies.

However, the need to fight against foreign economic and political influence and against political instability has resulted in the emergence of a highly centralised State. Since 1927 the country has been governed by what is virtually a one-party system. Such opposition parties as exist never gain enough votes to constitute any threat to the PRI - the Institutional Revolutionary Party. Nevertheless the system does allow sufficient divergence of views to avoid the periodic resurgences of authoritarianism which have scarred almost all other Latin American republics. In practice the President can be an autocrat through there are two major checks upon his power. The more important of these is that he may not be re-elected, and so a presidential change must come about every six years. The second is the independence of the Supreme Court, which frequently nullifies executive acts which have been found to be unconstitutional. By Latin American standards Mexico's army is small and politically weak. In the general elections of July 1976, the PRI candidate, José López Portillo, a former Secretary of Finance, was elected President with about 95% of the votes cast. He took office in December 1976 replacing President Luis Echeverria (1970-1976) for a six year term.

International Relations

Political relations with neighbouring states are generally good. However, there are considerable underlying tensions between Mexico and the USA, the giant shadow on its northern border. The large economic influence of the USA is resented and so is its cultural and political influence. Seventy-five per cent of Mexico's export trade and 65% of her import trade is with the USA and 80% of all foreign investment in Mexico is American. In 1975 the Mexican government signed trade and cooperation agreements with the EEC and the CMEA (Council for Mutual Economyc Assistance) in an effort to reduce its economic dependence on the USA.

On the southern border relations between Mexico and Guatemala parallel to some extent those between Mexico and the USA. Belize periodically presents a problem; Guatemala and Mexico both have territorial claims, which are kept in abeyance while Belize continues to be a British colony but which will raise problems when it becomes independent. Mexico has no foreign military bases on its territory and is not a member of any military alliance. Unlike other Latin American countries, it has not followed the American line upon Cuba, with which it has maintained unbroken relations. Mexico also has diplomatic relations with China, and in general Presdident Echeverria pursued a policy of strengthening links with countries of all political persuasions, especially Third World countries.

5 THE ECONOMY

Economic Situation

Mexico has diversified her economy from an agricultural base to develop industrial enterprises. The major area of economic growth in the late 1970s and early 1980s was petroleum extraction and associated petro-chemical industries. By 1980 Mexico had become the fourth largest petroleum producer in the world. Other areas of growth in the 1970s included fishing. However, the rate of economic growth – averaging 2.7% per annum – between 1960 and 1979, slowed down in the later 1970s.

The slowing of economic growth together with a deteriorating trade position meant that the public foreign debt increased leading to a major crisis in 1982 which in turn produced a series of economic austerity measures.

Agriculture

Agriculture now accounts for only 15% of GNP although it is still the most important sector of the economy employing about 39% of the active population. Only about 15% of the total land surface is cultivable and Mexican agriculture is almost wholly dependent upon irrigation in which the country has made substantial investment. By 1971 there were 3 million hectares of irrigated land. Average yields are low and any increase in production should come from new irrigation. The main crops are sugar, coffee, maize, beans, wheat and rice. These crops – especially cotton and coffee – represent about 38% of Mexico's exports. the beef cattle industry is also important. A National Farm Plan (1975-80) was launched with the aim of increasing the production of basic foodstuffs.

About half the agricultural land is worked in small private holdings while the rest belongs to the State which grants right of land to the peasant communities. A major problem is the inefficiency of the small holdings, of which 50% farm below subsistence level and 30% at subsistence level. In 1974 a programme of collectivisation of smallholdings began in an effort to increase productivity and improve rural living conditions. In the same year 18% of the total budget was set aside for agricultural and allied purposes. However, the government will not allow the re-emergence of large holdings, and the acreage of irrigated land allowed to one farmer is limited.

Fisheries

There are extensive though largely neglected fishery resources. However, about 3,600 million pesos were invested in the industry between 1971 and 1976 resulting in an increase in the catch of 197,000 tons (total 451,000 tons).

Natural Resources

Although only 10% of the country has been surveyed Mexico is one of the world's principal producers of silver and sulphur and also produces copper, zinc, lead and manganese. Large deposits of phosphorus and uranium have been discovered and there are large undeveloped coal reserves. Investment in mining was poor but in 1973 its value rose by 25% with the rise in world prices. Minerals account for 14% of the country's total export trade and mining produces about 1.5% of GNP.

Mexico was the first country to nationalise its hydrocarbon reserves. *Petroleos Mexicano* (PEMEX) is the decentralised government agency responsible for the exploitation and sale of oil, petroleum products and natural gas. Mexico became self-sufficient in oil in 1974 and by mid-1865 estimated reserves were 13,581 million barrels. Production reached one million barrels per day at the end of 1976 and at that time oil exports stood at about 200,000 barrels per day, having doubled since 1974.

Petroleum production (and estimates of reserves) expanded dramatically in the late 1970s. In 1979 output reached 1.6 million barrels a day.

Industry

There has been a very rapid industrialisation over the past 40 years and the expansion was approximately 9% per year for the last decade. Between 1960 and 1970 electric power capacity increased by 140% and sulphuric acid consumption by 350%. Mexico is now self-sufficient in most consumer goods, semi-manufactuered products and some capital goods, for example, boilers, transformers and railway rolling stock. Manufactured exports trebled between 1970 and 1974 and now account for about 42% of all exports. The government grants certain benefits to new industries and encourages decentralisation. There is considerable government investment in industry and in December 1976 a US$5,000 million industrial investment plan was announced covering petrochemicals, capital goods industries, vegetable oils, and the motor industry. The steel industry is expanding rapidly and in 1976 investment stood at US$1,600 million. The government also encourages more investment in the tourism industry (which accounted for 40% of foreign exchange earnings in 1974), through the National Trust for Tourism Development.

Incomes

The per capita annual income in 1979 was US$1,640, putting Mexico near the head of the league of developing countries. However, this average figure conceals a very uneven distribution of income. There is still a large economically marginal population - roughly 25% of the total - and the absolute size of this group seems to be diminishing a little. Amongst the wage-earning population agricultural workers are impoverished, whereas industrial workers, although they may not aspire to European standards, manage to maintain a better standard of life. At the other end of the spectrum, the upper middle classes are wealthier than their European counterparts, as are academics.

Employment

Unemployment and under-employment are serious and increasing problems. In the decade 1960-70, the total population rose by 39% but the number of employed by only 14%. The education system is reacting to this situation by an emphasis upon trade, agricultural and fisheries schools. There is also increasing concern about the shortage of middle-level manpower.

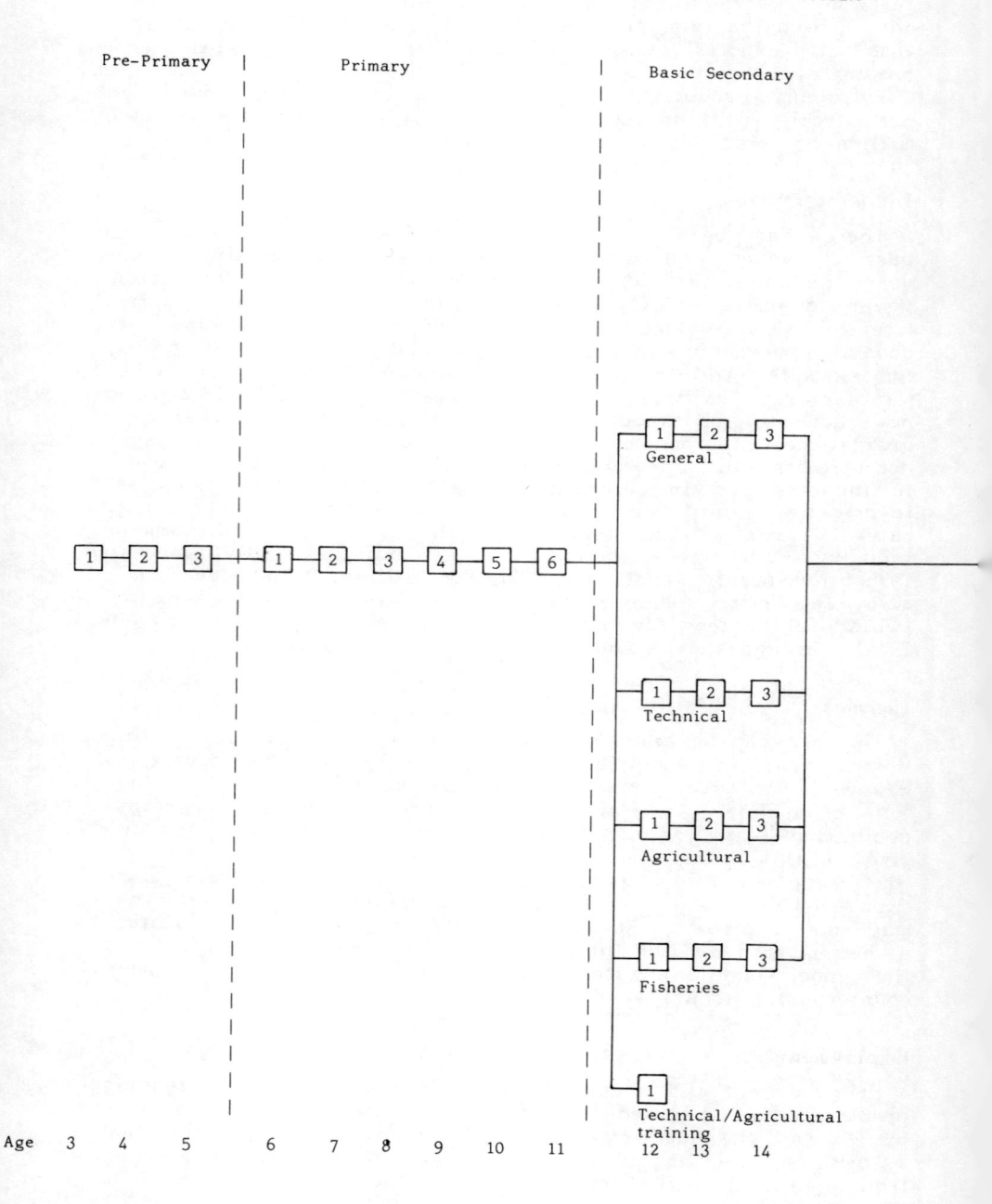

THE EDUCATION SYSTEM

Pre-Primary | Primary | Basic Secondary

General: 1 — 2 — 3
Primary: 1 — 2 — 3 — 4 — 5 — 6
Pre-Primary: 1 — 2 — 3
Technical: 1 — 2 — 3
Agricultural: 1 — 2 — 3
Fisheries: 1 — 2 — 3
Technical/Agricultural training: 1

Age 3 4 5   6 7 8 9 10 11   12 13 14

OF MEXICO

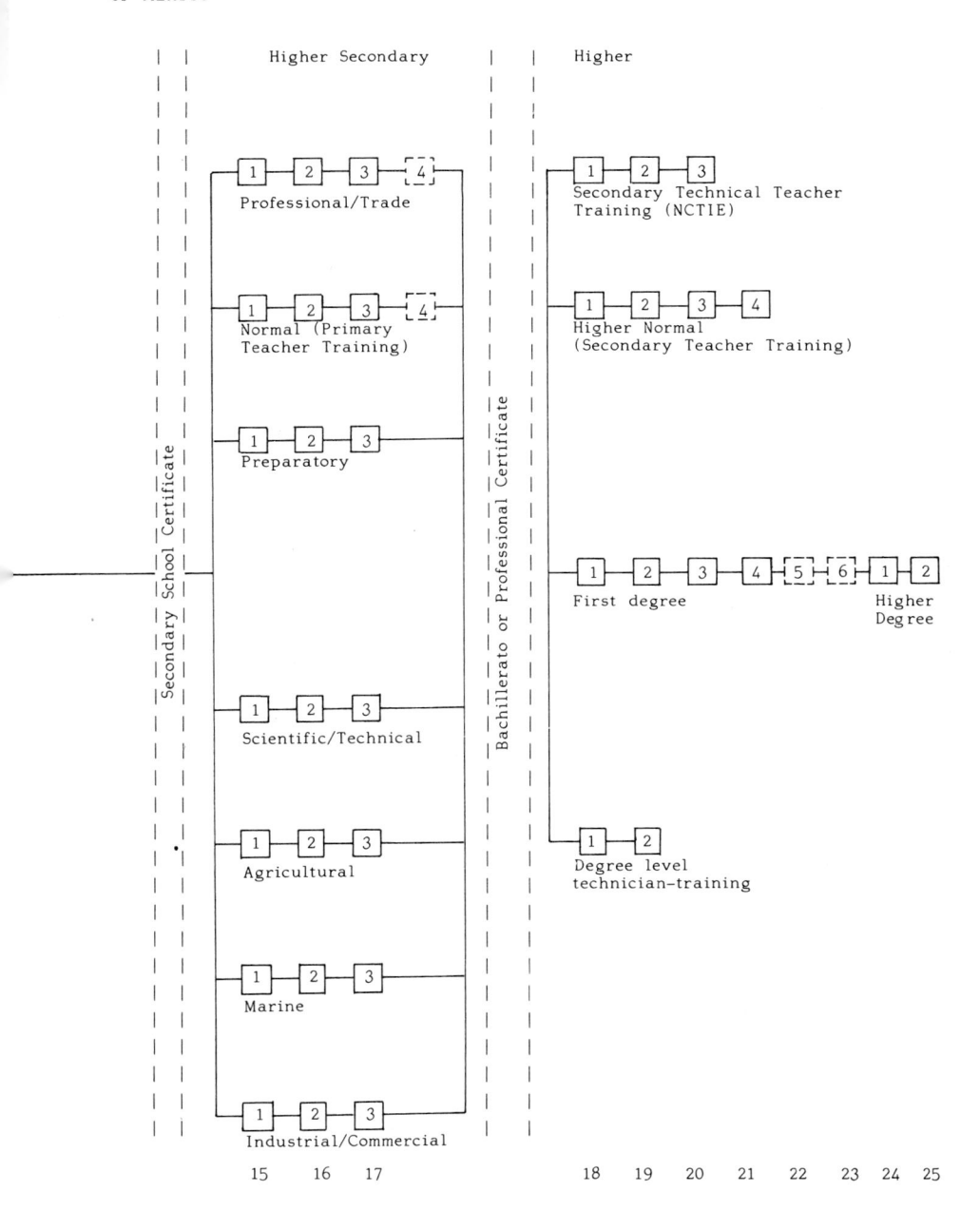

Higher Secondary

Professional/Trade: 1 — 2 — 3 — [4]

Normal (Primary Teacher Training): 1 — 2 — 3 — [4]

Preparatory: 1 — 2 — 3

Scientific/Technical: 1 — 2 — 3

Agricultural: 1 — 2 — 3

Marine: 1 — 2 — 3

Industrial/Commercial: 1 — 2 — 3

Higher

Secondary Technical Teacher Training (NCTIE): 1 — 2 — 3

Higher Normal (Secondary Teacher Training): 1 — 2 — 3 — 4

First degree: 1 — 2 — 3 — 4 — [5] — [6]   Higher Degree: 1 — 2

Degree level technician-training: 1 — 2

Secondary School Certificate

Bachillerato or Professional Certificate

15 16 17   18 19 20 21 22 23 24 25

6 THE EDUCATION SYSTEM

The Federal Education Law of 1973 decrees that the national system of education should consist of three levels: elementary, secondary and higher.

Academic Year

For all levels the academic year begins in September and ends in June/July. In the schools the year is divided into three terms with vacations in December and April; at higher levels the session is divided into two semesters with a break of about two weeks at the end of January for mid-year evaluation and examinations.

Elementary

Pre-primary education is voluntary and is provided for children from 0-4 years old. Schools are run by the Ministry of Education, the Ministry of Public Health and Welfare, the Mexican Social Security Institute, other Ministries and private institutions but the Ministry of Education is responsible for the provision of pedagogical advice. In 1979 there were 9,152 schools with 836,316 pupils. The majority of schools were controlled by the Federal government.

The proportion of the age group in pre-primary education increased considerably in the late 1970s and early 1980s. In 1976/77 15.3% of children aged 5 received pre-primary education. In 1980/81 this figure had increased to 35%.

Primary

Education is compulsory according to the Constitution for children between the ages of 6 and 14. The primary course lasts six years though there are pupils who stay longer. Some children over 10 years take an intensive three-year course in special centres. Primary is provided by both public and private agencies. Government primary schools are run either by the federal government or state governments. In 1979/80 there were almost 10 million pupils in federal primary schools (including government schools in Mexico City), 3.3 million in state and autonomous government schools and 0.7 million in private schools.

The curriculum, which went into operation in September 1969, is uniform throughout the country both for State and private schools; the language of instruction is Spanish. The aim is to relate school activities to life in the home and in the world outside, and to promote the study of the environment, an understanding of social life, skill in practical activities, etc.

There are nine areas of learning: Spanish; mathematics; natural sciences; social studies; art education; physical education; technological education; health education; and regional education (in specific areas).

Basic Secondary

The basic secondary cycle (commonly called secondary) covers three years of schooling, normally for boys and girls between the ages of 13 and 15, although it is not unusual for students to remain in school up to and even beyond the age of 20. In the capital and other big cities so-called 'schools for workers' are available for those who are already at work; in these there is a minimum age limit of 16 for student enrolment but no upper age limit. Spanish is the medium of instruction throughout the basic secondary cycle. English is taught as the foreign language in 95% of all secondary schools (French in 5%).

The outline of a new common core curriculum was agreed in 1974. Syllabi were drawn up in 1975 and the new programme of studies went into effect in all secondary schools throughout the country in September of that year. All students at this level follow a broadly based course, spread over 30 hours per week, consisting (like the primary curriculum) of areas of learning: Spanish language (an literature) mathematics, a foreign language, natural sciences (biology, physics and chemistry), social sciences (history and geography), and physical, artistic and technical education. On completion of the course students are awarded a Secondary School Certificate.

General

In general secondary schools pupils follow the common syllabus and normally take one or more options from arts and crafts, music, domestic science, etc. the majority of students in the basic cycle are in general secondary schools.

Vocational

As well as the general secondary schools there are other kinds of institutions offering courses at this level. The schools are:

(i) technical (industrial and commercial)

(ii) agricultural (opened in 1970)

(iii) fisheries (opened in 1972).

In addition there are still a relatively small number of training centres that provide one academic year of technical training for primary school leavers to prepare them for semi-skilled jobs in agriculture or industry. These one-year courses are also offered at some technical secondary schools and some higher technical institutions. Courses in vocational secondary schools follow the common syllabus outlined above. However, here the options available cover practical training in a wide variety of relevant specialist subjects, ranging from carpentry to dressmaking, from electronics to book-keeping. Where the schools are sited in rural areas many options are directed towards the requirements of the local peasant communities. In the technical secondary system a total of more than 90 optional subjects are available, as many as 15 to choose from in some of the largest schools.

Telesecundaria

In 1968 a programme of general secondary education by television was inaugurated after a one-year experiment with a closed circuit broadcasting system based on a single school in the capital. The system provided courses based on the general secondary school syllabi to students in the deprived urban and rural areas (mostly within beaming distance of the capital) where there were no regular secondary school installations. In the first year its broadcast to 6,500 pupils attending small community school halls in the urban areas and in the states of Hidalgo, Mexico, Morelos, Puebla, Tlaxcala and Veracruz. In 1971 the Minister of Education declared that all secondary studies pursued through the *Telesecundaria* programme would be considered valid throughout the country. By 1974 there was a student enrolment of over 40,000. In that year *Telesecundaria* expanded its coverage when the TCM (cultural television) began to broadcast the lessons. TCM has 45 relay stations throughout the country.

Television programmes are broadcast from 0800 – 1400 every weekday and each group of students receives the statutory 30 hours of tuition per week. Each broadcast lasts about 20 minutes and the remainder of the class-hour is devoted to follow-up, practice and preparation under the supervision of the class 'coordinator', a non-specialist ex-primary school teacher who has to cover all the subjects in the curriculum. Classes average 23 pupils (as opposed to 55 in the normal classroom). In 1972 a survey of the system by a team from Stanford University reported favourably on its cost-effectiveness as compared with the traditional system (25% cheaper).

Higher Secondary

The second cycle of secondary education has traditionally been administered by the universities and other institutions of higher education; it was called for a long time *preparatory* (i.e. leading to a university degree course) or *vocational* (i.e. leading to higher studies at an institute of technology). However, the term *vocational* can be misleading, including as it does education at this level that is terminal and aimed at the preparation of technicians and skilled craftsmen to work in the middle level of industry. Many of the vocational schools have now been renamed. The normal length of course at this level is three years leading to the *bachillerato* (or higher school graduation certificate), or a professional certificate.

Preparatory

As well as the normal three-year course some preparatory schools offer courses of two years only, which are then followed by a further 'prepedeutic' year when the student reaches university.

Nearly all the public universities in the country have their own dependent preparatory schools, graduates of which may proceed automatically to first degree courses in their respective universities. The model for all preparatory schools is that of the National University, established over 100 years ago and called the National Preparatory School. This organisation now consists of nine different schools in various parts of the capital which provide a broadly-based course for the first two years, with the following main subject options in the third: liberal studies, social sciences, economics and administration, chemical and biological sciences, fine arts and mathematics and physical sciences. Students choose to specialise in the branch they hope to follow at tertiary level. In 1971 the National University initiated an alternative system of preparatory education, called the College of Science and Humanities, working in five different schools, with rather more emphasis throughout the three-year course on applied studies; the first graduates of these schools entered university in 1975.

In addition to the preparatory schools directly dependent upon the state universities, there are many private establishments, most of them incorporated into the National University system, and a few schools administered directly by the federal government, particularly in deprived areas of the country where the state governments are unable to provide adequate facilities. A direct move by the federal government to become involved in non-technical education at this level saw in 1974 the creation of a new semi-autonomous decentralised body called the *Colegio de Bachilleres*, an administrative organisation designed to run preparatory schools throughout the country; five schools in Mexico City are now functioning as affiliates to this new system as well as three in the northern state of Chihuahua, and three new schools in the Federal District have now been authorised. In these institutions preparation for work is given the same weight as preparation for higher education and on completion graduates either receive the *bachillerato* or a professional certificate. It may be that this represents the prototype for the reform of existing institutions in providing more flexibility and independence in the upper secondary cycle.

Technical

Higher secondary education in technical subjects is provided by a wide variety of institutions. Just as the preparatory system developed out of a lead given by the National University, so the National Polytechnic Institute was the first to develop a dependent technical preparatory system in the form of 15 vocational schools, now renamed Centres for Scientific and Technical Studies. These schools provide three years of pre-university training in the following branches: engineering, mathematics and physical sciences, chemical and biological sciences, economics, commerce and administration.

Recently there has been increased federal government involvement in technical education marked by expansion at this level. The pattern of training established by the National Polytechnic Institute has been widely followed and the federal government has systematically developed a chain of technical colleges under the direct control of the Ministry of Education, also called Centres of Scientific and Technical Studies, sited in the industrial and agricultural areas. Many of them occupy the same premises as the technical and agricultural secondary schools. There are industrial, commercial and agricultural centres and since 1975 there have been centres for marine studies as well. Technical preparatory schools are also linked to new Regional Institutes of Technology in the provinces, and some of these institutions run their own technical schools which provide crafts and technician training at the higher middle level. such schools were also founded by universities before the expansion at this level and these are still in existence. In addition there are so called professional and trade schools (most of which are located in the capital) which prepare students for a recognised professional qualification over a period of three or four years or for entry to an appropriate first degree course in an institution of higher education.

Higher (Universities)

There are 40 universities in Mexico. Twenty-six of them are autonomous, that is, they are self-governing but financed by the federal government. Of the others, six are directly controlled by their State governments, albeit with considerable financial support from the federal authorities, and the remaining ten are privately owned, all of them either in the capital or in the two next largest Mexican cities of Guadalajara and Monterrey.

Far and away the most important university is the National Autonomous University of Mexico (UNAM) situated in the capital. It had more than 260,000 students following undergraduate and post-graduate courses in 1976. It has begun to decentralise, opening five new subsidiary campuses in industrial areas to the north and east of Mexico City. Thus the National University accounts for over one quarter of the total student population in higher education, which in 1979/80 was 848,875. The next largest universities are the State University of Guadalajara and the Autonomous University of Nueva Leon; followed by the Autonomous University of Puebla, the Autonomous University 'San Juan Nicolas de Hidalgo' of Michoacan and the University of Veracruz. Of the private universities the Autonomous University of Guadalajara is easily the largest. By contrast, many of the provincial universities are very small, some of them having less than 1,000 students.

Entrance

University entrance is open to students who have successfully completed courses at the higher secondary level and obtained a *bachillerato* of equivalent certificate. Those who have attended preparatory schools belonging to specific universities usually have direct access; other students have to take competitive, and often highly selective, examinations to secure places.

Courses

Most universities have faculties of arts, natural sciences, law and economics but the full range of options is only available in the largest institutions. Taught courses lead to first degrees *(licenciatura)* and in some cases to higher degrees *(maestria)* ; in the majority of fields post-graduate research or courses leading to a doctorate are only possible at the National University. Degrees are gained by passing a stated number of 'credit' courses, followed by the submission, and defence before a jury, of a short thesis or dissertation. Students may enrol each term for as many credit courses as they wish. As a result it normally takes from five to as many as seven or eight years to obtain a degree. There is no limit to the length of time during which a student may remain registered for a first or second degree. In all universities, when a student has finished all his taught credit courses, he obtains a certificate of completion of studies, which will enable him to obtain appropriate employment. For this reason a high proportion of students do not go on to submit dissertations and obtain formal degrees.

New System

The two most recent autonomous foundations, the Metropolitan University (opened in 1974) and the University of Chiapas, represent important departures from the traditional Mexican pattern. These universities are decentralised with a general administration and services unit and separate campuses. The campuses operate to an extent as individual institutions. Freshmen students at these universities enter divisions or 'areas of studies' (physico-mathematical sciences, social sciences, biomedical sciences) rather than specialised faculties and follow inter-disciplinary foundation courses. There are modular course structures with units of work taught in a range of ways.

Study Patterns

In the public autonomous or State-controlled universities tuition costs. are nominal and the majority of students are part time, working their way through college. The large universities work on a double shift, mornings and afternoons, Monday to Friday. The private universities which charge high fees for tuition, and which therefore exclude those less favoured on the social scale, have modelled their curricula and syllabi on public institutions and have adopted the shift system so that their students also study part time. Students spend most of their time in formal classes with little or no private study expected of them. Students in the new universities described above are encouraged to take responsibility for their own learning.

Academic Year

All universities except the National and the Metropolitan follow the same academic year as the rest of the education system i.e. from September to June. However, the Metropolitan University operates a three-term (or quarter) academic year, while the National University at present works a two-semester year from January to October, with its mid-year break falling in May; but it is gradually working towards the normal pattern.

Higher (Technical)

The National Polytechnic Institute in Mexico City occupies the same position in relation to technical education at the higher level as the National University does in the general system. After the National Polytechnic, the next largest technical institute is the Institute of Technology and Higher Studies of Monterrey, a prestigious and high quality private institution. There are also a few other private institutes of technology, mostly concentrated in the big cities, but the fastest growing network at present is that of the Regional Institutes of Technology, directly controlled by the federal government. As a result of a crash programme initiated in 1970, 21 institutes were opened in five years, bringing the total throughout the country to 41, including a National Centre of Technical and Industrial Education. Higher education is also available in the professional schools but most of these concentrate heavily on work at higher secondary level and have relatively few students taking degree level courses.

Entrance

As with universities, entrance is confined to students who have successfully completed higher secondary courses. Those who have attended secondary institutions attached to specific technical institutes usually have direct access. Otherwise it is necessary to sit an examination.

Courses

The National Polytechnic Institute offers a wide variety of courses leading to first and higher degrees in engineering, pure and applied sciences (including medicine), economics, commerce and administration. Similarly, the Technological Institute of Monterrey has a considerable range of options, but the private and Regional Institutes of Technology are for the most part limited to not more than two or three branches of engineering and applied science. Courses in the technological institutes follow the same pattern as in the universities, with students gaining credits towards their degree, which they subsequently receive upon submission and successful defence of an appropriate dissertation.

Study Patterns

The majority of students in these institutions study part time and degree courses are normally extended over a period of four or five years. The National Polytechnic operates a morning and afternoon shift system, whereas most of the Regional Institutes of Technology function only in the afternoons at the level of higher education. The academic year is similar to that of the universities.

Teacher Training

In Mexico teacher training is offered in separate kinds of institution for the different levels of education. Training for the higher levels requires higher entrance qualifications from prospective teachers and it is possible to enter training at various stages throughout the system.

Elementary (Normal)

Students wishing to train for teaching at pre-primary and primary levels may enter training after obtaining a Secondary School Certificate. In 1979/80 there were 180,200 students in Normal (and Higher Normal) Schools. Normal schools are run by the federal and state governments and by private organisations. There are schools or colleges for pre-primary, primary and physical education teachers as well as programmes for training instructors in vocational training centres. Colleges are federal, state-run or private and students follow a three- or sometimes four-year programme of general and educational studies. In 1975 a reform was initiated to strengthen the content of the normal school programme. Subjects studied are now arranged in three main areas: scientific-humanistic; physical artistic and technical; and specific professional (including teaching practice). Pre-school and primary school student teachers follow broadly the same programme with special adaptations. A Normal School Certificate can be acceptable for entrance to university.

Secondary (Higher Normal)

These schools provide four-year training courses for secondary and normal school teachers. The entrance qualification is a *bachillerato* or a Normal School Certificate.

The vast majority of students attending the Higher Normal Schools are practising teachers, who have already finished their training as primary school teachers and are working their way through college in order to obtain comparatively more remunerative positions in secondary schools. Many of these students complete their taught courses in the Higher Normal Schools after a period of four or five years and are then appointed to posts in secondary schools even though they have still not submitted their dissertations and obtained their formal professional qualifications; some of them complete the requirements many years later, while others never take the trouble to do so.

For primary school teachers living and working in areas in which there is no access to training colleges, most of the Higher Normal Schools offer six- to eight-week intensive summer courses in which students studying full time can obtain their qualifications after about six or seven consecutive summer sessions. There are six state-run and three private Higher Normal Schools which are only open in the summer for these intensive courses. The syllabi of the latter are exactly the same as those of the regular courses.

At the moment there is little special provision for the training of teachers for technical secondary schools or technical colleges or for corresponding agricultural or fisheries institutions; though the National Centre for Technical and Industrial Education does provide a three-year training course which caters for about 150 students a year. The federal government has recently founded two special training colleges, one each for teachers in technical and agricultural secondary schools and colleges. Teachers for special education are also trained at this level in two institutions.

Higher Secondary

The normal requirement for a teaching position in a preparatory or comparable higher secondary school is the possession of a first degree or at least a certificate of completion of university studies, and many degree-level syllabi now include one- or two-semester courses on methods and techniques of teaching the specialist subject; a number of institutions of higher education also have their own educational research and teaching centres through which in-service training courses are provided for their own faculty and preparatory school staff.

Higher

In 1972 the National Association of Universities and Institutions of Higher Education set up a national programme to train teachers for higher education under which university staff were given scholarships to take special courses in university teaching methods with a view to becoming teacher trainers for higher education. The Association claims that in the first three years 8,000 teachers were trained in this way. Universities are now being encouraged to establish their own teaching methods units, using microteaching techniques and employing closed circuit TV. The valuable contribution of educational technology is being recognised and a number of in-service courses are being offered in curriculum design, and the use of audio-visual aids and the mass media. Training has to be organised in this way as there is no money available to release teachers to take full time courses.

In-Service

In 1971 a department of in-service training was set up in the Ministry of Education to help teachers understand and implement reforms of the curriculum. In order to introduce newer, more active methods, vacation courses and seminars have been held throughout the country.

Extra Mural and Literacy Work

Non-formal education, including literacy work, is provided by a wide variety of official, charitable and private organisations as well as by the federal government. The Ministry of Education's departments of non-formal education in urban, rural and indigenous areas offer training in crafts and semi-skilled occupations as well as primary schooling, often by means of mobile units staffed by one or more qualified teachers. The Department of undamental Education runs literacy and primary level calsses for adults throughout the country.

In December 1975 the government passed a decree setting up a National Programme for Adult Education designed to coordinate public and private efforts to reduce functional illiteracy amongst the adult population and to provide primary and basic secondary education for those who lack it. The government openly admits to an illiterate adult population of 7 million (approximately 12.5%). Other estimates vary between 10% and 40%. A further 10 million people over the age of 15 have never managed to finish their primary education and there are 8 million more with incomplete secondary studies. The programme is based on home study and is designed to make the educated section of the community conscious of the deprivations suffered by their impoverished compatriots and consequently willing to act in a voluntary capacity as teaching assistants, working with groups or individuals in the factory, office or home. In this way it is hoped to reduce the total number of functional illiterates by half during the next six years and to stimulate the desire for self-instruction at higher levels on the part of those who are given this initial opportunity to further the education they have missed so far.

'Open' Systems

The major response to quantitative pressures now acting on Mexican education has been a sudden and speedy adoption of systems of 'open learning'. These are now operating at primary, secondary, higher secondary and higher levels. Open systems are also seen as a way of solving the in-service teacher training problems especially at higher level. Unlike the British OU, students on Mexican open courses are required to have the qualifications necessary to enter the appropriate level of edcuation. Learning is independent, with self-instructional pre-printed materials for use out of school, but with some kind of regular tuition in school. There is no correspondence element because of the difficulties of administering the postal system sufficiently reliably. The 1973 Education Act makes provision for a national system of certification which recognises as of equal validity qualifications obtained through formal and open systems.

The two oldest open systems date from 1972/73. One is at university level and run by UNAM - the Open University. Students attend the university campus on Saturdays. As with the OU the main medium of instruction is printed texts. (In fact this form of extra-mural teaching is now considerably more fashionable in Mexico than educational broadcasting). The other system is at higher secondary level and run by a decentralised government agency called CEMPAE (Centre for Study of Advanced Methods and Processes in Education). Its Open Preparatory School is sited at Monterrey and has its own TV channel in the city. However, the programmes transmitted are motivational rather than directly instructional and print does 90% of the teaching. Three thousand students are enrolled with an average age of 24.

The open primary and secondary systems set up in 1975 each have specially produced textbooks with accompanying books for the teachers who run the local study groups. The first books for the primary system were published in 1975 in editions of 500,000. the first secondary courses enrolled 13,000 students throughout the country in the first few months.

A national open system at higher secondary level has been developed by the *Colegio de Bachilleres*. The College's SEA *(Sistema de Ensenanza Abierta)* opened for applications in February 1976. Within three days 8,000 applications had been received for 5,000 places. In the pilot stage the open system is only available in Mexico City using the conventional preparatory schools as study centres. Business firms, unions and government organisations are being provided with teaching materials so that they can run their own open systems using their own tutorial/counselling staff and their own premises.

7 EDUCATIONAL ADMINISTRATION

Centralised Control

The system that has emerged is highly centralised. At primary and secondary levels curricula and detailed syllabi are provided by the Ministry of Education to all schools, public and private. The Ministry also prescribes which textbooks are to be used; in the case of primary schools obligatory texts for all subjects have been prepared under Ministry auspices since 1970 and by 1974/75 were being provided free of charge to all students attending public establishments. At secondary level the Ministry publishes lists of 'approved' textbooks for each subject. Schools dependent upon the state authorities, as well as all private schools incorporated into the federal government system, follow the same programme of studies. Evaluation is also organised nationally. A central government agency is responsible for the maintenance, building and equipping of schools.

From 1978 government has given stress to the decentralisation of educational administrations. This has meant giving officials at state level more autonomy in decision-making in terms of school provision and finance over federal educational institutions.

Responsibility for Provision

The responsibility for providing public education at primary and secondary level is devolved upon states, subject to the overall policies and plans laid down by the federal government. The state governments are required to establish and staff the schools and colleges in their territories. In practice few states have the necessary resources to provide a complete set of amenities, with the result that the federal government has set up a parallel network of educational establishments throughout the country, in addition to those for which it is responsible in the Federal District. In many of the poorest and least developed states, the federal authorities are responsible for pretty well the whole of the basic cycle of secondary education and in order to streamline its administration services the ministry set up in 1973 a chain of decentralised regional units; each one is responsible for the running of federal educational services in the area in which it is located.

Traditionally the higher levels of education have been administered by the universities and other institutions of higher education; but there has always been a certain amount of overlapping and now the distinction is becoming increasingly blurred as the federal authorities assume more direct responsbility for education at the higher middle level, particularly in technical and vocational training.

University Administration

Of the public universities those which are autonomous are constitutionally free from interference by the federal government even though the greater part of their finances are provided by direct government subsidy. An important part of the autonomous system is the so-called 'professional freedom' *(libertad de catedra)*. This means that although the universities publish syllabi for all their taught courses - sometimes in considerable detail - individual teachers are legally free to choose their own teaching methods and materials. Furthermore, once they have established their permanent right to teach certain subjects they cannot legally be dismissed. However, even the autonomous universities are subject to some degree of government control through their membership of the National Association of Universities and Institutes of Higher Education, a centralised body for planning. Recently announced proposals for a new National Education Plan include a reference to preserving the autonomy of the public universities while at the same time indicating a need to establish a commission to examine ways and means of coordinating standards in these institutions.

Ministry Organisation

In 1974 a new administrative structure was introduced in the Ministry of Education, whereby the minister is assisted directly by four under-ministers, who take full responsibility for such special activities as educational planning and coordination, and non-formal education and popular culture. Since the establishment of the new presidential régime considerable reorganisation has taken place within the ministry. However, a settled structure is not yet apparent and at the time of writing no organagram has been published even for the use of ministry staff.

8 EDUCATIONAL FINANCE

Financial Sources

Finance for public education is provided by both the federal and state authorities with the federal government providing most. Generally, specific educational taxes have not been levied but to support the expansion of secondary and higher education the government has introduced such a tax on salaries above a prescribed figure. Students attending public schools, colleges and universities pay either nothing at all or only nominal fees; private schools and universities, which do not qualify for government subsidies, charge high fees.

Education Budget

In 1980, 125 billion pesos were allocated by federal government to education, which represented 14.9% of federal government expenditure and 3.1% of GNP. The state governments spent 28 billion pesos on educastion and almost 9 billion pesos were spent by the private sector. These funds were allocated in the following proportions - 49% for basic education and 37% for secondary.

Foreign Cooperation

Mexico has a wide range of cultural conventions with foreign countries. Under these agreements, and usually with the major financial input coming from the foreign country concerned, a large number of expatriate teachers have been supplied to work in Mexico at tertiary level in a variety of disciplines. Most of these come from the USA but there are also substantial numbers from Britain, France and FDR. In the state system below tertiary level, expatriates are rarely found. With the exception of occasional gifts, for example of language laboratories by the Japanese and American governments, aid as such has given way to bilateral technical cooperation schemes. Major schemes are operated by the USA, Britain, France, FDR and Japan.

9 DEVELOPMENT AND PLANNING OF THE EDUCATION SYSTEM
Origins

The development of educational policy in Mexico has its origins in the long standing struggle for power and influence between an overtly liberal and anti-clerical government and the Catholic Church, seen as the representative of earlier colonial dominance and of the forces of elitism and conservation. Mexican independence arose in an atmosphere of liberalism that embraced not only philosophical thought and recognition of humanistic values, but also the provision of the conditions for developing such values. As a consequence a policy emerged in the nineteenth century which rejected education as an instrument of religious evangelism, as a privilege of the few or even as a special training for the civil and ecclesiastical bureaucracy, but saw it in the context of a liberal ideology as the right of every citizen to realise his personal development. As early as 1833 the religious foundation of the University of Mexico was abolished and replaced by a 'General Direction of Public Instruction for the Federal District and Territories', the main function of which was to issue regulations for instruction at different levels, the appointment of teachers and the selection of textbooks. At the same time the state governments were given the power to organise and expand education in their own territories.

Aims of the Reformists

To the liberal reformists the first element in the educational law was the idea of universal formal instruction as an absolute social need. The second was the idea of public education; instruction could not be left in private hands but the government as the legitimate representative of society should assume the total responsibility of providing educational opportunity to enable every citizen to achieve freedom, equality and personal development. As the reformists gained strength, new laws laying down a single system of public instruction were passed, free and compulsory primary education was introduced and religious instruction was forbidden in government schools, replaced by classes in moral and civic education without relation to religious principles.

1946 Education Act

These aims were consolidated upon the establishment of the Ministry of Public Education in 1905, and later formalised in the Constitution of 1917 and in the Education Act of 1946:

> "Access to formal instruction, primary, secondary and higher, shall be available to everybody. Education shall have no religious bias when given in official (= public) educational institutions, and the same conditions shall apply to primary, secondary and higher education offered by private establishments. No religious body nor minister of any sect shall found or direct schools for primary instruction. Private schools shall be established only if subject to official inspection. In official institutions primary instruction shall be available free of charge."

During the past few years, and particularly in the period of the previous government, these objectives have been formally restated and expanded.

Educational Reform

Recent developments in learning theory and teaching methods, the need to expand vocational training and to coordinate education and opportunities for employment, together with a deliberate policy of establishing non-formal systems parallel and equivalent to the formal, led in 1973 to the new Federal Education Act, and to educational reform (begun in 1971) which has so far completely revised and modernised the context of primary and secondary education without altering the social and moral basis of national educational objectives.

Planning Institutions

Within the framework of educational reform, a central advisory body, the National Technical Council for Education, has been made responsible for educational planning at primary and secondary levels; in higher education the National Association of Universities and Institutions of Higher Education has been given a substantial budget and wide-ranging powers to develop national policies; while of recent creation is the Council for the National System of Technical Education, intended in the next few years to coordinate policies for technical and vocational education at higher secondary and tertiary levels. All these bodies are funded directly by and answerable to the federal government, which thus manages to keep a tight rein on educational planning at all levels.

National Technical Council for Education

This organisation has undertaken the complete revision of the primary and secondary school curricula. The new curricula and the detailed syllabi which accompany them are more practical and realistic than the old, reflecting an integrated approach based on 'area' studies and on discovery methods and student activity in the classroom. A corollary of this reform has been the coordination of different systems of secondary education with the production of a common core curriculum.

Council for the National System of Technical Education

A similar coordinating role is expected from this institution in the planning of more realistic syllabi for technical and vocational training centres and in the integration of such establishments with the socio-economic needs of the local community.

National Association of Institutions of Higher Education

This institution is empowered by the federal government to play a similar unifying role in helping universities and higher technical institutes to develop courses relevant to local job opportunities and community development.

National Education Plan 1977

In the summer of 1977 the new government announced a National Education Plan drawn up by the National Technical Council for Education. As it stands the Plan is said to be 'no more than a point of departure for further analysis, dialogue and action' and is essentially a 'credo' consisting of general proposals grouped around four main objectives:

(i) to affirm the popular and democratic character of the education system

(ii) to improve the quality of education

(iii) to relate education more closely to the process of development

(iv) to obtain the full support of society for the national education effort.

The translation of these objectives into a specific plan of action may take some time. Meanwhile the following proposals are seen as long term aims consistent with the objectives outlined above:

(i) expansion of pre-primary education in flexible form with the support of local communities

(ii) provision of grants for students with limited financial resources

(iii) increased educational provision in rural areas by crash school building programmes, use of mobile units, mass media, and 'open' systems; with regional universities and other education establishments encouraged to assume a greater social role in service to the locality

(iv) development of adult education to allow people to develop their capabilities and receive a training that will help them to obtain productive employment

(v) development of open systems at all levels; apart from a valuable compensatory function this is seen as the only viable alternative to an even greater expansion of school based education which would be impractical and an impossible drain on the country's economic resources

(vi) secondary education to be made compulsory

(vii) increased research into curricula, teaching methods and materials

(viii) expansion and upgrading of teacher training and the creation of a National Pedagogic University whose primary function will be to educate the country's teacher trainers by providing degree courses in education up to doctoral level

(ix) devolution of some responsibility for educational administration to the provinces so that the objectives of national education policy are reconciled with the needs of the local community

(x) intensive development of vocational training with more emphasis on practical work and increased vocational content in all educational programmes

(xi) development of high level manpower planning structures to feed information to those involved in educational strategy

(xii) organisation of local participation in education by the creation of state education councils and local education committees.

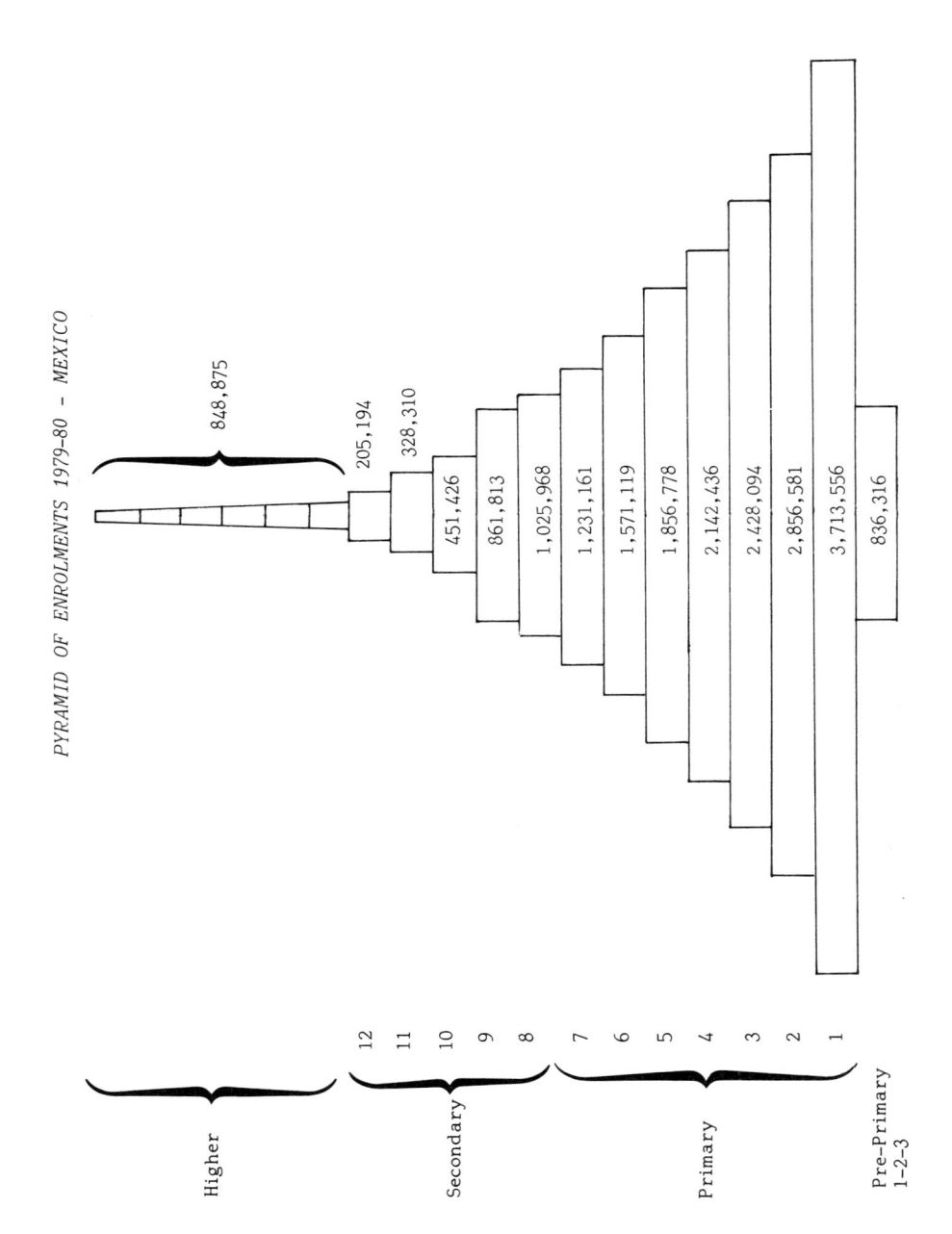

PYRAMID OF ENROLMENTS 1979-80 – MEXICO

Level	Grade	Enrolment
Higher		848,875
Secondary	12	205,194
	11	328,310
	10	451,426
	9	861,813
	8	1,025,968
Primary	7	1,231,161
	6	1,571,119
	5	1,856,778
	4	2,142,436
	3	2,428,094
	2	2,856,581
	1	3,713,556
Pre-Primary 1-2-3		836,316

MEXICO BASIC STATISTICS

Population

1960	1970	1980
36,046,000	50,690,000	67,405,700

Enrolment Ratios 1970 and 1979

Primary = Enrolments divided by the total population aged 6-11
Secondary = Enrolments divided by the total population aged 12-17
Higher = Enrolments divided by the total population aged 20-24

Year	Primary	Secondary	Higher
1970	104	22	6.1
1979	124	45	11.6*

* 1978

Schools, Teachers & Pupils 1975/76 and 1979/80

	Schools	Teachers	Pupils
Pre-primary			
1975/76	4,156	14,073	537,090
1979/80	9,152	24,983	836,316
Primary			
1975/76	55,618	255,939	11,461,415
1979/80	72,414	353,538	14,282,908
Secondary			
1975/76	7,943	141,730	2,516,014
1979/80	10,634	222,400	3,827,671

	Institutions	Teachers	Students
Teacher Training			
1975/76	296	8,396	111,502
1979/80	347	11,526	180,200
Higher			
1975/76	175	47,529	543,112
1979/80	813	69,582	848,875

Proportions of Students in Different Types of Institutions 1979/80

	Federal	State/Autonomous	Private
Pre-school	67%	25%	8%
Primary	71%	24%	5%
Secondary	55%	23%	22%
Teacher Training	25%	30%	45%
Higher Education	17%	69%	14%

Higher Education Students by Field of Study 1978

	Students	% Female
Education and Teacher Training	6,172	65
Humanities	9,856	53
Fine and Applied Arts	1,614	50
Law	58,396	28
Social and Behavioural Sciences	50,597	48
Commerce and Business	129,543	33
Mass Communications	14,838	46
Service Trades	5,200	52
Natural Science	18,318	43
Mathematics and Computer Science	6,069	28
Medicine and Related Fields	150,437	41
Engineering	99,832	12
Architecture	65,999	11
Crafts and Industrial Programmes	24,626	4
Agriculture	55,488	8
Other	1,156	2

Total Public Expenditure on Education

Year	As a % of Total Government Expenditure	As a % of GNP
1970	8.5%	2.6%
1980	14.9%	3.1%

Public Expenditure on Education by Level

Year	Pre-Primary	Primary	Secondary	Higher	Other & Not Distributed
1970	3.1%	47.7%	27.2%	10.4%	11.5%
1978	2.2%	36.7%	23.0%	25.2%	12.9%

Basic Social and Economic Data

GNP per capita 1979 - US$1,640

Annual average growth of GNP per capita 1960/79 - 2.7%

Life expectancy 1979 - 66

Proportion of the labour force employed in:

    Agriculture
      1960   55%
      1979   37%

    Industry
      1960   20%
      1979   26%

    Services
      1960   25%
      1979   37%

Peru

CONTENTS

1 Geography	756
2 Population	758
3 Society and Culture	759
4 History and Politics	762
5 The Economy	764
6 The Education System	766
7 Educational Administration	777
8 Educational Finance	779
9 Development and Planning of the Education System	783
10 The System in Operation	787

Peru is the poorest of the larger countries of South America. With its low per capita national income, reliance on primary product exports, the heavy concentration of its population in agriculture and the low rate of economic growth in the 1960s and 1970s, it is more similar in some ways to the under-developed countries of Africa and Asia than to the middle income states of South America. Also like African and Asian countries, but unlike the other large countries of Hispanic America, Peru has deep cultural divisions, based on the 40-40-20 distribution between Indians, Mestizos and 'Europeans' and on the widespread use of two languages – Spanish and Quecha.

In view of these economic and social conditions and in comparison with other South American countries, Peru's educational achievements have been considerable. Primary schooling has been made available for almost all children while the proportions of the population in secondary and higher education reached higher levels than in most other Latin America countries.

This educational advance can be associated with the strongly egalitarian and social welfare based policies of the reforming military government after 1968. After 1968 also Peru was in the forefront of the implementation of educational reforms which have been adopted, a little less forcibly, in other parts of the sub-continent. There were moves to achieve integrated and universal 'basic education' for children aged 6-15; decentralisation of educational administration to allow more local decision-making; a reform of the curriculum to give more attention to local economic and social needs as well as the diversity of pupil interests; a more vocationally orientated upper secondary education; and a greater place for Indian languages and culture in Peruvian education.

Peru's educational innovations have been ambitious. The momentum of reform slowed down after the mid-1970s and many of the planned changes have not been implemented. This may be associated with the loss of political initiative of the military government from the mid-1970s until it was replaced by a civilian government. But Peru's relative poverty and deep social divisions and lack of major economic development have also had a major obstructive effect on the continuation of educational change.

1 GEOGRAPHY

Topography

Peru extends from north to south through slightly more than 18° latitude, with its northern extremity almost touching the equatorial line. Its frontiers, all of which have at some time within the last century been the subject of dispute, are contingent with the neighbouring Andean Pact countries of Ecuador and Colombia in the north, Brazil and Bolivia to the east and south east, and Chile in the far south. The total land area is 269,760 sq km (469,000 sq miles) or approximately five times the size of Britain, of which well over 60% comprises the largely impenetrable jungle in the upper Amazon basin.

The three principal natural regions are parallel strips running from north to south:

(i) Sierra, the mountainous area of the Andes, which averages 3,900 metres (13,000 feet) and rises in places to over 6,000 metres (20,000 feet)

(ii) Selva, the tropical jungle to the east

(iii) Costa, to the west the coastal desert, which is 2,240 km long (1,400 miles) and is irrigated at intervals by some 50 rivers, most of them seasonal (December-April).

Two sub-regions are formed by the flat Peruvian/Bolivian *altiplano*, 3,600 metres high (12,000 feet) and covered in part by Lake Titicaca (8,300 sq km) and by the semi-tropical transitional slopes *(montaña)* to the east of the Andes.

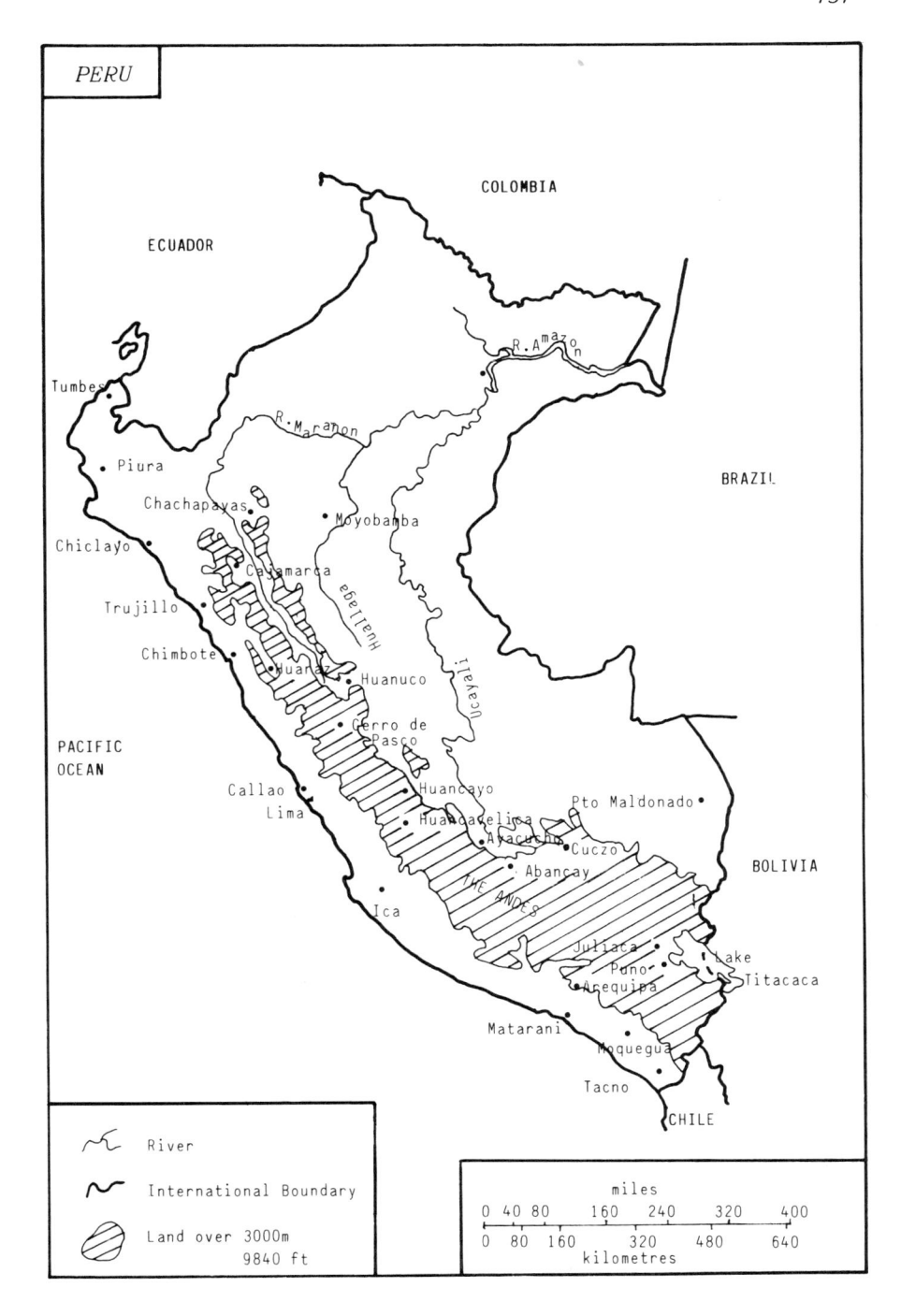

PERU

Climate

The Peruvian climate is determined less by latitude than by the two over-riding factors of the high Andes and the cold waters of the Humboldt current which sweeps almost the entire length of the coast. Much of the coastline is covered by a blanket of sea-mist for six months of the year (June-November), although there is negligible rainfall, and temperatures average 20°C throughout the year with little variation between the coldest month (August, 16.1°C) and the sunniest (February, 23.5°C). The climate of the sierra is varied and divided between dry and wet seasons. The driest parts are to the west of the Andes and the wettest to the north and east; in Cuzco rainfall ranges from 5 mm in June/July to 16.3 cm in January, although mean temperatures (9°-12°C) vary little with the seasons. The climate in the selva is constantly hot (27°-28°C) and humid (85-100%). Rainfall averages 200-300 cm but can even reach 450 cm per year in parts of the *montaña*.

Communications

Communications play a vital part in integrating the diverse areas of the country. Two broad gauge railways, constructed in the nineteenth century from Callao to Huancayo (346 km) and from Matarani to Cuzco (860 km) via Arequipa and the *altiplano* towns of Juliaca and Puno, were an important step towards the integration of sierra and costa. The road system was slower to develop and only in the last 30 years has motorised transport replaced the traditional mule trains in many parts of the sierra. At present there are approximately 45,000 km of roads, of which 17,000 km are made up, but only 4,500 asphalted. Iquitos and other cities in the selva are entirely dependent on air and water transport for communications with the outside world. The lack of an integrated transport system is a major factor retarding the social and economic development of the rural areas of Peru.

2 POPULATION

Growth

Although statistics are unreliable, it is evident that in common with other Latin American countries Peru is suffering a population explosion. The population grew from 8,170,000 in 1950 to 14,121,000 in 1972 which represented an annual increase of about 3% per annum. The population was estimated to be 17,297,000 in 1979 with an annual growth rate of 2.7% in 1978-79.

Distribution

Not only is the population growing but the cities are expanding disproportionately, reflecting massive migration from the provinces to urban centres on the coast and in the highlands. Moreover, since the cities are concentrated on the coastal strip, the flood of migration to the cities is creating even more profound regional imbalances of population density.

The major towns are Lima (2.8 million), Arequipa (0.3 million), Callao (0.3 million) and Trujillo (0.2 million).

Groups

Peru is a racially diversified society. The racial composition in 1972 was 41% indigenous (Indian), 39% mestizo (mixed blood), 19% white, and 1% oriental and negroid, though the figure for the white population appears rather high, depending on definitions of the term.

3 HISTORY AND POLITICS

Colonisation

The Spanish conquest of Peru was begun in 1532 although the territory was not finally pacified for about another 40 years. The elite of the indigenous Indian system was destroyed and Spanish civilisation was superimposed upon an Indian society which firmly resisted acculturation. Indian labour practices were modified to meet the Spanish need for gold, mercury and other metals, while choice land was parcelled out to the conquistadores and operated on a semi-feudal basis. Such was the impact of the conquest and colonisation that the Indian population declined from roughly 6-8 million in 1532 to 700,000 according to the 1798 census.

The peculiarity of the Spanish colonial system in Peru was that although labour practices were semi-feudal, differing only in intensity from those set up by the Incas, the products obtained were sold commercially on the world market. Thus the Spaniards redirected the objects of production without fundamentally changing Indian society. The colonial system of government clearly reflected the economic situation. The major government - the Viceroy, the High Court, and administrators - was responsible for administering the territory in the Spanish commercial interest, but the Indian population was ruled through the minor government - Indian chiefs put in charge of large groups of natives, a rough approximation to the original Inca system. Thus the colonial system created two distinct societies, differing economically, culturally, and racially. Indian society was preserved within a subsistence economy while a European orientated, commercial civilisation was slowly formed in isolated enclaves. In anticipation of this development, Pizarro moved the capital from Cuzco to Lima. It is not too fanciful to suggest that the contemporary migration to the cities represents the long delayed Indian response to that gesture.

Independence

The colonial period ended with the wars of independence. Since Lima had been a seat of Spanish government and had enjoyed corresponding privileges, there was more sympathy for the Spanish crown in Peru than elsewhere in Latin America. However, the influence of French and American revolutionary ideas, together with growing resentment of the Spaniards, who monopolised high office in the colonial administration, from the Creoles (Peruvians born of Spanish blood), led to the triumph of the independence movement. San Martin procalimed independence at Lima on 28 July 1821, although pro-Spanish troops were not finally defeated until January 1826. The republican period has been dominated by a series of military dictatorships interspersed with periods of democratic government. However, until recently the fundamental division between the European elite and the Indial masses has remained.

Present Régime

In 1968 the military régime overthrew the democratic government of President Belaunde (1964–68). Unlike other South American countries, there was a real social gulf between military and civilian elites. Typically army officers came either from military families or the provincial lower middle class (such as ex-president Velasco). Even more important was the general lack of participation by military officers in industrial or agricultural management. As a result the military régime was able to follow a policy of a distinctly different character to those of other Latin American military régimes. During 12 years of military power, the régime made a considerable number of major decisions and was able to rely upon its political base within the military to carry out its policies, often in opposition to powerful civilian forces.

In 1980 there was a return of civilian government after the military régime had failed to deal satisfactorily with continuing economic and political problems. President Belaunde returned to power for five years by popular election.

International Relations

Peru has been a prominent member of the Third World/Non-Aligned group of nations. After the military revolution of 1968, closer links were established with communist countries to maintain Peru's non-aligned stance. Since 1975 it has been government policy to concentrate more on Latin American affairs, and special efforts have been made to improve relations with Peru's neighbours, with two of whom, Ecuador and Chile, border problems persist. This shift of emphasis has been accompanied by the re-establishment of closer links with the West, particularly with the United States.

Andean Pact

In 1969 the Agreement of Cartagena (sub-regional agreement) was signed by Chile, Colombia, Ecuador, Peru and Bolivia, and later by Venezuela in 1973. The so-called Andean Pact was established with the object of promoting the balanced and harmonious development of the member states of the Latin American Association for Free Trade (ALALC), established by the Treaty of Montevideo 1960, and of promoting a continuous improvement in the standard of living of the inhabitants of the sub-region. (Chile has now withdrawn from the grouping.) Among measures discussed and agreed at subsequent meetings are the following:

(i) the harmonisation of economic and social policies of the different member countries by legislation where necessary

(ii) the collective planning and intensification of sub-regional industrialisation

(iii) the lowering of tariffs between member states with the aim of achieving a common tariff system

(iv) the planned acceleration of the development of the agricultural sector

(v) the canalisation of resources in and outside the sub-region to finance the investment necessary for the process of integration

(vi) preferential treatment for Bolivia and Ecuador (the most under-developed countries in the group).

Educational Cooperation

In 1970 the *Convenio Andrés Bello* was signed between Chile, Colombia, Venezuela, Peru, Ecuador and Bolivia for cooperation in education, science and culture. The five bases of the agreement are:

(i) the encouragement of good relations between the countries of the Andean region

(ii) the preservation of the cultural identity of their peoples within the framework of the Latin American heritage

(iii) the intensification of interchange of cultural riches between the countries

(iv) the joint development of their countries through education, science and culture

(v) the application of science and technology to raising the standard of living of the peoples of the region.

The Ministers of Education of the signatory countries meet regularly. The group has already agreed to recognise each others' primary and secondary studies. The group has also made a comparative study of the education system in each member country but its publication has been held up by the present Chilean government which wishes to make some changes to the system that existed under President Allende.

4 SOCIETY AND CULTURE

Social Patterns

Although the Spanish descended Peruvians *(criollos)* have been termed individualistic and even egocentric, the influence of the family is very strong. Family networks can be extensive and the influence of some rich families, though reduced in recent years, remains very great indeed. Personal relations are valued highly and personal contacts are often necessary in order to gain access to positions of influence and wealth. Generally speaking, contemporary Peruvian social values are a product of the geographical and racial diversity of the country, the colonial heritage, and the impact of twentieth century industrialisation. Social differentiation is based on a complex blend of racial, cultural and economic categories, a process that began with the first Inca-Spanish contact and has continued since then to the present day.

Colonial Groupings

Early colonial society consisted of three caste-like groups differentiated both on racial grounds and by economic functions. The *criollos* or Spanish descended whites *(blancos)* lived mostly on the coast in Lima and controlled all social, economic and political institutions. The *mestizos* (mixed blood) served the *criollos*, staffed the bureaucracy and were active commercially in the towns. The Indians did the manual labour on the *haciendas* and in the mines. Despite the current cult of the Indian, the object of the socially ambitious individual is still to distance himself as far as possible from Indian culture and to aspire to integration into the *criollo* culture. The logical extension of this process is a rather exaggerated regard for European and American models.

In a country as large as Peru and one suffering from such poor communications the gradual fusion of these three major groups has been a slow process and is still far from complete. For the Indian the process of acculturation is a complex one. First he has to learn Spanish. (According to the 1960 census only 67% of the population was Spanish speaking, the rest being restricted to Quechua and Aymara. This 33%, living principally in the southern sierra, was effectively enclosed in the Indian sub-culture and even today the areas in which educational attainment is weakest are precisely those where there is the greatest concentration of Quechua and Aymara speakers.) Next the Indian has to adopt the cultural patterns of *mestizos* and seek strategic links with those in the socially superior community. Most difficult of all, he has to find secure employment (usually involving migration) in order to be able to integrate economically and thus afford the lifestyle of culturally more prestigious groups. *Cholos* (Indians in process of acculturation) have not always been readily accepted by the urban *mestizos* and cultural conflicts between the two groups can cause problems for the schools, as when *Cholos* are called 'llamas' by their *mestizo* classmates. In the end, the prospects for assimilation will probably depend upon the somewhat uncertain financial future of the country.

Impact of Industrialisation

Despite these groupings Peru was never a true caste society and it was always possible for individuals to rise into higher cultural and economic groups. Industrialisation, which started in the 1920s, considerably accelerated this process by offering greater economic opportunities and providing the means for a greater diffusion of knowledge. A survey undertaken in 1970 revealed the impact of social change consequent to industrialisation. The survey revealed that 53% of heads of families hoped to educate their sons to become professionals or technicians, although only about 5% of the population was currently employed in those occupations. The corresponding figures for farming and livestock breeding were 17% and 47% respectively. Clearly a high proportion of the Peruvian population now wish, somewhat unrealistically, that their children will enjoy a substantial degree of upward mobility and view the purpose of the educational system as providing the means whereby these dreams may be realised.

Because of the development of better transport facilities and because industries have been increasingly concentrated on the coastal strip, particularly in Lima, industrialisation has occasioned considerable migration within the country, breaking down barriers of distance that existed in colonial times and to a lesser extent in the early republican period. The rapid if uneven development in parts of the coastal strip and isolated enclaves of the jungle and sierra have resulted in the establishment of educational facilities and the growth of social attitudes conducive to acceptance of education. Industrialisation, whether of the rural of urban variety, necessitated the development of basic literacy skills and aided the dissemination of Spanish, until recently the sole medium of instruction. By way of contrast, the undercapitalised traditional sectors lacked, and still lack, incentive to profit from formal school instruction which has been, in any case, orientated to vastly different social conditions and cultural assumptions.

Religion

Peru is very much a Catholic country and religion is one of the most important unifying factors, even though it is probable that only a minority of Peruvians are practising Catholics and amongst the practising minority very different conceptions of the nature and purpose of religion are entertained. The influence of the Church on both politics and education remains very strong, although very difficult to assess in concrete terms. It is probably fair to say that although the Church contains radical elements, it is slightly more conservative in orientation than, for example, the churches of Brazil, Chile or Mexico. It remains heavily dependent on foreign clergy and religious orders.

5 THE ECONOMY

Pattern of the Economy

The principal characteristics of the Peruvian economy are its dualism and the relatively dynamic and diversified nature of its export sectors with limited background linkages. The dualistic nature of the economy has led to extreme regional contrasts with the coastal strip being the advanced export sector and the sierra the backward traditional sector (except for a few mining enclaves). Consequently there exist extreme regional contrasts of income distribution and type of economic activity which may be summarised as follows:

(i) *Rural Sector*
Large areas of the coastal strip employ relatively advanced technology, produce for the domestic or international market and enjoy relatively high rates of employment but most of the sierra is characterised by under-capitalised subsistence agriculture and vast under-employment

(ii) *Non-Rural Sector*
The dualism of the rural sector is also present, if to a less marked degree, in urban areas in which a dynamic modern sector enjoying relatively high employment levels coexists with an under-employed sub-stratum concentrated most heavily in the service sector.

Agriculture and Fisheries

Agriculture occupies nearly half the workforce, but accounts for less than one fifth of the national product. Only 25% of the total territory is agricultural land, of which a mere 2% is arable, most of the rest being poor mountain pasture. In product terms, the sector can be divided between industrial crops, principally sugar and cotton grown on the coast, and foodcrops (maize, potatoes, rice etc.), these being respectively organised in large capitalised estates and peasant farms. About a quarter of the agricultural labour force is permanently employed on the estates with another 15% coming in as seasonal labour. Production on the large estates is highly organised and integrated into processing and exports, with good access to finance and inputs. Food production, by contrast, is technically backward, poorly organised and lacking in finance and inputs. Fishing is dominated by the fishmeal industry based on the exploitation of the anchovy but is dependent on the vagaries of the Humboldt current and subject to the problems accompanying over-exploitation.

Agrarian Reform

Under the Belaunde government an attempt at land reform was passed into law (1964), but there was no real attempt at implementation. The effect was to exacerbate rural tensions and the combination of weak agro-export prices, social disturbance and attractive investment opportunities in urban areas led to a decapitalisation of the rural sector leading to an absolute fall in agricultural production in 1967 and again in 1968. The Agrarian Reform Law, instituted in 1969, was the most radical in South America. Large estates were turned over to the workforce, creating a series of *Co-operativas Agrarias de Producción* (CAPs) on the coast and *Sociedad Agrícola de Interés Social* (SAIS) in the sierra. Low levels were set for private holdings, 150 hectares on the coast, 30-35 elsewhere. Just over 200,000 families working on 5 million hectares of land benefited from the reform. However, the bulk of the rural workforce, primarily those producing food for domestic consumption, were not affected because about 60% work their own plots and the 15% who work seasonally on the estates could not participate in the benefits of the cooperative or SAIS, the profits being restricted to the permanent workforce. Moreover the relative size of the holdings has not changed, nor have the structure and techniques of production.

Minerals

There is vast mineral wealth in the Andes, principally copper, lead, zinc, iron and silver, while oil deposits are being exploited in the Amazon region. Minerals have been managed by large corporations (CENTROMIN, MINEROPERU, PETROPERU) and ownership has passed from foreign capital to Peruvian state control since 1968. Although the mining sector is a small employer of labour, it is the principal generator of foreign exchange.

Industry

Industry is relatively under-developed. About a quarter of manufacturing output is concerned with processing export products (minerals, sugar, fishmeal), about half is in consumer goods (principally textiles and food processing), while the remaining quarter is in basic industry (especially steel, cement and fertilisers). Emphasis is now being placed on the development of this third sector of manufacturing production. Production is sharply divided between large capitalist or state enterprise which, using relatively sophisticated technology, accounts for two thirds of the output of the manufacturing sector, but employs only one third of the workforce, and artisan production (i.e. in firms of 5 employees or less) which tends to absorb the bulk of migrants from the rural areas.

It is clearly impossible to pass an overall judgement of the efficiency of Peruvian industry, but there are strong indications that there is considerable room for improvement.

Within the industrial sector the government since 1968 effected a considerable transfer of ownership nationalising large sectors of Peruvian industry at the expense of both private and foreign capital and experimenting with a variant of workers' control. In 1975 42% of industry was State-owned compared with 18% in 1963. During the same period foreign ownership declined from 34% to 13% and domestic from 48% to 35%, with 10% of industry owned by cooperatives. However, since 1975 there has been a steady drift to the right, although this does not necessarily mean that the State apparatus is being dismantled or replaced by private enterprise. While the initial policies of the régime gave priority to social-structural change through technological development, current policies are typically technocratic, emphasising rapid growth of productivity and concentration on the sectors most likely to achieve that end.

Employment

Levels of employment vary between urban and rural sectors. Although the levels of urban unemployment are relatively low (between 5% and 10%) the under-employed account for nearly one third of the urban population. Full data is not available but it is probably that there is a tendency for this proportion to rise. According to a report issued by the *Instituto Nacional de Planificación* the effective employment rate of the economically active rural population varied markedly according to region. While 90% of the labour force on the coast was employed in 1965, the situation in the sierra and selva was dramatically different with effective employment levels of only 36% and 48% respectively.

6 THE EDUCATION SYSTEM

Academic Year

The academic year runs from March to December with the long break taken in January and February. Term dates are variable.

Reforms in Progress

The pre-university system was changed as a result of the application of a General Education Reform Law passed in 1972. The traditional pattern of primary, secondary and higher education was replaced by a new tripartite structure, viz:

(i) initial education - the pre-primary stage for children under 6 years of age

(ii) basic education - for those aged between 6 and 15

(iii) higher education - which comprises three cycles: Higher Schools of Professional Education (ESEPs) and university studies at under-graduate and post-graduate level.

Pre-Primary

Attendance is voluntary though encouraged by the Ministry of Education. The percentage of 5 year olds enrolled in pre-primary education rose from less than 10% of the age group in 1972 to 17% in 1975. Of the 191,000 children attending pre-primary classes in 1976 89% lived in urban areas, the majority coming from middle class homes. There was a considerable growth of provision in the late 1970s with an increase of enrolments from 195,895 in 1977 to 286,000 in 1978.

Basic

Basic education consists of nine grades grouped in three cycles:

(i) first cycle of grades 1-4 (ages 6/7 - 9/10)

(ii) second cycle of grades 5-6 (ages 10/11 - 11/12)

(iii) third cycle of grades 7-9 (ages 12/13 - 14/15).

Primary (grades 1-6)

Every teacher working in the first six years of basic education should have received a manual issued by the Ministry of Education outlining the philosophy and practice of the reformed curriculum. The manual commences with a critique of the traditional pattern of Peruvian education, criticising it for its 'pure intellectuality', lack of connection with contemporary Peruvian reality, and its excessive concentration on past facts and abstract conceptions. Instead of the unilateral concentration on over-institutionalised curricula, the manual proposes that an 'integral curriculum' be established embodying a plurality of aims. Henceforth the school should attempt:

THE STRUCTURE OF THE

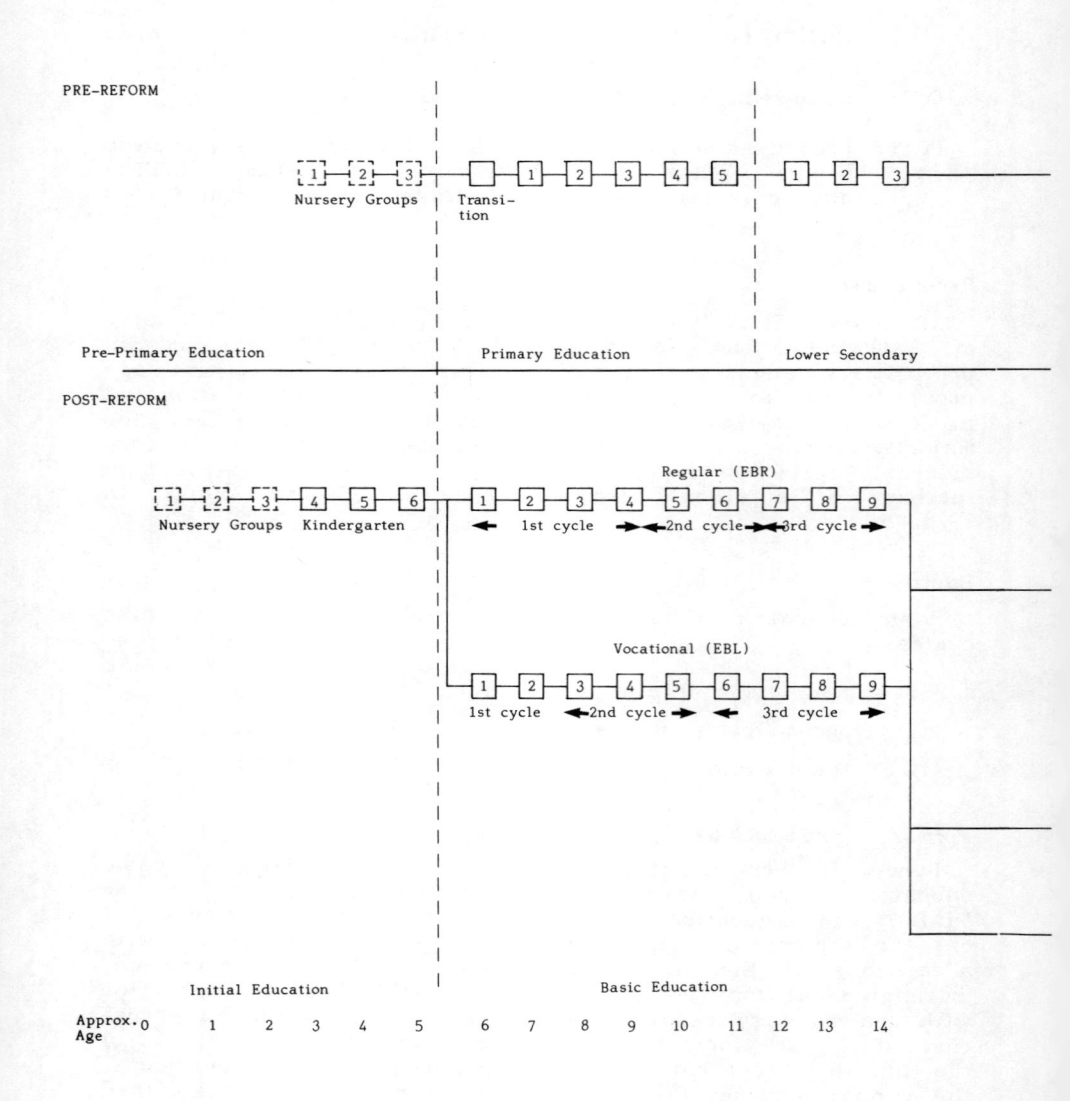

PRE-REFORM

| [1] [2] [3] | | 1 2 3 4 5 | 1 2 3 |
| Nursery Groups | Transi-tion | | |

Pre-Primary Education | Primary Education | Lower Secondary

POST-REFORM

[1] [2] [3] 4 5 6 | 1 2 3 4 5 6 7 8 9
Nursery Groups Kindergarten

Regular (EBR)
← 1st cycle → ← 2nd cycle → ← 3rd cycle →

Vocational (EBL)
1 2 3 4 5 6 7 8 9
1st cycle ← 2nd cycle → ← 3rd cycle →

Initial Education | Basic Education

Approx. Age: 0 1 2 3 4 5 6 7 8 9 10 11 12 13 14

PERUVIAN EDUCATION SYSTEM

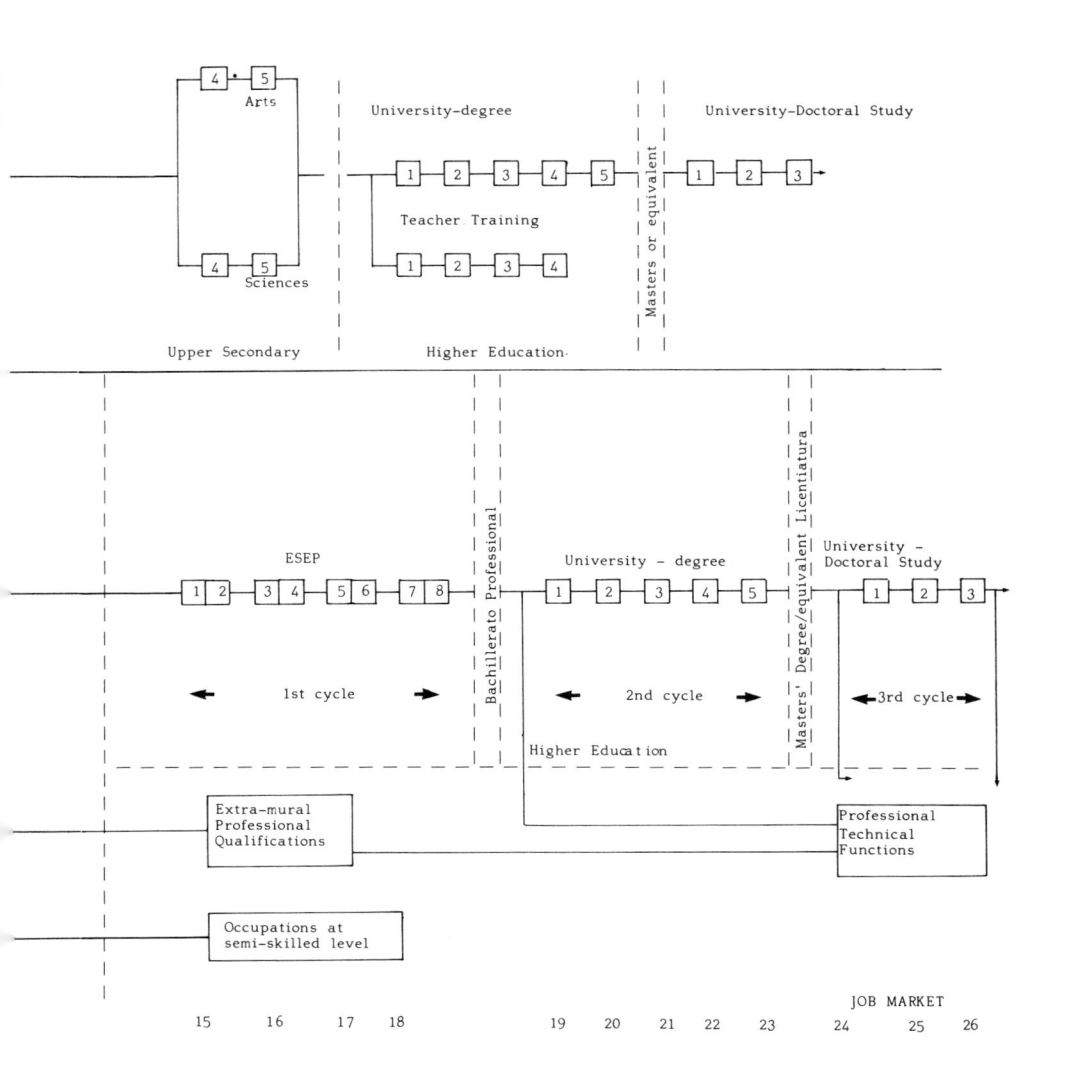

(i) to transmit both theoretical and practical knowledge, emphasising scientific facts and ways of thought
(ii) to enable each child to engage in physical activity
(iii) to equip each child for work by enabling him to acquire the symbolic and technical skills necessary for the different productive processes
(iv) to orientate the child by means of vocational and psychological support.

The reformed curriculum comprises the following subjects at primary level: language, mathematics, social sciences, natural sciences, art, physical education, vocational education, religion. The ministry has not laid down set timetables detailing the number of periods for each subject; each school is at liberty to devote as much time as is required to each subject provided that the aims laid down by the ministry are satisfied. However, the ministry has retained control of the educational process by laying down a series of objectives for each grade in each subject area. Each principal objective is divided into a series of secondary objectives designed to contribute to the realisation of the principal objective. A series of suggestions for the realisation of each secondary objective is also included in the teachers' manual.

Emphasis is also placed on the methodology of the teacher. To quote from the manual: "Educative work in the classroom on the part of both teacher and pupil must be an act of permanent creation to overcome the divorce that the traditional school effected between theoretical and practical aspects, between the school and life between some forms of knowledge and others, and between formal and informal activities."

Secondary (grades 7-9)

A similar reform programme as in primary schools has been introduced though the changeover occurred somewhat later. This replaced a traditional academic curriculum to which had been added subjects such as practical work and orientation and well-being.

Secondary education is still not available for all the age group though about 50% of 12-16 year olds were in secondary schools in 1978 compared to only a little more than 25% in 1970.

Promotion

Promotion from grade to grade is not necessarily tied to fixed chronological periods but is linked to the conditions and learning demands of the individual student. He may be promoted to the next grade automatically once he has achieved the experience and learning which constitute the appropriate minimum requisites. Therefore repetition of the grade is excluded. Each student has a single cumulative record card in which his overall performance is recorded. On completion of the basic level he is issued with a global certificate of studies.

Vocational

Secondary technical or vocational training schools, seek to prepare students for 'blue collar' careers by industrial, commercial, agricultural and craft programmes. Greatly increased enrolment in the wide variety of programmes offered by these establishments has followed as a direct consequence of vastly increased demand for technical school programmes. The number of students enrolled has jumped from 48,000 in 1963, to 96,000 in 1968 and to 257,000 in 1976, of which about two thirds were following full time day courses.

Higher Schools of Professional Education (ESEPs)

The Higher Schools of Professional Education is the first cycle of the higher education system and replaced the upper echelon of the former system of secondary education. The ESEPs were a keystone of the educational reform. They were designed to provide basically, but not exclusively, technical training and aimed to provide students with a professional qualification. This cycle is open to all students who have completed basic education and lasts from six to eight semesters depending on the option chosen. The special glossary at the end of the Educational Reform Law defines a semester as being 90 working days. A system of credits is used and certificates are awarded throughout the cycle, so that students can begin to work if they wish before completing their studies, which lead finally to the *Bachillerato Professional*.

In 1975 the first ten ESEPs were initiated and were located in Arequipa, Cuzco, Huancayo, Iquitos, Juliaca, Lima, Moquegua, Piura and Puno. A total 5,200 pupils were attending these ten schools. The pupils were taken out of the third and fourth year of 25 secondary schools. By the end of 1976, 13 ESEPs were functioning, including four in Lima, with a total attendance of 11,700 pupils.

A process of widening the curriculum scope of the ESEPs is being undertaken to include non-academic studies. The aim was that 40% of the students would follow non-academic courses though there have been difficulties in realising this aim.

Curricula

According to the General Education Law the ESEP curriculum will have an adequate proportion of general courses as well as those with a purely professional orientation. It is impossible to describe these general courses in national terms since the law allows for flexibility of curricula and it is the task of each ESEP to determine the relative weight that will be given to each subject within the general course area. However, each ESEP is expected to offer general courses in English, Spanish, natural sciences, physics, religious education, history and geography, which both represent an extension of basic education and a preparation for various types of university training.

In addition to the general courses, each ESEP will offer a series of specialist vocational options, the range of choice being determined by the specific socio-economic characteristics of the region in which the ESEP is situated. Each subject area is divided into a number of specialities permitting the student some small flexibility of vocational choice within his option. The options are as follows:

(i) rural husbandry (agricultural production, animal production)

(ii) petroleum studies (laboratory work, processing operations)

(iii) economics and administration (administration, accountancy and finance, executive secretaryship)

(iv) electricity and electronics (electricity, electronics)

(v) health (diseases, oral health)

(vi) mechanics (auto-mechanics, production mechanics)

(vii) forestry (forestry industries)

(viii) mining and metallurgy (foundry work and metallurgy, prospecting and mineral extraction)

(ix) construction and topography (construction, construction and topography)

(x) arts (graphic design).

Universities

There are 22 State and 11 private universities in Peru, the majority having been founded since 1955. A rapidly diversifying occupational structure brought about by the process of industrialisation has created a demand for the specialist academic skills provided by universities. Hence in recent years the university population has grown considerably from 30,983 in 1960 to 111,078 in 1970 and 186,511 in 1975, when 72% of students were in State universities, 28% in the private sector. Total enrolments rose fo 210,083 in 1978.

Entrance

Entrance is gained by passing an entrance examination set by the individual university. The number of those seeking admission has increased even more rapidly than the expansion of places. The number of candidates seeking admission to the University of San Marcos graphically illustrates the steeply rising demand curve:

1930	1950	1960	1968	1976
182	2,525	4,554	13,279	33,500

In 1976 there were only 3,090 vacancies. However, the fierceness of competition does not necessarily imply a high standard of entry, but is more a reflection of rising expectations and the narrowness of the career ladder, as well as the increasing importance attached to university qualifications for entry to the professions.

Courses

According to information published by the National Council of Peruvian Universities (CONUP), a total of 77 subject areas are offered by the Peruvian university system, of which 22 are in various fields of engineering. Within each area a wide variety of courses are offered.

A credit system based on American models is used as the basis of assessment. Each student takes a multiplicity of courses and is given a mark (out of 20) for each. Failure to attain the pass mark of 11 entails repetition of the course, and occasionally, the semester. If a student progresses satisfactorily and is not delayed by strikes he can expect to complete his university course in five years, although teacher training courses are shorter and a few subjects such as medicine require a more extended period of training.

Organisation

The administrative structure of the university system is complex. At the head of the university hierarchy is a Rector or the President of the Governing Commission, the latter post a relatively recent innovation intended to devolve power from the head of the university to a board. In theory, the President of the Governing Commission is regarded as primus inter pares with respect to other members of the commission whereas the Rector is usually granted ore extensive powers. In practice, personality is often a more important consideration. Rectors or Presidents are almost always academics and usually elected by faculty members. The organisational structure of universities varies but generally there are parallel academic and administrative hierarchies which find their unity in the Governing Commission.

Teacher Training

In the late 1960s deteriorating conditins accompanying rapid expansion drew congressional attention to the need for reform of teacher training. A plan was drawn up under which the number of teacher training institutes would be reduced from 78 to 39 in an effort to economise and prevent needless overlapping of human and material resources. Further reductions then occurred with the aim of having 20 institutions by 1980.

An increasing proportion of the teaching force is now being trained in the educational faculties of the universities, which were until recently reserved for those who intended to teach at secondary level. The number of primary school teachers now studying at the National Educational University should bring about a welcome rise in the standard of teaching in this sector. In 1973 the same university set up an adult education unit, enrolling just over 400 students in the first year of operation. However, the rise in numbers of those training in the universities has only partially offset the decline in the numbers of students registered as studying in teacher training institutes:

Year	Universities	Teacher Training Institutes
1965	9,500	15,400
1970	19,700	17,800
1975	23,111	9,400

Courses

Typically a trainee teacher has followed an encyclopaedic course in which the study of his academic speciality consumed only a small fraction of the time spent in training. A credit system, based on American models, is used to evaluate his progress. Until recently little emphasis was placed on teaching practice and many trainee teachers were allowed only 10 practice teaching periods during their time in training.

In-Service

The reorientation required by the 1972 General Education Law implies a complete retraining of the teaching profession. Since 1972 many teachers have gone on retraining courses, the vast majority of which have been of less than two months' duration.

Adult and Non-Formal

Peru provides an excellent example of a developing country where the combination of rapid, if uneven, modernisation combined with what was, and to a great measure still is, an inflexible archaic formal school system, has given rise to an impressive array of vocationally orientated courses, the vast bulk of which fall outside the formal school system. Non-formal adult education is concerned with two major areas of need, namely the eradication of illiteracy and the upgrading of work skills for those already in employment. There are also very limited programmes for providing vocational education to the unemployed. In 1972, 970,000 adults of 15 years and over were registered as regularly attending a course in adult education of whom more than 80% lived in urban areas. The vast majority were aged under 30 and about 60% were men. Although exact figures are not available it is likely that about half were taking courses that could be strictly defined as non-formal.

Adult Basic

A programme administered by the Ministry of Education is designed to provide basic training for adolescents and adults who have not followed the standard basic education courses. The principal objective of this mode of education is to eliminate illiteracy. Although 70% of adults responding to the 1972 census claimed that they could read and write, this figure is likely to be wildly optimistic. According to the same census about 30% of the adult population had never even entered primary school and of those who had, less than half had completed their fourth grade and were thus likely to be functionally illiterate.

Access is open to those over 15 years of age and no previous studies are required. The system consists of three cycles and nine grades. Graduation tests are employed to place prospective students in their appropriate grade at entry. The educational content does not necessarily coincide with that of standard basic education although sufficient basic educational skills are taught to enable students to function as semi-skilled workers after their studies have been completed. The core areas of the curriculum are the historico-social sciences, language, mathematics and natural sciences, though art, religion, physics and vocational skills are also studied. The vocational component is adapted to the characteristics of the population and the regions and organised to coincide with regional development plans. Each student has a record card in which his cumulative overall performance is described. On completing the nine grades, he is given a global certificate of studies with a specification of the vocational areas and training completed. Possession of this certificate will entitle a student to enter the first cycle of higher education (ESEP).

Vocational

In response to a growing demand for skilled labour, Peruvian industrialists banded together in 1961 to create their own non-formal sub-system canned SENATI – *Servicio Nacional de Arendizaje y Trabaje Industrial* (National Apprenticeship and Industrial Labour Service). Originally SENATI was not subsidised by the government but solely supported by a payroll tax collected from approximately 2,000 Peruvian firms employing 15 or more workers. However, in 1971 it was reorganised as a public decentralised institution under the Ministry of Labour (Ministry of Industry and Tourism in 1973). The serious lack of skilled labour was illustrated by a survey carried out by SENATI in 1975. Although the categories employed in the survey were fairly crude, the following table illustrates the scale of the problem. It should also be borne in mind that the industrial workforce accounted for only about 14% of the total workforce at the time the survey was commissioned, a similar figure obtaining today:

Work Category	% needed	% employed
Profession	5	1.5
Technicians	10	2.5
Executive and Clerical	18	16.0
Skilled workers	33	18.0
Semi-skilled workers	29	26.0

In the 15 years of its existence SENATI has achieved considerable success. Not all of those trained have been given direct vocational training, a proportion of the programme being devoted to general education, but there is widespread agreement that SENATI has maintained excellent links with local firms and is providing a training at approximately the right technological level. It is claimed that even those who have studied on the general education programme have improved their work efficiency as a consequence of their training.

In 1975 a decree law was passed to the effect that all manufacturing establishments must establish an in-service training unit. By September 1976, there were more than 400 in-service training units in the industrial sector and 800 in the commercial. The principal aim of the law was to improve industrial efficiency. Most in-service training units are giving directly vocational training in such areas as machine maintenance and industrial safety.

Training programmes for an extraordinary professional qualification are the responsibility of a special unit in the Ministry of Education. The programmes are open to adolescents or adults with or without employment who wish to take specifically vocational courses. The following types of programme are offered:

(i) training for specific occupations

(ii) upgrading of currently employed work skills

(iii) training of self-employed workers

(iv) retraining programmes.

The number of those following courses in extraordinary professional education rose from 64,000 in 1974 to 80,000 in 1976.

Other

The Department of Educational Extension in the Ministry of Education attempts to utilise the various modes of distance teaching: radio, television, correspondence courses, etc., in an effort to realise one of the principal aims of the Educational Reform Law, that of providing permanent education for the adult population of the country. The principal function of these programmes has been to aid the literacy campaigns undertaken by the local vocational education centres and to promote cultural and political awareness.

There are a whole range of other non-formal education institutes of which the most significant is probably the armed forces which teaches a variety of vocational skills, including literacy, to conscripts.

7 EDUCATIONAL ADMINISTRATION

Centralised Control

Educational administration in both the public and private sectors is closely controlled by the State authorities. Beneath the Minister and Vice-Minister, both of whom are army officers, are the Directors-General of the four principal administrative areas:

(i) initial and basic regular education

(ii) basic vocational education

(iii) higher education (excluding the universities but including the ESEPs)

(iv) extra-mural education.

These Directors are all professional educationalists, working in the Ministry of Education. At national level, the appropriate Director-General works closely with INIDE (National Institute of Educational Research and Development) in determining the objectives to be achieved within each grade, the basic structure of the curriculum, and the means of evaluation. INIDE undertakes educational research, prepares school textbooks and curricular and methodological grades and bears the responsibility for training teachers in the doctrines of the educational reform.

Within the ministry the Permament Committee for Coordination of Education, a committee composed of civilian educationalists, is concerned with liaison with other public sectors and internal bodies (and with the initiation of a more vocationally orientated curriculum there is a primary need for inter-sectoral cooperation at both local and national levels). In addition, the ministry receives advice from the Assessment Committee for the Ministry of Education (CAME) which is composed of military and civilian specialists and the inspectorate which fulfils a dual administrative and pedagogical role. Responsibility for coordinating Technical Cooperation Awards lay with the National Planning Institute until 1976 at which date the Scholarships Institute (INABEC) took over the programme. The National Planning Institute is still responsible for counterparts.

Devolution

Implementation of the policies initiated by the ministry in conjunction with INEDE rests with a network of decentralised institutions:

(i) there are 8 regions, each of which has a *unidad de co-ordinación técnica regional* whose task it is to coordinate the activities of the region and to provide the ministry with the regional data necessary for national planning

(ii) each region is divided into between three and five zones, each of which has its own *unidad de co-ordinación técnica pedagógica regional*. The task of the zonal officers is to ensure that the basic educational unit, the *nucleo educación communal* (NEC), is carrying out ministerial policy.

The *nucleos* were a creation of the Education Reform Law of 1972 and are the basic administrative unit of the education system at local level. The new structure was gradually set up between 1972 and 1975, there being 814 *nucleos* in the country. Each comprises a network of schools and informal education services and is responsible for the implementation of ministerial guidelines in its own locality. The administrative boundaries of the *nucleos* have usually been drawn to coincide with socio-economic boundaries. Thus each *nucleo* is intended to have only a limited range of social groups within its area in an effort to simplify the administrative problems of implementing a curriculum designed to provide a vocationally effective education. A flexibility with regard to timetabling permits each *nucleo* to emphasise different aspects of the general curriculum so that the content of education corresponds more closely with the peculiar socio-economic conditions obtaining in each nuclear area.

University Administration

Overall control of the university system lies with the National Council of Peruvian Universities (CONUP) which is a direct dependency of the Ministry of Education. This organisation fulfils a smilar function to the University Grants Committee and is responsible for university administration (including budgeting) and policy making. Its range of power reflects the centralised character of the Peruvian education system. Within CONUP membership of the Council of Rectors is restricted to the Rectors of the seven most prestigious universities - 5 public and 2 private (San Marcos, Trujillo, Cuzco, the National Engineering University, the Agrarian University, the Catholic University and Cayetano Heredia). Administrative power, however, is vested in the Executive Director, although a strong rector, particularly one from San Marcos, can influence the power situation considerably. In November 1976, CONUP was partially decentralised, certain of its functions devolving to regional councils set up in Arequipa, Ayachucho and Trujillo.

8 EDUCATIONAL FINANCE

Financial Administration

The administration of educational finance in Peru is extremely complex. In theory planning is conceived in both the long and the short terms. Within the framework established by the national long term plans, the Ministry of Economics and Finance, and National Planning Institute and the Council of Ministers are responsible for drawing up a national short term plan on the basis of which a global allocation is granted to the ministry. In cooperation with the Directors-General and the ministerial planning office, the minister has to distribute his allocation amongst the various sectors for which he is responsible, his final proposals being subject to the approval of the Ministry of Economics and Finance, the National Planning Institute and the Council of Ministers, after which the revised proposals are returned to the Directors-General for execution.

Education Budget

Peru devoted a high proportion of government expenditure and of national income to education in the late 1960s and early 1970s. However, both these proportions declined sharply in the later 1970s. Of total government expenditure in 1970, 18.8% went to education compared to 16.6% in 1975 and 10.5% in 1978. Similarly government educational expenditure as a percentage of GNP declined from 3.8% in 1970 and 4.0% in 1975 to 2.1% in 1979.

The way that the 1972 reforms were implemented firstly at primary level and then at secondary has meant that while the proportion of the education budget devoted to primary education rose from 39.8% in 1970 to 41.8% in 1977 it fell again to 38.1% in 1978. The proportion spent on secondary schooling has risen from 20.8% in 1975 to 26.5% in 1978.

ORGANISATION OF EDUCATIONAL

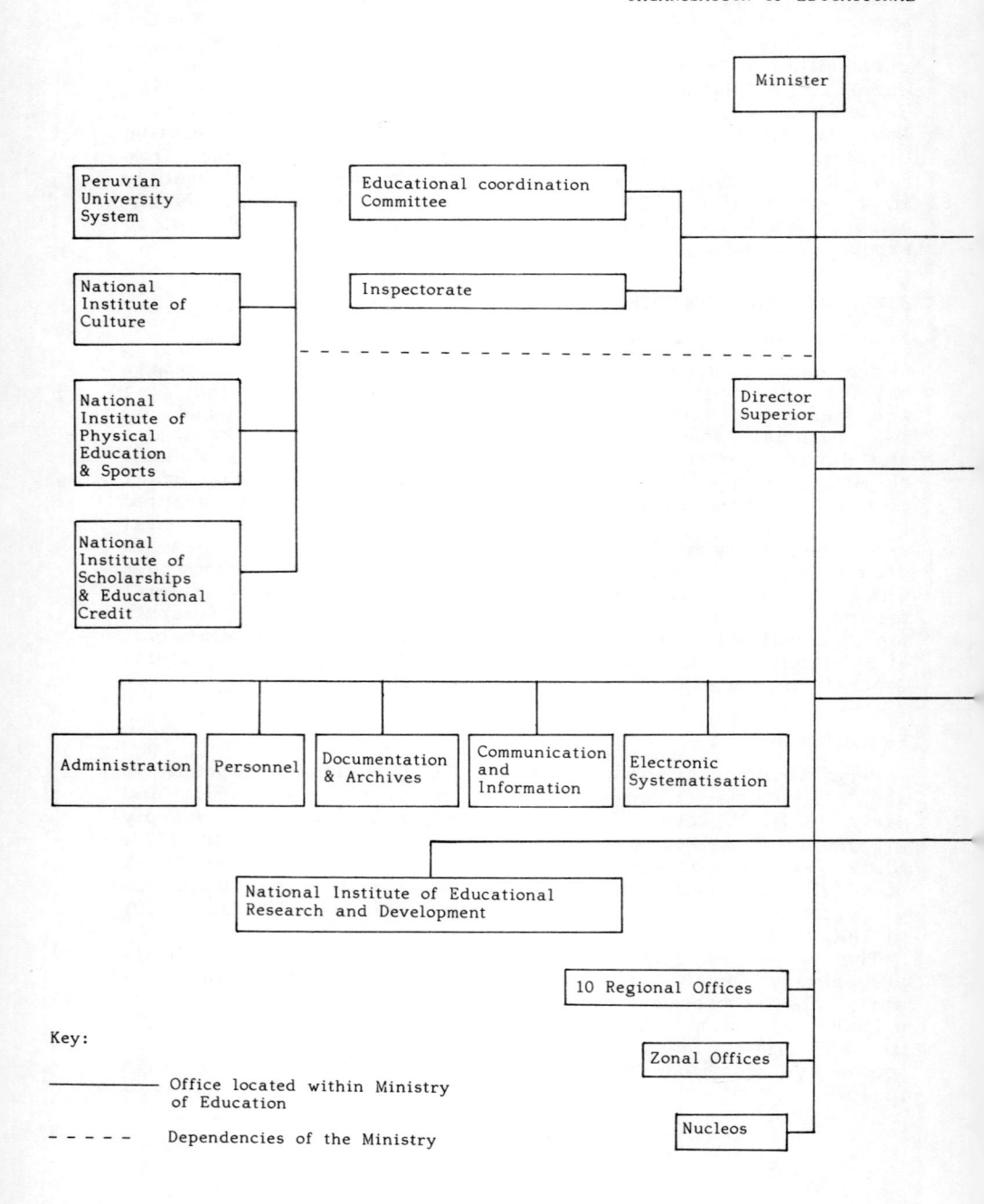

- Minister
- Peruvian University System
- National Institute of Culture
- Educational coordination Committee
- Inspectorate
- National Institute of Physical Education & Sports
- National Institute of Scholarships & Educational Credit
- Director Superior
- Administration
- Personnel
- Documentation & Archives
- Communication and Information
- Electronic Systematisation
- National Institute of Educational Research and Development
- 10 Regional Offices
- Zonal Offices
- Nucleos

Key:
─────── Office located within Ministry of Education
- - - - - Dependencies of the Ministry

ADMINISTRATION - PERU

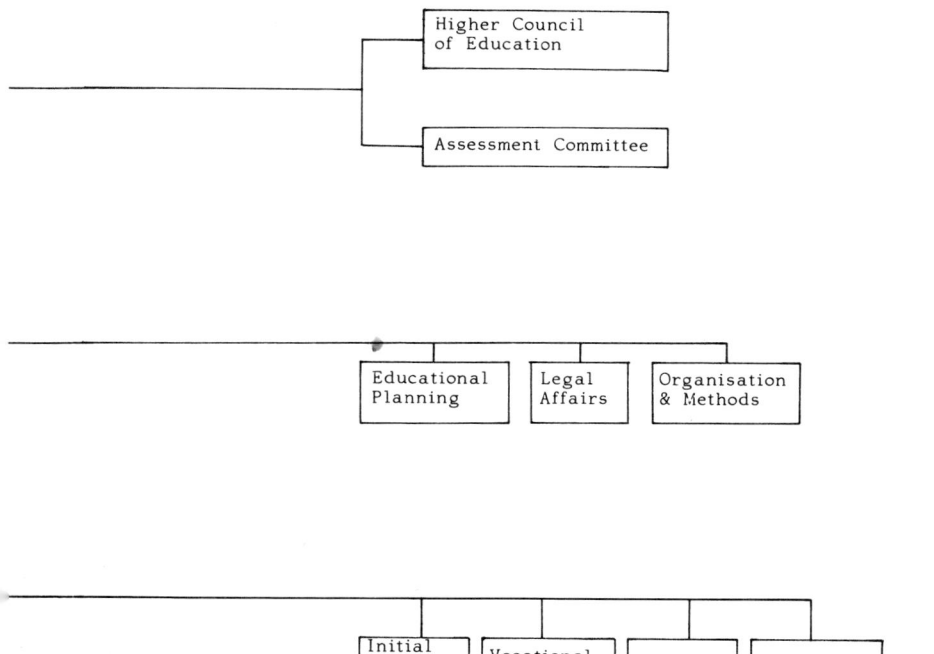

```
                    ┌──────────────────┐
                ────│ Higher Council   │
                │   │ of Education     │
                │   └──────────────────┘
                │   ┌──────────────────┐
                └───│ Assessment Committee │
                    └──────────────────┘
```

```
        ┌──────────────┐  ┌──────────┐  ┌──────────────┐
        │ Educational  │  │ Legal    │  │ Organisation │
        │ Planning     │  │ Affairs  │  │ & Methods    │
        └──────────────┘  └──────────┘  └──────────────┘
```

```
  ┌────────────┐ ┌────────────┐ ┌──────────┐ ┌────────────┐
  │ Initial    │ │ Vocational │ │ Higher   │ │ Educational│
  │ Basic      │ │ Education &│ │ Education│ │ Extension  │
  │ Regular    │ │ Calification│ │         │ │            │
  │ Education  │ │            │ │          │ │            │
  └────────────┘ └────────────┘ └──────────┘ └────────────┘

              ┌──────────────────────┐
              │ National Institute of│
              │ Tele-education       │
              └──────────────────────┘
```

Source: Ministry of Education

ORGANISATION OF CONUP

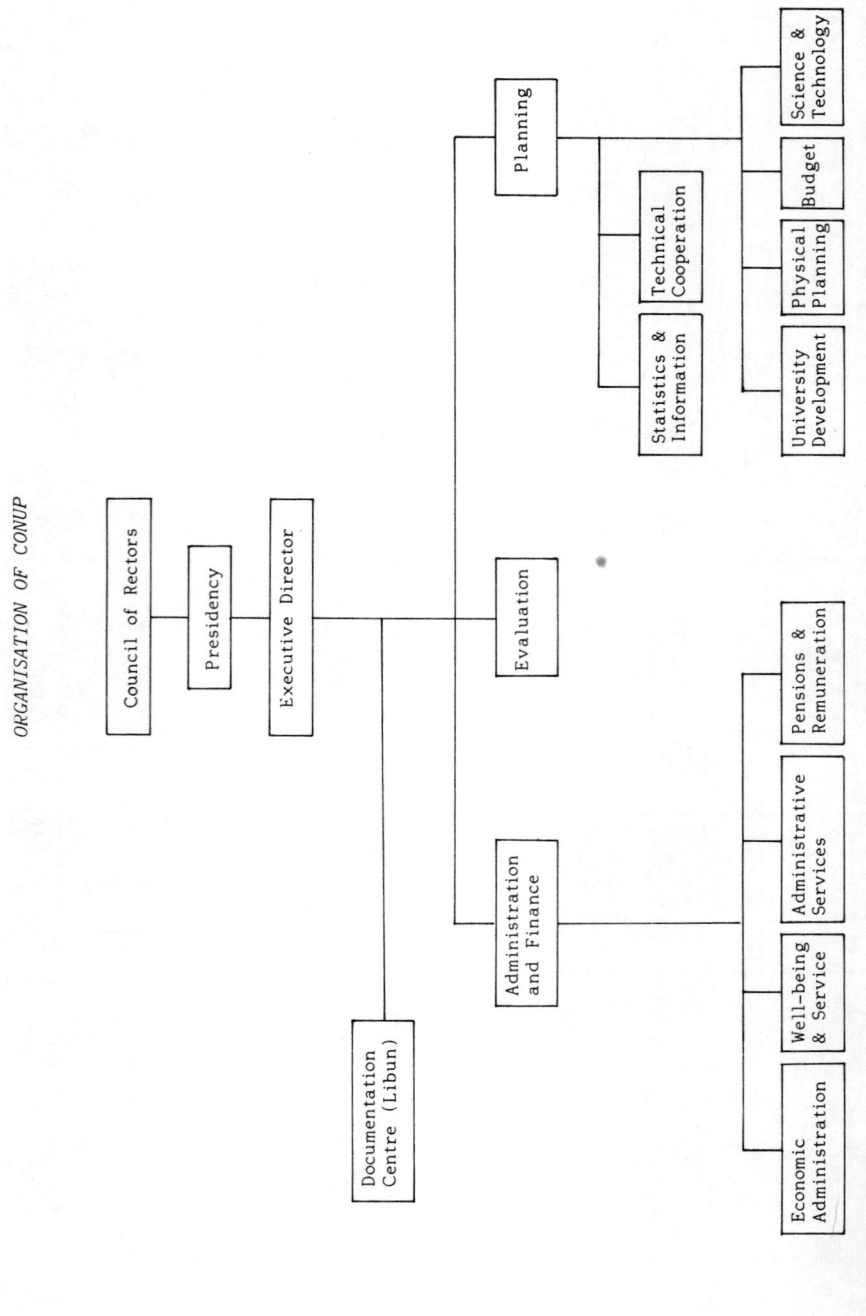

```
                    Council of Rectors
                           |
                       Presidency
                           |
                    Executive Director
        ┌──────────────────┼──────────────────┐
        │                  │                  │
  Administration       Evaluation          Planning
   and Finance                                 │
        │                           ┌──────────┴──────────┐
        │                    Statistics &          Technical
        │                    Information          Cooperation
        │
 ┌──────┼──────┬──────────┬──────────┐      ┌──────┬──────┬──────┬──────┐
Economic  Well-being  Administrative  Pensions &   University  Physical  Budget  Science &
Administration & Service  Services   Remuneration  Development Planning          Technology

  Documentation
  Centre (Libun)
```

Source: CONUP

Foreign Aid

A total of nine countries and ten agencies granted the Peruvian school system US$6.4 million in capital assistance in 1976 and US$9 million in 1977. Contributions in 1976 were dominated by FDR which spent over US$2 million in setting up a private German ESEP, and Canada which provided more than US$2 million of capital assistance to the ESEP system. In 1977 FDR was once again responsible for half the foreign capital assistance to the school system followed by UNESCO, Holland and Canada. In 1976 about 75% of all assistance was directed to the newly formed ESEP system, the proportion declining to about 12% in 1977. Other areas in which donors were interested included science, curriculum development, planning and bilingual education. In addition a large number of nations including Austria, Belgium, Britain, Denmark, FDR, Holland, Japan, Spain and Switzerland, as well as international organisations such as UNESCO and ILO have donated equipment, technical assistance, scholarships and funds for the main SENATI training centre in Lima and, to a lesser extent, the regional centres in Chiclayo and Arequipa.

Although it is difficult to assess the impact of Technical Cooperation Schemes the pool of available skilled manpower in Peru has been considerably augmented as a result of scholarships offered by the international community, and Peruvians are very well aware of the development potential inherent in Technical Cooperation scholarships. There is universal agreement that providing the candidates are well chosen and are specific in their training requirements the opportunity to study abroad is a valuable development tool.

9 DEVELOPMENT AND PLANNING OF THE EDUCATION SYSTEM

Origins

Incan education, totally destroyed in the conquest, is of historical interest only. In contrast, Spanish influence on Peruvian education remains largely visible today. Education under Spanish rule stressed Church control of a secondary and university education reserved for the dominant *criollo* group. With independence, the native *criollo* aristocracy, who had displaced those born in Spain, paid lip service to the ideals of the French Revolution, including the radical notion of universal schooling. However, throughout the nineteenth century over three quarters of the population, the Indians, remained outside the Spanish speaking culture and totally uninstructed. Schools and universities prepared the lawyers, doctors, priests and men of letters required by the high culture and the economy. The prevailing conception of education as aristocratic and humanistic grew as a logical result of economic and social realities and the philosophical basis of the Church.

The Twentieth Century

Twentieth century industrial progress has both required educational reform and partially given the means for achieving it. Educational reforms were attempted by Leguia (1908-12 and 1919-30), dependent largely on American expertise and capital. Although the first tentative steps were taken in this period towards the creation of a public education system, as late as 1940 the distribution of education was unequal in the extreme and symptomatic of the fact that Peruvian society was hardly ready to faced the demands which were to be made upon it by fairly rapid industrialisation. Only 3,007 of Peru's 29,246 towns had a primary school; there was one teacher for every 189 school age children (6-14 years) of whom only one third received any instruction. Children attending school were drawn almost exclusively from the *mestizo* and *blanco* groups. It is not, therefore, surprising to find that there were enormous regional variations in the rates of illiteracy, which varied from less than 9% in the constitutional department of Callao (Lima) to an average of 85% in the five departments making up the Indian heartland (Cuzco, Huancavelica, Ayachucho, Puno and Apurímac).

A comment made by the Peruvian educator, V A Belaunde, on the early American reform efforts reveals the attitudes to education amongst wide sections of the elite prior to and even after World War II. According to Belaunde the early American reform effort failed because:

> "It resulted in the introduction of the American high school with its egalitarian levelling emphasis that sacrificed the training of exceptional students for positions of leadership and substituted a programme of mass uplifting. To this error was added another in procedure; it believed that American methods could only be introduced by American personnel who were not always adapted to conditions in Peru."

Belaunde was certainly correct in issuing a warning against the uncritical introduction of foreign educational techniques into a society for which they were ill adapted. But his fears of a 'mass society', uttered contemporaneously with Ortega y Gasset and others in Europe, was itself ill adapted to a society which opted for rapid industrialisation after 1945.

Planning Institutions

Within the ministry the Higher Council for Education, composed of civilian educationists, is concerned with educational planning. However, overall planning responsibility lies with the National Planning Institute which is answerable to the National Council for Social and Economic Development and the Council of Ministers.

Educational Reform

Volume I of the NPI's National Plan 1971-75 (published May 1971) outlined global planning policy for the quinquenium, including basic guidelines for the proposed educational reform. These guidelines were later vastly expanded, with minor shifts of emphasis, in the Educational Reform Law 1972 which should not therefore be regarded as an isolated document but a significant part of an overall domestic and international strategy.

Reform Law 1972

The Law attempted to effect basic changes within the school system at three levels: organisational, curricular and methodological. But its objectives were conceived at varying levels of generality and were intended to be implemented over very different time spans. The first section of the Law (articles 1-29) set out the principles on which the educasctional reform was to be based. The basic purpose of Peruvian education was defined as "the complete formation of the human being"; it should be oriented towards creating "a new man, participating fully in a free, just and united society, developed for the creative and communal work of all its members". Stated in general terms the objectives were to prepare individuals for:

(i) specific tasks that are adapted to the development of the country

(ii) structural change and the permanent process of perfecting Peruvian society

(iii) the self-assertion and independence of Peru within the international community.

The State guaranteed freedom of education, the right of all to be educated and choose their form of education, and equality of educational opportunity. To this end, State education was to be free at all levels so that nobody would be excluded for economic reasons.

In more specific terms the reform aimed to achieve the following:

(i) to improve the administrative framework and increase financial provision

(ii) to reduce the bureaucracy and accelerate the process of decentralisation

(iii) to train and reorientate teachers at all levels; formalistic methods were to be discouraged and encouragement given to developing qualities of constructive criticism, creativity and cooperation

(iv) to coordinate educational reform with agrarian reform, with the aims of integrating and restructuring society

- (v) to include all sectors of the community, including the indigenous population, in the revolutionary process; accordingly education was to take into account the existence of different languages and cultures within the country and to protect their preservation and development; the whole population was to learn Spanish, but the process must respect the culture of different groups, and their own languages would be used as part of the educational process
- (vi) to eliminate illiteracy
- (vii) to improve the quality of technical education
- (viii) to further the idea of education as a continuing process from birth to death, by extending the education of infants and of educationally under-privileged adolescents and adults, by including criminals and handicapped people by means of special schools and extra-mural programmes, such as night classes and educational radio and television
- (ix) to broaden the bases of education, to include fine and performing arts, recreation and sport and to lay the foundation for an authentic Peruvian culture.

Tupac Amaru Plan

In February 1977 the government issued a new forward plan for 1977-80 - The Tupac Amaru Plan, a translation of the educational provisions of which is included as an appendix to this profile.

The Plan marks a reorientation of educational policy. In general terms, whereas the Education Reform Law wished to harness scientific modes of thinking and technological progress as a means of effecting social-structural change, the Tupac Amaru plan emphasised technical and vocational education as the means by which production may be increased. Whereas the 1972 Law envisaged Peruvian society as a rapidly changing process which the task of education was to accelerate, the Tupac Amaru Plan viewed society as a given structure which the educational system was to strengthen by more efficient allocation of future work roles through vocationally oriented education. The two plans concur in the emphasis placed on non-formal literacy campaigns and the ESEPs, the latter institutions being the only sector of the school system marked out for special attention.

Conclusion

It is therefore clear that the Educational Reform Law was only a starting point. The Peruvian education system has been, and remains, in a continuous state of transition since the promulgation of the guidelines in 1972.

10 THE SYSTEM IN OPERATION

The following account of the system in operation will attempt to capture the regional contrasts of educational attainment presented by the official statistics. The performance of the Peruvian education system is correlated to such a remarkable degree with the economic structure of the cousntry that economic and social factors must be given precedence when analysing the scope, distribution and efficiency of the system.

Education and Social Groupings

A peculiarity of the Peruvian education system is that each social stratum has historically come to be linked with a distinct educational sub-system. These sub-systems are closely tied to each of the four different social groups: the blancos, the mestizos, the cholos and the Indians. The following table presents a social and educational stratification model that includes typical attributes of members in each social stratum. It will be noted that the system of cultural stratification is closely linked to the economic structure as previously analysed.

Although the following table is evidently schematic and subject to numerous exceptions, the point is that the social class-linked educational structure both reflects and tends to perpetuate the hierarchical and social systems and in so doing obstructs educational rationalisation and development. It does so directly by helping maintain traditional inequalities of resource allocation since most of the educational bureaucracy are from mestizo or blanco stock and usually educate their own children at private or elite public schools. Indirectly the congruence of economic and social forces makes it extremely difficult for any government to contemplate a major shift of resource allocation in favour of the rural areas, without which it is unlikely that the rural school system will be able to improve significantly.

A study published in 1972 examined the social impact of education in rural areas. While the results of the study are hardly surprising, confirming studies made in other developing countries, they are worth recording here as indicative of the impact of the educational system in the new context. The principal findings were as follows:

(i) the curricula were heavily oriented towards urban values. Consequently one of the principal effects of extended education was the affirmation of individual autonomy at the expense of community consciousness

(ii) the impact of the education system has been to increase individual social mobility marginally. Individual social mobility is often accompanied by a tendency to move to the urban areas although the educational levels of migrants, while higher

	Blanco	Mestizo	Cholo	Indian
Social Class	Upper	Middle	Lower	Marginal
Location	Lima	Urban (Lima and Provinces)	Urban–rural (migratory)	Rural
Language	Spanish and European	Spanish	Indigenous and Spanish	Indigenous (some Spanish)
Occupation	Owner	Manager, professional skilled worker in rural or urban industry	Unskilled worker in petty urban tertiary sector, soldier	Agricultural labourer *Minifundistas*
School	Elite Private (usually Lima University)	Lesser private, good public school; often high school or university	Primary (some secondary in cities)	Incomplete primary or unschooled

Source: Rolland Paulston (1972). *Society Schools and Progress in Peru.*

than their rural counterparts, are lower than the average urban levels

(iii) the higher the educational level achieved by an individual, the less likely he is to own land. In other words, even in rural areas it is the non-farmers who have benefited most

(iv) education has facilitated entry into non-agrarian professions only to the extent that the occupational structure of the locality has become differentiated.

Enrolments

Although it is true that all statistics relating to education in Peru should be treated with caution, those relating to primary and secondary schools are more than usually open to criticism. The only statistics available, published by the Ministry of Education, are compiled by obtaining reports on school attendance on the first day of the academic year and take no account of what happens subsequently. It is certain that a considerable proportion of the school population enrol at the beginning of the academic year, subsequently drop out, and re-enrol for the same grade at the beginning of the next academic year. Since a system of automatic promotion and flexible timetabling is in operation, excluding repeaters by definition from the official statistics, analysis of the efficiency of the system cannot rely on global attendance figures.

Bearing the above caveat in mind, there has been a steady improvement in the percentage of children attending school at primary and secondary level (on the first day of the academic year):

Year	Total Population 8-14 (000s)	No. Attending Grades 1-9 (000s)	% Rate of Attendance
1960	2,642.1	1,489.5	56.4
1965	3,153.3	2,153.6	68.3
1970	3,744.5	2,734.6	73.0
1975	4,202.7	3,224.0	77.0

In 1972 separate figures were given (which do not quite tally with those immediately above) in which the school age population was broken down by sex and residence when approximately 55% of the population lived in urban areas.

	Urban		Rural		Urban enrolment as % of total
Age	Male (000s)	Female (000s)	Male (000s)	Female (000s)	
6– 7	187.7	181.2	83.0	68.0	71
8– 9	205.7	200.3	120.9	99.3	65
10–12	304.9	285.5	200.5	149.3	63
13–14	180.5	165.5	98.6	60.2	80
Total	878.8	832.8	703.0	376.8	

Since demand for education is highest in the cities, school enrolments there are increasing even more rapidly than the population. Naturally since migration to the cities and the demand for education form part of the same pattern of expectations. The figures show that the bulk of those not enrolled live in the rural sector with girls in rural areas being far and away the most disadvantaged group. Moreover, those who attend school in rural areas tend to enrol for the first time at a later age than their urban counterparts land tend to leave at an earlier age. The bias against girls is clearly shown by figures illustrating the male/female attendance ratios at each level of the education system in 1970:

	Primary	Secondary	Higher
Males	54%	58.8%	69.7%
Females	46%	41.2%	30.3%

Provision

There is a serious shortage and unequal distribution of educational facilities and materials which is correlated very highly with social and economic variables. According to official statistics the provision of schools would seem to be remarkably evenly distributed. However, schools are larger on the coast with schools in the department of Lima having an average of 380 pupils and 13 members of staff compared to an average of 200 pupils and five members of staff in the sierra. Rural schools are often ill constructed.

Books and equipment destined for the rural sector often either never arrive or arrive months late, hampering planning on the part of teachers. There is a strong suggestion that small schools with inadequate facilities and a limited range of staff skills are the norm in the sierra, but no really hard information is available. There are certainly far fewer schools with secondary facilities in the sierra, and this encourages the more dynamic families to migrate to the cities hampering still further the task of providing a greater range of educational facilities in the rural areas. However, again no comparative figures are available.

Teachers

There has been a steady improvement in the qualifications held by the teaching force. The Ministry of Education recognises three categories of teacher:

1st category: teachers who hold an educational degree or diploma

2nd category: teachers who do not hold a teaching qualification but have a professional degree or have completed their educational studies without obtaining the diploma

3rd category: teachers who hold none of the above qualifications.

The following table illustrates the improvement in quality that has taken place:

	Category 1	Category 2	Category 3
Primary			
1960	37.9	14.8	47.2
1965	45.2	8.8	45.8
1970	55.1	5.8	38.9
1976	79.0	3.0	18.0
Secondary			
1960	35.7	22.8	41.4
1965	35.8	22.9	41.2
1970	45.1	14.5	31.3
1976	83.0	7.0	10.0

However, it should be borne in mind that the poor quality of teacher training means that the improvement in the level of teachers' qualifications may be more apparent than real. Partly as a result of the enormous expansion of numbers enrolled in teacher training institutes the facilities necessary for instruction in all but a few have been notoriously inadequate and plan to reduce the number of teacher training institutes was a direct congressional response to this. The average product of a teacher training course lacked a grasp of his subject, a factor which contributed heavily to the emphasis placed on the rote memorisation of textbooks commonly found in Peruvian schools and which persists today. In addition the inadequacy of practice teaching periods deprived trainees of the practical guidance vitally necessary for the production of good professional teachers. Educational extension workers in such programmes as literacy, adult education and bilingual education have also lacked adequate training in their speciality.

Although teachers have been steadily improving their paper qualifications, they have been confronted by ever-increasing classes. The staff-pupil ratios in primary schools have worsened from 1:35 in 1960 to 1:40 in 1978, whilst in the secondary sector an even more rapid deterioration has occurred, the staff-pupil ratios rising from 1:12 in 1960 to 1:29 in 1978. The average teacher-pupil ratios are higher in the sierra (1:40 as against 1:30 in the coastal strip).

The growth in numbers of university teachers has not kept pace with the expansion of student numbers. The teacher-student ratios worsened from 1:9 in 1968 to 1:17 in 1976, the figures being the same for both public and private sectors. However, these statistics mask the differences that exist between the universities as illustrated on the next page.

Only one sixth of all university lecturers work full time; the figures in the following table include both full time and part time teachers and since the less well endowed institutions also have a lower proportion of full time staff, the differences illustrated in the table actually under-state the magnitude of the gap that exists between the best and least endowed universities. However, even the most prestigious institutions are beset by financial problems as they attempt to raise the quality of their teaching force. Even at the Catholic University, a well qualified engineer would only expect to receive between 19,000 and 30,000 soles a month, whereas the same individual could expect a starting salary of 30,000 a month in industry.

It is now recognised that there is a serious lack of trained personnel to teach the technical subjects that will form the basis of the ESEP system. In order to overcome this deficiency the forward plan proposed by the government proposes that salaries be made more attractive for the teachers of these subjects in an effort to attract trained professionals and that agreements be signed with local firms under which skilled technicians be released for specified periods to engage in teaching.

	1970			1974		
University	Students	Staff	Ratio	Students	Staff	Ratio
San Marcos	20,310	1,885	1:11	22,566	2,834	1:8
Agrarian	2,088	316	1:6.5	2,884	329	1:9
Engineering	6,319	599	1:11	10,859	657	1:17
Catholic	4,126	651	1:6.5	7,465	778	1:9.5
Cay. Heredia	628	569	1:1	1,018	636	1:1.5
Fed. Villareal	11,832	370	1:32	19,172	556	1:35
San Martin de Porres	7,252	229	1:32	11,028	256	1:43
San Antonio Abad (Cuzco)	5,097	481	1:11	7,125	328	1:22

Wastage

Although there are no figures quantifying the numbers who fail to complete a school year, a rough idea of the efficiency of the system can be obtained by following the progress of successive cohorts of students. Taking the number of students of a given age who enrol in a particular grade for the first time in any year, the rate of wastage can be roughly calculated by following the progress of the age cohort through the school system. Until approximately 1964 rates appear to have been gradually improving. Of the children who entered the first grade in 1955, only 11% succeeded in enrolling in the ninth grade in 1964, whereas the cohort of 1961-70 succeeded in enrolling 22% of its number. Although there are strictly comparable figures only up to 1970 it appears that there was little improvement in the efficiency of the system after 1964 until the implementation of the Educational Reform, which seems to be making a considerable impact with a significant drop in wastage rates. At university level the drop out rate is alarming, the pass rate at four selected universities (Engineering University, Educational University, Huacho and Cuzco) varying from 8% to 30% of the enrolment.

Regional Variations

It is impossible to capture fully the relation between economic structure and distribution of educational attainment by analysing at departmental level since all the more developed coastal departments include a section of underdeveloped sierra and even the most backward of the sierra departments, Ayachuco, includes at least one large regional centre where the levels of attainment are significantly higher than the surrounding countryside. However, the broad outlines can clearly be discerned. The following table illustrates the wastage rate of selected departments, the sixth grade being the terminal grade of primary education (see next page).

Even the enormous discrepancies revealed by the departmental statistics do not express the magnitude of the difference in wastage rates between the most advanced urban areas and backward rural ones. Moreover the base levels on which the figures are calculated are expressing different percentages of enrolment, those from the more advanced areas including a greater percentage of the age group in question. More seriously, the figures suggest that low wastage rates are simply a factor of urbanisation which would be to simplify the situation rather drastically.

Even within the rural sector, the areas of industrialised commercial agriculture enjoying high employment rates and employing relatively high intermediate inputs have comparatively low rates of school wastage. The following (p.796) figures are taken from a study of the huge sugar cooperative, CAP Cartavio located in the coastal strip in the north of the country (1972 figures). They show the maximum level of education achieved by the various age groups of the population.

	1963 - 1st grade enrolment	1966 - 4th grade enrolment (As % of cohort first enrolled in 1963)	1968 - 6th grade enrolment (As % of cohort first enrolled in 1963)	Urban population (% of total)
Coast				
Lima	100	89	80	90.0
Lambayeque	100	77	64	67.0
La Libertad	100	59	47	46.8
Sierra				
Cuzco	100	41	27	35.8
Ayacucho	100	29	18	37.7
Junin	100	45	42	53.2
Jungle				
Amazonas	100	46	31	39.2

Age group	Total	Initial	Primary	Secondary	Higher	No level	Non-determined
5-14	100	23	56	6	0	12	13
15-24	100	1	33	53	5	3	5
25-34	100	1	58	24	8	6	3
35-44	100	2	66	11	4	15	2
45-54	100	3	58	4	2	31	2

In some respects the figures given in the preceding table are astonishing. They illustrate rapidly improving educational levels, clearly highly connected with the increasing sophistication of the local economy since the improvement is far more dramatic than any found in the sierra provinces. Secondly the levels attained by the 15-24 age group, roughly coterminus with the 1961-70 cohort discussed above are far superior to the national average despite the fact that CAP Cartavio is a purely rural zone.

Within urban areas it is impossible to present the educational statistics in a way which would illustrate the differences in educational attainment of different sectors of the urban population. The census definition is unhelpful in that an urban area is defined as any locality that has a population cluster of 1,500 or more persons, whereas the lowest rates of wastage are to be found in the largest cities, almost irrespective of where they are located. However, there is a correlation between levels of urban under-employment and educational attainment as the figures (1970) on the following page show. Although these figures take no account of the rates of migration nor the levels of achievement by age group, they are at least indicative of the fact that where rates of unemployment and underemployment are higher (indicating the presence of a large service sector) the level of educational attainment is lower. Further disaggregation would undoubtedly reveal huge discrepancies in educational attainment between sectors.

Causes of Wastage

The only survey to have investigated the causes of desertion strongly indicates the economic situation of the family as the principal determinant of school attendance, although fully 20% of the sample indicated that their attendance lapsed after moving house, showing that the heavy internal migration rates are at present a factor contributing to high drop-out rates. At university level the problem may be ascribed, in part at least, to the inadequate provision and low quality of teachers and a paucity of natural resources.

Private Schools

On average, the private sector enjoys slightly better teacher:pupil ratios than State schools and is about 20% more efficient in terms of overall wastage rates. However, such generalisations are misleading since the private sector embraces a multitude of schools operating at castly different levels of efficiency. At the pinnacle are the foreign bilingual schools such as the British type schools, Markham College and San Silvestre, which are patronised by the Lima elite. Standards in these schools are high with the majority of pupils gaining university entrance, either in Peru or abroad, prior to following what is normally a business rather than public sector or military career. Also of a high standard

	National	(Coast) Lima	(Sierra) Arequipa	(Jungle) Iquitos	Levels of Employment Lima	Arequipa	Iquitos	(OECD Definition)
Without Instruction	24	5	10	7	69	59	54	Fully Employed
Primary	48	43	48	58 }	27	34	36	Under-Employed
Secondary	23	41	34	30 }				
Superior	5	11	13	5	4	7	10	Unemployed

are numerous Church schools which similarly send a disproportionate number of their graduates to university. Unlike the foreign private schools, the high quality Church schools are located in all the principal centres of the country. Below the Church schools are a multitude of private establishments, often very small and of variable quality.

Universities

The universities are currently in a state of crisis. We have seen that enormous expansion has been accompanied by inadequate numbers and low quality of teachers and high drop out rates. In addition a proliferation of overlapping departments has led to unproductive duplication of physical and human resources which the financial structure of the university system is unable to accommodate. The number of administrative personnel has grown alarmingly in recent years at the structure of each university has become more complex. At the University of Cuzco, for example, the number of administrative staff has grown from 9 in 1960 to 246 in 1976, and proliferating departments has led to a situation where salaries take up to 98% of the university budget in the State sector. The amount devoted to books amounted to only 0.02% of the university budget in 1975 and capital equipment fared little better. Surface symptoms of crisis are clearly discernible. Endemic political unrest results in numerous striked so that the years allotted to completing a given course have become purely notional in the majority of universities.

The roots of the crisis appear to be found in two factors. Firstly, as will all other institutions in Peru, the current state of the university system is a response to the impact of modernisation on a traditional society. The varied response which modernisation met with amongst educated groups in Peru finds its expression in the division of the university system within which different institutes can be conveniently described as confessional, secular/technocratic or radical. Although these labels could no doubt be substituted by others, the Peruvian university system certainly is beset by internal rivalries of an ideological nature. Ideological rivalry has heavily contributed to the fragmentation of the university system.

Secondly, the growth of the university system has been connected with the rise of modern industry which created unemployment opportunities for its products. Initially demand for university education was closely correlated with the growth of the modern sector but the rapid rise in university enrolments has by now outstripped the capacity of local industry to absorb the ever increasing supply of graduates. Since about 1964 the percentage of the total economically active population employed in manufacturing has remained roughly constant at 13-14% representing an annual increase of between 3% and 4%, far below the increase in university enrolment figures. Although the State bureaucracy has expanded tremendously in recent years the point seems to have been reached when the limited tax base cannot support further growth of this sector, so that alternative employment opportunities have not been forthcoming.

Administration

The political instability that seems to be a permanent feature of Peru is reflected in the politicisation of the Ministry of Education where most high ranking personnel are political appointees. This does not necessarily mean that those appointed have little or no experience of educational problems, but does lead to a situation in which personnel are substituted en bloc when the government significantly reorientates its education policy. In the first two months of 1977, the rightward drift of the military government resulted in a purge of ministry personnel, a few departments losing up to 90% of their employees and even the research based institution INIDE losing half of its existing staff. Such intense politicisation and lack of permanent career structure is clearly inimical to long term implementation of educational policy.

The quality of administration is also low despite, or perhaps because of, the enormous expansion of administrative personnel attached to the education system in recent years. In particular, the quality of the university system could be rapidly improved if administration were more effective. Given the social and economic context in which education is administered, it is hardly surprising to find that maladministration reinforces the divisions that already exist between the advanced and backward sectors of the educational system. For example, rural educational programmes often require the participation of other public sector bodies Ministries of Agriculture, Food, Health, Housing). Unfortunately many such programmes are carried out with little or no coordination and with much duplication and waste of effort.

Relevance

The 1972 Decree on which the current educational system is based had to take into account expectations of social advancement through education while recognising that one of the most important tasks of contemporary educational systems is to try to ensure that school graduates are able to find employment appropriate to the development of the country. Thus the question of what constitutes relevance is by no means easy to answer since the economic structure of the country is such that what is relevant to the individual student (the financial prospects on terminating a particular course) is not necessarily congruent with development needs. A certain ambivalence therefore pervades the Reform Law, and the Educational Reform in general, in which the desire to confer the traditional humanistic benefits of education on the whole population is somewhat at odds with the realistic recognition of the necessity to prepare children for specific occupational roles.

Nevertheless, the Educational Reform Law initiated a process whereby the emphasis of Peruvian education would be placed more on vocational education and the prestige formerly accorded to academic subjects would be diminished. The creation of the ESEPs was undoubtedly the most positive move in this direction. Hitherto, the secondary vocational system has been extremely inefficient. Over 80% of all technical schools have not had the facilities to meet their objectives and partly as a consequence of this situation the curricula have been heavily weighted in favour of cultural humanistic courses. Moreover only about one fifth of technical school teachers possess the necessary qualifications. Consequently existing industrial firms have been unable to absorb the growing over-production of poorly prepared graduates and have preferred to upgrade the skills of workers already employed or to hire untrained primary school graduates at a lower wage. There are now some promising signs. Certain of the ESEPs are establishing good contacts with local industry, but there is a serious doubt whether national manpower planning techniques are sufficiently developed to permit a wholehearted vocational emphasis in the schools. For this reason, it is important to note that although more emphasis is rightly being placed on the inculcation of appropriate vocational skills and attitudes, general education has not been neglected. It remains to be seen whether the correct balance can be struck.

It has been argued in this Profile that the development of the Peruvian education system has been essentially a response to the modernisation process resulting from industrialisation, encouraged by the concentration of investment and the creation of jobs in the export sector. There is as yet no sign of a fundamental shift of resource allocation towards rural subsistence areas. Accordingly it is unlikely that satisfactory employment opportunities will grow to any great extent in the backward traditional areas so that the provision of educational courses oriented to this sector is bound to meet with disaster unless educational programmes are coordinated with long term investment plans. First indications from the ESEPs are that the courses in management are proving extremely popular so that it is possible that the new vocational orientation will merely confirm traditional prestige patterns. In the absence of marked changes in employment opportunities and the distribution of income, this is only to be expected.

Impressive as the figures are for adult education, they give no indication of the depth of coverage, nor of the vocational utility of the courses in practice. Moreover, although the urban areas are well covered, only 150,000 adults are attending adult education courses in the country which suggests that the basic effect of the adult education programmes has been to upgrade vocational skills in the urban industrial areas rather than develop more literacy campaigns in the countryside. However, the courses are, on paper, supplementing real deficiencies in the educational experience of a large number of adults and should prove a good investment once firmly established. Distance teaching and bilingual education programmes and adult literacy campaigns are being initiated in rural areas, while instruction units are being set up in industrial enterprises. Expansion of these programmes would seem to be an excellent means of raising productivity, but success in the rural sector will depend upon improved coordination between different planning bodies.

Finally, the university system has yet to criticise the type of skilled manpower it is turning out. Instead of producing adequate numbers of individuals trained with appropriate skills it has hitherto concentrated on producing the largest pool of skills with insufficient regard to their possible employment in society. This does not necessarily imply that the universities should immediately reorientate their activities towards agriculture which are present is woefully catered for. Unfortunately, the low numbers of agricultural specialists being produced by the universities is a reflection of the limited demand for qualified personnel in the largely under-capitalised agricultural sector. In this respect the pronounced urban orientation of university courses is a rational response to the economic structure of the country.

APPENDIX

THE TUPAC AMARU PLAN
Translation of the Clauses Relating to Education

EDUCATION

Objective

Better levels of education, enlargement of its coverage and reduction of illiteracy, implementation of the Educational Reform.

Policy Guidelines

1. To reduce illiteracy with the support of the population and public bodies

2. To intensify the application of non-academic programmes within the various levels and modes of organisation of the system of education

3. To enlarge, improve and equip educational centres, to promote the participation of the community and to employ communal infrastructural resources suitable for educational use

4. To reinforce education at work and for work at the appropriate levels and modes (of the education system) linking (these) with the work of the community

5. To promote the effective participation of the community in educational management through the

6. To push the application of the first cycle of higher education adapting it to the requirements of the country and the structure of production

7. To ensure that the preparation of skilled personnel is adequate for the occupational requirements of the country, and that studies of these said requirements are kept up to date

8. To promote the participation of the teaching force in the application of the Reform and in the planning and solution of the problems that appertain to it

9. To pass a teachers law and other legal measures regulating work norms in the education sector

10. To promote through the education system the preparation of personnel capable of scientific and technological research

11. to pass and progressively implement legal measures with respect to the civil service of graduates

12. To promote a policy which reaffirms, promotes and diffuses national and universal culture in all its forms

13 To intensify the implementation of the national system of recreation, physical education and sports

14 To intensify inter-sectorial participation in the application of the Educational Reform

15 To ensure the obligatory contribution of firms to the financing of education for workers and their families

16 To deepen the reform of educational administration and to try to obtain financial resources from sources other than the public purse

17 To encourage the creation and development of educational centres which will share the task of education with the State (private schools, cooperative schools, participation of companies) in accord with the General Educational Law.

THE PERUVIAN UNIVERSITY

Objective

Universities that truly constitute high centres of education in which culture may be preserved and the support of study and research encouraged and which, functioning within the university system, contribute effectively to the progress of the country.

Policy Guidelines

1 To regularise university life so that the universities conform to norms of their environment and those ruling the country

2 To create a well functioning university system with an efficient administration

3 To support research, academic work, extra-mural activities and the promotion of culture linked with regional plans with the aim of raising university productivity

4 To press for the planning and rationalisation of the university system and of each university

5 To encourage the preparation, training and tenure of university professors

6 To regulate the activity of university study organisations by means of measures designed to ensure their orientation towards educational, cultural, social and sporting ends

7 To promote in the different sectors of the university community the full identification with the authentic aims of the university and a complete fulfilment of their obligations and responsibilities.

PERU BASIC STATISTICS

Population

1960	1970	1979
10,025,000	13,586,000	17,297,000

Enrolment Ratios

Primary = Enrolments divided by the total population aged 6-11
Secondary = Enrolments divided by the total population aged 12-16
 (1970 12-17)
Higher = Enrolments divided by the total population ages 20-24

	Primary	Secondary	Higher
1970	103%	30%	11.1%
1978	112%	54%	16.5%

Schools, Teachers and Pupils 1970 and 1978

	Schools	Teachers	Pupils
Pre-Primary			
1970	639	2,016	74,318
1978	2,553*	5,552	286,600
Primary			
1970	18,439	65,965	2,341,068
1978	19,420	77,844	2,126,000
Secondary			
1970	–	31,587	546,183
1978	–	37,383	1,090,200

* = 1977

Public Expenditure on Education

Year	As a % of total government spending	As a % of GNP
1970	18.8%	3.8%
1979	10.5%	2.1%

Higher Education Students by Field of Study 1978

Education and Teacher Training	11,349
Humanities	2,593
Law	11,721
Social and Behavioural Sciences	33,169
Commerce and Business	38,643
Natural Science	6,960
Mathematics and Computer Science	3,076
Medicine and Related Fields	3,076
Engineering	43,862
Agriculture	18,054
Other	20,917

Public Expenditure on Education by Level

Year	Pre-Primary	Primary	Secondary	Other
1970	1.1%	39.8%	20.8%	38.3%
1978	2.3%	38.1%	26.5%	33.1%

Basic Social and Economic Data

Gross National Product per capita 1979 – US$730
Average annual growth of GNP per capita 1960-1979 – 1.7%
Life expectancy 1979 – 58 years
Proportion of the labour force engaged in:

Agriculture
1960   53%
1979   38%

Industry
1960   19%
1979   20%

Services
1960   28%
1979   42%

Venezuela

CONTENTS

1 Geography 808
2 Population 810
3 Society and Culture 812
4 History and Politics 813
5 The Economy 816
6 The Education System 817
7 Educational Administration 830
8 Educational Finance 831
9 Development and Planning of
   the Education System 832

Venezuela has economic, social and political conditions which should support a highly developed and cohesive education system. The country has the highest national income per capita in Latin America, based largely on the export of petroleum. There has been a democratic system of government since 1958 which is responsive to popular demand for education. Venezuela has a high degree of cultural unity founded on its hispanic traditions.

Educational provision in Venezuela expanded rapidly in the 1970s. however, despite the legal requirement of compulsory education reinforced by the Education Law of 1980 which extended its length to nine years, an imbalance has developed between the various levels of edudcation. Primary education is available for almost all children but there are problems of drop-outs and wastage. Only about half the relevant age group was enrolled in secondary schools at the end of the 1970s. Higher education provision expanded faster than any other kind of education in the 1970s and the participation rate was not only the highest in Latin America but was also higher than that of many industrialised countries. Over 40% of government educational expenditure was allocated to higher education by the early 1980s.

This uneven provision has been the response to popular demand which the government, control over which has alternated at five-year intervals between the two major political parties, has been unable to resist. At the same time, there has still be inadequate provision of lower level education especially in the more remote areas and for the poorer classes.

Educational policies have been introduced since the late 1960s to reorientate the character of primary and secondary education to give them a more vocational and technical orientation and to try to weaken the traditional conception that all education leads ultimately to conventional university studies and membership of one of the traditional professions. New types of higher education have also been introduced which are aimed at other kinds of occupation.

But popular demand is still for a traditional higher education so that it is the older universities that have expanded most. There is also a major private sector operating at all levels of education which can also frustrate intentions to reorientate the character of Venezuelan education. As long as petroleum based income is plentiful and government allows wide personal choice in education the proposed changes in education will encounter important obstacles.

1 GEOGRAPHY

Topography

The Republic of Venezuela is located at the northern tip of the South American continent and is bounded by the Caribbean to the north, Guyana to the east, Brazil to the south, and Colombia to the south west and west. Venezuels also has a number of Caribbean islands. It covers an area of 352,150 square miles (approximately twice the size of Spain), and lays claim to 58,000 square miles of territory at present in Guyana. The name of the country comes from 'little Venice', because the first Spanish explorers on seeing the native houses built on stilts over water were reminded of Venice.

There are four main regions. The largest in terms of population comprises the temperate mountainous zones (the coastal mountains with peaks up to 9,000 feet [2,770 metres] and the Venezuelan Andes with peaks up to 16,000 feet [4,924 metres]). The coastal mountains are to be found just inland and parallel to the Caribbean coast and this area includes Caracas (the largest city, the commercial, industrial and government centre), Valencia (the agricultural centre), Maracay (a cattle centre), Barquisimeto (a growing industrial centre). In the western part some maize and coffee are grown. The Andean mountains include snow-capped peaks but most of the population is to be found at the altitudes between 3,000 and 6,000 feet. In this area most of the coffee copy is grown (the chief export crop). It also includes the Tachira area which produced the series of ruthless dictators which governed Venezuela for much of the first half of the twentieth century.

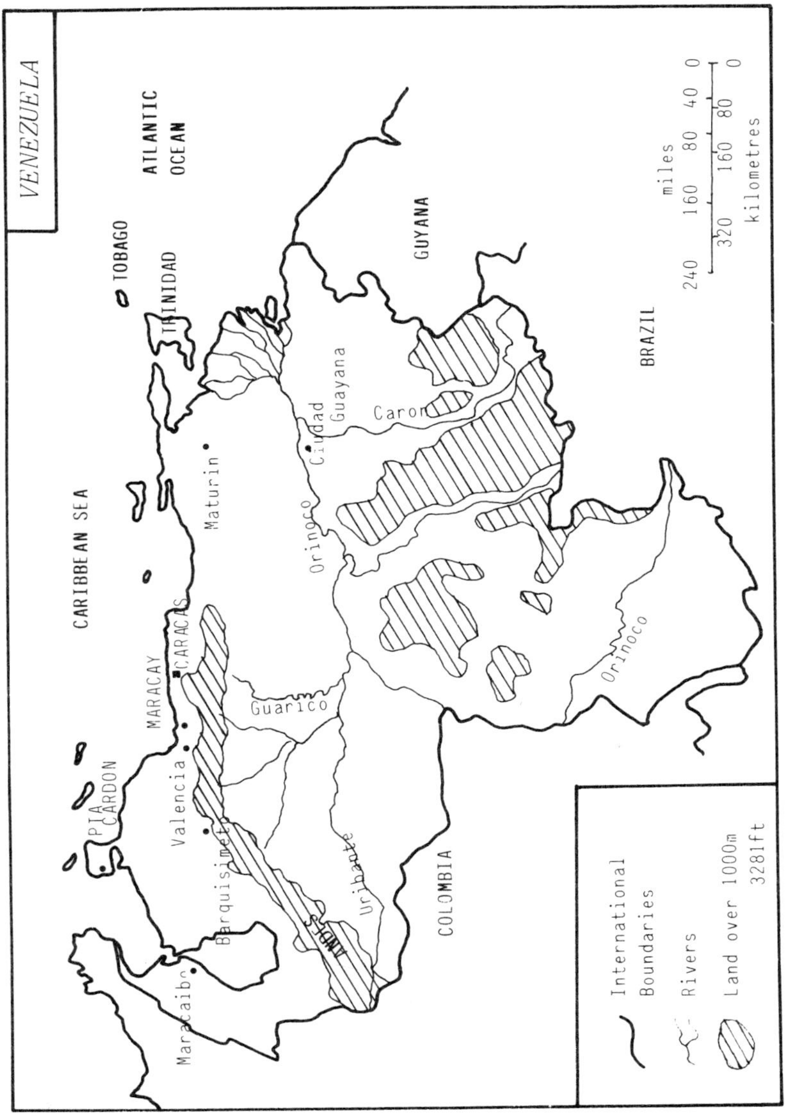
VENEZUELA
ATLANTIC OCEAN
TOBAGO
TRINIDAD
CARIBBEAN SEA
GUYANA
BRAZIL
COLOMBIA
CARACAS
MARACAY
Valencia
PTA CARDON
Barquisimeto
Maracaibo
Maturin
Ciudad Guayana
Caroni
Orinoco
Guarico
Uribante
ANDES
miles
240 160 80 40 0
320 160 80 0
kilometres
International Boundaries
Rivers
Land over 1000m 3281ft

Climate

The coastal zone is a narrow belt of hot humid land between the mountains and the Caribbean broadening at the west, where the oil-rich Maracaibo Basin is to be found, and at the eastern end which comprises the Orinoco delta. This is a populous zone (18% of the population) and produces cocoa, bananas and fish, but is largely known for its petroleum industry centred on Maracaibo, Amuay, and Punta Cardon and for its iron and oil industries centred on Ciudad Guayana.

The area between the mountains and the Orinoco is made up of low treeless plains which cover about a quarter of Venezuela's total territory. It is an area of great seasonal variation: from April till October there are heavy rains and floods and from November to March it is exceedingly dry. The heat, insects and lack of communications in the rainy season have meant that it has remained sparsely populated. The plains are traditionally a cattle centre but oil exists in vast, deep sedimentary deposits throughout the region. Recently agriculture has increased with the opening in 1956 of a dam across the Guarico River, controlling floods and providing irrigation. The plains drain into the Orinoco which is navigable from the Caribbean up to the Colombian border for shallow draft vessels.

The fourth area, the Guayana Highlands, is to be found to the south of the Orinoco and although it makes up 45% of Venezuela's territory it contains only some 2% of its population. The highlands rise to some 9,000 feet and the Indian population is little known. The discovery of gold in this area in the nineteenth century enticed a small number of adventurers into the area and the El Callao mine was for some time the chief gold producer in the world. In 1926 diamonds were discovered of a good quality, but not numerous or large. Huge deposits of almost pure iron have been found in the north eastern part of the region and recently a large iron-ore industry has begun to be established mainly through large American steel corporations.

Communications

Air communications are highly developed and there are good principal roads (35,000 miles, 70% all weather, 30% dirt). Ninety eight per cent of Venezuela's exports leave the country by sea, and ports are well developed. There is also a highly developed system of inland water transportation on the Orinoco and on Lake Maracaibo.

2 POPULATION

Venezuela's population has doubled in the past 25 years and is continuing to grow at an extraordinarily rapid rate. At the time of the 1950 census, the population was 5,034,838. The population in the 1981 census was 16.5 million. This increase is attributable largely to improved living conditions causing a drop in mortality rate and a significant rise in the birth rate. In spite of this population explosion, however, the average density is only 15 inhabitants per square kilometre.

The current average growth rate (which stood at 3.2% per annum in 1979) makes Venezuela one of the fastest growing countries in the world. The nation thus has an extraordinarily young poplation: 44% of the people are under the age of 15 and a further 21% are under 25. There is no official government policy on birth control but the government does assist family planning programmes run by private organisations and has recently taken over the running of 123 family planning clinics from one of the latter.

The distribution of people is very uneven since the recent increase in population has coincided with a rapid process of urbanisation brought about by large scale migration from rural areas. Thus 83% of Venezuelans lived in urban areas in 1980 as opposed to 54% in 1950 and 35% in 1936. The metropolitan region of Caracas has proved a particularly powerful magnet with the result that it has increased in size from 1.28 million in 1961 to an estimated 3.1 million in 1980. It thus dominates the country in every respect especially since the nation's next largest cities, Maracaibo, Barquisimeto, Valencia and Maracay have populations only half the size or smaller. Since these cities are concentrated in the northern part of the republic, nine tenths of the nation's poulation lives in this area. By contrast the south is sparsely populated particularly in the jungle areas near the Brazilian and Guyanan borders.

Although the roots of Venezuela's language, religion and culture are Spanish, the blood of its people is of varied origin. Over two thirds of the population is of mixed blood, or Mestizo, a product of the fusion of three races: the aboriginal, the white and the black. Of the remainder about 20% are white, 9% Negro and about 2% Indian. Whilst the Mestizos are dispersed throughout the republic, the pure races tend to be concentrated in certain areas – the whites in the major urban centres and the Andes, the Negroes along the coast and the Indians in the remote forests of the Amazon territory. It is hard to ascertain exact numbers of the latter but they probably do not exceed 40,000. In any case they are becoming fewer as they are gradually incorporated into the mainstream of Venezuelan life.

There was no sizeable immigration until after World War II when a government sponsored immigration and land settlement programme coupled with the existence of millions of displaced persons in Europe brought in more than half a million people, mainly from Spain, Italy and Portugal. This flow continued until the end of the 1950s when it began to tail off. Since then the most numerous and constant immigration has been from Colombia. It is estimated over one million Colombians live and work in Venezuela, nearly three quarters of them illegally. Now with its massive oil wealth and political stability, Venezuela is beginning to attract other Latin

Americans, notably from those countries experiencing economic and political difficulties such as Argentina, Chile and Uruguay. These groups number some 50,000. (Interestingly since 1929, Negro immigrants have been barred from Venezuela by law.) In selecting new arrivals, the government gives preference to those people who have professional and technical skills, particularly agriculturalists. The number of registered foreigners in Venezuela in 1977 was 1.1 million.

The national language is Spanish: it is spoken by nearly all Venezuelans except some of those of Indian origin living in some of the remotest areas of the country. The Indian population is linguistically very diverse, having some 150 distinct languages and dialects. With their decline in numbers however, many languages are becoming extinct. English is unofficially recognised as the country's second language but it cannot be said that it is widely used. It is a compulsory language in all schools from seventh grade, i.e. from the start of the Basic Cycle.

3 SOCIETY AND CULTURE

Venezuelan society has undergone profound changes during the past 50 years, principally on account of economic factors – notably the discovery of petroleum and the subsequent effect this has had of transforming the national economy from its agrarian base to a primary dependence on the export of mineral resources and more recently, on a growing manufacturing sector.

Other changes have affected the basic structure of society. As late as the 1920s, the fabric of the nation's social system was a little different from what it had been in colonial times – in other words the population was divided into two classes, a minority class in possession of wealth, education and power and a majority who were marked by illiteracy, menial occupations and poverty. With the expansion of the economy following the discovery of petroleum, however, there arose a genuine middle class and industrial proletariat. A large proportion of the country's wealth from oil has been used to expand and develop the nation's educational system with the result that ambitious members of the poorer classes now have better opportunities to acquire higher status and more remunerative occupations.

Change has also come to the rural areas, albeit at a slower rate – improvement in communications, construction of roads, establishment of schools: all these things have begun to have visible effects in changing old attitudes.

Family and kinship patterns have been affected by all these transformations. Small family units replace extended families as a consequence of urban living and economic change.

Religious Background

The vast majority of people in Venezuela are Roman Catholics: only about 1% are Protestant, and the number of Jews in the population is smaller still. There is no official state religiou although ties between the government and the Roman Catholic Church are close and in recent years have become increasingly cordial as well. The government exercises the right of patronage over high church officials. It also subsidises the lower clergy and helps to pay church maintenance costs.

Ecclesiastical influence over the government is slight having been eroded progressively over the years ever since the country became independent. This fact is demonstrated in public schools where Catholic instruction may be given only at the express request of the parent.

An acute shortage of clergy men has plagued the Venezuelan church through most of its history. Because of this the country has come to rely on foreign clergy with the result that currently more than 50% of Venezuelan priests come from abroad - notably Spain. Thus in many church-run schools a fair number of the teachers are Spanish.

There has been a growing concern on the Church's part in recent years about the country's social problems. This has been shown for example in the large number of schools which have been set up by the priests in some of the shanty areas of big cities. In spite of this new image, however, religious indifference is growing in urban areas although traditional Catholic belief still remains strong in some country areas.

4 HISTORY AND POLITICS

Christopher Columbus discovered what is now Venezuela in 1498 during the third voyage to the New World. Though the first of Spain's New World mainland colonies to be discovered, Venezuela was nevertheless one of the last to be conquered and developed. Indeed for most of its colonial history, it was regarded by the mother country as a very marginal political entity largely because of the paucity of its human and material resources.

Freedom from the Spanish yoke finally came in June 1821 after a ten-year struggle spearheaded by the nation's criollos population (native-born whites) led by Simon Bolivar. Once independence had been won, there followed a period of political experimentation when Colombia and Ecuador were fused with Venezuela to form the new Republic of Gran Colombia. The experiment was short lived, however, and in 1830 an autonomous Venezuelan nation came into being led by General Jose Antonia Paez.

From 1830 until very recently, Venezuelan history had been substantially a history of a succession of dictators overthrowing one another and grabbing the Presidency. New constitutions succeeded each other with similar rapidity and were in essence usually designed to safeguard the position of the incumbent President. The balance between centralism and federalism also varied according to whoever was in power.

Except for a brief interlude of liberal democracy from 1945 to 1948, the Venezuelan nation was controlled for the first 58 years of this century by five successive military strong men from the Andean State of Tachira - General Cipriano Castro 1899-1908; Juan Vincente Gomes 1908-1935; General Eleazar Lopez Contreras 1936-1941; General Isias Medina Angarita 1941-1945; and General Marcos Perez Jimenez 1952-1958. Of these five, Castro, Gomes and Perez Jimenez governed in the true 'Caudillo' tradition having little regard for anything other than preserving their own power and amassing a personal fortune. Under Contreras and Medina, however, the first tentative steps were taken to restore some measure of honesty and efficiency in government and to introduce plans for economic and social development.

During the terms of Contreras and Medina, many revolutionaries who had fled the country after the student revolt of 1928 against Gomez, returned to organise new political parties and prepared to take power. Hence the civilian-military coup of October 1945 which brought to power a mixed junta, headed by Romulo Betancourt and dominated by Accion Democratica, a party of moderate left political persuasions. AD's sweeping programme of reform provoked reaction from conservative forces and in November 1948 the Army seized power. Betancourt and his supporters were sent into exile and a three-man military junta took over the rule. Perez Jimenez, one of the original three members of the junta, soon established himself as supreme dictator and abandoned AD's reform programme in favour of modernising Caracas and enriching himself and his army of associates. Finally popular opposition to his government led to the three armed forces combining to overthrow him in January 1958. A civilian-military junta then ran the country for one year, after which Betancourt was elected President.

Since 1958 the country has had a democratic form of government and power has not only passed from one President to another but also from one party to another.

The political system is federal, but real power is concentrated in the national government. Within the government the President's position is supreme. Presidential support is necessary for the success of any government initiative. The President is elected for a five-year term of office after which he must stand down. Given the concentration of power in his hands and the large number of appointments which accompany a new presidency, each five-year period is a self-contained unit. Planning cannot realistically span more than one President's term of office and a change of President, even when it does not involve a change of party, represents a marked break in continuity. Results are therefore looked for in the short term and little long term planning takes place.

The second Betancourt administration (1959-1964) which was a coalition of AD and COPEI (the Christian Democratic Party) was considerably more conservative than the first but in spite of this, important developmental progress was made. The government was plagued throughout its term of office, however, by political unrest (caused by groups of the extreme Left and Right and various sectors of the Army) and these problems were compounded by an economic depression which caused widespread unemployment.

The December 1963 Presidential Elections, held in an atmosphere of great political tension, were narrowly won by the AD candidate, Raul Leoni. His administration (1964-1969) was able to restore a good measure of political calm. The Christian Democrats withdrew from the governing coalition but they were replaced by the labour-leftist Union Republicana Democratica. A return to prosperity accelerated the industrial, agrarian, educational, housing and health development programmes begun in the early 1960s. But the opposition Christian Democratic Party continued to grow in strength and its Presidential candidate, Rafael Caldera, won the 1969 Presidential Elections. The COPEI administration followed a more left wing line than its AD predecessor but in the elections of December 1973, its presidential candidate Lorenzo Fernandez was overwhelmingly defeated by the AD candidate Carlos Andres Perez. The latter pursued a more left wing course than was originally expected of him, including the nationalisation of the country's oil industry, as well as iron and aluminium extraction. As a result of the 1978 elections, Luis Herrera Camperis (COPEI) became President.

International Relations

Venezuela is an active supporter of OPEC and is the third largest oil exporter in OPEC. Venezuela has used some of its increased oil revenue to provide foreign aid and investment.

Recently, Venezuela has joined the Andean group, which should provide a larger market for the products of its industrial expansion. Venezuela, especially under Carlos Andres Perez, saw itself as the leader of Latin America in world affairs.

Venezuela has border disputes with all her neighbours particularly with Guyana and Colombia and does not accept the nineteenth century allocation of a large area of territory to British Guiana, as it then was. This almost uninhabited area contains considerable mineral wealth. This dispute is a source of continuing conflict. Since the discovery of offshore oil in the Gulf of Venezuela, Colombia has laid claim to a number of small islands which would entitle her to exploit the nearby undersea deposits. The large number of illegal Colombian immigrants in Venezuela and difficulties in controlling smuggling across the border are irritants in Venezuelan-Colombian relations.

Relations with Cuba improved from the 1970s.

5 THE ECONOMY

With a population of some 16 million and an area of nearly one million square kilometres, Venezuela is lightly populated. It has, however, an abundance of raw materials, notably oil, natural gas, iron and coal. Apart from oil, the economy is under-developed. Manufacturing is only just becoming established. Until 1972 the steady fall in real terms of oil prices reduced Venezuela's growth rate to 4.5%, that is, hardly any increase at all in real per capita terms. The sharp rise in oil prices in the 1970s improved Venezuelan economic prospects and led to a growth rate of 7.5%. Venezuela is heavily urbanised. Although 20% of the population is engaged in agriculture, it only represents 7% of national income and foodstuffs have to be imported. Venezuela has monetary and exchange stability and its rate of inflation was low until the massive increases in expenditure created by increased oil revenue.

Oil dominates the Venezuelan economy, representing 97% of the value of exports and 86% of government revenue (1974). Intensive exploration is taking place and further reserves exist in the Orinoco tar belt. Output was cut back from 3.7 million barrels per day in 1970 to 2.8 million barrels per day in 1975. The Venezuelan Government recognises that its economy must move away from the overwhelming dependence on oil, and alternative development plans are being drawn up which the vastly increased oil revenues will help to finance.

The present government's economic strategy aims to develop a strong domestic industrial sector by capitalising on Venezuelan raw materials, and by increasing the competitiveness of Venezuelan manufactured goods. The government has started to dismantle the long established high cost low volume production maintained by subsidies and has liberalised import controls. Very little of Venezuela's manufacturing industry has found an outlet outside the country, exports having been inhibited by the over-valuation of the currency relative to local production costs and the absence of the administrative machinery to handle exports.

Legislation was passed in 1976 by which foreign petroleum and iron mining companies' concessions reverted to the State. Nationalisation was carried out carefully in order to ensure the continuing goodwill of the companies after nationalisation since Venezuela is short of technical expertise.

Development plans in the major areas of expansion (iron, steel, aluminium, shipbuilding, power supply, communications and new town developments) demand from education an enormously increased supply of trained manpower. The demand is for higher general standards of education amongst the work force as well as technical and management skills. The capacity of the Venezuelan educational system to provide the necessary manpower is the major problem if her ambitious development plans are to be realised.

6 THE EDUCATIONAL SYSTEM

Aims

Article 80 of Venezuela's 1961 Constitution states: "The aim of education is the full development of personality, the formation of citizens equipped for life and for democracy, who will be able to contribute to our cultural tradition and further a spirit of human solidarity".

At greater length the 1958 Education Law declares: "Public education aims to form and develop the intellect of the people and to contribute to their moral and physical improvement. This aim goes hand in hand with the intention to educate citizens who will be conscious of Venezuela's historic destiny and will contribute to fulfilling this destiny within the principles of our democratic tradition and in a spirit of international cooperation". A national development plan for education is in preparation, but since 1961 there have been a series of National Plans which have had considerable implications for educational development.

During the long period of military dictatorships the pressure for education was resisted. When democracy was introduced, this demand exploded with all the greater force, and Venezuela's democratic governments have had a natural sympathy for this demand. Coupled as it has been with a rapidly expanding population, the education system has grown enormously. This growth has recently been further encouraged by the increased revenue from oil and the emphasis on technically trained manpower to realise Venezuela's industrial potential.

The current government's stated objectives are:

(i) continued expansion of the education system, placing emphasis on the "extensive gaps in the pre-school branch and at the post-graduate level" and on "the training of specialists" (Carlos Andres Perez 1973). The 1980 Education Law planned to provide complete coverage at the primary level and to extend compulsory education from a period of six to nine years under the title of 'Basic Education'

(ii) improvement in the quality of education using the latest developments in teaching methodology and technology

(iii) to establish "a genuine equality of opportunity . . . for all the children and youth of Venezuela", to use education as a means to achieve "mobility and social advancement", and to cut drop-out rates by ensuring that the economic needs of pupils are looked after

(iv) to tidy the legal structure of Venezuelan education and to introduce a decentralised administration.

The conflicting demands made upon this education system in Venezuela are characteristic of the ineluctable tensions of development. The wish to preserve a measure of parental choice, which favours academic courses and the access they provide to professional status, conflicts with centralised manpower planning aimed at providing the middle and lower ranges of technical skills. The same tension is at work in administration, between the need for both centralisation and decentralisation. As in other rich developing countries, the generous investment in national development plans has quickly outrun the capacity of the educational system to supply enough of the right kind of manpower to maintain them.

Planning

Planning of education in Venezuela first began in 1959 with the creation of the Integrated Educational Planning Office, better known as EDUPLAN. This office, which has been renamed simply as the Directorate of Planning, is directly responsible to the Ministry of Education and very closely linked with CORDIPLAN (the Central Office of Coordination and Planning) which is the semi-autonomous agency responsible for drawing up four-year national plans for development. Whilst CORDIPLAN decides what the national priorities for education shall be, the Planning Directorate elaborates plans for fulfilling these objectives.

The function of discussing and approving education plans falls to a Planning council which is presided over by the Minister and composed of directors in the Ministry, a representative of CORDIPLAN and the Ministry's leval adviser.

Besides drafting plans the Planning Directorate is also responsible for carrying out research, providing technical advice for the execution of plans, coordinating the participation of various educational departments, evaluating the results of plans, etc. etc.

The first national Educational Plan was introduced in 1976.

Before 1980 the structure of education had four levels: pre-primary, primary, secondary (divided into two cycles) and higher. The 1980 Education Law when extending compulsory education from six years (covering the primary course) to nine years, decreed a new structure: basic education (primary and lower secondary), middle education (upper secondary) and higher education.

However, since this law was still in the process of implementation in 1982, the old system will be described.

Pre-Primary

This is voluntary for children between the ages of 4 and 6. It is estimated that over 2 million children are in this age bracket and yet of these only 328,927 were enrolled in kindergartens in 1978.

It was common until very recently for the majority of kindergartens to be privately operated. Between 1969 and 1974 the percentages were 54% privately owned and 46% provided by the public sector. The situation has now been reversed, however, with the public sector prodiving 80% of places in 1978. The growth of the public sector can be attributed largely to an increasing interest on the part of the Ministry of Education in improving and expanding this sector of education.

Primary

Primary education is compulsory for all children from the age of 7 and is free in public sector schools. A course of 6 years is provided. Promotion of a pupil from one grade to the next is largely automatic, based on his or her teacher's evaluative report, except in the last year when an examination set by the teacher of the Sixth Grade must be taken. If the pupil passes this, he is awarded a Certificate in Primary Education, which gives him access to secondary education if he wishes to proceed to this.

There are four types of primary school – national, state, municipal or private – depending on the sources of financial support. The majority (56%) are provided by the central government with the states providing 26% and the municipalities only 6%. Total provision by the public sector therefore amounts to 88%, with the remaining 12% being provided by the private sector (mostly run by the Roman Catholic Church). Rural schools which generally consist of one room/one teacher and as such as known as *unitarias* are provided by a multiplicity of agents (autonomous entities such as INCE (Instituto Nacional de Cooperacion Educativa), various ministries, central government, states, etc.).

Syllabi and curricula are prescribed by the Ministry and are therefore uniform in all schools. Similarly all teachers must be registered by the Ministry. The academic year runs from September to July.

Enrolments have increased significantly in recent years, from 1,459,652 in 1965/66 to 2,456,203 in 1979. Only around 60% of these, however, actually complete the full six-year course.

In 1978 there were 82,226 teachers working in primary schools throughout the country. The national average pupil/teacher ratio is 29:1. The highest number of pupils per teacher is in the main urban regions of the country – the metropolitan area of Caracas, central region and Zulia. The lowest concentration is in the Andean and southern regions. The proportion of total expenditure spent on education at the primary level has been falling steadily, mainly because enrolments at this level have not risen as dramatically as at other levels.

In addition to the above, there are three special categories of primary education worthy of mention.

Rural Education

Here two innovations have taken place in recent years. First is the amalgamation of *unitarias* into small groups known as rural nuclear systems and second is the establishment of farm and pre-vocational schools. Whilst the latter (which are residential) are intended to provide instruction in rural skills as well as a general primary education, the idea behind the rural nuclear systems is to improve the possibilities of being able to provide primary education beyond the third grade which is all that the *unitarias* were able to offer.

Education in Frontier Areas

This is aimed primarily at the many small groups of tribal Indians living in the frontier regions, particularly in the Amazon and Guayana areas. Thirty-two special schools for approximately 6,000 children have been built in various parts of these regions in an attempt to provide education for this particular sector of Venezuelan society.

Special Education for Handicapped People

This not surprisingly is virtually non-existent. Of the estimated $1\frac{1}{4}$ million people included in this category, only about 6,000 have access to the special educational facilities that they need.

Secondary

The government is currently under far greater pressure to expand secondary (and higher) education than schooling at primary level). Accordingly in an attempt to meet this demand, the proportion of the educational budget spent on secondary education has increased.

Enrolment figures almost doubled in the 1970s. In 1970 there were 525,146 pupils in all types of secondary education. In 1979 this had increased to 820,233. Around 80% are in public schools. As with primary education, there is a high wastage rate.

Curriculum, syllabi and texts at the secondary level are strictly controlled by the Ministry. Teaching methods tend to be dogmatic and routine based and provide little opportunity for open discussion or questioning and even less for stimulating creativity and initiative. Because classes are large it is difficult to establish a close teacher/pupil relationship and in any case teachers traditionally keep their distance. However, conditions are often much better in private schools which mainly have a higher status than government schools.

Secondary education normally takes place between the ages of 13 and 18. In public schools tuition is free. Fundamentally it is made up of two cycles - a basic common cycle of three years followed by a diversified cycle of two (sometimes three) years. It is more usual for each cycle to be offered in separate institutions although there are a number of schools (especially private ones) which offer a combination of the two. Both cycles were established by presidential decree on 13 August 1969 and constitute key elements in the general reform of the educational system begun at that time.

Basic Common Cycle

The basic common cycle was introduced primarily with a view to providing a common standard of education at the intermediate level without any particular vocational orientation. As such it replaced the old system whereby students had to follow specialist courses of study from the first year of their secondary education. The new system began in the academic year 1969/70.

The 1980 Education Law extended compulsory education to include the basic cycle of secondary schooling. The common curriculum for the cycle is as follows (see table on following page).

Both in the basic common cycle and in the diversified cycle, promotion from one year to the next is dependent on the average marks a student has received for work done during the year and on the results of his end of year examinations (taken in July). The former count for 60% of the overall total: the latter for 40%. Marks are always out of 20, 10 being taken as the pass mark. Exemption may be given from taking end of year examinations if the student has obtained an average of 16 or over for work done during the school year (this does not apply, however, in the case of the third year of the basic cycle and last year of the diversified cycle). Examinations are set and marked by the teacher of the subject in question but in the case of the third year of the common cycle and the last year of the diversified cycle a panel of three people must by law prepare and adjudicate each examination.

The 1980 Law proposed a certificate to be awarded at the end of Basic Education (i.e. the end of the Basic Common Cycle).

In order to help students choose their specialist course of study in the diversified cycle, 'orientation services' have been established in a number of basic cycle schools and a few also in schools offering both the basic and diversified cycles.

Diversified Cycle (from 1980 Middle Education)

The diversified cycle, which was first put into effect in October 1972, offers three specialised branches of study — academic, technical and pedagogic. All three branches offer two-three year courses leading to the title *bachillerato* which is the qualification giving access to higher education. This is in contrast to the previous system whereby only the academic branch led to the *bachillerato* and was therefore

	Year 1		Year 2		Year 3	
	Hours per week		Hours per week		Hours per week	
	Theory	Practice	Theory	Practice	Theory	Practice
Spanish language & literature	5		5		4	
Mathematics	4		3		3	
Geography & History	4		6		6	
Biology	4	2	4	2	4	2
Chemistry					3	1
Physics					4	1
English	4		3		3	
Civics	1		2			
Art	2		3			
Child culture					2	
Physical Education	2		2		2	
Manual skills *	4		4		4	

*The latter, which cover a variety of areas including industrial, commercial, agricultural, domestic and aesthetic skills, have been introduced as part of the latest reform to complement the primarily academic content of the rest of the courses and to develop vocational interests among students.

the sole gateway to university. Whereas formerly it was possible to obtain a *bachillerato* in two areas, sciences or humanities, now this title is awarded in five other fields also: industry, commerce, agriculture, primary school teaching and social work. Furthermore within these fields students can now choose between a number of specialisms - 38 in all. Thus if a student opts for the industrial field of study specialising in technical drawing, he emerges with the title of 'industrial *bachillerato* with a specialism in technical drawing". Broadly speaking in theory, therefore, a student may opt between 38 different types of *bachillerato* under this system.

All students, whatever their branch of study, follow a number of basic subjects in common during the first year of the diversified cycle. These are Spanish language and literature (3 hours per week), mathematics (4 hours per week), contemporary Venezuelan history and geography (4 hours per week), physical education (2 hours per week) and English (3 hours per week). English and physical education are also continued into the second year. Only in their second year do students really begin to concentrate on their specialism properly.

Generally speaking the different branches of study are taught in separate institutions. This of course is a consequence of the old system but gradually a mixing of the branches is taking place.

Academic

This is by far the most popular branch of upper secondary education mainly because it is the gateway to the traditionally popular courses in universities which lead in turn to the traditionally prestigious careers in Venezuelan society, e.g. medicine, law and engineering.

More than 90% of the total numbers of students in the diversified cycle choose this branch. The majority then choose sciences rather than humanities.

Both the science and humanities courses normally last two years. During this period, besides their basic common subjects, humanities students must study the following:

	Year 1	Year 2
Spanish language and literature	–	5
Mathematics	–	3
Philosophy	4	4
French	4	4
History of Art	3	–
Sociology	–	5
Latin & Greek	3	3
Optional subjects	3	3
Grand total (inc. basic common subjects)	33	34

The specialist timetable of science students is as follows:

	Year 1		Year 2	
	Theory	Practice	Theory	Practice
Spanish language & literature			2	
Physics	4	2	4	2
Chemistry	4	2	4	2
Biology	4	2	4	2
Earth Sciences	–		3	2
Drawing	2			
Philosophy	3			
Mathematics				
Grand total including basic common subjects	33		29	

Upon successful completion of their course, students receive the title of *bachillerato* in sciences or humanities according to whichever field they studied. In fact only 45% of all students in the academic branch reach a successful conclusion of their studies.

Technical

In spite of Venezuela's crying need for more technicians to develop and diversify her economy, the technical stream of secondary education fails to attract any significant proportion of students in the diversified cycle. The reason for this is exactly the reverse of that given for the popularity of the academic stream – namely that technical education lacks prestige.

In addition to the agricultural and industrial areas of study, commerce and social work are offered under the technical branch of upper secondary education. With the exception of the social work field, the number of specialisms offered in each of these areas is very large – 18 in the industrial and 7 in the commercial field.

The commercial field of study is the only one in this branch which offers courses lasting only two years. In the remainder the average length of course is three years.

Providing they successfully complete their courses, students are awarded the title of *bachillerato* in whatever particular area they studied.

Wastage and drop out rates are extremely high in this sector – over 80%.

Pedagogic (Docente) Branch

This provides teacher training at the primary level.

Courses normally last three years and as in other branches, during the first year students must study certain basic common subjects and only begin to specialise properly in their second year. Even then the training given is very general. The opportunity for teaching practice (usually 15 hours per week) is not given until the third year.

Successful students, on completion of their course, emerge with the title of *maestro*, the equivalent of a *bachillerato* in primary school teaching.

Vocational Training

Apprenticeship programmes and job related training are provided by INCE (Instituto Nacional de Cooperacion Educativa) which was founded in 1959 in an attempt to turn the large pool of unemployed and under-educated youths into the trained manpower needed to feed the country's economic development. INCE operates 54 centres throughout the country (including three fully residential agricultural centres), as well as mobile units servicing rural areas. Classes theoretically are not more than 12/15, though in practice occasionally are as large as 25. Drop-out rates, averaging just over 10%, are very low by Venezuelan standards.

The provision of vocational training is based on the manpower surveys INCE conducts, and on consultations with employers and unions. Courses are free and so is all the support material (books, equipment, protective clothing, etc.). INCE entirely supports residential students and assists day students.

Apprenticeship programmes started in 1965. They typically last three years (but may last a considerably shorter period), beginning with an initial period in an INCE centre to introduce practical skills and the minimum necessary theoretical background. This is followed by supervised and systematic work in industry. Apprentices must have completed their primary school education and be aged between 14 and 18. Unless an employer's work force includes at least 3% apprentices, he is subject to financial penalties. If an apprentice has not reached a level suitable to start his training programme, special courses are available to bring him up to that level.

Full time vocational training is available for 16 to 26 year olds. Students undertaking such training are generally more highly motivated, older, and have higher career expectations than apprentices. Part time courses are available for employees aged 18 or more to improve their job skills.

Instructor training programmes and courses for workers responsible for apprentices are provided by INCE. Instructors' salaries are not fully competitive and it is difficult to recruit the best skilled workers into vocational training. Instructors, therefore, are frequently in full time professional employment and only work for INCE several hours per week. Responsibility for placing trainees in employment falls to the Ministry of Labour. There is evidence of some lack of coordination between INCE and the Ministry of Labour leading to trainees not obtaining employment.

To finance its operations INCE collects directly from all firms employing more than five people a levy of 2% of their total wages bill. Additionally workers contribute ½% of their annual bonus (a minimum bonus is one week's pay) which is deducted by the employer. The government then contributes 20% of the contributions collected from employers and employees. This financial arrangement has given INCE a degree of independence from the government as well as an ample supply of funds to support its programmes.

Higher Education

There is a very high participation rate in higher education in Venezuela compared to other non-industrialised countries (22% of all 20-24 year olds in 1980). This growth has occurred mainly in the 1970s (the participation rate was 8.5% in 1968).

Higher education in Venezuela is provided by universities and by higher education instutites. There are three main types of university. The five autonomous universities (government supported but largely self-governing) are the oldest and largest – they account for over 80% of all university enrolments. The largest and oldest is the Central University of Venezuela in Caracas founded in 1721, which had over 65,000 students in 1980. The other autonomous universities are the Universities of Los Andes, Zulia, Carabobo and Oriente.

The second kind of university is government controlled (often termed experimental). These universities (of which there were eight in 1982) were established mainly in the 1970sm Some, such as Simon Bolivar in Caracas, have become more prestigious and selective than the older and overcrowded autonomous universities. Thirdly there are private universities, six in 1982. The oldest (Andres Bello) is Catholic but the others are secular and were mainly established in the 1970s. Some are highly selective, expensive and elitist (such as the Metropolitana) while others are cheaper, popular and less prestigious (e.g. Santa Maria).

Until recently large, publicly financed autonomous universities were the sole providers, with the Teacher Training Institute in Caracas, of higher education. A Venezuelan who has obtained his *bachillerato* has a legal right to a place in higher education and this has led to a rapid growth of traditional universities in response to the growth of secondary education. Unselected entry means that the first year is used to weed out those unsuitable for university study. This, and the fact that an estimated two thirds of the first year students at the Central University come from socio-economic backgrounds which are unable to support them for a full five-year course, means that drop-out rates are high. University departments thus find themselves concentrating a very high proportion of their energies on first year students, the majority of whom will not graduate. Uncompetitive salaries for university lecturers in a society short of well-qualified personnel, and frequent political disturbances have reduced the effectiveness of university work. The result has been declining standards of university education.

Traditional university education in Venezuela has emphasised medicine and law (53% of graduates from the Central University 1900-1959) and when subjects more relevant to society's needs have been taught a theoretical, academic approach has invariably been adopted. The percentage of failures in science and technology has, moreover, been above average. The failure of traditional university education to meet the demands for suitably qualified graduates has led to the development of non-university higher education and the creation of 'experimental' and private universities.

In the 1970s non-university institutions of higher education (university colleges, university institutes of technology, polytechnics, military colleges, pedagogical institutes) grew in number (from 3 in 1968 to 60 in 1980). However the enrolments at 85,260 in 1980 were only 27% of total higher education student numbers.

The role of the non-university institutes is uncertain because they have been created with two objectives in mind - to provide the technical courses between graduate and school level required by industrial development and to relieve universities of some of the pressure for places in higher education. For instance, Institutes of Technology (IUTs) offer shorter, more practical courses but since the three years' study in an IUT can be credited as three years of study towards a five-year degree course in an IUP, the IUTs may become the initial stage in a programme, the ultimate objective of which is a degree. IUT courses consist of a general first year course common to all non-university higher education institutions followed by increasing specialisation in the subsequent two years. Courses include a short practical attachment and lead to the qualification *tecnico superior*. Junior Colleges are very similar to IUTs, though tending to offer a broader range of subjects.

Venezuela's first Polytechnic (IUP) opened with UNESCO assistance in Barquisimeto in 1953, offered four-year *tecnologo* courses closely related to industrial requirements. The original *tecnologo* is no longer offered. IUPs have a five-year degree course similar, though not as theoretical, to a university engineering course. The new IUP in Caracas allows a student on the five-year degree programme to opt out if he so wishes after three years with the *tecnico superior* qualifications, so combining IUT and IUP type programmes.

The decline in status of the Central University in the 1960s was one of the reasons which encouraged wealthier parents concerned about the standards of their children's university education to turn to the private sector. Although they account for only just over 10% of university enrolment in some private universities, the quality of their programmes and their comparatively low wastage rates (though the number of entrants who finally graduate is still under 40%) means that private university education currently has a very sound reputation.

Since 1970 all higher education, public and private, has been subject to tight policy and budgetary control by the Ministry of Education. For universities this is through the National Universities Council and for non-university higher education the Higher Education Institutions Council.

However, the growth in number of students has been matched by an increase in the teaching staff so that the staff:student ratio was only 1:11 in 1980 compared to 1:9 in 1968.

Effectively two systems of higher education exist side by side with different objectives. On the one hand the large state universities, IUPs, IUTs and the Junior Colleges are providing higher education for the masses. They are providing, that is, the places in higher education which Venezuelans have the right to demand. On the other hand, private universities, some of the 'experimental' universities, together with some specialist, selective faculties within the traditional university system, are providing quality higher education. Since the latter has a very much lower wastage rate and its product is related more closely to national requirements, it can be seen as a more efficient system of higher education.

To enter higher education a student must have obtained his *bachillerato*, but since, having done this, he has a right to higher education he is placed in higher education rather than selected for it. Placing is conducted through a central computer operated system. When this system was first operated in 1974 only a small percentage of all applicants failed to receive an offer related to their request, they were automatically given top priority for placing the following year. The waiting period for less qualified applicants has extended often to two years from the late 1970s and more are allocated to the less popular universities or to non-university institutions. Private universities, some of the 'experimental' universities, and a few of the high prestige faculties in the traditional universities operate an additional selection procedure.

Teachers in higher education are rarely full time academics holding post-graduate qualifications (only 25% of university lecturers have post-graduate degrees), though the position is better in the 'experimental' and private universities. A lecturer is usually someone actively engaged in a profession who through a small number of classes tries to transmit his expertise to those who will follow him in that profession. This has led to generally low standards of teaching emphasising memorisation and formal examination and has inhibited the development of research and post-graduate programmes (in which Venezuela is notably weak). Libraries in consequence are poorly stocked and poorly administered.

Teacher Training

Secondary school teacher training programmes are provided in teacher training institutes and schools of education in Universities or Junior Colleges. There are three teacher training institutes, of which the oldest, largest and most prestigious is the Institute in Caracas founded in 1936 on a Chilean/German model. A second was created in Barquisimeto in 1959 and recently further institutes have been established. They operate outside the university system but are officially accorded equal status. Education courses are also included in the programme of some universities and Junior Colleges.

Primary school teachers are currently trained separately within the secondary school system in normal schools. Ninety per cent of trainees are women. Present policy is to bring primary teacher training within the sphere of higher education. To enter primary teacher training, students will have to hold the same entrance requirements as secondary level teacher trainees, although their courses will last only two years.

To enter secondary teacher training a student must have obtained his *bachillerato*. At an Institute the student normally spends two thirds of his time taking a main and subsidiary subject, the rest of the time being devoted to teaching methodology and general background. Additionally one semester is devoted to teaching practice. Some 20% of the students complete their courses without extending the time spent on them by repeating courses. Drop-out rates at 25% are low by Venezuelan higher education standards. Institute graduates normally spend their entire career in teaching.

The education courses in universities and Junior Colleges provide a broad range of studies, together with an aspect of education (education administration, education technology, etc.), and a small amount of teaching methodology and practice. They do not provide detailed preparation in a main and subsidiary subject area as in Institutes. While most university-prepared educationists teach in secondary schools, many enter administration and by taking some additional courses the university educationist is qualified to teach higher education.

There is a shortage of trained secondary school teachers. The teacher training system does not meet the demand. It particularly fails to meet the demand in some areas (mathematics, physics, chemistry) while providing an adequate supply in others (Spanish, English, geography, history, biology).

Some in-service teacher training programmes are provided. A small secondary level technical teacher training programme is offered at the Institutes in Barquisimeto and Maturin.

Teachers' Unions are organised along the major divisions of the system, thus there are separate unions for primary and secondary teachers.

Non-Formal Education/Illiteracy

Non-formal education in Venezuela is largely the responsibility of the Division of Adult Education in the Ministry of Education, although other bodies such as INCE, IAN (Instituto Agrario Nacional) and municipalities run their own education programmes for adults. In the early part of the 1960s, the main emphasis of these was on literacy and courses were given in more than 300 centres of cultural extension throughout the country. This work continues but its importance has diminished as literacy has spread.

The focus of adult training has accordingly shifted to other fields. In 1969 a presidential decree called for the establishment of educational training facilities for adults within the ordinary national educational system. Thus it is now possible for adults to receive primary and secondary schooling at an accelerated rate (four years at primary level, five years at secondary). Courses may be followed through night schools in the public system or through courses by radio, TV, or correspondence.

Besides academic study programmes, there are also a number of adult vocational programmes run by the Ministry of Education and other organisations. These are usuallly organised in conjunction with primary school training and include such specialities as barbering, dressmaking, draughts-manship and agricultural techniques.

Correspondence education has existed in Venezuela since 1939, and job related correspondence courses have been offered by INCE since 1966. INCE's 33 correspondence courses are generally very short (some only last two weeks) and are mostly designed to provide theoretical background to practical skills. They cover general subjects as well as technical subjects, largely in the field of car mechanics. The drop-out rate is high (nearly 50%). Whenever possible correspondence course students are allocated to a local coordinator through whom correspondence material is usually distributed to avoid problems with the postal system.

The *Instituto de Mejoramiento de Profesores* has offered correspondence courses to allow unqualified practising teachers to obtain their teacher's certificate. These courses include a six-week residential period during the school holidays. In practice the correspondence part of this training programme has been ineffective and the attempt to compress a one-year programme into the six-week residential course has led to low standards. The programme has been graduating some 50 students a year.

An open university using correspondence methods and providing technical/vocational courses as well as general education was established in the late 1970s.

7 EDUCATIONAL ADMINISTRATION

Responsibility for the administration of education in Venezuela rests primarily in the hands of the Ministry of Education.

Since, however, the country has a federal system of government, some administrative authority is exercised by state governments and in some cases by municipalities as well.

In common with all Venezuelan ministries, the Ministry of Education operates a highly centralised system of control: choice of textbooks and curricula supervision and approval of examinations, recognition and accreditation of teachers, all these are functions of the Ministry. In addition, it has the authority to inspect and supervise the activities of private schools. Accordingly private education is unrestricted only in matters of internal management.

To cope with the reforms and changes in the education system, the Ministry has undergone a reorganisation. The purpose was to decentralise some of the Ministry's functions as part of a more general policy of regionalisation decreed by the government in 1969. Under this, it was proposed that the 23 states of the country should be grouped into eight regions and each region should have its own regional office of education which would in effect be a regional section of the central Ministry. To date, however, there has been no real delegation of power to the regions and consequently such regional education offices as were established have proved ineffective. The day to day execution of the Ministry's policy therefore continues to be carried out for the time being through its old system of supervisors operating in 21 zones.

8 EDUCATIONAL FINANCE

Although the financing of public education in Venezuela is theoretically a collective function of all three levels of government: Central State and Municipal, in fact most of the funds come from central government and the remainder from state and muncipal governments, principally the former. Most of the central government's money originates from the Ministry of Education but other Ministries, such as Public Works, Defence and Agriculture, account for the remainder. It should be noted that contributions from the States towards educational services depend largely on the annual contribution by the National Executive to the States according to the provisions laid down by law.

Expenditure on public education in relation to the total budget has increased dramatically over the past 15 years - in 1960 it accounted for 16.67% of the GNP: by 1974 this figure had risen to 24.34%. Of the various sectors of government involved in the provision of education, by far the largest increased contributions to the rise in public expenditure on education has come from the Ministry of Education itself - its contribution has quadrupled whereas that of the state governments ·and other ministries has doubled only.

Within the structure of the education system, expenditure on higher education has been rising steadily in recent years. In contrast, although the total spent on primary education has been growing, as a proportion it has been falling gradually (from 37.4% in 1970 to 17.2% in 1977). This is largely in response to enrolment demands.

Private educational institutions normally finance their capital investment and operating costs from their own income. They can, however, under certain circumstances, apply to the Ministry of Education for financial aid and if the Ministry approves their request, it can make recommendations accordingly to the Ministry of Finance.

9 DEVELOPMENT AND PLANNING OF THE EDUCATION SYSTEM

During Venezuela's long period of political dictatorship education was neglected. With political change in 1958 came increasing attention to education but the remarkable period of growth which followed, and still continues, took place in an uncoordinated way. To a remarkable degree, therefore, Venezuelan education cannot be seen as a single system of education. Reforms have often been hastily introduced in response to particular pressing needs without careful consideration of the full implications of change. More often than not the one crucial factor which is overlooked by Venezuela's education planners is whether the appropriate trained personnel exist to carry out the reforms they propose. Thus, for example, the idea of introducing manual skills and orientation classes into the curriculum of the basic cycle, though basically sound, has been applied inefficiently in practice for lack of qualified staff. Similarly in the diversified cycle, there is a serious discrepancy between the theory and practice regarding the number of specialisms offered under the technical branch of study - again for lack of adequate personnel.

In terms of curricula and administration education in Venezuela is highly centralised. Each educational unit's lines of communication are almost exclusively with Caracas. Coordination between units in one location does not take place. Each level of education is a separate centralised system with minimal communication between the different levels. So, for example, there is little contact between a primary school and the secondary school which most of its pupils will subsequently attend.

In this centralised system the role of the teacher is often seen as no more than that of an intermediary between centralised expertise and the pupil. Teaching is in consequence formal and this, combined with the immense respect in which purely academic achievement is held, has created an educational system in Venezuela which aims for the most part to develop theoretical and academic skills. Since a university degree is the key to an assured social status and high salary, it is the goal which parents wish their children to reach. As a non-academic course at school virtually rules out the possibility of university education, parents understandably press eagerly for their children to take academic options.

As one would expect, students at each step of the educational ladder come from more privileged backgrounds, the *barrio* child and the child in the country often leaving the system before completing primary school, while the university graduate normally comes from an educated and well-off family.

Continuity is impaired by the wholesale change of personnel within the Ministry of Education and within institutions which follow political changes. The new appointee invariably feels obliged to strike out a new policy for his institution. Students at the higher levels of education are very active politically and student politics can seriously impair the educational efficiency of an institution.

Although the curricula are centralised, there are considerable variations in standards. School buildings and equipment are generally good. For quality of teaching staff and buildings national schools are usually best, followed by state and last of all by municipal schools. Naturally a centralised administration tends to think principally in terms of the needs of the urban majority: as a result the curricula and the design of buildings are not always appropriate to a rural environment.

The outstanding weakness of the system is the shortage of good teachers at all levels. The uneven distribution of teachers contributes significantly to a disparity of educational standards. While nearly 90% of primary school teachers have been trained, the Ministry of Education estimates that only 40% of secondary school teachers have teaching qualifications, with a concentration of trained teachers in Caracas and a dearth in remote areas. The demand for teachers is outstripping the current supply, and although a small in-service programme exists to enable practising teachers to qualify, at its present level of operation it can have no impact on the supply of qualified teachers. Similarly, the programmes of short in-service training for qualified teachers are offered in such small numbers as to have no influence on teaching standards. Many teachers are part time, some because they work in several schools as a means of increasing their salaries, and some because they spend part of the day in other employment or are themselves students within higher education. The overall picture, therefore, is one of great shortages of qualified teachers, particularly aggravated in rural areas and in some subjects.

An educational system characterised by a formal academic approach and a shortage of good teachers is ill-equipped to satisfy an explosive demand for technically trained manpower. This, together with the lack of any efficient mechanism to direct pupils into courses related to their abilities and national requirements means that education in Venezuela is failing to sustain the economic development envisaged by the National Plan.

Venezuela has long been short of trained manpower. In the past this has partly been solved through substantial immigration, but immigration is no longer the flood it was. The possibility of obtaining technical manpower through immigration has itself inhibited the development of Venezuela's own technical education. Current and projected development, however, is far outstretching Venezuela's ability to supply the necessary manpower in many technical fields. Organisations like SIDOR, for example, the government's gigantic steel development in Ciudad Guayana, cannot operate with the minute supply of 10/12 metallurgists which Venezuelan education graduates each year and is forced to advertise throughout Latin America for qualified staff. In many fields the supply of graduates is unrelated to needs: only a handful of the geologists, metallurgists and mining engineers needed to exploit Venezuela's natural resources are produced each year, while the demand for 1000 humanities graduates 1971 to 1985 will according to CORDIPLAN estimates, be over-supplied by the production of 15,200 graduates. The shortage of technically trained personnel below the university level is particularly acute. Technical education in schools and in higher education has yet to prove itself an attractive alternative to academic studies and this situation is unlikely to change while the rewards for the holder of an academic qualification are substantially higher. Since education does not produce the quantities demanded by the labour market, and since teachers' salaries are not competitive, the educational system does not absorb enough of its own products to improve standards.

The educational system can therefore be said to be inefficient in the sense that it is not fulfilling the demands which the national plan is making upon it. This has perhaps been most clearly recognised by the Ayacucho programme to train massive numbers of Venezuelans overseas in priority development areas where supply from the Venezuelan educational system is inadequate: shipbuilding, fisheries, agriculture, metallurgy, technically trained personnel for industrial development in iron and steel, oil, and petrochemicals, together with teaching and research. Venezuela's resort to immigrants previously, and currently to programmes of overseas training, can be seen as avoiding the reform of its own educational system to supply its own needs. And this in turn may mean that the failure of the educational system will prevent Venezuela from achieving its aim of reducing dependence for industrial development on imported technology.

The following problems can be identified in the Venezuelan education system:

Internal Efficiency

   (i)   There is a shortage of qualified teachers, particularly acute in some parts of the country and in some subject areas

   (ii)   Teacher training frequently does not provide practical teaching skills and teaching methodology is poor

   (iii) The demand for education is explosive, straining the education system to the limits

(iv) Although Venezuela does not lack the financial resources to support education, it is seriously short of administrative expertise within education

(v)   The system has a low productivity rate with a large number of drop-outs and repeaters

(vi) Large numbers of students obtain places in higher education with a necessarily high failure rate in consequence

(vii) Provision of educational facilities is uneven with a concentration of the best in Caracas.

External Relevance

(i)   The curriculum is academic and irrelevant to development needs

(ii) Personal and parental aims frequently do not coincide with national requirements

(iii) The supply from the education system is not closely related to the manpower needs of Venezuelan development.

Trends and Possibilities

Population pressures, popular demand and the government's desire to use oil money to develop and diversify the economy have led to massive educational expansion supported by a massive increase in funds.

Deficiencies are commonly acknowledged by Venezuelans involved in education, but no systematic, coordinated solutions have been found.

The following developments are planned.

(i)   Although theoretically compulsory, some Venezuelan children do not attend primary school and others do not complete the full six-year programme. The government is committed to extending the coverage of primary school education

(ii) Until the mid-1970s specialisation began at the start of secondary education. The introduction of the three-year general studies programme at the secondary school level has delayed the point at which specialisation begins. It is now planned under the 1980 Education Law that the whole period of general studies (that is, nine years, covering primary school and the basic cycle at secondary school) should be compulsory, not just the six years of primary education as has been the case

(iii) Distance education is being seriously looked at in Venezuela with a view to its widespread use. It is seen as a means of meeting the enormous demands for education at all levels. Particular attention is being given to the possibility of using distance education for programmes of training and retraining of primary school teachers as well as to the expansion of the Open University

(iv) The training of primary school teachers is being taken from the school sector to become part of higher education. The wider implications of such a change have not been delat with. For example, at present a primary teacher's salary is approximately half that of a secondary school teacher. If both primary and secondary teacher training have the same entry requirements, it would be natural for many to choose to train to become secondary teachers since the rewards are so much greater. The change has important implications for teacher supply as well as teacher differentials.

Reforms have been taking place with such rapidity that it is recognised that it is now time for consideration and retrenchment. It is acknowledged by the President that it is time to concentrate on improving the quality and not just the quantity of education.

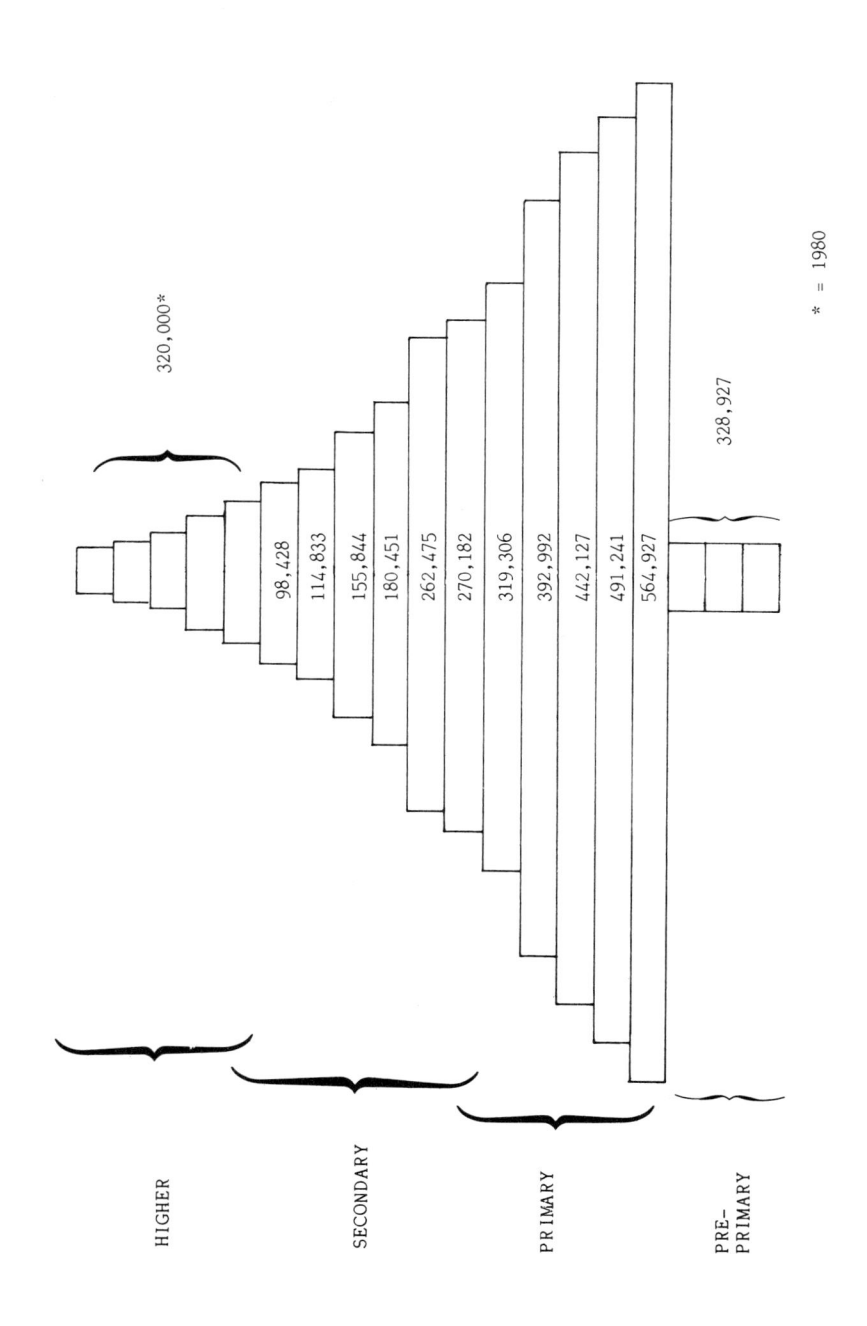

PYRAMID OF ENROLMENTS 1978-79 - VENEZUELA

HIGHER: 320,000*

SECONDARY:
98,428
114,833
155,844
180,451

PRIMARY:
262,475
270,182
319,306
392,992
442,127
491,241
564,927

PRE-PRIMARY: 328,927

* = 1980

ORGANISATIONAL STRUCTURE OF

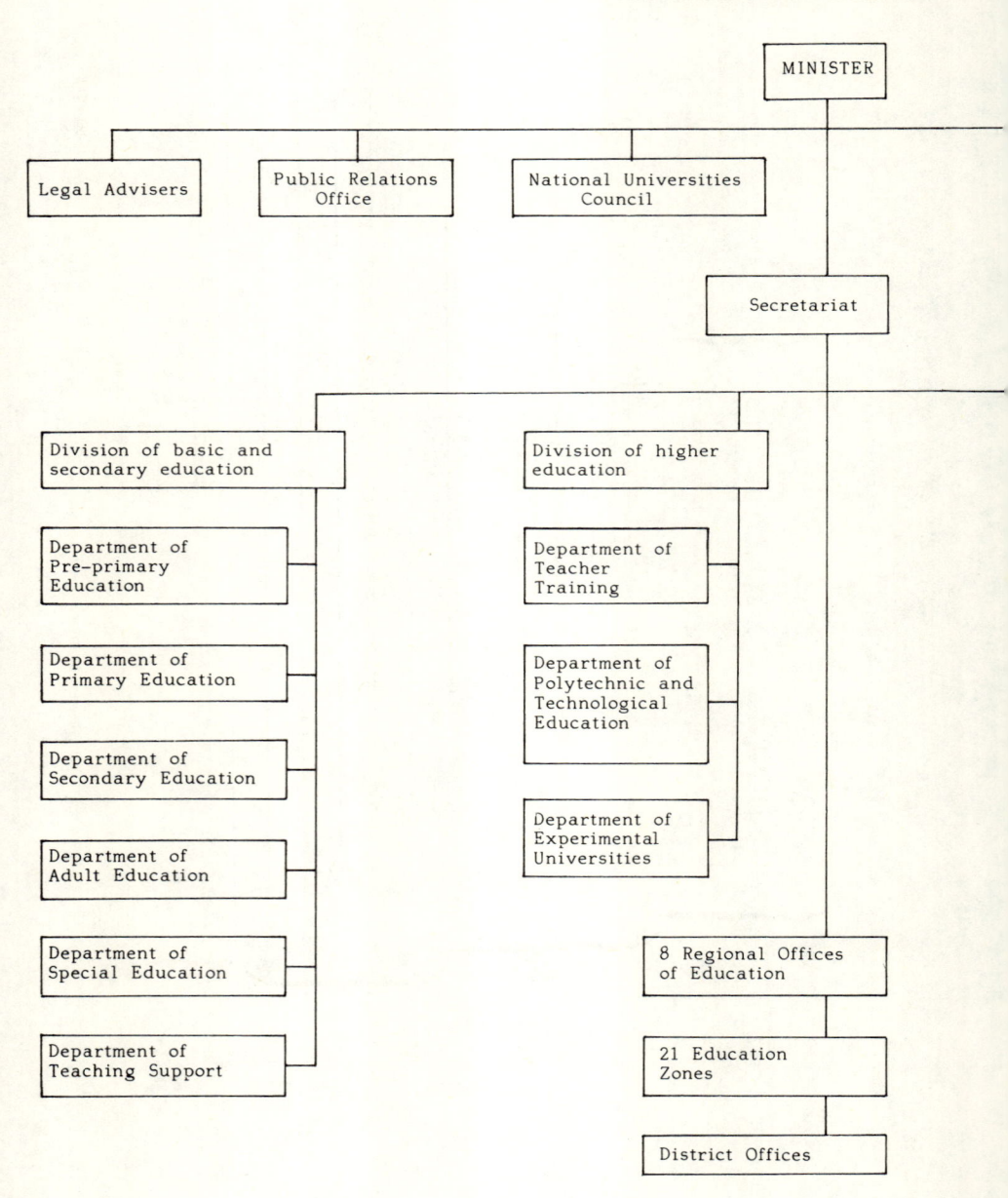

- MINISTER
  - Legal Advisers
  - Public Relations Office
  - National Universities Council
  - Secretariat
    - Division of basic and secondary education
      - Department of Pre-primary Education
      - Department of Primary Education
      - Department of Secondary Education
      - Department of Adult Education
      - Department of Special Education
      - Department of Teaching Support
    - Division of higher education
      - Department of Teacher Training
      - Department of Polytechnic and Technological Education
      - Department of Experimental Universities
    - 8 Regional Offices of Education
      - 21 Education Zones
        - District Offices

THE MINISTRY OF EDUCATION

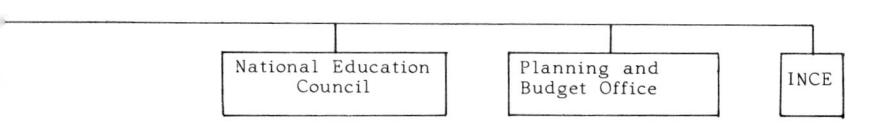

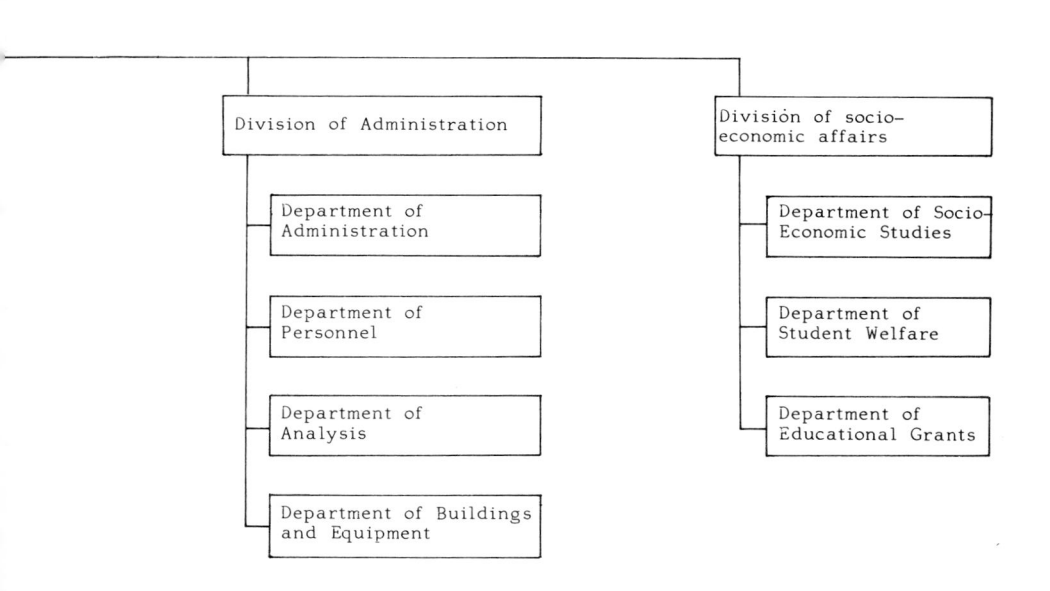

- National Education Council
- Planning and Budget Office
- INCE

- Division of Administration
  - Department of Administration
  - Department of Personnel
  - Department of Analysis
  - Department of Buildings and Equipment
- División of socio-economic affairs
  - Department of Socio-Economic Studies
  - Department of Student Welfare
  - Department of Educational Grants

THE STRUCTURE OF THE

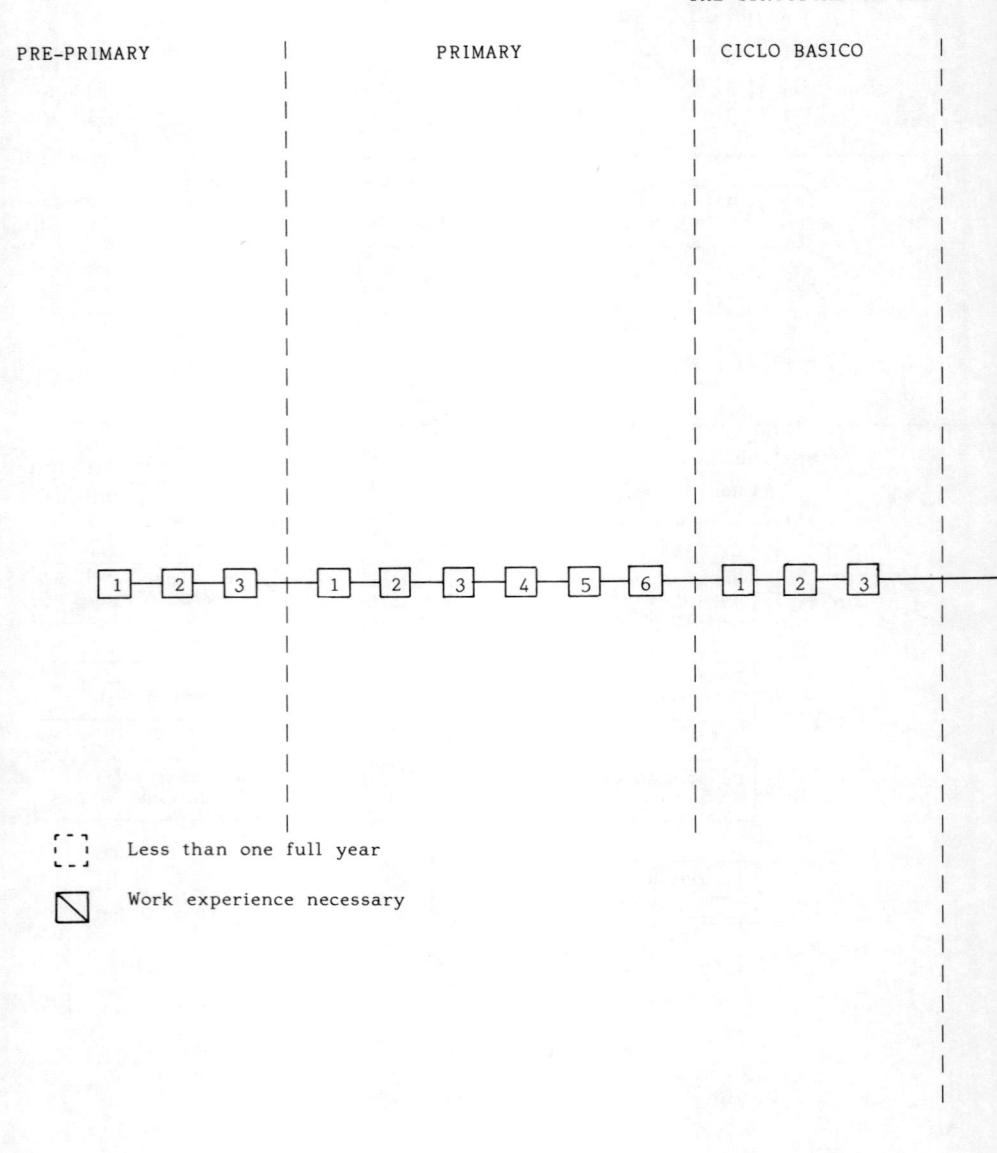

PRE-PRIMARY | PRIMARY | CICLO BASICO |

| 1 |—| 2 |—| 3 | | 1 |—| 2 |—| 3 |—| 4 |—| 5 |—| 6 | | 1 |—| 2 |—| 3 |

```
[ ]  Less than one full year

[◺]  Work experience necessary
```

Age   4   5   6   7   8   9   10   11   12   13   14   15

VENEZUELAN EDUCATION SYSTEM

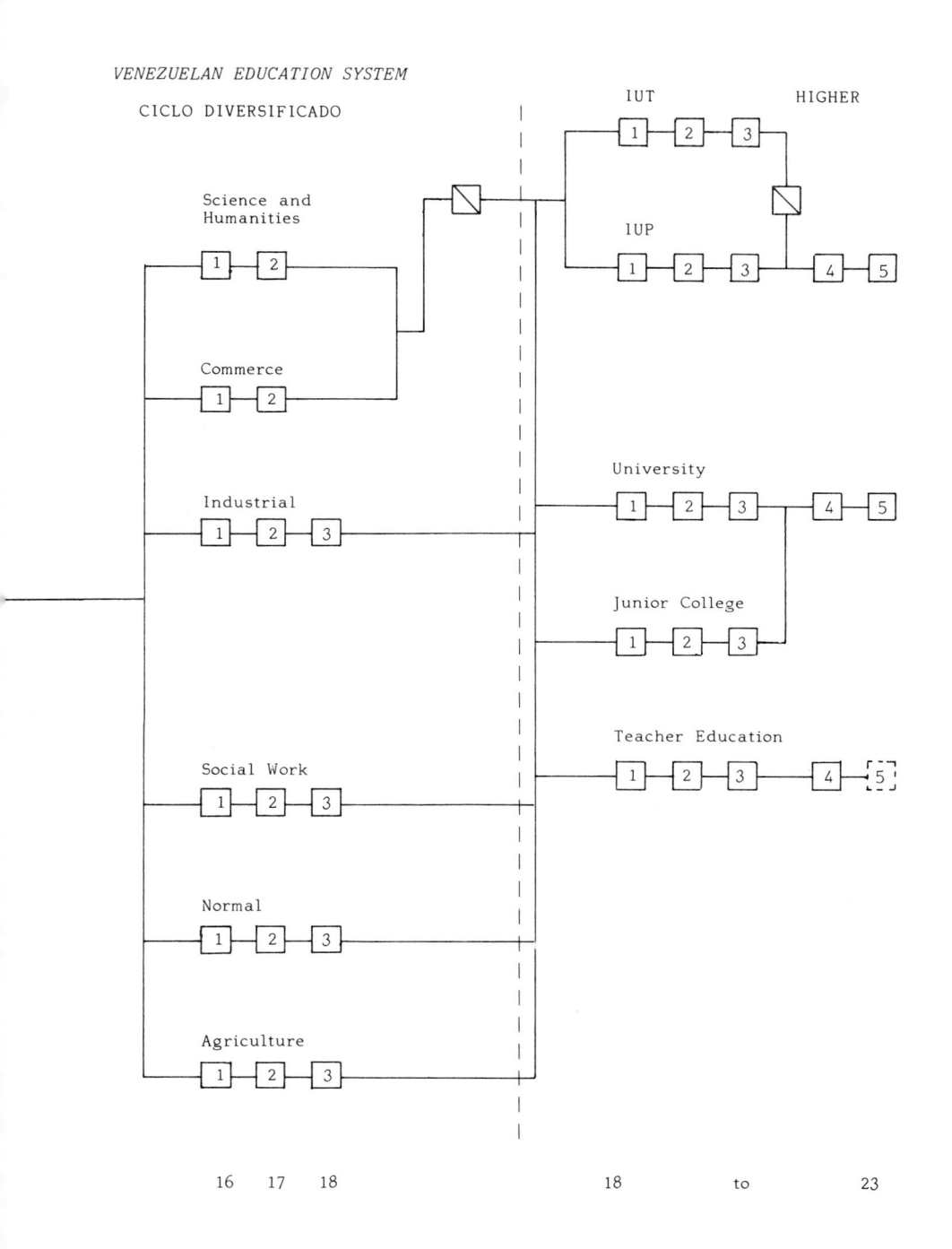

CICLO DIVERSIFICADO

Science and Humanities: 1 — 2

Commerce: 1 — 2

Industrial: 1 — 2 — 3

Social Work: 1 — 2 — 3

Normal: 1 — 2 — 3

Agriculture: 1 — 2 — 3

HIGHER

IUT: 1 — 2 — 3

IUP: 1 — 2 — 3 — 4 — 5

University: 1 — 2 — 3 — 4 — 5

Junior College: 1 — 2 — 3

Teacher Education: 1 — 2 — 3 — 4 — [5]

16 17 18   18   to   23

Population

1961	1971	1981
7,523,999	10,721,522	17,686,000

Enrolment Ratios
Primary = Enrolments divided by the total population aged 7-12
Secondary = Enrolments divided by the total population aged 13-18
Higher = Enrolments divided by the total population aged 20-24

Year	Primary	Secondary	Higher
1970	94%	34%	11.6
1979	110%	40%	21.6*

* 1980

Higher Education Students by Field of Study 1978

Education and Teacher Training	46,352
Humanities	3,357
Law	15,845
Social and Behavioural Science	11,819
Commerce and Business	25,197
Home Economics	9,940
Natural Science	3,833
Mathematics and Computer Science	6,103
Medicine and Related Fields	25,022
Engineering	27,377
Architecture	4,318
Transport	6,978
Agriculture	10,864
Other and Non-specified	85,069

Institutions, Teachers and Pupils

	Schools	Teachers	Pupils
Pre-Primary			
1970	–	1,444	50,159
1979	–	9,158*	328,927*
Primary			
1970	10,509	50,822	1,769,680
1979	12,753*	82,226*	2,456,203
Secondary			
1970	–	22,983	425,146
1979	–	47,996*	820,233

	Institutions	Teachers	Students†
Universities			
1968	10	6,387	58,674
1980	19	19,931	221,873
Other Institutions			
1968	3	478	3,775
1980	60	8,121	85,260

* 1978
† Full time

Government Expenditure on Education

Year	As a % of Total Government Spending	As a % of GNP
1968	13.3%	4.8% (1970)
1982	15.7%	5.1% (1978)

Government Expenditure on Education by Level

	Primary	Secondary	Higher	Other
1970	38.3%	20.6%	25.5%	15.5%
1975	21.1%	18.4%	37.0%	22.4%
1982	–	–	40.5%	–

Basic Social and Economic Data

    Gross National Product per capita 1979 – US$3,120
Average annual growth of GNP per capita 1960–79 – 2.7%
        Life expectancy 1979 – 67 years
    Proportion of the labour force employed in:

                Agriculture
                1960   35%
                1979   19%

                Industry
                1960   22%
                2979   27%

                Services
                1960   43%
                1979   54%